HUMAN RIGHTS

HUMAN RIGHTS

Current Issues and Controversies

EDITED BY

Gordon DiGiacomo

UNIVERSITY OF TORONTO PRESS

MIX
Paper from responsible sources
FSC® C013483
FSC www.fsc.org

www.utppublishing.com

Library and Archives Canada Cataloguing in Publication

Human rights (University of Toronto Press)
Human rights : current issues and controversies / edited by Gordon DiGiacomo.

Includes bibliographical references and index.

Issued in print and electronic formats.

ISBN 978-1-4426-0954-9 (bound).—ISBN 978-1-4426-0953-2 (paperback).—
ISBN 978-1-4426-0955-6 (pdf).—ISBN 978-1-4426-0956-3 (html).

1. Human rights. 2. Human rights—Canada. I. DiGiacomo, Gordon, author, editor II. Title.

JC571.H769428 2016 323 C2015-904423-5

C2015-904424-3

We welcome comments and suggestions regarding any aspect of our publications—please feel free to contact us at news@utphighereducation.com or visit our Internet site at www.utppublishing.com.

North America
5201 Dufferin Street
North York, Ontario, Canada, M3H 5T8

2250 Military Road
Tonawanda, New York, USA, 14150

ORDERS PHONE: 1-800-565-9523
ORDERS FAX: 1-800-221-9985
ORDERS E-MAIL: utpbooks@utpress.utoronto.ca

UK, Ireland, and continental Europe
NBN International
Estover Road, Plymouth, PL6 7PY, UK
ORDERS PHONE: 44 (0) 1752 202301
ORDERS FAX: 44 (0) 1752 202333
ORDERS E-MAIL: enquiries@nbninternational.com

The University of Toronto Press acknowledges the financial support for its publishing activities of the Government of Canada through the Canada Book Fund.

Printed in the United States of America.

I dedicate this book to the memory of Paul McRae, friend, teacher, and member of Parliament for Thunder Bay–Atikokan from 1972 to 1984.

It would be difficult to overstate the importance of Paul in my life. He died suddenly a number of years ago, but hardly a day goes by when he does not enter my thoughts. A young man could not ask for a better elder. The opportunities he made possible led to some of the happiest, most fulfilling times of my life. He was a physically big man who exuded energy, optimism, and good feeling. A visit to his rural home was an opportunity to recharge one's batteries, filled as it inevitably was with colleagues, friends, relatives, visitors, food, and political chatter.

The range of Paul's interests befitted his size. He was a human rights champion in the broadest sense of the term. His politics was the politics of ideas, of just solutions to the issues in his riding, his country, his world. Pierre Trudeau had no more loyal MP, but the last thing Paul aspired to be was a party hack.

My education in serious politics began with Paul. Whether tagging along on tours of his riding or talking environmental policy in his Ottawa office, I learned that the politics of meaning is not about opinion polls or spin but about ideas, and converting those ideas into policies. So, Paul, through this dedication, I honour your memory and pay tribute to your work on earth.

It is fitting that I also dedicate this book to the numerous hard-working and motivated upper-level undergraduates whom I have had the pleasure of teaching.

In the subjects I taught in my teaching life—political science, constitutional law, and labour relations—I am privileged to have had many ambitious students who were eager to learn, accepted my assignments with enthusiasm, and fearlessly assumed responsibility for getting the maximum from my classes.

I am very happy to be able to recognize here several remarkable former students from both the University of Ottawa and Carleton University: Amaila Bhatti, Russell Burgess, Laura Clements, Ryan Curran, Yolanda Elias Cux, David Davis, Michael DeLuca, Emma Dolan, Ashley Donald-Tebbutt, Marissa Blake Gibson, Victoria Ho, Jane Houser, Amanda Iarusso, Susan Kim, Sarah Kirby, Monika Lemke, Victoria Lennox, Ryan Mallough, Mercedes Mueller, Sara Munkittrick, Ashley Pereira, Sarah Poxton, Will Samson-Doel, Lauren van Leeuwen, Mitchell Warner, Andrea Westcott-Lacoursière, and Reem Zaia.

I wish the very best for these and the other exceptional young people who took my courses. I deeply hope that I was to them just a little of what Paul McRae was to me.

Contents

Acknowledgements

I WOULD LIKE TO EXPRESS MY DEEP GRATITUDE to the contributors to this volume. It was a pleasure to work with such experienced, knowledgeable, and accommodating scholars. A special thanks to the contributors who came on board late in the game to replace others who had to drop out.

I want to recognize also the considerable assistance of the staff at the University of Toronto Press with whom I worked, namely Natalie Fingerhut, Megan Pickard, Mark Thompson, Anna Del Col, and Ashley Rayner, and of freelance copy editor Gillian Watts. Their professionalism, hard work, patience, encouragement, and upbeat attitude are hugely appreciated.

I want to say thanks so much to Ashley Donald-Tebbutt and Ashley Pereira, who did an enormous amount of work to help me put the volume together. Thanks too to the anonymous reviewers who carefully read the volume and offered thoughtful comments.

Last but by no means least, I wish to express my heartfelt thanks to Patricia Zito for being an invaluable source of support and advice.

Contributors

Sam Adelman is a legal theorist in the School of Law of the University of Warwick, United Kingdom. He has degrees from the University of the Witwatersrand, Harvard University, and the University of Warwick. He was banned and exiled during the struggle against apartheid. His main areas of research are climate change, law and development, and human rights.

Melanie Adrian is currently on the faculty of the Department of Law and Legal Studies at Carleton University in Ottawa. Her work critically examines the tensions that arise when a general religious right is applied in a specific context, and what this application signifies for national identity and cultural norms. In her writing, she looks at minority rights and their manifestation in relation to international and national human rights norms and respect for national values. Her book *Religious Freedom at Risk: The EU, French Schools, and Why the Veil Was Banned* takes up these issues in France and the wider European context.

Caroline Andrew is Director of the Centre on Governance at the University of Ottawa. From 1997 to 2005 she was Dean of the Faculty of Social Sciences. For the past 40 years she has been doing research on building inclusive cities for women and girls in all their diversity and on the integration of recent immigrants. In 2013, Caroline received the Order of Ottawa and in 2014 she was appointed to the Order of Canada. Caroline was Chair of the Task Force on Respect and Equality at the University of Ottawa, which recently submitted its report, *Ending Sexualized Violence.*

Tanya Basok is Professor in the Department of Sociology, Anthropology, and Criminology at the University of Windsor, Ontario. She has published widely in the area of migrant rights and social justice. She is the co-author of *Issues in Social Justice: Citizenship and Transnational Struggles* (2013) and of *Rethinking Transit Migration in Mexico: Precarity, Self-Making, and Mobility* (2015).

Roland Burke is a lecturer in history at La Trobe University, Melbourne, Australia, and author of *Decolonization and the Evolution of International Human Rights* (University of Pennsylvania Press, 2010). His research has focused on the 1948 Universal Declaration of Human Rights (*Journal of Global History*), the contested evolution of economic and social rights, and the New International Economic Order (*Humanity, Journal of World History, Humanity, Human Rights Quarterly, History Australia*). He has published chapters in collections on human rights, empire, and humanitarianism. Currently he is engaged in completing a monograph on shifting visions of the Universal Declaration of Human Rights, entitled *Human Rights in Eclipse*.

Karen Busby is Professor of law and Director of the Centre for Human Rights Research at the University of Manitoba. She has worked on numerous cases and law reform projects through the Women's Legal Education and Action Fund (LEAF) and Egale Canada.

Tara M. Collins is Assistant Professor, School of Child and Youth Care, Ryerson University, Toronto. She has a PhD from the University of London and has worked on international human rights since 1996. Her professional experience includes work for universities in Canada and Ireland, the Canadian government and parliament, and a national non-governmental organization. Research interests include monitoring human/child rights, child and youth participation, child protection, international development, and rights-based approaches.

Gordon DiGiacomo obtained his doctorate in political science in 2010 from Carleton University, Ottawa. Most of his career, prior to entering the academic world in 2003, was devoted to working on issues pertaining to labour rights. His introduction to rights and rights instruments came in the early 1980s, when, like other ministerial assistants at the time, he was engaged in promotion of a constitutionally entrenched charter of rights for Canadians. Among the courses he teaches at the University of Ottawa is the Politics of Human Rights.

Christine Gervais is Associate Professor of criminology in the Faculty of Social Sciences and a member of the Interdisciplinary Research Laboratory on the Rights of the Child (IRLRC) in the Faculty of Law at the University of Ottawa. Her interdisciplinary studies have been published in *Children and Society, Journal of Youth Studies, Signs, Canadian Woman Studies, Journal of International Women's Studies, Criminologie, Sociology of Religion, Religions*, and *Review of Religious Research*.

Brooke Jeffrey is Professor of political science and Director of the Master's Program in Public Policy and Public Administration at Concordia University,

Montreal. A former senior public servant, she first worked in the Human Rights Program of the former Department of the Secretary of State (now Canadian Heritage), where she was the principal author of Canada's first reports to the United Nations on the two international human rights covenants. She later worked on the constitutional reform process that resulted in adoption of the *Constitution Act, 1982*, and served as research advisor for the House of Commons Special Committees on Visible Minorities (1984) and Equality Rights (1985).

Susan L. Kang is Associate Professor in the Department of Political Science at John Jay College of Criminal Justice, City University of New York. Her research focuses on labour rights, trade unions, social movements, and general resistance to neoliberalism. She is the author of *Human Rights and Labor Solidarity: Trade Unions in the Global Economy* (2012).

John Kincaid is the Robert B. and Helen S. Meyner Professor of Government and Public Service and Director of the Meyner Center for the Study of State and Local Government at Lafayette College, Easton, Pennsylvania. He is an elected fellow of the National Academy of Public Administration, recipient of the Distinguished Scholar Award from the American Political Science Association's Section on Federalism and Intergovernmental Relations, and recipient of the Distinguished Scholar Award from the American Society of Public Administration's Section on Intergovernmental Administration and Management. He is the author of various works on federalism and intergovernmental relations, co-editor most recently of *The Covenant Connection: From Federal Theology to Modern Federalism* (2000), *Constitutional Origins, Structure, and Change in Federal Countries* (2005), and the *Routledge Handbook of Regionalism and Federalism* (2013), and editor of *Federalism* (4 volumes, 2011).

James Kirby is a PhD student in history at La Trobe University in Melbourne, Australia. After attaining first-class honours in 2012, James was awarded an Australian Research Council scholarship to begin a PhD in 2013. In 2014, two university grants were awarded for research trips to Botswana and the United Kingdom. James's broader research interests include the history of human rights in the twentieth century, with a focus on the context of Africa and the wider decolonization movement. Based on extensive archival material, his thesis is a study of Botswana's foundational narrative as a success story for non-racial democracy in southern Africa.

Thomas R. Klassen is Professor in the Department of Political Science and the School of Public Policy and Administration at York University,

Toronto. He has written extensively on retirement and aging. His recent books include *Retirement in Canada: Choices, Challenges, and Prospects* (2013) and *Retirement in Japan and South Korea: The Past, the Present, and the Future of Mandatory Retirement* (2015).

Mahmood Monshipouri is Professor of international relations at San Francisco State University. He is also Visiting Professor at the University of California, Berkeley. His recent books include *Inside the Islamic Republic: Social Change in the Post-Khomeini Iran* (2015) and *Information Politics, Protests, and Human Rights in the Digital Age* (forthcoming).

Kelley O'Dell is a graduate in Arabic and Middle Eastern studies from the University of California, Berkeley. She is presently pursuing an MA in Middle Eastern studies at New York University, where she is focusing on transnational feminisms and postcoloniality.

Trevor Purvis is Assistant Professor in the Department of Law and Legal Studies and the Institute of Political Economy at Carleton University, Ottawa. He teaches courses in international law and the law of armed conflict, and has published in the areas of citizenship studies, nationalism, ideology studies, and the legal implications of the global war on terror.

Jennifer Rutledge is Assistant Professor in the Department of Political Science at John Jay College of Criminal Justice, City University of New York. Her work focuses on comparative social policy, food politics, and social rights. Her most recent publication is *Feeding the Future: The Emergence of School Lunches as Global Social Policy* (2015).

Tracie Scott is currently an adjunct lecturer at Murdoch University, Dubai, United Arab Emirates. She has published several articles on Aboriginal self-government in Canada, as well as the book *Postcolonial Sovereignty: The Nisga'a Final Agreement* (2012).

Sara L. Seck is Associate Professor at the Faculty of Law, Western University, London, Ontario. A graduate of the University of Toronto's Faculty of Law, she received her PhD from Osgoode Hall Law School in 2008, having joined Western Law the previous year. Sara has published extensively in areas that include corporate social responsibility; international environmental, human rights, and sustainable development law; climate change; and indigenous law, often with a focus on extractive industries. Her research often explores aspects of international and transnational legal theory, notably the relationship between Third World approaches to international law and international legal process theories that are informed by constructivist understandings of international relations.

Valerie Steeves is Associate Professor in the Department of Criminology at the University of Ottawa. She has written extensively on human rights and technology issues, with a special emphasis on privacy and surveillance. She is also the author of a series of award-winning multimedia games designed to teach young people how to protect their human rights in a networked environment. Her recent books include *eGirls, eCitizens, and Transparent Lives: Surveillance in Canada*. She has a JD from the University of Toronto and a PhD in communications from Carleton University, Ottawa.

Kirsten Stefanik is a PhD candidate in the Faculty of Law at Western University. She holds an LLM from Western University, for which she received the Governor General's Academic Gold Medal in 2013. She earned her law degree and BA degree from the University of British Columbia. She currently holds a doctoral fellowship from the Social Sciences and Humanities Research Council of Canada. Her areas of focus are the law of armed conflicts, international criminal law, international human rights, and transitional justice and post-conflict reconstruction. Her current research focuses on the protection of civilians and the environment in armed conflict, with a particular emphasis on the participation of non-state actors.

Deborah Stienstra held Nancy's Chair in Women's Studies at Mount Saint Vincent University, Halifax, Nova Scotia, from 2013 to 2015 and is Professor in disability studies at the University of Manitoba. She researches and writes in the areas of disability policy, gender and intersectionality, and disability and global development. In 2012 she published *About Canada: Disability Rights*, which explores the landscape of disability rights in Canada through the stories and voices of women, men, girls, and boys with disabilities.

David Zarnett is a PhD candidate in the Department of Political Science at the University of Toronto. He has written on realist international relations theory and Western solidarity activism. His most recent work is forthcoming in *Foreign Policy Analysis*.

Introduction

GORDON DIGIACOMO

THE IDEA FOR THIS BOOK EMERGED from my experiences as an instructor of a fourth-year political science course at the University of Ottawa, titled the Politics of Human Rights. I came to see the need for a book, prepared mainly by Canadians but usable internationally, that discusses a broad range of contemporary issues in human rights, is comprehensible to the target groups, and acknowledges the role of political institutions in rights protection. The number of human rights volumes that meet these criteria is limited. I am delighted, therefore, to be able to offer this volume to human rights instructors and students.

The book is intended primarily for upper-level undergraduate students in the social sciences, but master's level and law students should also find it useful. It seeks to introduce students to current human rights concerns and controversies, and in so doing familiarize them with the major human rights instruments—provincial, national, and international—that protect Canadians. Collectively, the chapters provide in-depth treatment of rights issues that affect particular segments of the population and of what we might call cross-cutting rights issues that affect all citizens.

Rights Definitions

The commonly used definition of *human rights* was popularized by the human rights scholar Jack Donnelly,[1] among others, and is repeated by Reeta Tremblay and her co-authors in their Canadian text: "Rights are claims or entitlements to be treated in particular ways ... Human rights are rights that are held by all human beings by virtue of being human. Human rights are universal, held equally by all people. They are 'inalienable,' meaning that although they may be violated, a person's rights cannot be surrendered or erased."[2] The statement that human rights are entitlements that people may claim simply because they are human seems somewhat vague and incomplete, too general. However, it appeals because of its point that one does not have to earn rights; a person has rights simply because he or she inhabits the planet.

Another scholar of human rights, Michael Haas, agrees that there is no consensus on the precise meaning of *human rights*, but "nearly everyone agrees that human rights involve the ability to demand and enjoy a minimally restrictive yet optimal quality of life with liberty, equal justice before law, and an opportunity to fulfill basic cultural, economic, and social needs."[3] This definition certainly makes clear what having rights makes possible, but it does not actually say what is a right.

Yet another human rights scholar, Alison Brysk, refers to human rights as "a set of universal claims to safeguard human dignity from illegitimate coercion, typically enacted by state agents."[4] This definition is more specific, but again the term *universal claims* does not really say in a precise way what a right is.

The prominent American legal scholar Cass Sunstein defines rights as "legally enforceable instruments for the protection of their claimants."[5] This is a legal positivist definition, and it raises the question of whether rights exist outside of legal documents. Does a right exist only because a judge or legal document says it does? The right to privacy is not set out in the Canadian Charter of Rights and Freedoms, so are we to conclude that such a right does not exist? Some rights found in a charter may exist for some but, because of the need or desirability of circumscribing those rights, do not exist for others. The right to vote is a case in point: that right is in the Canadian Charter but the age requirement for exercising the right means that the right does not exist for those below the stipulated age.

In his work, Michael Ignatieff says that human rights are about protecting human agency, that is, "the capacity of individuals to set themselves goals and accomplish them as they see fit."[6] In other words, rights are guarantors of human agency. This formulation has appeal because it is more specific about what is to be protected, namely the qualities necessary for human agency. But there is a serious flaw in the definition, as pointed out by James Griffin, a leading advocate of the agency definition of rights:[7] if human rights are about protecting human agency—that is, the capacity for autonomous action—then it follows that those who lack this capacity—for example, infants, coma patients, those with advanced dementia, and the severely mentally disabled—are not entitled to human rights protection.

Given the foregoing, perhaps it is possible to say simply that rights are the attributes of personal and collective freedom, the expression of which requires both legal protection and state support and leads to a life of human dignity.

Types of Rights

Bills of rights may contain different types of rights, including civil, political, socioeconomic, cultural, and environmental rights. Borrowing from the *Stanford Encyclopedia of Philosophy*, we may say that civil rights, in the modern sense, are the basic rights "needed for free and equal citizenship."[8] They would include what the Canadian Charter of Rights and Freedoms calls fundamental freedoms (s. 2), such as freedom of thought and expression; legal rights (ss. 7–14), such as the right to life and liberty and the right not to be arbitrarily detained or imprisoned; and equality rights (s. 15), the right to equality before and under the law. Political rights are the rights the individual needs to participate in the political life of the country, such as the right to stand for election to the House of Commons or the provincial legislative assemblies.[9]

Socioeconomic rights (also known as economic and social rights) aim to help citizens, vulnerable to the vagaries of a market-based economy, maintain an acceptable standard of living and quality of life. Examples of socioeconomic rights can be found in the International Covenant on Economic, Social and Cultural Rights (ICESCR). They include the right of everyone to an opportunity to gain a living by work that is freely chosen or accepted; the right to just and favourable conditions of work; the right to housing; the right to form and join trade unions; the right to free primary education; and the right to social security.[10]

Cultural rights are defined by Haas as "claims to observe a group's long-standing customs, language, and/or religion."[11] The United Nations Declaration on the Rights of Persons belonging to National or Ethnic, Religious and Linguistic Minorities sets out cultural rights. Article 2, for instance, states, "Persons belonging to national or ethnic, religious and linguistic minorities (hereinafter referred to as persons belonging to minorities) have the right to enjoy their own culture, to profess and practise their own religion, and to use their own language, in private and in public, freely and without interference or any form of discrimination."

Environmental rights refer to the right of every person of present and future generations to live in a natural environment adequate for their health and well-being.[12] Several constitutions contain clauses protecting the right to a healthy (or healthful) environment. Some scholars in Canada argue that the Charter's guarantee of the right to life in section 7 should be interpreted to include environmental rights. As discussed in Chapter 17 of this volume, there is increasing interest in reframing environmental rights from their individual focus to an Earth- or nature-oriented focus. In 2008, for example, Ecuador was the first to codify the rights of nature in its constitution. Articles 10 and 71–74 recognize the inalienable rights of ecosystems to exist and flourish, create a right to petition on behalf of ecosystems, and oblige the state to remedy violations of these rights.

Two ways of distinguishing among human rights are, first, between positive and negative rights, and second, between individual and collective or group rights. With respect to the former, negative rights are those that require the state to refrain from intruding into the life of the individual; governments are required *not* to do something. Positive rights, on the other hand, require the state to act; governments need to do something to implement a right. Disagreement exists as to whether positive rights—or at least some of those rights—are justiciable, that is, able to be addressed by the courts.

Individual rights are those that apply to individuals, such as the right to equality and the rights to free speech and freedom of religion. Collective or group rights are defined by the University of Minnesota Human Rights Resource Center as "the rights of groups to protect their interests and identities."[13] This definition suggests two applications. First, it can be interpreted to mean the rights of individuals collectively applied. For instance, section 20 of the Charter ensures the right of Canadians to communicate with the Government of Canada in either English or French; the right applies to particular communities but it is exercised by individuals. Alternatively, the definition can refer to rights that can be exercised only by a collectivity. These are sometimes also called group rights. For instance, the right of workers to collective bargaining is exercised by a labour union on behalf of the membership.

Also, in *Mahé v. Alberta* (1990), the Supreme Court of Canada ruled that the Charter allowed for some management and control over education by the francophone minorities in Canada: "In some cases, this would require the establishment of an independent minority language school board; in other cases, guaranteed representation and certain exclusive authority within the majority board would be sufficient."[14] Here the francophone collectivity was assured of the right to self-governance, or a measure of self-governance, on educational matters. Similarly, section 25 of the Canadian Charter of Rights and Freedoms, as well as section 35, which is outside the Charter but within the constitution, has been interpreted by Canadian governments as embracing Aboriginal peoples' inherent right to self-government. This is not an individual right but a right that is exercised by a structure of some sort on behalf of the community.[15]

Some Major Criticisms of Rights Instruments and Rights Discourse

While accepting the need for human rights instruments, several commentators have levelled serious criticisms at those instruments and at rights discourse. Mary Ann Glendon is one such critic. One of her criticisms is that the focus on rights promotes excessive individualism. Rights discourse in her view, at least in the United States, neglects the dimension of sociality and helps to create isolated, self-absorbed individuals, always ready to assert what is theirs rather than participate in communal life. She writes, "The exceptional solitariness of the American rights-bearer is but one aspect of the hyperindividualism that pervades our American rights dialect."[16] The emphasis on individual autonomy has pushed to the background other American traditions, such as hospitality and community concern.

Sunstein disagrees and observes that there is no easy opposition between rights and the collective entity. Many rights, he says, "deserve to exist because of their collective consequences."[17] For instance, freedom of assembly and association may be described as individual rights, but they are intended to protect collective action. Freedom of speech, the quintessential individual right, may be intended for individuals but "it is a precondition for a highly social process, that of democratic deliberation."[18] Similarly, "the right to subsistence and the right to environmental quality—whether or not these should be codified in law—do not seem to promote selfishness. Both rights might be products of altruism, and may promote altruism and even feelings of responsibility."[19]

Glendon devotes a chapter of her book to an examination of the right to property and court decisions on this right. It might perhaps have been more to the point if Glendon had pursued this line of thinking rather than rights discourse, if her concern is excessive individualism. That is to say, one can make a strong argument that the values inherent in a market-based economic system have contributed a great deal more to the development of excessive individualism than has rights talk.

Another criticism articulated by Glendon is that rights talk causes people to focus on what they are entitled to, not on what their responsibilities are or what it is right to do. She states, "In its silence concerning responsibilities, [rights discourse] seems to condone acceptance of the benefits of living in a democratic social welfare state, without accepting the corresponding personal and civic obligations."[20] This is the civic republican criticism of rights. Civic republicanism, a strand of liberalism, stresses civic virtue, that is, each individual's responsibility to one's neighbour and one's nation. For civic republicans, the focus on rights and not responsibilities is problematic. So troubled is Glendon by this neglect of responsibilities in rights discourse that she proposes that governments enact legislation imposing a legal duty on citizens to come to the aid of another in peril.

Again Sunstein addresses Glendon's argument. He points out that some rights also have features associated with responsibilities. The right to vote, for instance, is intended to protect an individual democratic right. But exercise of the right partially fulfills a responsibility of the individual to be a good citizen. Further, Sunstein notes, rights and duties imply one another: "To say that someone has a right is usually to say that someone else has a duty."[21]

For instance, if Jane has a right to property, other people have a duty not to trespass on what she possesses. Conversely, Jane has a responsibility to respect others' property. If Joe has a right to be free from racial discrimination in employment, employers and managers have a duty to ignore the colour of Joe's skin.[22]

Some rights documents include duties and responsibilities. Article 29 of the Universal Declaration of Human Rights, for instance, states, "Everyone has duties to the community in which alone the free and full development of his personality is possible." Similarly, article 25 of the International Covenant on Civil and Political Rights, though phrased as a right, can also be construed as a responsibility. It reads, "Every citizen shall have the right and the opportunity … to take part in the conduct of public affairs, directly or through freely chosen representatives." So rights and duties are intricately bound up with one another. Indeed, as Sunstein writes, "Glendon's discussion comes close to an argument not only for a new duty, but also for a new right: a right to assistance, to be granted to vulnerable people and held by them against both other people and the government."[23]

A third criticism has to do with socioeconomic rights, alluded to earlier. Some scholars argue that a major deficiency of the Canadian Charter is the absence of explicit socioeconomic rights provisions and the reluctance of the Supreme Court to read such rights into the Charter. This criticism is made even though Canada has a well-developed social security infrastructure that, while flawed, is very comprehensive. This infrastructure came about well before the Charter.

While the Supreme Court of Canada has indeed been reluctant to read socioeconomic rights into the Charter, this does not mean that the justices have totally ignored them. In *Health Services and Support—Facilities Subsector Bargaining Assn v. British Columbia* (2007), the Court upheld the right of workers to collective bargaining. This was based on the freedom of association, but it can be interpreted as a social right. Another BC case upheld the right of deaf persons to have sign language interpretation covered under the province's health-care insurance plan.[24] This was a victory under section 15, equality rights. The tools seem to be there, so to speak, for the Court to get into socioeconomic rights. Further, it is possible to suggest that the thinking of the justices may be changing. The Court's willingness to pronounce on health care in the *Chaoulli* case indicates a greater willingness to involve itself in social policy.[25]

In addition, the Supreme Court has long recognized that international human rights obligations are a relevant factor in Charter interpretation. Former Chief Justice Brian Dickson argued that "the Charter should generally be presumed to provide protection at least as great as that afforded by similar provisions in international human rights documents which Canada has ratified."[26] The takeaway message from this is that the Court will not ignore what international human rights instruments have to say about socioeconomic rights.

Legal scholar Aoife Nolan and her colleagues point out that concerns about the justiciability[27] of socioeconomic rights rest on three assumptions: that socioeconomic rights are inherently different from civil and political rights; that it is inappropriate for the courts to intrude into social and economic policy; and that the courts lack the capacity to properly adjudicate and enforce socioeconomic rights.[28] In their reply, they review international jurisprudence and conclude that

> the argument that economic and social rights lack the qualities of justiciability cannot, therefore, be sustained in the face of any reasonable survey of jurisprudence at the national and international level. ... In a surprising number of cases from a variety of legal systems, courts have demonstrated that they are capable of identifying the relevant legal standards to apply in cases concerning alleged violations of economic and social rights, while at the same time respecting their limits in relation to the distinctive role and competencies of governments.[29]

On the other hand, some scholars argue that the constitutionalization of socioeconomic rights is not likely to have the desired effect in terms of reducing income inequality. Hirschl and Rosevear point out that Sweden, Finland, and Denmark, three nations noted for their social welfare policies, have long subscribed to an "egalitarian conception of distributive justice" but have been less than enthusiastic "toward the notion of constitutional rights and judicial review." Conversely, in Brazil and India, where "constitutional support for social welfare rights can be discerned," the degree of income inequality parallels that in the United States, where support for the constitutionalization of socioeconomic rights is almost non-existent.[30] "Clearly, then," the authors conclude, "the constitutionalization of socio-economic rights per se—however morally compelling its premise is or however significant its symbolic value may be—is limited in its independent capacity to alleviate pre-existing inequalities in living conditions."[31]

A fourth criticism, directed at international rights instruments, comes from Tony Evans. He adopts a political economy approach to the analysis of international human rights and takes issue with the emphasis on international human rights treaties as the principal way to advance international human rights. He asks: what role does the global political economy play in securing or denying access to the means for protecting human rights? Is international law the most effective way of promoting all human rights? And what is the future of human rights in the age of globalization? He argues that, "While on one hand international law is presented and promoted as the solution to problems of human rights, on the other, the practices of market discipline continue to provide the context in which human rights are violated. International law might therefore be seen as a 'mask' that conceals the true causes of many human rights violations."[32]

In an age of globalization, the state has less capacity to protect and advance rights, and the application of legal norms cannot address the violations committed by the global economic order. Evans also writes, "investigations into the causes of human rights violations seldom go beyond the assumption that all violations can be explained by reference to the wilful acts of evil, brutal, despotic and cruel individuals, excluding the possibility, for example, that the principles of international politics, the rules that govern world trade or the principles of the global economic order itself may also lead to human rights violations."[33] The preference is to try to protect rights by emphasizing "post-violation redress" rather than to see "the structures of the global political economy" as possibly containing the causes of the violations.

Under the conditions of globalization, the victims of social rights violations tend, in fact, not to be seen as victims. Indeed, "As economic development is understood increasingly as the central aim of all governments, the deprivations suffered by those whose environment is degraded, culture devastated, freedom to protest peacefully suppressed, and traditional ties with the land forcibly severed are seen less as the victims of human rights violations and more as the unfortunate citizens who must bear the cost of economic progress for the good of the wider community."[34]

The case presented by Evans is a powerful one and is something of a corrective to the tendency to pin the hope for a more rights-respecting global order on human rights law. To grasp the point, Canadians need only look to the situation in which Canadian labour unions now find themselves. Once a strong and vigorous force in Canadian society that consistently was able to advance the rights of working people, Canadian labour is now a shadow of its former self, unable to do the work it was intended to do—a direct result of the onset of globalization. Although labour rights were upheld by a couple of important Supreme Court of Canada decisions,[35] no one would seriously suggest that labour has regained its former strength, and it is not likely to do so as long as governments are preoccupied with the competition for investment.

A final criticism is that judicial decisions arising from the Charter of Rights and Freedoms may infringe on the jurisdiction of the provincial governments. When former Prime Minister Pierre Trudeau was making the case for the Charter, he acknowledged that "an entrenched bill of rights" would place "some restrictions on the theory of legislative sovereignty." It would "restrain" the power of the federal and provincial governments "in favour of the Canadian citizen."[36] In other words, both levels of government would have to govern in conformity with the rights of citizens. There obviously would be some hedging in of jurisdictional autonomy, but neither level of government would gain powers at the expense of the other. Both would be subject to the rulings of the judiciary.

Nevertheless, some scholars insist that the Charter's erosion of the powers of provincial governments is highly problematic. Professor Jose Woehrling is one. He has argued that the Charter has exerted both a centralizing effect and a standardizing effect.[37] He says, for instance, that when the Supreme Court invalidated the Canadian citizenship requirement for admission to the BC Bar Association in *Andrews v. Law Society of BC* (1989), all the provinces amended their legislation to ensure consistency with the decision. Similarly, when in *Eldridge v. British Columbia* (1997), referred to earlier, the Court prescribed the kind of sign language interpretation a BC hospital had to provide in order to comply with section 15, all the other provinces had to follow suit. According to Woehrling, many other examples could be given.

The examples that Woehrling provides do not seem to represent onerous burdens on the provinces or heavy detractions from the provincial diversity benefit of federalism. They seem to be reasonable attempts to ensure some uniformity with respect to equality rights in a country that, while federal, is still one country.

F.L. Morton is another scholar concerned about the impact of the Charter on provincial autonomy. He argues that governments have been reluctant to adopt certain policies for fear of a Charter challenge. In other words, the Charter has had a "preemptive impact." All governments in Canada have lawyers, perhaps sections within departments of justice, that assess legislation in terms of its impact on the Charter. Charter screening processes, sometimes involving legislatures as well, ensure that the Charter's provisions are taken into account at the earliest stages of the policy and legislative process. In this way, the Charter's impact on federalism has been pronounced.[38]

The impact may be pronounced but one cannot conclude that restrictions on provincial policy autonomy have resulted in an enlargement of federal power. Rather, they may be said to have enlarged citizens' power. Further, it is not clear why Morton would object to a legislative drafting process that includes an assessment of a bill's ability to withstand a rights challenge. Why he would want the process to allow for passage of a bill that would possibly violate an individual's right is not clear.

Morton contends that the Charter has enabled certain groups, particularly the official-language minority groups but including, among others, women's rights, Aboriginal, and ethnocultural groups, "to use the courts to do an end-run around unfriendly provincial policies."[39] As a result, the de facto authority of the federal government has been strengthened while provincial autonomy has been reduced. This process was helped along by federal funding support of language and equality rights litigation. Thus the Charter "represents an institutional loss of policy autonomy for the provinces and a corollary empowerment of social interests favoured by the federal government."[40]

Morton's paper highlights the contestation between rights concerns and provincial autonomy concerns. On this there is room for honest disagreement. Morton is clearly on the side of provincial autonomy, but he conveys an uncompromising stance when he acknowledges the "various provinces' restrictive and unfriendly treatment of official language minority groups"[41] but does not at the same time allow that there are limits to provincial autonomy—limits that can be legitimately defined by a rights charter.

Rocher and Gilbert's criticism of the Charter's impact on provincial autonomy is directed at the relationship between the Supreme Court and federal politicians. They write,

> Furthermore, in the long run, the Court, whose members are appointed by the federal government without any provincial input, favours an increase in the political legitimacy of the central government's powers on account of the organic and institutional ties that bind members of the Supreme Court and federal politicians. Guy Laforest continues in the same vein: "The 1982 Charter deterritorializes conflicts, removes them from their provincial realms in order to place them in a pan-Canadian politico-judicial arena in which they are adjudicated by a Supreme Court that is an arm of the central state."[42]

The criticism is that the Supreme Court favours the federal government in Charter disputes for three reasons. One has to do with the lack of involvement of provincial governments in Supreme Court appointments. A second has to do with the ties between federal politicians and the Court. The third has to do with the Court as an "arm" of the central state.

With respect to the first reason, it is not accurate to say that the provincial governments have no input into the appointment of Supreme Court justices, as the following comment by Ian Peach explains:

> One must also realize that, while there is no formal process by which appointments to the Supreme Court of Canada are reviewed, an *informal but extensive process of consultation* and review of potential candidates has already developed in recent decades. Currently, when the federal minister of Justice wishes to identify a short list of candidates to fill a vacancy, he or she consults with the chief justice of the Supreme Court of Canada (and sometimes the other justices), *the chief justice(s) of the court(s) from the region with the vacancy, the attorney(s) general of the province(s) with the vacancy*, and at least one senior member of the Canadian Bar Association and the Law Society or societies of the province(s) with the vacancy.[43]

Here Peach makes clear that the attorney general of the relevant province is consulted, as well as the chief justice of the court from the relevant province. For the past several years, federal MPs have been involved, thus making possible further opportunities for provincial input into the appointment process.

The second reason identified by Rocher and Gilbert for the Court's alleged tendency to favour the federal government is based on the organic ties "that bind members of the Supreme Court and federal politicians." The authors do not make clear their meaning of "organic ties." The word *organic* is defined by *Webster's Universal College Dictionary* as "inherent" or "fundamental." If the authors are suggesting that Supreme Court justices and federal politicians share a similarity of outlook regarding federal power, notwithstanding occasional outbursts of judicial contrariness, that could be considered a generally positive thing. Deep, irreconcilable differences between federal political leaders and the high court would be indicative of an unhealthy level of divisiveness in the country.

In addition, if the works of Shapiro[44] and Bzdera[45] have any predictive value, one could argue that the ties that would bind the political elite and the judicial elite in a newly sovereign Quebec would also be "organic." The relationship between senior politicians and high court judges in an independent Quebec would likely be no different from the relationship that presently exists between them in Canada.

That said, it is also inaccurate to declare that the Supreme Court invariably favours the federal government. According to James Kelly, a scholar who specializes in the Charter, during the first five years of the Charter's existence, a higher percentage of provincial laws were invalidated because they infringed on a Charter right. However, from 1990 to 1997 that figure was reversed; a higher percentage of federal laws were invalidated. Since then, the balance has been generally even. As a result, Kelly concludes, "it has not been demonstrated empirically or substantively that Charter review has resulted in further centralization of the Canadian federation."[46] He adds, significantly: "Recent analysis suggests that the Supreme Court has demonstrated an appreciation of federal values such as diversity, and that this appreciation has significantly influenced the Court's approach in Charter cases."[47]

One factor not mentioned by Rocher and Gilbert is the impact of international human rights norms on rights issues in Canada. Consider, for instance, the dispute concerning the Quebec sign law. In *Ford v. Quebec* (1988), the Supreme Court of Canada struck down the sections of a Quebec law prohibiting the use of languages other than French on public signs, because they violated both the Canadian Charter of Rights and Freedoms and the Quebec Charter of Human Rights. In the view of the Court, a total restriction on other languages "could not be justified." The Quebec government, with the approval of the legislature, then invoked section 33 of the Charter (the so-called notwithstanding clause), which enables a federal or provincial government to enact a law even though it violates section 2 or sections 7–15 of the Charter if parliament or the legislature approves; the legislative override expires after five years but may be renewed, again if parliament or the legislature approves.[48]

Subsequently the Quebec law was considered by the United Nations Human Rights Committee, the treaty body that monitors compliance with the International Covenant on Civil and Political Rights. Like the Supreme Court of Canada, the Committee found the law to be an unreasonable infringement of freedom of expression. It stated, "A State may choose one or more official languages, but it may not exclude, outside the spheres of public life, the freedom to express oneself in a language of one's choice."[49]

The UN committee's comments show the Supreme Court ruling to have been a reasonable restriction on the policy autonomy of the Quebec government, one that served to protect a human right, not to enlarge the reach of the federal government. Further, assuming that a sovereign Quebec would accede to UN human rights treaties, the Committee's findings demonstrate that even an independent Quebec would not have unlimited policy autonomy.

With respect to Laforest's depiction of the Supreme Court as an "arm of the central state," it should be understood that (1) no high court is going to facilitate or preside over the dismantling of the state of which it is a part, and (2) no state is going to give a high court the power to break it up. As Martin Shapiro wrote, "No regime is likely to allow significant political power to be wielded by an isolated judicial corps free of political restraints."[50] As suggested earlier, an independent Quebec state, like other independent states, would doubtless seek to ensure that its judicial branch subscribed to the same set of political values as its executive and legislative branches.

Both Laforest's comment and Rocher and Gilbert's general criticism do not factor in the Supreme Court's opinions in two critically important reference cases, the Patriation Reference and the Secession Reference.[51] The stakes in both were exceptionally high, and in both the stance of the Court makes it difficult to accept that it is merely an "arm of the central state." In the Patriation Reference, the justices put the brakes on Prime Minister Trudeau's efforts to achieve his long-cherished goal of patriating the constitution and inserting a charter of rights into it. And it did so on highly questionable grounds—grounds that prompted the former prime minister to deliver a scathing denunciation of the decision in a public speech in 1991.[52] In the Secession Reference, the Court was asked to respond to three specific questions. It not only responded to those questions but also went on to lay out a path for secession! In yet another case, the Securities Reference (2011), the Court articulated a provincialist interpretation of Canadian federalism that I have argued elsewhere is not consistent with the constitution.[53]

The Chapters

The 19 chapters in this book have been written by 24 scholars drawn from political science, law, sociology, international relations, history, and anthropology. The selection of topics was based on two criteria. First, I wanted to include issues that were topical, such as the rights of migrant workers and freedom of religion, and those that were emerging, such as ageism, privacy, and human rights and climate change. Second, I wanted to de-emphasize the legal perspective on rights; hence the diversity in scholarly backgrounds, the three chapters on political institutions, and the inclusion in other chapters of discussions of the influence of political factors on the shaping of rights instruments and rights protection.

The collection is divided into four sections. Part One consists of two chapters that "set the table" for the remaining contributions; that is, they describe how the national and international rights instruments that protect Canadians came to be. Chapter 1, by Brooke Jeffrey, traces the evolution of human rights protection in Canada. She identifies some of the appalling rights-related episodes in Canadian history and traces the growing commitment of the country to human rights protection, beginning after the Second World War and highlighted by entrenchment of a charter of rights in the constitution in 1982. Chapter 2, by Roland Burke and James Kirby, provides an account of the origins of the UN's International Bill of Rights.[54] They argue that it had diverse origins and benefited significantly from non-Western contributions. Further, the drive for universal human rights that gained momentum from anti-colonialist, civil rights, and social democratic forces had to overcome much Western resistance, including American opposition to racial equality and economic and social rights.

In Part Two, the authors show the relationship between certain political institutions and rights protection. In Gordon DiGiacomo's chapter, the focus is on the controversy surrounding constitutional judicial review, as well as the rights-protective potential of executive structures, electoral systems, and political parties. In John Kincaid's, the focus is on federalism; he concludes that federalism can add value to rights protection by providing for the protection of both individual and communitarian rights. And in David Zarnett's contribution, the discussion centres around non-governmental human rights organizations. One of the difficult questions he addresses is this: how do such organizations exert influence in an international system replete with apparently more powerful actors, including states, international organizations, multinational corporations, and armed militant groups?

Part Three is the lengthiest section. Here the nine chapters address rights issues pertaining to specific communities. Chapter 6, by sociologist Tanya Basok, deals with the rights of temporary migrant workers in Canada. Basok outlines the forms of rights violations that these migrants experience and then discusses two legal frameworks—the citizenship rights framework and the international human rights framework—employed by migrant-rights activists to redress these violations.

Chapters 7 and 8, by Tara Collins and Christine Gervais and by Thomas Klassen respectively, pertain to the rights concerns of those on either end of the age spectrum. Collins and Gervais analyze the Convention on the Rights of the Child and, in a fascinating discussion, show the impacts on children of knowing their rights. In Chapter 8, Klassen sheds considerable light on ageism, particularly as it is practiced in the workplace. He points out that ageism is unique among the various grounds for discrimination: barring an early death, everyone will one day join the group of "old people," even though not all individuals will be members of a particular racial, religious, or ethnic group or of the same gender.

In Chapter 9, Gordon DiGiacomo and Tracie Scott distinguish between the right of self-government and the right of self-determination in the context of Aboriginal rights. They analyze an innovative model of the former, namely the Nisga'a Final Agreement, signed by representatives of the Nisga'a nation and the federal and British Columbia governments.

Chapter 10 is about the rights of persons with disabilities. Contributed by Deborah Stienstra, the chapter argues that, despite significant human rights protection, people with disabilities continue to experience disproportionately high levels of exclusion. She asks why this disparity between lived experience and human rights standards exists, and the extent to which human rights can be used to address the disparity.

In Chapter 11, Caroline Andrew points out the increasing complexity of our understanding of women's human rights, largely because of the growing importance of intersectionality[55] and the multiplicity of identities. Andrew looks at two policy areas—employment and violence against women—because in these two areas debates about intersectionality have been clearly present.

Chapter 12, by Karen Busby, explores how Canadian law reconciles religious rights claims and queer equality rights claims. She addresses two difficult questions: first, if one feels compelled by religious belief to speak out against homosexuality, should such expression be immune from hate expression laws? And should religiously mandated schools be compelled to permit gay–straight alliance groups to form and meet on their premises?

Chapter 13 is by Mahmood Monshipouri and Kelley O'Dell. It is a reflection on events in the Middle East, principally Egypt, Tunisia, Bahrain, and Syria. The authors point out that the growing impoverishment and inequality in the Middle East and North Africa will make emergence of human rights values very difficult, as citizens will naturally prioritize economic security. The temptation to support autocratic leaders who emphasize economic priorities at the expense of liberty will be very strong, and perhaps irresistible.

The final chapter of Part Three is by Melanie Adrian. In it she confronts the issue of religious freedom. After showing it to be one of the centrally protected rights guaranteed in several rights instruments, Adrian criticizes the European Court of Human Rights for failing to uphold religious freedom in three landmark decisions, in the process contradicting the way religious freedom has historically been understood.

In Part Four, the authors of the five chapters write on transversing rights issues: issues that affect most or all citizens. In Chapter 15, Susan Kang and Jennifer Rutledge wrestle with the existence of contradictory trends in socioeconomic rights: on the one hand there has been a reaffirmation of the importance of these rights, while on the other, financial crises and market forces have made states reluctant to take the necessary measures to protect them. In Chapter 16, Sara Seck and Kirsten Stefanik focus on human rights violations committed not by the state but by transnational corporations (TNCs). They identify the kinds of mechanisms that could be employed to prevent rights violations and to provide victims with a remedy. One interesting option is to expand the mandate of the International Criminal Court (ICC) to allow for prosecution of TNCs that do not conduct their activities in accordance with human rights norms.

The expansion of the ICC's mandate is also mentioned in Chapter 17, by Sam Adelman. His concern is with the effects of climate change on rights. Among other things, he assesses the idea of making ecocide—large-scale environmental destruction—a crime under the treaty that created the ICC. He concludes by predicting that human rights law will increasingly be called upon to provide justice to those affected by climate change.

In Chapter 18, Trevor Purvis looks at the way state measures to prevent terrorism have affected citizens' rights. For Purvis, the post-9/11 retreat from human rights commitments in the name of security represents a dangerous trajectory for the future of human rights. He contrasts the seismic reactions of Western governments to the 3,000 tragic and untimely deaths on 9/11 with their somewhat subdued reaction to the 30,000 deaths on the same day—and every day since—caused by hunger and poverty.

The book's final chapter, by Valerie Steeves, analyzes the impact on the protection of privacy rights of the bureaucratic desire to maximize efficiency and the commercial monetization of personal information. Steeves is highly critical of the anemic way by which governments seek to protect privacy rights.

Notes

1. J. Donnelly, *Universal Human Rights in Theory and Practice*, 3rd ed. (Ithaca, NY: Cornell University Press, 2013), 7.
2. R. Tremblay, J. Kelly, M. Lipson, and J.-F. Mayer, *Understanding Human Rights: Origins, Currents, and Critiques* (Toronto: Nelson, 2008), 3. Regarding the last sentence in the quotation, obviously convicted prisoners would have to surrender some of their rights.
3. M. Haas, *International Human Rights: A Comprehensive Introduction* (New York: Routledge, 2008), 3.
4. A. Brysk, "Introduction: Transnational Threats and Opportunities," in *Globalization and Human Rights*, ed. A. Brysk (Los Angeles: University of California Press, 2002), 3.
5. C. Sunstein, "Rights and Their Critics," *Notre Dame Law Review* 70, no. 4 (1995): 739.
6. M. Ignatieff, *The Rights Revolution* (Toronto: House of Anansi Press, 2007), 23.
7. J. Griffin, *On Human Rights* (Oxford: Oxford University Press, 2008), 95.
8. A. Altman, "Civil Rights," in *The Stanford Encyclopedia of Philosophy* (Summer 2013), ed. E.N. Zalta, http://plato.stanford.edu/entries/civil-rights.
9. Another right that may be described as a political is the right of self-determination. This right is the first one listed in both the International Covenant on Civil and Political Rights (ICCPR) and the International Covenant on Economic, Social and Cultural Rights (ICESCR). It is discussed at length in Chapter 9.

10. The right to own property may be referred to as a socioeconomic right, although Dominique Clément describes it as a civil right. See D. Clément, *Canada's Rights Revolution: Social Movements and Social Change, 1937–82* (Vancouver: UBC Press, 2008), 6.
11. Haas, *International Human Rights*, 354. For an interesting discussion of cultural rights, see L. Reidel, "What Are Cultural Rights? Protecting Groups with Individual Rights," *Journal of Human Rights* 9, no. 1 (2010): 65–80.
12. Taken from article 1 of the Aarhus Convention on Access to Information, Public Participation in Decision-Making and Access to Justice in Environmental Matters, 1998.
13. University of Minnesota Human Rights Resource Center, *Human Rights Here and Now: Celebrating the Universal Declaration of Human Rights*, ed. N. Flowers (Minneapolis, MN: Amnesty International USA, Human Rights Resource Center, and Stanley Foundation, 1998), http://www1.umn.edu/humanrts/edumat/hreduseries/hereandnow/Part-5/6_glossary.htm.
14. R. Sharpe and K. Roach, *The Charter of Rights and Freedoms*, 4th ed. (Toronto: Irwin Law, 2009), 368.
15. For an insightful analysis of individual and collective or group rights within the context of a discussion on cultural rights, see Reidel, "What Are Cultural Rights?" Another interesting discussion of group rights is offered by Sujit Choudhry in "Group Rights in Comparative Constitutional Law: Culture, Economics, or Political Power?" in *The Oxford Handbook of Comparative Constitutional Law*, ed. M. Rosenfeld and A. Sajó (Oxford: Oxford University Press, 2012).
16. M. Glendon, *Rights Talk: The Impoverishment of Political Discourse* (New York: Free Press, 1991), 75.
17. Sunstein, "Rights and Their Critics," 737.
18. Ibid., 745.
19. Ibid., 744.
20. Glendon, *Rights Talk*, 14.
21. Sunstein, "Rights and Their Critics," 746.
22. Ibid.
23. Ibid., 747.
24. *Eldridge v. British Columbia*, [1997] 3 S.C.R. 624.
25. *Chaoulli v. Quebec*, [2005] 1 S.C.R. 791.
26. *Reference re Public Service Employees Relations Act (Alta.)*, [1987] 1 S.C.R. 313, at para. 59.
27. This term refers to whether or not disputes about a right can be dealt with by the judiciary.
28. A. Nolan et al., "The Justiciability of Social and Economic Rights: An Updated Appraisal," Working Paper no. 15 (New York: Center for Human Rights and Global Justice, 2007), 6.
29. Ibid., 19–20. Another commentary in support of judicial recognition of socioeconomic rights is contained in L. Arbour and F. LaFontaine, "Beyond Self-Congratulation: The Charter at 25 in an International Perspective," *Osgoode Hall Law Journal* 45, no. 2 (2007).
30. R. Hirschl and E. Rosevear, "Constitutional Law Meets Comparative Politics: Socio-economic Rights and Political Realities," in *The Legal Protection of Human*

Rights: Sceptical Essays, ed. T. Campbell, K.D. Ewing, and A. Tomkins (Oxford: Oxford University Press, 2011), 213–14.

31. Ibid., 216.
32. T. Evans, *The Politics of Human Rights: A Global Perspective* (London: Pluto Press, 2005), 53.
33. Ibid., 31.
34. Ibid., 116.
35. Most notably in *Health Services and Support—Facilities Subsector Bargaining Assn v. British Columbia,* [2007] 2 S.C.R. 391.
36. Quoted in S. LaSelva, *The Moral Foundations of Canadian Federalism: Paradoxes, Achievements, and Tragedies of Nationhood* (Montreal: McGill-Queen's University Press, 1996), 89.
37. J. Woehrling, "The Canadian Charter of Rights and Freedoms and Its Consequences for Political and Democratic Life and the Federal System," in *Contemporary Canadian Federalism: Foundations, Traditions, Institutions*, ed. A.-G. Gagnon (Toronto: University of Toronto Press, 2009).
38. F.L. Morton, "The Effect of the Charter of Rights on Canadian Federalism," in *Publius* 25, no. 3 (Summer 1995): 177. The Harper government had been accused of using a less than rigorous process in assessing whether proposed legislation can withstand a Charter-based challenge. The accuser is a former Department of Justice official, and the Federal Court of Canada has agreed to hear his claims.
39. Ibid.
40. Ibid., 178.
41. Ibid.
42. F. Rocher and M.-C. Gilbert, "Re-federalizing Canada: Refocusing the Debate on Centralization," in *The Case for Decentralized Federalism*, ed. R. Hubbard and G. Paquet (Ottawa: University of Ottawa Press, 2010), 132–33.
43. I. Peach, "Legitimacy on Trial: The Appointment of Supreme Court Judges in Canada," *Optimum Online* 35, no. 1 (March 2005): 26, http://www.optimumonline.ca/article.phtml?e=mesokurj&id=219&page=1; emphasis added. See also I. Cotler, "An Unknown But Not a Secret Process: Appointment of Supreme Court Justices," *Canadian Parliamentary Review* 27, no. 2 (Summer 2004); and Standing Committee on Justice, Human Rights, Public Safety and Emergency Preparedness, *Improving the Supreme Court of Canada Appointments Process* (Ottawa: House of Commons, 2004).
44. M. Shapiro, *Courts: A Comparative and Political Analysis* (Chicago: University of Chicago Press, 1981).
45. A. Bzdera, "Comparative Analysis of Federal High Courts: A Political Theory of Judicial Review," *Canadian Journal of Political Science* 26, no. 1 (March 1993).
46. J. Kelly, "The Courts, the Charter, and Federalism," in *Canadian Federalism: Performance, Effectiveness, and Legitimacy*, 2nd ed., ed. H. Bakvis and G. Skogstad (Toronto: Oxford University Press, 2008), 46.
47. Ibid. If this is the case, one might legitimately wonder if it is a good thing. Is it in the best interests of citizens to have federalism concerns trump rights concerns?
48. The Quebec government did not renew use of the notwithstanding clause and adopted the formula suggested by the Supreme Court.

49. *Ballantyne, Davidson, McIntyre v. Canada*, communications 359/1989 and 385/1989, UN Doc. CCPR/C/47/D/359/1989 and 385/1989/Rev. 1 (1993), para. 11.4.
50. Shapiro, *Courts*, 34.
51. Formally known respectively as *Reference re Amendment of Constitution of Canada*, [1981] 1 S.C.R. 753, and *Reference re Secession of Quebec*, [1998] 2 S.C.R. 217.
52. The speech is contained in P.E. Trudeau, *Against the Current: Selected Writings 1939–1996*, ed. G. Pelletier (Toronto: McClelland and Stewart, 1996), 246–61.
53. See DiGiacomo, "The Supreme Court of Canada's Federalism as Expressed in the Securities Reference and the Secession Reference," *Journal of Parliamentary and Political Law* 8, no. 1 (March 2014).
54. The Bill consists of the Universal Declaration of Human Rights, the International Covenant on Civil and Political Rights, and the International Covenant on Economic, Social and Cultural Rights.
55. *Intersectionality* refers to the interplay of race, ethnicity, gender, class, and other axes of identity in reinforcing patterns of domination.

PART ONE

1
The Evolution of Human Rights Protection in Canada

BROOKE JEFFREY

Learning Objectives

- To become familiar with the historical development of the human rights institutions that protect Canadians
- To understand why those human rights institutions emerged

This chapter examines the way in which the concept of human rights evolved and was given effect in Canada through the introduction of federal and provincial legislation, the entrenchment of a Charter of Rights and Freedoms in the constitution, and the country's accession to numerous international human rights conventions. In doing so, it will highlight the difficulties caused by the original lack of a constitutionally entrenched bill of rights and amending formula, as well as the complications posed by the federal nature of the political system.

The chapter begins with an analysis of early formal discrimination on the part of federal and provincial governments, despite a relatively high degree of societal tolerance, before turning to the implementation of provincial and federal human rights legislation and the creation of human rights commissions in the postwar era and the introduction of a statutory bill of rights. A fourth section outlines Canada's increasing commitment to international human rights instruments such as declarations, covenants, and conventions, and the fifth part demonstrates how this, along with internal pressures related to federalism, led to eventual entrenchment of the Charter of Rights and Freedoms in the Constitution Act, 1982. A sixth section explores some of the implications of the Charter's coming into force, while a final section outlines new and emerging rights issues in Canada.

Early History: Tolerance and Official Discrimination

Unlike most Western democracies, Canada did not have a formal bill of rights entrenched in its constitution at the outset, primarily because of its British colonial heritage. Although some scholars argued for the existence of an implied bill of rights, based on the claim that our constitution was similar in nature to that of Britain, the argument did not prove compelling in terms of court decisions, and the fact remained that the lack of an entrenched bill of rights posed significant constraints. Moreover, given the absence of an amending formula, the possibility of retroactively entrenching such a bill of rights in the constitution was long viewed as extremely unlikely.

There were, however, a number of specific guarantees in the Constitution Act, 1867, regarding language and religion, which constitutional scholar Peter Hogg has described as a "small bill of rights" and which were a significant factor in the evolution of the concept of human rights in Canada.[1] For example, section 133 guaranteed language rights, inasmuch as it provided for bilingualism in the federal parliament and the provincial legislature of Quebec, as well as allowing for records to be kept in both languages and authorizing bilingualism in federal and Quebec courts. This provision has also been cited for the requirement that all statutes and delegated legislation must be in both languages and have equal force. Similarly, assigning to the provinces exclusive jurisdiction for education and guaranteeing government support for Catholic school systems (s. 93), as well as ensuring that three of the nine seats on the Supreme Court came from Quebec (with its civil law rather than British common law base), were considered important indicators of early rights protection. Indeed, given the period and the British military victory that resulted in the takeover of New France, the concessions to minority rights have been rightly described by former Quebec premier Jean Charest as remarkably tolerant.[2]

Nevertheless there were few concrete guarantees of civil rights for the first century after Confederation, and in keeping with the times, those few that did exist were typically sanctions found in the Criminal Code. The use of other human rights instruments, and in fact the broader concept of human rights itself, developed only after the Second World War, as discussed below.

Still, as a New World democracy with a significant immigrant population, Canada was viewed almost from its inception as a tolerant pluralist society. For example, with the abolition of slavery in the British Empire in 1833, Canada became a well-known refuge for black slaves fleeing the United States via the Underground Railway. Similarly, the guarantees of religious freedom and the provision of state funding for Catholic schools were viewed at the time as a model of accommodation.[3] This image of tolerance was heightened when immigration was actively encouraged by early federal governments as a means of settling the west, to establish Canadian hegemony over vast stretches of country between the original eastern colonies and British Columbia.

But this settlement was not always achieved without friction, as evidenced by the Riel Rebellions of 1885 and 1869. Moreover, incidents such as the Orange–Catholic riots in Toronto in 1858, and the presence of Ku Klux Klan chapters in southern Saskatchewan and Alberta during the Great Depression of the 1930s, demonstrate that there were limits to societal tolerance. Indeed, these limitations were evident from the beginning, with respect to the prejudicial treatment of Aboriginal peoples and in the unequal status accorded to black Loyalists arriving in Atlantic Canada. And, as with virtually all Western democracies of the time, women were relegated to the status of second-class citizens in society until well into the twentieth century. For example, women were not eligible to vote in federal elections until 1918, and it was not until the Persons Case of 1929 that women were legally considered to be persons under the constitution and consequently eligible for appointment to the Senate. (Meanwhile, although status Indians were allowed to vote after Confederation, they could do so only if they renounced their status, a situation that was not remedied until 1960.) It must therefore be recognized that both the federal and provincial governments were guilty of enacting discriminatory legislation in those early years, although incidents resulting from such formal government policy were relatively few in comparison with many other Western democracies of the day.

One of the most significant examples of official government discrimination was the introduction of the Chinese head tax, a measure introduced after more than 15,000 "temporary" workers from China had been recruited for the arduous task of building the transcontinental railroad to British Columbia. The workers were paid less than half the wage of their Canadian counterparts, and many died during the construction. Nevertheless, when the railroad was completed, their continued presence in BC—where roughly 3,000 of the railway survivors resided—was viewed as a particular threat, since they represented almost 10 per cent of the total population. In response to provincial pressure, the Government of Canada passed the 1885 Chinese Immigration Act. This legislation required any potential immigrant from China to first pay a $50 fee, later known as a head tax. The amount was designed to be prohibitive and to discourage future immigration from China. Nevertheless, enough hopeful immigrants were able to pay the tax that the government was obliged to increase the amount repeatedly; it reached a maximum of $500 in 1903. (By the time it was abolished the government had collected some $23 million—roughly $308 million in 2014 dollars—from 81,000 head-tax payers.) The legislation was patently racist, particularly as it came during a time when the federal government was deliberately recruiting "white" immigrants from Europe to settle the west, including a record 400,000 in 1913 alone. The head tax was finally repealed in 1923, but only because the government had passed the Chinese Immigration Act, which eliminated virtually all immigration from China. That legislation in turn was not repealed until 1947.

A second example of the federal government's discriminatory behaviour toward Asian immigrants can be found in its treatment of some 375 Sikhs and a small number of Muslims, who arrived in Canada in 1914 from the Punjab aboard a Japanese ship, the *Komagata Maru*. Unlike the Chinese, Indian citizens were British subjects and could not be refused entry outright. As a result, some 3,000 Sikhs had already immigrated from the Punjab to British Columbia, and the federal government was under considerable pressure from the provincial government and citizen groups to stem the tide. As a result it had introduced regulations in 1908 that prohibited the immigration of persons who had not come to Canada directly from their home country or who had not purchased their entire passage before leaving their home country. This refinement was aimed directly at Indians from the Punjab, who, because of the great distance, would almost invariably have to proceed in stages. But in 1913 a group of 38 Sikh immigrants had arrived in Canada and successfully challenged the so-called Asian exclusion legislation in the courts. This led a wealthy entrepreneur, Gurdit Singh, to try to do the same. He leased the *Komagata Maru* and arranged for it to sail from Hong Kong to Vancouver after collecting passengers in various Indian cities. However, when the ship arrived in Vancouver in May 1914, it was prevented from entering the harbour by federal immigration officials, urged on by local politicians. The vessel spent two months anchored off the coast while Singh and others continued their efforts to obtain the right to land. In July the government used military troops to force the *Komagata Maru* to depart, citing its non-compliance with the exclusion regulations. On its return to Calcutta, several of the passengers were arrested by British troops, a riot ensued, and many passengers were killed.

Both of these incidents have recently been the subject of redress claims and demands for official apologies from the federal government. Although previous governments offered collective measures such as monuments or museums, they had expressed concern about setting a precedent if individual compensation were offered. Several court decisions confirmed that the government was under no legal obligation to do so. Nevertheless, in June 2006 Prime Minister Stephen Harper fulfilled an election commitment by offering an apology for the head tax in the House of Commons and providing financial compensation for survivors or their spouses. In August 2008, Harper also issued an apology for the government's handling of the *Komagata Maru* incident, "on behalf of the government of Canada," while attending an event at a Sikh temple in British Columbia. His government also provided some $2.5 million to the Indo-Canadian community to erect commemorative symbols.

A third noteworthy example of government-sponsored discrimination involved the rejection of Jewish refugees during the Second World War. As revealed in numerous accounts of official activities, anti-Semitism was relatively common among Canadian bureaucrats and politicians of the day.[4] Indeed, Canada accepted only 5,000 Jewish refugees between 1933 and 1948, the lowest number of any Western country. The most blatant example of such anti-Semitism was the Canadian government's 1939 decision to refuse entry into Halifax of MS *St. Louis*, a German vessel carrying some 937 Jewish refugees from Nazi Germany. The ship was forced to return to Europe, where many of the passengers perished during the Holocaust. No official apology was ever requested, but the Canadian government and the Canadian Jewish Congress recently unveiled a monument to the *St. Louis* at the national immigration museum, Pier 21, in Halifax.

A final important example of official discrimination also occurred during the Second World War. More than 22,000 Japanese Canadians, 14,000 of whom had been born in Canada, were arbitrarily interned without hearing after the Japanese entered the war by bombing Pearl Harbor in December 1941. A large Japanese-Canadian community had developed in British Columbia in the previous two decades; many individuals were prosperous fishermen and businessmen. But lingering racism had prevented them from being allowed to vote, and their economic success was widely resented. The federal government was again pressured to take action, despite reports from the RCMP that these individuals did not pose a security threat. On 24 February 1942, regulations were passed as part of the Defence of Canada Regulations of the War Measures Act that gave the federal government the power to intern all "persons of Japanese racial origin" and established a "protected" strip 100 miles wide along the Pacific coast. Initially all men of Japanese origin between the ages of 14 and 45 who were living in the area were removed, but soon their families were obliged to follow. Their forcible detention and displacement to communities in the BC interior and the prairies continued until 1949, when they were released but not compensated for their lost property, which had been confiscated and sold to pay for their internment.[5] In 1988 the Brian Mulroney government officially apologized for those earlier federal actions and offered a combination of individual and community compensation. In 1997 the Canadian Race Relations Foundation was established as part of the compensation agreement between the Mulroney government and the Association of Japanese Canadians.

Meanwhile a number of legal cases also arose from accusations of discrimination in provincial legislation in the era before the Second World War.

Perhaps the most well-known and significant involved the government of the province of Manitoba and its attempts to eliminate various guarantees of religious and linguistic rights in the late nineteenth century. These efforts were motivated primarily by changing demographics, the result of an influx of anglophone Protestants from Ontario and a dramatic decline in francophone Catholic Métis, who had left the province to move westward. The provincial government's initial removal of provisions for a publicly financed Catholic education system and for French as an official language caused outrage in the province and political upheaval both in Quebec and at the federal level. A series of conflicting decisions by the Canadian Supreme Court and the British Judicial Committee of the Privy Council (the JCPC, the ultimate court of appeal until 1949), based exclusively on jurisdictional concerns, further complicated the situation. The result was a political crisis that was resolved only by informal negotiations between Prime Minister Wilfrid Laurier and Manitoba Premier Thomas Greenway.[6] Certainly the so-called Manitoba schools crisis demonstrated once again the importance of these minority rights in the evolution of Canadian thinking on human rights in general. (In addition, the approach taken in the compromise solution arguably foreshadowed the wording of the 1969 federal Official Languages Act, which required provision of bilingual services "where numbers warrant.")

Then, in the early twentieth century, several western provinces introduced discriminatory legislative measures directed primarily against Asian immigrants, most of which were found by the courts to be constitutional. For example, in the case of *Cunningham v. Homma* (1903), BC legislation prohibiting people of Japanese descent from voting was declared constitutional because it fell within provincial jurisdiction. Similarly, in *Quong Wing v. R.* (1914), a Saskatchewan law preventing Chinese businesses from hiring "white" women was ruled valid for the same reason. There were also several noteworthy cases of religious discrimination, epitomized by the treatment of Jehovah's Witnesses in Ontario and Quebec, as well as the "Padlock Law" (1937), which outlawed communism, and various statutes authorizing mandatory commercial closures on Roman Catholic holidays.[7]

As all of these cases demonstrate, in the absence of a constitutional bill of rights, most court decisions were still based solely on jurisdictional legitimacy. As a result, the federal nature of the Canadian political system again posed an additional constraint on the evolution of rights legislation. Indeed, one decision specifically noted that "both Parliament and the provinces could validly limit freedom of worship providing they did so in the course of legislating on some other subject which lay within their respective powers."[8]

The Adoption of Modern Provincial and Federal Human Rights Mechanisms

Both public opinion and the attitudes of governments changed significantly in the aftermath of the Second World War. During the war, the Allies had identified the defence of "four freedoms" as their underlying purpose, namely freedom of speech, freedom of religion, freedom from fear, and freedom from want. With the creation of the United Nations in 1945, its charter "reaffirmed faith in fundamental human rights, and dignity and worth of the human person," and committed all member states to promote "universal respect for, and observance of, human rights and fundamental freedoms for all without distinction as to race, sex, language, or religion."

Nevertheless, many believed it was necessary to spell out the specific rights that were considered inherent for all individuals and encompassed by the terms *human rights* and *fundamental freedoms* in the organization's charter. These rights were subsequently included in a document drafted by Canadian law professor John Peters Humphrey (then director of human rights at the UN Secretariat) and his team. The Universal Declaration of Human Rights contained some 30 articles covering political and legal (civil) rights and economic, social, and cultural rights.

In December 1948 the UN member states, including Canada, overwhelmingly voted to adopt the Universal Declaration of Human Rights. It soon became the foundational text on which numerous international human rights conventions, regional treaties, and even national constitutions were based. Perhaps its most significant contribution was the fact that it altered thinking on human rights issues, first by expanding the range and context of rights protection, and second by promoting a proactive approach to rights. In addition to the pre-existing use of the courts and criminal sanctions—the common approach in Canada and elsewhere before the war—legislation *promoting* various rights and freedoms was increasingly becoming an accepted part of the human rights infrastructure.

It was in this climate of enhanced social consciousness and growing awareness of human rights issues that the Ontario government introduced the Racial Discrimination Act of 1944 and the Saskatchewan government tabled the Bill of Rights Act in 1947. Although both were important, they were nevertheless quasi-legal statutes that once again declared certain acts to be illegal and imposed sanctions, most notably fines. However, the BC government's introduction of the Social Assistance Act of 1945 took another direction. In effect it marked the beginning of the modern era of human rights protection in Canada, when both the federal and provincial governments began to adopt a variety of proactive mechanisms to protect and promote human rights outside of the Criminal Code.

While the adoption of a constitutionally entrenched charter of rights—one that would provide protection for citizens from the discriminatory actions of governments—was still considered an unlikely development, the immediate postwar era saw Canadian governments introduce statutory human rights legislation that would protect citizens from discriminatory acts on the part of the private sector. Based on a model introduced in the state of New York in 1945, the province of Ontario introduced the Fair Accommodation Act (1951) and the Fair Employment Practices Act (1954).[9] Over the next 15 years virtually all the other provinces followed suit. Over time, additional provincial acts were introduced to cover such areas as the provision of services, property rental, and occupancy. These measures were all well-received. As early as 1947, national public opinion polls demonstrated that some 64 per cent of Canadians approved of this type of legislation.[10]

Within a decade, the existence of so many disparate pieces of legislation led to the inevitable conclusion that both efficiency and efficacy would be heightened if the various acts were consolidated. Again Ontario led the way, with the introduction of a Human Rights Code in 1962. Within little more than a decade, all the provinces had taken the same approach, creating human rights acts or codes covering the full range of anti-discrimination legislation: Alberta (1972), British Columbia (1973), Manitoba (1975), New Brunswick (1973), Newfoundland (1970), Nova Scotia (1969), Prince Edward Island (1975), Quebec (1975), and Saskatchewan (1972).

In addition, all the provinces created a body to administer these acts. Most established a human rights commission, some created a human rights tribunal or agency, and others provided for both mechanisms. As the first chair of the Ontario Human Rights Commission, Dr. Dan Hill, once noted, the purpose of these mechanisms was twofold: first, to enforce anti-discrimination legislation and impose sanctions when necessary; and second and equally important, to educate, inform, and persuade—essentially to bring about attitudinal change.[11] As a result, the operation of the various provincial commissions and tribunals was very similar. An aggrieved individual would lay a complaint and the appropriate commission would first determine whether there were grounds to proceed. If so, the most common approach was conciliation, followed only if necessary by adjudication and, ultimately, legal measures such as financial compensation orders, penal sanctions, or injunctions. However, legal measures were seen as a last-ditch option and rarely used. Most complaints were, and are still, resolved through mediation and conciliation.

Two specific issues should be noted with respect to these provincial mechanisms. First, the specific grounds for an individual to lay a claim were not standardized, and this continues to be the case, since the legislation falls under provincial jurisdiction. For example, some jurisdictions include political beliefs, disability, or marital status as prohibited grounds of discrimination, while others do not. At present the Quebec Charter of Human Rights and Freedoms is unique among Canadian (and North American) human rights documents because it includes not only the fundamental civil and political rights but also several social and economic rights.[12] As a result, the list of prohibited grounds is the most extensive in Canada, including the traditional grounds, such as race, colour, ethnic or national origin, religion, sex, language, handicap, sexual orientation, marital status, and age, as well as pregnancy, civil status, political conviction, and social condition. It should also be noted that in 1977, Quebec became the first jurisdiction in North America to recognize sexual orientation as a prohibited ground.

At the same time it is important to underline that the grounds covered by the provincial legislation in almost all jurisdictions have expanded over time. In several instances, a particular case has served to draw attention to a legal lacuna or an emerging issue. One noteworthy example was the case of a gay racing steward, John Damien, who was fired by the Ontario Jockey Club immediately after it learned of his sexual orientation. Several legal opinions concluded that the existing ground of gender did not cover the situation, and as a result the additional ground of sexual orientation was added to the Ontario Human Rights Code in 1986.

A second issue that has been raised in virtually all jurisdictions is that of legal exceptions. For example, the concept of a bona fide occupational requirement has become a well-accepted legal principle. The decisions in a number of specific cases have defined the scope and application of the term. One of the most well-known is *Bhinder* (1985), which involved the requirement to wear a hard hat for safety reasons, a requirement that was upheld. Two more recent well-known cases were *Meiorin* (1999), a case involving the physical requirements for firefighters in BC, which the Supreme Court ruled were not reasonable or essential, and *Grismer* (1999), which involved physical disability restrictions that the court also rejected. The two decisions clearly established the principle of the "duty to accommodate" as part of human rights protection in Canada.

Meanwhile, at the federal level, the government initially continued to pursue additional rights protection through the Criminal Code. For example, in 1966 the Special Committee on Hate Propaganda (also called the Cohen Committee), which had been established by the federal government, issued its report. The recommendations of the Cohen Committee led to the introduction of several Criminal Code amendments prohibiting incitement to genocide and hatred, as well as the distribution of hate propaganda.

The changes were made in response to the growing presence in Canada of white supremacist and neo-Nazi groups originating in the United States that were distributing anti-Semitic and anti-black material. However, the threshold for charges under the provisions was high, and little practical use was made of these measures.[13]

Then in 1977 the Canadian Human Rights Act was introduced. Like its provincial counterparts, it provided protection from discrimination by private-sector actors, in this case in areas falling under federal regulation, such as transportation, telecommunications, and banking. The Act also established a Human Rights Commission, to investigate and offer redress to complainants through mediation and conciliation, and a Human Rights Tribunal, to adjudicate cases that could not be resolved through the Commission process. In addition, the Act provided for the Commission to administer section 13, which prohibited telephone communications that were "likely to expose a person or persons to hatred or contempt by reason of the fact that that person or those persons are identifiable on the basis of a prohibited ground of discrimination." This alternative to the Criminal Code approach to hate literature was considered far more successful, and a number of cases were handled by the Commission and the Tribunal over the next two decades.

Over time the Canadian Human Rights Commission also developed an extensive research capability as part of its ongoing efforts to identify new and emerging areas of discrimination and rights conflicts. Some areas explored in recent reports include mental illness, family status, and the situation of Aboriginal Canadians. The Commissioner, as an officer of parliament, is also mandated to table an annual report in parliament, and these reports have contained both statistical analysis of complaints and detailed surveys and reports on specific issues, all of which arguably expanded both governmental and public understanding of human rights. Several commissioners, including the first Chief Commissioner, Gordon Fairweather, urged the adoption of amendments to the Act to expand the grounds for claims. Currently the Act prohibits discrimination on 11 grounds, namely race, ethnic origin, colour, religion, age, sex, sexual orientation, marital status, family status, disability, and a conviction for which a pardon has been granted or a record suspended.

A recent issue that gained considerable attention is the alleged conflict between the anti-hate-speech provision of the Act (s. 13) and the concept of freedom of speech.[14] Originally introduced in the 1977 legislation, the scope of section 13 was expanded by Parliament in 1996 to capture technological advances such as the Internet and developments in the mass media. Since 2007, several court cases have dealt with challenges to the Commission based on the issue of rights conflict, and the Commission itself solicited expert opinion. The Canadian Bar Association and numerous academics argued in favour of retaining the provision, albeit with certain modifications, and the Supreme Court ruled unanimously in *Whatcott* (2013) that similar restrictions on free speech in the corresponding Saskatchewan Human Rights Act were justified. However, a 2012 private member's bill was tabled in the House of Commons that moved to strike section 13 from the Canadian Human Rights Act. The bill passed in both the House and the Senate, and, in July 2013, section 13 was repealed.[15]

A second current issue relates to the Commission's role in administering and enforcing the Employment Equity Act in federally regulated industries. Under the Act, the Commission is responsible for promoting equality in the workplace for four designated groups—women, Aboriginal peoples, persons with disabilities, and members of visible minorities—by conducting compliance audits to ensure that employers meet the requirements of the Act. Recently, however, the role and procedures of the Commission have been criticized, and the scope of the Act itself, although already quite narrow (affecting an estimated 6 per cent of the workforce), has been further limited through government amendments reducing the number of businesses captured under the federal contractors' provisions.

The Canadian Bill of Rights

While the early efforts to establish human rights legislation described above were being carried out in various provinces to protect citizens from the actions of the private sector, the federal government of Prime Minister John Diefenbaker was intent on providing Canadians with protection from the activities of governments themselves. No doubt influenced by both the Saskatchewan Bill of Rights of 1947 (Diefenbaker represented a Saskatchewan riding) and the adoption of the Universal Declaration of Human Rights by the United Nations the following year, Diefenbaker was determined to introduce a federal bill of rights. In 1950, as an opposition MP, he had already given a speech in which he declared that such a bill was needed "to take a forthright stand against discrimination based on colour, creed or racial origin."[16]

Recognizing the difficulties of achieving a constitutionally entrenched bill, however, he decided to proceed with what he considered to be a "quasi-constitutional" statute. The result was the Canadian Bill of Rights, which came into effect in 1960. The Bill applied to federal jurisdiction. It was intended to protect numerous traditional civil and political rights—such as freedom of speech and religion—and enumerated grounds against discrimination that included those mentioned in Diefenbaker's 1950 speech, many of which are now entrenched in the Charter of Rights and Freedoms.

It also contained a section guaranteeing property rights, which is not in the Charter, and an exclusion clause that arguably formed the basis of the notwithstanding clause in the Charter.

Unfortunately, a number of seminal court decisions soon demonstrated that the Bill had serious limitations. First and foremost, of course, it was not embedded in the constitution and therefore was not automatically supreme. As a result, its status vis-à-vis other statutes was in question, despite Diefenbaker's belief that it would take precedence. In addition, it neither amended existing statutes that were found to be in conflict nor explicitly provided that conflicting statutes should be understood to operate notwithstanding the Bill. In such situations the courts were often inclined to fall back on the conventional judicial interpretation, which typically favoured the older statute and would consider the newer one to intend only minimal change. Nevertheless, the courts were not obliged to follow that pattern; lacking clear direction in the legislation, they could also decide to interpret provisions literally.

Three cases clearly demonstrated this difficulty. In *Drybones* (1969), a provision of the Indian Act regarding the consumption of alcohol was struck down by the Supreme Court because it was considered to discriminate on the basis of race, and therefore was in violation of the Canadian Bill of Rights. But in the second and third cases, *Lavell* and *Bédard* (1974), the Court decided that section 12(1)(b) of the Indian Act did not violate the respondents' right to "equality before the law" under section 1(b) of the Canadian Bill of Rights. The two respondents, Lavell and Bédard, had argued that the section was discriminatory because it deprived status Indian women of their status when they married non-Indians but did not do the same for Indian men. Here the court ruled that the Indian Act took precedence. As legal scholar Robert Kerr concluded, "Obviously these cases are logically inconsistent. ... In consequence they lead to the conclusion that judicial interpretation of the right to equality before the law under the Canadian Bill of Rights at the present time is not merely in a state of uncertainty, which is likely to be a perpetual condition in view of the inherent vagueness of the concept, but indeed in a state of profound confusion."[17] This confusion was heightened with the decision in *Bliss* (1979), when the Supreme Court found that the Unemployment Insurance Act did not discriminate on the basis of sex, since only a subcategory of women—those who were pregnant—was affected by a certain provision.

All these decisions were controversial. Needless to say, they also reinforced the belief that only a constitutionally entrenched bill of rights could provide the hoped-for protection. Even then it would clearly be necessary to pay close attention to the wording of the Court's decisions in these cases to avoid similar results. But during the 1970s the federal government was not contemplating any action on that front. Instead it was actively proceeding with negotiations with the provinces in order for Canada to become a signatory to international human rights covenants and protocols introduced at the United Nations. These documents represented completion of the basic human rights instruments originally envisaged by the drafters of the Universal Declaration of Human Rights, namely a four-part international bill of human rights consisting of the Universal Declaration; the International Covenant on Economic, Social, and Cultural Rights; the International Covenant on Civil and Political Rights; and the optional protocols. The General Assembly had adopted the two Covenants in 1966, but they did not come into force until 1976, when they had been ratified by a sufficient number of individual nations.

Accession to International Human Rights Covenants and Conventions

Immediately following the Second World War, Canada and other UN member states ratified the Convention on the Prevention and Punishment of Genocide (1952), which for obvious reasons was not considered controversial, nor was it considered problematic in terms of domestic legislation. However, with the UN's adoption of the International Human Rights Covenants on Political and Civil Rights and Economic, Social, and Cultural Rights in 1966, Canada was again challenged by institutional constraints, this time with regard to the federal nature of the system. Both conventions covered a much broader and less clear-cut range of rights that could potentially have a significant impact on domestic laws and practices; this concern was especially prevalent in terms of the economic, social, and cultural rights covenant.[18] Although the signing of foreign treaties was clearly the prerogative of the federal government, it was also true that the federal government could not guarantee compliance of all provincial legislation with these international treaties, since the provinces were masters of their own legislation in their areas of exclusive jurisdiction. And, unlike the earlier conventions, these instruments not only had potential implications for Canadian legislation but also required preparation of regular progress reports by member states.

It should be noted that the federal government's concerns about the need for provincial consultation and cooperation were well-founded. Before the JCPC was removed as the final court of appeal, it rejected various efforts by the federal government to establish elements of an American-style "New Deal" as being *ultra vires.* While the JCPC clearly stated that the federal government had the authority to sign treaties, it also concluded that the federal government could not force provinces to implement legislation in their areas of jurisdiction. The so-called Labour Conventions Case of 1936–37 resulted in a lengthy delay in Canada's adoption of many programs of the welfare state, and an abiding caution on the part of the federal government about venturing into areas of possible provincial jurisdiction.

In addition, it is important to note that Canada—like Germany and many other Commonwealth countries—has adopted a "dualist" legal approach to international human rights treaties. Rather than incorporating the treaty directly into domestic legislation, this approach focuses on ensuring that the existing panoply of legislation and programs, taken together, will achieve the objectives of the treaty, and, if necessary, on removing any legislation that may be considered a hindrance to compliance. As a result, a thorough examination of existing legislation at both the federal and provincial levels becomes an essential element of the process of human rights treaty ratification and implementation in Canada.[19]

Two alternative approaches to treaty ratification were consequently debated within the federal government by an interdepartmental committee that included officials from the Departments of Justice, Foreign Affairs, and Secretary of State (now Canadian Heritage) before signing the two international human rights covenants. Either the federal government could sign the treaties and then work toward achieving full compliance, or it could conduct negotiations with the provinces to ensure their full cooperation and legislative compliance before ratification. In the end, the latter route was chosen.

Federal-provincial cooperation was then facilitated by holding a Federal-Provincial Conference of Ministers Responsible for Human Rights in 1975. On 12 December 1975 the ministers agreed to establish specific provisions for ratifying, implementing, and reporting on these international human rights instruments. First, they agreed that prior consultations would take place before the signing of any such instrument. Second, they agreed that Canada's reporting on any instrument would consist of a federal report and 10 reports prepared independently by each province. Although Canada would have the responsibility for presenting the reports to the United Nations, they also agreed that any province would be entitled to assign a representative to the Canadian delegation for meetings where the report would be discussed. And finally, they agreed that, in the event of international criticism of a provincial law or institution, the province in question would have the opportunity to defend that law or institution itself. (This condition was put into practice when the UN Human Rights Committee criticized the Government of Ontario's support for a separate Catholic school system.) The conference also established the Continuing Committee of Officials on Human Rights, to be chaired by the Secretary of State (later Heritage) Department, which had the lead role on human rights domestically and was where the Human Rights Program was located. This program continues to act as the permanent secretariat for the Committee and the facilitator of information exchange.

As a result of these negotiations, Canada was among the last member states to ratify the two conventions, which it did in May 1976. Since then Canada has ratified five other major UN human rights instruments, including the Convention on the Elimination of All Forms of Discrimination Against Women (1981), the Convention on the Rights of the Child (1991) and its Optional Protocol (2005), the Convention Against Torture (1987), the Convention Against Racial Discrimination (1970), and the Convention on the Rights of Persons with Disabilities (2010).

Canada has also played a positive role within the United Nations itself for much of the past 60 years. In particular, several prominent Canadians have served in a variety of senior administrative capacities in human rights agencies. For example, from 2004 to 2008, former Supreme Court Justice Louise Arbour served as the UN High Commissioner for Human Rights. Likewise, former Canadian human rights commissioner Max Yalden served on the United Nations Human Rights Commission from 1996 to 2004. Earlier, Maurice Strong, a former president of the Canadian International Development Agency, had served as the first executive director of the United Nations Environmental Program (UNEP), from 1973 to 1975.

In a similar vein, Canadian foreign affairs minister Lloyd Axworthy was instrumental in obtaining international support for an independent, permanent International Criminal Court. The Rome Statute, adopted in July 1998, established the legal basis for the court, which is located in the Hague. Its first president was Canadian bureaucrat Philippe Kirsch, who served from 2003 to 2009. In June 2000, Canada became the first country to adopt the Crimes Against Humanity and War Crimes Act, an atypical but necessary precondition for ratification of the Rome Statute, to which Canada acceded in July 2000.

However, in recent years the application of some UN conventions to situations in Canada has become unexpectedly controversial. For example, in their arguments regarding the case of Omar Khadr (a Canadian citizen and child soldier imprisoned at Guantánamo for many years), numerous lawsuits made reference not only to the obligations of the federal government under the Charter of Rights and Freedoms but also to the obligations flowing from its accession to the Convention on the Rights of the Child.[20] Similarly, the government's handling of prisoners during the Afghan war led to concerns about its commitments under the Convention Against Torture, while recent legislation introduced by the federal government concerning what it has termed "bogus" refugees and "queue jumpers" has been criticized for potential conflict with the Convention Relating to the Status of Refugees. However, as noted above, while such treaties have considerable influence through moral suasion, they do not have the force of law in Canada and consequently have little or no direct impact on judicial decisions; a government is essentially free to ignore such implications.

Meanwhile, Canada's federal system has played an ongoing role in the federal government's reluctance to accede to several other UN conventions, most notably the Migrant Workers' Convention and the Enforced Disappearance Convention, both of which are opposed by several provinces. Similarly, Canada has signed relatively few of the International Labour Organization (ILO) treaties, in large measure because of provincial opposition, although here the reluctance can also be attributed to the fact that economic and social rights are primary concerns.[21]

At the same time, Canada's participation in various international human rights organizations and accession to a number of international human rights treaties has played an important role in the development of its own most recent domestic human rights instrument, as the following section demonstrates.

The Charter of Rights and Freedoms

The most recent human rights mechanism to be introduced in Canada is, of course, the Charter of Rights and Freedoms, which is part of the Constitution Act, 1982. As discussed above, the entrenchment of a bill of rights in the constitution was considered unlikely for more than a hundred years after Confederation. Indeed, an earlier attempt by Prime Minister Pierre Elliott Trudeau to entrench the narrower concept of language rights in the constitution, as part of the Victoria Charter negotiations with provinces on constitutional amendment issues, had ultimately failed despite a promising start. Not surprisingly, when this agreement collapsed, the issue of constitutional reform was placed on the back burner indefinitely. However, with the emergence of separatist pressures from Quebec and the defeat of the 1980 referendum on Quebec sovereignty in May, Trudeau again made constitutional reform a priority.

Trudeau's emphasis on language rights at the time of the Victoria Charter negotiations was already a response to the increasingly aggressive positions articulated by Quebec nationalists. Although Canada had adopted the Official Languages Act in 1969, Trudeau was of the view that this important minority right should be clearly guaranteed in the constitution. As a result, when he introduced a constitutional reform package in October 1980, it not only contained a proposed constitutional amending formula but included the Official Languages Act within the proposed Charter of Rights and Freedoms.

Trudeau's decision to propose a more comprehensive bill of rights in 1980 is a clear indication of the evolution of thinking on human rights issues that had taken place in the previous decade, during which domestic human rights instruments were being introduced and Canada was becoming a signatory to the various United Nations human rights conventions. Indeed, the final language incorporated in the Charter—after a lengthy consultation and citizen participation process, which included televised hearings of a special joint parliamentary committee, extensive parliamentary debate, a Supreme Court reference, and two formal First Ministers' Conferences—was based in large measure on the text of the UN human rights conventions. In addition, the Canadian Bill of Rights served as a model, both in terms of content and in terms of the cautionary legal lessons. In fact, the language used in certain sections of the Charter was a direct response to problems encountered in specific cases involving the Bill, notably gender bias (s. 28).

The Charter contains sections on fundamental freedoms (s. 2), democratic rights (ss. 3–5), legal rights (ss. 7–14), and equality rights (s. 15), as well as official languages (ss. 16–22). Section 15(2) further ensured that affirmative action programs such as employment equity would not be considered discriminatory. In addition, certain sections were added during the consultation process specifically to ensure that Charter rights would not be interpreted by the courts in a way that would negate or limit pre-existing Aboriginal rights (ss. 25, 35, and 36) or the multicultural nature of Canada (s. 27). Similarly, and in keeping with commitments made in the Constitution Act, 1867, concerning minority education, as discussed above, the Charter also contained specific sections guaranteeing minority education rights (ss. 23 and 29). In addition, and reflecting the federal nature of the country, the Charter contained a specific section guaranteeing mobility rights (s. 6).

It should be noted that Trudeau had originally intended the Charter to apply to the federal government alone, fearing that considerable opposition from provincial premiers could derail the entire package, but he was persuaded during internal discussions in cabinet and caucus to expand its application to provincial governments as well (s. 32). Nevertheless, section 31 of the Charter specifically states that "nothing in this Charter extends the legislative powers of any body or authority." Indeed, as Trudeau often said, the Charter's purpose was to limit the powers of both levels of government insofar as they would not be able to enact legislation that violated the fundamental human rights of any citizen. To that end, section 24 provided for judicial remedy in the event of Charter violations. At the same time, Trudeau made it clear in early negotiations with the premiers that the Charter was a non-negotiable item in the constitutional patriation package. As he declared in a televised address to the nation at the start of the negotiations, when several premiers were demanding that the scope of negotiations be broadened to include issues other than patriation, rights, and an amending formula (such as amendments to jurisdictional authority concerning fisheries, energy, and telecommunications), "I will not trade rights for fish."[22]

While there was initial provincial opposition to the proposed amending formula contained in the Constitution Act, 1982, and, to a lesser extent, to the process laid down by the federal government, it should be underlined that a widespread consensus existed with respect to the general content of the Charter, on the part of the premiers, the opposition parties, and the general public. Debate on its contents centred almost exclusively on the wording of specific provisions and was largely intended to strengthen the text. That said, the decision to apply the Charter to provincial jurisdiction did in fact lead to some resistance, as Trudeau had feared.

One important substantive point concerning the Charter was raised by Premiers Blakeney of Saskatchewan and Lyon of Manitoba, who focused on the relationship between the Charter (and hence the courts that would interpret it) and parliament or the provincial legislatures. Their concern for the principle of parliamentary supremacy ultimately led to introduction of the "notwithstanding clause" (s. 33)—despite the presence of section 1, which already provided for exceptions and exclusions based on "such reasonable limits prescribed by law as can be demonstrably justified in a free and democratic society." This additional clause allowed either level of government to declare that a legislative measure it had introduced was to be in force "notwithstanding a provision in section 2 or section 7 to 15." (The clause, as mentioned above, appears to be based on a provision in the Bill of Rights; it is in any event unique internationally.) However, a sunset provision was also placed in section 33 that required a government to re-invoke section 33 every five years. At the time, Trudeau indicated that he would never invoke the clause. He also thought it unlikely that any premier would do so, given that such a move would be an admission that provincial legislation was in violation of Charter rights. As the discussion below demonstrates, this did not prove to be as much of a deterrent as he had hoped. Trudeau often indicated that he regretted having acceded to the premiers' request, although it is unlikely that he would have been able to proceed without it.[23]

Second, it must be noted that support for the Charter was not unanimous. Some groups of Aboriginal Canadians continued to oppose provisions that they felt did not adequately protect inherent Aboriginal rights, while the separatist government of Quebec did not sign the agreement.[24] However, with the support of nine provincial governments, both opposition parties in the House of Commons, and overwhelming public support both nationally and within Quebec, the federal government proceeded to repatriate the constitution.

As a result, after a two-year process of consultation and negotiation, the Constitution Act, 1982, which included an entrenched bill of rights, came into force in April 1982. However, the application of section 15 was delayed for three years, by unanimous consent, in order to allow all jurisdictions to ensure that their legislation and programs were in compliance. Once again a consultative approach was taken—borrowed directly from the process used for accession to international treaties—as both levels of government examined their respective legislative regimes. At the federal level, this process involved the striking of a special parliamentary subcommittee on equality rights, chaired by MP Patrick Boyer, to determine what changes were required.

Application of the Charter

A number of positive benefits have flowed from the introduction of an entrenched charter of rights, as well as certain unanticipated consequences. Perhaps most important, the Charter has enjoyed overwhelming popular support and quickly became an important symbol of Canadian identity. Interestingly, this positive perception, as indicated by countless public opinion polls over time, is shared almost equally across the country, including Quebec.

An immediate consequence of the introduction of the Charter was the decision of Quebec premier René Lévesque and his successor, Robert Bourassa, to invoke the notwithstanding clause as a blanket measure covering all provincial legislation in Quebec, although Bourassa subsequently revoked its application in 1987. With the adverse decision of the Supreme Court in *Ford* (1988) regarding language rights, Quebec again employed section 33 with respect to Bill 178, which restricted the posting of commercial signs in languages other than French. However, in 1993, when Bill 178 was criticized by the United Nations Human Rights Committee, the law was rewritten to conform to the Charter and the notwithstanding clause was removed, an important but unusual example of the influence of international treaties on Canadian legislation.

The province of Alberta twice attempted to employ section 33, albeit unsuccessfully. In the first instance, which involved potential lawsuits related to the government's past practice of forced sterilization under the defunct Alberta Eugenics Board, public pressure forced the government of Premier Ralph Klein to withdraw its intended application. In the second, the government attempted to employ section 33 to protect Bill 202, an act that amended the province's marriage act to limit the definition of marriage to opposite-sex couples. In this case a Supreme Court reference found the provincial use of the notwithstanding clause to be *ultra vires* because marriage fell under federal jurisdiction, and the effort was abandoned.

Meanwhile, Trudeau had declared that the federal government would never avail itself of section 33. As a result, a directorate was established within the federal Department of Justice that was tasked with evaluating all proposed federal legislation, in advance of its tabling in the House of Commons, to ensure compliance with the Charter. For more than two decades the guidelines for this legal unit required it to approve only legislation that its staff considered to be more than 95 per cent certain of compliance with the Charter. However, a recent court case alleged that in recent years those guidelines had been altered to require only a 5 per cent likelihood of compliance.[25] The information revealed in the Federal Court lawsuit, filed by a Department of Justice lawyer working in the unit, has gone a considerable distance toward explaining a recent string of Supreme Court decisions that have found a number of federal legislative initiatives to be unconstitutional.[26]

Similarly, Trudeau had originally expanded the work of the pre-existing legal challenge support program regarding language rights, to cover all aspects of the Charter. The Court Challenges Program was designed to provide financial assistance to individuals or groups who were considered to have legitimate complaints of potentially national significance concerning legislative violations of Charter rights, in order to allow them to be able to pursue legal redress as guaranteed under the Charter's section 14. However, this financial support program to encourage test cases was eliminated by the Mulroney government. Subsequently reinstated by the Chrétien government, it was once again eliminated by the Harper government in 2006, leading a number of observers to express concern that the pursuit of Charter rights cases may be unaffordable for many future potential litigants.[27]

Among the equality rights cases flowing from the Charter's implementation were decisions related to gender bias, notably in favour of women in the military, the allocation of pension benefits, and equal opportunity legislation. With respect to sexual orientation, the case of *Vriend* (1998) provided confirmation that this must indeed be considered a ground for non-discrimination. Another significant decision affecting sexual orientation was the Supreme Court's reference affirming the constitutionality of same-sex marriage, a decision that many scholars consider to have flowed logically from *Vriend*.

However, without question the most significant impact of the Charter has fallen, somewhat unexpectedly, within the sections dealing with legal rights. According to Justice Marc Rosenberg in his analysis of the first 25 years of Charter jurisprudence, "the impact of the Canadian Charter of Rights and Freedoms is most visible in the field of criminal law. It has changed the way crime is investigated in this country. It has changed the way offences are prosecuted. It has changed the way that criminal law is practised. And, it has changed the way that due process is valued in society."[28]

Current and Emerging Issues

A number of concerns have been expressed recently about government actions that appear to have cast doubt on the image of tolerance and support for diversity that has long been a cornerstone of Canadian identity. For example, in contrast with the acceptance of more than 100,000 Vietnamese refugees in the late 1970s and the positive reception shown toward more than 150 Tamil refugees found drifting off the coast of Newfoundland in 1986, the Harper government responded negatively and aggressively to the arrival of some 490 Tamil asylum-seekers on the west coast in 2010. In addition, it has introduced several restrictive legislative measures, some of which have been found unconstitutional, and a variety of programs that appear to be at odds with international commitments.

Meanwhile in Quebec, the introduction of the Charter of Quebec Values by the Marois government in 2013 called into question the commitment to rights outlined in the Quebec Charter of Human Rights and Freedoms, and once again raised the spectre of perceived conflict between individual and collective rights. The Quebec Human Rights Commission delivered a 21-page critique of the Values proposal, which it described as a "clear violation of personal freedoms guaranteed under the Canadian Charter of Rights and Freedoms, Quebec's own Charter enacted 38 years ago, and international law."[29] Despite having earlier argued that the Values document would not be found unconstitutional, Bernard Drainville, the minister responsible for democratic institutions and active citizenship, later declared that the Parti Québécois (PQ) government would invoke the notwithstanding clause if necessary to ensure the supremacy of the Values charter. However, the defeat of the PQ government in the 2014 election appeared to have derailed the Values charter, which incoming premier Philippe Couillard vigorously criticized.

One important emerging issue relates to implementation of the economic, social, and cultural rights that are included in the second UN human rights convention, to which Canada is a party. Although a proposal to include a "social charter" was put forward by then-Ontario Premier Bob Rae, during discussions of the Charlottetown Accord constitutional amendment package of 1992, this was quickly abandoned once the Accord failed. Since then, as legal scholar Martha Jackman has outlined, little progress has been made and these rights have continued to be viewed more as "policy objectives" than guaranteed human rights. Jackman nevertheless argues that they can (and should) be read into section 15 of the Charter, as well as various provincial human rights acts.[30] Her argument was reinforced by the second periodic report on Canada by the Committee on Economic, Social, and Cultural Rights (1993), which specifically noted in its concluding remarks that Canada's failure to be in compliance with various rights outlined in the convention was strikingly at odds with its relative wealth and stable political system.

Flowing from this, and undoubtedly the most serious human rights challenge facing Canada today, is the situation of Aboriginal peoples, an issue that has been identified by successive Canadian Human Rights Commission reports and which was recently the subject of two separate United Nations fact-finding missions, leading to highly critical reports, as well as a scathing report by Amnesty International.[31] Despite the numerous guarantees found in law and in the Charter of Rights and Freedoms, the continuing struggle of Aboriginal peoples remains a significant challenge for federal, provincial, and municipal levels of government. With Third World standards prevalent on many reserves and little progress being made on either the treaty claims or self-government negotiations of First Nations, and with a recent Supreme Court ruling that the federal government was negligent in its dealings with Métis peoples under the Manitoba Act more than a century ago, as well as the ongoing revelations of the Truth and Reconciliation Commission concerning the legacy of residential schools, the Canadian record with respect to Aboriginal peoples is both lamentable and seemingly intractable.

In addition, in 2007 the Harper government refused to support the UN's International Declaration on the Rights of Indigenous Peoples, making Canada one of only four member states that did not do so. Five years later, although the government issued a statement in support of the Declaration, it also reiterated its concerns about various provisions of the Declaration dealing with lands, territories and resources, self-government, intellectual property, and "the need to achieve an appropriate balance between the rights and obligations of Indigenous peoples, States and third parties," concerns that it stressed were ongoing. The federal government's subsequent failure to consult with First Nations over plans to construct an energy pipeline across Aboriginal lands suggests that these concerns continue to take precedence over constitutional obligations, as indicated by former Indian affairs minister Jim Prentice.[32]

Similar concerns were raised in the UN Human Rights Committee report on Canada's compliance with the International Covenant on Civil and Political Rights (reports are issued on a regular basis as part of the oversight mechanism for countries that have ratified the covenant). The report, issued in July 2015, was the first to cover the period following election of the Harper government in 2006. In addition to the deplorable situation of Aboriginal Canadians, the report identified seven other areas of significant concern: (1) the uneven state of women's rights; (2) lack of corporate accountability (for example, of Canadian mining companies operating abroad); (3) the treatment of refugees and migrants; (4) the lack of support for Canadians subject to human rights violations abroad; (5) the "shrinking space" for advocacy and dissent in civil society; (6) the lack of adequate safeguards for security and intelligence agencies; and (7) the government's "lack of engagement" with the multilateral human rights system. However, numerous government spokespersons rejected the report's negative findings and insisted that Canada's human rights record continues to lead the world.

Conclusion

Although Canada's reputation as a champion of human rights and tolerance of diversity was established soon after Confederation, a number of specific instances of formal discriminatory government policy in the early years demonstrate that the image was not entirely accurate. Since the Second World War, however, Canada's progress in implementing human rights legislation and other rights instruments has been significant, and in some cases ground-breaking. For example, Canada is now one of the very few Western democracies to officially recognize same-sex marriage, and progress on equality rights, as well of those of the disabled, has been noteworthy, if not as substantial as proponents may have hoped.

Certainly the human rights instruments now in place in Canada are, in theory, at the cutting edge of rights protection internationally. At the same time, political will is required for the respect, implementation, and application of legally recognized rights, as is the education of jurists and legislators. In the end, the promotion and protection of human rights requires continual vigilance and a continuous process of adaptation and improvement. Canada, despite its long-established reputation for respect of human rights, is no exception. Although in many respects the reputation was well-deserved, a number of unresolved and emerging issues threaten to challenge the validity of that image. And, as numerous public opinion polls have demonstrated, Canadians continue to overestimate the impact and security of those formal rights, despite considerable evidence to the contrary.

Takeaway Messages

- Canada's federal and provincial human rights commissions are designed to address discrimination in the private sector, while the Charter of

Rights and Freedoms is designed to protect citizens from the actions of governments.

- In Canada's dualist legal approach, international treaties that have been ratified by the federal government do not automatically have the force of law, but they may be considered an important form of moral suasion.
- The modern definition of human rights consists of both civil and political rights and economic, social, and cultural rights.

Study Questions

- In what ways has the federal system of government influenced the development of human rights instruments in Canada, either positively or negatively?
- In what way do you think Canada could best recognize economic, social, and cultural rights more directly?

Issues for Debate or Roundtable

- Following on the arguments of Martha Jackman and Bob Rae, do you agree that poverty should be considered grounds for non-discrimination under the Charter? Are there other grounds that should be read into the Charter?

Additional Reading

Ignatieff, Michael. *The Rights Revolution.* Toronto: Anansi, 2000.

Miron, Janet. *A History of Human Rights in Canada: Essential Issues.* Toronto: Canadian Scholars' Press, 2009.

Wolman, Andrew. "The Relationship between National and Subnational Human Rights Institutions in Federal States." *International Journal of Human Rights* 17, no. 4 (2013): 445–62. http://dx.doi.org/10.1080/13642987.2012.762507.

Websites

Canadian Human Rights Commission. http://www.chrc-ccdp.ca/eng.

Foreign Affairs, Trade and Development Canada. http://www.international.gc.ca/rights-droits/policy-politique.aspx.

Heritage Canada. http://www.pch.gc.ca/eng/1355765048274/1355765626167.

United Nations. http://www.un.org/en/sections/what-we-do/protect-human-rights/index.html.

United Nations. Human Rights Council. http://www.ohchr.org/EN/HRBodies/HRC/Pages/HRCIndex.aspx.

Notes

1. Peter Hogg, *Constitutional Law of Canada*, 5th ed. (Toronto: Carswell, 2007).
2. Jean Charest, "Remarks on the Introduction of Don Tapscott," Forum of Federations International Conference on Federalism, Mont Tremblant, Quebec, October 1999.
3. In modern times, however, Canada's constitutional guarantees on the funding of religious education have faced increasing criticism due to evolving rights concepts and competing rights claims. For example, a 1999 decision of the United Nations Human Rights Committee found that Ontario was in violation of the International Covenant on Civil and Political Rights because it funded Catholic schools and not other faith-based schools. Meanwhile, both Quebec and Newfoundland have abolished religion-based schools through constitutional amendments.
4. Walter Stewart, *But Not in Canada* (Toronto: Macmillan, 1976); Irving Abella and Harold Troper, *None Is Too Many* (Toronto: Lester and Orpen Dennys, 1983).
5. For more detail see, for example, N.F. Dreisziger, "7 December 1941: A Turning Point in Canadian Wartime Policy toward Enemy Ethnic Groups?" *Journal of Canadian Studies* (Spring 1997): 93–111.
6. For a comprehensive discussion, see Gordon Bale, "Law, Politics, and the Manitoba School Question: Supreme Court and Privy Council," *Canadian Bar Review* 63, no. 461 (1985): 467–73.
7. See, for example, *Chaput v. Romain* (1949) and *Saumur v. the City of Quebec* (1953).
8. Peter Russell, *Leading Constitutional Decisions* (Toronto: McClelland and Stewart, 1973), 194.
9. Interestingly, Ontario Premier Leslie Frost had been lobbied to adopt such legislation for several years by a coalition of labour and civil liberties associations, as well as the Canadian Jewish Congress, but when he announced the Act he referred instead to the Universal Declaration of Human Rights as the primary incentive and justification. For more detail, see James Walker, "Decoding the Rights Revolution: Lessons from Canada," in *Taking Liberties: A History of Human Rights in Canada*, ed. D. Goutor and S. Heathorn (Toronto: Oxford University Press, 2013).
10. Poll results first published in the *Toronto Star*, 19 June 1947.
11. Cited in B. Jeffrey and P. Rosen, "The Protection of Human Rights in Canada," *Canadian Parliamentary Review* 2, no. 2 (1979).
12. For further details, see the discussion below on the international human rights conventions to which Canada is a signatory.
13. For more detail, see P. Rosen, "Hate Propaganda," publication no. 85–6E, Parliamentary Information and Research Service, 24 January (Ottawa: Library of Parliament, 2000). For historical background, see W. Kaplan, "Maxwell Cohen and the Report of the Special Committee on Hate Propaganda," in *Law, Policy, and International Justice: Essays in Honour of Maxwell Cohen*, ed. W. Kaplan and D. McRae (Montreal: McGill-Queen's University Press, 1993).
14. See Pearl Eliadis, *Speaking Out on Human Rights* (Montreal: McGill-Queen's University Press, 2013), 203–39.

15. For a detailed account of the issue, see Pearl Eliadis, "The Controversy Entrepreneurs," *Maisonneuve* 29 (August 2009).
16. "John Diefenbaker and the Canadian Bill of Rights," *Citizens' Forum*, CBC Radio, 16 March 1950, http://www.cbc.ca/archives/categories/politics/prime-ministers/john-diefenbaker-dief-the-chief-the-canadian-bill-of-rights.html.
17. R.W. Kerr, "The Canadian Bill of Rights and Sex-Based Differential in Canadian Federal Law," *Osgoode Hall Law Journal* 12, no. 2 (1974): 357–87.
18. Debate at the UN itself over the definition and relative importance of the various rights had been so significant that in the end it was decided to separate the two categories of rights into separate covenants. While social democratic regimes such as those in Eastern Europe prioritized economic and social rights, Western liberal democracies were instead more comfortable with and likely to prioritize the civil and political rights identified in the first covenant.
19. There are several implications of the two systems. In the monist system—adopted notably by the United States—international law does not need to be translated into national law. The act of ratifying an international treaty automatically incorporates that treaty into national law, and the international treaty therefore can be directly applied and adjudicated in national courts. One consequence of this approach is that countries such as the United States are reluctant to sign many international treaties. On the other hand, countries that adopt the dualist approach may sign treaties secure in the knowledge that there is no direct implication for national law unless a government decides it shall be so. For more on the treaty-making and treaty-implementing process in Canada, see G. Van Ert, "Canada," in *The Role of Domestic Courts in Treaty Enforcement: A Comparative Study*, ed. D. Sloss and D. Jinks (Cambridge: Cambridge University Press, 2009).
20. See, for example, Phillips Gill LLP, "Omar Khadr: Why This Case Matters," 21 November 2013, http://www.phillipsgill.com/2013/11/21/omar-khadr-why-this-case-matters/.
21. For a list of international human rights instruments to which Canada has become a party, see Appendix 1.
22. For Trudeau's account of his views on the package and negotiations, see *Memoirs* (Toronto: McClelland and Stewart, 1993). For another and more detailed insider's perspective on the negotiations, see also Jean Chrétien (minister of justice during the negotiations), "Bringing the Constitution Home," in T. Axworthy and P.E. Trudeau, *Towards a Just Society: The Trudeau Years* (Toronto: Viking, 1990), 282–311.
23. The Supreme Court reference of November 1981 made it clear that, while constitutionally correct, the federal government would be in violation of established constitutional convention if it decided to proceed unilaterally to London with the package without the approval of a greater number of premiers than it had achieved at the time.
24. A comprehensive analysis of the process can be found in R. Graham, *The Last Act: Pierre Trudeau, the Gang of Eight and the Fight for Canada* (Toronto: Allen Lane, 2011). For an interesting perspective on the rationale for Quebec Premier Lévesque's determination to reject any constitutional accord, see his autobiography, *Attendez que je me rappelle* [*Memoirs*] (Toronto: McClelland and Stewart, 1986).

25. B. Curry, "Judge Raps Justice Department for Treatment of Whistleblower," *Globe and Mail*, 16 January 2013.
26. S. Fine, "Harper's Judicial Losing Streak Reveals Limits of Government Action," *Globe and Mail*, 27 April 2014.
27. W. Mackay, D. McGruder, and K. Jennings, "Why the Government Was Wrong to Cancel the Court Challenges Program," in *Contemporary Political Issues*, 6th ed., ed. P. Barker and M. Charlton (Toronto: Nelson, 2009). For a detailed chronology of events, see also Voices-Voix Coalition, "Court Challenges Program," http://voices-voix.ca/en/facts/profile/court-challenges-program.
28. M. Rosenberg, "Twenty-Five Years Later: The Impact of the Canadian Charter of Rights and Freedoms on Criminal Law," *Supreme Court Law Review*, 2nd ser., 45 (Markham, ON: LexisNexis Canada, 2009).
29. As cited in L. Perreaux, "Proposed Quebec Values Charter Violates Rights, Commission Says," *Globe and Mail*, 17 October 2013.
30. M. Jackman, "Constitutional Contact with Disparity in the World: Poverty as a Prohibited Ground of Discrimination under the Canadian Charter and Human Rights Law," *Review of Constitutional Studies* 2, no. 1 (1994).
31. For a detailed analysis, see B. Farber, "Canada Should Reflect on Its Human Rights Record," *Globe and Mail*, 18 March 2013.
32. J. Prentice, "Canada Must Look Beyond U.S. to Strengthen Access to Global Energy Market," speech at the University of Calgary School of Public Policy, 28 September 2012.

2
The Genesis and Evolution of the Postwar Human Rights Project

ROLAND BURKE AND JAMES KIRBY

Learning Objectives

- To gain an understanding of the historical evolution of the modern human rights regime and its constituent ideas
- To understand the political and intellectual contexts that shaped and reshaped what constituted international human rights
- To appreciate the contentions and controversies within the history of human rights

In recent years, human rights has emerged as one of the premier subjects for historians. A whole generation of foundational works, notably Paul Gordon Lauren's remarkably comprehensive *Evolution of International Human Rights*, has been sharply revised by a collection of "new histories," most notably that from Samuel Moyn.[1] These new histories have been, for the most part, defined by their skepticism as to the continuity of progress and the relative homogeneity of the concept assumed in the rights narratives of the older historians. Where Lauren found an essentially continuous, if punctuated, lineage of proto–human rights movements extending for centuries into the past, the newer historians have instead emphasized a radical rupture between preceding emancipatory movements and the modern human rights idea.

By emphasizing the distinctive features of the contemporary human rights movement, particularly in the form it has adopted since the 1970s, these new accounts have challenged orthodox verities of gradual progress toward genuine universality. Their contributions have instead revealed a process that was much more complex—and markedly more contradictory—than the established linear narrative of incremental evolution.[2]

This chapter is informed by these new accounts of the provenance and progress of the human rights idea, but it eschews the more maximal propositions of total rupture and a de novo genesis of human rights in the 1970s. The history of human rights is far from unitary; it is a history with both meaningful sinews of continuity and moments of dramatic rupture. This chapter will chart the fractured arc of rights in the second half of the twentieth century, from the foundational decades of the postwar human rights enterprise as it emerged from the United Nations, and its subsequent interactions with the myriad emancipatory struggles that followed across Asia, Africa, and Europe, to the post–Cold War renaissance of human rights activism. Yet this explosion of human rights into a global lingua franca was also coincident with an increasingly bitter contest about what constituted rights, and in many cases a serious paring back of the ambition and optimism that defined the vision of the 1948 Universal Declaration. By the 1990s, human rights had become a universal language for moral legitimacy—but one that was almost as universally contested in its content.

The Ecosystem of Rights Before "Human Rights": Humanitarians, Minority Protections, and "Self-Determination"

A generation of scholars from legal, historical, and philosophical disciplines tended to assign a long origin to the rights movement, typically identifying a catalogue of waypoints or "precursors" that expressed the partial, unfinished spirit of human rights. Prominent on this list were early Enlightenment sentimentalism, the Atlantic revolutions, abolitionism, Romantic nationalism, pre- and interwar humanitarianism, Wilsonian self-determination, and—as herald to the "world made new" proper—the 1941 Atlantic Charter. For historians Lynn Hunt and Paul Gordon Lauren, these were intermediate nodes in a complicated but basically continuous tradition.[3] Their account of the modern human rights order is defined by its expansiveness and inclusivity; it encompasses all manner of emancipations, even those that made significant dissonance with the ultimate expression of "human rights" in the postwar twentieth century.

Revolutions in France and the United States, and the ideas that animated them, are almost the default foundational moment in the historiography of human rights. Their most celebrated formal expressions, the 1776 Declaration of Independence and the later Bill of Rights, the 1789 Declaration of the Rights of Man and the Citizen and its more radical 1793 sequel, are almost inescapable comparators to the 1948 Universal Declaration of Human Rights (UDHR). Each proclaimed popular sovereignty, a government that derived its legitimacy solely from the people, and a state that existed to secure the rights of its citizens. Each enumerated specific lists of rights that inhered (notionally) in all individuals, including almost all the modern civil and political rights of conscience, expression, assembly, political participation, legal equality, and integrity of aspects of the person. Jacobin political thought, in its 1793 Declaration, augmented this with some gestures of recognition of economic and social rights. Universalism was apparent in the philosophies of both Declarations, albeit much more explicitly in the

French case. In revolutionary France, the concept of the "rights of man" exceeded the borders of national citizenship, if only (like many features of the Revolution) spiritually and rhetorically. Rights were explicitly recognized as maximally universal and applicable to an "all, all the time, and everywhere" that was never defined with much specificity.[4]

Nineteenth- and early twentieth-century humanitarians cast wide their conscience and included peoples from across the world as worthy objects for popular concern.[5] They presupposed that especially severe abuses, often in distant lands, required intercession from a wider community, principally middle-class and often with a Christian inflexion. This humanitarianism was certainly international insofar as it extended to territories far outside metropolitan Britain, most notably the Belgian Congo—administered by King Leopold as a source of personal enrichment—with its grotesque treatment of the Congolese people.[6] The chief standard-bearers for the cause of the Congo were Edmund Dene Morel and Roger Casement. In an increasingly interconnected and technologically advanced world, external witnesses with knowledge and evidence of such abuses held greater capacity for launching public action on a global scale. By 1904, as a result of Casement's graphic written account and Morel's photographic expositions, their Congo Reform Association inspired global publicity and indignation over the human suffering experienced by Belgium's colonial subjects.

Regardless of distance, for the humanitarian movement, concern for human life and basic freedoms transcended both colour lines and colonial borders. Humanitarians bestowed these protections from a position of superiority, and while this could produce very substantial improvements in welfare, it was a much less radical moral language than the idea of fully equal humans with fully symmetrical inherent rights. Despite some similarity, human rights was not a latent future possibility within this movement, even if concern about universal human suffering animated both.

In the early twentieth century, another crusade, one of self-determination, emerged as another attempt at universal reform. Most famously expounded by US President Woodrow Wilson and codified (very weakly and inconsistently) in the post–First World War settlement under the League of Nations, the idea of self-determination accorded a collective right to national freedom for recognized (or recognizable) peoples.[7] The granularity of the right was coarse; it inhered in a national people, with only implied freedom for the constituent individuals that existed within it. National freedom and self-determination might very well be won without doing much to advance the position of the people within the nation. Self-determination represented, at best, half of the admixture of liberty.

Alongside national self-determination, and conceived as the complement to it, was another kind of right, that of the minority. It was cognizant of the likelihood that mono-ethnic states were unrealistic in much of Europe, and especially so in territories that had a dynamic history of borders and sovereigns. Given the risk that pure ethnic majoritarianism would allow severe discrimination within a "self-determined" nation-state, the League of Nations leavened the preference for nations with a makeshift set of Minority Treaties. These would confer a degree of supranational protection, institutionalized within the League itself, for recognized minorities, who could then appeal on the basis of the treaty for redress against their own national government. As was the case with much of the League's efforts, the record of the Minorities regime was modest. It nevertheless did produce at least some minor forms of redress in Upper Silesia, notably for Franz Bernheim, a citizen who had his complaint against the German government upheld.[8] Although limited to very particular circumstances, and apportioned on the basis of belonging to a specific minority community rather than membership in humankind, the Minority Treaties were the first systematized legal effort at a system of redress for individuals against their own state.[9] They were a partial precursor to the mode of operation later attempted under the UN human rights treaty system and its various optional protocols, which allowed personal petition to an international body when all domestic remedies had been exhausted.

These were all philosophies and systems that held some conceptual affinity with the ideas that came to mean human rights in the postwar period, without being usable prototypes. Humanitarianism sought to alleviate the gravest forms of suffering. Its operation was almost invariably asymmetrical, with the healthy, powerful, and "civilized" dispensing assistance to the most desperate. It lacked any intrinsic recognition of all human individuals as equal agents, and it was perfectly compatible with liberal imperialism and overt racial discrimination. Both national self-determination and its close interwar contemporary, minority rights, did allow for a kind of parity between humans, but only when they were organized into collective peoples defined along essentialist ethnic lines of identity. The modern human rights movement could not be readily superimposed on any of these preceding systems of global welfare and rights, even if it overlapped with some of their components.

The Universal Declaration of Human Rights: A Global Charter for Nation-States and National Citizenship

The terminal phases of the Second World War, and the deliberations on the shape of the new postwar world at Dumbarton Oaks (1944) and San

Francisco (1945), saw a flourishing enthusiasm for rights, which were increasingly cast as "human rights."[10] After 30 years of almost unbroken international crisis, widespread revulsion at the atrocities of the most total war in humanity's history, and fear of renascent totalitarianism, human rights became one of the pillars of the new postwar settlement. Although markedly less direct in its influence than has been supposed, the horror of the Holocaust was part of the milieu of human misery from which the impulse to a standard of international human rights arose.[11] What the term *human rights* actually meant was not altogether clear, in spite of its prominent place in the 1945 UN Charter. Among the great powers, it was certainly less of a lodestar for the postwar settlement than international stability and an orderly system of sovereign nation-states. The fact that Field Marshal Jan Smuts, the prime minister of South Africa and an avowed proponent of racial segregation, co-drafted the Charter and embraced the term *human rights* suggested that its meaning remained highly ambiguous even after the war had concluded.[12]

From 1946 onward, and especially from 1947, the new United Nations and its Commission on Human Rights commenced a long and fraught series of debates on what precisely constituted "human rights," and the means by which they might be realized. A constellation of outstanding individuals, drawn from across the world, drove the project forward.[13] Most famous was Eleanor Roosevelt, the "First Lady to the World" and the chair for many of the Commission's sessions.[14] Philosophical weight was provided by Lebanese Thomist scholar Charles Malik and Confucianist Peng Chung-Chang. Hansa Mehta, a leading Indian feminist and parliamentarian, provided a practical approach to the challenges of universal rights for societies outside the Western world. Carlos Romulo, a Pulitzer Prize–winning essayist from the Philippines, advocated the case for those countries not yet independent, and warned against any differentiation in rights between the "civilized" and the "backward." René Cassin, a French lawyer and future Nobel laureate for his work on the UDHR, carefully framed the language of the text and a number of its key articles (Cassin had lost his family in the Holocaust). Canadian lawyer John Humphrey, who led the UN's Human Rights Division, drove himself to near collapse trying to sustain the program and achieve adoption of a meaningful text. Countless other figures, drawn from a worldwide catchment of traditions and political and religious dispositions, made significant contributions, from William Hodgson of Australia to Émile Saint-Lot of Haiti.

The adoption of the Universal Declaration of Human Rights on 10 December 1948 crystallized the postwar spirit. It boldly extended the latent logic of the long catalogue of rights charters that had been proclaimed across the Western world in the eighteenth and nineteenth centuries.[15] At least in form, and formally, it eliminated almost all the exceptions and inconsistencies that inhered in the French, American, and British traditions, and for the first time, it brought all humans within the realm of rights. In its articles on social and economic rights, it furnished the material basis for enjoying civil and political freedoms, codifying a century of activism from social democratic, trade union, Catholic, and Christian democrat reformers across the Western and Latin American world.[16] It departed from the more archaic phrasing of the "rights of man" and was informed, albeit perhaps insufficiently, by meaningful engagement from liberal feminist representatives. In its maximalist universalism, the UDHR was at once a sequel and a novelty. Previous rights charters had been defined by their limits on the bounds of equal humanity and their exclusions. The hallmark of the UDHR was the absence of any such limits.

While often lauded as the expression of soaring supranational ambition, the UDHR was in many ways a universalized expression of the sort of liberal nationalism that had animated the eighteenth-century Atlantic revolutions and their nineteenth-century European sequels. The logic of its architects, almost all of them avowed liberal internationalists, was of a world order defined by nation-states and populated with rights-bearing national citizens. In key respects, the notion of rights that defined so much of the drafting debate around the UDHR was hyper-conventional, a retreat even from the timid supranational quality implied in the weak interwar system of the League of Nations. The UDHR soon became the touchstone for countless emancipatory struggles, but its vision was not one that presupposed the kind of radical transnational mobilization that later emerged, primarily in the mass growth of human rights non-governmental organizations (HRNGOs) in the 1970s.[17] It instead took the model of a national state as the means for protecting individual rights, an idea that was at least as old as 1776, and renovated it into a universal banner for all peoples and all nations—or at least eventually, all peoples and nations.

The emergence of anti-colonial nationalism through the 1940s and early 1950s radically expanded the deployment of human rights while conserving, and slowly consolidating, its emphasis on the nation-state.[18] A wave of liberal anti-colonial leaders embraced human rights language to frame the cause of collective emancipation. Their approach was profoundly disruptive in manner, and it spread the purported realm of rights to peoples and territories in much bolder terms than those countenanced by the imperial powers. But their fidelity to the basic contours set down in 1948 was, for the most part, maintained.[19] The main lines of Asian and African nationalism mounted arguments that operated within the reasoning set down by the architects of the UDHR: of the state being the essential means for securing individual liberties. Their innovation was one of expansiveness, wielding the logic of Western democratic nationalism in places well outside the conceptual and geographical West.

Such sweeping universality produced a configuration that was in some ways counterintuitive. Western imperial powers, which had long claimed to be the bearers of universal civilization, recoiled from the prospect of extending the full panoply of rights to their overseas territories.[20] They counselled for a glacial gradualism and feigned deference to cultural particularities that rendered immediate realization of rights both unrealistic and potentially counterproductive. For Britain and France, human rights were universal, but only when considered across almost geologic time. For key anti-colonial leaders in the 1950s and into the early 1960s, human rights were both the instrument for and the ultimate end of national emancipation. Over time it would become apparent that many anti-colonial nationalists were reliable champions of sovereignty and only transient enthusiasts for human rights, but not before they had catalyzed dramatic expansion of the UN's human rights system.

Covenants, Conventions, and Committees: Building the Human Rights System

Across the four decades spanning 1950 to 1990, an impressively comprehensive edifice of international legal instruments was proposed, advanced, debated, and adopted, bringing precision to the sweeping aspirational norms of the UDHR. Each of these human rights conventions provided a model and a precedent for the next tranche of rights protection. This was most striking in the commonalities of the monitoring and enforcement systems, almost all of which had a common origin in the first major human rights convention, passed in the early 1960s. Much of the initial momentum for the birth of this legal structure was provided by the newer states, which began to reshape the agenda to match their own priorities. The first of these legally binding sequels to the UDHR was the 1965 International Convention on the Elimination of All Forms of Racial Discrimination (ICERD), a project pressed forward primarily by the newer nations and steered through the shoals of narrow anti-colonial extremism by Ghanaian representative George Lamptey. The ICERD was the culmination of a decade-long shift in the disposition of the United Nations, and indicative of the sharply altered balance of forces within the General Assembly and its accessory forums.

While the UDHR had approached equality in a general sense, with race as a specifically cited criterion, the ICERD took this one aspect of non-discrimination as the most urgent and most privileged right. It was the first to be thus enshrined in a comprehensive international human rights treaty. The text itself was reasonably balanced, aided by the adept diplomacy of moderate Asian and African delegations, but the very fact that its introduction, iteration, and passage occurred in less than two years was telling in terms of how the UN was disposed to apportion its energies.[21] Work on the human rights covenants—the full legal sequels to the UDHR—had commenced more than 15 years before the ICERD, and were ultimately adopted a year after it was concluded.

The Covenants themselves had a bitterly contested history.[22] Begun in the late 1940s and originally designed to produce a single, unitary treaty, in the 1950s the endeavour was consumed by both Cold War and anti-colonial politics. After a torturous effort to retain both categories of rights—the civil and political and the economic, social, and cultural—in a shared text, the draft was split into two separate covenants in 1952.[23] While, in the aspirational design of the UDHR, it had been possible to conceive of the body of human rights as an organic and interdependent entity, it proved impossible to draft a treaty that kept them together.

The logic of the split between economic and social rights and the civil/political group was most persuasively advanced by Indian representative Hansa Mehta.[24] Mindful of the severe resource constraints within her own country, Mehta borrowed from the example of the Indian constitution. Under its terms, civil and political rights were protected by law. Economic and social rights—to health, housing, and welfare—were placed in a different class. These were objectives that would guide India's government, but they could not immediately be implemented in full. Instead they were to be achieved progressively as development allowed. Mehta's interventions in the debate, and the Indian example, provided a means around a key impasse.[25] The fact that India, rather than the Western democracies, was now among the leaders of the drafting process was emblematic of the sharp shift in the balance of power within the UN's human rights enterprise.

By the mid-1950s, the flagship of the UN's human rights project was lacking any energetic Western patronage, making Asian and Arab engagement vital to the eventual passage of the Covenants. The United States, which had, in the figure of Eleanor Roosevelt, lent support to the UDHR, in 1953 openly abandoned participation in the Covenant drafting process. The Western imperial powers, wary of the liabilities a legally binding human rights convention would pose to the administration of their colonies, sought to exempt colonial territory from its reach. Britain and France drafted a clause for the Covenant that made ratification binding for their metropoles but required additional agreement from the colonial administrations to spread its protections to those zones. The optimistic universalism of the late 1940s, already waning by the conclusion of the UDHR, had largely departed.

Enthusiasm was found instead in the newer states, many of which had recently secured independence. Yet to lose the hopeful orientation that accompanied their birth as independent states, Asian, Arab, and, by the later 1950s, African representatives seized leadership of the foundering Covenants. While not radical in their revisions to the substance of the articles, the newer states were insistent in their effort to fuse human rights with anti-imperialism. The proposed colonial clause, which separated the treatment of metropolitan citizens from that of colonial subjects, was voted down. In its place a very different colonial clause was adopted, one that expressly demanded automatic application of the Covenant to all territories of the signing state. If the United Kingdom signed, the residents of Lagos would enjoy the same rights as those of London; if France signed, Conakry would be formally under the same system as Chamrousse. The incipient "Third World" was militantly anti-imperialist and, as a consequence, more emphatically universalist than almost all the other contributors that shaped and reshaped the Covenants.

The anti-imperialist orientation of the Covenants was rendered unmistakable with the inclusion of a right to self-determination. As early as 1950, the assertive Arab and Asian delegations attempted to inscribe self-determination—defined broadly as freedom from alien rule and the realization of national sovereignty—as the preeminent right in the whole catalogue of freedoms protected under the draft Covenant. It was a measure that provoked howls of outrage from the Western European powers, who complained about the cynical politicization that lay behind the self-determination article. For their part, the more eloquent defenders of the right, including (privately) the chief of the UN's Human Rights Division, John Humphrey, argued that popular sovereignty and the dissolution of colonial empires was an essential requirement for the effective pursuit of all the other rights. Their logic was classically liberal, and not obviously distinct from that of the American revolutionaries of 1776. Collective national freedom was the natural companion of, and the gateway to, individual liberty. After years of ferocious battles over the content and meaning of this self-determination, the right was firmly inscribed as the very first article in both of the Covenants.[26] By the time of their passage, in 1966, there was little of the British and French empires left to dissolve. More depressingly, with the emergent pattern of repression by post-colonial rulers, it had also become apparent that national independence was by no means a guarantee of human rights.

In the wake of the burgeoning international network of human rights and women's rights NGOs, the late 1970s and 1980s witnessed a second wave of conventions, driven less by the optimism of states than the energy of activists. In 1979, after a rapid drafting effort, women's rights were set out in the Convention on the Elimination of All Forms of Discrimination Against Women (CEDAW).[27] The CEDAW was a massive renovation of the only previous convention that was explicitly dedicated to women's rights: the decidedly austere 1952 Convention on the Political Rights of Women (CPW). While the CPW, drafted at the dawn of the postwar period, spoke only to the most restrictive standards of formal legal equality and had no enforcement mechanisms, the CEDAW approached the protection of women's rights as a much more complex task that required more than equal suffrage.[28] It was perhaps the first example of a treaty that entailed more than imposing discrete legal obligations upon governments, instead setting out a program of full-scale social transformation. Social and cultural practices, and the violations practiced by one group of citizens against another, were clearly within the ambit of the CEDAW. In its recognition that violations of women's rights could stem from sources other than state policy, the CEDAW was a convention with a much more impressive appreciation of the problems of securing human rights. Rights required more than formalistic promises and a scrawled signature on the UN treaty register. As bold as its vision was, the CEDAW struggled to find meaningful support; numerous ratifications were accompanied by statements of reservation, statements that often undercut the very essence of the protections that had supposedly been agreed on.[29] Fortunately, women's rights NGOS and transnational leverage were among the more effective features that (albeit slowly) infused the CEDAW with life.[30]

After a decade-long campaign by various NGOs, notably Amnesty International, and the apparent epidemic of torture across large swaths of the world, the UN haltingly moved toward the Convention Against Torture (CAT).[31] Unlike the CEDAW, a treaty that reflected an ambitious and hopeful vision of full human rights for women, the CAT was defined by its pessimistic outlook. With the full set of human rights enumerated by the UDHR and the two Covenants seemingly out of reach by the late 1970s, torture was cast as a human-rights violation that could potentially be universally outlawed with some degree of normative consensus.[32] Even states that might well dispute the freedoms of association and expression generally balked at openly contesting the validity of a ban on torture. The CAT was a treaty that reflected the lowered horizons of the 1970s and 1980s, when making the world a marginally less evil place was the best that could be hoped for. Eleanor Roosevelt's famous phrase on the birth of the UDHR, about seeking "a world made new," now seemed not merely utopian but fantastical.

Driven forward by an at-times incongruous coalition of Communist, European, Oceanic, American, Asian, and African states, UNICEF, and assorted NGOs, the 1989 Convention on the Rights of the Child (CRC) resurrected a priority that had been essentially moribund for three decades. The Declaration on the Rights of the Child, adopted in 1959, had been an almost orphaned text.[33] While the revival of the children's rights agenda, which commenced with a Polish initiative at the 1978 session of the Commission on Human Rights, was an important addition to the corpus of human rights laws, it again reflected a lowered ambition.[34] Children, as a uniquely vulnerable group, were afforded special human rights protections because there was so little faith in the general-case human rights promised by the ICCPR and the ICESCR. It was, in a way, a form of thematic triage; this was a group that might perhaps be saved from the worst abuses. Even then, the refusal of the United States to ratify was hardly auspicious.

In other ways the CRC was less promising still. Among its lead advocates was Adam Lopatka, a Polish jurist and loyal defender at the UN of General Jaruzelski's military government.[35] As Lopatka was declaiming the importance of the rights of children, the Polish dictatorship was arresting thousands of parents and systematically violating the civil and political rights of its citizens. Signatures from myriad dictatorships on the CRC were less than encouraging, given the manifest hollowness of their preceding promises to adhere to the ICERD, the two Covenants, the CEDAW, and the CAT.

Whatever the cynicism of the signatory governments, the treaties would, ever so slowly, have some impact. Regular reporting to specialist (and admirably independent) panels of experts did provide a potential source of embarrassment for governments.[36] A striking example of the power of hard questions was the appearance of the delegate from the Islamic Republic of Iran to defend his country's report to the Human Right Committee (HRC). The HRC has been created to monitor compliance with the ICCPR, a treaty that Iran had signed while under the rule of the Shah. Displeased with the dissimulation of the report and of Iran's representative, Sayed Hadi Khosroshahi, a substantial section of the HRC panel challenged the Islamic Republic on numerous points. The questions produced pages of invective and venom from the Iranian delegation, much of it revealing of the new republic's disposition toward universal human rights.[37] UN scrutiny had unmasked the authoritarian character of the new government. There was no capacity for sanction or enforcement, but via exposure and attention, bodies such as the HRC furnished ample material for the growing human rights movement to publicize, and another nucleus around which to mobilize international public opinion. For the victims of repression it was unlikely to mean freedom, except in especially rare instances, but it was a major step forward from silence.

This was especially so for those that had accompanying individual petition mechanisms, which were in various ways provided for in all the major covenants except the ICESCR. While it was entirely optional, many states did accede to the individual petition processes that were attached to the ICERD, ICCPR, CEDAW, CAT, and CRC. If all domestic avenues had been exhausted, a complaint could be submitted to the UN bodies responsible for these treaties in hope of supranational redress. The efficacy of petitioning was far from clear, but it did deliver meaningful outcomes for a number of individuals. Admittedly, many of those successes tended to involve citizens whose states had reasonably good human rights records. Signatories to the optional protocols were more frequently countries that presumed they had little to fear from additional attention, for instance, the social democratic countries of Western and northern Europe, Canada, Australia, and New Zealand. Equally, their citizens were sufficiently free to consider a petition without fear of state retribution. As a consequence, the petition mechanism improved the status of human rights in the places that were least in need of improvement.

Nevertheless, even quite liberal states were forced by petitions to do better, especially when it came to vulnerable groups that were not necessarily treated with sympathy by their fellow citizens. In Australia, a federal state, the Commonwealth government compelled one of its constituent states, Tasmania, to reform laws that discriminated against homosexuality, following a petition in late 1991.[38] In the absence of a domestic human rights charter, the various UN treaties provided a distant umbrella of protection when government, society, and the courts had failed. Layered and imperfect, the haphazard collage of treaties and protocols incrementally lent added safety nets, each providing a potential shield or remedy against human rights abuses. It was not elegant, but to those it assisted, the incoherent design of the treaty system was an inconsequential flaw.

By the close of the 1980s, this haphazard patchwork of treaties and procedures formally encompassed a huge expanse of themes. The terms of these texts were often impressive for their precision and fine calibration between competing traditions and imperatives. There was precious little wrong with the provisions of any of the grand catalogue of covenants and conventions, which promised to secure almost every right enumerated in the soaring aspiration of 1948, and in cases, notably the CEDAW and the CRC, went beyond the original aspiration. A raft of solemn signings and ratifications accrued, from the Nordic democracies to Nigeria. If the status-of-treaties register of the UN's Human Rights Centre had reflected reality, the state of human rights would have been healthy indeed.[39] The problem was that it did not, even remotely, accord with the actual situation in many of the signatory countries.

There were signs that the UN was, if anything, eager to insulate its human rights apparatus from the wider world. It moved many of its human rights operations to Geneva in 1974, and, privately, the decision was explained as a means of diminishing activity in the program. Crucially, it placed the sessions of the Commission on Human Rights an ocean away from the concentration of human rights NGOs that had set up their base in New York. At certain points, the UN Secretariat appeared to be actively pursuing countermeasures against communication with the victims of human rights abuses, notably with the 1969 instruction from Secretary-General U Thant that UN offices should refuse any correspondence presented by Soviet citizens. Thant's edict was a reaction to a petition from the Initiative Group on Human Rights, which had delivered a detailed protest against Soviet human rights violations, provoking a minor furor. Despite the institutional and logistical barriers, however, the world poured into New York and Geneva as plaintive letters asking for help. By the late 1960s, a very select handful of those complaints were actually being studied, after two decades of officially mandated indifference.

A Breakthrough? The Renascent and Refashioned Human Rights of the 1970s

In the wreckage of anti-colonialism, widespread disillusionment with both Western democratic and Soviet communist systems, and chronic dysfunction in the institutional human rights forums of the United Nations, a new source of energy was found. Anti-bureaucratic, anti-statist, and non-governmental, the assorted nodes of the 1970s human rights "breakthrough" resided beneath and outside the state, in the emergence of a substantial popular human rights NGO (HRNGO) movement. As an expression of mass moral sentiment, the HRNGOs of the late 1960s and 1970s were arguably peerless.[40] The new-generation NGOs that rose to prominence in the 1970s harnessed the less articulate moral sentiment of ordinary citizens. In so doing, they cultivated a mass organization that drew upon inchoate outrage and nebulous humanitarian sentiment. Amnesty International, and later Human Rights Watch, constructed a network of affiliated satellite groups, a web of engagement with human rights questions that was vastly more embedded in reality than the ethereal legalism of UN deliberations. At one point in the 1970s, Amnesty grew so precipitously that it lacked the logistical capacity to absorb and process all its would-be subscribers; mass enthusiasm for human rights advocacy was literally overwhelming its office staff.[41]

Paradoxically, the same Cold War polarization that did so much to damage progress on human rights within the UN, and that facilitated so many of the gross human rights violations of the second half of the twentieth century, also helped to seed this NGO-led revival. On both sides of the Cold War, although without substantial transnational connections before 1975, the critiques of local activists resulted in an efflorescence of civic activism and domestic concern for human rights. By December 1965, human rights groups within the USSR were challenging the entire framework of the society, questioning the ideology that justified one-party rule and its Marxist emphasis on economic and social rights. As Martin Luther King Jr. called on the US government to respect the rights of all citizens as accorded to them in the constitution, his counterparts within the USSR undertook a similar campaign calling for the party leadership respect the political and civil rights outlined under the Soviet constitution.[42]

Beyond the freedoms to be claimed under domestic law, in May 1969 the Initiative Group for the Defence of Human Rights in the USSR appealed to the United Nations to examine violations of the UDHR by the totalitarian state.[43] The United Nations largely ignored the organization to avoid the potential risks of antagonizing the USSR. Nonetheless, for the wider movement at home, the Initiative Group demonstrated the efficacy of human rights as a political tool. Such principles, proclaimed to have a universal character that crossed ideological divides, were used to undermine the rationale for repression by the regime and attract international supporters to the dissident cause. The Initiative Group demonstrated the moral worth of organizing and campaigning for human rights, despite the danger associated with such political ventures within a totalitarian society. As the regime began arresting supporters of the organization, the Initiative Group found itself able to write about abuses committed against its own members. Perversely, their persecution proved the case for human rights violations in the Soviet Union, but at the ultimate cost of survival of the organization past the middle of the 1970s.[44]

Revivification of the Soviet human rights movement rested, ironically, on a new multilateral treaty that was enthusiastically supported by the Soviet state. Seeking to reduce the risk of direct conflict, the two blocs entered into negotiations in the 1973 Conference on Security and Cooperation in Europe (CSCE) in Finland, developing a formal treaty to ensure greater stability and cooperation.[45] Thirty-five states, including the two superpowers, signed the Helsinki Final Act on 1 August 1975, upholding a mutual respect among all signatories for territorial integrity and collaborative action on common economic and social goals. Both Washington and Moscow expected far more stability than radical change as a result of the Final Act. However, the delegations of the Western European governments succeeded in agreeing to include a set of human rights provisions that entailed much greater transformative power than was acknowledged by any state at the time.

Within Principle VII of Basket I, the Final Act established a commitment to uphold "human rights and fundamental freedoms, including the freedom of thought, conscience, religion or belief, for all without distinction as to race, sex, language or religion."[46] The US government, regardless of the favourably Western orientation of the human rights provisions, saw limited value in the Final Act, perceiving it as a more successful outcome for the USSR.[47] Despite having initial reservations about the inclusion of human rights, the regimes of the Soviet Union and the Eastern bloc came to believe that the benefits outweighed any perceivable costs.[48] They would attain their long-awaited goal of broader recognition of their national sovereignty while encountering no enforceable mechanism to ensure their adherence to the human rights enshrined in the Final Act.

However, in the years following the signing of the Final Act, the priority of improving East–West relations and the aspiration for protection of human rights in the USSR became increasingly recognized as interdependent. Just as the repression by the Soviet regime succeeded in leading to dissolution of the Initiative Group, the organization's successors throughout the USSR—which included the Moscow Helsinki Watch Committee and Czechoslovakia's Charter 77—used the Final Act as a standard by which to hold their governments to account.[49] Transnational networks between East and West developed under the freer flows of information, ideas, and people provided for in Basket III.[50] Clampdowns on civic actors had proven to be an effective device for political control; however, the totalitarian governments were trapped by their own signatures, tying their regimes to international obligations to protect citizens from such excessive use of power by the state.[51] As a result of the "Helsinki Process," the USSR found its domestic human rights abuses becoming a global political issue, exceeding the grasp of the state and empowering local dissenters.

As its economy crumbled and its leadership ossified, the Soviet regime was simultaneously delegitimized by its manifest failings in the realm of human rights. The greater the exposure of human rights violations, as provided by dissidents and the wider transnational movement, the weaker became the Soviet Union's claim to ideological superiority. Human rights became less a concept that the Soviet regime could contest and reformulate, in accordance with its self-empowering Marxist-Leninist ideology, than a clearly defined set of standards, as laid out in the Final Act, by which to subvert its claim to power.[52] Brave Soviet citizens and the seemingly realist and coldly strategic Helsinki Accord had produced a result that the dedicated UN treaties failed to deliver: the USSR was among the first to sign and ratify the UN's human rights covenants.

A World Made New: The 1990s and the Very Modest Triumph of a Universal Human Rights System

In terms of sheer textual volume, the UN program of the 1960s minted human rights instruments at an impressive rate. Yet all this activity was an imperfect proxy for any substantive triumph of human rights. The proliferation of intricately balanced articles and interlocking freedoms sat at odds with a world composed of regimes with fragile—and rapidly diminishing—enthusiasm for the vision of 1948. The 1970s NGO mobilization and the emergence of Soviet human rights dissent were transformative phenomena, but they never fully recaptured the hopes of the immediate postwar moment. Human rights in their new, 1970s form were appreciably less ambitious than the sort of wholesale social and political reformation of the world enunciated by the early champions of the UDHR. Instead, the HRNGOs re-authored a minimalist vision of the most basic freedoms. Even this less ambitious goal—of diminishing the worst human rights abuses—did not appear to win much immediate success.

Submerged by an intensification of the Cold War during the first half of the 1980s, the significance of this geographically dispersed and chronologically erratic assortment of human rights movements was hard to discern. The worsening violence in apartheid South Africa, which spent much of the 1980s under various states of emergency, was testament to the decidedly modest powers and reach of international civil-society mobilization. While the international anti-apartheid movement exercised substantial (but invariably insufficient) pressure on the apartheid regime, perhaps more important was the domestic revival of rights within the South African freedom movement.[53] After a decade of valourizing armed struggle and drifting to new, emancipatory forms of Africanism and black consciousness, the movement now coalesced around the 1955 Freedom Charter, a document that set out most of the rights under the UDHR. Dormant for years, the Freedom Charter was raised again as the guiding document for the multiracial, society-wide coalition of the United Democratic Front, established in 1983. It would provide the spiritual blueprint for the new "rainbow nation," born in the first multiracial democratic elections in 1994.

At the Second World Conference on Human Rights, held in Vienna in June 1993, the distance between the 1960s and the dawning post–Cold War era was vividly rendered. NGOs monopolized the basement floor of the host venue, their professional displays and information videos being studied by state legations that ventured up and down the escalators. Above all, the subterranean network of women's rights NGOs emerged as perhaps the best organized, most transnational, and most eloquent and persuasive bearers of human rights discourse. It was clear that the NGO dimension of UN activity was now nearly equal to that of the sovereign states. Both were housed in the same building, the Vienna Convention Centre. Both held press conferences. Neither group could contain or silence the other, and both alternately irritated or cooperated with the other. It was a telling demonstration of how the official, state-dominated UN now related to the vigorous collection of transnational NGOs.[54]

Perhaps the signature clash between these two groups at Vienna was over the question of "Asian values." A set of authoritarian governments, predominantly from the Asian region, openly contested the universality of human rights, citing cultural differences. Led by China and the Islamic Republic of Iran, these states' elites pressed for a compromised universalism, citing social and cultural patterns and economic conditions. While the philosophical principle of universality ultimately survived Vienna, it did so in the language of diplomatic compromise. What best ensured its survival were the voices of NGOs from the Asian region. In their joint communiqué, the assembled NGOs had openly dissented from the idea of a monolithic set of "Asian values" that stood apart from universal human rights.

Vienna also produced, after 30 years of failed proposals, a firm decision to create the Office of the High Commissioner for Human Rights (OHCHR). The idea of a high commissioner empowered to lead the monitoring of human rights had been suggested from the mid-1960s onward. Each time, the initiative was blocked by authoritarian states. With the slow tide of democratization throughout the 1980s and early 1990s, plus NGO lobbying, the OHCHR at last had a majority behind it. From 1994 onward, the figure of the HCHR became a visible presence for human rights, providing regular appraisal of human rights situations and a permanent UN voice for human rights. The role called for more than a mere media commentator with authority. Sérgio Vieira de Mello, the third person to hold the High Commissioner position, would be murdered in August 2003 by insurgents while carrying out his duties, seeking to assist the people of Iraq.

For the gravest and most massive human rights abuses, international legal protection was radically bolstered in 1998 with the adoption of the Rome Statute, which created the International Criminal Court (ICC). Building upon the two ad hoc tribunals enacted to respond to the genocides in Rwanda and former Yugoslavia, the ICC would be a permanent institution, and a durable international court of criminal justice for the most appalling human rights violations. While the ICC arrived too late to provide an effective system for the two gravest abuses of the 1990s, and remained inconsistent in its application, it did provide some recourse, especially once its operations became more established in the mid-2000s. It also served as another node for NGO mobilization, in popular campaigns for prosecutors to investigate particular abuses. The abuses in Darfur, around which a large coalition of NGOs and private citizens rallied, were accompanied by demands that Sudanese president Omar al-Bashir face justice.[55]

All the while during the 2000s, the broader UN system continued to evolve. The new Human Rights Council, which represented a modestly upgraded replacement for the Commission on Human Rights, introduced the Universal Periodic Review (UPR). Under the UPR, every country was examined; their official government presentations were supplemented by NGO reports, which often read rather differently from those of the state. The fabric of human rights treaties became stronger and wider, with new optional protocols to established conventions and new areas of concern. The umbrella of treaty protection spread to persons with disabilities in 2006, with the adoption of the Convention on the Rights of Persons with Disabilities.[56] Again it fell to domestic civil society to make these undertakings real, increasingly using the tools of social media to pressure their governments.

Conclusion

More than 60 years after the close of the Second World War, the human rights order was a patchwork, one being constantly renovated with new patches of protection. It was neither the "world made new" of the utopian postwar vision nor the "slightly less wicked place" of the 1970s transnational revival.[57] It was, instead, both and neither of these visions. The grand hopes of the Universal Declaration remained only partially realized, despite more than half a century of effort since the euphoric evening of its adoption on 10 December 1948. Yet despite—or perhaps because of—decades of disappointment, the hope persisted, quoted by countless activists across the world. Equally, the transnational NGO network, which had lost faith in the state and appealed to citizens directly, had reached a modus vivendi with the state-centric and often bureaucratic institutions of the United Nations. All the accumulated covenants and conventions could not ensure human rights of themselves, but they furnished new spaces for advocacy and activism. The "shadow reports" of local NGOs now jostled for attention alongside those from governments.

Sovereign states had built the postwar human rights architecture, but slowly they had been forced to share it with these non-governmental representatives. Conventions that were signed without thought to consequences found life when wielded by local activists. Governments made promises at the United Nations, and their citizens, aided by a web of global allies, held those governments to account. This complementary relationship was not by design, but its powers were increasingly apparent by the 1990s. Human rights had not triumphed but they had survived, dispersed to smaller entities and advocacy groups. The myriad treaties may have been dead letters for a time, but with each success and each appeal, they acquired a life beyond the sterile surrounds of Geneva and New York. States built the UN treaty system. It fell to their citizens to give it meaning.

Takeaway Messages

- The emergence of the contemporary vision of human rights was a protracted and fiercely contested process, not the enunciation of a single consensual vision agreed upon by all at a single moment in time.
- Modern human rights ideas share a partial affinity with concepts and visions that extend back centuries, notably through the Atlantic revolutions. However, there are very significant extensions and divergences between the "human rights" of the 1790s and those of the 1940s, and even between the human rights of the 1940s and the late 1970s.
- Human rights are a project that involves state, civil society, and international and transnational elements. It was not a vision that encompassed the straightforward, unmediated transcendence of the state in the near term, but one that relied on the reconstruction of sovereignty to ensure the protection of individual rights.
- Different historical actors, governmental and non-governmental, led the struggle for human rights at various points during the century; there was no single, consistent source of leadership or reliable champion of universality.

Study Questions

- Were human rights born in 1948? To what extent did the Universal Declaration of Human Rights represent a rupture or radical break with the previous traditions of rights?
- Were anti-colonialism and the struggle for collective national freedom and sovereignty (self-determination) a human rights–oriented movement?
- What are the differences between the vision of human rights that was proclaimed in 1948 and that advanced by the transnational human rights movement that ascended in the 1970s?

Issue for Debate or Roundtable

- Were the architects of the Universal Declaration of Human Rights more interested in transcending the state or reforming it? Consider the text of the UDHR, its drafting debates, and the historical and political context of its production.

Additional Reading

Ishay, Micheline. *The History of Human Rights: From Ancient Times to the Globalization Era*. Berkeley: University of California Press, 2008.

Websites

Amnesty International. http://amnesty.org/en/.
International Commission of Jurists. http://www.icj.org.
Human Rights Watch. http://www.hrw.org.
Office of the High Commissioner for Human Rights. http://www.ohchr.org/EN/Pages/WelcomePage.aspx.
United Nations. Universal Periodic Review (UPR). http://www.ohchr.org/EN/HRBodies/UPR/Pages/UPRMain.aspx.
United Nations Human Rights Council. http://www.ohchr.org/EN/HRBodies/HRC/Pages/HRCIndex.aspx.
US Department of State. Human Rights Country Reports.
http://www.humanrights.gov/reports.

Notes

1. P.G. Lauren, *The Evolution of International Human Rights: Visions Seen* (Philadelphia: University of Pennsylvania Press, 2003), 1–3; S. Moyn, *The Last Utopia: Human Rights in History* (Cambridge, MA: Belknap/Harvard University Press, 2010), 7–8; R. Afshari, "On Historiography of Human Rights: Reflections on Paul Gordon Lauren's *The Evolution of International Human Rights: Visions Seen*," *Human Rights Quarterly* 29, no. 1 (February 2007): 65. See also S.-L. Hoffmann, "Genealogies of Human Rights," in *Human Rights in the Twentieth Century*, ed. S.-L. Hoffmann (Cambridge: Cambridge University Press, 2011), 2–3.
2. K. Cmiel, "The Recent History of Human Rights," *American Historical Review* 109, no. 1 (February 2004): 117–35.
3. Lauren, *Evolution of International Human Rights*; L. Hunt, *Inventing Human Rights* (New York: Norton, 2007).
4. K. Baker, "The Idea of a Declaration of Rights," in *The French Idea of Freedom*, ed. D.Van Kley (Stanford, CA: Stanford University Press, 1997), 154–96; K. Tunstall, *Self-Evident Truths? Human Rights and the Enlightenment* (New York: Bloomsbury, 2012).

5. M. Barnett, *Empire of Humanity: A History of Humanitarianism* (Ithaca, NY: Cornell University Press, 2011).
6. A. Hochschild, *King Leopold's Ghost: A Story of Greed, Terror and Heroism in Colonial Africa* (New York: Houghton Mifflin, 1999).
7. E. Manela, *The Wilsonian Moment: Self-Determination and the International Origins of Anticolonial Nationalism* (New York: Oxford University Press, 2007), 10.
8. G. Burgess, "Human Rights Dilemma in Anti-Nazi Protest: The Bernheim Petition, Minorities Protection, and the 1933 Sessions of the League of Nations," CERC Working Paper Series 2 (Melbourne, Australia: Contemporary Europe Research Centre, 2002), 1–56.
9. M. Mazower, "The Strange Triumph of Human Rights," *Historical Journal* 47, no. 2 (2004): 379–98; M. Mazower, "Minorities and the League of Nations in Interwar Europe," *Daedalus* 126, no. 2 (Spring 1997): 47–64.
10. J.H. Burgers, "The Road to San Francisco: The Revival of the Human Rights Idea in the Twentieth Century," *Human Rights Quarterly* 14, no. 4 (1992): 447–77. See also, on the American role in the nascent postwar human rights settlement, E. Borgwardt, *A New Deal for the World* (Cambridge, MA: Harvard University Press, 2005); and G. Mitoma, *Human Rights and the Negotiation of American Power* (Philadelphia: University of Pennsylvania Press, 2013). Compare T. Evans, *US Hegemony and the Project of Universal Human Rights* (London: Macmillan, 1996).
11. M. Duranti, "The Holocaust, the Legacy of 1789 and the Birth of International Human Rights Law: Revisiting the Foundation Myth," *Journal of Genocide Research* 14, no. 2 (2012): 159–86.
12. S. Dubow, "Smuts, the United Nations and the Rhetoric of Race and Rights," *Journal of Contemporary History* 43, no. 1 (January 2008): 45–74.
13. S. Waltz, "Universalizing Human Rights: The Role of Small States in the Construction of the Universal Declaration of Human Rights," *Human Rights Quarterly* 23, no. 1 (February 2001): 44–72.
14. M.A. Glendon, *A World Made New: Eleanor Roosevelt and the Universal Declaration of Human Rights* (New York: Random House, 2001).
15. J. Morsink, *The Universal Declaration of Human Rights: Origins, Drafting and Intent* (Philadelphia: University of Pennsylvania Press, 1999).
16. M.A. Glendon, "The Forgotten Crucible: The Latin American Influence on the Universal Human Rights Idea," *Harvard Human Rights Journal* 16 (Spring 2003): 27–39.
17. R. Normand and S. Zaidi, *Human Rights at the UN: The Political History of Universal Justice* (Bloomington: Indiana University Press, 2008), 142.
18. A.W.B. Simpson, *Human Rights and the End of Empire* (Oxford: Oxford University Press, 2001), 300.
19. R. Burke, *Decolonization and the Evolution of International Human Rights* (Philadelphia: University of Pennsylvania Press, 2010).
20. Charles Parkinson, *Bills of Rights and Decolonization* (Oxford: Oxford University Press, 2007), 32–33.
21. For a précis of the ICERD's provisions, see E. Schwelb, "The International Convention on the Elimination of All Forms of Racial Discrimination," *International and Comparative Law Quarterly* 15, no. 4 (1966): 966–1068.
22. See, generally, C. Robertson, *The Contentious History of the International Bill of Human Rights* (New York: Cambridge University Press, 2015).

23. D. Whelan, *Indivisible Human Rights: A History* (Philadelphia: University of Pennsylvania Press, 2010).
24. R. Burke, "Some Rights Are More Equal Than Others: The Third World and the Transformation of Economic and Social Rights," *Humanity* 3, no. 3 (Winter 2012): 427–48.
25. M. Bhagavan, *India and the Quest for One World: The Peacemakers* (New Delhi: HarperCollins, 2012).
26. S. Morphet, "Article 1 of the Human Rights Covenants: Its Development and Current Significance," in *Human Rights and Foreign Policy: Principles and Practice*, ed. D. Hill (Basingstoke, UK: Macmillan, 1989).
27. For a brief overview of the text and its precursors, see "Short History of CEDAW Convention," UN Women, http://www.un.org/womenwatch/daw/cedaw/history.htm.
28. M. Freeman, C. Chinkin, and B. Rudolf, eds., *The UN Convention on the Elimination of All Forms of Discrimination Against Women: A Commentary* (Oxford: Oxford University Press, 2012).
29. "Reservations to CEDAW," UN Women, www.un.org/womenwatch/daw/cedaw/reservations.htm.
30. See, generally, R. Cook, "State Accountability under the Convention on the Elimination of All Forms of Discrimination Against Women," in *Human Rights of Women National and International Perspectives*, ed. R. Cook (Philadelphia: University of Pennsylvania Press, 1994), 228–56.
31. J.H. Burgers, *The United Nations Convention Against Torture* (Boston: Martinus Nijhoff, 1988); M. Nowak and E. McArthur, *The United Nations Convention Against Torture* (New York: Oxford University Press, 2008). See also, for a general summary of the CAT's provenance and character, H. Danelius, "The Convention Against Torture," UN Audiovisual Library of International Law, http://legal.un.org/avl/ha/catcidtp/catcidtp.html.
32. For the mobilization around torture in the late 1960s and 1970s, see B. Keys, "Anti-Torture Politics: Amnesty International, the Greek Junta, and the Origins of the Human Rights 'Boom' in the United States," in *The Human Rights Revolution: An International History*, ed. A. Iriye, P. Goedde, and W.I. Hitchcock (Oxford: Oxford University Press, 2012), 201–21; S. Snyder, "The Rise of Human Rights During the Johnson Years," in *Beyond the Cold War: Lyndon Johnson and the New Global Challenges of the 1960s*, ed. F.J. Gavin and M.A. Lawrence (New York: Oxford University Press, 2014), 237–60; A.M. Clark, *Diplomacy of Conscience: Amnesty International and Changing Human Rights Norms* (Princeton, NJ: Princeton University Press, 2001), 37–68.
33. S. Detrick, *A Commentary on the United Nations Convention on the Rights of the Child* (Boston: Martinus Nijhoff, 1999).
34. On the drafting history, see "Convention on the Rights of the Child," UN Audiovisual Library of International Law, http://legal.un.org/avl/ha/crc/crc.html.
35. B. Nossiter, "U.N. Chief to Hold Inquiry on Rights in Poland," *New York Times*, 21 December 1982, 6; *Summary Records of the Commission on Human Rights*, 57th meeting (1982), 10 March 1982, E/CN.4/1982/SR.57.
36. C. Heyns and F. Viljoen, *The Impact of the United Nations Human Rights Treaties on the Domestic Level* (Dordrecht, Netherlands: Martinus Nijhoff, 2002).

37. *Summary Records of the Human Rights Committee*, 364th, 365th, and 366th meetings, 15–16 July 1982, Geneva, annex to CCPR/C/SR.364, SR.365, SR.366.
38. Australian Human Rights Commission, "Complaints about Australia to the Human Rights Committee," https://www.humanrights.gov.au/human-rights-explained-case-studies-complaints-about-australia-human-rights-committee. See also Parliamentary Library, Commonwealth of Australia, "Strange Bedfellows: The UN Human Rights Committee and the Tasmanian Parliament," Current Issues Brief no. 6 (1994), http://parlinfo.aph.gov.au/parlInfo/download/library/prspub/8VN10/upload_binary/8VN10.pdf;fileType=application%2Fpdf#search=%22bedfellows%20+%20tasmanian%22. When the HRC ruled the complaint valid in 1994, to bring Australia into compliance with its obligations under the ICCPR, the Commonwealth government passed legislation that superseded the Tasmanian state law. Because the ICCPR had been an undertaking to the international community by the Commonwealth, the external affairs powers in the federal constitution enabled intervention in what was otherwise normally the sphere of state law.
39. United Nations, "Status of Treaties," Office of the High Commissioner for Human Rights, http://www.ohchr.org/Documents/HRBodies/HRChart.xls.
40. J. Eckel, "The International League for the Rights of Man, Amnesty International, and the Changing Fate of Human Rights Activism from the 1940s Through the 1970s," *Humanity* 4, no. 2 (2013): 183–214; J. Eckel and S. Moyn, ed., *The Breakthrough: Human Rights in the 1970s* (Philadelphia: University of Pennsylvania Press, 2013).
41. B. Keys, *Reclaiming American Virtue* (Cambridge, MA: Harvard University Press, 2014).
42. L. Alexeyeva, *Soviet Dissent: Contemporary Movements for National, Religious, and Human Rights* (Middletown, CT: Wesleyan University Press, 1985), 267–69.
43. R. Horvath, "Breaking the Totalitarian Ice: The Initiative Group for the Defence of Human Rights in the USSR," *Human Rights Quarterly* 36, no. 1 (February 2014): 156–57.
44. Ibid., 164–75.
45. T. Fischer, "'A Mustard Seed Grew into a Bushy Tree': The Finnish CSCE Initiative of 5 May 1969," *Cold War History* 9, no. 2: 177–79.
46. "Conference on Security and Co-operation in Europe, Final Act, Helsinki," 1975, http://www.osce.org/mc/39501?download=true; C.P. Peterson, *Globalizing Human Rights: Private Citizens, the Soviet Union, and the West* (New York: Routledge, 2012), 7; D. Thomas, *The Helsinki Effect: International Norms, Human Rights, and the Demise of Communism* (Princeton, NJ: Princeton University Press, 2001), 257–58; D. Thomas, "Human Rights Ideas, the Demise of Communism, and the End of the Cold War," *Journal of Cold War Studies* 7, no. 2 (Spring 2005): 124; A. Wenger and V. Mastny, "New Perspectives on the Origins of the CSCE Process," in *Origins of the European Security System: The Helsinki Process Revisited, 1965–75*, ed. A. Wenger, V. Mastny, and C. Nuenlist (Abingdon, UK: Routledge, 2008), 18–19; J. Suri, "Détente and Human Rights: American and West European Perspectives on International Change," *Cold War History* 8, no. 4 (November 2008): 537.
47. J.M. Hanhimäki, "'They Can Write It in Swahili': Kissinger, the Soviets, and the Helsinki Accords, 1973–75," *Journal of Transatlantic Studies* 1, Suppl. 1 (2003): 40; M.C. Morgan, "The Seventies and the Rebirth of Human Rights," in *The Shock of the Global: The 1970s in Perspective*, ed. N. Ferguson, C.S. Maier, E. Manela, and

D.J. Sargent (Cambridge, MA: Belknap/Harvard University Press, 2010), 247–48; R. Davy, "Helsinki Myths: Setting the Record Straight on the Final Act of the CSCE, 1975," *Cold War History* 9, no. 1: 4; W. Korey, *The Promises We Keep: Human Rights, the Helsinki Process, and American Foreign Policy* (New York: St. Martin's Press, 1993), xix–xxiii.

48. Thomas, *Helsinki Effect*, 264, 268–69.
49. S. Snyder, *Human Rights Activism and the End of the Cold War* (New York: Cambridge University Press, 2011), 13.
50. Thomas, *Helsinki Effect*, 21–22, 280–81, 284–85.
51. Alexeyeva, *Soviet Dissent*, 17–18.
52. Peterson, *Globalizing Human Rights*, 14, 182, 186.
53. S. Dubow, *South Africa's Struggle for Human Rights* (Athens: Ohio University Press, 2012), 87–126.
54. For the rise and impact of transnational NGOs and their interactions with international institutions, see, generally, M. Keck and K. Sikkink, *Activists Beyond Borders: Advocacy Networks in International Politics* (Ithaca, NY: Cornell University Press, 1998); J. Quataert, *Advocating Dignity: Human Rights Mobilizations in Global Politics* (Philadelphia: University of Pennsylvania Press, 2010); T. Risse, T. Risse-Kappen, S. Ropp, and K. Sikkink, eds., *The Persistent Power of Human Rights: From Commitment to Compliance* (Cambridge: Cambridge University Press, 2013); A. Neier, *The International Human Rights Movement: A History* (Princeton, NJ: Princeton University Press, 2012), 233–57; Clark, *Diplomacy of Conscience*, 9–20.
55. cf. M. Mamdani, *Saviors and Survivors: Darfur, Politics, and the War on Terror* (New York: Doubleday, 2010).
56. "Convention on the Rights of Persons with Disabilities," UN Audiovisual Library of International Law, http://legal.un.org/avl/ha/crpd/crpd.html.
57. Moyn, *Last Utopia*, 147.

PART TWO

3
Political Institutions and the Protection of Human Rights

GORDON DIGIACOMO

Learning Objectives

- To understand the part that certain political institutions can play in the protection of human rights
- To become familiar with the concept of constitutional judicial review

It must sometimes appear to citizens that the burden of protecting their rights falls mainly to judicial institutions. Certainly it is true that in a number of countries the courts are empowered to strike down enactments and executive decisions (or parts of enactments and executive decisions) that are judged to be in violation of a constitutionally entrenched human right. But this is only part of the story. Political institutions too have a critically important function in rights protection. Indeed, many scholars prefer a more prominent role for political institutions, most especially legislatures and parliaments.

The objective of this chapter is to show how certain political institutions can protect human rights. It opens by discussing the practice of constitutional judicial review, an issue that divides those who support a strong role for the judiciary and those who see the value and importance of political institutions in protecting citizens' rights. The following section discusses the potential for rights protection by executive systems, electoral systems, and political parties.[1] The choice of political institutions to include in this chapter was based on my interest in the impact of these institutions and on their fundamental importance to democracy and rights protection. In other chapters in this volume, the authors discuss the relationship between rights and other political institutions, namely federalism and advocacy groups.

Other scholars, it should be noted, would have a different list of political institutions. For Tom Campbell, K.D. Ewing, and Adam Tomkins, "the protection of human rights ultimately depends on the capacities of political institutions, such as parliaments, political parties, the trade union movement, and interest groups."[2] Canadian political scientist Janet Hiebert believes that, in order for governments to feel "compelled to justify or amend decisions involving rights," a number of institutional reforms would have to be made, including "electoral reform, to prevent government domination of parliament, a large enough parliament (to ensure sufficient numbers of members who view their role as parliamentarians, rather than through the lens of their party-political aspirations), and/or effective bicameralism, to provide more independence from the governing party."[3] In her comparative analysis of constitutional review in Europe, legal scholar Maartje de Visser looks at the roles of these political institutions in constitutional review: councils of state and chancellors of justice (advisory bodies that review bills); parliaments and parliamentary committees; heads of state; and "the people," by which she means public opinion, the media, and academia.[4]

Judicial Review

Like most of the world's states,[5] Canada has a constitution that contains a comprehensive set of rights. The Canadian Charter of Rights and Freedoms comprises the first 34 sections of the Constitution Act, 1982. The insertion of these rights provisions into the Canadian constitution greatly expanded the scope of what is called constitutional judicial review.

Constitutional judicial review refers to the power of the courts to examine government enactments and decisions and determine if they are consistent with the constitution. If an enactment or decision, from any government, is determined to be inconsistent with the constitution, the courts may strike it down or, in some countries, notify the legislators that it is incompatible with human rights provisions.[6]

The eminent American constitutional scholar Mark Tushnet has distinguished between "strong-form" and "weak-form" judicial review. Of the United States, which practices strong-form judicial review, Tushnet writes: "The US system of judicial review ... insists that the courts' reasonable constitutional interpretations prevail over the legislatures' reasonable ones. Courts exercise strong-form judicial review when their interpretive judgments are final and unrevisable. The modern articulation of strong-form judicial review is provided in *Cooper v. Aaron*, where the U.S. Supreme Court described the federal courts as 'supreme in the exposition of the law of the Constitution,' and inferred from that a duty on legislatures to follow the Court's interpretations."[7]

In the US, every court is able to judge whether a law is unconstitutional and to declare it null and void. In weak-form judicial review, on the other hand, "judicial interpretations of constitutional provisions can be revised in the relatively short term by a legislature."[8] In other words, the legislative branch has the last word on the constitutionality of an enactment. Tushnet classifies Canada as a country with weak-form judicial review. He is not a fan of judicial review. In his view, "giving judges the power to enforce constitutional limitations can threaten democratic self-governance."[9]

The Canadian judiciary has always had the power of judicial review because of the federal nature of the Canadian state. Courts can invalidate a law if it is judged to be beyond the constitutional authority of the government that enacted it. Since 1982, the courts have had another basis on which to strike down a law: the Canadian Charter of Rights and Freedoms. If a law is judged to be in violation of the Charter, a court can invalidate it, or parts of it, unless the government invokes section 33 of the Charter, known as the notwithstanding clause or "legislative override." This section allows a government, federal or provincial, to enact a law even though it may have been found in violation of section 2 (fundamental freedoms), sections 7–14 (legal rights), or section 15 (equality rights). However, the relevant legislative branch must approve of the invocation, which is in effect for five years, after which it must be renewed by that legislative branch. It is the presence of section 33 in the Charter that enables Tushnet to classify constitutional judicial review in Canada as being weak-form, with respect to Charter cases. In reality, the section has been very rarely used, and it has never been used by the federal government.

Section 52(1) of the Constitution Act, 1982, authorizes constitutional judicial review. It states: "The Constitution of Canada is the supreme law of Canada, and any law that is inconsistent with the provisions of the Constitution is, to the extent of the inconsistency, of no force or effect." Since, as Peter Hogg points out, "it inevitably falls to the courts to determine whether or not a law is inconsistent with the Charter [or the distribution-of-powers sections in the Constitution Act, 1867], s. 52 (1) provides an explicit basis for judicial review of legislation in Canada."[10]

Strong-form constitutional judicial review on Charter rights grounds has been subject to serious criticism by Canadian scholars. As suggested by Tushnet above, the principal criticism has to do with the perceived undemocratic nature of judicial review. Any society that aspires to be democratic, Janet Hiebert writes, "should resolve the most important priorities through its elected legislatures rather than in courts."[11] In a system of judicial review, the argument goes, a small group of unelected, unrepresentative, unaccountable justices makes decisions on vitally important issues that ought to be made by the elected representatives of the citizens. Conversely, judges should not have the power to strike down decisions made by a democratically elected legislature.

A number of variants of this criticism have been advanced. Morton and Knopff argue that women's rights groups and minority groups have been able to achieve through the courts what they were not able to achieve through democratically elected majorities in parliament and the legislatures.[12] "From this viewpoint, judicial decisions under the Charter tend to show preference to minority interests and thus exhibit an anti-majoritarian tendency."[13] Another variant of the democracy criticism comes from Peter Russell. He suggests that the Charter and judicial review could weaken rather than strengthen the democratic character of the citizenry. He has written, "The danger here is not so much that non-elected judges will impose their will on a democratic majority, but that the questions of social and political justice will be transformed into technical legal questions and the great bulk of the citizenry who are not judges and lawyers will abdicate their responsibility for working out reasonable and mutually acceptable resolutions of the issues which divide them."[14] In other words, judicial review turns important social and political questions into legal queries, thereby transforming citizens into bystanders rather than active participants in the resolution of those issues.

Judicial review, of course, has its defenders. One argument in support of judicial review is that the rights of citizens should not be subject to political winds. In any society at any time, majorities may feel negatively toward certain groups and elect politicians who share those views. If parliaments and legislative assemblies had the last word on rights, the rights of those groups could be imperilled. Certainly the history of Canada does not lead one to conclude that parliament and the provincial legislatures have been attentive to the rights issues of particular communities such as Aboriginal peoples, Asian Canadians, and women.

The argument is also made that judicial review is necessary to protect democratic government. An independent judiciary is a bulwark against any attempt to unreasonably curtail our democratic rights and fundamental freedoms. Freedom of the press, of assembly, of expression, and the right to vote—these and other rights are all necessary for a democracy to flourish. The judiciary exists to uphold these rights against legislative assemblies that might be tempted to infringe on them unreasonably. So, while it is true that judges are unelected, judicial review's supporters say it can protect the country's democracy.[15]

Dominic DiFruscio points out additionally that it was elected officials, representing a majority of Canadians, who approved the Charter, and it was their clear intention to grant an independent judiciary the power to strike down legislation inconsistent with the values embedded in the Charter. He also recalls that the constitutional patriation process "involved open parliamentary committee hearings."[16] He quotes legal scholar Lorraine Weinrib, who described the process as "exemplary." DiFruscio includes in his defence of the Charter and judicial review reference to public opinion polls, which have consistently shown substantial citizen support across the country for the Charter and the role of the courts in protecting rights.

It cannot be denied though, that, throughout history, the courts too have upheld discriminatory and anti-democratic legislation and practices. The lesson appears to be that the responsibility for rights protection lies not only with the judicial institutions but also with the political institutions and an active civil society.

Of the 10 countries with the highest scores on *The Economist*'s 2013 Democracy Index—Norway, Sweden, Iceland, Denmark, New Zealand, Australia, Switzerland, Canada, Finland, and Luxembourg—only Canada comes close to practicing strong-form judicial review. In the Nordic region, Ran Hirschl writes, "variations on a combination of well-established, *ex ante* parliamentary review and restrained *ex post* judicial review have proven effective in … ensuring an alternative, non-juristocratic way of going about protecting rights."[17] In Finland, a parliamentary committee called the Constitutional Law Committee, comprising members of parliament and advised by constitutional experts, reviews bills whose constitutionality is in doubt prior to enactment.[18] Australia does not have a bill of rights, although it does have a number of rights-related enactments and a human rights commission. New Zealand has only a statutory bill of rights. Judges cannot invalidate legislation but they are able to add or delete words to ensure compatibility with the New Zealand Bill of Rights Act. The onus is on the attorney general and the ministry of justice to draft legislative initiatives that are consistent with the Act. In the United Kingdom, which adheres to the principle of parliamentary supremacy, a parliamentary committee is a significant player in the work of ensuring compatibility between legislation and human rights.

It should be mentioned here that several countries around the world assign the task of constitutional judicial review to specialized constitutional courts. Among those countries are Germany, Italy, Spain, South Korea, South Africa, Chile, and Hungary. Eighteen of the 27 countries of the European Union have created constitutional courts. Constitutional courts differ from the Canadian and American model in that they address only constitutional issues and typically possess a monopoly on constitutional adjudication. They also differ in the way that they undertake judicial review. For instance, the German Constitutional Court uses three review procedures.[19] One is called "abstract review," when a bill is reviewed before it is enacted or comes into effect. It is usually politically initiated; various authorities are able to refer bills to the Court for constitutional review (this type of review is not unlike the Canadian reference procedure). A second procedure is "concrete review," when judges of ordinary courts send questions of constitutionality to the Court during litigation. Proceedings are suspended until the Court renders its decision. A third procedure is called the "constitutional complaint," under which individuals, firms, and groups can petition the Court if they believe their rights have been violated.

Constitutional courts vary in their functions and powers. What is important, of course, is their effectiveness, and various scholars have identified criteria for effectiveness.[20] For Alec Stone Sweet, the most effective constitutional courts are in Colombia, the Czech Republic, Germany, Hungary, Indonesia, Poland, Slovenia, South Africa, and South Korea.[21] From the perspective of this chapter, what is important is their effectiveness at protecting rights. In ranking Colombia and Hungary among the most effective constitutional courts, Stone Sweet was doubtless thinking about certain of their features that are of considerable interest to rights scholars.

In Colombia, for instance, any individual whose rights are being threatened can request any judge to protect his or her rights. Citizens may file a claim without an attorney, and the judge, who is legally bound to give priority attention to such requests, must reach a decision within 10 days. The judge can order the adoption of any measure necessary to protect the threatened right, even before issuing a final decision. All these decisions can be reviewed by the Constitutional Court, and indeed it has used this provision to expand the catalogue of protected rights.[22]

In Hungary until 2012, citizens had access to a mechanism called the *actio popularis*—the right of an individual, citizen or not, to initiate abstract review regardless of his or her specific legal interest in the case. As a result of people's use of this procedure, several important laws were invalidated, including the death penalty. Restrictive rules of standing were not applied because the individual who launched an *actio popularis* was considered a "trustee of the public good" rather than an aggrieved complainant. Not surprisingly, the workload of the Hungarian Constitutional Court became unmanageable.[23] In 2012 the *actio popularis* was replaced with a somewhat more restrictive procedure.

Political Institutions and the Protection of Rights

Executive Types and Rights

Democratic governments typically consist of three branches: an executive branch, a legislative branch, and a judicial branch. Determining the degree to which each is separated from the others—referred to as the separation of powers[24]—is a central task of constitutional designers. The executive branch initiates and implements laws and manages the government on a day-to-day basis. The legislative branch makes laws, monitors the executive branch, and represents citizens. The judicial branch interprets the laws and adjudicates disputes about questions of law.

Scholars have identified three types of executive systems: the parliamentary system, the presidential system, and the hybrid or mixed system. In what follows, the three types are briefly described and the contours of the debate among scholars about which is most rights-protective are outlined.

Parliamentary government, or parliamentarism, is a structure of government in which "a collective executive is accountable to an elected legislative chamber."[25] If the executive loses the confidence of the chamber, through what is called a vote of no confidence, the executive falls, in which case an election is held or another party (or coalition of parties) is called upon to form a government. Parliamentarism is the most common form of democratic government; among the countries with such a system are Canada, the United Kingdom, India, Norway, South Africa, Japan, and Jamaica.

In a parliamentary system, the separation of powers is not as rigid as it is in presidential systems. This is because the members of the executive, including the head of government—the prime minister—are drawn from the legislative branch. There is then some degree of fusion between the executive and legislative branches. Prime ministers are indirectly elected. Voters cast their ballots in electoral districts for a candidate of a party that has already selected its leader. If the party wins the election, the leader becomes the prime minister. Parliamentary systems typically have a symbolic head of state: a president or monarch; the powers associated with this position are largely ceremonial.

Baranger and Murray make the important point that the need for the executive to retain the confidence of parliament does not mean that parliament is dominant. Indeed, the opposite is often the case. With a majority of the members belonging to his or her party, the prime minister has considerable law-making power. In addition, members do not readily vote to bring down a government, since to do so is to place their own positions at risk. Nevertheless, the prime minister has to keep the cabinet ministers and members onside or face the prospect of an election or the wrath of the parliamentary party. Margaret Thatcher of Britain and Jean Chrétien of Canada were highly successful politicians who delivered consecutive majority governments for their respective parties, but they were inelegantly pushed out of office by their own parties because of internal dissatisfaction.

Generally speaking, parliamentary systems do not have fixed election dates as presidential systems do. This is because parliamentary governments may sometimes be in a minority situation, where the total number of opposition seats is greater than the number of government seats. In such circumstances a government could face a vote of no confidence at virtually any time and a fixed election date would be meaningless. It would, of course, work in a majority government situation.

The British model is not the only model of parliamentarism. In South Africa, for example, the president is head of both the executive and the state. The legislative assembly elects the president from among its members, but once elected the president leaves the assembly. Still, the basic feature of parliamentarism remains, namely "the accountability of a collective executive to the legislature."[26] In sum, then, a parliamentary regime is a system of mutual dependence, in that "the chief executive power must be supported by a majority in the legislature and can fall if it receives a vote of no confidence," and the executive "has the capacity to dissolve the legislature and call for elections."[27]

In contrast, a presidential type of executive is a system of mutual independence. The separation of executive, legislative, and judicial functions is much more rigid than it is in parliamentary systems. Both the president and the members of the legislative branch are directly elected, giving both independent sources of legitimacy. Examples of states with presidential executives are the United States, Brazil, Argentina, the Philippines, South Korea, Nigeria, Chile, and Costa Rica.

The president is both head of government and head of state. The members of the president's cabinet may or may not be members of the legislative branch. Mostly they are not, in keeping with the separation-of-powers principle. As mentioned, in parliamentary systems, cabinet ministers are largely drawn from the legislative branch. Presidential executives have fixed election dates. Thus, a president can be removed only by a lengthy process of impeachment, which is undertaken not for reasons pertaining to policy disagreement but for reasons of competence, integrity, or behaviour. An impeachment process, Pippa Norris points out, entails "a major constitutional crisis and a period of serious political instability and uncertainty."[28]

Party discipline, which refers to the requirement that the legislators vote as directed by the party leadership, is much weaker in presidential systems. Thus legislators in presidential democracies are freer to cast their votes according to their own views or according to the views of their constituents. In presidential executives, the party leadership exerts pressure on legislators to vote in a certain way, but the consequences for legislators of not doing so are not as severe as they are in parliamentary systems.

In presidential systems, the legislative agenda is set by the legislative branch. Members can and do introduce bills, with or without the support of the executive. In parliamentary systems, the executive controls the legislative agenda and legislators rarely have their proposed bills debated, let alone enacted. Representatives from both the executive and legislative branches in a presidential executive may collaborate in the formulation of bills and in the setting of the agenda, but the legislature and its members have considerably more clout than they do in parliamentary systems.

Baranger and Murray note that, while the American presidential model has been frequently adopted around the world, particularly in Latin America, many countries have deviated significantly from the US example: "In many South American and African countries, the powers of the President are substantially greater than those of the US President and checks and balances weaker."[29] For example, the president may be given broad powers to issue decrees, that is, laws that are not submitted to the legislature for approval. Emergency powers, including the power to cease the operation of human rights enactments, may also be given to the president. The impact of the use of these powers on democratic government is obvious.

The third type of executive/legislative arrangement is the mixed or hybrid model. This system features a dual executive, with a president sharing power with a prime minister. Depending on which office has more power, a hybrid system may be termed semi-presidential or semi-parliamentary. The president in a hybrid arrangement is elected directly by popular vote and may be given important constitutional powers. While the prime minister and cabinet ministers are accountable to parliament, as in parliamentary systems, the president is not. The president cannot be removed from office prior to the end of his or her term.

The system most often cited as an example of a hybrid model is the system used in France. There the president retains significant powers, including the authority to nominate the prime minister and to choose his or her own cabinet.[30] Legislation is initiated and drafted mostly by the president, the ministers, and the bureaucracy. The president also conducts foreign policy on behalf of the government. Day-to-day management of the government is left to the prime minister. Other countries with hybrid systems are Portugal, Taiwan, and Nicaragua. Norris reports that, as of 2003, 92 countries used the hybrid model. One of the "most striking developments in new constitutions has been the popularity of this form of regime, for example, throughout Central Europe."[31]

A country with a dual executive may end up with a president from one political party and a prime minister and parliamentary representatives from another. On occasion this has happened in France. In this circumstance, Baranger and Murray point out that "the President's formal constitutional powers are intact, but his/her political authority is diminished. The French system then functions as a classic 'monistic' parliamentary government, in which the Prime Minister sets the political agenda and is accountable only to the majority in Parliament."[32] The arrangement may not always work out so neatly. If the ideological and policy divisions between the president and prime minister are significant, the president may be tempted to use emergency or decree powers to get around the prime minister and his or her majority. In such a context, Cindy Skach writes, "the design flaw of semi-presidentialism ... becomes apparent."[33] The consequences for rights also become apparent.

Political actors in deeply divided societies may be drawn to hybrid models because they make possible a degree of power-sharing. Representatives from different segments of society can occupy the executive positions. If both parties are able to collaborate, the dual executive can be effective. Of course, from a rights perspective, it is critical that both positions be open to all citizens of a country, regardless of ethnicity, religion, region, or nationality.[34]

The question before us now is this: which of the executive types is the most rights-protective? A number of scholars have discussed the relationship between executive type and democracy.[35] Among them is Juan Linz, who took a strong stand against presidential systems. In an oft-quoted article, Linz notes that the vast majority of stable democracies in the world are parliamentary democracies. Indeed, "the only presidential democracy with a long history of constitutional continuity is the United States."[36] The problems with presidential types, Linz argues, stem from the "democratic legitimacy" that both the executive branch and the legislative branch can claim (since both are directly elected) and the fixed terms of presidential executives. These institutional features frequently produce deadlocks that tempt presidents to use extraordinary measures or the armed forces to intervene. The fixed terms mean that there is no readily accessible way to remove an unpopular leader between elections; the cumbersome tool of impeachment is the only way to do so. By contrast, prime ministers can dissolve parliament and call an election to break prolonged stalemates. As Stepan and Skach write, "the executive's right to dissolve parliament and the legislature's right to pass a vote of no confidence are deadlock-breaking devices."[37] In addition, as noted previously, in parliamentary systems an unpopular leader can be forced out of office by members of his or her own party.

Other scholars have taken a less categorical stance on presidential systems. Donald Horowitz, for instance, believes that a presidential system can be beneficial in divided societies. He has a qualification, however, and it is one that is demonstrated in the case of Nigeria: in order to win, a presidential candidate needs to obtain at least 25 per cent of the vote in at least two-thirds of all Nigeria's states.[38] From a rights perspective, it can be argued that the requirement could translate into greater sensitivity and responsiveness to citizens outside the candidate's ethnic group, home base, or religious community, which in turn could lead to enhanced rights protection.

José Antonio Cheibub concedes that parliamentary systems have higher survival rates than presidential systems, but this is because presidential systems have emerged more frequently in countries where the probability of democratic breakdown is high. Presidentialism is not inherently flawed; rather, the fragility of presidential systems is a function of "the inhospitable environments in which such systems have been established. In these environments, any executive type would demonstrate fragility."[39] Cheibub is favourable to the type of condition laid out by Horowitz.

Norris has examined the impact of political institutions in her book *Driving Democracy: Do Power-Sharing Institutions Work?* She uses four scales, or sets of indicators, to assess which political institutions most effectively serve democracy and rights. For our purposes, the most pertinent scale of the four is the Freedom House scale, which measures a country's performance with respect to political rights and civil liberties. Among the institutions Norris analyzes are electoral systems, federalism, and type of executive.

Norris tested Linz's thesis in her quantitative analysis of the effects of executive type on rights and democracy. She looked at four types of executive used worldwide: parliamentary monarchies, presidential republics, mixed republics, and military states. Her research results confirm that, as Linz argues, presidential republics are associated with lower levels of democracy and rights protection than parliamentary democracies. Notably, presidential republics are more often associated with political crisis—such as coups d'état, major constitutional changes, general strikes, and purges of opposition—than parliamentary monarchies. In the latter, Norris writes,

> there are multiple checks and balances on political leaders. The dual executive divides the ceremonial monarch as the symbolic head of state from the prime minister, functioning as the effective head of government. The government faces the electorate at regular intervals, and between these contests, the cabinet remains collectively accountable in their daily actions to the scrutiny of the legislature, and, if they lose the confidence and trust of their backbenchers, they pay the ultimate penalty and lose office. The flexibility in the prime minister's tenure, so that the leadership can be replaced without a major constitutional crisis if he or she loses support, provides an additional safety valve.[40]

For advocates of human rights, the preferred option appears to be parliamentary systems.

Electoral Systems and Rights

An electoral system is "the set of rules that structure how votes are cast at elections for a representative body and how these votes are then converted into seats in that assembly."[41] The association between electoral systems and human rights may not be obvious but it does exist. It is perhaps one reason why countries take seriously their choice of electoral system. About 20 per cent of countries, including Kenya, Ireland, Austria, and Italy, specify the electoral system for the lower house of the national legislature in their constitution.[42]

The following briefly describes the main electoral systems[43] and then discusses which is generally believed to be the most rights-protective. Scholars of electoral systems have identified four families of such systems: the plurality family, the majoritarian family, the proportional representation family, and the mixed family.

The most popular electoral method in the plurality family is the first-past-the-post (FPTP) system, also known as the single-member plurality (SMP) or single-member district (SMD) system.[44] According to the International Institute for Democracy and Electoral Assistance (IDEA), as of 2004, 23.6 per cent of 199 countries and territories of the world used the FPTP system.[45] Examples are Canada, Britain, the United States, Botswana, India, and Malaysia. In the FPTP method, the "district magnitude"—that is, the number of representatives elected from an electoral district— is one. The winner is the candidate who gets the most votes.

The majoritarian family has two electoral methods, the two-round system and the alternative vote. The distinguishing feature of majoritarian methods is the requirement that the winner get 50 per cent plus one of the votes cast. In both methods, one member is elected from each electoral district. In the two-round system, if no candidate gets a majority of the votes, a second round of voting is held, usually between the top two finishers of the first round. In the alternative-vote method, voters are able to rank their preferences on the ballot. In the first count, if no candidate gets a majority of the votes, the last-place finisher is dropped and his or her second preferences are distributed accordingly. These counts are continued until a candidate gets a majority of the votes.

The objective of the proportional representation (PR) systems is to ensure a congruence between the percentage of votes that a political party wins and the percentage of seats that the party is given: if a party gets 30 per cent of the vote, it should get 30 per cent of the seats. The main PR methods are list PR and the single transferable vote (STV). About 36 per cent of 199 countries and territories in the world use some form of proportional representation.[46]

In the list PR system, each political party presents a list of candidates to voters in a multi-member district, that is, an electoral district that has more than one representative. When voters enter the voting booth, they vote for a party, not a candidate. Each party receives seats in proportion to its overall share of the vote in the district. Winning candidates are taken from the lists in order of their position on the lists. In some countries that use list PR, voters can rank the candidates on the party list according to their preferences. The ranking of candidates is referred to as preferential voting.

The STV method also features multi-member districts, but voters are able to vote for individual candidates and, as with the open list PR method, they can rank their preferences. Significantly, political parties can run more than one candidate in each district. This method is distinctive in the way ballots are counted. It is a complicated process, which may be one reason why it is used in very few countries—namely Ireland, Malta, and Australia (for elections to the federal senate). Nevertheless, this system was recommended by the British Columbia Citizens' Assembly on Electoral Reform in 2004.

The fourth family is called the mixed family, and it features two electoral methods, mixed-member proportional and mixed-member parallel. Germany and New Zealand are among the relatively few countries that use the mixed-member proportional system, and Japan and South Korea are among the countries that use the mixed-member parallel method. In 2007 the Ontario Citizens' Assembly on Electoral Reform recommended the mixed-member proportional system for the province of Ontario. In each of the mixed systems, two methods are used, the objective being to capture the advantages of the list PR method and those of either the FPTP system or the alternative-vote method. The distinguishing element of the mixed methods is that voters are able to vote both for an individual candidate and for a political party. It is, therefore, possible for a voter to select an individual candidate who does not belong to the party that he or she chooses.

Some countries use another method to enhance the fairness of elections: reserving seats for specific communities. Reserved seats have been defined as "seats in which a determinable criterion such as religion, ethnicity, language or gender is a requirement for nomination or election."[47] Andrew Reynolds has identified 32 countries or autonomous territories that reserve seats for certain minority groups. Among them are New Zealand, which has seven seats reserved for Maori citizens, and Lebanon, which has 64 seats reserved for Christian representatives and an equal number reserved for Muslim representatives. He also lists the countries that use special mechanisms to ensure the representation of minorities, such as the United States, which employs explicit race-conscious districting, and four countries, including Denmark and Finland, that over-represent defined ethnic communities.[48]

Which of the electoral methods is the most rights-protective? For an answer to that question, we turn again to the work of Pippa Norris. In her analysis of electoral systems, Norris uses both large-N cross-national time series analysis and case studies. She concludes that "countries using list PR electoral systems consistently rate as significantly the most democratic."[49] Further, "the results confirm that PR electoral systems are more democratic than majoritarian systems, *a pattern replicated irrespective of the choice of indicator used*, and a pattern that was particularly marked in divided societies."[50] In other words, the electoral method that promoted and protected rights and democracy most effectively was the list PR system.

List proportional representation tends to be more rights-protective than other systems because of the freedom that political parties have in whom they can appoint to the party lists. The competition for votes gives parties an incentive to appoint women candidates, as well as candidates from politically salient minority groups, to the lists that are presented to the electorate. This results in greater numbers of women and minority candidates being elected to legislatures around the globe. The theory posits that, with greater representation in a country's legislature, women and minorities will have the strength to be an effective voice for the protection of the rights of the members of their respective communities.

The data do indicate that PR systems facilitate the entry of women and minorities into the world's law-making bodies. For instance, Norris has pointed out that "today around the globe roughly twice as many women get elected to national parliaments under PR (19.6%) than under majoritarian electoral systems (10.5%)." Mixed systems "fall between these poles (13.6%)."[51] The website of the Inter-Parliamentary Union contains additional revealing data. It shows, for instance, that as of February 2014, the percentage of women sitting in the world's national parliaments (both houses) was 21.7 per cent. In the lower houses it was slightly higher: 22.1 per cent. However, in the five Nordic countries (Denmark, Finland, Iceland, Norway, and Sweden)—all of which have list PR systems—the percentage was 42.1 per cent.[52]

With respect to ethnic minorities, Karen Bird argues that they are more likely to benefit from PR systems with open lists (where voters can rank the candidates on the list) than from any other system, as well as from electoral systems that feature multi-member districts. She has written:

> This method of election [SMD] can be advantageous for ethnic minorities—but only where areas of very high ethnic concentration correspond with electoral districts. Where ethnic groups are dispersed throughout the population and across electoral districts, their capacity to convert political mobilization

> into effective representation is limited. As a general rule, electoral lists and PR—especially with preferential voting—appear more likely to yield representative assemblies. Furthermore, in elections with larger district magnitudes (i.e., where parties select a large number of candidates for a large, multi-member district) parties are less reluctant to nominate political outsiders or other non-typical candidates to the list. Under Canada's SMD system, with a district magnitude of only one, choosing a visible minority as the candidate means not choosing a typical white male candidate.[53]

PR systems are considered to be the most rights-protective for another reason. Basing the percentage of seats awarded on the percentage of votes won makes it comparatively easy for a political party to get a seat or seats in the parliament. It is true that in PR systems—and mixed systems—a party has to reach a certain level of support before it is given a seat. In Israel, for instance, a party must get at least 3.25 per cent of the vote in order to gain a seat; in Turkey, it is 10 per cent. However, even with the threshold requirement, it is still much easier for a party to get representation in parliament than in a plurality or majoritarian system. What this means from a rights-protection perspective is that an aggrieved or victimized group of citizens can establish its own political party and make it into parliament, and perhaps even into a coalition government. They are then in an advantageous position to advocate for the rights of their community and its members.

Despite Norris's findings, criticisms of PR systems remain. Norris herself notes Tsebelis's point that PR arrangements may reinforce and perhaps freeze the stances of parties along narrow ethnocultural, religious, and linguistic lines "rather than promoting a few major catch-all parties that gradually facilitate group cooperation within parties."[54] Meisburger points out that, because candidates depend on the party or its executive to get on the party list, their focus of loyalty becomes the party, not the constituents, with consequences for constituency service. He points out further that, while it is true that ethnic communities can more easily establish political parties under a list PR system to advance their rights, it is also true that right-wing extremists can do the same. Meisburger favours the alternative-vote method, which, because of the need to attract a majority of voters, requires candidates to reach out to voters beyond their comfort zone and convince them of their ability to represent groups other than their own. This necessity forces candidates and parties to moderate their positions.[55]

Like Karen Bird, Melanie Hughes points out that, if a minority is regionally concentrated, it can do well in an SMD system. She also notes that "minority women may face particular obstacles to election in PR systems; in particular, religiously based ethnic political parties elect fewer women only in these systems."[56] It should also be mentioned that an electoral system that allows for district representation, such as the alternative-vote, first-past-the-post, and mixed-member proportional systems, may make it easier for individuals and groups who have had their rights violated to get the attention of the politicians.

Political Parties and Rights

Article 25 of the International Covenant on Civil and Political Rights (ICCPR) declares, "Every citizen shall have the right and the opportunity, without any of the distinctions mentioned in article 2 and without unreasonable restrictions: (a) To take part in the conduct of public affairs, directly or through freely chosen representatives; (b) To vote and to be elected at genuine periodic elections which shall be by universal and equal suffrage and shall be held by secret ballot, guaranteeing the free expression of the will of the electors."

One of the mechanisms through which this right is expressed is the political party. Political parties thus assume a critically important role in democratic development and, hence, in rights protection. Yet Joo-Cheong Tham has observed from his reading of the literature that two themes are evident: either "a neglect of political parties and the role they can play in protecting rights [or] a jaundiced view of political parties that views them as either indifferent to questions of rights or, worse, tending to undermine the protection of rights."[57] Courts, Ronald Dworkin famously said, are the "forum of principle," while political institutions such as parliaments and political parties are seen to be places where decisions are not based on principle but on responses to majority will.

Reviewing the histories of specific political parties leaves one wondering how it is possible to conclude that political parties are indifferent to rights. In Canada, for instance, the Liberal Party under Pierre Elliott Trudeau vigorously sought the entrenchment of the Charter of Rights and Freedoms in the constitution, which was finally achieved in 1982. The African National Congress was the principal force behind the dismantling of South Africa's apartheid. Other parties have demonstrated a keen interest in specific rights, for example, labour parties and the rights of workers; green parties and environmental rights; and conservative parties and private property rights. Of course, there are also political parties that seem to be willing to trample on the rights of certain groups of citizens. Certainly in Canada, before the constitutional reforms of the early 1980s, no political party distinguished itself in the advancement and protection of Aboriginal citizens' rights.

Generally, political parties have two ways of responding to issues related to human rights. One way is through the positions they take on public rights issues and controversies. On balance, do their public declarations and actions reflect a rights-protective orientation? Do those declarations and the party's positions demonstrate knowledge of rights and rights issues? To what degree does a party insist on national compliance with the international human rights treaties the state has ratified? To what degree does the party seek to represent those with rights concerns? In this regard, Mark Tushnet has asked an important question: under what conditions will a political party—or its leadership, or a party faction of large enough size, or backbenchers with a significant base of support within the party—orient itself to rights protection? Under what conditions will it take protecting rights as an important priority of the party's political agenda?[58]

Answering his own question, Tushnet identifies three structural conditions. One is the electoral system. Tushnet favours a system of proportional representation (PR) because it tends to produce many parties. He argues that the "effective number of significant political parties is important because some parties in a true multiparty system can take rights protection … as the main element in their platforms." However, in a two- or three-party system, "party platforms necessarily range across public policy generally, with rights issues being no more than one of many to which the party addresses itself."[59] Tushnet's second structural condition is the party's candidate-selection mechanism. He favours systems in which party leaders have control of, or a great deal of influence over, candidate selection, because they will be able to place rights-oriented candidates in favourable positions or ridings. It is clear that Tushnet's preference is for closed list PR systems.

The third condition identified by Tushnet has to do with the methods by which political parties raise funds. Publicly financed political parties are free to take whatever position they want on rights matters, whereas parties that depend on donors will shape their policies according to the views of those donors. Such views may or may not be rights-protective. As an example, Tushnet points out that in the United States, "large donors from the entertainment industry have had an important effect in making the rights of gays and lesbians a significant priority for the Democratic Party."[60]

On this matter of party support, Tushnet refers to the influence of rights-oriented NGOs, namely the American Civil Liberties Union and Amnesty International. He suggests that their influence is negligible except in elections that are expected to be particularly close. In Canada, some NGOs have considerable influence with particular parties; labour unions and the New Democratic Party (NDP) are one example, and environmental groups and the Green Party constitute another. One could also add the relationship between official-language minority groups and the federal Liberal Party. When these NGOs speak, certain political parties take note.

We might add another condition to Tushnet's three: the degree to which the legislative branch is structurally able to examine legislation and determine its consistency with rights instruments. As noted earlier, the United Kingdom, Finland, and Australia have parliamentary committees that serve this function. Such committees afford representatives of political parties an opportunity to demonstrate their party's rights-protective orientation.

The second way political parties respond to issues related to human rights is through their internal rules, procedures, and communications. Understandably, democratic states are reluctant to impose rules on the internal functioning of political parties. The UN Human Rights Committee also demonstrated an unwillingness to be too directive in its comments on internal party affairs, urging only that states ensure "that, in their internal management, political parties respect the applicable provisions of Article 25."[61] It has indeed been critical of states that impose too many restrictions on political parties. However, an exception to the norm, pertaining to the role of women in political parties, is evident. The UN body that monitors the Convention on the Elimination of All Forms of Discrimination Against Women has interpreted article 7 of the Convention as imposing obligations on political parties. That article says:

> States Parties shall take all appropriate measures to eliminate discrimination against women in the political and public life of the country and, in particular, shall ensure to women, on equal terms with men, the right:
>
> (a) To vote in all elections and public referenda and to be eligible for election to all publicly elected bodies;
> (b) To participate in the formulation of government policy and the implementation thereof and to hold public office and perform all public functions at all levels of government;
> (c) To participate in non-governmental organizations and associations concerned with the public and political life of the country.

The UN monitoring body has interpreted this article as requiring that political parties "embrace the principles of equal opportunity and democracy and endeavour to balance the number of male and female candidates."[62] Further, it has declared that political parties "also have a responsibility to ensure that women are included in party lists and nominated for election in areas where they have a likelihood of electoral success."[63] Reinforcing the message, the body stated that "political parties have an obligation to demonstrate their commitment to the principle of gender equality in their constitutions, in the application of those rules and in the composition of their membership."[64] This obligation could be broadened: to what degree do party leaders attempt to instill a basic rights consciousness—"Charter values," if you will?

Disagreement exists about the wisdom of allowing narrowly focused political parties such as ethnically based parties. The defining feature of an ethnically based party is that "its only real appeal is to members of that group, and its only real mission is to advance the interests of members of that group."[65] The concern is that such parties may incite hatred toward ethnic communities that are different from their own; at the very least, they may neglect the needs and legitimate interests of those other ethnic communities. If ethnically based parties achieved positions of power, they would be well placed to implement their agenda, thus threatening the rights of citizens from different ethnic communities: "The ethnic party's particularistic, exclusivist, and often polarizing political appeals make its overall contribution to society divisive and even disintegrative."[66]

Some states have sought to deal with ethnic parties, as well as other narrowly focused parties, by banning them or imposing conditions. In the Indian constitution, for instance, there is a provision requiring that national political parties exist in more than four of the country's states. The objective appears to be to encourage parties to demonstrate a national focus and not be too regionally fixed. Similarly, article 91 of the Kenyan constitution states:

> (1) Every political party shall—
> (a) have a national character as prescribed by an Act of Parliament;
> [...]
> (e) respect the right of all persons to participate in the political process, including minorities and marginalised groups;
> (f) respect and promote human rights and fundamental freedoms, and gender equality and equity;
> (2) A political party shall not—
> (a) be founded on a religious, linguistic, racial, ethnic, gender or regional basis or seek to engage in advocacy of hatred on any such basis.

Indonesia is another country that imposes conditions on political parties. In order to lessen the influence of the country's most salient cleavages—ethnicity, religion, and region—and therefore the likelihood of rights abuses, the country requires for election to its lower house that each party exceed a 3.5 per cent vote threshold. Also, each party must have chapters in all provinces; in no less than 75 per cent of all regencies and municipalities in each of the provinces; and in no less than 50 per cent of all districts in each of the regencies and municipalities. To win the presidency, a candidate must obtain not only an absolute majority vote but also at least 25 per cent of the vote in more than half of the provinces. The party rules appear to have had the intended effect. In his assessment, Geoffrey Macdonald concludes, "The weakening of particularistic politics is at least partly explained by Indonesia's party rules and changing electoral system, which have progressively encouraged parties to target latent crosscutting cleavages instead of identity groups during elections."[67]

The advantages of broadly based parties over those with narrow focuses were noted by the International Institute for Democracy and Electoral Assistance in a discussion of electoral systems and political parties. The authors of the discussion write, "Most experts also agree that the electoral system should encourage the development of parties which are based on broad political values and ideologies as well as specific policy programmes, rather than narrow ethnic, racial or regional concerns. As well as lessening the threat of societal conflict, parties which are based on these broad 'cross-cutting cleavages' are more likely to reflect national opinion than those which are based predominantly on sectarian or regional concerns."[68] Significantly, the authors prefer that broadly based parties come about as an effect of the electoral system rather than through government legislation. Such legislation could be seen as an infringement on the right to freedom of association.

Indeed, the Human Rights Committee has stated, "The right to freedom of association, including the right to form and join organizations and associations concerned with political and public affairs, is an essential adjunct to the rights protected by article 25."[69] Similarly, the UN Declaration on the Rights of Persons Belonging to National or Ethnic, Religious and Linguistic Minorities states in article 2 that "persons belonging to minorities have the right to establish and maintain their own associations."[70] In a recent paper on the regulation of political parties, the Organization for Security and Cooperation in Europe (OSCE) and the Venice Commission state that rights instruments, such as the UN Declaration, "fully guarantee the right to form and associate with political parties to all members of minority groups within a country's jurisdiction."[71] The paper also opposes the prohibition of political parties based on geographic considerations.[72]

One can understand why an ethnic minority with a justified sense of grievance should be able to create a political party to protect its rights. But in a context where particularistic politics have the potential to result in conflict, violence, and domination, many may also understand such measures as being reasonable limits on that freedom. And indeed, the OSCE/Venice Commission paper identifies the incitement of ethnic, social, or religious hatred and the threat to use violence as being legitimate grounds for the prohibition of political parties.[73]

Conclusion

This chapter began by briefly explaining the concept of constitutional judicial review and adumbrating the arguments for and against its practice. It then attempted to show how executive systems, electoral systems, and political parties affect rights. The research does seem to indicate that parliamentary systems and list PR electoral systems are more supportive of human rights than the alternatives. However, the type of systems chosen will depend on the particular circumstances of each country. Canada, for instance, which has never used the list PR electoral system, nevertheless is among the 10 highest-ranking countries in *The Economist*'s Democracy Index 2013. It has also consistently received Freedom House's highest possible score for the protection of political rights and civil liberties. The section on political parties discussed the rights-protection potential of parties, pointing in particular to Tushnet's conditions under which a political party will orient itself to the protection of rights. It also discussed the pros and cons of banning political parties; the concern is that narrowly focused parties will demonstrate intolerance toward citizens outside of their group.

The challenges to citizens' rights at this time in history are considerable. The use of information and communications technologies, state actions to deal with terrorism, widespread environmental destruction, economic inequality—all these and other issues give rise to concerns about citizens' rights and about just how seriously state actors take people's rights and the commitments made to the various UN human rights treaties. In sum, then, citizens need to insist that all three branches of government, as well as political parties, involve themselves in rights protection in a committed way, and that political institutions such as the electoral system are designed with the goal of rights protection in mind.

Takeaway Messages

- Constitutional judicial review refers to the power of the judiciary to review legislation and, in some countries, to invalidate legislation. There are persuasive arguments for and against judicial review.

- Political institutions have an impact on human rights, and the effective protection of rights requires attention to those institutions as well as to judicial institutions.

Study Questions

- What are the arguments for and against judicial review?
- Do you accept that the parliamentary system is more rights-protective than the presidential system?
- What are the essential features of the various electoral systems?
- Should political parties ever be banned?

Issues for Debate or Roundtable

- Section 33 should never have been inserted into the Canadian Charter of Rights and Freedoms.
- Canada should make use of reserved seats in the House of Commons to advance the rights of women and Aboriginal citizens.

Additional Reading

Campbell, T., J. Goldsworthy, and A. Stone, eds. *Protecting Rights Without a Bill of Rights: Institutional Performance and Reform in Australia*. Burlington, VT: Ashgate Publishing, 2006.

Goodhart, Michael, ed. *Human Rights: Politics and Practice*. Oxford: Oxford University Press, 2009.

Jhappan, Radha. "Charter Politics and the Judiciary." In *Canadian Politics in the 21st Century*, 6th ed., ed. Michael Whittington and Glen Williams. Toronto: Nelson, 2004.

Volcansek, M., and Charles Lockhart. "Explaining Support for Human Rights Protections: A Judicial Role?" *Journal of Human Rights* 11, no. 1 (2012): 33–50. http://dx.doi.org/10.1080/14754835.2012.648149.

Websites

Clément, Dominque. "Canada's Human Rights History." http://www.historyofrights.com.

Freedom House. http://www.freedomhouse.org.

Human Rights Internet. http://www.hri.ca.

International Journal of Constitutional Law and ConstitutionMaking.org. *I-CONnect* [blog]. http://www.iconnectblog.com.

Open Global Rights. www.opendemocracy.net/openglobalrights.

Notes

1. In the 2013 edition of *The Economist's* Democracy Index, 8 of the 10 countries with the highest scores have parliamentary systems, 7 are unitary states, and 7 use a list PR (proportional representation) electoral system.
2. T. Campbell, K.D. Ewing, and A. Tomkins, "Introduction," in *The Legal Protection of Human Rights: Sceptical Essays,* ed. T. Campbell, K.D. Ewing, and A. Tomkins (Oxford: Oxford University Press, 2011), 9.
3. J. Hiebert, "Governing Like Judges?," in *The Legal Protection of Human Rights: Sceptical Essays,* ed. T. Campbell, K.D. Ewing, and A. Tomkins (Oxford: Oxford University Press, 2011), 65.
4. M. de Visser, *Constitutional Review in Europe: A Comparative Analysis* (Oxford: Hart, 2014).
5. W. Sandholz, "Treaties, Constitutions, Courts, and Human Rights," *Journal of Human Rights* 11, no. 1 (2012): 17.
6. As of 2005, more than three-quarters of the countries of the world had some form of constitutional judicial review, including several countries with undemocratic governments. See D. Horowitz, "Constitutional Courts: A Primer for Decision Makers," *Journal of Democracy* 17, no. 4 (October 2006): 125.
7. M. Tushnet, *Weak Courts, Strong Rights: Judicial Review and Social Welfare Rights in Comparative Constitutional Law* (Princeton, NJ: Princeton University Press, 2008), 21.
8. Ibid., 24.
9. Ibid., 20.
10. P. Hogg, *Constitutional Law of Canada,* student ed. (Toronto: Carswell, 2009), 882.
11. Quoted in N. Stephanopoulos, "The Case for the Legislative Override," *UCLA Journal of International Law and Foreign Affairs* 10 (2005): 262. http://chicagounbound.uchicago.edu/journal_articles.
12. F.L. Morton and R. Knopff, *The Charter Revolution and the Court Party* (Peterborough, ON: Broadview Press, 2000).
13. D. DiFruscio, "Patriation, Politics and Power: The State of Balance Between the Supreme Court and Parliament after Thirty Years of the Charter," *Journal of Parliamentary and Political Law* 8, no. 1 (March 2014): 44.
14. P. Russell, "The Political Purposes of the Canadian Charter of Rights and Freedoms," *Canadian Bar Review* 61, no. 1 (March 1983): 52.
15. For more on the relationship between judicialization and democracy, see L. Vanhala, "Civil Society Organizations and the Aarhus Convention in Court: Judicialization from below in Scotland?" *Representation* 49, no. 3 (2013); and R. Cichowski, "Mobilization, Litigation and Democratic Governance," *Representation* 49, no. 3 (2013).
16. DiFruscio, "Patriation, Politics and Power," 51.
17. R. Hirschl, "Epilogue: Courts and Democracy Between Ideals and Realities," *Representation* 49, no. 3 (2013): 363.
18. K. Tuori, "Judicial Constitutional Review as a Last Resort," in *The Legal Protection of Human Rights: Sceptical Essays*, ed. T. Campbell, K.D. Ewing, and A. Tomkins (Oxford: Oxford University Press, 2011). However, Maartje de Visser points out that, while Parliament is still considered to be chiefly responsible for "ensuring respect for the constitution," Finland did choose "to allow all its

courts to enforce the constitution against the legislature when it adopted a new constitution in 2000." See de Visser, *Constitutional Review in Europe*, 7.

19. A. Stone Sweet, "Constitutional Courts," in *The Oxford Handbook of Comparative Constitutional Law,* ed. M. Rosenfeld and A. Sajó (Oxford: Oxford University Press, 2012), 823.
20. Ibid., 825.
21. Ibid., 826.
22. M.J. Cepeda-Espinosa, "Judicial Activism in a Violent Context: The Origin, Role, and Impact of the Colombian Constitutional Court," *Washington University Global Studies Law Review* 3, no. 4 (2004): 552–53.
23. W. Sadurski, *Rights Before Courts: A Study of the Constitutional Courts in Postcommunist States of Central and Eastern Europe* (Dordecht, Netherlands: Springer, 2005), 6.
24. Not to be confused with the term *division of powers*, which refers to the distribution of competencies to the central and regional governments in a state with a federal structure.
25. D. Baranger and C. Murray, "Systems of Government," in *The Routledge Handbook of Constitutional Law*, ed. M. Tushnet, T. Fleiner, and C. Saunders (New York: Routledge, 2013), 76.
26. Ibid., 78.
27. A. Stepan and C. Skach, "Constitutional Frameworks and Democratic Consolidation: Parliamentarism versus Presidentialism," *World Politics* 46, no. 1 (October 1993): 3.
28. P. Norris, *Driving Democracy: Do Power-Sharing Institutions Work?* (New York: Cambridge University Press, 2008), 144.
29. Baranger and Murray, "Systems of Government," 80.
30. Austria and Iceland use a hybrid system in which the president has significant constitutional powers. However, in practice they are rarely used. See R. Elgie, *Semi-Presidentialism: Sub-Types and Democratic Performance* (Oxford: Oxford University Press, 2011), 85–86, 157–60.
31. Norris, *Driving Democracy*, 146.
32. Baranger and Murray, "Systems of Government," 79.
33. C. Skach, "The 'Newest' Separation of Powers: Semipresidentialism," *International Journal of Constitutional Law* 5, no. 1 (January 2007): 103.
34. For a detailed study of Bosnia-Herzegovina's attempt to restrict its three-person presidency to Serbs, Croats, and Bosniaks, see C. McCrudden and B. O'Leary, *Courts and Consociations: Human Rights versus Power-Sharing* (Oxford: Oxford University Press, 2013).
35. *Democracy* and *rights*, of course, do not mean the same thing, but the relationship is tight. Rights make a healthy democracy possible and a healthy democracy can ensure that rights are protected. In *The Economist*'s 2013 Democracy Index, 5 of the 10 top-ranked countries, including Canada, have the highest possible score (10) in the protection of civil liberties. Only 2 countries outside the top 10 scored 10 on the protection of civil liberties: Ireland and Uruguay. The United States ranked nineteenth on the democracy index and its civil liberties score was 8.53. For more on the relationship between rights and democracy, see D. Beetham, "Democratization and Human Rights: Convergence and Divergence," in *The Routledge Handbook of Democratization*, ed. J. Haynes (New York: Routledge, 2012).

36. J. Linz, "The Perils of Presidentialism," *Journal of Democracy* 1, no. 1 (Winter 1990): 51–52.
37. Stepan and Skach, "Constitutional Frameworks," 18.
38. See Baranger and Murray, "Systems of Government," 83.
39. J.A. Cheibub, *Presidentialism, Parliamentarism, and Democracy* (New York: Cambridge University Press, 2007), 136.
40. Norris, *Driving Democracy*, 155–56.
41. M. Gallagher and P. Mitchell, "Introduction to Electoral Systems," in *The Politics of Electoral Systems*, ed. M. Gallagher and P. Mitchell (Oxford: Oxford University Press, 2005), 3.
42. Z. Elkins, T. Ginsburg, and J. Melton, *The Endurance of National Constitutions* (Cambridge: Cambridge University Press, 2009), 51–52.
43. For a thorough explanation of electoral systems, see D. Farrell, *Electoral Systems: A Comparative Introduction* (New York: Palgrave, 2001). See also L. Johnston, *From Votes to Seats: Four Families of Electoral Systems* (Toronto: Ontario Citizens' Assembly on Electoral Reform); and H. Milner, ed., *Making Every Vote Count: Reassessing Canada's Electoral System* (Peterborough, ON: Broadview Press, 1999).
44. Other systems under the plurality umbrella are the block vote, the party block vote, and the cumulative vote.
45. A. Reynolds et al., *Electoral System Design: The New International IDEA Handbook* (Stockholm: International IDEA, 2005), 30.
46. Ibid.
47. Ibid., 181.
48. A. Reynolds, *Electoral Systems and the Protection and Participation of Minorities* (London: Minority Rights Group International, 2006), 15–19.
49. Norris, *Driving Democracy*, 117.
50. Ibid., 130 (emphasis added). In her categorization of electoral systems, Norris combines the plurality and majoritarian families.
51. P. Norris, "The Impact of Electoral Reform in Women's Representation," *Acta Politica* 41 (2006): 201.
52. See Inter-Parliamentary Union, http://www.ipu.org/parline-e/parlinesearch.asp.
53. K. Bird, *Comparing the Political Representation of Ethnic Minorities in Advanced Democracies*, paper presented at the Annual Meeting of the Canadian Political Science Association, Winnipeg, MB, 3 June 2004, 27, http://www.cpsa-acsp.ca/papers-2004/Bird.pdf. In a personal email (26 April 2014), Professor Melanie Hughes, who studies women's political representation, noted that there are differences in the electoral chances of minority men and minority women. She stated, "I found that minority women do not do any better or worse (in absolute terms) by electoral system. However, minority *men* tend to be better represented in SMD systems than in PR systems" [emphasis in original].
54. P. Norris, "Ballots Not Bullets: Testing Consociational Theories of Ethnic Conflict, Electoral Systems, and Democratization," in *The Architecture of Democracy: Constitutional Design, Conflict Management, and Democracy*, ed. A. Reynolds (Oxford: Oxford University Press, 2002), 213. It should be noted that South Africa, after two national elections with a list PR system, created a task force in 2002 to review the electoral system. It recommended creation of a more constituency-based system that would allow for more accountability while retaining the proportionality feature. Its recommendation was not acted on.

55. T. Meisburger, "Getting Majoritarianism Right," *Journal of Democracy* 23, no. 1 (January 2012): 156–58.
56. M. Hughes, "Intersectionality, Quotas, and Minority Women's Political Representation Worldwide," *American Political Science Review* 105, no. 3 (August 2011): 608.
57. J.-C. Tham, "Reclaiming the Political Protection of Rights: A Defence of Australian Party Politics," in *The Legal Protection of Human Rights: Sceptical Essays*, ed. T. Campbell, K.D. Ewing, and A. Tomkins (Oxford: Oxford University Press, 2011), 312.
58. M. Tushnet, "The Political Institutions of Rights Protection," in *The Legal Protection of Human Rights: Sceptical Essays*, ed. T. Campbell, K.D. Ewing, and A. Tomkins (Oxford: Oxford University Press, 2011), 302.
59. Ibid., 303.
60. Ibid., 304.
61. UN Human Rights Committee, *General Comment No. 25: The Right to Participate in Public Affairs, Voting Rights and the Right of Equal Access to Public Service (Art. 25)*, 7/12/1996, para. 26.
62. UN Committee on the Elimination of Discrimination against Women, *CEDAW General Recommendation No. 23: Political and Public Life*, UN Doc. A/52/38, 12 August 1997, para. 22.
63. Ibid., para. 28.
64. Ibid., para. 34.
65. R. Gunther and L. Diamond, "Types and Functions of Parties," in *Political Parties and Democracy*, ed. L. Diamond and R. Gunther (Baltimore, MD: Johns Hopkins University Press, 2001), 23.
66. Ibid., 24.
67. G. Macdonald, *Election Rules and Identity Politics: Understanding the Success of Multiethnic Parties in Indonesia*, IFES Hybl Democracy Studies Fellowship Paper (Washington, DC: International Foundation for Electoral Systems, 2013), 9.
68. Reynolds et al., *Electoral System Design*, 13.
69. UN Human Rights Committee, *General Comment No. 25*, para. 26.
70. Significantly, in article 8 the Declaration makes clear that "nothing in the present Declaration may be construed as permitting any activity contrary to the purposes and principles of the United Nations, including sovereign equality, territorial integrity and political independence."
71. OSCE (Office for Democratic Institutions and Human Rights) and Venice Commission, *Guidelines for Political Party Regulation* (Warsaw: 2011), para. 54, www.osce.org/odihr.
72. In a 1995 volume, Human Rights Watch also took a position against prohibitions on religiously or ethnically based political parties. "Such groups," it wrote, "should be protected by the right of free association." But the organization cautioned that, if a party with a religious, ethnic, or racial agenda makes it into government, it is "obligated to protect the rights of everyone." See Human Rights Watch, *Slaughter among Neighbors: The Political Origins of Communal Violence* (New Haven, CT: Yale University Press and Human Rights Watch, 1995), 9. See also O. Protsyk, *The Representation of Minorities and Indigenous Peoples in Parliament*, a report prepared for the Inter-Parliamentary Union and the United Nations Development Programme (2010).
73. OSCE and Venice Commission, *Guidelines*, para. 96.

4
Federalism and Rights: The Case of the United States, with Comparative Perspectives

JOHN KINCAID

Learning Objectives

- To learn how federalism does and does not advance rights
- To learn the difference between federal protections of individual and communitarian rights
- To learn the advantages and disadvantages of federalism for rights protection

Overall, federal forms of government have stronger records of democratic performance and rights protection than non-federal governments.[1] Indeed, modern federalism and rights protection are siblings: the founders of the United States invented modern federalism in 1787 in order to protect the natural rights of life, liberty, and property widely recognized by Enlightenment thinkers such as John Locke and Thomas Hobbes. The social-compact theories of those secular philosophers had roots in the covenant or federal theology of Reformed Protestantism, dating back to Huldrych Zwingli (1484–1531) and Heinrich Bullinger (1504–75). Like all siblings, though, federalism and rights have both friendly and antagonistic relations. Consequently there are exceptions to the positive connection between federalism and rights, and factors other than federalism affect rights protections.

This chapter focuses on federalism and rights in the United States but illuminates that case with comparative perspectives. This focus does not mean that the United States is exceptionally good or bad at protecting rights. The focus is warranted because the founders of the United States invented both modern federalism and constitutional declarations of rights. The US was the world's first nation founded on the principle of natural rights, with governments obligated to protect those rights. The Massachusetts Constitution of 1780 and US Constitution of 1789 are the oldest written constitutions still in effect in the world; the Virginia Declaration of Rights of 1776 was the first of its kind and a model for the later French Declaration of the Rights of Man and of the Citizen (1789) and the US Bill of Rights (1791), which in turn became models for contemporary charters such as the Universal Declaration of Human Rights (1948). The US case also provides a 226-year record of positive and negative aspects of federalism and rights.

Federalism and Individual Rights Protection

The word *federal* comes from the Latin *foedus*, meaning "treaty, contract, or covenant." When Protestants following in the wake of Martin Luther (1483–1546) confronted the Roman Catholic Church and the "divine right" claims of monarchs, they found in the biblical idea of covenant and in the political uses of covenanting in the Hebrew Bible an alternative way of understanding human relationships, as voluntary agreements.[2] Reformed Protestants emphasized rights of conscience and consent and of education for informed consent, as well as human equality and a right of revolution against oppressive governments (for example, the *Vindiciae contra tyrannos* of 1579).[3] They sought to protect such rights, especially religious rights, by grounding all relationships in covenants—from individuals' relations with God to individuals entering marriage, individuals and families forming congregations and selecting their own pastors, congregations federating to create larger religious bodies, families and congregations forming towns and electing their officers, and towns federating to establish larger secular polities and electing representatives to a common legislature.[4] The first secular political philosophy of covenanting was *Politica*, published in 1614 by Johannes Althusius,[5] an important figure in European federalism.[6]

The first systematic political ideas articulated in what is now the United States were derived from the Puritans' covenant or federal theology. Later, Huguenots and other Reformed Protestants arrived with covenant theologies, such that individuals culturally associated with Reformed Protestantism made up a sizable portion of the US population, which was 98 per cent Protestant (including Anglicans) in the 1780s. The first written constitution and federal polity based on these covenant ideas was the Fundamental Orders of Connecticut (1639), which united three towns in a "Combination and Confederation." An important objective of this confederation was to protect religious liberty. These covenant ideas also found expression in the Massachusetts Constitution of 1780 and its declaration of rights, the first article of which states, "All men are born free and equal, and have certain natural, essential, and unalienable rights; among which may be reckoned the right of enjoying and defending their lives and liberties; that of acquiring, possessing, and protecting property; in fine, that of seeking and obtaining their safety and happiness."

Wary of religious strife, the leading founders of the United States eschewed theology and adapted ideas from such secular theorists as Hugo Grotius, whose *De iure belli ac pacis libri tres* appeared in 1625; Hobbes, whose *Leviathan* was published in 1651; and Locke, whose *Two Treatises of Government* appeared in 1689. The covenant idea is secularized in the works of these social compact theorists, who treated the protection of natural rights as government's fundamental duty.

The founders also studied history for lessons, especially ancient Greece and Rome. Alexander Hamilton and James Madison argued in *The Federalist*[7] that the Articles of Confederation (1781–89) were grounded in ancient federalism that could not protect rights because, like the Achaean and Lycian leagues, the American confederation was not a real government authorized to govern and tax individuals directly. Absent a real government, individuals are vulnerable to rights deprivations from internal and external aggressors. A confederation cannot, therefore, extricate individuals from the state of nature, which Hobbes and Locke characterized as a war of all against all. The founders sought to correct this fatal flaw of ancient federalism by dividing sovereignty, so that the new federation government[8] and the continuing state governments could each independently legislate for individuals, levy taxes, and protect rights within their respective spheres of constitutional authority.[9]

Madison saw federalism as part of a double security for rights protection against oppressive government:

> In a single republic, all the power surrendered by the people, is submitted to the administration of a single government, and usurpations are guarded against by a division of the government into distinct and separate departments [i.e., the separation of legislative, executive, and judicial powers]. In the compound republic of America [i.e., a republic having both national and confederal characteristics], the power surrendered by the people, is first divided between two distinct governments [i.e., federal and state], and then the portion allotted to each, subdivided among distinct and separate departments. Hence, a double security arises to the rights of the people. The different governments will control each other; at the same time that each will be controuled by itself.[10]

Most American founders believed rights could best be protected by a properly structured federal and republican form of government.

Declarations and Bills of Rights

Written bills of rights were also central to the American federal founding. These were developed indigenously during the colonial era and first found their fullest modern expression in the 1776 Virginia Declaration of Rights, which was a model for the US Bill of Rights added to the federal Constitution in 1791. Although Magna Carta (1215), the English Petition of Right (1628), and the English Bill of Rights (1689) are often seen as precursors of the rights in the American documents, only 5[11] or 7[12] of the 27 rights listed in the US Bill of Rights can be traced back to the English documents. Instead, these rights were derived from many bills of rights written by the colonists, beginning with the Massachusetts Body of Liberties (1641), which set forth 16 of the 27 rights later lodged in the US Bill of Rights.[13] States began enacting written constitutions in 1776. Seven of the 13 states prefaced their constitution with a declaration of rights; four others cited rights throughout their document.

Some founders opposed adding a bill of rights to the US constitution, but the addition was demanded by many of the constitution's opponents, especially backcountry farmers, artisans, and other lower- and middle-class Americans. Such a bill would be redundant, argued some, because states adequately protected rights and the new federation government had little power to trample rights. Hamilton contended that a bill of rights would imply that the federation government had more power than was the case and would encourage expansion of the federation's powers. Bills of rights, moreover, are merely "parchment barriers" to oppression. Rights are better protected, asserted Madison, by a proper constitutional structuring of government and by social diversity that spawns competing organizations, such as citizen associations, religious institutions, and news media.[14]

The US Bill of Rights contains mostly negative rights, namely rights against government misdeeds, such as freedom of speech and protection against unwarranted government searches and seizures, rather than positive rights, namely rights to government guarantees such as education, health care, and housing. However, the idea of positive rights emerged after the 1780s and appeared in US state constitutions. For example, about 80 per cent of the world's national constitutions today proclaim a right to education; the US constitution contains no such right.[15] But this comparison is misleading because it is the state constitutions in the United States that mandate free public education for all children. Indeed, during the nineteenth century, US states pioneered what became the right to education now found in so many national constitutions.[16] Many state constitutions contain other positive rights, such as the rights to organize trade unions, enjoy a clean environment, fish and hunt, and play bingo.[17] Furthermore, most positive rights in national constitutions are not justiciable, while all rights in US constitutions are justiciable. Thus, comparing the national constitutions of federal and non-federal countries is misleading because the distribution of powers in a federal polity can leave the national constitution silent about rights protected by the constituent political communities.

Not every federal constitution has a bill of rights (Australia, for example), and some bills were added long after federation (such as Canada's 1982 Charter of Rights and Freedoms). Yet these federal countries have excellent rights-protection records, suggesting that Hamilton and Madison may have been correct in their contention that more is needed to protect rights than a parchment barrier. Today, though, nearly all federal constitutions contain a bill of rights, and some sub-national constitutions (in countries that have them) include rights too.

Bills of rights ordinarily acknowledge the need for certain forms of government regulation that may impinge upon rights, but they do not admit exceptions or overrides, except for the unusual notwithstanding clause in Canada's Charter of Rights and Freedoms. Many provinces feared the Charter would give the courts too much power to negate acts of elected parliaments. The clause, therefore, allows a federal, provincial, or territorial legislature to declare an action or law operational for five years in spite of a contrary Charter right or freedom. However, the clause can be used to override only some, not all, Charter rights, and it has not significantly affected rights protections.

The US founders did not expect the courts, especially the federation's courts, to play the major role in protecting rights. But during the course of American history, the US Supreme Court asserted an ever larger role in protecting individual rights, even declaring itself the final arbiter of federal constitutional rights.[18] Most other federal countries have followed suit. Today the supreme court or constitutional court in most federations significantly affects rights, although high courts in less democratic federations have weak rights-protection records. However, a concern in some federal countries—including Canada and the United States—is that high-court interpretations of constitutional rights can foster centralization as the court mandates equality and uniformity of ever more rights across the entire country.[19]

Federalism and Individual Rights Dereliction

Federalism is not always or necessarily a good protector of rights.[20] Most obvious was the legality of slavery in 8 of the 13 original US states in 1789. Disconnects between federalism and rights arise mainly from three sources: (1) federal bargains that include and exclude some people, (2) struggles for recognition of new participants, and (3) countries with weak traditions of rights protection adopting federalism.

Exclusion

Federal constitutions promulgated before 1945 usually excluded certain groups from coverage. For example, the Anglo immigrant federations—Australia, Canada, and the United States—long excluded indigenous peoples and some non-Anglo immigrants such as Asians from equal rights protection. Latin American federations also excluded indigenous peoples and others. Exclusions have been less common since 1945 because of rising international norms endorsing human equality and rights, although some of the new Muslim federations (for example, Pakistan and the United Arab Emirates) diminish non-Muslim inclusion because they accord the Koran supremacy over secular constitutional and statutory law.

Comparatively, the American federal system has protected the rights of the included rather well; therefore, struggles for inclusion have been defined as struggles for "equal rights," even though some struggles—such as that for African-American inclusion—required centuries. The quality of rights protection in many western hemisphere federations has been sufficiently high to induce most excluded groups to seek inclusion or, in the case of indigenous peoples, inclusion with some territorial autonomy, rather than exit from the federation. The North American exception is separatism in Quebec, advanced by those who believe they cannot fully express their "national" identity inside Canada.

In many federal systems, exclusions are not system-wide. Even if the federal constitution excludes certain groups, some constituent political communities may enact inclusionary policies to the extent of their authority. These policies may diffuse to other states and eventually overturn the federal exclusion. For example, about 11.5 million illegal immigrants reside in the United States. Federation policies are largely exclusionary, as are some state policies, but many states have enacted inclusionary policies such as access to health care, state universities, and driver's licences, thus treating illegal immigrants in those respects about equally with state citizens.

In an effort to preserve their culture, Swiss voters enacted exclusionary national policies banning new minaret construction in 2009 and restricting immigration in 2014. Because of their linguistic and religious diversity, the Swiss are a *Willensnation* that constantly re-covenants to live in unity with diversity.[21] "Together, we defend the right to remain different"[22] and, thus, to exclude others who are too different.

The trend in Western developed federal countries has been toward inclusion, including efforts to keep Quebec in the Canadian federation. However, as discussed below, some groups, such as the Basques and Catalans in Spain, resist inclusion. The other side of the exclusion coin is the extent to which included communities joined the federation voluntarily.

Recognition

There also are struggles for recognition of groups excluded not because they were seen as potential participants but because they fell outside the prevailing cultural ambit of inclusion. For example, a few women's rights advocates agitated during the 1780s,[23] but they received little recognition because women, like children, were seen as falling under the care of men. Only after considerable agitation did women gain the basic political right to vote in all elections nationwide: in 1908 in Australia, 1920 in the United States, 1940 in Canada, and 1990 in Switzerland. However, in each federation, various constituent political communities[24] extended the franchise to women before those dates; in Australia, Canada, and Switzerland, women could vote in federation government elections before they could do so in all constituent state elections. Because of this history, the contemporary women's movement is ambivalent about federalism. On the one hand, when the federal government fails to act, constituent states often advance women's rights, although not universally; on the other hand, when the federal government acts, it does so for the whole country.[25] By contrast, in a unitary system the protection of any particular right is all-or-nothing.

Persons with disabilities are another example of struggles for recognition, and recognition of LGBT rights is a further example. After millennia of exclusion, there has been rapidly growing recognition in most Western and developed countries of disability and gay rights. The US Americans with Disabilities Act was enacted in 1990, and Australia passed its Disability Discrimination Act in 1992.

On gay rights, eight provinces and one territory in Canada recognized the right of gay marriage before passage of the federal Civil Marriage Act (2005).[26] As of June 2015, when the US Supreme Court legalized same-sex marriage nationwide by accepting advocates' arguments for "marriage equality," 11 US states, Washington (DC), and 22 Indian tribes had already legalized same-sex marriage. In addition, lower federal courts had struck down gay-marriage bans in 19 other states and four state courts had ruled gay-marriage bans unconstitutional. Because of a 2013 US Supreme Court ruling,[27] for purposes of federal benefits the federal government already recognized same-sex marriages solemnized in states that permitted them.

In Australia, which had not legalized same-sex marriage as of mid-2015, the High Court in 2013 declared marriage law an exclusive federal power; states therefore cannot legalize gay marriage.[28] However, the federation government has enacted laws equalizing many matters for same-sex couples, and most states have addressed gay rights within the limits of their authority. By contrast, India's Supreme Court in 2013 overturned a lower court ruling that had invalidated a British colonial-era law making homosexual sex a crime punishable up to life in prison.[29] Only the central parliament, opined the court, can change this old law. As these examples suggest, some constituent states in democratic federations often advance rights recognitions that spread to some other states and then lead to federal constitutional or statutory changes. Following federal action, some constituent states comply more vigorously than others.

The above examples highlight another feature of some federal systems: forum shopping. In pursuing rights claims, individuals and groups turn alternately to the federation and the constituent governments, and also to different constituent governments most amenable to protecting their desired rights at particular times. Shopping for rights protections among the constituent political communities is called voting with one's feet. Millions of black Americans fled from southern states to northern states during the first half of the twentieth century for better rights protections, while their civil rights organizations litigated mostly in the federal courts because southern state courts were hostile to their rights claims.

Federalism Adoptions by Weak Rights Protectors

A third source of federalism–rights disconnects has been the adoption of federal forms of government by countries with weak records of rights protection, such as Iraq, Pakistan, Russia, and Venezuela. Table 4.1 lists the world's 28 nominally federal and quasi-federal countries. Half of them, including most of the long-established and best-functioning federations, are labelled "free" by Freedom House and have high scores for protecting political rights and civil liberties. The eight "partly free" countries include those that are nominally but not very functionally federal and susceptible to authoritarian rule. The six "not free" countries have consistent records of authoritarian rule and weak or non-existent democracy. The free federal countries also score higher (66.6 average) than partly free countries (55.6) on a measure of economic freedom that emphasizes property rights and low government regulation. Insufficient data are available for the not-free countries.

Put differently, 50 per cent of the federal countries are free, compared to 45 per cent of the world's non-federal countries. The partly free proportion (29%) of federal countries is close to the 30 per cent of partly free non-federal countries, while 21 per cent of the federal countries are not free, compared to 25 per cent of non-federal countries. Overall, federal countries have slightly better rights-protection records than non-federal countries.

Table 4.1 Freedom, Rights, and Religious Affiliations in Federal Countries

Country	Freedom	Political Rights	Civil Liberties	Economic Freedom	Rights Institutions	Protestant (%)	Catholic (%)	Muslim (%)
Australia	free	1	1	81.4	F/S	39	25	2
Austria	free	1	1	71.2	F/S	5	63	6
Belgium	free	1	1	68.8	F	1	73	6
Canada	free	1	1	79.1	F/S	27	39	3
Germany	free	1	1	73.8	F/S	35	30	5
Micronesia	free	1	1	49.6	N	42	50	0
St. Kitts and Nevis	free	1	1	N/A	N	85	N/A	0
Spain	free	1	1	67.6	F/S	1	71	2
Switzerland	free	1	1	80.5	S	37	39	6
United States	free	1	1	76.2	S	52	24	1
Argentina	free	2	2	44.1	F/S	7	77	3
Brazil	free	2	2	56.6	S	21	65	0
South Africa	free	2	2	62.6	F	73	7	2
India	free	2	3	54.6	F/S	2	2	15
Mexico	partly free	3	3	66.4	F/S	8	8	0
Comoros	partly free	3	4	52.1	N	0	2	96
Nepal	partly free	3	4	51.3	F	0	0	4

(continued)

Table 4.1 Freedom, Rights, and Religious Affiliations in Federal Countries

Country	Freedom	Political Rights	Civil Liberties	Economic Freedom	Rights Institutions	Protestant (%)	Catholic (%)	Muslim (%)
Bosnia and Herzegovina	partly free	4	3	59.0	F	0	15	42
Malaysia	partly free	4	4	70.8	F	4	3	61
Nigeria	partly free	4	5	55.6	F	38	14	48
Pakistan	partly free	4	5	55.6	N	1	1	96
Venezuela	partly free	5	5	34.3	F	10	79	0
Ethiopia	not free	6	6	51.5	N	19	1	34
Iraq	not free	6	6	N/A	N	0	1	99
Russia	not free	6	6	52.1	F/S	2	1	12
United Arab Emirates	not free	6	6	72.4	N	1	5	76
South Sudan	not free	7	6	N/A	N/A	N/A	N/A	N/A
Sudan	not free	7	7	N/A	N/A	2	N/A	71

Sources: **Columns 1–3:** Freedom House, Freedom in the World 2015, https://freedomhouse.org/report/freedom-world-2015/table-country-ratings#.VZ7xk-2DIGlN; **Column 4:** Heritage Foundation, 2015 Index of Economic Freedom, http://www.heritage.org/index/; **Column 5:** A. Wolman, "The Relationship Between National and Sub-national Human Rights Institutions in Federal Countries," *International Journal of Human Rights* 17:4 (2013): 445–62. **Column 6:** Pew Research Center, Religion and Public Life Project, Christian Population as Percentages of Total Population by Country, 2010 estimate, http://www.pewforum.org/2011/12/19/table-christian-population-as-percentages-of-total-population-by-country/; **Column 7:** en.wikipedia.org/wiki/Catholic_Church_by_country; **Column 8:** Pew Research Center, Religion and Public Life Project, Muslim Population by Country, 2010 estimate, http://www.pewforum.org/2011/01/27/table-muslim-population-by-country/.

Most federal countries have human rights institutions.[30] Sixteen have an internationally accredited institution established by the federation government (denoted as F in Table 4.1); nine of those countries also have rights institutions established by some or all of their constituent states (F/S); and three have rights institutions only in some or all states (S). Eight have no federation or constituent-state institution (N). The tally is misleading, however, because two of the most rights-protecting countries—Switzerland and the United States—have no internationally accredited rights institution established by the federation government, while several federations with weak rights records have such an institution.

One reason for the weak rights performance of half the federal systems is that many of those federations, such as Ethiopia, Iraq, Nigeria, and Pakistan, were established to promote peace and national unity by accommodating territorially based ethnic, religious, linguistic, or cultural differences that might splinter the country. Federalism was deemed more a necessity than a virtue; protecting rights and promoting democracy were secondary objectives at best. Some observers argue that these less democratic federations are not really federal because federalism requires freedom, rule of law, and rights protections for individuals and political communities to engage with one another in a system of self-rule and shared rule.[31] The free countries characterized by federal cultural accommodations, such as Belgium, Canada, India, Spain, and Switzerland, either had democratic and rights-protective systems from the outset or developed democratic and rights-protective institutions simultaneously with their federalization (for example, India and Spain).

Many observers contend that the essence of federalism "lies not in the institutional or constitutional structure but in [the attitudes of] society."[32] Overlaying federal institutions on a society not historically or culturally attuned to rights will not protect rights. The latter was true of the United States. Slavery and racial prejudice were deeply rooted in American culture, especially the culture of the South.[33] As observers such as Alexis de Tocqueville noted,[34] the tragic irony of the commitments to equality and unalienable rights expressed in the American Declaration of Independence of 1776 is that slavery's supporters resolved the contradiction between slavery and equality by defining slaves as nonpersons.[35] As a result, federalism and racism have been intertwined in US history, to the point where political scientist William H. Riker famously declared during the 1950s–1960s struggle for racial equality that if "one approves of Southern white racists, then one should approve of American federalism."[36]

The information in Table 4.1 suggests two cultural patterns. First, 46 per cent of the 28 federal countries are former British colonies.[37] Forty-two per cent of the free, 38 per cent of the partly free, and 67 per cent of the not-free federations were British colonies. The United Kingdom, a predominantly Protestant country, is itself a multinational polity with some federal features and a thread of federalist thinking about its empire and commonwealth.[38] British policymakers considered federalism an option for many of their multinational and multicultural colonies that achieved independence after the Second World War. Although the Latin American federations were not influenced by Britain, they modelled their federal constitutions after the US constitution. By contrast, the only former French colony that has a federal form is the Union of the Comoros, although two short-lived federations—the Mali Federation (1960) and the Senegambia Confederation (1982–89)—were among former French colonies. Europe's other colonial powers fostered no federalism.

Second, there is an apparent influence of religion. Religion is a rough proxy for culture. Among the free federal countries, the average Protestant population in 2010 was 30 per cent and the Muslim was 4 per cent. In the partly free federal countries, the Protestant population was 8 per cent and the Muslim population 44 per cent; the proportions were 4 per cent and 58 per cent respectively in the not-free countries. Put differently, 57 per cent of the free federations have a Protestant population that exceeds 25 per cent, while only one partly free federation (Nigeria) and no not-free federation has such a Protestant population. Five of the six oldest free and continually democratic federations have a Protestant population above 25 per cent. The exception is India, although its formation was influenced by Protestant Britain. Six (43 per cent) of the free federations have a Catholic population of 50 per cent or more, as do 25 per cent of the partly free federations. However, all four of the Latin American federations are predominantly Catholic, and all have experienced long periods of authoritarian civilian or military rule. Of the remaining four Catholic federations, two (Belgium and Spain) are experiencing significant separatist strains, Austria is one of the most centralized federations,[39] and the Federated States of Micronesia is affiliated with the United States through a compact of free association.

Democracy and federalism took root in substantially Protestant countries more so than in non-Protestant countries, and Protestant influence has been important in the development of liberal democracy and strong civil societies since the Second World War.[40] Generally, "countries with more Protestants are more democratic and have more stable democratic transitions."[41] Islamic countries are less democratic and less supportive of the rule of law, judicial independence, and rights, especially for women.[42] This is not to imply that Islamic countries cannot be democratic—Indonesia and Senegal are arguably democratic—but that most contemporary political expressions of Islam are not conducive to democratic federalism.[43]

In summation, federalism plays an important positive role in rights protection in countries that are too large and/or too multicultural to be governed in a unitary manner, but federalism is not sufficient for rights protection without the support of an underlying culture of democracy, rule of law, and rights sensitivity.[44] Absent such a cultural underpinning, federalism may foster internal peace and national unity but not necessarily rights protection—although domestic peace does protect life and gives citizens some liberty to pursue happiness.

Federalism's Unique Rights Challenges and Opportunities

Federalism poses some unique challenges and opportunities for protecting individual rights. Rights can be protected equally well by the federation and its constituent governments or equally poorly by each government. As Canada's former chief justice Bora Laskin observed, before adoption of the 1982 Charter of Rights and Freedoms, the "basic constitutional question" in Canada "was which jurisdiction should have the power to work the injustice, not whether the injustice itself should be prohibited."[45] Alternatively, the federation government might protect rights better than the constituent states, or the constituent states might protect rights better than the federation government. In a dualistic federation such as the United States, moreover, the federation and state governments might have responsibility for protecting different rights. State declarations of rights contain many rights pertaining to privacy, labour, women, environmental protection, political participation, and other matters that are not in the US constitution. At least in the free democratic federations (Table 4.1), both the federation and constituent governments protect rights rather well.

An important challenge for federalism is that rights are ordinarily conceived to be universal, a concept embedded in the United Nations Universal Declaration of Human Rights. Hence, rights ought to be uniform nationwide rather than subject to the variable preferences of diverse majorities. Supporters of a right to abortion, for instance, believe it ought to be available to all women in a federation, not to women in only some constituent political communities. Yet fundamental to federalism is the notion of achieving unity while preserving diversity. Can rights be included in this diversity, or does rights universalism demand uniformity?

Rights Diversity

In fact, rights diversity exists in many federal systems for several reasons. The founders of the United States distinguished between natural, civil, and political rights. They viewed natural rights (such as life, liberty, and property) as universal and not legitimately subject to jurisdictional diversity.[46] The framers of the US constitution therefore prohibited the federation government from suspending access to writs of *habeas corpus* unless rebellion or invasion required suspension; prohibited both the federation and the states from enacting any bill of attainder or ex post facto law or granting any title of nobility; and prohibited states from "impairing the obligation of contracts" (because contracts are primarily a state law responsibility). These rights are in the body of the constitution, not the Bill of Rights added in 1791. Civil rights, such as freedoms of speech, press, and religion, however, were subject to legitimate jurisdictional variation. For example, while the US Bill of Rights prohibits the federal government from establishing a tax-supported religion, several states continued to support an established church beyond 1791. Political rights, such as the right to vote, were also seen as legitimately subject to variation. Thus states had different voting ages until the US constitution was amended in 1971 to make 18 the universal voting age for federal elections. State and local governments can set a lower voting age, however. Nineteen states allow 17-year-olds to vote in primary elections and caucuses if they will be 18 by the later general election. In 2013, Takoma Park, Maryland, became the first US jurisdiction to lower its municipal election voting age to 16. (In 1996, Germany's Lower Saxony reduced its voting age to 16 for local elections, and Catalonia and Scotland allowed 16-year-olds to vote in their 2014 secession referendums.)

The voting age example illustrates another reason for rights diversity. It is difficult, perhaps impossible, to agree on the ideal equitable voting age, at least between the ages of about 15 and 25. If the voting age varies among a federation's constituent jurisdictions within such parameters, is that diversity an injustice? At the same time, other voting matters are said to involve more fundamental rights; hence states can no longer bar women or any racial or ethnic group from voting. One distinguishing criterion is that the latter characteristics are deemed to be unchangeable, while eventually a 15-year-old will presumably reach age 18.

A federal bargain usually includes agreement to disagree on certain matters, which may include certain rights. Residents of the various constituent political communities may have different values and views that produce irreconcilable differences, along the lines of Pascal's famous aphorism "Truth on this side of the Pyrenees, error on the other side."[47] One function of federalism is not only to preserve diversity up to certain mutually agreed points but also to diffuse conflict over fundamental cultural issues across the constituent political communities, so as to avoid the white heat of political firestorms that can erupt when the national government endorses one side over another side in a cultural conflict. The US Supreme Court's 1973 ruling granting a broad right of abortion under certain circumstances triggered such a firestorm.[48] Even though a majority of Americans (peaking at 61 per cent in 1997) have generally supported the Court's position since 1975,[49] anti-abortion forces mobilized vigorously, thereby distorting the national political process, fostering national polarization, and giving rise to the current conservative backlash represented by the Tea Party.

This firestorm is one reason why the US Supreme Court declined to choose sides on other divisive cultural issues such as capital punishment. After suspending all executions nationwide in 1972, the Court reinstated the death penalty in a series of 1976 rulings after states had addressed the court's constitutional concerns. As of mid-2015, 32 states and the federation government had the death penalty, although Texas has conducted 37 per cent of all executions since 1976, and Oklahoma and Virginia account for another 16 per cent. (As of mid-2015, 1,412 individuals had been executed since 1976.) By contrast, capital punishment is prohibited in 18 US states, all of Canada (where capital punishment is a federal responsibility), and all member states of the European Union.

Similarly, in 1997 the US Supreme Court refused to declare physician-assisted suicide to be a fundamental right under the US constitution.[50] To have done so would have added fuel to the firestorm ignited by the Court's 1973 abortion decision. Instead, the Court left the right to physician-assisted suicide to be decided by the democratic processes of the states. As of mid-2015, physician-assisted suicide had been legalized in Oregon (in 1994), Washington (2008), and Vermont (2013). In 1986 the US Supreme Court upheld anti-sodomy laws then in effect in 29 states, arguing that the right of privacy did not extend to homosexual sex.[51] In 2003, however, the Court overturned its 1986 ruling; only 13 states (mostly southern) still had such laws.[52]

Sometimes the Supreme Court allows variation in rights applications. For example, the Court has held that obscenity is not a protected right, but so long as states enact obscenity laws that adhere to the Court's general guidelines, and thus do not intrude unduly on free speech, the exact standard of obscenity can vary across communities.[53] What is deemed obscene in Iowa City might be deemed normal in New York City. By contrast, in Australia the states allow the national government to determine standards nationwide.[54]

Another reason for rights diversity is that the constituent political jurisdictions differentially implement statutes and court rulings promulgated by the federation. For example, despite the differences between the American and Canadian federal systems, implementation of the right to abortion by the states and provinces displays similar asymmetrical patterns in both countries.[55] States and provinces where there is strong opposition to abortion find ways to limit abortions. In the United States, 46 states allow health-care personnel to refuse to participate in an abortion; 42 prohibit abortions after a certain point (usually fetal viability); 39 require abortions to be performed by a licensed physician; 38 require some form of parental involvement in a minor's decision to have an abortion; 26 require a woman to wait for a certain period, usually 24 hours, between receiving counselling and an abortion; 19 prohibit "partial birth" abortion; and 17 states mandate that women be given pre-abortion counselling that includes information on purported links between abortion and breast cancer (5 states), ability of a fetus to feel pain (12 states), or long-term mental health consequences for the woman (8 states).

This example illustrates the complexity of implementing rights in a federation. As a result, some observers criticize federalism for failing to enforce rights adequately.[56] However, this critique misses key issues. First, most constitutional statements of rights are abstract. The devil is in the details of their implementation in both federal and unitary systems. In a federal system, those details—using abortion as the example—might be established by the constituent political communities and thus apply only to women in those jurisdictions. In a unitary system, the same political forces that produce variable details across a federation's constituent political communities would produce comparable but uniform details within a national implementation policy that would apply to all women in the country. For instance, a 24-hour waiting period mandated by a unitary national government would apply to all women; in the American system, the waiting period applies only to women seeking abortions in 26 states. Thus proponents as well as opponents of any given right may have legitimate and rational reasons for supporting or opposing various implementation details.

Second, in some federations a woman can escape restrictions by obtaining an abortion in a constituent state that has few or no restrictions; in a unitary system there is no escape from restrictions imposed by the national government. Third, because federalism is itself a constitutional value, it should not necessarily have to give way to another constitutional value. Instead, federalism may require accommodation of both values. Hence a continuing national dialogue may be needed to reach an agreeable balance—a dialogue that could facilitate greater public acceptance of both values.

Laboratories of Rights Experimentation

Rights diversity will exist as well where the constituent political communities can be laboratories of democracy that create new rights. The states, for example, were the first to enact laws protecting privacy and consumer rights on the Internet. In 1777 Vermont was the first state to constitutionalize a right to hunt and fish. No state followed suit until Alabama did so in 1996; now 18 states recognize this right. In 1980, Wisconsin was the first state to enact a crime victims' bill of rights. Today 33 states have crime victims' rights embedded in their constitutions, while 17 states and the federation government have crime victims' rights statutes. These rights include, among others, rights to information, privacy, protection, and restitution; to be present and heard at criminal justice proceedings; and to be informed of the release or escape of a convicted offender. In May 2014, Colorado enacted the country's first "right to try" law. It broadens the access of terminally ill patients to experimental drugs not yet approved by the US Food and Drug Administration. States have also legislated for such things as sperm-donor rights. The rise of solar power has required state and local governments to define access rights to sunshine, and voters in two states recently approved a constitutional right to farm.

A prominent example has been enactment of rights to use marijuana for medical purposes in 23 states. In 2012 voters legalized a right to use recreational marijuana in Colorado and Washington; Alaska and Oregon voters followed suit in 2014. Although these state laws violate the US Controlled Substances Act, neither Congress nor presidents have believed it politically advisable to assail them. President Barack Obama sought to accommodate these state laws because many supporters of his party, the Democratic Party, champion marijuana rights.

The marijuana example illustrates an unusual feature of American federalism, namely the right of voters in many states to place rights issues on the ballot. Through initiative and referendum processes, voters both expand and contract rights over time.

Problems of Diversity

Rights diversity does, however, produce inequalities across constituent political communities. This troubles critics of federalism who believe equality should prevail countrywide. Such inequalities are not necessarily undesirable, insofar as they arise for important purposes such as accommodating fundamental disagreements, giving certain individuals refuge in constituent political communities that are supportive of their rights, and allowing for the development of new rights that might eventually benefit everyone countrywide.

Of course, the ultimate question is: how far can diversity go before it becomes rights suppression? For example, since 1999, sharia has been instituted in nine of Nigeria's northern Muslim states and in parts of three states with large Muslim populations. In 2002 a Muslim court in Katsina sentenced a woman to be stoned to death for adultery and for conceiving a child with a man who broke his promise to marry her. International outrage helped ensure overturning of the woman's conviction by an appellate court, but the case illustrates the difficult normative and political challenges of drawing lines between acceptable and unacceptable rights diversity. It may be impossible to draw clear lines; the line drawing is ultimately a political question that must be revisited continually as a federation confronts changing conditions.

Individual and Communitarian Rights

As the above discussions suggest, federalism aims to protect not only the rights of individuals but also the rights of constituent political communities to exercise self-rule independently of the federation government. Most secular federal thought from Althusius onward has emphasized prevention of centralized domination. Such autonomy is especially important in federations that have territorially based racial, ethnic, national, linguistic, and/or religious communities, such as Flanders and Wallonia in Belgium, Quebec in Canada, Amhara and Oromia in Ethiopia, and the Basque Country and Catalonia in Spain. In some cases self-rule is vital for the very right to life. Under Iraq's federal arrangement, for example, Kurds seek to prevent a recurrence of the genocidal killings perpetrated by former dictator Saddam Hussein.

Thus, protecting communitarian rights indirectly protects individual rights by preventing one group from unilaterally imposing burdens on individuals of another group or of depriving those persons of their lives, rights, property, or historic identity. Every government that suppresses individual rights must also suppress communitarian rights.

At least 17 (61 per cent) of the federal countries in Table 4.1 have communitarian diversity; another three consist of two or more islands with autonomy interests. For example, Ethiopia's nine states and other administrative subdivisions are organized to represent the country's nations, nationalities, and peoples; India's 28 states are organized along language lines; Nigeria's states were increased from 3 in 1960 to 36 by 1996 in order to give more ethno-religious groups a constituent state; and 17 of Switzerland's 26 cantons have German as their official language, 4 have French, 1 has Italian, and 4 host two or three official languages.

In principle, federalism aims to protect communitarian rights through

1. voluntary consent of all the member communities to form or join the federal union;
2. consent, often super-majority consent, of the member communities to alter the federal union;

3. a written constitution specifying and protecting the terms of union;
4. constitutional guarantees of autonomous self-government for the constituent political communities;
5. diffusion of powers to prevent formation of a tyrannical central government;
6. guarantees of participation by constituent governments in the federation government's makeup and operation; and
7. guarantees of territorial integrity for the constituent communities (as an example, there can be no alteration of US state boundaries without the states' consent).

Not all federal systems incorporate all of the above elements; consequently, some constituent political communities are not willing partners to the federal covenant; they desire separation. The former Socialist Federal Republic of Yugoslavia was an extreme example of partners unwillingly yoked together. After autocrat Marshal Josip Tito died in 1980, the federation disintegrated violently during the ensuing 25 years, especially after Slovenia and Croatia declared independence in 1991. In 2008, Kosovo became the last independent republic formed from Yugoslavia. By contrast, in Quebec many residents desire separation, although majorities of voters rejected separatist referendums in 1980 and 1995. In Spain, the Basque Country and Catalonia are reluctant partners in the quasi-federal "state of the autonomies" established during the democratic revolution of 1978. Catalonia planned an official vote on independence in November 2014; the Constitutional Court of Spain suspended the referendum, but Catalans voted for independence anyway.

A Right of Secession?

An important communitarian rights question in some federal systems is: should constituent political communities have a right to secede and, if so, for what reasons and under what conditions? For Americans, secession is anathema because 11 southern states seceded in 1860–61 in order to protect slavery. One of President Abraham Lincoln's key arguments against southern secession—an argument that "remains at the center of" Lincoln's "international reputation" today[57]—is that a people cannot declare self-determination or cultural autonomy if they intend to use their autonomy to oppress other people.

Catalonia, the Basque Country, Quebec, and some other separatist communities today are quite different. They are democratic, mostly nonviolent, and rights-respecting; they meet Lincoln's non-oppression criterion. Yet the only federal constitution that explicitly provides for secession is that of

Ethiopia. Article 39 of Ethiopia's constitution declares a number of communitarian rights, beginning with section 1: "Every Nation, Nationality and People shall have the unrestricted right to self-determination up to secession."[58] Procedures are set forth for secession, although no state has sought to secede and the country's authoritarian government would likely thwart any secession request. Canada recognizes a statutory right of secession contingent on mutual negotiations between the federation and the separatist province, after approval by a clear majority of the residents of the separatist province of a clear question on secession.[59] Some public-choice theorists argue that a right of secession should be constitutionally available and feasible for any constituent political community of any democratic federation, because such a right offers powerful leverage against a federation government bent on oppression.[60]

However, secession raises difficult normative and practical questions. Can a federation survive and function effectively if the constituent political communities have too easy a right of secession? What is a clear question? What is a clear majority—50 per cent plus one? 66 per cent? 75 per cent? What are the rights of minority political communities, such as African Americans or First Nations, that vote against secession, especially if the "clear majority" is predominantly of European settler descent? Should every distinct nation or people have a right to its own state? Could the world manage thousands of independent micro-states? At an international conference on federalism in Canada in 1999, President Bill Clinton advised against secession: "When a people thinks it should be independent in order to have a meaningful political existence, serious questions should be asked: Is there an abuse of human rights? Is there a way people can get along if they come from different heritages? Are minority rights, as well as majority rights, respected? What is in the long-term economic and security interests of our people? How are we going to cooperate with our neighbors? Will it be better or worse if we are independent, or if we have a federalist system?"[61]

Another tension involves obligations that the federation and constituent political communities may or may not owe each other with respect to social and economic rights. Virtually all federations engage in fiscal equalization in order to ensure uniform or approximately equal living standards federation-wide. The United States is an exception, preferring instead to redistribute resources directly to poor persons rather than to poor places.[62] Fiscal equalization usually depends on the nature of the federation. Federations that have one or more culturally distinct constituent political communities ordinarily engage in fiscal equalization in order to foster solidarity and compensate for low levels of interjurisdictional citizen mobility. Germany is a notable exception; its rigorous equalization is partly a response to the country's Nazi past.

Fiscal equalization, however, has the anti-rights attributes of bribery and extortion in some federations; that is, the federation offers equalization payments to quell regional discontent or separatism, while some constituent political communities extort payments from the federation as the price of union. In Nigeria, one reason for the creation of 33 new states since independence has been the desire of various ethno-religious groups to have a state eligible to receive federation payments.

There is, however, significant tension between individual and communitarian rights. As suggested by the example of abortion rights discussed above, should the right to abortion trump communitarian rights to restrict it, or should communitarian rights trump an unfettered right to abortion? Thus the exercise of individual rights can reduce communitarian rights, and the exercise of communitarian rights can reduce individual rights. One ongoing controversy in Quebec, for example, has been French-language signage laws. Such laws are a vital element of the maintenance of French identity in Quebec. However, what rights belong to non-French-speakers in the province who wish to post non-French signage that is equally as public and prominent as French-language signs? Should a cultural majority be able to curtail the rights of cultural minorities?

The American Revolt Against States' Rights

The most egregious American example of communitarian rights (commonly called "states' rights" in the United States) suppressing individual rights was slavery. Despite opposition to slavery in northern states, including the southern slave states in the federation was the necessary price of union.[63] Southern states defended the right of each state to legalize or prohibit slavery. The US constitution, which does not use the words *slave* and *slavery*, contains provisions that opponents of slavery hoped would foster slavery's demise, but the institution survived until the South was defeated in the Civil War (1860–65). After the war, southerners again used states' rights to establish racial segregation, which lasted until the 1960s.

In contrast to federations where federalism is seen as a means of liberation from centralized oppression (as in Germany and Spain), many Americans came to see federalism as a key source of non-centralized oppression that required strong federation countermeasures. Beginning with the post–Civil War amendments to the US constitution (XIII, XIV, and XV) —which abolished slavery, authorized Congress to intervene in states to protect individual rights, and extended the right to vote to non-whites—increasing rights protection has entailed increasing centralization and even coercive federalism, whereby the federation compels errant states to respect rights.[64]

Especially important has been the Fourteenth Amendment (1868), which prohibits state deprivation of individual rights and authorizes federation intervention to protect rights. Initially, political forces enabled both the Congress and the Supreme Court to ignore the amendment; consequently, southern states institutionalized racial segregation. In 1896 the Supreme Court upheld racial segregation by ruling that separate but allegedly equal accommodations for blacks and whites did not violate the Fourteenth Amendment's rule that no state shall "deny any person within its jurisdiction the equal protection of the laws."[65] Not until 1954 did the Supreme Court reverse course and rule that the Fourteenth Amendment required speedy desegregation, in that case of public schools.[66] This ruling triggered a civil rights revolution that involved massive federation interventions in states, including some military and police interventions, to enforce rights.

Thus, for 165 years neither the federation nor most states adequately protected the rights of black Americans. Likewise, neither the federation nor most states protected the rights of the indigenous people. After the Civil War, the federation government, which had sole responsibility for relations with the tribes in the western territories, engaged in genocidal policies. With respect to white Europeans included in the federal covenant, rights were long protected dualistically. In 1833 the Supreme Court ruled that the US Bill of Rights applied only to the actions of the federation government, not those of state and local governments (which were subject to their own state constitutional declarations of rights).[67]

In 1897, however, the Court ruled that the Fourteenth Amendment "incorporated" at least one provision of the US Bill of Rights, thus making it applicable to state and local governments.[68] The Court incorporated 6 more provisions before 1961, 11 more in 1961–71, and 1 in 2010, thereby incorporating most of the Bill of Rights. Through hundreds of cases, the US Supreme Court has substantially nationalized and liberalized rights protection and has required states to adhere to its interpretations of the details of rights protection. The most recent incorporation recognized a fundamental national, constitutional right of individuals to own and carry firearms.[69] The 5–4 ruling exposed thousands of state and local laws regulating guns to legal challenges and strengthened the ability of gun-rights advocates to attain new state laws liberalizing the rights of individuals to own, carry, and use firearms in everyday life. It will require decades for the Supreme Court to sort out the details of this new national right.

The New Judicial Federalism

This right-to-bear-arms case also reflects a somewhat conservative trend on the Supreme Court that began when President Richard Nixon appointed a conservative chief justice in 1969. Nixon's 1968 election represented, in part, a public backlash against the Court's liberalization of rights, especially the rights of criminal defendants. The Court began to retrench in some rights areas, especially criminal rights. Liberals reacted to the retrenchment by realizing that state constitutional declarations of rights offered opportunities to strengthen rights protections in areas of federal court retrenchment. In 1977 a sitting justice, William J. Brennan, argued that US Supreme Court interpretations of the US Bill of Rights established only a national floor of rights protection, not a ceiling. States, therefore, had the authority under their state constitutions to grant higher or more rigorous rights protections than those recognized under the national Bill of Rights.[70] This sparked a movement termed "the new judicial federalism," in which many state supreme courts issued hundreds of rulings that offered higher rights protection.[71] Likewise, state legislatures can enact laws granting higher rights protection and also protecting rights not recognized by the US Bill of Rights. In 1986 the US Supreme Court ruled that such state court rulings are immune from its review, so long as the state courts base their rulings entirely on "adequate and independent" state constitutional grounds.[72]

An early example occurred after the US Supreme Court ruled in 1976 that individuals do not have a right to freedom of speech on someone else's private property, such as a shopping mall.[73] In 1979, however, the California Supreme Court ruled that the state's declaration of rights protects freedom of speech in shopping malls, in this case an attempt by high school students to solicit signatures on a protest petition in the Pruneyard mall.[74] Pruneyard appealed the California ruling to the US Supreme Court, arguing that it contradicted the Court's previous ruling. The Court, however, upheld the California court, opining that the US Supreme Court's prior ruling on this matter did "not *ex proprio vigore* limit the authority of the State to exercise its police power or its sovereign right to adopt in its own Constitution individual liberties more expansive than those conferred by the Federal Constitution."[75] The supreme courts of Colorado, Massachusetts, and New Jersey followed the California court's precedent, although about 13 state high courts rejected it. In 2003 the European Court of Human Rights considered but refused to follow California's *Pruneyard* precedent.[76]

In another example, the US Supreme Court held that police do not need a court-issued warrant to search trash placed outside one's home for municipal disposal.[77] However, the supreme courts of California, Hawaii, New Jersey, Vermont, and Washington have ruled that police do need a warrant to search people's trashcans. Consequently, in those five states, federal law-enforcement officials such as FBI agents do not need a warrant to search curbside trash, because they are governed by the US Supreme Court's ruling, but state and local police do need a search warrant. What is to prevent state police from asking federal agents to conduct a warrantless search and give them the incriminating evidence? State courts have ruled that such evidence will almost always be excluded from trial in their courts.

In sum, a new form of communitarian rights, or states' rights, has emerged in the United States whereby the constituent political communities can define rights for themselves so long as they are more protective than national rights standards. This applies to local governments too, such as New York City's Local Civil Rights Restoration Act (2005), which makes it easier for residents to sue employers for workplace sexual harassment than under the comparable state and federal laws. Hence the new judicial federalism has added considerable diversity to rights protection across the country's 50 states and 89,476 local jurisdictions.

Human Rights Treaties

Human rights treaties raise other tensions. Exercise of treaty power is a major issue in many federations because ratification of treaties by a federation government can reduce the self-rule powers of the constituent political communities. For instance, in 1913 Congress enacted a law limiting the hunting of migratory birds. Courts deemed the law an unconstitutional intrusion upon states' powers to regulate hunting within their borders. In 1916 the United States concluded a treaty with Great Britain to protect various birds migrating between Canada and the United States. In 1918 Congress passed the Migratory Bird Treaty Act. The US Supreme Court upheld the Act in 1920 on the ground that a law enacted pursuant to a treaty pre-empts conflicting state laws, even if it nullifies traditional state powers.[78]

As a consequence of this doctrine, as well as concerns about US national sovereignty, the United States has declined to ratify many human rights treaties and does not recognize compulsory jurisdiction of the International Court of Justice (ICJ). Opponents of such treaties argue that introducing the sometimes vague and aspirational norms of international human rights conventions into domestic law would be anti-democratic and destructive of federalism. More recently though, the US Supreme Court held that even if an international treaty constitutes an international commitment, it is not binding domestic law unless Congress enacts statutes to implement it or the treaty is self-executing. The Court also opined that ICJ decisions are not binding domestic law and that without authority from Congress or the constitution, the US president cannot enforce international treaties or ICJ rulings.[79]

In 2014 the Court again addressed the extent to which a treaty can override state powers, by allowing Congress to enact implementing laws that exceed its constitutionally enumerated powers. Carol A. Bond had placed toxic chemicals on the car, mailbox, and doorknob of a woman friend who had had a child from an affair with Bond's husband. The woman experienced a minor burn easily treated with water; local police did not pursue serious criminal charges. The US government, however, charged Bond with criminal violation of a federal statute that enforces the Chemical Weapons Convention, a treaty ratified by the US Senate in 1997. A key question was whether Bond's prosecution was permitted by the Court's broad 1920 interpretation of the treaty power. The unanimous Court issued a narrow ruling that the federal statute did not specifically criminalize Bond's action. The justices declined to roll back the 1920 doctrine, although they opened a crack in the doctrine by implying that the treaty power might be challenged if it intrudes too deeply into local matters.[80]

In Australia, which has no domestic bill of rights, the federation government can enact statutes implementing treaties even if their subject matter lies outside federation jurisdiction. This has occasioned complaints from states that the federation government has used treaties to expand its powers, including powers over rights. In Canada, the federation cannot implement treaties whose subject matter falls within provincial jurisdiction. Because human rights involve shared federation and provincial powers, the federation executive ordinarily ratifies human rights treaties only after obtaining support from the provinces and territories. Thus, ratification of such treaties cannot be done easily. Furthermore, human rights treaties are usually not incorporated into domestic law; nevertheless, there has been a trend on the Canadian Supreme Court to acknowledge international human rights treaties and conventions as tools for interpreting domestic legislation and the constitution.

Recently, international rights treaties and covenants have played a role in improving rights protections in many countries. Also, some federal constitutions acknowledge the authority of international law. For example, section 233 of South Africa's constitution provides: "When interpreting any legislation, every court must prefer any reasonable interpretation of the legislation that is consistent with international law over any alternative interpretation that is inconsistent with international law." In the United States, there have been strong objections to US Supreme Court efforts to do the same, although in its 2015 case on same-sex marriage, supporters of gay marriage urged the Supreme Court to acknowledge "an emerging global consensus among liberal democracies" in support of same-sex marriage, while opponents urged the court to recognize that only 17 of the 193 member states of the United Nations have legalized same-sex marriage.[81]

Conclusion

A well-structured federal system can protect rights insofar as it frustrates centralized tyranny, but its rights-protecting capability is limited in the absence of an underlying culture of democracy, rule of law, and respect for rights. However, the same can be said of unitary systems. Worldwide, federalism has a better record of rights-respecting democracy than other systems. It also can add value to rights protection by protecting both individual and communitarian rights. These two types of rights often conflict, but democratic federal processes can strike a balance between the two in accordance with prevailing public preferences for one or the other.

Federalism also allows for diversity of rights protection. Such diversity not only manages disagreements about rights but also allows individuals to move to jurisdictions that are more compatible with their rights expectations and, in turn, allows the constituent political communities to develop new rights protections when the federation is unwilling or slow to do so. The new American judicial federalism also represents an interesting experiment in one-way federalism, in which rights protections offered by state and local governments can only go up, not down.

Takeaway Messages

- Federalism has a better record of rights protection than other systems, but institutions of federalism are not sufficient to protect individual rights without appropriate cultural underpinnings such as democracy, rule of law, and respect for rights.
- Rights vary across the constituent political communities of a federation for important and rational reasons, but the difficult normative challenge of distinguishing between acceptable and unacceptable rights diversity is ultimately a political question.
- Federalism aims to protect both individual and communitarian rights and must continually negotiate tensions between the two.

Study Questions

- What factors enhance or reduce rights protection in federations?
- What unique challenges and opportunities confront federalism in rights protection?
- How does federalism seek to both protect communitarian rights and resolve tensions between individual and communitarian rights?

Issues for Debate or Roundtable

- In what ways is a federal system superior and inferior to a unitary system for protecting rights?
- Under what circumstances should individual rights prevail over communitarian rights, and vice versa?
- What kinds of rights should be allowed to vary across constituent political communities, and how? What kinds of rights should not be allowed to vary across constituent jurisdictions?

Additional Reading

Elazar, Daniel J. *Exploring Federalism.* Tuscaloosa: University of Alabama Press, 1987.
Kincaid, John. "Values and Value Tradeoffs in Federalism." *Publius* 25 (Spring 1995): 29–44.
Morley, Felix. *Freedom and Federalism.* Chicago: Henry Regnery Co., 1959.
Neumann, Franz L. "Federalism and Freedom: A Critique." In *Federalism: Mature and Emergent*, ed. Arthur W. MacMahon. New York: Doubleday, 1955.
Tran, Luan-Vu N. Human Rights and Federalism: A Comparative Study on Freedom, Democracy, and Cultural Diversity. The Hague: Martinus Nijhoff, 2000.
White, Linda A. "Federalism and Equality Rights Implementation in Canada." *Publius* 44 (Winter 2014): 156–82.

Websites

American Civil Liberties Union. https://www.aclu.org/.
Forum of Federations. http://www.forumfed.org/en/index.php.
Foundation for Individual Rights in Education. https://www.thefire.org/.
International Association of Centers for Federal Studies. http://www.iacfs.org/.

Notes

1. P. Norris, *Driving Democracy: Do Power-Sharing Institutions Work?* (Cambridge: Cambridge University Press, 2008); J. Kincaid, "Federalism and Democracy: Comparative Empirical and Theoretical Perspectives," in *Federal Democracies*, ed. M. Burgess and A.-G. Gagnon (London: Routledge, 2010), 299–324.
2. D.J. Elazar, *Covenant and Polity in Biblical Israel* (New Brunswick, NJ: Transaction, 1995).
3. See, for example, J.H. Franklin, ed. and trans., *Constitutionalism and Resistance in the Sixteenth Century: Three Treatises by Hotman, Beza, and Mornay* (New York: Pegasus, 1969).
4. D.J. Elazar and J. Kincaid, eds., *The Covenant Connection: From Federal Theology to Modern Federalism* (Lanham, MD: Lexington Books, 2000).
5. J. Althusius, *Politica*, ed. and trans. Frederick S. Carney (Indianapolis: Liberty Fund, 1995).

6. T. Hueglin, "Johannes Althusius: Medieval Constitutionalist or Modern Federalist?" *Publius* 9 (Fall 1979): 9–41.
7. J.E. Cooke, ed., *The Federalist* (Middletown, CT: Wesleyan University Press, 1961).
8. The term *federation government* is used here to refer to what various federations call the federal, national, or central government.
9. J. Kincaid, "*The Federalist* and V. Ostrom on Concurrent Taxation and Federalism," *Publius* 44 (Spring 2014): 275–97.
10. Cooke, *The Federalist*, no. 51, 351.
11. B. Schwartz, *The Great Rights of Mankind: A History of the Bill of Rights* (New York: Oxford University Press, 1977), 197.
12. D.S. Lutz, "The State Constitutional Pedigree of the US Bill of Rights," *Publius* 22 (Spring 1992): 19–45.
13. P.T. Conley and J.P. Kaminski, eds., *The Bill of Rights and the States: The Colonial and Revolutionary Origins of American Liberties* (Madison, WI: Madison House, 1991).
14. Contemporary research seems to confirm Madison. See A.S. Chilton and M. Versteeg, "Do Constitutional Rights Make a Difference?" http://papers.ssrn.com/sol3/papers.cfm?abstract_id=2477530.
15. C. Jung, R. Hirschl, and E. Rosevear, "Economic and Social Rights in National Constitutions," *American Journal of Comparative Law* 62 (Fall 2014): 1043–93.
16. See E. Zackin, *Looking for Rights in All the Wrong Places: Why State Constitutions Contain America's Positive Rights* (Princeton, NJ: Princeton University Press, 2013).
17. Bingo is a game of chance, invented in 1929, that is played with randomly drawn numbers that players match against numbers printed on five-by-five matrices. Usually the winner shouts "Bingo!" Some churches and nonprofits use bingo to raise money.
18. *City of Boerne v. Flores*, 521 U.S. 507 (1997).
19. See, though, J.B. Kelly, "Reconciling Rights and Federalism during Review of the Charter of Rights and Freedoms: The Supreme Court of Canada and the Centralization Thesis," *Canadian Journal of Political Science* 34 (June 2001): 321–55.
20. W.H. Riker, *Federalism: Origin, Operation, Significance* (Boston: Little, Brown, 1964).
21. N. Schmitt, "Swiss Confederation," in *Constitutional Origins, Structure, and Change in Federal Countries*, ed. J. Kincaid and G.A. Tarr (Montreal: McGill-Queen's University Press, 2005), 348.
22. D. de Rougemont, *La Suisse ou l'histoire d'un people heureux* (Lausanne: L'age d'homme, 1990), 18.
23. See, for example, M. Wollstonecraft, *A Vindication of the Rights of Woman with Strictures on Political and Moral Subjects*, ed. M.B. Kramnick (Harmondsworth, UK: Penguin, 1972).
24. The phrase "constituent political communities" is used here to refer to what various federations call cantons, *Länder*, provinces, regions, or states.
25. See, for example, J. Vickers, "Is Federalism Gendered? Incorporating Gender into Studies of Federalism," *Publius* 43 (Winter 2013): 1–23.
26. Pew Research, "Gay Marriage Around the World," 19 December 2013, http://www.pewforum.org/2015/06/26/gay-marriage-around-the-world-2013/; CBC News, "Timeline: Same-Sex Rights in Canada," 12 January 2012, http://www.cbc.ca/news/canada/timeline-same-sex-rights-in-canada-1.1147516.
27. *United States v. Windsor*, 570 U.S. 12 (2013).

28. *The Commonwealth of Australia v. The Australian Capital Territory*, (2013) HCA 55. See also G. Williams, "Can Tasmania Legislate for Same-Sex Marriage?" *University of Tasmania Law Review* 31 (2012): 117–33.
29. *Suresh Kumar Koushal v. Naz Foundation*, Civil Appeal no. 10972 of 2013.
30. A. Wolman, "The Relationship Between National and Sub-National Human Rights Institutions in Federal Countries," *International Journal of Human Rights* 17, no. 3 (2013): 445–62.
31. I.D. Duchacek, *Comparative Federalism: The Territorial Dimension of Politics* (Lanham, MD: University Press of America, 1987).
32. W.A. Livingston, "A Note on the Nature of Federalism," *Political Science Quarterly* 67 (March 1952): 84.
33. W.J. Cash, *The Mind of the South* (New York: A.A. Knopf, 1941).
34. A. de Tocqueville, *Democracy in America*, ed. J.P. Mayer, trans. G. Lawrence (Garden City, NJ: Doubleday Anchor, 1969).
35. *Dred Scott v. Sandford*, 60 U.S. 393 (1857).
36. Riker, *Federalism*, 155.
37. These are Australia, Canada, India, Iraq, Malaysia, Nigeria, Pakistan, St. Kitts and Nevis, South Africa, South Sudan, Sudan, United Arab Emirates, and United States.
38. M. Burgess, *The British Tradition of Federalism* (London: Leicester University Press, 1995).
39. A. Gamper, "Republic of Austria," in *Legislative, Executive, and Judicial Governance in Federal Countries*, ed. K. Le Roy and C. Saunders (Montreal: McGill-Queen's University Press, 2006), 72–100; J. Erk, "Austria: A Federation Without Federalism," *Publius* 34 (Winter 2004): 1–20.
40. R.D. Woodberry, "The Missionary Roots of Liberal Democracy," *American Political Science Review* 106 (May 2012): 244–74; R.F. Tusalem, "The Role of Protestantism in Democratic Consolidation among Transitional States," *Comparative Political Studies* 42 (2009): 882–915; A. Hadenius, *Democracy and Development* (Cambridge: Cambridge University Press, 1992).
41. Woodberry, "Missionary Roots," 245.
42. J. Gutmann and S. Voight, "The Rule of Law and Constitutionalism in Muslim Countries," 2014, http://ssrn.com/abstract=2434793; A. Karatnycky, "Muslim Countries and the Democracy Gap," *Journal of Democracy* 13 (January 2002): 99–112.
43. See also W.B. Hallaq, *The Impossible State: Islam, Politics, and Modernity's Moral Predicament* (New York: Columbia University Press, 2012).
44. R.D. Putnam, *Making Democracy Work: Civic Traditions in Modern Italy* (Princeton, NJ: Princeton University Press, 1993).
45. Quoted in I. Cotler, "Can the Center Hold? Federalism and Rights in Canada," in *Federalism and Rights*, ed. E. Katz and G.A. Tarr (Lanham, MD: Rowman & Littlefield, 1996), 177. See also T.R. Berger, *Fragile Freedoms: Human Rights and Dissent in Canada* (Toronto: Clarke, Irwin, 1981).
46. For an alternative list, see W.J. Talbott, *Which Rights Should Be Universal?* (Oxford: Oxford University Press, 2005).
47. B. Pascal, *Pensées* [1670], trans. A.J. Krailsheimer (Harmondsworth, UK: Penguin Books, 1966), section V, 294.
48. *Roe v. Wade*, 410 U.S. 113 (1973).

49. L. Saad, "Public Opinion about Abortion: An In-Depth Review," Gallup Poll, 22 January 2002, http://www.gallup.com/poll/9904/Public-Opinion-About-Abortion-InDepth-Review.aspx.
50. *Washington v. Glucksberg*, 521 U.S. 702 (1997); *Vacco v. Quill*, 521 U.S. 793 (1997).
51. *Bowers v. Hardwick*, 478 U.S. 186 (1986).
52. *Lawrence v. Texas*, 539 U.S. 558 (2003).
53. *Miller v. California*, 413 U.S. 15 (1973); *Paris Adult Theatre I v. Slaton*, 413 U.S. 49 (1973).
54. B. Harris, "Censorship: A Comparative Approach Offering a New Theoretical Basis for Classification in Australia," *Canberra Law Review* 8 (2005): 25–58.
55. R. McKeever, "Abortion, the Judiciary and Federalism in North America," in *The Federal Nation*, ed. I.W. Morgan and P.J. Davies (London: Palgrave Macmillan, 2008), 223–39.
56. H.A. Palley, "Canadian Abortion Policy: National Policy and the Impact of Federalism and Political Implementation on Access to Services," *Publius* 36 (Fall 2006): 565–86.
57. P. Abbott, "The Lincoln Propositions and the Spirit of Secession," *Studies in American Political Development* 10 (1996): 103–29.
58. See also A. Habtu, "Multiethnic Federalism in Ethiopia: A Study of the Secession Clause in the Constitution," *Publius* 35 (Spring 2005): 313–35.
59. *Reference re Secession of Quebec*, [1998] 2 S.C.R. 217; Clarity Act (2000). Secession of a province would require an amendment to Canada's constitution. This would require negotiations with the governments of all the provinces as well as the federal government.
60. J.M. Buchanan, "Federalism as an Ideal Political Order and an Objective for Constitutional Reform," *Publius* 25 (Winter 1995): 19–27.
61. W.J. Clinton, "Address by William Jefferson Clinton," *Publius* 29 (Fall 1999): 23–32.
62. D.A. Kenyon and J. Kincaid, "Fiscal Federalism in the United States: The Reluctance to Equalize Jurisdictions," in *Finanzverfassung im Spannungsfeld zwischen Zentralstaat und Gliedstaaten*, ed. W.W. Pommerehne and G. Ress (Baden-Baden: Nomos Verlagsgesellschaft, 1996), 34–56.
63. H. Agar, *The Price of Union* (New York: Houghton Mifflin, 1950).
64. J. Kincaid, "From Cooperation to Coercion in American Federalism: Housing, Fragmentation, and Preemption, 1780–1992," *Journal of Law and Politics* 9 (Winter 1993): 333–433.
65. *Plessy v. Ferguson*, 163 U.S. 537 (1896).
66. *Brown v. Board of Education*, 347 U.S. 483 (1954).
67. *Barron v. Baltimore*, 32 U.S. (7 Pet.) 243 (1833).
68. *Chicago, Burlington & Quincy Railroad Co. v. City of Chicago*, 166 U.S. 226 (1897).
69. *McDonald v. Chicago*, 561 U.S. 3025 (2010).
70. W.J. Brennan Jr., "State Constitutions and the Protection of Individual Rights," *Harvard Law Review* 90 (1977): 489–504.
71. J. Kincaid, "Foreword: The New Federalism Context of the New Judicial Federalism," *Rutgers Law Journal* 26 (Summer 1995): 913–48.
72. *Michigan v. Long*, 463 U.S. 1032 (1983).
73. *Hudgens v. NLRB*, 424 U.S. 507 (1976).
74. *Robins v. Pruneyard Shopping Center*, 592 P.2d 341 (1979).

75. *Pruneyard Shopping Center v. Robbins*, 447 U.S. 74, 81 (1980).
76. *Appleby and Others v. the United Kingdom* (2003) 37 EHRR 783.
77. *California v. Greenwood*, 486 U.S. 35 (1988).
78. *Missouri v. Holland*, 252 U.S. 416 (1920).
79. *Medellín v. Texas*, 552 U.S. 491 (2008). In 2004 the ICJ ruled that the United States had violated the Vienna Convention on Consular Relations by not allowing 51 Mexican nationals in US state prisons to consult their consulate. Medillín was on death row in Texas and was executed in 2008. Governor Rick Perry rejected pleas from Mexico and the federation government to delay the execution, citing the torture, rape, and strangulation of two teenage girls in Houston 15 years earlier as the ground for execution.
80. *Bond v. United States*, 572 U.S. ___ (2014).
81. A. Liptak, "Supreme Court Is Asked to Look Abroad for Guidance on Same-Sex Marriage," *New York Times*, 7 April 2015, A13.

5
Human Rights NGOs

DAVID ZARNETT

Learning Objectives

- To distinguish human rights NGOs from other non-state actors
- To understand an NGO's source of influence and the conditions under which NGOs are most effective in curbing human rights abuse
- To learn about "discrimination" and selectivity in NGO activism
- To identify common critiques made of the NGO sector

Consider how you might answer some of the following questions: Why does the United Nations Charter include a series of human rights provisions? Why was the Universal Declaration of Human Rights drafted and ratified? How do the international human rights norms set out in these and other UN treaties influence the domestic policies of states? Who provides information on human rights abuses and crises taking place on the other side of the world? Who provides humanitarian relief to the people victimized by such abuse?

Many scholars investigating these and other, related questions have pointed to the important role played by human rights non-governmental organizations (NGOs). In this view, to understand many different aspects of contemporary politics, one must look beyond the state and consider the role played by human rights NGOs in shaping the ways in which international and domestic politics are practised. These NGOs have sought to exert influence by raising awareness of new problems, suggesting solutions to problems, generating sufficient interest in order to put these solutions into practice, and ensuring sustained commitment to their implementation.

This chapter offers an introduction to the politics of human rights NGOs. With a focus on international human rights NGOs in particular, it seeks to address a number of questions. What is a human rights NGO? Why did scholars of world politics begin to study them? How do human rights NGOs exert influence in an international system replete with apparently more powerful actors, including states, international organizations, multinational corporations, and armed militant groups? Under what conditions have human rights NGOs contributed to the improvement of human rights practices in various countries? How do human rights NGOs decide which issues are most deserving of their scarce resources? And what are some of the criticisms of human rights NGOs' work? Below, the existing literature on human rights NGOs will be consulted in order to shed light on these questions.

What Is a Human Rights NGO?

Understanding what a human rights NGO is requires being clear on two questions: What are human rights? And what are NGOs? The first question refers to a set of objectives, while the second refers to a type of organization.

There is little consensus as to what constitutes a human right.[1] This controversy has implications for how we understand human rights NGOs. In the existing literature on NGOs, there is a tendency to distinguish human rights NGOs from other types of NGOs. For instance, in their analysis of the growth of the international NGO sector during the second half of the twentieth century, Kathryn Sikkink and Jackie Smith distinguish human rights NGOs from those that work on peace, women's rights, the environment, international law, and development.[2] If we understand the concept of human rights to be contested, then it is not immediately clear on what grounds these distinctions are being made. Is the right to be free from torture or arbitrary arrest any more of a human right than the right of access to clean drinking water or land free of limb-shredding landmines? Does Amnesty International's focus on prisoners of conscience make it more of a human rights NGO than Greenpeace's efforts to protect communities whose land is being polluted by multinational oil corporations?

While it is important to distinguish NGOs that focus on different issue areas, such as children in armed conflict, indigenous rights, arms control, or water security, there is no compelling reason to treat these NGOs as anything but human rights organizations. In this sense, the term *human rights NGO* is best understood as an umbrella category that includes a wide range of actors who work in some way to improve the lives of different segments of aggrieved human populations. This definition therefore includes a wide range of NGOs, such as those that seek to defend human rights worldwide like Amnesty International and Human Rights Watch, as well as those that work on behalf of specific aggrieved populations like the International Campaign for Tibet or the Palestine Solidarity Campaign. It also includes NGOs that focus on legal norms and judicial process (e.g., the International Commission of Jurists), that provide humanitarian relief to refugees and internally displaced persons (e.g., CARE), that work to provide security to civilians in conflict zones (e.g., Peace Brigades International), and that seek to curb environmental degradation associated with economic development (e.g., Friends of the Earth). Excluded from this definition, of course, would be those organizations that work to advance the rights of non-human subjects. For instance, NGOs such as the Toronto Humane Society, the Society for the Prevention of Cruelty to Animals, and the World Society for the Protection of Animals would not be considered human rights NGOs, but rather animal rights organizations.

In short, while most people think of organizations like Amnesty International and Human Rights Watch when they think of human rights NGOs, there is no reason to see them as any more human rights–focused than many other NGOs that seek to improve the quality of life for aggrieved populations around the world. Adopting a narrow conception of human rights can blind us to the myriad human rights objectives pursued by various international NGOs (INGOs), and to the many and varied methods employed in pursuit of those rights.

Defining an NGO's objectives, in this case human rights, is not sufficient to let us say what an NGO is. After all, many organizations—including the UN Human Rights Council, the European Court of Human Rights, and the human rights division of the US State Department, among numerous others—also work to advance human rights as they see them. However, these actors are not NGOs.

Just as the term *human rights* is contested, so too is the meaning of the term *non-governmental organization*. Developing a comprehensive definition of *NGO* is not a simple task. The problem, according to Peter Willets, is that "there is no such thing as a typical NGO."[3] However, common characteristics can be discerned. Drawing on the existing literature, there appear to be four core aspects of what constitutes an NGO: it is formally organized, non-profit, non-violent, and non-state. These attributes are relevant to all types of NGOs, both human rights and non–human rights, but the former will be emphasized in the discussion below.

Formally Organized

Human rights NGOs are often considered to be formal organizations with internal hierarchies, decision-making processes, and agreed-upon budgets. In this sense, NGOs provide well-defined job descriptions to their staff, which can be either professional, volunteer, or a combination of the two. By contrast, other civil society actors who may also seek to advance human rights, such as social movements or transnational advocacy networks (TANs), tend not to develop the same type of internal governing structures as NGOs do. These types of actors are more broad-based and in many ways are better understood as coalitions of actors who are united around shared goals.

But distinguishing human rights NGOs from other civil society actors with a human rights focus in this way does raise certain challenges. First, NGOs themselves vary in organizational structure, ranging from highly centralized to those that are more decentralized.[4] Second, it is not always clear when a domestic social movement or TAN becomes an (I)NGO, especially when a coalition of actors begins to implement more formalized structures and routines.[5] Despite some of these complexities, however, NGOs can be usefully distinguished from social movements and TANs by the fact that they are single organizations that tend to have higher levels of internal coordination.[6] More specifically, NGOs are often one type of actor within larger social movements and TANs.

Non-Profit

In addition to being more formally organized, human rights NGOs are often considered to be non-profit.[7] That is, their reason for being is not to accrue wealth for themselves and their shareholders but rather to advance specific non-material goals, such as the cessation of torture, the freeing of prisoners of conscience, or equal rights for minority groups. In this way, human rights NGOs are distinct from businesses and multinational corporations. Although corporations are often associated with undermining and abusing human rights, some have adopted strategies to promote them instead.[8] In these cases, a human rights NGO may not seem distinct from a corporation in its work to promote human rights, especially if that corporation engages in lobbying or public advocacy work to publicize its human rights initiatives. What does distinguish a human rights NGO from a corporation that adopts corporate social responsibility (CSR) practices is the ways in which an interest in human rights fits within the organization's broader set of interests. For corporations that adopt CSR practices, the pursuit of human rights objectives is often secondary to the pursuit of profit, or is done in such a way as to be made supportive of it. By contrast, for human rights NGOs the advancement of human rights is an end in itself.[9]

While the non-profit status of human rights organizations adequately distinguishes them from corporations that practise CSR, there are two complexities that arise when thinking about these types of NGOs as non-profit actors. First, the non-profit status is often conflated with being "left-wing" or "progressive," and thus associated with the advancement of certain types of human rights. This tendency is clear in the international rights literature on transnational activism, which emphasizes the efforts made by NGOs to promote compliance with international norms on personal integrity rights, arms control and weapons bans, and environmental protection.[10] According to this view, NGOs are non-profit principled actors pushing the world in a more progressive and humane direction. As such, they are seen to be agents of a certain type of moral progress. This perspective, however, arbitrarily delimits the universe of NGOs that operate in the international system, by imposing value judgements on what constitutes a human rights NGO's stated goals. What constitutes a "progressive" cause? What constitutes a "regressive" cause? In reality, the NGO sector also includes right-wing NGOs that seek to advance their own understandings of human rights, on such matters as gay rights, abortion, and the possession of firearms.[11]

Because of the varied nature of human rights NGO objectives and the difficulties in distinguishing progressive from regressive value systems, some have argued against defining human rights NGOs in terms of the presumed nature of their objectives. According to Willets, a human rights NGO's "values may be of any type: whether progressive, conventional or reactionary; religious or secular; nationalist or cosmopolitan."[12] In short, while a key characteristic of human rights NGOs is that it is value-driven, we should not presume anything about the nature of those values.

Second, it is important to understand that the non-profit status of NGOs does not mean that they operate free from material interests and incentives. The non-profit frame has not only enabled a "good norm" bias in scholarship on transnational activism, it has also tended to obscure the fact that NGOs are organizations like any other, with material and instrumental goals that can conflict with their stated normative ambitions. Recent research on advocacy organizations has suggested that much can be learned about the internal workings of NGOs by adopting what Prakash and Gugerty refer to as the "firm analogy." This analogy suggests not seeing NGOs as identical to firms (which they are not), but rather seeing them as organizations that have material concerns related to basic issues of survival and success.[13]

As non-profit actors, human rights NGOs must rely on funding from governments, international organizations, foundations, and/or individuals in order for them to do their work. While these NGOs can influence their donors, they are also in turn influenced by them. They must strategize and act in ways that consider the interests and needs of those funders, lest they fail to attract adequate funding. This particular dynamic between human rights NGO behaviour and funder influence has been documented in the humanitarian relief sector, in which NGOs have prioritized obtaining renewed contracts to do their work at the expense of adopting strategies that more effectively serve the people they were created to help.[14] While human rights NGOs are rightly understood as distinct from profit-seekers, the term *non-profit* should not be understood to mean that they do not take material concerns seriously. In fact, those concerns play an important role in determining the issues they focus on and the ways in which they work on those issues.[15]

Non-Violent

In addition to being formally organized, non-profit organizations, NGOs are also widely seen as actors that adopt solely non-violent tactics to achieve their objectives. Human rights NGOs engage in actions that are more associated with that of civil society: the non-violent and democratic pursuit of interests.[16] In terms of tactics, in some cases human rights NGOs will lobby governments and international organizations to act on particular problems. In so doing, they may suggest solutions or they may identify non-compliance with international law and norms. Human rights NGOs can "name and shame" violators of human rights norms in order to pressure them to alter their practices. In contrast to armed groups that may also be driven by human rights concerns, NGOs seek to change behaviour through the power of the pen and spoken word rather than through the power of the sword. In other cases, human rights NGOs may function as service providers, themselves implementing solutions through practical provision of goods and services to affected populations, as is the case with soup kitchens and international humanitarian relief organizations.

But complications arise in thinking about the relationship between NGOs and non-violence. Some types of human rights NGOs may not actively engage in violence but they might support groups that do. For instance, a number of Tamil diaspora NGOs in Canada that seek to promote the rights of Tamils in Sri Lanka have been charged with being organizational fronts for the Liberation Tigers of Tamil Eelam (LTTE), a group identified as a terrorist organization by numerous Western governments.[17] The same is said of some Kurdish diaspora organizations operating in Germany that are said to be key supporters of the militant Kurdistan Workers' Party (PKK).[18] Similarly, non-diaspora solidarity NGOs may also support groups, directly or indirectly, that are involved in armed struggle. For instance, leading individuals in the UK-based Palestine Solidarity Campaign have been criticized for building links with leaders of Hamas in Gaza. Less directly, and as discussed in more detail below, critics of Darfur advocacy NGOs in the United States have suggested that their work has helped to embolden Darfuri rebels to continue and step up their attacks against the Sudanese government, thereby increasing the violence in the region.

When considering the issue of non-violence and NGOs, it is worth reflecting on whether the NGO in question directly or indirectly supports or encourages other, militant organizations, and whether some members of the NGO have sought to build personal ties with militant group leaders. In some cases there is a more complex relationship between certain human rights NGOs and violence than the term *non-violent* suggests.

Non-State

Last, central to any comprehensive definition of a human rights NGO is its status as a non-state actor. This distinguishes NGOs from organizations created by states that may act as NGOs but are in fact state-led actors. These are commonly referred to as government-organized NGOs (GONGOs). GONGOs are used by states to advance their national interests within the wider NGO community. Thomas Weiss indicates that the Soviet Union and its satellites, as well as "Third World" autocrats and the US government, have all employed the strategy of creating GONGOs.[19] Because of their close ties with governments, GONGOs should not be understood as NGOs in the true meaning of the term.

However, this distinction between GONGOs and NGOs should not obscure the fact that the latter often have complex and varying relationships with states. Just as human rights NGOs can have close relations with armed groups, they can also have close relations with governments. This point can sometimes be missed because of the tendency in the existing literature to depict NGOs as challengers of state power, either through direct opposition to state policies or behaviour, or by taking on roles traditionally performed by states, especially in instances of state failure. According to some, the emergence and growth of an NGO sector raised questions about the future dominance of the state in the international system.[20] Felice Gaer refers to the confrontational politics that occur inside the United Nations between NGOs and states, while Kathryn Sikkink depicts human rights NGOs as working to challenge and reform common understandings of state sovereignty.[21] This adversarial dynamic between human rights NGOs and states is echoed in other works that consider the roles NGOs play in conforming the domestic policies of states to international legal norms, as well as those that consider the effectiveness of NGO attempts to curb the abuses committed by states through naming and shaming.[22] Thus a common theme in the literature on international NGOs is the effort expended to compel states to take actions they do not want to, and to hold states accountable to their own stated commitments.

While the frame of NGOs as adversaries of states captures a good deal of what NGOs do, the relationship they have with states and international organizations is more complex than that. This relationship is multifaceted and varies under different settings. As noted above, many NGOs receive considerable funding from states, both directly and through international institutions.[23] Furthermore, INGOs can play an active role in implementing state foreign policies abroad, whether through the nature of their advocacy and selection of targets or issue areas, or through their work in development and aid relief. Some have suggested that Western NGOs are part of a broader political project to extend a Western understanding of human rights, and thus are players in a liberal imperialist project.[24] Abby Stoddard has shown how humanitarian NGOs in the United States and Europe have different relationships with their home governments. She refers to Wilsonian NGOs in the US that work in solidarity with their governments and Dunantist NGOs in Europe that take active steps to distance themselves from state power.[25] Similarly, while some NGOs, such as Amnesty International and Human Rights Watch, receive no funding from governments, others, such as the International Crisis Group, receive approximately half of their budget from various, mostly Western, governments.[26] Whatever the specific relationship is to the state, NGOs are ultimately independent non-profit organizations that work to pursue their own principled and material interests. This can put them either at loggerheads with governments or in bed with them.

In sum, there are four core characteristics that define an NGO, and each has inherent complexities. Taken literally, the term *NGO* refers to the entire universe of non-governmental actors; however, it is widely used to refer to a particular type of actor that is formally organized, non-profit, non-violent, and non-state. While these terms should provide some clarity as to what is and what is not an NGO, it is important to recognize the questions that arise in applying these terms.

The next sections of this chapter take a closer look at the politics of human rights NGOs. Before doing so, however, it is worth briefly outlining how the study of human rights NGOs emerged within the context of international relations.

The Origins of the Study of Human Rights NGOs in International Relations

Historically, the study of international relations (IR) focused on how states interacted with other states. It was only in the 1990s that scholars began to take a closer look at human rights NGOs and the ways in which they mattered for world politics.[27] Today, human rights NGOs are the subject of a vast and growing body of literature. What explains this shift? Why have scholars been paying increasing attention to this particular type of non-state actor?

The increased attention given to human rights NGOs is the result of two significant changes, one empirical and the other theoretical. Empirically, the second half of the twentieth century saw a rapid proliferation of international NGOs, many of them dedicated to advancing human rights. According to Sikkink and Smith, the number of social- or political-change INGOs working on matters of human rights, broadly defined, grew from 110 in 1953 to 685 in 1993.[28]

In explaining the growth of the NGO sector, scholars have focused on demand-side factors, such as state and market failures to adequately respond to grievance and deprivation,[29] as well as supply-side factors, namely the increasing levels of funding and political access to NGOs from national governments as well as international institutions. These provided the material and political conditions conducive to NGO formation.[30]

Yet the proliferation of international NGOs on its own was not enough to attract considerable scholarly attention, even if it made it more likely. Increased interest in human rights NGOs must be situated within the gradual shift that began in the 1970s, away from state-centrism and toward a greater appreciation of non-state actors in world politics.[31] In addition, the interest in human rights NGOs was propelled by what has been called the "constructivist turn" in IR theory. This shift facilitated greater attention to the normative underpinnings of international order and the ways in which new norms and ideas can change political practice. If, as constructivists argued, material reality is shaped by prevailing inter-subjectively held norms, than scholars of international politics ought to pay closer attention to the origins of these norms and be sensitive to the ways in which they may change. Human rights NGOs were deemed to be key actors driving change in the international system, and thus they became a key focus of IR scholarship.

Alongside the proliferation of international NGOs and the constructivist turn in IR theorizing came an increased focus on the study of the causes of human rights abuse. As Emilie Hafner-Burton has outlined, 50 years ago the study of human rights was not a primary focal point for social science research. The landscape today is much different. The literature on human rights, as Hafner-Burton puts it, is "vast, encompassing every methodology and facet of research imaginable."[32] Part of this research examines the conditions under which human rights abuses occur.[33] However, another part has addressed the question of how to curb such abuses. This particular aspect of the human rights NGO literature will be the focus of the next two sections.

What Are the Sources of Human Rights NGO Influence?

The proliferation of international NGOs over the course of the twentieth century raises important questions: Were the individuals behind the formation of these NGOs engaged in a fool's errand, or did they have the potential to meaningfully contribute to the ways in which domestic and international politics were practised? How was it possible that an organization with relatively few resources, no military capacity, and little economic leverage could exert influence in a world dominated by ostensibly more powerful states, international organizations, multinational corporations, and armed groups? Despite these material limitations, human rights NGOs are said to derive their influence from three non-material sources.

First, like epistemic communities, NGOs can gain influence by being perceived as providers of objective knowledge.[34] The role of expert activists has been documented in the field of arms control and security, as well in environmental protection and development. In these areas, NGOs have been able to gain access to official decision-making bodies by virtue of their expertise on specific matters of importance to states and international organizations.[35] This type of access can provide NGOs with opportunities to influence decision-making processes.

For NGOs that engage in human rights advocacy work, influence is said to come also from the perceptions of their role as credible reporters of human rights violations.[36] Frequently Amnesty International reports will state explicitly that its work does not take sides in political disputes; it only documents violations of existing international legal and human rights norms committed by all conflict actors, whether state or non-state. Maintaining this reputation is important for an NGO's standing in the global human rights community, as well as among states and international institutions. As David Lake and others document, NGOs will often go to great lengths to maintain their credibility.[37]

Second, NGOs also derive influence from being perceived as legitimate political actors. Legitimacy in international relations can be an important source of power. Human rights NGOs are often seen as legitimate actors by virtue of the representation and voice they provide on behalf of communities that feel excluded from global decision-making processes. An NGO's legitimacy can be tied to the extent to which it accurately represents those on whose behalf it purports to work. NGOs may lose legitimacy when they begin to distance themselves from those they say they represent and instead tailor their work more closely to the interests of their donors.

Third, in addition to expertise and political legitimacy, NGOs also derive influence from being perceived as moral agents. For human rights–advocacy NGOs, this perception enables them to wield a moral stick in their efforts to persuade targets to change their practices. This stick is most often deployed through naming and shaming, which involves identifying rights violations committed and the party guilty of the violations. Often naming and shaming is contrasted with the coercive material power of the state. However, moral authority should also be understood as a source of power. The ability to wield a moral stick provides an NGO with a potential source of leverage over its targets. Risse, Ropp, and Sikkink argue that, over time, attempts at moral suasion can help to socialize target states to adopt and internalize international human rights norms and build them into their domestic political institutions.[38]

Importantly, however, NGOs are not equally influential under all conditions. Not all rights-abusing states are as vulnerable as some to NGOs' naming and shaming work. The following section outlines the conditions under which human rights NGO advocacy is most likely to lead to improvements in a state's human rights record.

When Does NGO Naming and Shaming Work?

On the question of whether or not human rights naming and shaming is effective, or whether it is just "cheap talk," some have argued that there is no scholarly consensus. In 2009, Emilie Hafner-Burton and James Ron suggested that while qualitative scholars argued that NGO naming and shaming was effective in improving rights protections, quantitative scholars argued that it was not.[39] This claim of a methodological divide has since been echoed in more recent work on the topic.[40] However, at the time Hafner-Burton and Ron's article was published, and since then, a number of quantitative studies have suggested positive effects of NGO naming and shaming on the human rights records of targeted states.[41] Thus it is now reasonable to suggest that there is a consensus that NGO campaigning can be effective in improving the human rights practices of states.[42] The debate, however, revolves around the conditions under which this positive effect takes place. The literature suggests three important conditions.

First, states with a local organized domestic opposition are said to be more vulnerable to transnational advocacy efforts. In these cases, foreign NGOs partner with local actors to form a transnational network to pressure local authorities from "above" and from "below."[43] In Keck and Sikkink's view, the international advocacy efforts of local actors—which they refer to as "boomerangs"—are crucial to the formation of a TAN. Without local actors reaching out for international support and making their grievances known to the international community, a rights-abusing state is less likely to be the subject of international pressures to reform.[44]

The relationship between local and transnational actors is symbiotic. Local actors are a key source of information that transnational actors can use in their international advocacy efforts. Given that NGOs' influence is conditional on their ability to provide reliable information, the presence of local information sources on the ground is vital. Without them, NGOs may be more likely to advance erroneous claims.[45] At the same time, local actors need transnational NGOs for both material and psychological support. Material support can come in the form of direct financial aid as well as training on how to more effectively mobilize and campaign domestically.[46] Psychological support can come from international legitimation of a group's struggle, which can encourage local actors to stay the course against more powerful foes.[47] As Amanda Murdie and David Davis have shown, international human rights NGO advocacy work is most effective when it is paired with domestic activism and mobilization inside the target state.[48]

However, local sources of opposition are not always present, often because state authorities actively prevent oppositional forces from establishing an independent civil society. This points to a second condition that can make some states more vulnerable to transnational pressure than others. Existing research suggests that states with leaders who are sensitive to their international reputations are more likely to succumb to international NGO naming and shaming. Conversely, leaders who do not care about tarnished reputations are far less likely to reform their domestic practices in response to transnational campaigns.[49] There are two distinct reasons why a state leadership sensitive to reputational costs might agree to domestic reforms. First, a tarnished reputation can have material costs. Under these conditions, reforms are the outcome of a cost-benefit analysis. State leaders calculate that diminished international standing may hurt their ability to receive foreign aid or to sign international trade agreements, particularly with Western democratic states.[50] In addition, a tarnished reputation may also impact the decisions of foreign investors, especially if by investing in projects in a norm-violating state they undermine their own domestic reputation and thus alienate their consumer base or shareholders.[51] Second, behavioural change as a result of reputational concerns can be the result of the psychological pressure that naming and shaming puts on the identities that state leaders have adopted. If leaders believe themselves to be democratic and concerned about human rights abuse but are repeatedly shown to support policies that contradict these self-perceptions, the resultant psychological costs may spur reforms over time.[52]

A third condition that affects the vulnerability of a state to transnational activist pressures has to do with the domestic institutional design of the target. Thomas Risse and his colleagues find that the effectiveness of transnational coalitions of actors, including international NGOs, is conditioned by the structure of the target state. Transnational coalitions that target more centralized states will find it harder to access policymaking channels, but once they do, they are more likely to affect policy change. By contrast, transnational coalitions that target more decentralized states will have an easier time accessing relevant policymaking channels but will find it harder to realize their goals once inside the system.[53] These findings are echoed in Joshua Busby's recent work on transnational "moral movements" targeting G8 states. Like Risse, he argues that looking at the extent to which the target state grants policy vetoes to more actors can capture variation in the success of these movements. Target states that provide fewer policy vetoes are more likely to change their policies in response to pressure than states that afford more vetoes.[54]

"Discrimination" in INGO Activism

In order to establish the importance of transnational activism in the study of international relations, scholars initially focused on identifying the conditions under which INGO activism was effective. The cost of this approach, however, was that it tended to obscure a logically prior issue: how do these human rights NGOs select which issues to mobilize around and which to ignore? Although the second half of the twentieth century saw rapid expansion of the transnational human rights community, significant advocacy gaps remain. Not all human rights issue areas or aggrieved populations attract the same amount of attention and support. "For most groups suffering violations," Bob observes, "the chief response of the international community is not action but indifference."[55]

Understanding why this might be the case is fairly straightforward. Despite the significant increase in the number of INGOs, the demand for foreign support and assistance exceeds its supply. In other words, the community of human rights NGOs does not have enough resources to assist all affected populations at the same time. This imbalance forces actors who initially may have been guided by universal principles of justice to select which causes or groups of people are "most worthy" of their scarce resources.[56] The reality is that only a portion of the wider universe of human rights abuse generates much concerted advocacy attention. If NGOs' advocacy matters for the curbing of human rights abuses, as we saw above, then the decisions they make about which issues to focus on have life-and-death consequences for victimized populations.[57]

The question of what makes some issues global *causes célèbres* but not others is, however, more difficult to answer. One early perspective suggested that the characteristics of an issue itself determine its chances of being the target of transnational advocacy efforts and campaigning. Keck and Sikkink argue that issues that involve bodily harm, clear causal chains between perpetrators and victims, and/or the legal denial of equal opportunity are most likely to generate transnational advocacy attention.[58] However, more recent research has cast some doubt on this hypothesis.[59]

Consider the case of Darfur. In the early 2000s, in response to attacks launched by rebel groups in the Darfur region of Sudan, the Sudanese government and local pro-government militias engaged in a counter-insurgency campaign that resulted in huge losses of life and civilian displacement. Numerous human rights INGOs responded. In March and May 2003, the London-based NGO Justice Africa began expressing concern for the safety of Darfuri citizens. Later that year, Amnesty International and the International Crisis Group published reports on the spiralling violence in the region.[60] In 2004 the United States Holocaust Memorial Museum's Committee on Conscience issued a "genocide warning" in response to events in Darfur, which was then upgraded to a "genocide emergency" a few months later.[61] In addition to NGO advocacy, Western media outlets, including the *New York Times*, the *Washington Post*, and *Le Monde*, among others, began reporting on Darfur, with many articles reiterating the claim of genocide.[62] US officials echoed these claims as well. In July 2004, the US Congress passed a resolution referring to genocide in Darfur.[63] In September, the State Department, drawing on a study conducted by the International Commission of Jurists, reiterated the genocide charge.[64] This environment provided the conditions for more widespread civil society mobilization, which resulted in creation of the Save Darfur movement; some have suggested that this was one of the largest social movements to emerge since the anti-apartheid movement of the 1980s.[65]

Although casualty figures were contested and in flux,[66] the labelling of the conflict as a genocide and its involving hundreds of thousands of refugees made activism on the issue appear to be uncontroversial. However, the matter was not so clear-cut. At the same time as the violence in Darfur was peaking, equally grave human rights crises were unfolding in neighbouring Uganda and the Democratic Republic of Congo. Yet the responses to these conflicts were vastly different. No "Save Uganda" or "Save Congo" movements were formed.[67] As Jan Egeland, then UN Undersecretary General for Humanitarian Action in 2004, stated, "I don't know why one place gets attention and another not ... It's like a lottery, where there are 50 victimized groups always trying to get the winning ticket, and they play every night and they lose every night. I myself have said that the biggest race against the clock is Darfur, but in terms of numbers of people displaced, there are already more in Uganda and eastern Congo."[68]

The question Egeland raised has become a key topic of interest among scholars of transnational human rights activism. The early literature emphasized the role played by "norm entrepreneurs," who were said to be vital to the process of norm development.[69] However, all too often, norm entrepreneurs fail to gain much traction and support for their particular cause.[70] More recent research has instead come to focus on the influence of "gatekeeper" NGOs, whose advocacy decisions determine what "makes it" onto the transnational human rights agenda and what does not.[71] Scholars have shown gatekeeper NGOs to play a powerful role in turning a number of issues into popular transnational causes. These include the local struggles of the Ogonis in Nigeria, the Zapatistas in Mexico, and the Dalits in India, as well as the use of anti-personnel landmines, the violation of LGBT rights, and aid to those suffering from the effects of HIV/AIDS.[72] In taking up an issue, gatekeepers signal to the wider human rights community that the issue is "safe" for advocacy.

It is worth noting that the tendency of NGOs to follow the lead of gatekeepers may also contribute to advocacy gaps and "discrimination" in the INGO sector. While it may help to produce larger coalitions of actors working on the same cause, it also results in a concentration of resources around certain issue areas or regions that can come at the expense of advocacy coverage. This raises a question: why are gatekeeper NGOs so influential? Three closely related factors shape the level of influence an NGO has over its broader advocacy network. The first is reputation and expertise. According to Bob, gatekeeper power stems from "reputations for credibility and clout, reputations earned through years of work in the field."[73] As discussed above, providing information that is trusted is a key source of NGO influence.

The second factor has to do with an organization's position within an advocacy network. Bob notes that gatekeepers often have the ability to reach wider audiences with their work. Carpenter refers to this idea as "network centrality." She suggests that organizations that hold central or hub-like positions within a network are given disproportionate influence over network behaviour. As hubs, gatekeeper NGOs have the most links to other actors in the network. This position makes their advocacy choices more visible to the rest of the network, thereby increasing the chances that other NGOs will follow suit.[74]

The third factor is the extent to which an NGO has exclusive ties to actors or groups of actors in its own network and the extent to which it has ties to actors outside of its network. Exclusive ties, like network centrality, provide an NGO with influence. Similarly, NGOs derive influence from their links with outside actors, which may include ties with NGOs that are working in other issue areas or links to governments or international institutions. These ties give an NGO the ability to build larger coalitions to support its campaigns, as well as to interact with outside decision makers whose support is crucial for norm development and implementation.[75]

That said, the literature does tend to exaggerate the influence of these gatekeeper NGOs. For instance, Bob suggests, "central to network formation are gatekeepers, whose decisions to back a movement activate other organizations and individuals across the world."[76] However, in many instances gatekeeper NGO advocacy has fallen flat and has not sparked wider mobilization. This has particularly been the case when it comes to Amnesty International's work to expose violations committed by states against various groups around the world. For instance, Amnesty has devoted considerable resources to documenting abuses by the Sri Lankan and Turkish governments against Tamils and Kurds respectively. However, thus far neither group has elicited much solidarity in Western activist circles. Further research is required on these and others cases to identify the conditions under which gatekeeper advocacy is most influential.

If the choices made by NGO gatekeepers shape which issues are more likely to "make it," then an understanding of how these NGOs make choices is important. Research on this question has come in two forms. First, scholars have investigated why Amnesty International devotes more of its advocacy resources to abuses occurring in some countries but not in others. Ron, Rodgers, and Ramos find that the severity of abuses in a country does affect Amnesty's decisions to publish press releases and background reports; however, this is not the only factor that matters. Certain states in which some of the worst conflicts and abuses occur—including Afghanistan, Somalia, Myanmar, Burundi, Brazil, and the Democratic Republic of Congo—are not among the top targets of Amnesty's naming and shaming efforts. Other factors matter too: states that are stronger militarily and economically, receive higher levels of military aid from the United States, and are prominently featured in Western media coverage are found to receive more attention from Amnesty International.[77] These three factors help to make a country more visible in international politics. By tailoring their work to public visibility, Amnesty seeks to serve key organizational interests such as improving its own public image, increasing the charitable donations it receives, and strengthening its volunteer ranks. The cost of this approach is that less attention is given to more obscure human rights issues.[78]

Further research on the question of gatekeeper advocacy choice has identified additional factors of importance. In examining Amnesty's urgent actions, Meernik, Alois, Sowell, and Nichols find that states with more domestic human rights NGOs receive more critical attention from Amnesty. As they explain, "since [urgent actions] depend upon the timely communication of information, only those states with groups that are numerous and sufficiently skilled to disseminate their stories are likely to arouse the interest of an organization like AI."[79] The implications of this finding are significant. Individuals or groups in more repressive societies who are unable to form their own organizations, as well as those that have low levels of communication linkage with the West—caused by factors such as poor infrastructure, lack of Internet availability, or geographic distance—are less likely to receive attention and support, despite the fact that they may be among the most vulnerable populations on the planet.

In their study of gatekeeper choice, Cullen Hendrix and Wendy Wong attempt to explain not why some countries receive more attention than others from Amnesty International but why some countries receive different types of advocacy attention. As suggested above, Amnesty's naming and shaming repertoire consists of three types of advocacy documents: background reports, press releases, and urgent actions. "INGOs," Hendrix and Wong explain, "do not approach every human rights violation, or every country, in the same way."[80] While some are handled with background reports, others are the subject of more urgent actions and press releases. By varying their advocacy packages in this way, Amnesty seeks to balance its principal vision—"for every person to enjoy all the rights enshrined in the Universal Declaration of Human Rights and other international human rights treaties"[81]—with its material concerns of organizational survival and growth. In other words, Amnesty produces different types of advocacy items in order to speak to the interests of its various audiences. States with higher levels of military and economic linkage to the United States are the subject of more press releases and urgent actions, because those links make the state more salient for Amnesty's donor and volunteer base. Conversely, states with lower levels of US linkage tend to be dealt with through background reports, not only to raise awareness of more obscure rights issues but also to maintain Amnesty's reputation as an objective NGO, working to curb all human rights abuses wherever they occur.[82]

The second area of research on this question looks at a slightly different issue than country targeting; instead it asks why gatekeeper NGOs mobilize around some issue areas but not others. The literature on transnational activism contains a number of potential answers to this question. As mentioned above, Keck and Sikkink argue that issues that involve certain characteristics are more likely to attract attention from transnational advocacy networks.[83] Richard Price suggests that the issues more likely to attract attention are those that can be easily grafted onto existing norms.[84] Finnemore and Sikkink refer to this grafting as an "adjacency claim."[85] Ron and Cooley point to the powerful role that donors and the media can play in pushing advocacy work toward some issues and away from others.[86] In examining these three perspectives in the area of child rights in armed conflict, Carpenter finds each of limited explanatory power. She argues that hypotheses that focus on issue characteristics, adjacency claims, and donor and media influence all fail to explain why NGOs working on child rights in armed conflict have failed to take up the issue of children born of wartime rape. The reason for this, Carpenter suggests, is that this particular issue bridges different advocacy networks, including those working on children in armed conflict and those working on gender-based violence. This overlap has created confusion as to who "owns" the issue and has resulted in a tendency to pass the responsibility on to others. The end result has been issue non-adoption.[87]

While the existing literature has greatly improved our understanding of how gatekeepers make choices about which issues to focus on, more research is still required. In particular, although we know more about how Amnesty International allocates its advocacy resources to different countries, we know less about the decision-making processes adopted by other gatekeeper INGOs, such as Human Rights Watch, the International Crisis Group, and the International Commission of Jurists. Do their reporting patterns follow similar trends to Amnesty's? If not, what might explain this variation? Furthermore, additional research is required on understanding issue-adoption by gatekeeper NGOs.[88]

INGOs and Their Critics

For all their hard work and efforts to improve world politics as they see it, human rights NGOs have been the target of important criticisms. These critiques touch on a variety of issues, including how INGOs allocate their resources, their level of transparency and accountability, the tactics they use to name and shame states, and the types of rights they promote. This section outlines some of these challenges to the NGO sector.

Selectivity

As discussed in the previous section, INGOs, because of material limitations and interests, do not dedicate the same amounts or types of resources to all issue areas. In some cases, INGO selectivity has been particularly controversial. Such controversy has been seen in the case of Human Rights Watch's coverage of the Middle East. In October 2009, Robert Bernstein, one of the founders of HRW, took to the pages of the *New York Times* to criticize his organization for failing to allocate its resources in a way that more accurately reflected what he saw to be the patterns of abuse across the region. He noted that HRW was assisting "those who wish to turn Israel into a pariah state."

"The region," he continued, "is populated by authoritarian regimes with appalling human rights records. Yet in recent years Human Rights Watch has written far more condemnations of Israel for violations of international law than of any other country in the region."[89] Human Rights Watch has not been alone in being criticized for its coverage of the Middle East. Amnesty International's reporting patterns have also been criticized, both in the scholarly literature and by other NGOs.[90] According to Gerald Steinberg, founder of *NGO Monitor*, NGOs such as Human Rights Watch, Amnesty International, Christian Aid, the International Commission of Jurists, and Oxfam are involved in a "war against Israel."[91] These charges of bias and selectivity can be damaging to NGOs that rely on a reputation of objectivity and trustworthiness. They can also be damaging to NGOs that actively seek to represent themselves as neutral in political struggles.

Tactics

In addition to the issue of allocation of resources, critics have raised questions about the tactics NGOs adopt in their attempts to curb human rights abuses. For some, the practice of public naming and shaming abusive states can make things worse. Hafner-Burton finds that in some cases the level of political terror committed by a state can increase in response to human rights NGO naming and shaming work. She posits that international pressure can provide incentive for local leaders to step up their repression in response to growing challenges to their power. She also suggests that an increase in abuses can result when emboldened resistance movements calculate that adopting strategies that provoke increased state repression might invite even greater international action and levels of intervention.[92]

Discussions about the effects of the Save Darfur movement on the violence in Darfur have raised the question of whether the movement, however well-intentioned, has had adverse effects on the ground. Alex de Waal, for instance, has suggested that claims of genocide and other hardline rhetoric against the Sudanese government have made Khartoum less likely to negotiate. As to Darfuri rebels, support from Western NGOs may have encouraged them to hold out longer in the hopes of gaining a Kosovo-style military intervention by NATO.[93] As Alan Kuperman has put it, "because of the Save Darfur movement … the rebels believe that the longer they provoke genocidal retaliation, the more the West will pressure Sudan to hand them control of the region."[94]

In contrast to this line of argument, others have suggested that NGOs adopt tactics that are too meek and thus largely ineffective. INGO naming and shaming language is often highly legalistic as it urges targeted states to ensure that their policies meet international law, and that any abuses suspected to have occurred be investigated by domestic courts in order to hold perpetrators accountable. In her study of Human Rights Watch's advocacy on Chechnya in the 1990s, Bridget Conley-Zilkic finds that this approach reflected a failure to "speak plainly" about the abuses committed by the Russian government and thus failed to produce any meaningful positive results for Chechens.[95] Kenneth Cain makes a similar charge against Amnesty International and Africa Watch (which in 1988 became part of Human Rights Watch) in their advocacy work on Liberia. In his view, these NGOs advocated "human rights goals that had no hope of actually being implemented in the real world." They engaged in principled advocacy but demonstrated little concern for advancing a realistic and pragmatic path for change. "In the process," Cain writes, "it is difficult to ascertain precisely how victims of human rights abuses are actually served by fanciful references to the international covenants and whimsical human rights cheerleading."[96]

Undemocratic Structure

A final criticism of NGOs has to do with where they derive their moral authority. Part of a human rights NGO's legitimacy comes from its ability to accurately represent those they purport to work on behalf of. Concerns have been raised about the extent to which an NGO's internal structure is democratic and accountable, and the extent to which they adequately represent the interests of the global South.[97] According to Sikkink, "although most NGOs stress democracy and democratization, many are not themselves internally democratic." Part of the problem is a lack of clarity within an NGO about who the decision makers ought to be: "their staff, their boards, their volunteers, their members, those who provide funds, or those on whose behalf they organize?"[98] Others have suggested a strong Western bias in the nature of human rights NGO advocacy work. Makua Matua, for instance, suggests that INGOs are the proponents of a particular type of political ideology, liberal democracy that privileges a Western understanding of rights. This entails emphasizing the rights laid out in the International Covenant on Civil and Political Rights rather than those in the International Covenant on Economic, Social, and Cultural Rights. As Matua puts it, "no one should be expected to believe that the scheme of rights promoted by INGOs does not seek to replicate a vision of society based on the industrial democracies of the North."[99]

Conclusion

Over the past half-century, international human rights NGOs have shown themselves to be important players in domestic and international politics.

As formally organized, non-profit, non-violent, and non-state actors, NGOs have been able to exert considerable influence over ostensibly more powerful actors. The source of NGOs' influence does not stem from their material capabilities, which are slight compared to most states, international organizations, and multinational corporations. Rather, their influence comes from their role as experts and providers of trustworthy information, perceptions of their role as legitimate political actors faithfully representing the interests of affected populations, and from being perceived as moral agents able to shame others into ceasing their norm-violating behaviour. However, the influence of human rights NGOs in doing this type of work varies under different conditions. Some states are more vulnerable than others to human rights NGO advocacy work. As the existing research suggests, states with mobilized local opposition movements, with leaders concerned about their international reputation, and/or with more centralized decision-making processes are most likely to respond positively to NGO naming and shaming.

For all their successes, however, human rights NGO activism does suffer from "discrimination" and selective patterns of advocacy. Despite their rapid proliferation during the twentieth century and their claims to promote rights universally, it has been shown that INGOs do not mobilize with the same energy or in the same way in response to all human rights issues. In some respects this is largely a result of the fact that the demand for advocacy exceeds its supply. But while capacity issues contribute to advocacy gaps, so too does the tendency of NGOs to get on the bandwagon with gatekeeper NGOs, by following and supporting their advocacy choices. This tendency may produce larger NGO coalitions working together on a single issue or targeting a single state, but it does come at the cost of coverage and may exacerbate the problem of selectivity in the human rights NGO sector.

The existence of these advocacy gaps has exposed the NGO sector to claims of discrimination and bias, but these are not the only criticisms lobbed at NGOs. They have also been criticized for making things worse on the ground for those they purport to want to protect, for engaging in meaningless "human rights cheerleading" that constitutes little more than cheap talk, and for being undemocratic and unaccountable to their constituents.

While the literature on human rights NGOs has grown substantially over the past two decades or so, new lines of research still need to be pursued. As suggested above, we need to know more about how gatekeeper NGOs make choices about how to allocate resources. The study of which countries garner more INGO attention than others has received considerable attention, but far less scholarship has been devoted to issue selection. Furthermore, greater attention needs to be paid to specifying the conditions under which gatekeeper NGOs are most influential in shaping the transnational human rights agenda and when they are not. These issues, among myriad others, promise to keep international rights scholars interested in NGOs busy for the foreseeable future.

Takeaway Messages

- Defining the term *nongovernmental organization* is not straightforward and raises conceptual issues.
- NGOs are important actors in the international system, but not everyone sees the active NGO presence in the international system as a positive development.

Study Questions

- What is an NGO? How does it differ from other non-state actors?
- What are the sources of NGO influence?
- Under what conditions are NGOs most able to curb human rights abuses?

Issues for Debate or Roundtable

- Is the proliferation of NGOs in the international system a benign or a malignant development? What are the pros and cons of this phenomenon for world politics?
- Why do NGOs pay more attention to some human rights issues and not others?

Additional Reading

Clark, Ann Marie. *Diplomacy of Conscience: Amnesty International and Changing Human Rights Norms*. Princeton, NJ: Princeton University Press, 2001.

Hopgood, Stephen. *Keepers of the Flame: Understanding Amnesty International*. Ithaca, NY: Cornell University Press, 2006.

Neier, Aryeh. *The International Human Rights Movement: A History*. Princeton, NJ: Princeton University Press, 2012. doi: http://dx.doi.org/10.1515/9781400841875.

Stroup, Sarah. *Borders among Activists: International NGOs in the United States, Britain, and France*. Ithaca, NY: Cornell University Press, 2012.

Websites

Amnesty International. http://www.amnesty.org/en.
Human Rights Watch. http://www.hrw.org/.
NGO Monitor. http://www.ngo-monitor.org/.

Notes

1. W.H. Wong, *Internal Affairs: How the Structure of NGOs Transforms Human Rights* (Ithaca, NY: Cornell University Press, 2012), 1–3; A. Acharya, "Human Security: East versus West," *International Journal* 56, no. 3 (Summer 2001): 442–60.
2. K. Sikkink and J. Smith, "Infrastructures for Change: Transnational Organizations, 1953–1993," in *Restructuring World Politics: Transnational Social Movements, Networks and Norms*, ed. S. Khagram, J. Riker, and K. Sikkink (Minneapolis: University of Minnesota Press, 2002), 30. Also see C. Bob, *The Marketing of Rebellion: Insurgents, Media, and International Activism* (New York: Cambridge University Press, 2005), 18–19.
3. P. Willetts, *Non-Governmental Organizations in World Politics: The Construction of Global Governance* (New York: Routledge, 2011), 31. Also see S. Tarrow, "Transnational Politics: Contention and Institutions in International Politics," *Annual Review of Political Science* 4, no. 1 (2001): 12; P.R. Baehr, *Non-Governmental Human Rights Organizations in International Relations* (London: Palgrave-MacMillan, 2009), 2; P.J. Simmons, "Learning to Live with NGOs," *Foreign Policy* 112 (Autumn 1998): 83.
4. Wong, *Internal Affairs.*
5. N. Shawki, "Organizational Structure and Strength and Transnational Campaign Outcomes: A Comparison of Two Transnational Advocacy Networks," *Global Networks* 11, no. 1 (2011): 97–117; S. Staggenborg, "The Consequences of Professionalization and Formalization in the Pro-Choice Movement," *American Sociological Review* 53, no. 4 (August 1988): 585–605; R.C. Carpenter, "Vetting the Advocacy Agenda: Network Centrality and the Paradox of Weapons Norms," *International Organization* 65 (Winter 2011): 69–102.
6. Tarrow, "Transnational Politics," 11–13.
7. K. Sikkink, "Human Rights, Principled Issue–Networks, and Sovereignty in Latin America," *International Organization* 73, no. 3 (June 1993): 412; T. Weiss, "NGOs and Internal Conflict," in *International Dimensions of Internal Conflict,* ed. Michael Brown (Cambridge, MA: MIT Press, 1996), 437; Willetts, *Non-Governmental Organizations in World Politics,* 8.
8. For instance, see Walmart's Global Responsibility Report, http://corporate.walmart.com/global-responsibility/environment-sustainability/global-responsibility-report. Also see C. Thauer, "Goodness Comes from Within: Intra-Organizational Dynamics of Corporate Social Responsibility," *Business and Society,* 24 April 2013, doi: 10.1177/0007650313475770.
9. S. Khagram, J. Riker, and K. Sikkink, "From Santiago to Seattle: Transnational Advocacy Groups Restructuring World Politics," in *Restructuring World Politics: Transnational Social Movements, Networks and Norms*, ed. S. Khagram, J. Riker, and K. Sikkink (Minneapolis: University of Minnesota Press, 2002), 11.
10. T. Risse, S.C. Ropp, and K. Sikkink, eds., *The Power of Human Rights: International Norms and Domestic Change* (Cambridge: Cambridge University Press, 1999); R. Price, "Reversing the Gun Sights: Transnational Civil Society Targets Land Mines," *International Organization* 52, no. 3 (Summer 1998): 613–44; Carpenter, "Vetting the Advocacy Agenda"; P. Wapner, "Politics Beyond the State: Environmental Activism and World Civic Politics," *World Politics* 47, no. 3 (April 1995): 311–40.

11. C. Bob, "Packing Heat: Pro-Gun Groups and the Governance of Small Arms," in *Who Governs the Globe?* ed. D. Avant, M. Finnemore, and S. Sell (Cambridge: Cambridge University Press, 2010), 183–201; C. Bob, *The Global Right Wing and the Clash of World Politics* (New York: Cambridge University Press, 2012).
12. Willetts, *Non-Governmental Organizations in World Politics*, 30.
13. A. Prakash and M.-K. Gugerty, eds., *Advocacy Organizations and Collective Action* (New York: Cambridge University Press, 2010).
14. A. Cooley and J. Ron, "The NGO Scramble: Organizational Insecurity and the Political Economy of Transnational Action," *International Security* 27, no. 1 (Summer 2002): 5–39.
15. C. Hendrix and W. Wong, "Knowing Your Audience: How the Structure of International Relations and Organizational Choices Affect Amnesty International's Advocacy," *Review of International Organizations* (September 2013).
16. R. Price, "Review: Transnational Civil Society and Advocacy in World Politics," *World Politics* 55, no. 4 (July 2003): 580–81.
17. D. Byman, P. Chalk, B. Hoffman, W. Rosenau, and D. Brannan, *Trends in Outside Support for Insurgent Movements* (Santa Monica, CA: RAND, 2001), 41–60.
18. International Crisis Group, "Turkey: The PKK and a Kurdish Settlement," Europe Report no. 219 (11 September 2012), 18–19.
19. Weiss, "NGOs and Internal Conflict," 440; Willetts, *Non-Governmental Organizations in World Politics,* 14.
20. H.V. Milner and A. Moravcsik, eds., *Power, Interdependence and Nonstate Actors in World Politics* (Princeton, NJ: Princeton University Press, 2009); R.D. Lipschutz, "Reconstructing World Politics: The Emergence of Global Civil Society," *Millenium: Journal of International Studies* 21, no. 3 (1992): 389–420; J. Boli and G. Thomas, *Constructing World Culture: International Nongovernmental Organizations Since 1875* (Palo Alto, CA: Stanford University Press, 1999), 19.
21. F.D. Gaer, "Reality Check: Human Rights Nongovernmental Organizations Confront Governments at the United Nations," *Third World Quarterly* 16, no. 3 (1995): 389–404; Sikkink, "Human Rights, Principled Issue–Networks."
22. B. Simmons, *Mobilizing for Human Rights: International Law in Domestic Politics* (Cambridge: Cambridge University Press, 2009); E. Hafner-Burton and J. Ron, "Seeing Double: Human Rights Impact Through Qualitative and Quantitative Eyes," *World Politics* 61, no. 2 (April 2009): 360–401.
23. K. Reimann, "A View from the Top: International Politics, Norms and the Worldwide Growth of NGOs," *International Studies Quarterly* 50 (2006): 45–67.
24. M. Mutua, "Human Rights International NGOs: A Critical Evaluation," in *NGOs and Human Rights: Promise and Performance*, ed. C.E. Welch (Philadelphia: University of Pennsylvania Press, 2001), 151–163.
25. A. Stoddard, *Humanitarian Alert: NGO Information and Its Impact on US Foreign Policy* (Bloomfield, CT: Kumarian Press, 2006), 7–8.
26. For a breakdown of ICG's funding sources, see http://www.crisisgroup.org/en/support/who-supports-crisisgroup.aspx.
27. To the best of my knowledge, one exception is P. Willetts, ed., *Pressure Groups in the Global System: The Transnational Relations of Issue-Oriented Non-Governmental Organizations* (London: Frances Pinter, 1982).
28. Smith and Sikkink, "Infrastructures for Change," 30; see also E. Werker and F.Z. Ahmed, "What Do Nongovernmental Organizations Do?" *Journal of Economic*

Perspective 22, no. 2 (Spring 2008); W. Korey, *NGOs and the Universal Declaration of Human Rights: "A Curious Grapevine"* (New York: St. Martin's Press, 1998); A. Cooley and J. Ron, "The NGO Scramble: Organizational Insecurity and the Political Economy of Transnational Action," *International Security* 27, no. 1 (Summer 2002): 5–39; and P.J. Simmons, "Learning to Live with NGOs," *Foreign Policy* 112 (Autumn 1998).

29. Prakash and Gugerty, "Advocacy Organizations and Collective Action: An Introduction," in *Advocacy Organizations and Collective Action*, ed. Prakash and Gugerty, 8; A.M. Florini, ed., *The Third Force: The Rise of Transnational Civil Society* (Washington, DC: Carnegie Endowment for International Peace and Brookings Institution Press, 2000).
30. Reimann. "View from the Top."
31. R.O. Keohane and J. Nye, eds., *Transnational Relations and World Politics* (Cambridge, MA: Harvard University Press, 1971).
32. E. Hafner-Burton, "A Social Science of Human Rights," *Journal of Peace Research* 51, no. 2 (2014): 274.
33. For example, see S.C. Poe and N. Tate, "Repression of Human Rights to Personal Integrity in the 1980s: A Global Analysis," *American Political Science Review* 88, no. 4 (1994): 853–900.
34. P. Haas, "Introduction: Epistemic Communities and International Policy Coordination," *International Organization* 46, no. 1 (Winter 1992): 1–35; M. Evangelista, *Unarmed Forces: The Transnational Movement to End the Cold War* (Ithaca, NY: Cornell University Press, 1999).
35. Evangelista, *Unarmed Forces*; S. Khagram, "Restructuring the Global Politics of Development: The Case of India's Narmada Valley Dams," in *Restructuring World Politics*, ed. Khagram, Riker, and Sikkink, 206–30; P. Nelson, "Agendas, Accountability, and Legitimacy among Transnational Networks Lobbying in the World Bank," ibid., 142.
36. J. Ron, H. Ramos, and K. Rodgers, "Transnational Information Politics: NGO Human Rights Reporting, 1986–2000," *International Studies Quarterly* 49, no. 3 (September 2005): 559.
37. P.A. Gourevitch, D.A. Lake, and J.G. Stein, eds., *The Credibility of Transnational NGOs: When Virtue Is Not Enough* (Cambridge: Cambridge University Press, 2012).
38. Risse, Ropp, and Sikkink, *Power of Human Rights.*
39. Hafner-Burton and Ron, "Seeing Double."
40. C.S. Hendrix and W.H. Wong, "When Is the Pen Truly Mighty? Regime Type and the Efficacy of Naming and Shaming in Curbing Human Rights Abuses," *British Journal of Political Science* (October 2012): 4.
41. J. Franklin, "Shame on You: The Impact of Human Rights Criticism on Political Repression in Latin America," *International Studies Quarterly* 58 (2008): 187–211.
42. More recent positive quantitative assessments include A. Murdie and D.R. Davis, "Shaming and Blaming for Change: An Event-Data Study on the Impact of Human Rights INGOs on Human Rights Practices," *International Studies Quarterly* 56 (2012): 1–16; M. Krain, "J'Accuse! Does Naming and Shaming Perpetrators Reduce the Severity of Genocides and Politicides?" *International Studies Quarterly* 56 (2012): 574–89; Hendrix and Wong, "When Is the Pen Truly Mighty?"

43. A. Brysk, "From Above and Below: Social Movements, the International System, and Human Rights in Argentina," *Comparative Political Studies* 26 (1993): 259–85.
44. M. Keck and K. Sikkink, *Activists Beyond Borders: Advocacy Networks in International Politics* (Ithaca, NY: Cornell University Press, 1998).
45. D. Hill, W. Moore, and B. Mukherjee, "Information Politics versus Organizational Incentives: When Are Amnesty International's 'Naming and Shaming' Reports Biased?" *International Studies Quarterly* 57, no. 2 (June 2013): 219–32.
46. A. Murdie and T. Bhasin, "Aiding and Abetting: Human Rights INGOs and Domestic Protest," *Journal of Conflict Resolution* 55, no. 2 (2011): 163–91.
47. Risse, Ropp, and Sikkink, *Power of Human Rights.*
48. Murdie and Davis, "Shaming and Blaming."
49. S. Burgerman, *Moral Victories: How Activists Provoke Multilateral Action* (Ithaca, NY: Cornell University Press, 2001); D.G. Hawkins, *International Human Rights and Authoritarian Rule in Chile* (Lincoln: University of Nebraska Press, 2002).
50. Franklin, "Shame on You."
51. L. Patey, "Against the Asian Tide: The Sudan Divestment Campaign," *Journal of Modern African Studies* 47, no. 4 (2009): 551–73.
52. Price, "Review: Transnational Civil Society," 593.
53. T. Risse, ed., *Bringing Transnational Relations Back In: Non-State Actors, Domestic Structures, and International Institutions* (New York: Cambridge University Press, 1995).
54. J. Busby, *Moral Movements and Foreign Policy* (New York: Cambridge University Press, 2010).
55. C. Bob, "Overcoming Indifference: Internationalizing Human Rights Violations in Rural Mexico," *Journal of Human Rights* 1, no. 2 (2002): 247.
56. C. Bob, *The Marketing of Rebellion: Insurgents, Media, and International Activism* (New York: Cambridge University Press, 2005), 20; C. Bob, "The Market for Human Rights," in Prakash and Gugerty, *Advocacy Organizations and Collective Action*, 133–54.
57. R.C. Carpenter, *Forgetting Children Born of War: Setting the Human Rights Agenda in Bosnia and Beyond* (New York: Columbia University Press, 2010), 40.
58. Keck and Sikkink, "Activists Beyond Borders."
59. R.C. Carpenter, "Studying Issue (Non)-Adoption in Transnational Advocacy Networks," *International Organization* 61 (Summer 2007): 643–47.
60. A.F. Gryzb, "Media Coverage, Activism, and Creating Public Will for Intervention in Rwanda and Darfur," in *The World and Darfur: International Response to Crimes Against Humanity in Western Sudan*, ed. A.F. Gryzb (Montreal: McGill-Queen's University Press, 2009), 78; International Crisis Group, "Sudan's Other Wars," June 2003, http://www.crisisgroup.org/~/media/Files/africa/horn-of-africa/sudan/B014%20Sudans%20Other%20Wars.pdf; Amnesty International, "The Looming Crisis in Darfur," July 2003, https://www.amnesty.org/en/library/asset/AFR54/041/2003/en/4dc587da-d6d2-11dd-ab95-a13b602c0642/afr540412003en.pdf.
61. See the United States Holocaust Memorial Museum's press release, http://www.ushmm.org/information/press/press-releases/united-states-holocaust-memorial-museum-declares-genocide-emergency-in-sudan.
62. D. Murphy, "Narrating Darfur: Darfur in the US Press, March–September 2004," in *War in Darfur and the Search for Peace*, ed. A. de Waal (Cambridge, MA: Global Equity Initiative, Harvard University, 2007), 314–36.

63. See http://news.bbc.co.uk/2/hi/africa/3918765.stm.
64. See http://www.washingtonpost.com/wp-dyn/articles/A8364-2004Sep9.html.
65. D. Lanz, "Save Darfur: A Movement and Its Discontents," *African Affairs* (2009): 669.
66. M. Mamdani, *Saviours and Survivors: Darfur, Politics, and the War on Terror* (Cape Town, South Africa: HSRC Press, 2009), 25–39.
67. A. Brysk, *Speaking Rights to Power: Constructing Political Will* (New York: Oxford University Press, 2013), 99–105.
68. Quoted in Bob, "Market for Human Rights," 138.
69. M. Finnemore and K. Sikkink, "International Norm Dynamics and Political Change," *International Organization* 52, no. 4 (1998): 887–917.
70. Carpenter, "Vetting the Advocacy Agenda," 71.
71. R.C. Carpenter, "Governing the Global Agenda: 'Gatekeepers' and the 'Issue Adoption' in Transnational Advocacy Networks," in *Who Governs the Globe?* ed. D. Avant, M. Finnemore, and S. Sell (Cambridge: Cambridge University Press, 2010), 209.
72. Bob, *Marketing of Rebellion*; C. Bob, "'Dalit Rights and Human Rights': Caste Discrimination, International Activism, and the Construction of a New Human Rights Issue," *Human Rights Quarterly* 29, no. 1 (Feb 2007): 167–93; Carpenter, "Vetting the Advocacy Agenda"; C. Bob, ed., *The International Struggle for New Human Rights* (Philadelphia: University of Pennsylvania Press, 2009).
73. Bob, *Marketing Rebellion*, 18.
74. Carpenter, "Vetting the Advocacy Agenda," 74.
75. Ibid., 74–75.
76. Bob, *Marketing of Rebellion*, 18.
77. Ron, Ramos, and Rodgers, "Transnational Information Politics."
78. Ibid., 573.
79. J. Meernik, R. Aloisi, M. Sowell, and A. Nichols, "The Impact of Human Rights Organizations on Naming and Shaming Campaigns," *Journal of Conflict Resolution* 56, no. 2 (2012): 248.
80. C. Hendrix and W. Wong, "Knowing Your Audience: How the Structure of International Relations and Organizational Choices Affect Amnesty International's Advocacy," *Review of International Organizations* (September 2013): 32.
81. See http://www.amnesty.org/en/who-we-are.
82. Hendrix and Wong, "Knowing Your Audience."
83. Keck and Sikkink, *Activists Beyond Borders.*
84. Price, "Reversing the Gun Sights."
85. Finnemore and Sikkink, "International Norm Dynamics."
86. Cooley and Ron, "The NGO Scramble."
87. Carpenter, "Studying Issue (Non)-Adoption."
88. Carpenter, "Vetting the Advocacy Agenda," 99.
89. R. Bernstein, "Rights Watchdog, Lost in the Mideast," *New York Times*, 19 October 2009, http://www.nytimes.com/2009/10/20/opinion/20bernstein.html?_r=1&.
90. D. Habibi, "Human Rights and Politicized Human Rights: A Utilitarian Critique," *Journal of Human Rights* 6, no. 3 (2007): 3–35, http://www.ngo-monitor.org/.
91. G. Steinberg, "Soft Powers Play Hardball: NGOs Wage War Against Israel," *Israel Affairs* 12, no. 4 (October 2006): 748–68.
92. E. Hafner-Burton, "Sticks and Stones: Naming and Shaming the Human Rights Enforcement Problem," *International Organization* 62 (Fall 2008): 692.

93. "Darfur Experts Debate Conflict," *Newsweek*, 7 November 2007, http://www.newsweek.com/darfur-experts-debate-conflict-96887; M. Haeri, "Saving Darfur: Does Advocacy Help or Hinder Conflict Resolution?" *PRAXIS: The Fletcher Journal of Human Security* 23 (2008): 33–46.
94. A. Kuperman, "Strategic Victimhood in Sudan," *New York Times*, 31 May 2006, http://www.nytimes.com/2006/05/31/opinion/31kuperman.html.
95. B. Conley-Zilkic, "Speaking Plainly about Chechnya: On the Limits of the Juridical Model of Human Rights Advocacy," *Nongovernmental Politics*, ed. M. Feher, G. Krikorian, and Y. McKee (New York: Zone Books, 2007), 72–81.
96. K. Cain, "The Rape of Dinah: Human Rights, Civil War in Liberia, and Evil Triumphant," *Human Rights Quarterly* 21, no. 2 (1999): 297.
97. Nelson, "Agendas, Accountability, and Legitimacy," 141; Price, "Review: Transnational Civil Society," 590.
98. Sikkink, "Restructuring World Politics," 306.
99. Mutua, "Human Rights International NGOs," 159.

PART THREE

6
Temporary Migrant Workers in Canada: Protecting and Extending Labour Rights

TANYA BASOK

Learning Objectives

- To gain knowledge about the working conditions of various streams of temporary migrant workers in Canada
- To learn how rights can be claimed under two legal frameworks: citizenship and international human rights
- To understand limitations in the application of the two frameworks in the case of migrant workers in Canada
- To understand and be able to assess the role of activism in advancing migrant workers' rights

Every year several hundred thousand migrants come to Canada on temporary contracts to fill jobs in sectors that are presumably experiencing labour shortages. Most of them are expected to return home once their contracts expire. Canada is not unique in its reliance on temporary workers. In fact, throughout the world more and more countries are adopting programs and policies that supply migrant labour to specific employers who claim to be unable to meet their labour demands through local supply. Among global policymakers, temporary migration is touted as an ideal, or "triple win," form of labour mobility; on the one hand, it helps host states to meet their labour needs and, on the other, it benefits the migrants themselves, as well as their home countries. For the sending countries, temporary migration is presumed to promote development through the skills and remittances migrants bring or send back to their home communities.

This growing reliance on temporary (as opposed to permanent) migration has raised serious concerns among migration scholars and migrants' rights activists, who question whether the rights of migrant workers are sufficiently protected. This chapter will explore current trends in Canadian immigration policy toward a greater reliance on temporary migration. It will pay particular attention to the diversity of programs that make it possible for temporary migrants to work in Canada. Focusing on lower-skilled temporary migrants, the chapter will outline the various forms of rights violations these migrants experience. It will then explore two moral/legal frameworks for redressing these violations.

The first framework is citizenship rights. It is based on the Canadian Charter of Rights and Freedoms and provincial human rights provisions, as well as such legally binding documents as the provincial employment standards acts and health and safety acts. Even though temporary migrants in Canada are not citizens, most of the citizenship framework nevertheless applies to them. However, as non-citizens they are excluded from the citizenship framework protections in one fundamental way: their freedom of movement is curtailed. As will be argued in this chapter, without the freedom to change employers, migrants have a limited ability to claim their rights.

The chapter then proceeds to question the effectiveness of the human rights framework for protecting non-citizens. It is argued that the human rights instruments have been largely ineffective in advancing migrants' rights in Canada, since the Canadian government has been reluctant to ratify migrant-specific treaties. Nevertheless, as suggested in this chapter, values expressed in international law can influence interpretations of Canadian laws and policies. Because of their vulnerability, temporary migrants are hardly in the position to assert rights. As illustrated in the chapter, it is pro-migrant advocates who have the greatest potential to redress some of the migrants' rights violations by drawing on the citizenship and international human rights frameworks.

The Evolution of Temporary Labour Migration in Canada

The history of temporary labour migration to Canada dates back to the 1960s, when the domestic worker and seasonal agricultural worker programs were introduced. Before then, mostly European domestic workers were authorized to work and settle in Canada permanently. This provision changed when Jamaican women started displacing their European colleagues. Unlike their predecessors, Jamaican domestic workers admitted through what is currently known as the Live-in Caregiver Program (LCP) were authorized to remain in Canada on a temporary basis.[1] At the same time, another temporary migration program, the Seasonal Agricultural Workers' Program (SAWP) was launched. Introduced in 1966, again for Jamaican workers, this program was subsequently extended to migrants from other Caribbean countries and Mexico.[2]

The year 1973 marked another important stage in the evolution of the Canadian Temporary Foreign Worker Program (TFWP), when, in an effort to attract skilled professionals such as academics, business executives, and engineers, Canada introduced a temporary work visa. Under pressure from employers in a wide range of economic sectors, the TFWP began to expand again in 2002 to include workers in a wide range of lower-skill occupations, such as construction work, meat packing, hospitality, agricultural work, and others.[3] This pilot project, currently known as the Stream for Lower-Skilled Occupations Program, or SLSOP, targeted jobs defined as requiring skills classified at the C and D levels in the National Occupational Classification (NOC). The highest educational requirement for admission into this program is a high school (secondary school) diploma or two years of occupation-specific training, for NOC C jobs, or on-the-job training for jobs classified as NOC D.[4]

Since then, temporary labour migration has experienced a steady rise, outstripping the inflow of economic immigrants admitted as permanent residents (see Figure 6.1). The various streams that make up Canadian temporary migration vary in terms of their country of origin, composition, and entitlements. Whereas skilled temporary migrants are predominantly from the United Kingdom, European countries, the United States, and Australia, migrants from Asia, the Pacific, and Latin America are admitted mostly in the lower-skilled categories.[5] Whereas the migrants admitted as skilled workers are allowed to bring their families and apply for permanent residency, these rights are denied to most lower-skilled temporary migrants. The LCP is an exception: this program does offer an opportunity to domestic workers to apply for permanent settlement, although this is possible only after they have met certain requirements, including completion of a minimum period of continuous employment, as discussed below. This chapter focuses on the rights of lower-skilled workers; their admission and working conditions are outlined in the next section.

The Seasonal Agricultural Workers' Program (SAWP) is administered through bilateral agreements (or memoranda of understanding) between the sending countries participating in the program and Canada. The recruitment for this program is handled by government agencies in Mexico and the Caribbean. Workers are authorized to work in Canada for a maximum of eight months per year. They are allowed to reapply and are admitted for as long as their employers request them, or they can be matched with other employers. Workers usually live on the farm but not in the same houses as the growers.[6] The live-in caregiver program, on the other hand, is distinct from the SAWP in that caregivers are required to live in their employers' homes. Recruited by private agencies, these mostly female workers—largely from the Philippines—are allowed to apply for permanent residency as long as they have worked for 24 months during a 36-month period. Finally, the Stream for Lower-Skilled Occupations Program (SLSOP) opens possibilities for migrants from a wide range of countries to work in a variety of

Figure 6.1 Working Conditions and Social Protections for Temporary Workers in Canada

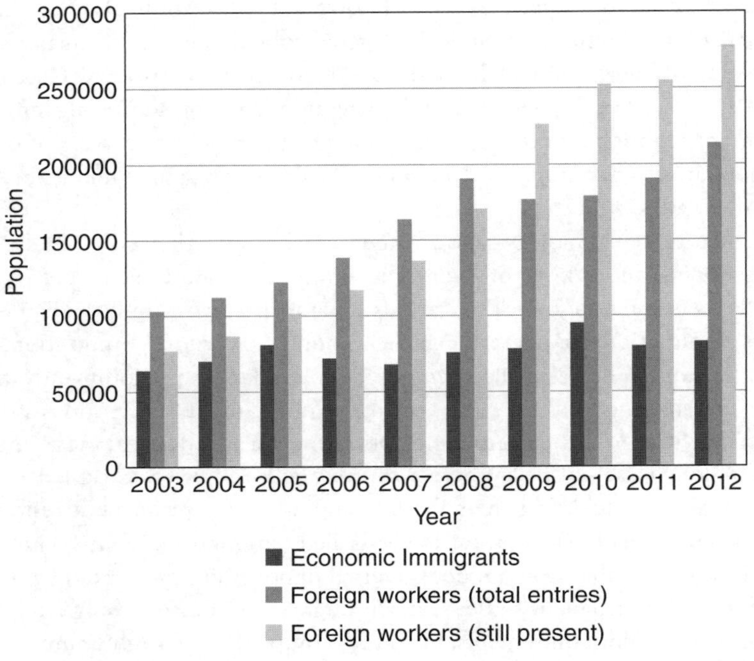

Source: Citizenship and Immigration Canada. Canada Facts and Figures: Immigration Overview, Permanent and Temporary Residents 2012 (Ottawa: CIC).

Note: Since temporary employment visas are granted for up to four years, the CIC report uses two sets of data to estimate the number of temporary foreign workers: total entries and the total number of temporary foreign workers still present in the country.

occupations. Workers in this program are also recruited by private agencies, and they are allowed to renew their contracts every year for up to four years. After four years of work in Canada, however, they must wait for another four-year period before they are allowed to work in Canada again.[7]

Employers interested in hiring temporary workers are required to prove that no Canadians are available to fill the jobs. For economic sectors with chronic labour shortages, expedited procedures are put in place to facilitate speedy delivery of requested workers.[8] In each stream, workers are authorized to work for a specific employer. While in theory it is possible for workers to transfer to another employer, in practice such mobility is virtually unattainable; the approval process is too lengthy, and/or it relies on a request from the current employer.[9]

Each of the three streams of workers has experienced problems with their working conditions in Canada, despite the fact that the provincial employment standards acts or codes apply to them. SAWP workers have faced threats of deportation, exposure to dangerous chemicals, excessive demands by employers, and inadequate housing and transportation.[10] Moreover, although SAWP migrants are eligible to receive workers' compensation when injured, they tend to significantly under-report accidents.[11] The live-in caregivers have also faced abusive working conditions, such as long and unpaid hours of work, sexual and racial harassment, inadequate living quarters, demands to perform tasks that fall outside their contract, insufficient nourishment, dismissal without sufficient cause, and non-compliance with employment and health and safety standards.[12] For SLSOP workers, problems also include receiving lower wages than promised, housing difficulties, demands for inappropriate personal services, racism, and threats of deportation.[13] With the exception of SAWP workers, who are recruited by government agencies, temporary migrants often fall victim to abusive recruitment practices, including excessive recruitment fees (as high as $10,000) and misinformation about the wages to be earned or the kinds of jobs they will be expected to perform. In some extreme cases, workers find upon arrival that there is no job for them, or that the job's duration is considerably shorter than anticipated.[14]

Even though temporary migrants pay premiums to the employment insurance plan, they are unable to collect insurance payments when their contracts end. SAWP workers are returned to their home countries upon termination of their contracts (even in cases of premature termination). Because they are not present in Canada, they cannot engage actively in a search for another job, which is a precondition for receiving unemployment insurance benefits. Many workers do not satisfy the qualifying period required to be entitled to benefits. Furthermore, since temporary workers' authorization to work in Canada is tied to a specific employer, in technical terms they are not considered "available to work" for other employers if they become unemployed.[15]

Finally, migrants are often destined for economic sectors that have the lowest levels of legal protection in Canada—agriculture and domestic work. For instance, in Alberta and Ontario, the two provinces that receive the greatest numbers of agricultural workers, these workers are still denied the right to collective bargaining and they are excluded from such benefits as overtime pay, maximum hours of work, and statutory holidays. Agricultural workers in Alberta continue to be excluded from coverage by the provincial occupational health and safety legislation; it was only in 2006 that such coverage was extended to agricultural workers in Ontario, as a result of a legal challenge advanced by the United Food and Commercial Workers Union,[16] as discussed below.

How can migrant workers ensure that their rights are properly enforced and new rights and protections are extended to them? There are two extant legal frameworks that make it possible for marginalized people to assert their rights: the citizenship rights framework and the international human rights framework. Although these two frameworks are rooted in the same moral principles, the mechanisms for claiming rights in each framework are different, as discussed in the next two sections.

The Citizenship Framework and Temporary Migrants

The first rights framework is citizenship. Rooted in the principles of the French Revolution, the notion of modern citizenship brings together national belonging, political participation, and rights. Within this framework of citizenship, non-citizens residing in the territory of the nation-state are generally excluded from many benefits, although they may be granted some. The citizenship framework incorporates the principles of civil rights (such as the right to freedom of expression and property rights), political rights (such as the rights to political participation and freedom of association), and social rights (social welfare rights, such as the rights to health care, education, and unemployment insurance).[17] These principles are entrenched in such legal documents as the Canadian Charter of Rights and Freedoms and provincial human rights codes, as well as such legal protections as the federal employment insurance act, provincial employment standards acts or codes, and provincial health insurance acts.

Those who feel that their civil, political, or social rights are being denied rely on these legal documents to claim their rights in a court of law, in a human rights tribunal, or by launching a complaint to the corresponding body—for example, through the ministry of labour, the ministry of health, occupational health and safety contact centres, labour relations boards, or union representatives. While the Charter cannot be used to assert violations of rights by private individuals such as employers, it can be used to challenge government policies that exclude some groups of individuals from established protections and benefits. By contrast, provincial human rights codes establish enforceable standards that apply to public policies and the social and political conduct of government representatives, as well as to the social and economic conduct of private individuals in a variety of settings.[18] Part 1 of the Ontario Human Rights Code asserts that all persons are entitled to equal treatment without discrimination in five social areas: provision of services, goods, and facilities; accommodation; contracts; employment; and vocational associations.[19]

As discussed below, both the Charter of Rights and Freedoms and provincial human rights codes have been used to redress exclusions and violations experienced by migrants. The Charter has been used to change public policies, while provincial codes have been used to challenge provincial policies and seek compensation from employers. Temporary migrant workers are a peculiar category of non-citizens. Although they are not granted permission to reside permanently in Canada, they are nevertheless covered by the citizenship framework.[20] The rights in sections 2, 7, and 15 of the Charter apply to "everyone" and "every individual," and therefore migrant workers are entitled to protection under these provisions, despite being admitted on temporary visas to work and live in Canada.

At the same time, temporary migrants are excluded from two important citizenship rights: the right to "enter, remain in and leave Canada" and the right "to pursue the gaining of a livelihood in any province." Consequently, laws and policies that confine temporary migrants to the specific provinces where they are authorized to live and work do not constitute a violation of Charter rights.[21] Furthermore, not only are temporary migrants prevented from moving from one province to another, they cannot change employers. Since a condition of their work visa is the promise of an employment contract from a specific employer, it would be a violation of their admission condition to change employers. It is this restriction that distinguishes migrant workers from Canadian citizens and permanent residents. Being tied to a specific employer renders migrants impotent to launch complaints against them, as discussed in more detail below. As a consequence, advocacy for migrants' rights has come from a variety of labour and civil society organizations rather than from the temporary migrants themselves.[22]

The International Framework for Migrants' Rights

The second framework that can be employed to advance migrants' rights is the international human rights framework. The notion of human rights as "inalienable rights of man" was originally elaborated by the Enlightenment era philosophers. Similarly to citizenship rights, the human rights expressed in the Universal Declaration of Human Rights (UDHR) and the treaties and declarations that followed identify civil, political, and social rights, including labour rights. In addition, labour rights are elaborated in International Labour Organization (ILO) conventions. While the content of rights is in many ways the same for citizenship and human rights, unlike citizenship rights, the human rights principles transcend national borders. The set of principles expressed in the UDHR and its related treaties applies universally to all human beings, merely by virtue of their membership in humankind.

The UDHR is "the first international authoritative affirmation that all humans are human."[23]

The vast majority of fundamental human rights are inscribed in the following treaties:

- International Convention on the Elimination of All Forms of Racial Discrimination;
- International Covenant on Civil and Political Rights;
- International Covenant on Economic, Social and Cultural Rights;
- Convention on the Elimination of All Forms of Discrimination against Women;
- Convention against Torture and Other Cruel, Inhuman or Degrading Treatment or Punishment;
- Convention on the Rights of the Child; and
- Convention on the Rights of Persons with Disabilities.

By virtue of their universality, the rights expressed in these international treaties apply to migrants. Similarly, the ILO's Declaration on Fundamental Principles and Rights at Work (1998) entrenches the universal applicability of labour rights.

The power of international treaties varies from one country to another. A treaty may be on par with domestic constitutional law, stand above it, or fall somewhere between domestic constitutional law and domestic statutory law. It may also lack validity, if not ratified. In Canada, unless the terms of treaties are incorporated into domestic law, they cannot be legally enforced.[24] Yet even when they are not legally binding, international treaties can be and have been invoked when interpreting provisions of the Canadian Charter.[25] In 2007 the Supreme Court of Canada reaffirmed that "it is a well-established principle of statutory interpretation that legislation will be presumed to conform to international law," and that, *notwithstanding its ratification or incorporation*, international law provides a source of interpretation in court.[26]

While the ILO's Declaration on Fundamental Principles and Rights at Work is not a legally enforceable instrument, it is an expression of commitment by the ILO and its member states to respect and promote four fundamental principles, regardless of whether the state has ratified fundamental ILO conventions. The four principles are freedom of association and the effective recognition of the right to collective bargaining; the elimination of forced and compulsory labour; the abolition of child labour; and the elimination of discrimination in respect of employment and occupation.[27]

One limitation of the above-mentioned treaties is that they do not mention migrants explicitly, and it is not clear whether the principles of universality are to be applied in the migrants' home countries or in the territories of host states. By contrast, other conventions, such as the UN Convention on the Protection of the Rights of All Migrant Workers and Members of Their Families (CRMW) of 1990 and two ILO conventions on migrants—numbers 97 (1949) and 143 (1975)—spell out the rights of migrants who live and work in countries other than their own.

The labour rights of migrants were first addressed by two ILO conventions. Convention 97, on Migration for Employment (1949), and Convention 143, on Migrants in Abusive Conditions and the Promotion of Equality of Opportunity and Treatment of Migrant Workers (1975), set out principles of non-discrimination for legally admitted migrant workers. They included such issues as guarantees of security of employment, provision of alternative employment, relief work, and retraining. Shortly after Convention 143 was adopted, a working group was established to draft a United Nations convention on migrants' rights. About half of the UN member states participated in this process, and the International Convention on the Protection of the Rights of All Migrant Workers and Members of Their Families was adopted on 18 December 1990.[28] It took almost 13 years to gather the 20 signatures required for the Convention to enter into force. Since it was first adopted, this Convention has faced political obstacles; even today, no major migrant-receiving countries of the global North have ratified it,[29] but at a symbolic level, the migrants' rights convention provides a useful resource. Finally, in 2011, the ILO approved the Domestic Workers Convention (number 189),[30] which recognized that many domestic workers are migrant women and that domestic work is not covered by national or regional labour standards. The convention extends to domestic workers the same protections enjoyed by other workers.

Some of the principles expressed in the migrant-specific conventions include responsibilities placed upon the governments of migrant-receiving countries to (1) ensure that migrant workers are provided with accurate information about the conditions of their employment prior to departure from their countries of origin; (2) regulate the process of recruitment and placement of migrant workers; (3) oversee the contracts between employers and employees; (4) ensure the application of domestic laws without discrimination to migrant workers, in terms of remuneration, membership in trade unions and the benefits of collective bargaining, accommodation, social security, and employment taxes; and (5) ensure protection against all forms of abuse, harassment, and violence.[31]

Canada has not ratified any of the migrant-specific conventions. However, these conventions "provide important policy guidance,"[32] and Canadian judges draw on the principles and values expressed in them when they justify decisions on legal challenges involving migrant workers.[33] Thus there are two rights frameworks that people who experience various forms of exclusion can draw on to advance their rights: the citizenship framework and the international human rights framework. How have temporary migrants in Canada resorted to these frameworks to improve their access to various protections and benefits? This question will be addressed in the next two sections.

Enforcing Migrants' Rights through the Citizenship Framework

As mentioned earlier, the Temporary Foreign Workers Program is under federal government jurisdiction. It is therefore reasonable to expect that the federal government would oversee the conditions under which foreign nationals, once admitted, are treated on Canadian soil. But it is the provinces that are responsible for governing employment rights, occupational health and safety protection, health care, and housing in Canada. Thus, because of this jurisdictional split, each of these players feels constrained to address the problems that emerge.[34] Although the SAWP is regulated by memoranda of understanding between the sending states and Canada, in reality these agreements are not legally enforced.[35]

Employers and the employees are required to sign a contract before Human Resources and Skills Development Canada (HRSDC) initiates the work visa authorization process. The contract stipulates the type of job that the migrant will perform, as well as the duration of employment, work schedule, wages, deductions, the employer's responsibility for covering transportation costs, health benefit coverage, and registration for workers' compensation plans, as well as the minimum notice required for contract termination. However, HRSDC has no authority to enforce these contracts. In fact, no one does. As Fudge and MacPhail observe, these contracts are a form of "soft law," which sets important principles but cannot be legally enforced.[36]

All provincial employment standards acts set out complaint procedures, as do the occupational health and safety acts, yet very few migrant workers launch complaints against their employers. While language barriers and lack of information about the procedures may prevent low-skilled migrants from attempting to submit a complaint to the ministry of labour, the main reason why most migrant workers do not complain about their working conditions is the precarious nature of their employment. As mentioned earlier, temporary migrants are authorized to work for a specific employer. If they are dismissed, they lose their authorization to work in Canada and must return home. Employers often use threats of deportation to discipline their workers to increase productivity and accept their working conditions, as numerous researchers have documented.[37]

Preibisch and Hennebry point out that vaguely worded employment contracts make it possible for employers to arbitrarily dismiss workers without the right of appeal.[38] In 2001, for instance, some 50 Mexican workers walked off the job, demanding better working conditions; in retaliation, the employer sent 20 "ringleaders" back to Mexico.[39] The case of Rol-Land Farms presents another vivid illustration of migrants' deportability. On 6 December 2008 about 70 temporary workers contracted from Mexico and Jamaica to work at Rol-Land Farms, a mushroom-growing operation near Guelph, Ontario, were unexpectedly laid off. Although they had all signed two-year contracts, they lost their jobs after eight months, and they were given no explanation for the termination of their contracts. The UFCW and other analysts suspect that the decision to fire the workers was triggered by an Ontario Court of Appeal decision on 17 November 2008 to strike down the ban on farm unions in the province.[40]

In the case of SAWP workers, deportation means not only immediate dismissal and repatriation but also the fear of being barred from participating in the program in the future. The program allows migrants to reapply as long as their employers approve of their work. At the end of the season, each employer submits worker evaluations to the relevant authorities in the workers' countries of origin. The workers are highly dependent on their employers not only for current employment and daily necessities but also for future opportunities to work in Canada.[41] This vulnerability makes it virtually impossible for the workers to launch complaints about their working conditions. Furthermore, recruitment organizations such as the International Organization for Migration (IOM) strongly discourage migrants from asserting their rights.[42]

Many temporary migrants employed in low-skilled occupations in Canada face poverty in their home countries. In addition, some of them incur large debts to pay their recruiters. These migrants are highly dependent on their jobs in Canada and are willing to accept their working conditions rather than risk being removed from the program. Thus their lack of mobility in the labour force and their dependence on employers, in combination with desperate conditions in their country of origin, force SAWP and other temporary workers to accept exploitation and exposure to occupational hazards without questioning or challenging these practices.[43]

Therefore it is hardly surprising that very few workers launch complaints against their employers. In 2007 the former British Columbia Ministry of Employment, Immigration, and Industry acknowledged that there was a "real disincentive" for temporary foreign workers to lodge complaints; it reported that only 18 out of the 4,000 complaints being investigated had been filed by temporary foreign workers in that province.[44] One other requirement further complicates an already risky process in some provinces. In British Columbia and Alberta, for instance, before making a complaint to an employment standards officer, workers are required to fill out and submit a "self-help kit" to the employer as a first attempt to resolve the situation.[45] As Nakache and Kinoshita point out, although this step is not a formal requirement, an officer can turn down the worker's request to investigate a claim if the prescribed procedure is not followed.[46]

While very few migrants are in a position to launch lawsuits against their employers, in some exceptional circumstances it is possible, as the following case illustrates. In the first class-action suit advanced by temporary migrant workers in Canada, a Filipina temporary worker, Herminia Vergara Dominguez, alleged on behalf of herself and 50 other temporary workers that the Northland Properties Corporation, in charge of a Denny's Restaurant, failed to provide them with the amount of work promised in their contracts, to pay them overtime—despite the fact that British Columbia has legislation mandating a certain level of pay for overtime work—and to reimburse them for certain expenses, including recruitment and travel costs. The $10,000 law suit was settled on 8 February 2013. The settlement included payment to the workers of any shortfall in hours; payment of overtime, vacation pay, and interest; reimbursement for airfare to Canada and return costs (exceptions included those who were permanent residents of Canada); payment of agency fees by Denny's (up to $10,000); a payment of $80,000; and the workers' legal fees. A fee of $2,500 was also to be paid to Dominguez as representative plaintiff.[47]

While most temporary migrants are reluctant to confront their employers or to launch formal complaints for fear of being deported, various civil society organizations have attempted to assist temporary migrants and/or advocate on their behalf. Among them are Justicia for Migrant Workers; the Agriculture Workers Alliance; KAIROS: Canadian Ecumenical Justice Initiatives; the Philippine Women's Centre of British Columbia; PINAY: Filipino Women's Organization in Quebec/Organisation des femmes Philippines du Québec; Migrante Ontario; Quebec's human rights commission, the Commission des droits de la personne et des droits de la jeunesse; and the Canadian Refugee Council, as well as labour organizations such as the Canadian Labour Congress, UFCW Canada, the Alberta Federation of Labour, and the British Columbia and Yukon Territories Building and Construction Trades Council.[48] These actors have pursued one of three main strategies. First, using section 15 of the Charter of Rights and Freedoms—which refers to the right to be treated equally, without discrimination—they have challenged the exclusion of migrant workers (or the entire occupational sectors in which they are concentrated) from certain protections. Second, they have lobbied the Canadian government to introduce policy changes to make working and living conditions fairer for migrant workers. And third, they have represented in court individual migrant workers who have experienced unfair treatment by their employers.

UFCW Canada has launched four constitutional challenges in the Supreme Court, two of which were successful and two unsuccessful. The first challenge involved the exclusion of agricultural workers (both migrant and resident) from the Ontario Health and Safety Act (OSHA). As a result of this challenge the Ontario government changed its policy, and now agricultural workers are covered by OHSA provisions; that is, they have the rights to refuse unsafe work and to receive safety training and information on potential workplace hazards.[49] The second constitutional challenge, known as *Fraser v. Canada (Attorney General)*, concerns the right of Ontario workers to unionize and bargain collectively. The UFCW argued that agricultural workers' exclusion from the Ontario Labour Relations Act was unconstitutional because it violated the workers' Charter rights to freedom of association and equality, as well as section 15 of the Charter. Ruling in favour of the UFCW, the Supreme Court ordered the Ontario government to make changes. In response, Ontario passed the Agricultural Employees Protection Act, which permits migrant workers to "form associations" but not to bargain collectively.[50] The third Charter challenge concerned the applicability of the Employment Insurance Act to migrant workers, on the grounds that they were effectively unable to collect some of the benefits available under the Act.[51] This challenge was also unsuccessful.

The fourth challenge involved the exemption of farms with less than three continuously employed workers from the Quebec Labour Code's standards. On 10 July 2008, the UFCW deposited a petition under the Labour Code to be certified as the bargaining agent for workers on a Quebec farm. The employers, L'Écuyer and Locas, contested the motion on the basis of paragraph 5 of section 21 of the Code, which specifies that persons employed in the operation of a farm shall not be deemed employees unless at least three of them are "ordinarily and continuously" employed. Although the Commission des relations du travail (Labour Relations Commission) acknowledged that L'Écuyer and Locas were engaged in the operation of the farm that did not ordinarily and continuously employ three persons, in a decision rendered on 16 April 2010, it proceeded to certify the UFCW as a bargaining agent of the farm workers. In order to do so, the Commission declared paragraph 5 unconstitutional and contrary to both section 2(d) of the Canadian Charter of Rights and Freedoms and article 3 of the Quebec Charter of Human Rights and Freedoms—sections that recognize freedom of association as a fundamental right in our society.

L'Écuyer and Locas then asked the Quebec Superior Court to declare that the Commission had exceeded its jurisdiction in declaring paragraph 5 unconstitutional and inoperable. The presiding judge, Thomas Davis, recognized the peculiarity of seasonal farming and how it impinged on the workers' rights to unionize:

> The requirement that farm workers may only be organized if they are employed on farms that "ordinarily and continuously" employ three or more employees means that, under the current legislative regime, the employees of many of these farms will never be able to benefit from their right to free association and the right to collective bargaining. … The seasonal nature of production means that a vast number of these farms, while they ordinarily employ many more than three employees, do not do so on a continuous basis.

Thus, on 11 March 2013, the Court declared that paragraph 5 of section 21 of the Quebec Labour Code was unconstitutional.[52] Following this decision the Province of Quebec revised its labour code, extending the same rights to all agricultural workers.[53] However, this victory was short-lived; in October 2014 the Quebec government passed a law that once again denied the right to form unions and bargain collectively to agricultural workers on farms employing fewer than three workers. The UFCW expressed outrage and committed itself to doing everything in its power "to fight against this draconian piece of legislation."[54]

The second strategy pursued by various civil society and trade union organizations is to lobby the provincial and federal governments to make policy changes based on collected evidence of abuses. One of the issues identified by supporters of migrants' rights is the abusive behaviour of unscrupulous recruitment agents. As discussed above, some migrants pay excessive recruitment fees and others are deceived by recruiters about the nature of the work they will perform or the salaries they will receive. Various migrants' rights advocates have raised concerns about recruitment agencies. In response, some provinces have introduced measures to regulate the recruitment of migrant workers. For instance, since 2009 it has been illegal for recruiters to charge fees to workers arriving in Manitoba. In order to ensure that this regulation is enforced, Manitoba employers are required to register with the province before recruitment of temporary foreign workers begins. The employers are then made liable for recruitment fees charged to a worker by an unlicensed recruiter or if they recruit directly. Recruitment agencies are also required to register and provide a letter of credit in the amount of $10,000 prior to obtaining a licence. If they charge fees to a worker, this amount is used to reimburse the worker. The province retains the right to refuse or revoke a licence if employers or recruiters are found to be engaging in illegal fee collection.[55]

In addition, the four western provinces have signed memoranda of understanding with the Philippines to provide guidelines for recruiting low-skilled workers contracted to work in those provinces.[56] Similarly, in Ontario, Bill 210 was introduced to protect live-in caregivers (although no other low-skilled temporary workers) from recruiter abuse. While Bill 210 bans recruitment fees, as in Manitoba, Ontario has not put in place any mechanisms to ensure that employers and recruiters comply with this ban. Instead, it is only when migrants themselves complain about their recruiters that an investigation will take place.[57] This provision seriously undermines the effectiveness of the bill.

Migrants' rights advocates have also lobbied the Canadian government to introduce and/or strengthen mechanisms required to protect migrant workers from abusive employers. Some moderate changes have been introduced by the federal government, although most critics see them as a smokescreen. For instance, in October 2009 the federal government announced that employers found to have violated the workers' contracts with respect to their wages, working conditions, or occupation would be ineligible to access the TFWP for two years and would be listed on the program website. However, no mechanisms to inspect the workplaces were introduced; instead, this policy was to rely on complaints filed by the migrant temporary workers themselves.[58] As discussed above, this was highly unlikely to happen. On 31 December 2013 the federal government introduced changes that would make contract enforcement somewhat more reliable; the new regulations granted powers to federal authorities to inspect workplaces. According to the Employment and Social Development Canada spokesperson, Eric Morrissette, "these changes to the TFWP demonstrate the Government of Canada's ongoing commitment to protect vulnerable foreign workers from the risk of abuse and exploitation."[59] It remains to be seen how these provisions will be enforced.

The third strategy involves assisting individual migrants claiming compensation for wrongful dismissal or employer-perpetrated abuses, as the following two cases illustrate. In 2009 a St. Lucian migrant worker, Adrian Monrose, came to the town of Leamington, in southwest Ontario, to work at Double Diamond Acres Ltd. Monrose and some of his fellow workers on the farm were called "monkeys" by both the owner and a supervisor. Monrose complained to the owner about the monkey comments, and the owner fired him and sent him back to St. Lucia little more than a week later. Adrian was sponsored by his fiancée to return to Canada. Then, with the help of Justicia for Migrant Workers, he retained a lawyer and launched a complaint with the Ontario human rights tribunal, alleging discrimination in employment and reprisal under section 34 of Part IV of the Human Rights Code. In 2013 he was awarded $23,500 by the tribunal, which included $3,000 compensation for damages to his dignity, feelings, and self-respect.[60]

The second case concerns the Construction and Specialized Workers' Union (CSWU), Local 1611. This union filed a representative complaint before the British Columbia Human Rights Tribunal on behalf of a group of temporary workers from Costa Rica, Colombia, and Ecuador who had been employed for construction of a tunnel on the Canada Line project in Vancouver. The CSWU alleged that the respondents discriminated against the Latin American workers on the basis of their race, colour, ancestry, and place of origin in respect of the terms and conditions of their employment, contrary to section 13 of the British Columbia Human Rights Code. The workers alleged that, unlike their temporary migrant co-workers from Europe who were also employed by the company, they experienced various forms of discrimination: their wages were lower; they received the poorest housing, which was also farthest away from the worksite; their meal plan was worse; and their expense allowance was considerably lower (an average of $76 as opposed to $300 for the European workers). While the company argued that the European workers had more experience, the tribunal found this not to be the case. The panel ruled in favour of the Latin American workers and ordered the company to pay each worker the difference between the salary paid to them and the average salary paid to members of the comparative group, or $10,000.[61]

International Human Rights and Migrants' Rights in Canada

As mentioned earlier, international treaties cannot be legally enforced in Canada unless their terms are incorporated into domestic law. However, the values and principles entrenched in international treaties can be employed in rights discourse and frames by rights activists. Not surprisingly, Canadian trade unions and grassroots organizations advocating on behalf of temporary migrant workers have drawn inspiration from and engaged with international human rights to frame their claims and advance migrants' rights. For instance, in its advocacy campaigns, the UFCW has made explicit references to the UDHR, particularly its guarantees of effective access to remedy by national tribunals for acts violating fundamental rights and entitlement to full equality and to fair and public hearings by an independent and impartial tribunal, as well as the right of everyone to safe and healthy working conditions.[62]

Other migrant rights' organizations draw on the international human rights treaties to argue for stronger protections for migrant workers. In its report to the UN Committee on Economic, Social, and Cultural Rights on Canada's compliance with the ICESCR, the Canadian Council for Refugees, a non-profit organization, contends that denying seasonal agricultural workers the rights to family reunification and collective bargaining constitutes a clear violation of two ICESCR articles. Article 8.1(a) guarantees all persons the right "to form trade unions and join the trade union of his choice, subject only to the rules of the organization concerned, for the promotion and protection of his economic and social interests." Article 10.1 states that "the widest possible protection and assistance should be accorded to the family, which is the natural and fundamental group unit of society, particularly for its establishment and while it is responsible for the care and education of dependent children."[63]

Different courts of law also engage the international human rights framework to provide interpretations of the Charter of Rights and Freedoms. In the *Fraser* case, the Supreme Court cited a number of international human rights instruments—such as ILO Convention No. 87, concerning freedom of association and protection of the right to organize; ILO Convention No. 11, concerning the rights of association and combination of agricultural workers; and ILO Convention No. 141, concerning organizations of rural workers and their role in economic and social development—in order to reach a decision that denial of the right to form a trade union was a violation of the workers' basic right to freedom of association.[64] Even the International Convention on the Protection of the Rights of All Migrant Workers and Members of Their Families, a treaty that Canada has not ratified, was invoked in the ruling that permitted the UFCW to represent SAWP workers following their legal challenge on unemployment insurance benefits, discussed above.[65]

Conclusion

In their article "Numbers vs. Rights: Trade-Offs and Guest Worker Programs," Martin Ruhs and Philip Martin argue that the more rights are granted to migrants in host countries, the fewer migrants will be invited to work there. They explain this seeming paradox in the following manner: from the employers' point of view, labour costs increase because of additional employment rights such as minimum wage increases, unionization, and occupational health protection. Thus, when migrants have the full rights outlined in ILO and UN conventions, including the right to equal wages and all work-related benefits, their cost is high and thus employers will request fewer workers. On the other hand, more limited migrant rights result in lower costs for employers and, therefore, more migrants will be employed.[66] As this chapter illustrates, temporary migration has expanded in Canada; in fact, it has become popular among many employers precisely because migrants are denied many labour rights. While employers have enjoyed this access to an inexpensive and docile labour force, for many labour organizations, grassroots activists, and human rights organizations, this denial of rights to migrant workers is unacceptable. The universality of workers' rights principles, as expressed in both international and Canadian human and labour rights documents, makes it imperative that migrant workers' rights be protected and extended.

Takeaway Messages

- Lower-skilled migrant workers in Canada experience various kinds of abuses and rights violations.
- Because migrants are too vulnerable to claim their own rights, migrants' rights advocates have been instrumental in protecting and extending their rights using either the citizenship or the international human rights frameworks.
- Both rights frameworks have limitations; however, by employing both rights frameworks, migrants' rights advocates have been able to bring about improvements in migrant workers' working conditions.

Study Questions

- What are the similarities and differences between the citizenship and human rights frameworks?
- What are the main problems that lower-skilled temporary migrants have faced in Canada?
- What strategies have activists used to protect and advance the rights of migrant workers in Canada? Have they been successful? Why or why not?

Issues for Debate or Roundtable

- Do you believe it is possible (and desirable) to extend all nationally and internationally recognized labour rights to migrant workers authorized to work in Canada on a temporary basis?
- Do you believe that migrant rights should be restricted in order to serve labour market needs in Canada?

Additional Reading

de Guchteneire, Paul, Antoine Pécoud, and Ryszard Cholewinski, eds. *Migration and Human Rights: The United Nations Convention on Migrant Workers' Rights*. Cambridge: Cambridge University Press, 2009.

Lenard, Patti Tamara, and Christine Straehle, eds. *Legislating Inequality: Canada's Temporary Migrant Worker Program*. Montreal: McGill-Queen's University Press, 2012.

Websites

International Convention on the Protection of the Rights of All Migrant Workers and Members of Their Families. http://www2.ohchr.org/english/bodies/cmw/cmw.htm.

International Labour Organization. http://www.ilo.org/global/lang--en/index.htm.

UFCW Canada. http://www.ufcw.ca/index.php?lang=en.

Notes

1. P. Daenzer, *Regulating Class Privilege: Immigrant Servants in Canada, 1940–1990s* (Toronto: Canadian Scholar's Press, 1993); A. Macklin, "Foreign Domestic Worker: Surrogate Housewife or Mail Order Servant?" *McGill Law Journal* 37, no. 3 (1992): 681–760; A. Bakan and D. Stasiulis, "Foreign Domestic Worker Policy in Canada and Social Boundaries of Modern Citizenship," *Science and Society* 58, no. 1 (1994): 7–33; R. Cohen, "A Brief History of Racism in Immigration Policies for Recruiting Domestics," *Canadian Women's Studies* 14, no. 2 (1994): 197–215.
2. V. Satzewich, *Racism and the Incorporation of Foreign Labour: Farm Labour Migration to Canada since 1945* (London: Routledge, 1991); T. Basok, *Tortillas and Tomatoes: Mexican Transmigrant Harvesters in Canada* (Montreal: McGill-Queen's University Press, 2002); K. Preibisch, "Local Produce, Foreign Labor: Labor Mobility Programs and Global Trade Competitiveness in Canada," *Rural Sociology* 72, no. 3 (2007): 418–49; F. Faraday, *Made in Canada: How the Law Constructs Migrant Workers' Insecurity* (Toronto: Metcalf Foundation, 2012), 35–41.
3. N. Sharma, *Home Economics: Nationalism and the Making of Migrant Workers in Canada* (Toronto: University of Toronto Press, 2006); Faraday, *Made in Canada*, 25–26.
4. J. Fudge and F. MacPhail, "The Temporary Foreign Worker Program in Canada: Low-Skilled Workers as an Extreme Form of Flexible Labour," *Comparative Labor Law and Policy Journal* 31, no. 5 (2009): 22; D. Nakache and P.J. Kinoshita, "The Canadian Temporary Foreign Worker Program: Do Short-Term Economic Needs Prevail over Human Rights Concerns?" IRPP Study no. 5 (May 2010), 5.
5. Sharma, *Home Economics*, 129; R. Trumper and L. Wong, "Canada's Guest Workers: Racialized, Gendered, and Flexible," in *Race and Racism in 21st-Century Canada: Continuity, Complexity, and Change*, ed. S. Hier and B. Singh (Peterborough, ON: Broadview Press, 2007), 150–60; Nakache and Kinoshita, "Canadian Temporary Foreign Worker Program," 6.
6. Basok, *Tortillas and Tomatoes.*
7. The four-year-maximum regulation went into effect on 1 April 2011 (see www.cic.gc.ca, for instance). This regulation has been enforced since 1 April 2015; see *Toronto Star*, "Temporary Foreign Workers Warned to Leave Canada as

Required," 1 April 2015, http://www.thestar.com/news/canada/2015/04/01/foreign-workers-warned-not-to-dodge-deportation.html.

8. Faraday, *Made in Canada*, 27–30; Fudge and MacPhail, "Temporary Foreign Worker Program in Canada," 25–26; Nakache and Kinoshita, "Canadian Temporary Foreign Worker Program," 5.
9. J.L. Hennebry and K. Preibisch, "A Model for Managed Migration? Re-examining Best Practices in Canada's Seasonal Agricultural Worker Program," *International Migration Review* (2010): 22, Faraday, *Made in Canada*, 40; D. Nakache, "The Canadian Temporary Foreign Worker Program: Regulation, Practices and Protection Gaps," in *Producing and Negotiating Non-citizenship: Precarious Legal Status in Canada*, ed. L. Goldring and P. Landolt (Toronto: University of Toronto Press, 2013), 78.
10. Basok, *Tortillas and Tomatoes*; Preibisch, "Local Produce"; J. Hennebry and J. McLaughlin, "The Exception That Proves the Rule: Structural Vulnerability, Health Risks and Consequences for Temporary Migrant Farmworkers in Canada," in *Legislating Inequality: Canada's Temporary Migrant Worker Program*, ed. P.T. Lenard and C. Straehle (McGill-Queen's University Press, 2012), 117–38; L. Binford, *Tomorrow We're All Going to the Harvest: Temporary Foreign Worker Programs and Neoliberal Political Economy* (Austin: University of Texas Press, 2013); UFCW [United Food and Commercial Workers' Union] Canada, *Report on the Status of Migrant Workers in Canada* (Ottawa: UFCW, 2011).
11. T. Basok, "Post-National Citizenship, Social Exclusion, and Migrants' Rights: Mexican Seasonal Workers in Canada," *Citizenship Studies* 8, no. 1 (2004): 47–64; UFCW Canada, *Report on the Status of Migrant Workers*, 15–16; Hennebry and McLaughlin, "The Exception That Proves the Rule"; J. McLaughlin, *Trouble in Our Fields: Health and Human Rights among Mexican and Caribbean Migrant Farm Workers in Canada*, PhD dissertation, University of Toronto, 2009.
12. D. Stasiulis and A. Bakan, *Negotiating Citizenship: Migrant Women in Canada and the Global System* (London: Palgrave Macmillan, 2003); Bakan and Stasiulis, "Foreign Domestic Worker Policy in Canada"; H. Zaman, *Breaking the Iron Wall: Decommodification and Immigrant Women's Labor in Canada* (Lanham, MD: Lexington Books, 2006); G. Pratt and Philippine Women Centre, *From Migrant to Immigrant: Domestic Workers Settle in Vancouver, Canada*, Research on Immigration and Integration in the Metropolis Working Paper no. 03-18, (Vancouver: RIIM, 2003).
13. Y. Byl, *Entrenching Exploitation: The Second Report of the Alberta Federation of Labour Temporary Foreign Worker Advocate* (Edmonton: AFL, 2009); K. Flecker, *Canadian Temporary Foreign Worker Program (TFWP): Model or Mistake?* (Ottawa: Canadian Federation of Labour, 2011); Fudge and MacPhail, "Temporary Foreign Worker Program in Canada"; Nakache and Kinoshita, "Canadian Temporary Foreign Worker Program."
14. Byl, *Entrenching Exploitation*; Nakache and Kinoshita, "Canadian Temporary Foreign Worker Program," 13–14.
15. Nakache and Kinoshita, "Canadian Temporary Foreign Worker Program," 19–21; Nakhache, "Canadian Temporary Foreign Worker Program"; UFCW Canada, *Report on the Status of Migrant Workers*, 33–34.
16. Fudge and MacPhail, "Temporary Foreign Worker Program in Canada," 31; T. Basok and E. Carasco, "Advancing the Rights of Noncitizens in Canada: A Human Rights Approach to Migrant Rights," *Human Rights Quarterly* 32,

no. 2 (2010): 342–66; UFCW Canada, "UFCW Canada Gains Health and Safety Coverage for Ontario Farm Workers," 2006, http://www.ufcw.ca/index.php?option=com_content&view=article&id=547&catid=5&Itemid=99&lang=en.

17. T.H. Marshall, *Citizenship and Social Class, and Other Essays* (1950; reprint, Cambridge: Cambridge University Press, 1965).
18. Faraday, *Made in Canada*, 47–52; M. Carpentier, *Systemic Discrimination Towards Migrant Workers*, cat. no. 2120-7.29.2 (Quebec: Commission des droits de la personne et des droits de la jeunesse, 2011), 11.
19. Faraday, *Made in Canada*, 50.
20. Ibid., 49; Carpentier, *Systemic Discrimination*, 10–11.
21. Faraday, *Made in Canada*, 49; Carpentier, *Systemic Discrimination*, 15.
22. K. Preibisch, "Globalizing Work, Globalizing Citizenship: Community–Migrant Worker Alliances in Southwestern Ontario," in *Organizing the Transnational: Labour, Politics, and Social Change*, ed. L. Goldring and S. Krishnamurti (Vancouver: UBC Press, 2007), 97–114; C. Gabriel and L. Macdonald, "Citizenship at the Margins: The Canadian Seasonal Agricultural Worker Program and Civil Society Advocacy," *Politics and Policy* 39, no. 1 (2011): 45–67; G. Valarezo and C. Hughes, "Pushed to the Edge: Political Activism of Guatemalan Migrant Farmworkers," *Global Justice: Theory, Practice, Rhetoric* 5 (2012): 94–119; UFCW Canada, *Report on the Status of Migrant Workers*.
23. G. Teeple, *The Riddle of Human Rights* (Aurora, ON: Garamond Press, 2004), 139.
24. Basok and Carasco, "Advancing the Rights of Noncitizens," 351.
25. Carpentier, *Systemic Discrimination*, 12.
26. *R. v. Hape*, [2007] S.C.C. 26, at paras. 53 and 56, cited in Carpentier, ibid., 12.
27. ILO [International Labour Organization], "ILO Declaration on Fundamental Principles and Rights at Work," http://www.ilo.org/declaration/lang--en/index.htm.
28. A. Pécoud and P. de Guchteneire, "Migration, Human Rights and the United Nations: An Investigation of the Obstacles to the UN Convention on Migrant Workers' Rights," *Global Migration Perspectives* no. 3 (Geneva: Global Commission on International Migration, 2004).
29. T. Basok and N. Piper, "Justice for Migrants: Mobilizing a Rights-Based Understanding of Migration," in *Mobilities, Knowledge, and Social Justice*, ed. S. Ilcan (Montreal: McGill-Queen's University Press, 2013), 263–64.
30. ILO, "C189: Domestic Workers Convention, 2011 (No. 189)," http://www.ilo.org/dyn/normlex/en/f?p=normlexpub:12100:0::no::p12100_instrument_id:2551460.
31. Faraday, *Made in Canada*, 55–56.
32. Ibid., 54.
33. Carpentier, *Systemic Discrimination*, 12.
34. Nakache and Kinoshita, "Canadian Temporary Foreign Worker Program," 8; J. Hennebry, "Who Has Their Eye on the Ball? 'Jurisdictional *Fútbol*' and Canada's Temporary Foreign Worker Program," *Policy Options* 26 (July–August 2010).
35. Hennebry and Preibisch, "A Model for Managed Migration?" 19.
36. Fudge and McPhail, "Temporary Foreign Worker Program in Canada," 29–30.
37. See, for instance, T. Basok, "Free to Be Unfree: Mexican Guest Workers in Canada," *Labour, Capital and Society* 32, no. 2 (1999): 205, 210–12; Basok, *Tortillas and Tomatoes*, 110–12; T. Basok, D. Bélanger, and E. Rivas, "Deportability, Discipline,

and Agency: Migrant Agricultural Workers in Southwestern Ontario," *Journal of Ethnic and Migration Studies* 40, no. 9 (2014): 1394–1413, doi: http://www.tandfonline.com/doi/abs/10.1080/1369183X.2013.849566; Binford, *Tomorrow We're All Going to the Harvest*, 50; K. Preibisch, "Migrant Agricultural Workers and Processes of Social Inclusion in Rural Canada: *Encuentros* and *Desencuentros*," *Canadian Journal of Latin American and Caribbean Studies* 29, no. 57/58 (2004): 212; J.J. McLaughlin, "Classifying the 'Ideal Migrant Worker': Mexican and Jamaican Transnational Farmworkers in Canada," *Focaal* 57 (2010): 85, K. Preibisch and E. Encalada, "The Other Side of *el Otro Lado*: Mexican Migrant Women and Labor Flexibility in Canadian Agriculture," *Signs* 35, no. 2 (2010): 305–6; Valarezo and Hughes, "Pushed to the Edge," 101–102.

38. K. Preibisch and J. Hennebry, "Buy Local, Hire Global: Temporary Migration in Canadian Agriculture," in *Legislating Inequality: Canada's Temporary Migrant Worker Program*, ed. P.T. Lenard and C. Straehle (Montreal: McGill-Queen's University Press, 2012), 55.
39. Basok, *Tortillas and Tomatoes*, 58–59.
40. CBC News, "Temporary Workers Fired Without Cause, Says Union," 8 December 2008; UCFW, "Fired Foreign Agriculture Workers at Rol-Land Farms Speak Out," 8 December 2011, http://www.ufcw.ca/index.php?option=com_content&view=article&id=621:fired-foreign-agriculture-workers-at-rol-land-farms-speak-out&Itemid=6&lang=en; A. Truscott, "Foreign Workers Decry 'Harsh' Dismissals from Farms," *Globe and Mail*, 12 December 2008.
41. See, for instance, Basok, *Tortillas and Tomatoes*; K. Preibisch, "Pick-Your-Own Labor: Migrant Workers and Flexibility in Canadian Agriculture," *International Migration Review* 44, no. 2 (2010): 404–41.
42. Basok, Bélanger, and Rivas, "Deportability, Discipline, and Agency."
43. Basok, *Tortillas and Tomatoes*; Preibisch, "Local Produce, Foreign Labor"; Binford, *Tomorrow We're All Going to the Harvest*; Hennebry and McLaughlin, "The Exception That Proves the Rule."
44. Cited in Nakache and Kinoshita, "Canadian Temporary Foreign Worker Program," 24.
45. BC Ministry of Jobs, Tourism and Skills Training, "Employment Standards Complaint Submission," www.labour.gov.bc.ca/esb/forms/esb_comp.htm.
46. Nakache and Kinoshita, "Canadian Temporary Foreign Worker Program," 24.
47. *Dominguez v. Northland Properties Corporation*, 2012 B.C.S.C. 328; Canadian Press, "Denny's Restaurants Settle Foreign Workers Lawsuit," *Huffington Post British Columbia*, http://www.huffingtonpost.ca/2013/03/06/dennys-restaurant-foreign-workers-lawsuit-settlement_n_2817814.html.
48. Basok, "Post-National Citizenship"; Preibisch, "Local Produce, Foreign Labor"; C. Gabriel, C. Macdonald, and L. Macdonald, "Citizenship at the Margins: The Canadian Seasonal Agricultural Worker Program and Civil Society Advocacy," *Politics and Policy* 39, no. 1 (2011): 45–67.
49. Basok and Carasco, "Advancing the Rights of Noncitizens," 357n78; S. Raper and K. Preibisch, "Forcing Governments to Govern in Defence of Noncitizen Workers: A Story about the Canadian Labour Movement's Alliance with Agricultural Migrants," in *Organizing the Transnational: Labour, Politics, and Social Change*, ed. L. Goldring and S. Krishnamurti (Vancouver: UBC Press, 2007), 115–28.

50. Basok and Carasco, "Advancing the Rights of Noncitizens," 359; Raper and Preibisch, "Forcing Governments"; F. Faraday, J. Fudge, and E. Tucker, eds., *Constitutional Labour Rights in Canada: Farm Workers and the Fraser Case* (Toronto: Irwin Law, 2012).
51. Basok and Carasco, "Advancing the Rights of Noncitizens," 357–58; Raper and Preibisch, "Forcing Governments."
52. *L'Écuyer c. Côté*, 2013 Q.C.C.S. 973.
53. C. Sampson. "Droit à la syndicalisation pour tous les travailleurs agricoles du Québec," *Le Soleil*, 5 March 2014, http://www.lapresse.ca/le-soleil/affaires/agro-alimentaire/201403/05/01-4744994-droit-a-la-syndicalisation-pour-tous-les-travailleurs-agricoles-du-quebec.php.
54. UFCW Canada, "UFCW Canada Denounces Bill 8, Demands Quebec Government Stop Discriminating Against the Most Vulnerable," 24 October 2014, http://ufcw.ca/index.php?option=com_content&view=article&id=30301:ufcw-canada-denounces-bill-8-demands-quebec-government-stop-discriminating-against-the-most-vulnerable&catid=9563&Itemid=98&lang=en.
55. Nakache, "Canadian Temporary Foreign Worker Program," 15; Faraday, *Made in Canada*, 60–72; Fudge and MacPhail, "Temporary Foreign Worker Program in Canada," 32–33.
56. Faraday, *Made in Canada*, 74; Fudge and MacPhail, "Temporary Foreign Worker Program in Canada," 35.
57. UFCW Canada, *Report on the Status of Migrant Workers*, 13; Faraday, *Made in Canada*, 66.
58. Nakache and Kinoshita, "Canadian Temporary Foreign Worker Program," 29.
59. D. Black, "New Regulations to Temporary Foreign Worker Program Called a 'Smokescreen,'" *Toronto Star*, 3 January 2014, www.thestar.com/news/canada/2014/01/03/new_regulations_to_temporary_foreign_worker_program_called_a_smokescreen.html.
60. *Monrose v. Double Diamond Acres Limited*, 2013 HRTO 1273; J.R. Learn, "Migrant Worker Wins Human Rights Case after He and Co-workers Called 'Monkeys'," CTV News, http://www.ctvnews.ca/canada/migrant-worker-wins-human-rights-case-after-he-and-co-workers-called-monkeys-1.1388326.
61. *CSWU Local 1611 v. SELI Canada and Others (No. 10)*, 2009 BCHRT 237.
62. Basok and Carasco, "Advancing the Rights of Noncitizens," 354–55.
63. Ibid., 355.
64. Ibid., 358–59.
65. Ibid., 361.
66. M. Ruhs and P. Martin, "Numbers vs. Rights: Trade-Offs and Guest Worker Programs," *International Migration Review* 42, no. 1 (Spring 2008): 252–55.

7
Children's Rights: Their Role, Significance, and Potential

TARA COLLINS AND CHRISTINE GERVAIS

We are the world's children.
We are the victims of exploitation and abuse.
We are street children.
We are the children of war.
We are the victims and orphans of HIV/AIDS.
We are denied good-quality education and health care.
We are victims of political, economic, cultural, religious and environmental discrimination.
We are children whose voices are not being heard: it is time we are taken into account.
We want a world fit for children, because a world fit for us is a world fit for everyone.[1]

Learning Objectives

- To learn what children's rights are
- To understand why children's rights are important
- To explore child participation in social and political action and in research in order to understand the significance of child rights

After hundreds of years of being considered the property of others, children are now considered not only the adults of the future but also existing persons in the present.[2] Children's rights have played an important role over time in advancing understandings about them, the priorities of child protection, and then their roles in society. Nevertheless, child rights continue to pose a challenge for full implementation around the world, including in Canada.

Children's rights are an essential component of international human rights law and are included in numerous international and regional instruments. The primary instrument, the Convention on the Rights of the Child, is the most successful international human rights treaty ever, with 195 states parties.[3] Children's rights are an essential part of the international human rights corpus, but they have much more than legal significance. These rights are also important because they should guide state policies and programs and influence society and individuals in various ways. We argue that children's participation is an essential rights-based practice so that they may contribute to improving understanding of their realities. Various examples of children's contributions, from Bolivia, Canada, Ireland, and South Africa, are highlighted.

This chapter first briefly introduces the history of and rationale for children's rights. The role and significance of the primary children's rights instrument, the United Nations Convention on the Rights of the Child (CRC), are then considered. Before the chapter concludes, children's participation in political action and research is explored.

History

There is a long history of children's rights. After seeing how children suffered terribly in the First World War, a founder of the Save the Children movement, Eglantyne Jebb, led a successful effort to include children's rights in international law.[4] Consequently, the fifth Assembly of the League of Nations adopted the Geneva Declaration.[5] Van Bueren notes, "Despite the historical diplomatic invisibility of children this instrument was the first human rights Declaration adopted by any inter-governmental organization, and preceded the Universal Declaration of Human Rights [UDHR] by twenty-four years."[6] The Declaration's five points do not create state obligations but outline the general adult responsibility to provide to children the means to develop, relief, and protection from exploitation.[7]

The Polish author and pediatrician Janusz Korczak is another pioneer who contributed greatly to the development of children's rights from the 1930s until 1942. His efforts included writing, training, and running an orphanage that respected children's rights and capacities[8] in the Warsaw ghetto. When the Nazis expelled everyone to the Treblinka concentration camp, Korczak refused offers to secure his own safety; he stayed with the 200 children with whom he had lived and died with them in the gas chamber.[9] His writings have inspired many activists about how and why to respect children's rights.

After the Second World War, the successor to the League of Nations, the United Nations, advanced human rights as other chapters in this book explore. While most major UN human rights treaties are not child-specific,[10] they are applicable to every individual, with some specific provisions for children. As examples, the International Covenant on Economic, Social, and Cultural Rights (ICESCR)[11] and the International Covenant on Civil and Political Rights (ICCPR)[12] identify children to a limited extent.

The Convention on the Rights of Persons with Disabilities includes children with disabilities.[13]

The UN specifically elaborated children's rights in its Declaration on the Rights of the Child, adopted in 1959.[14] In its 10 points, the Declaration recognizes that, *inter alia*, children should have special protection according to their "best interest" and be entitled to a name and a nationality; social security; special treatment, education, and care for children with disabilities; education; and non-discrimination. The Declaration advances children's rights by including entitlement language by which children can "enjoy the benefits of" their rights.[15] In general, however, the references to children in the Declaration—and in the UDHR, ICCPR, and ICESCR—all maintain the perception that children need protection. They are relegated to being objects of international law rather than subjects, and the child's own perspective is ignored.[16]

Other international and regional organizations have also been concerned with human and children's rights. For instance, the International Labour Organization (ILO) attempts to redress child labour through its conventions on minimum working age and against the worst forms of child labour.[17] The UN Educational, Scientific, and Cultural Organization (UNESCO) advances the right to education, among other issues.[18] The UN fund for children, UNICEF, refers to the CRC and the Convention on the Elimination of Discrimination Against Women (CEDAW) in its work, and annually produces *The State of the World's Children*.[19] Children make up almost half of the world's refugee population,[20] so there is much opportunity for the UN High Commissioner for Refugees (UNHCR) to address children's rights.

The UN Security Council has traditionally preoccupied itself with "hard" issues of international peace and security, but its approach now incorporates child rights. In 1999, for the first time, the Security Council adopted a resolution on children in armed conflict.[21] It recognizes that the issue of children in armed conflict corresponds to UN Charter article 24(1), mandating "primary responsibility for the maintenance of international peace and security." Regional organizations have also elaborated human rights, including the Organization of American States (OAS), the Council of Europe (CoE), and the African Union (AU).[22] Activities include creation of the African Committee of Experts on the Rights and Welfare of the Child, to monitor the specific African instrument for children's rights, and the Council of Europe's programming.[23]

Rationale for Children's Rights

The development of children's rights follows rationales similar to those that exist for general human rights. The main goal of human rights is to recognize the "inherent dignity" and the "equal and inalienable rights of all members of the human family."[24] As Hart describes, "the concept of human rights seems to express a shared sense of the natural, inherent, and inalienable rights of human beings, emanating from the intrinsic property of persons and given philosophical, social and political policy support throughout history."[25] In general, human rights are internationally affirmed to be the "foundation of freedom, justice and peace in the world."[26]

The philosophical question of whether children are capable of possessing rights has been much discussed.[27] The traditional approach to rights envisions a direct relationship of the individual with the state, which is problematic for the child, who has varying autonomy over time and both direct and indirect (through the parents) relations with the state.[28] Consequently, Van Bueren argues, we should respect the current autonomy of children in accordance with Lowy: "In truth human rights, from which many of the rights of the child are derived, is concerned with both the protection of the individual from the state and the creation of societal conditions by which all individuals can develop to their fullest potential."[29]

Thus children's rights are simply human rights for children, which exist for many reasons, including

- children's entitlement to equal respect and concern, without discrimination;
- recognition of children's need for protection and their place within family and society, including their right to participate; and
- consideration of children as persons,[30] not the property of their parents or caregivers.

Children's rights, as Freeman explains, "are important because those who have them can exercise agency. Agents are decision-makers. They are people who can negotiate with others, who are capable of altering relationships or decisions, who can shift social assumptions and constraints."[31]

Children's rights inform understanding and should guide responses to a wide spectrum of issues and populations. Further, rights are universal and pertinent not just for children in "developing" countries. For instance, child poverty is an issue around the world, including in Canada, where almost one in seven children lives in poverty: 967,000 children live in families below Statistics Canada's "low-income measure."[32] "While the number of children living in poverty is of great concern, so too is the depth of poverty. A majority of low-income households with children live far below whatever measure is used as the poverty line."[33]

Moreover, 4 in 10 indigenous children in Canada live in poverty.[34] In fact, the situation of Aboriginal children, as the Canadian Council of Youth and

Child Advocates describes, is a "crisis."[35] Prime Minister Harper acknowledged historical attempts by some "to kill the Indian in the child."[36] The Senate Human Rights Committee recognizes that "Aboriginal children make up one of the most marginalized and vulnerable categories of children in Canada, overrepresented in a wide variety of areas," including "disproportionately living in poverty and involved in the youth criminal justice and child protection systems. Aboriginal children also face significant health problems in comparison with other children in Canada, such as higher rates of malnutrition, disabilities, drug and alcohol abuse, and suicide."[37]

Children with disabilities are particularly vulnerable around the world; hence "surviving and thriving can be especially difficult for children with disabilities."[38] Heshusius and Nussbaum suggest that, when in contact with human variation, people continue to reflect "exclusionary fear."[39] Historically this fear has led to the seclusion and institutionalization of vast numbers of children.[40] The disability rights movement has highlighted that the problem is society, in terms of its attitudes toward and access for persons with disabilities or impairment.

Violence against children can result in disabilities, among other impacts. As the UN Study on Violence Against Children highlighted, there are various settings of violence, including the home and family, schools, care and justice systems, work, and community: "Reports of cruel and humiliating punishment, genital mutilation of girls, neglect, sexual abuse, homicide, and other forms of violence against children have long been recorded, but the grave and urgent nature of this global problem has only recently been revealed."[41] Violence includes armed conflict, which also affects children around the world, including, for example, the kidnapping of 230 schoolgirls in Nigeria in April 2014 by the terrorist group Boko Haram.[42] Katherine Covell and Brian Howe describe violence against the child at an interpersonal level, including the effects of various toxic substances and experiences upon the child in utero, parenting styles, corporal punishment, abuse, intimate partner violence, and maternal depression.[43] For instance, abuse or neglect negatively affects children's physical, mental, and emotional well-being, potentially influencing them throughout their lives.[44]

Typical approaches to children and such issues as violence tend to focus on harm to individuals and less often on rights violations. Children's rights require a reorientation of our understanding of and responses to issues that face children. The boys and girls affected by the various aforementioned issues (and others) are not "problems";[45] they need opportunities to develop and grow, to participate, to be respected and protected. Jaap Doek explains that violence, for instance, "is not only morally and socially unacceptable, but a violation of her/his fundamental right to respect for and protection of her/his inherent human dignity and physical and mental integrity and to equal protection under the law."[46] Consequently, children's rights not only demand concern about children but also require responses to the issues they face. In order to be effective, these responses should include child participation, as discussed later in the chapter.

Implementation of children's rights falls primarily on parents, who help the child to exercise his or her rights. Only when parents fail does the state intervene directly, creating a relationship between the child and the state. The state can also intervene indirectly, by helping the parents to care for their child (for example, with financial help). Governments are the duty-bearers that must implement and respect their obligations to support children's rights. Moreover, policy makers, professionals, and practitioners need to understand children as rights-bearers. Thus, as examples, caregivers are obligated to report concerns about harm such as abuse and neglect, and governments should respond to domestic and international trafficking of children. The Canadian Coalition for the Rights of Children enunciates that full implementation of child rights not only reflects a moral and legal obligation but also represents a good economic and social investment.[47] They provide a valuable framework for guiding efforts to support progress with children and youth.

International cooperation is also important to support progress around the world, through resources, assistance and collaboration, and exchange of knowledge, and it can involve bilateral or multilateral assistance. Various areas of activity are valuable, including child rights awareness; child rights as a priority in the planning, policies, and programming of international cooperation; budgetary allocations and expenditures; technical assistance; and cooperation with civil society. For example, child soldiering has attracted much international attention and responses by various organizations, including naming a former child soldier, Ishmael Beah, as UNICEF Advocate for Children Affected by War, to support his awareness-raising about the devastating effects of armed conflict on children.[48]

In sum, children's rights have had significant impact. There is now greater awareness of children and their particular issues and concerns. Consequently, international child rights law and measures have been developed.

Convention on the Rights of the Child

In order to celebrate the International Year of the Child in 1979, the government of Poland proposed that the UN declaration be adopted as a convention on the rights of the child. There were several reasons for this proposal, as Van Bueren explains.[49] First, a convention would clarify international legal obligations for states, as declarations can be more voluntary; a convention would be internationally binding and inspire action. Second, existing international protection for children was spread across 80 different instruments, so there was a need for a comprehensive, consistent legal text. Third, there had been improvements in understanding about children since the 1959 declaration, including psychological needs and the right to express views. However, the effort to adopt a convention took much longer than the one year that the Polish government had expected. In fact it involved 10 years of negotiations among UN member states, with contributions from UN agencies and nongovernmental organizations (NGOs). This participatory approach is reflected in the resulting language, which recognizes those organizations' important implementation roles.[50] Because of the historically traditional approach to international human rights negotiations, children themselves were not included in the process.[51]

After the UN General Assembly's adoption of the Convention on the Rights of the Child (CRC) on 20 November 1989,[52] children's rights developed significantly in international law, beyond concerns for their protection and care. Although other international and regional instruments exist, the CRC is the primary tool for children's rights. The CRC inspires much progress beyond the legal sphere and advances understanding of how the child should be respected as a human being. The 195 states party to the CRC are obligated to implement it and to report regularly on their progress to the international treaty monitor, the UN Committee on the Rights of the Child (hereafter UN Committee). The only country that has not yet ratified or acceded to the CRC, for various reasons, is the United States.[53]

The CRC is the first international legal instrument to incorporate all five categories of human rights: civil, political, economic, social, and cultural rights. The CRC rights are often summarized as the "three Ps"—provision, protection, and participation—to reflect the various rights categories.[54] Similar to other international legal instruments, all rights in the Convention are understood as indivisible, interrelated, and interdependent; each is equally important and fundamental to the child's dignity. The CRC also involves domestic obligations and international cooperation.

Article 42 of the CRC requires that children and adults learn about these rights. Consequently, the Convention has inspired useful educational tools created by various organizations around the world, including a Jeopardy game—a youth version called Say It Right—and an online video.[55]

Contributions of the CRC

The CRC defines a child as "every human being below the age of eighteen years unless, under the law applicable to the child, majority is attained earlier."

As a child is always changing, the nature and scope of the "direction and guidance" to the child from caregivers should change over time, as article 5's principle of the evolving capacities of the child recognizes.

The UN Committee has designated four CRC articles as important general principles that are relevant to the implementation of all other CRC rights.[56] First, in article 2, non-discrimination requires that children's rights "not be hindered by discrimination or distinction of any kind." Discrimination is a significant issue for both individuals and groups of children around the world. For example, Canada's challenges are evidenced by the Canadian Human Rights Tribunal's consideration of claims that Aboriginal children are not receiving the same level of child protection services as non-Aboriginal children, which Canada's auditor general has confirmed.[57] Moreover, African-Canadian children also experience discrimination and are disproportionately affected by "issues such as poverty, literacy, health, education and criminal justice."[58] Non-discrimination is pertinent to all CRC rights for children around the world.

Second, in CRC article 3, the best interests of the child are "a primary consideration" in all actions concerning children. This principle has inspired a debate caused by tension between the exercise of autonomy and the duty of others to guide, care, and protect.[59] While there is no "fundamental conflict between parental rights and the rights of children," tensions often result "from different perspectives on what is in the best interests of children. In general, this understanding of the relationship between the rights of parents and the rights of children is upheld in Canadian law and Supreme Court decisions."[60] Nevertheless, confusion about this principle and the lack of consistency in decision making persist, highlighting the need for clarity in measures.

The third general principle, stated in article 6, is that survival and development should be ensured "to the maximum extent possible." In addition to supporting the child's right to life, physical and mental health and emotional, cognitive, social, and cultural development are necessary. According to the Canadian Coalition for the Rights of Children (CCRC), key issues include health inequities and socioeconomic conditions; early childhood development; prevention of abuse and neglect; mental health services; promotion of healthy living; and injury prevention.[61] Implementation of this provision must improve in the Canadian context.

The fourth general principle, in article 12, provides for the views of the child or child participation, as discussed later. These four general principles support full understanding of the scope of children's rights and should guide implementation and monitoring.[62]

CRC Implementation and Monitoring

After signing a treaty, states consider its requirements and determine their course of action. Ratification or accession means that the party agrees to be bound by the instrument's obligations. CRC article 4 specifies that "all appropriate legislative, administrative, and other measures" are necessary for implementation. As primary duty-bearers, states determine their own implementation. Governments should pursue various means of implementation, including constitutional or legislative provisions, case law, policies, programs, and practice.

The CRC's general measures of implementation, which the UN Committee has identified as a foundational part of the framework of action, provide guidance to states.[63] As Collins and Wolff outline, the CRC requires attention in the architecture of governance, both through governance structure and rights-based accountability and through law reform, national human rights institutions, budgeting, monitoring, child rights awareness, education, and training.[64] Even measures that may not seem related to children's rights, such as tax policy, often impact children. In this way the CRC has great implications for governance and for society as a whole.

Enforcement is based on *pacta sunt servanda*: "Every treaty in force is binding upon the parties to it and must be performed by them in good faith."[65] Progress is supported through the CRC's mandate for the UN Committee in article 44, which requires regular reporting by states parties. The Convention's specific provision for the role of other actors, including UNICEF and "other competent bodies," was revolutionary and provides for broad participation.[66] Many actors are important for implementation and monitoring, at various levels. For example, at the international level, the UN, UNICEF, and the Office of the High Commissioner for Human Rights advise and support the strengthening of the institutional capacity for domestic human rights around the world. At the regional level, inter-American, European, and African organizations make valuable contributions. At the domestic and local levels, actors include governments, civil society, the corporate sector, community organizations, and individuals. In Canada, for example, such organizations as the Canadian Council on Child and Youth Advocates, the CCRC, the First Nations Child and Family Caring Society, the African Canadian Legal Clinic are important.[67] These organizations and others provide essential insight into the situation of child rights within the jurisdiction. Consequently, the UN Committee is often described as a "monitor of monitors."[68]

Critiques of CRC

There are different critiques of children's rights. One common concern is a perceived tension with the family, and particularly parental rights. Some question, for example, whether "children need rights or that speaking in terms of 'rights' is even good for children."[69] Moreover, citing problems with disciplining children, violence, and cultural concerns, Akua Djanie believes that it is possible to "fall into the child rights trap."[70] Yet she also argues that "Our children have the right to be treated as human beings. They have the right not to be beaten, mentally, physically, or sexually abused." This understanding is essentially the goal of children's rights, which highlights some confusion. Despite misapprehensions, the CRC confirms the role of parents and the state in a child's life. Nevertheless, the child is "a subject, a person who is in the process of growing up [and] also has the right to decide" about his or her own welfare.[71] It must be enunciated that "child rights are not realized at the expense of the family."[72]

However, the text of the Convention has some weaknesses. In relation to armed conflict, the CRC inadequately protects child soldiers and civilians, a flaw—based on feasibility, not necessity—caused by CRC negotiation challenges. There is also inadequate detail with respect to child sexual exploitation and lack of a complaints mechanism. All three areas have since been strengthened by optional protocols to the Convention,[73] which require state ratification for them to be in force in a jurisdiction. This evolution reflects the ongoing development of child rights to reflect global demands for progress.

The Convention also has some other gaps, reflecting that it is an imperfect instrument. For instance, it does not include the issue of social media or medical experimentation on children, and it inadequately considers the role of the environment. But, while the CRC does not detail all these issues, its language is broad and flexible, much like a national constitution, in order to address the range of circumstances that children experience around the world and emerging issues.

Some may argue that there cannot be universal child rights in light of perceived conflict(s) with cultural, religious, and other considerations.[74] Freeman explains the challenge for some: "For the powerful, and as far as children are concerned adults are always powerful, rights are an inconvenience. The powerful would find it easier if those below them lacked rights. It would be easier to rule, decision-making would be swifter, cheaper, more efficient, more certain."[75] Yet children's rights are necessary in order to protect and support children; their rights should be balanced with those of others in relation to particular contexts in order to achieve the best outcome for all involved.[76]

The essential point is that children's rights can no longer be ignored in the decision making that concerns children.

Canada and the CRC

Canada is considered an international leader in children's rights. The country ratified the CRC on 13 December 1991; it then ratified the optional protocols on armed conflict and the sale of children in 2000 and 2005 respectively, both of which it helped to draft.[77] At the time of writing, however, Canada has yet to ratify the more recent optional protocol on communications.

Notwithstanding, the UN Committee reviewed Canada's progress with the Convention at its sixty-first session,[78] in late September 2012, and produced comments about Canada called "concluding observations."[79] The Committee noted that Canada has made progress in several areas, including ratification of the Convention on the Rights of Persons with Disabilities and the National Action Plan to Combat Human Trafficking;[80] these efforts make important contributions to support children's rights. The Committee also identified various concerns that Canada should address, including but not restricted to

- "all necessary measures" to address concerns from previous Committee reviews;
- discrimination affecting Aboriginal children, African-Canadian children, and other populations;
- violence against children;
- the role of business;
- assistance for parents and guardians and attention to children deprived of a family environment;
- mental health;
- child poverty;
- early childhood education and care;
- asylum-seeking and refugee children;
- economic exploitation;
- juvenile justice; and
- the sale, trafficking, and sexual exploitation of children.[81]

These recommendations highlight essential areas in which to advance children's rights in Canada.

This UN review was important to Canada for several reasons. It demonstrates how the CRC is a very significant elaboration and articulation of child rights. It also shows that CRC implementation remains a challenge even in a prosperous country like Canada: "In recognizing that they are holders of legal rights, the CRC has transformed the status of children, yet it has not sufficiently influenced ways in which governments promote and implement children's rights."[82] Public awareness and action are required for progress.

As we have shown, the Convention is a significant articulation of child rights. While there have been some criticisms and weaknesses, children's rights have advanced greatly around the world, thanks to the CRC. The next section considers some implications of children's rights.

When Children Know Their Rights

A CRC obligation in article 42 requires that adults and children alike be informed of child rights. While the frequency and depth of children's rights initiatives are not yet as universal or as widespread as they should be, it is important to recognize that child rights education among children occurs across a variety of political, economic, social, and cultural terrains. While child rights consultations remain relatively rare, recent efforts to respect children's rights both to be informed and to be heard have been taking place in both state and non-state domains.[83] When children themselves learn about their human rights, there is a great impact across far-reaching sectors, as the following discussion explores.

Positive Outcomes of Child Rights Education among Children

In this section we highlight the advantages of children's participation in child rights education. We shed particular light on children's learning and discoveries, on the benefits to children's personal development, and on children's agency and commitment to child rights. The examples below are based mainly on inclusive projects that we, as children's rights researchers, have undertaken with children[84] or on consultation processes that we have been affiliated with,[85] because we believe that consulting children about their rights is an essential practice when engaging in research and advocacy with children.

Children's Discovery and Awareness of Their Rights

As consultation-based research in Bolivia, Canada, Ireland, and South Africa has shown, rights-based education can provide children and youth with pivotal opportunities to become informed in meaningful and life-changing ways.[86] In fact, the discovery and use of international human rights instruments, including the CRC, by the very individuals (in this case, children) whose lives those standards are intended to protect and enhance can be a life-changing learning process, filled with encouragement, expectation, and engagement.[87] As the following quotations illustrate, young people's discovery of their rights can lead to significant, epiphany-like revelations.

> I see that the rights I have protect me and help in my life and that we all have the same rights. (Bolivian male, 16)
>
> I now know that people exist to help me make my rights respected. (Bolivian female, 17)
>
> [Child rights are the] most important rights of all, [because children] are going to have to deal with what comes next. (Irish male, 13)
>
> I have the right … to be treated like a human. (Canadian youth)[88]
>
> I was educated on laws that actually affect me … It was really an incredible experience that was so beneficial to me in the way I was educated and found a lot of encouragement. (Canadian youth)[89]

As children and youth have come to these rights-based realizations through supportive educational contexts, they have felt excited, grateful, and motivated about the possibilities opened up by such knowledge. The corresponding comfort and affirmation are highlighted below.

Benefits to Children's Personal Development

As the following quotations illustrate, children's and youth's awareness of their rights has the potential to equip them with greater confidence and capacity to address their own struggles and the plight of others.

> Now I consider that I am a somebody in life. (Bolivian male, 17)
>
> Before I was very negative with myself and I had very low self-esteem but now I do not. (Bolivian female, 15)
>
> I have learned to be conscious that I have a voice. (Bolivian female, 16)
>
> I feel more secure, and with more value and power to confront what comes. (Bolivian female, 17)

These comments demonstrate how learning about children's rights can engender feelings of self-worth and dignity among children. For some children, the esteem-building benefits derived from rights-based education and consultation serve as one of the few sources of comfort and strength they can draw upon to overcome adversity that they may encounter, in their present lives or in the future. Regardless of any rights-oriented reforms that may or may not be occurring on a structural level, children's personal moments of discovery of their rights and the resulting confidence-building must be recognized as worthwhile accomplishments in and of themselves, because of the ways in which they may help to sustain children's survival and success on a personal level. As the next section explores, the aforementioned rights-based empowerment can enable children to translate their new-found knowledge into action in pursuit of their rights.

Children's Agency and Commitment to Human Rights

The empowerment fostered by rights-based education and consultation among children enables young people to exercise their rights, and therefore to recognize their own capacities to think and act assertively and proactively in the protection of their rights. The following quotations reflect such rights-based progress on a personal level:

> I have a little more protection because I do not let anyone trample on my rights. (Bolivian male, 16)
>
> I feel more secure because now I have my rights respected and if someone violates them I can denounce them. (Bolivian male, 16)
>
> With my new knowledge, I can defend my rights. (Bolivian female, 14)
>
> I investigate more ... I analyze the problem and then I dialogue. (Bolivian female, 16)

Other researchers have observed similar progress among children and youth in other contexts throughout the world. For example, Patel and colleagues noted how a combination of traditional teachings and contemporary education furthered children's rights and protections, especially regarding sexual health in the context of war.[90] Similarly, Howe, Covell, and McNeil found that when children in England were made aware of their rights and responsibilities, there was a substantial decline in bullying and violent behaviours.[91] In that case, since violence in the school was viewed as a violation of human rights, children developed rights-based mechanisms to protect their own rights as well as those of their classmates. As we explore in the next section, such outcomes are consistent with many instances when children come to know their rights: they often attempt to safeguard the rights of others, not just their own.

Participation

When children know their rights and have gained courage and strength from that knowledge, they often express an interest in taking action in order to make a difference, both for themselves and for others. Accordingly, it is clear that participation is not an activity but a process.[92] Thus some children become involved on the social, political, and research levels in order to contribute to progress.

The Participation of Children in Social and Political Action

> Little people can do big jobs and you don't have
> to be a grown-up to make a difference.
> —*Ryan Hreljac*[93]

Ryan Hreljac's words[94] remind us that children are current, not futuristic, citizens who have both the capacity and the right to express their views, as well as to be given opportunities to be heard and to engage socially and politically—as provided by articles 12 to 15 of the CRC. Many child activists have exercised these rights in order to advance child rights within a variety of contexts. While Craig and Marc Kielburger[95] may be among the most renowned Canadian child rights activists, others such as Shannen Koostachin[96] and Wesley Prankard[97] must be recognized for their valuable contributions to indigenous children's rights within Canada. Still others, such as war-affected child rights and peace advocates Ishmael Beah, Grace Akallo, Mariatu Kamara, and Emmanuel Jal have worked to improve the lives of children distressed by conflict in Africa.[98] Most recently, renowned child and gender rights activist—and currently the youngest Nobel Peace Prize winner—Malala Yousafzai has inspired countless people to uphold children's, and especially girls', rights.[99]

While the efforts of renowned child activists are important to highlight because they represent ongoing sources of inspiration, we believe that it is essential to draw attention to lesser-known examples of children's engagement with human rights on social and political terrains. They also reveal much about how children exercise their rights in both informal and formal settings.[100] To this end, we feature a few examples below.

Various studies and initiatives among children from North and South America, Africa, and Europe shed light on children's capacities to contribute to political action and social programming. For example, while Quijada has drawn attention to active social agency among Latino youth in the United States,[101] Silva and Salles Souto's study on democracy and citizenship sheds light on the potential of youth social and political participation in Brazil.[102] Similarly, in her Brazilian study, Sapiro found that "One of the most impressive displays of children's political agency is found in Barra Mansa, Brazil, where children have been organized and involved in a series of projects in which they study and deliberate municipal budget issues in council and communicate their findings to the adult forums."[103] Thus meaningful children's participation can lead to political and social action at local, national and international levels.

Children's Commitments to Respecting the Rights of Others

It has been shown that when children are informed of their rights, they not only focus on their own gains but also become attentive to the rights and needs of others.[104] For example, in a participation-oriented project in Senegal, Maclure found that girls showed leadership in their efforts to inform themselves and others on issues of family violence, corruption, drug trafficking, forced marriage, and the sexual harassment of female workers.[105] Among children in South Africa, Cook and Du Toit observed similar effects, whereby rights-educated and dialogue-supported children showed a greater propensity to act as protagonists in actions aimed at improving their own and others' welfare.[106]

Comparably, the following statements, collected in Gervais's study among Bolivian youth, demonstrate more specifically how, for some children, this sensitivity to others' rights is born out of a realization that as citizens, children have both rights and responsibilities to others.

> I have many rights and just as many duties as a citizen. (Bolivian male, 16)
> I have a duty to respect. (Bolivian male, 13)
>
> Before I was always right and I was very egocentric; only my opinion mattered. Now I know that I have to respect the rights of other people. (Bolivian male, 17)

In Gervais's study, 96 per cent of the Bolivian boys reported significant changes in their understanding and attitudes about females.[107] A 17-year-old male explained the pro-equality change he had experienced as a result of his involvement with rights-oriented education: "I had a different vision about women's rights but with my participation in the workshops, I have come to understand that all that I had thought before was wrong because I thought that women did not have the same rights as men but now I know that it is not that way and that we all have the same rights." Other boys in the same study became focused on child rights: "I would like to get more of these human rights started because I do not want to listen anymore about abuses against children" (Bolivian male, 15).

Collins found similar attentiveness to other children's rights among Irish youth.[108] In a focus group, two 16-year-old females and one 17-year-old male expressed concern about the rights of other children affected by social distinctions that impede their effective participation in society: "We are all really well taken care of but if you look at other children of ethnic minorities ... they aren't as well taken care of by the government and by the constitution."

Similarly, in an atmosphere of both rights-based education and consultation during the 2012 Shaking the Movers conference, young Canadian participants exemplified their growing thoughtfulness about youth who were struggling with mental health concerns. A 16-year-old Canadian female participant expressed her commitment to advocacy: "I would like to start a program at my school where myself and other students in my school stand up for mental health and allow all students to come and talk to us if they need someone to talk to—it will be sort of like a hall monitor idea where we will be identified as a 'safe' person."[109]

Such statements are indicative of the impressive potential of rights-informed children and youth to initiate and support rights-oriented progress for other children, and they thus point to the importance of investing early in rights-based education and consultation among children.

The Participation of Children in Research

As children have human rights, they also have "the right to be properly researched."[110] However, in practice, researchers are not consistently respecting children. Research about children has been adversely affected by the objectification of children, whereby the emphasis has been placed on *what* rather than *who* children are.[111] Such objectification stems in part from adultism, which is "a belief system based on the idea that the adult human being is in some sense superior to the child or of greater worth, and thus the child, by default, inferior or of lesser worth. These beliefs find support in a persistent view of the child as an object, and not a human rights holder."[112]

When the adult perspective in research is superior, children can become the objects rather than the subjects of studies. This approach is problematic for children's rights; it manifests itself in a variety of ways, including state-based and expert-dominated studies that are conducted solely by adults and are thus devoid of children's input.[113] Thus it is essential to move beyond adult-generated views and presumptions about children's rights, which tend to analyze children as objects and intervene *for* children, but without dialoguing *with* children and obtaining input *from* children.[114]

Prioritizing children's voices ensures that it is they who define their views about and experiences with human rights, rather than have these considerations interpreted for and about them.[115] Listening to the voices of children within the research process corresponds with CRC expectations, including respecting children's rights to be heard (art. 12), to freedom of expression (art. 13), to freedom of thought (art. 14), and to provide input into decisions that directly affect their lives and are made in their "best interest" (art. 3). As the next section illustrates, such rights can be upheld when children are given opportunities to participate in research.

Participation-Oriented Children's Rights Research Practices

Many children's rights scholars take children's views seriously. In fact, for many researchers, children's views constitute the very subject of their studies.[116] They seek not only to respect children's rights but also to garner more accurate understandings of childhood.[117] Children's rights researchers draw on a variety of data collection methods in order to privilege children's voices and to respect their rights. Across a wide range of studies, children and youth have shared their views through in-person and online written surveys, oral interviews, focus groups, and action-oriented meetings, as well as through age-appropriate fun and safe activities.[118]

Children's rights research also coincides with the considerations of Mander, Pittaway, and colleagues that a study's participants are more than research subjects or statistics.[119] Rather, they are real, living people and capable research partners who deserve to be listened to and included fully in the research process. In an effort to ensure that the voices and experiences of children are central to the research, and out of respect for the potential of young participants to contribute to the generation of knowledge,[120] some researchers train child and youth participants to become leaders in the research process.[121] In these studies, participant-leaders have co-created research instruments and have assisted with recruitment for and facilitation of questionnaires and focus group sessions.[122] The involvement of participant-leaders has been found to improve the relevance, accessibility, and authenticity of the knowledge produced.[123]

Some researchers extend the opportunities for inclusion by involving children not only in collection of the data but also in its analysis and presentation. To this end, children give their opinion on how their own words are interpreted and prepare the results, either on their own or with the principal researchers, in a child-friendly manner.[124] Child participants' purposeful engagement in the research activities proves to be both educational and empowering for them; it not only values their views (art. 12) but also validates their capacities (art. 5) to enhance research.[125] By integrating children's leadership and participation in the research process, inclusive approaches not only adhere to the principle of respect for the views of the child, they also enable children to exercise their own rights.[126] Overall, child participation in research can yield more accurate understandings of childhood and children's rights, and consequently the research results and their implementation will ultimately be more effective.

As this section on participation has shown through children's voices, the greatest assets in efforts concerning young people are the children themselves. While they have diverse abilities and varied stages of commitment,[127] children are the vanguard of human rights initiatives.[128] When children are provided with sufficient information, rights-based support, and appropriate opportunities to participate, they become capable of sharing their knowledge and insights, empowered to increase understanding of their realities, and able to enhance various measures, including policies and programs intended to improve their lives.[129] While children often depend upon the adults around them to advance child rights,[130] it must be recognized that children's unquestionably significant contributions to human rights are a testament to the merit of investing early in rights-based education, consultation, participation, and research among children.

Conclusion

> We are not the sources of problems; we are the resources that are needed to solve them.
> We are not expenses; we are investments.
> We are not just young people; we are people and citizens of this world.
> Until others accept their responsibility to us, we will fight for our rights.
> We have the will, the knowledge, the sensitivity and the dedication.
> [...]
> We are the children of the world, and despite our different backgrounds, we share a common reality.
> We are united by our struggle to make the world a better place for all.
> You call us the future, but we are also the present.[131]

The necessity of implementing children's rights cannot be overemphasized. Children around the globe continue to face unrelenting and overwhelming adversity, including disease, poverty, illiteracy, malnourishment, homelessness, abuse, exploitation, and armed conflict.[132] Such conditions render children more vulnerable and jeopardize their rights,[133] particularly their needs-based rights.[134] As the children identify above, they are not so much "future concerns" as they are persons in the present, experiencing various issues that require effective response. Furthermore, studies have shown that the majority of children across the world are neither familiar with their rights nor aware of how to exercise them.[135] We must involve them in our efforts to redress the world's problems, as the children describe above.

In this light, the pursuit of children's rights remains an ongoing endeavour to which legal, political, social, economic, and human resources must be consistently allocated. Freeman explains their significance well: "Rights are important because they recognise the respect their bearers are entitled to. To accord rights is to respect dignity: to deny rights is to cast doubt on humanity and on integrity."[136] As this chapter has underscored, the dignity, humanity, and integrity of children must be the utmost consideration for all.

And, as the influential scholar John Eekelaar states in relation to the Convention on the Rights of the Child, children's rights are significant not only for children but also "for all people": "It would be a grievous mistake to see the Convention applying to childhood alone. Childhood is not an end in itself, but part of the process of forming the adults of the next generation. The Convention is for all people. It could influence their entire lives."[137] Thus it is up to all of us to respond, respect, and advocate children's rights.

Takeaway Messages

- Children are rights-bearers and citizens capable of participating in matters of concern to them.
- Child participation in research can support more accurate understandings of childhood and children's rights.
- Child participation in social and political action can lead to significant changes in the lives of other children.

Study Questions

- How have children's rights evolved over time?
- Why are children's rights significant?
- What is the difference between a declaration and a convention? What implication does this difference have in the international effort to uphold children's rights?
- How can children's rights influence children themselves?

Issues for Debate or Roundtable

- In light of John Eekelaar's aforementioned comment, how is the Convention on the Rights of the Child beneficial not only for children but for all people, and how can it influence people's entire lives?
- Following up on the insistence of some children's rights researchers that children should not only be consulted but also become co-disseminators

of research results in studies involving them, how could such an approach possibly counter children's rights?

Additional Reading

Canadian Coalition for the Rights of Children. *Right in Principle, Right in Practice: Implementation of the Convention on the Rights of the Child in Canada.* Ottawa: CCRC, 2011. http://rightsofchildren.ca.

Eekelaar, John. "The Importance of Thinking That Children Have Rights." In *Children, Rights and the Law*, edited by Philip Alston and Stephen Parker, 221–35. Oxford: Oxford University Press, 1992. http://dx.doi.org/10.1093/lawfam/6.1.221.

Freeman, Michael. "The Rights of Children Who Do Wrong," In *The Rights and Wrongs of Children.* London: F. Pinter, 1983.

Gervais, Christine. "From Education to Equality? Bolivian Adolescent Males' Understandings in the Wake of Gender Sensitivity Workshops." In *Children's Rights and International Development: Lessons and Challenges from the Field*, edited by M. Denov, R. Maclure, and K. Campbell (New York: Palgrave Macmillan, 2011), 175–92.

Hart, Stuart. "From Property to Person Status: Historical Perspective on Children's Rights." *American Psychologist* 46, no. 1 (January 1991): 53–59. http://dx.doi.org/10.1037/0003-066X.46.1.53.

Parliament of Canada, Senate Human Rights Committee. "Children: The Silenced Citizens—Effective Implementation of Canada's International Obligations with Respect to the Rights of Children. Final Report of the Standing Senate Committee on Human Rights." Ottawa: Parliament of Canada, April 2007. http://www.parl.gc.ca/Content/SEN/Committee/391/huma/rep/rep10apr07-e.pdf.

Pearson, Landon, and T.M. Collins. *Not There Yet: Canada's Implementation of the General Measures of the Convention on the Rights of the Child.* Florence: UNICEF Innocenti Research Centre and UNICEF Canada, 2009. http://www.unicef-irc.org/publications/pdf/canada_nty.pdf

United Nations. *Bulletin of Human Rights* 91, no. 2: *The Rights of the Child* (1992).

Websites

First Nations Child and Family Caring Society of Canada. "Shannen's Dream." http://www.fncaringsociety.ca/shannens-dream.

Funky Dragon (Children and Young People's Assembly for Wales). "UNCRC History." YouTube video, 5:09. Posted 1 June 2009. https://www.youtube.com/watch?v=bACQN4xFXlM.

UNICEF. "Ishmael Beah Calls for Protection of Children in Armed Conflict." YouTube video, 6:32. Posted 19 March 2012. http://www.youtube.com/watch?v=OljO2okPdb0.

Notes

1. "A World Fit for Us," a Children's Forum message drafted, debated, and agreed on by 400 child delegates, part of the United Nations Special Session on

Children, 8–10 May 2002, and delivered by children to the General Assembly of the United Nations on 8 May 2002, http://www.unicef.org/specialsession/press/cfmessage.htm.

2. S. Hart, "From Property to Person Status: Historical Perspective on Children's Rights," *American Psychologist* 46 (1991): 53–54.
3. United Nations, Convention on the Rights of the Child, UN Doc. A/RES/44/25, 20 November 1989, http://www2.ohchr.org/english/law/pdf/crc.pdf; United Nations Treaty Collection, Convention on the Rights of the Child, https://treaties.un.org/Pages/ViewDetails.aspx?src=TREATY&mtdsg_no=IV-11&chapter=4&lang=en.
4. Save the Children Canada, "Save the Children International," http://www.savethechildren.ca/international.
5. UN Documents, Geneva Declaration of the Rights of the Child, http://www.un-documents.net/gdrc1924.htm.
6. G.Van Bueren, *The International Law on the Rights of the Child* (Dordrecht, Netherlands: Martinus Nijhoff, 1998), 6.
7. Ibid., 7–8.
8. M.Wolins, Preface, in *Selected Works of Janusz Korczak*, trans. J. Bachrach (Warsaw: Scientific Publications Foreign Cooperation Center, 1967), 6–7, http://www.januszkorczak.ca/legacy/1_Introduction.pdf.
9. E.R. Codell, Introduction, in J. Korczak, *King Matt the First* (1923; reprint, London:Vintage, 2005), viii.
10. The Convention on the Rights of the Child is the only exception.
11. United Nations, International Covenant on Economic, Social and Cultural Rights, UN Doc. A/RES/2200 A (XXI), 16 December 1966. The ICESCR refers to families in articles 7(a)(ii), 10(1), 10(2), 11, and 13(3), and to children who require "special measures of protection and assistance" without discrimination, including protection from economic and social exploitation, access to education, and state support for the right to the highest standards of health in articles 10(3), 12, and 13.
12. United Nations, International Covenant on Civil and Political Rights, UN Doc. A/RES/2200 A (XXI), 16 December 1966. Further to provisions about families and parents, specific articles for children in the ICCPR pertain to juvenile justice; legal matters, including birth registration, name, nationality, and guardianship; and the right to protection, in articles 6(5), 10(2)(b) and 10(3), 14(1)(4), 23(4), and 24(1), (2), and (3).
13. United Nations, Convention on the Rights of Persons with Disabilities and Optional Protocol, UN Doc. A/RES/61/106, 13 December 2006, article 7, http://www.ohchr.org/EN/HRBodies/CRPD/Pages/ConventionRightsPersonsWithDisabilities.aspx. The Convention came into force on 3 May 2008.
14. United Nations, Declaration of the Rights of the Child, UN Doc. Resolution 1386 (XIV), 10 December 1959, http://www.ohchr.org/EN/ProfessionalInterest/Pages/CRC.aspx.
15. Van Bueren, *International Law*, 12n6.
16. G.Van Bueren, *International Documents on Children*, 2nd ed. (Amsterdam: Kluwer, 1998), xv.
17. ILO [International Labour Organization], Convention on Minimum Age (No. 138), 26 June 1973 (entered into force 19 June 1976); ILO, Convention Concerning the Prohibition and Immediate Action for the Elimination of the Worst Forms of

Child Labour (No. 182), 17 June 1999 (entered into force 19 November 2000). It is noted, however, that both children and researchers debate the ILO approach; see M. Bourdillon, D. Levison, W. Myers, and B. White, *Rights and Wrongs of Child Work* (New Brunswick, NJ: Rutgers University Press, 2010).

18. UNESCO, "Introducing UNESCO," http://en.unesco.org/about-us/introducing-unesco.
19. As examples, see UNICEF, "Human Rights-Based Approach to Programming: Introduction," 2014, http://www.unicef.org/policyanalysis/rights/; UNICEF, *The State of the World's Children 2014 in Numbers*, http://www.unicef.org/sowc2014/numbers/.
20. UNHCR, "Children," http://www.unhcr.org/pages/49c3646c1e8.html.
21. United Nations, Resolution 1261, UN Doc. SC/RES/1261, 1999.
22. Organization of American States, American Declaration on the Rights and Duties of Man, OEA/Ser.L/V.11.71, at 17, 1988, Res.30, 2 May 1948; American Convention on Human Rights (Pact of San José), OASTS 36, OAS Off.Rec.OEA/Ser.L/V/11.23, doc. 21, rev.6, 1979, 22 November 1969 (entered into force 18 July 1978); Council of Europe, European Convention for the Protection of Human Rights and Fundamental Freedoms, 213 UNTS 222; European Social Charter, 529 UNTS 89; ETS 35, 18 October 1961 (entered into force 26 February 1965); Organization of African Unity, African Charter on Human and Peoples' Rights, OAU Doc.CAB/LEG/67/3/Rev.5, June 1981 (entered into force 26 October 1986).
23. Organization of African Unity [now African Union], "African Committee of Experts on the Rights and Welfare of the Child," http://acerwc.org/; Council of Europe, "Building a Europe for and with Children," http://www.coe.int/t/dg3/children/.
24. UN Committee on Economic, Social and Cultural Rights, General Comment No. 13 (Twenty-First Session, 1999), Right to Education (article 13): "Compilation of General Comments and General Recommendations Adopted by Human Rights Bodies," UN Doc. HRI/GEN/1/Rev.4, 2000; United Nations, Convention on the Rights of the Child, UN Doc. A/RES/44/25, 20 November 1989, preamble, para. 1.
25. Hart, "From Property to Person Status," 55.
26. This language is affirmed in the preambles of various instruments, including the CRC and the Universal Declaration of Human Rights, UN Doc. A/RES/217 A (III), 10 December 1948, http://www.un.org/en/documents/udhr/.
27. See J. Eekelaar, "The Importance of Thinking That Children Have Rights," in *Children, Rights and the Law*, ed. P. Alston, S. Parker, and J. Seymour (Oxford: Oxford University Press, 1992), 221; M. Freeman, "The Rights of Children Who Do Wrong," in *The Rights and Wrongs of Children* (London: F. Pinter, 1983).
28. Van Bueren, *International Law*, chap. 1.
29. Ibid., 4.
30. Melton (1983b), cited in Hart, "From Property to Person Status," 55.
31. M. Freeman, "Why It Remains Important to Take Children's Rights Seriously," *International Journal of Children's Rights* 15 (2007), 8.
32. See Campaign 2000, *Canada's Real Economic Action Plan Begins with Poverty Eradication: 2013 Report Card on Child and Family Poverty in Canada* (Toronto: Family Service Toronto, 2013), 3, http://www.campaign2000.ca/reportCards/national/2013C2000NATIONALREPORTCARDNOV26.pdf.

33. Canadian Coalition for the Rights of Children [CCRC], *Right in Principle, Right in Practice: Implementation of the Convention on the Rights of the Child in Canada*, (Ottawa: CCRC, 2011), 32, http://rightsofchildren.ca/resources/childrens-rights.monitoring/
34. Canadian Centre for Policy Alternatives and Save the Children Canada, cited in Campaign 2000, *Canada's Real Economic Action Plan*, 3; C. Blackstock et al., cited in J. Rae, *Indigenous Children: Rights and Reality. A Report on Indigenous Children and the U.N. Convention on the Rights of the Child* (Ottawa: First Nations Child and Family Caring Society of Canada, 2006), 61, http://www.fncfcs.com/sites/default/files/docs/ISGReport.pdf.
35. Aboriginal peoples are described more specifically as Indian, Métis, or Inuit; Aboriginal rights are guaranteed by Canada's Charter of Rights and Freedoms (1982). See Canadian Council of Child and Youth Advocates [CCCYA], *Aboriginal Children: Canada Must Do Better—Today and Tomorrow*, 2011, 2, http://www.rcybc.ca/sites/default/files/documents/pdf/reports_publications/20111101_cccya_aboriginal_children.pdf.
36. CBC News, "Prime Minister Stephen Harper's Statement of Apology," 11 June 2008, http://www.cbc.ca/news/canada/prime-minister-stephen-harper-s-statement-of-apology-1.734250.
37. Parliament of Canada, Senate Human Rights Committee, "Children: The Silenced Citizens—Effective Implementation of Canada's International Obligations with Respect to the Rights of Children. Final Report of the Standing Senate Committee on Human Rights," April 2007, 170–71, http://www.parl.gc.ca/Content/SEN/Committee/391/huma/rep/rep10apr07-e.pdf.
38. UNICEF, *The State of the World's Children 2013: Children with Disabilities* (New York: UNICEF, 2013), 1. "Persons with disabilities include those who have long-term physical, mental, intellectual or sensory impairments which in interaction with various barriers may hinder their full and effective participation in society on an equal basis with others"; United Nations, Convention on the Rights of Persons with Disabilities, UN Doc. A/RES/61/106, 13 December 2006, article 1, http://www.un.org/disabilities/convention/conventionfull.shtml. The CRC identifies children with disabilities in article 23.
39. Cited in D. Hartas, *The Right to Childhoods* (London: Continuum Books, 2008), 24.
40. See the photo of a child in India tied to a post, International Disability and Human Rights Network, " Disability Is a Human Rights Issue," http://www.daa.org.uk/index.php?page=left-human-rights.
41. United Nations, *Report of the Independent Expert for the United Nations Study on Violence Against Children*, UN Doc. A/61/299 29, August 2006, 8, http://www.unicef.org/violencestudy/reports/SG_violencestudy_en.pdf.
42. F. Karimi and C. Carter, "Boko Haram: A Bloody Insurgency, a Growing Challenge," CNN World, 22 April 2014, http://www.cnn.com/2014/04/17/world/africa/boko-haram-explainer/index.html.
43. K. Covell and B. Howe, *Children, Families and Violence: Challenges for Children's Rights* (London: Jessica Kingsley, 2009).
44. K. Dorning, "Child Abuse and Neglect," in *A Safe World for Children*, ed. M. Gow (Monrovia, CA: World Vision, 2001), 17–27.
45. UNICEF, *State of the World's Children 2013*, 1.

46. J. Doek, "The CRC 20 Years: An Overview of Some of the Major Achievements and Remaining Challenges," *Child Abuse and Neglect* 33 (2009): 776.
47. CCRC, *Right in Principle*, 1.
48. UNICEF, "Ishmael Beah Calls for Protection of Children in Armed Conflict," YouTube video, 6:32, posted 19 March 2012, http://www.youtube.com/watch?v=OljO2okPdb0.
49. Van Bueren, *International Law*, 13–14.
50. M. Santos Pais, "The Convention on the Rights of the Child," in *Manual on Human Rights Reporting* (Geneva: United Nations, 1997), 495.
51. The negotiations for the more recent Convention on the Rights of Persons with Disabilities demonstrates the evolution of this process to a more participatory one, engaging states, NGOs, and advocates among others; United Nations Enable, "Frequently Asked Questions Regarding the Convention on the Rights of Persons with Disabilities," http://www.un.org/disabilities/default.asp?id=151#neg2.
52. 20 November is celebrated in Canada as National Child Day.
53. See J. Becker, "Dispatches: Will US Be Last to Endorse Child Rights Convention?" 26 November 2013, http://www.hrw.org/news/2013/11/26/dispatches-will-us-be-last-endorse-child-rights-convention.
54. B. Howe and K. Covell, "Child Poverty in Canada and the Rights of the Child," *Human Rights Quarterly* 25, no. 4 (2003): 1067–87. The CRC is also summarized by Van Bueren as having four Ps; *International Law*, 15.
55. See Children's Rights in Canada, https://jeopardylabs.com/play/childrens-rights-in-canada; CCRC, "Say It Right!" 2009, http://www.landonpearson.ca/uploads/6/0/1/4/6014680/say_it_right.pdf. Funky Dragon, "UNCRC History," YouTube video, 5:09, uploaded 1 June 2009, https://www.youtube.com/watch?v=bACQN4xFXlM.
56. UN Committee on the Rights of the Child, *Guidelines for Initial Reports of States Parties*, UN Doc. CRC/C/58, 1991, 3.
57. See First Nations Child and Family Caring Society [FNCFCS], "I Am a Witness: Canadian Human Rights Tribunal Hearing," http://www.fncaringsociety.ca/i-am-witness; FNCFCS, "Standing with First Nations Children to Achieve Culturally Based Equity," http://www2.ohchr.org/english/bodies/crc/docs/ngos/Canada_FNC_Caring_Society_of_Canada_CRC61.pdf; CCCYA, *Aboriginal Children*.
58. African Canadian Legal Clinic, "Disaggregated Data Collection (Race-Based Statistics): Policy Paper," 22, http://www.aclc.net/wp-content/uploads/Policy-Papers-1-11-English-FINAL.pdf; African Canadian Legal Clinic, "Canada's Forgotten Children," July 2012, http://www2.ohchr.org/english/bodies/crc/docs/ngos/Canada_African_Canadian_Legal_Clinic_CRC61.pdf.
59. Freeman, "Why It Remains Important," 14.
60. CCRC, *Best Interests of the Child: Meaning and Application in Canada* (CCRC, 2009), 17, http://rightsofchildren.ca/wp-content/uploads/bic-report-eng-web.pdf.
61. CCRC, *Right in Principle*, 42–43.
62. See T. Collins, "The Monitoring of the Rights of the Child: A Child Rights-Based Approach," PhD dissertation, University of London, 2007.
63. UN Committee on the Rights of the Child, "General Comment No. 5: General Measures of Implementation of the Convention on the Rights of the Child," UN Doc. CRC/GC/2003/5, 2003, http://tbinternet.ohchr.org/layouts/treatybody-external/Download.aspx?symbolno=CRC%2fGC%2f2003%2f5&Lang=en.

64. T.M. Collins and L. Wolff, "Canada's Next Steps for Children's Rights? Building the Architecture for Accountability Through the General Measures of Implementation of the CRC," in *Children Matter: Exploring Child and Youth Human Rights Issues in Canada*, ed. E. Murray (Calgary: Mount Royal University, 2012).
65. United Nations, Vienna Convention on the Law of Treaties, UN Doc. A/CONF. 39/26, 23 May 1969 (entered into force 27 January 1980), a.27.
66. Santos Pais, "Convention on the Rights of the Child," 495.
67. CCCYA, *Aboriginal Children*; CCRC, *Right in Principle*; FNCFCS, http://www.fncaringsociety.ca; African Canadian Legal Clinic, http://www.aclc.net.
68. T. Hammarberg, "The Work of the Expert Committee on the Rights of the Child," unpublished paper, UNICEF House, New York, 24 March 1993.
69. M. Guggenheim, *What's Wrong with Children's Rights?* (Cambridge, MA: Harvard University Press, 2005), xi; B.C. Hafen and J.O. Hafen, "Abandoning Children to Their Autonomy: The United Nations Convention on the Rights of the Child," *Harvard International Law Journal* 37 (1996): 449–91.
70. A. Djanie, "My Problem with Giving Children Their Rights" *New African*, May 2009, 52–53.
71. A. Lopatka, "Importance of the Convention on the Rights of the Child," in *The Rights of the Child*, Bulletin of Human Rights 91/2 (New York: UN Centre for Human Rights, 1992), 62.
72. See further in T.M. Collins, "International Child Rights in National Constitutions: Good Sense or Nonsense for Ireland?" *Irish Political Studies* 28, no. 4 (2013): 607, http://www.tandfonline.com/doi/full/10.1080/07907184.2013.838951.
73. United Nations, Optional Protocol to the Convention on the Rights of the Child on the Sale of Children, Child Prostitution and Child Pornography, UN Doc. A/RES/54/263, 25 May 2000 (entered into force 18 January 2002); United Nations, Optional Protocol to the Convention on the Rights of the Child on the Involvement of Children in Armed Conflict, UN Doc. A/RES/54/263, 25 May 2000 (entered into force 12 February 2002); United Nations, Optional Protocol to the Convention on the Rights of the Child on a Communications Procedure, UN Doc. A/RES/66/138, 19 December 2011 (entered into force 14 April 2014).
74. For example, see Djanie, "My Problem."
75. Freeman, "Why It Remains Important," 8.
76. This balancing is explored in M. Sengupta, "Human Rights and Cultural Difference: The Case of Sagarika Bhattacharya vs. Norway's Child Protection Services," Annual Conference of the International Studies Association, Toronto, 26 March 2014.
77. United Nations Treaty Collection, Chapter IV: Human Rights, https://treaties.un.org/pages/Treaties.aspx?id=4&subid=A&lang=en.
78. United Nations, CRC: Convention on the Rights of the Child, 61 Session (17 September 2012—5 October 2012), http://tbinternet.ohchr.org/_layouts/treatybodyexternal/SessionDetails1.aspx?SessionID=368&Lang=en.
79. UN Committee on the Rights of the Child, "Consideration of Reports Submitted by States Parties under Article 44 of the Convention: Concluding Observations – Canada, UN Doc. CRC/C/CAN/CO/3–4, 5 October 2012. Canada also submitted its first report on the optional protocol to the CRC on the sale of children, which the Committee responded to in specific concluding observations.
80. Ibid., 2.

81. Ibid., 2–21.
82. Collins and Wolff, "Canada's Next Steps," 15.
83. Article 42 of the CRC requires that "States parties undertake to make the principles and provisions of the convention widely known." However, many governments do not fulfill this responsibility. Fortunately, many nongovernmental and charitable organizations assume the responsibility to benefit children throughout the world. Improvements in child participation are occurring in some governments, courts, and civil society organizations at the municipal, national, and international levels (CCRC, *Right in Principle*), including consultation-based initiatives such as the City of Ottawa's Youth Summit Action Plan (http://ottawa.ca/en/youth-summit-action-plan); the national consultations for the UN Special Session; and conferences. On these last two, see Save the Children Canada, *A Canada Fit for Children: A Report on the Realities for Young People in Canada Today* (Toronto: Save the Children Canada, 2001); and G. Cockburn, *Meaningful Youth Participation in International Conferences: A Case Study of the International Conference on War-Affected Children* (Hull, QC: Canadian International Development Agency, 2001).
84. The examples from Bolivia are drawn from Christine Gervais's studies, based on data collected through written questionnaires and focus group sessions between June 2006 and October 2008 among 116 adolescent girls and 69 adolescent boys, aged 13 to 17, who were voluntary participants in a human rights training program in a women's community outreach centre in Cochabamba, Bolivia. For more information, see C. Gervais, "Boys Meet Girls' Rights: Bolivian Adolescent Males' Claims of Commitment to Gender Equality," *Children and Society* 26, no. 5 (2012); C. Gervais, "On Their Own and in Their Own Words: Bolivian Adolescent Girls' Empowerment Through Non-Governmental Human Rights Education," *Journal of Youth Studies* 14, no. 2 (2011). The quotations from Canada (except those from the "Shaking the Movers" conference), Ireland, and South Africa are affiliated with Tara Collins's studies, which involved a variety of approaches, including questionnaires, focus groups, and interviews with children and youth in various countries in order to ascertain their knowledge, garner their input, and respect their rights; see Collins, "Monitoring the Rights" and "International Child Rights." The quotations are drawn from different studies and reports, and not all reports included the participants' ages or sex; age and sex are thus provided based on available information.
85. As members of the Child Rights Academic Network who are involved in reviewing the annual "Shaking the Movers" conference, sponsored by the Landon Pearson Resource Centre for the Study of Childhood and Children's Rights, we also include quotations from the conference's youth participants.
86. Collins, "Monitoring the Rights"; Collins, "International Child Rights"; Gervais, "On Their Own"; Gervais, "Boys Meet Girls' Rights."
87. While its positive potential is being emphasized here, it is understood that the pursuit of human rights is often filled with struggles and that not all children involved in rights-based projects and research benefit, whether fully or partially, given the adversity they face. For more on the limitations, see Gervais, "On Their Own"; Gervais, "Boys Meet Girls' Rights"; R. Maclure, "The Dynamics of Youth Participation: Insights from Research Fieldwork with Female Youth in Senegal," in *Children's Rights and International Development: Lessons and Challenges from the Field*, ed. M. Denov, R. Maclure, and K. Campbell (New York: Palgrave-Macmillan, 2011), 155–73.

88. A. Del Monte and L. Akbar, *Shaking the Movers V. Divided We're Silent, United We Speak: Standing Up for Youth Justice. CRC Articles 37 and 40* (Ottawa: Landon Pearson Resource Centre for the Study of Childhood and Children's Rights, 2012), 19.
89. L. Akbar, *Shaking the Movers VI: Standing up for Children's Mental Health* (Ottawa: Landon Pearson Resource Centre for the Study of Childhood and Children's Rights, 2012), 31.
90. S. Patel, P. Spittal, H. Muyinda, G. Oyat, and N.K. Sewankambo, "The Wayo Program in Northern Uganda: Building on Traditional Assets in Supporting Acholi Young Women and Girls in the Context of War and HIV," in *Children's Rights and International Development: Lessons and Challenges from the Field*, ed. M. Denov, R. Maclure, and K. Campbell (New York: Palgrave Macmillan, 2011), 195–219.
91. K. Covell, R.B. Howe, and J.K. McNeil, "If There's a Dead Rat, Don't Leave It: Young Children's Understanding of Their Citizenship Rights and Responsibilities," *Cambridge Journal of Education* 38, no. 30 (2008): 334, 336.
92. T. Barber, "Participation, Citizenship, and Well-Being: Engaging with Young People, Making a Difference," *Young* 17, no. 1 (2009): 28.
93. E. Rubli, "A Very 'Beau' Christmas with Our Youngest Volunteer Yet!" Ryan's Well Foundation, 9 January 2014, https://www.ryanswell.ca/a-very-beau-christmas-with-our-youngest-volunteer-yet/.
94. Ryan Hreljac's statement is in keeping with the message from the 400 child delegates of the Children's Forum, "A World Fit for Us" (see note 1).
95. Founders of Free the Children, www.freethechildren.com.
96. The late Shannen Koostachin was a youth education advocate for First Nations children in Canada; http://www.fncaringsociety.ca/shannens-dream.
97. Wesley Prankard advocates the right to play (article 31 of CRC) for First Nations children in Canada; www.northernstarfish.org.
98. For more information on each advocate: Ishmael Beah, www.beahfound.org; Grace Akallo, www.africanwomenrights.org; Mariatu Kamara, http://www.unicef.ca/en/article/mariatu-kamara; Emmanuel Jal, http://emmanuel-jal.webs.com/warchildproject.htm.
99. Malala Fund, www.malala.org.
100. Gervais, "On Their Own"; Gervais, "Boys Meet Girls' Rights."
101. D. Quijada, "Reconciling Research, Rallies, and Citizenship: Reflections on Youth-Led Diversity Workshops and Intercultural Alliances," *Social Justice* 35, no. 1 (2008): 76–90.
102. I. Silva and A.L. Salles Souto, eds., *Democracy, Citizenship and Youth: Towards Social and Political Participation in Brazil* (London: I.B. Tauris, 2009).
103. V. Sapiro, "Not Your Parents' Political Socialization: Introduction for a New Generation," *Annual Review of Political Science* 7 (2004): 17–18.
104. Gervais, "On Their Own"; Gervais, "Boys Meet Girls' Rights"; Akbar, *Shaking the Movers VI*; Collins, "International Child Rights"; Maclure, "Dynamics of Youth Participation."
105. Maclure, "Dynamics of Youth Participation," 164.
106. P. Cook and L. Du Toit, "Circles of Care: Community-Based Child Protection in South Africa," in *Children's Rights and International Development: Lessons and Challenges from the Field*, ed. M. Denov, R. Maclure, and K. Campbell (New York: Palgrave Macmillan, 2011), 289.

107. Gervais, "On Their Own"; Gervais, "Boys Meet Girls' Rights."
108. Collins, "International Child Rights."
109. Akbar, *Shaking the Movers VI*, 16.
110. Knowing Children, *The Right to Be Properly Researched: How to Do Rights-Based, Scientific Research with Children* (Bangkok: Knowing Children, 2010), vol. 1, 12.
111. T.M. Collins, "Improving Research of Children Using a Rights-Based Approach: A Case Study of Some Psychological Research about Socio-economic Status," *Frontiers in Psychology* 3, art. 293 (2012): 1, doi: 10.3389/fpsyg.2012.00293. See such examples as T. Schapiro, "What Is a Child?" *Ethics* 109, no. 4 (1999): 715–38, http://www.jstor.org/stable/10.1086/233943; and W.S. Rogers, "What Is a Child?" in *Understanding Childhood: An Interdisciplinary Approach*, ed. M. Woodhead and H. Montgomery (Milton Keynes, UK: Open University, 2003).
112. H. Shier, "What Does Equality Mean for Children in Relation to Adults?" CESESMA Global Thematic Consultation, October 2012, 9, https://www.worldwewant2015.org/node/284010.
113. M. Santos Pais, "The Study of the UNICEF Innocenti Research Centre on the General Measures of Implementation of the Convention on the Rights of the Child," in *Rights of the Child: Proceedings of the International Conference*, ed. T. Collins et al. (Montreal: Wilson and Lafleur, 2008), 477–89; S. Harris-Short, "International Human Rights Law: Imperialist, Inept and Ineffective? Cultural Relativism and the UN Convention on the Rights of the Child," *Human Rights Quarterly* 25, no. 1 (2003): 130–81.
114. J. Amoah, "At the Crossroads of Equality: The Convention on the Rights of the Child and the Intersecting Identities of GRACE, an African Girl Child," in *Rights of the Child: Proceedings of the International Conference*, ed. T. Collins et al. (Montreal: Wilson and Lafleur, 2008), 313–37; T. Collins, "Monitoring: More Than a Report," in ibid., 1–14; Gervais, "On Their Own"; Gervais, "Boys Meet Girls' Rights"; B. LeFrançois and V. Coppock, "Psychiatrised Children and Their Rights: Starting the Conversation," *Children and Society* 28, no. 3 (2014): 165–71; Santos Pais, "Study of the UNICEF Innocenti Research Centre," 477–89; H. Shier, "Pathways to Participation: Openings, Opportunities and Obligations—A New Model for Enhancing Children's Participation in Decision-Making, in Line with Article 12.1 of the UN Convention on the Rights of the Child," *Children and Society* 15, no. 2 (2001): 107–17.
115. Amoah, "At the Crossroads of Equality."
116. For example, P. Cook and L. Du Toit, T. Collins, M. Denov, C. Gervais, and R. Maclure, among others.
117. Children are involved in research to varying degrees; not all researchers are fully inclusive; Shier, "Pathways to Participation," 107–17.
118. Cook and Du Toit, "Circles of Care"; Gervais, "On Their Own"; Gervais, "Boys Meet Girls' Rights"; Maclure, "Dynamics of Youth Participation"; Quijada, "Reconciling Research"; M. Ruiz-Casares, D. Rousseau, J. Morlu, and C. Browne, "Eliciting Children's Perspectives of Risk and Protection in Liberia: How to Do It and Why Does It Matter?" *Child and Youth Care Forum* 42 (October 2013): 425–37.
119. H. Mander, "'Words from the Heart': Researching People's Stories," *Journal of Human Rights Practice* 2, no. 2 (2010): 252–70; E. Pittaway, L. Bartolomei,

and R. Hugman, "'Stop Stealing Our Stories': The Ethics of Research with Vulnerable Groups," *Journal of Human Rights Practice* 2, no. 2 (2010): 229–51.

120. B. Mayall, *Towards a Sociology for Childhood: Thinking from Children's Lives* (Buckingham, UK: Open University Press, 2002); Save the Children, *So You Want to Involve Children in Research?* (Stockholm: Save the Children Sweden, 2004).
121. M. Denov and C. Gervais, "Negotiating (In)Security: Agency and Resistance among Girls Formerly Associated with Sierra Leone's Revolutionary United Front," *Signs* 32, no. 4 (2007): 885–910; Gervais, "On Their Own"; Gervais, "Boys Meet Girls' Rights"; Maclure, "Dynamics of Youth Participation."
122. Save the Children, *So You Want to Involve Children.*
123. Denov and Gervais, "Negotiating (In)Security"; Gervais, "On Their Own"; Gervais, "Boys Meet Girls' Rights"; Maclure, "Dynamics of Youth Participation."
124. Cook and Du Toit, "Circles of Care"; Maclure, "Dynamics of Youth Participation."
125. Denov and Gervais, "Negotiating (In)Security"; Gervais, "On Their Own"; Gervais, "Boys Meet Girls' Rights."
126. P. Alderson, *Young Children's Rights: Exploring Beliefs, Principles and Practice* (London: Jessica Kingsley, 2008); Save the Children, *So You Want to Involve Children*; N. Thomas, ed., *Children, Politics and Communication: Participation at the Margins* (Bristol, UK: Policy Press, 2009); C. Campbell and J. Trotter, "'Invisible' Young People: The Paradox of Participation in Research," *Vulnerable Children and Youth Studies* 2, no. 1 (2007): 32–39; UN Treaty Collection, Convention on the Rights of the Child.
127. S. Kaiser, "To Punish or to Forgive? Young Citizens' Attitudes on Impunity and Accountability in Contemporary Argentina," *Journal of Human Right* 4, no. 2 (2005): 171–96.
128. K. Campbell, M. Denov, R. Maclure, and I. Solomon, "Introduction," in *Children's Rights and International Development: Lessons and Challenges from the Field*, ed. M. Denov, R. Maclure, and K. Campbell (New York: Palgrave Macmillan, 2011), 1–14.
129. Maclure, "Dynamics of Youth Participation"; Mayall, *Towards a Sociology for Childhood*; Alderson, *Young Children's Rights*; Thomas, *Children, Politics and Communication.*
130. Campbell et al., "Introduction."
131. Children's Forum message (see note 1).
132. Campbell et al., "Introduction."
133. Cook and Du Toit, "Circles of Care"; Campbell et al., "Introduction."
134. Needs-based rights emphasize the importance of protecting children from conditions in which they are vulnerable; they are sometimes contrasted with capacity-based rights; see Campbell et al., "Introduction," 2. While we acknowledge the debate surrounding the alleged distinction between needs-based and capacity-based rights, we intend neither to raise nor to resolve it in this chapter.
135. As examples, see Patel et al., "The Wayo Program," and CCRC, *Right in Principle*, 9.
136. Freeman, "Why It Remains Important," 7.
137. Eekelaar, "Importance of Thinking," 234.

8
Age, Age Discrimination, and Ageism

THOMAS R. KLASSEN[1]

Learning Objectives

- To understand the extent to which age is used in public policy (for example, the legal age to engage in activities such as consuming alcohol, driving a car, and voting) and the impact of age-based restrictions in laws
- To appreciate the role of age in the labour market and workplace, and how laws and attitudes limit employment opportunities for members of particular age groups
- To comprehend the tensions between legislators and the courts, and between generations, that arise in considerations of age-based rights

Introduction

Chronological age is a key characteristic of individuals. The media often report the age of public figures such as athletes, politicians, performers, and criminals. Age is used to limit the rights of individuals to engage in a variety of activities, from getting married to drinking a glass of beer or voting in an election.[2]

Governments in Canada, and other nations, use age to determine when children must start elementary school and when teenagers and young people may have sex,[3] sign a contract, and many other activities. In later life, age determines eligibility for retirement pensions, old age security benefits, subsidized drug care, and keeping a driver's licence. The Canadian government uses a points system in selecting immigrants, with applicants between the ages of 18 and 35 being allocated 12 points, and those older than 35 receiving fewer points; no points are awarded as of age 47. As well, there is a separate youth justice system in Canada that applies to those aged 12 to 17 who get into trouble with the law.

The common use of age discrimination—denial of privilege or other unfair treatment based solely on chronological age—may seem at odds with laws such as the Canadian Charter of Rights and Freedoms. The Charter, in section 15, explicitly states "Every individual is equal before and under the law and has the right to the equal protection and equal benefit of the law without discrimination and, in particular, without discrimination based on race, national or ethnic origin, colour, religion, sex, *age* or mental or physical disability."[4]

Notwithstanding that the constitution prohibits discrimination based on age, this type of discrimination is widespread in Canada, in both laws and private contracts. Movie theatres offer lower-priced entry tickets to children and to those 65 or older. Public transit systems do the same. Some youth employment programs require that applicants be of a particular age to apply; the Canada Summer Jobs program, for example, accepts only those between the ages of 15 and 30. Some universities waive tuition for people who are 65 and older. Insurance companies charge more to insure young drivers than older ones, although they also charge more to insure very old drivers. The cost of private health insurance—such as for international travel—is significantly higher for some age groups than for others.

Using age to discriminate both for and against in programs, services, and contracts is permitted under the constitution: section 1 of the Charter allows limits on rights and freedoms that "can be demonstrably justified in a free and democratic society."[5] In other words, using age to discriminate is legal if there is a justifiable explanation or rationale.

Using age as a criterion—that is, discriminating against particular age groups—is usually justified on two grounds. First, limitations based on age are designed to encourage a particular activity among an age group because the activity is a public good, a benefit to society. Alternatively, they are used to prohibit or discourage an activity among an age group because the activity poses risks and dangers to individuals, as well as more widely. Laws prohibiting high school students (with some exceptions) from dropping out until reaching a specific age (usually 18) mean that all citizens have a basic level of formal education. On the other hand, placing age limits on activities such as access to bars, cars, cigarettes, and voting booths is also designed to protect the public good (such as users of roads, with respect to driver's licences), as well as reducing harm to individuals of a particular age group.

Second, giving preference in goods and services for some groups (such as the very young or old) reflects the fact that those groups typically have little or no employment income. For instance, elementary and high school students and those who are retired are not likely to work full-time (or even part-time); they may in fact be legally unable to earn employment income or may be physically incapable of driving. Thus, reduced public transit fares are thought to be fair. Free tuition for undergraduate programs for those 65 and older is justified in that it assists people who did not have the opportunity to study while young to do so later in life.

Age limits are not absolute; they change over time as politicians revise laws or as decisions of the courts interpret age-based rights. Nor are they uniform. Some jurisdictions (countries or sub-national jurisdictions) permit the consumption of alcohol at age 16, while others prohibit it until age 21. Some countries have no legal drinking age at all. In Canada the legal drinking age was 21 until the early 1970s, as was the voting age.

This chapter has three major objectives, each of which takes up a section of the pages that follow. The first objective is to analyze how age discrimination in employment, particularly in the form of mandatory retirement at age 65, has been legislated and interpreted by the Supreme Court of Canada. The case of mandatory retirement highlights many of the tensions between legislators and the courts—and between different generations—that arise in age discrimination in other contexts. The second objective of the chapter is to analyze illegal (rather than legal) age discrimination and how it arises from ageism. Third, the chapter examines how the social exclusion of some age-based groups has resulted in the recent rise of an age-based rights movement.

The chapter now turns to an examination of legal age discrimination in the workplace. Specifically, the next section analyzes several decades of jurisprudence and political debate on whether employees should be forced to retire at age 65.

Legal Age Discrimination in the Workplace

Where using age as a marker is most prominent—and most problematic—is in the workplace. This is because the right to work is one of the most fundamental human rights. Earning income from employment is critical for the economic security and well-being of the vast majority of Canadians.

Age discrimination in the workplace takes two forms. The first is legal discrimination, in that laws permit and require age-based distinctions. For instance, with certain exceptions, laws prohibit children under the age of 14 from being hired by employers, and employers are prohibited from employing children under the age of 16 during school hours. Students under the age of 18 can legally be paid a lower minimum wage than workers 18 and over.[6]

A more pervasive form of age-based discrimination is the illegal kind. For example, employers may refuse to hire someone who "looks too young" but not explicitly say so when turning away the applicant. Or an employer may pass over an older worker for computer training because "she's not going to get it," couching the decision as "There were only so many training spots." This type of discrimination is examined in the next section of this chapter.

Until recently the most widespread form of legal age discrimination in Canada was mandatory retirement at age 65—that is, using chronological age as the one and only marker to make decisions about employment. Mandatory retirement at 65 for reasons unrelated to workplace performance is clearly discriminatory, yet it was until recently legal.

When human rights laws, such as the Canadian Human Rights Act and provincial human rights statutes, were crafted during the 1960s and 1970s, protection from discrimination in employment was limited to those aged between 18 and 64.[7] Ontario's human rights code, enacted in 1962, stated in section 4(1) [now s. 5(1)], "Every person has a right to equal treatment with respect to employment without discrimination because of race, ancestry, place of origin, colour, ethnic origin, citizenship, creed, sex, sexual orientation, *age*, record of offences, marital status, same-sex partnership status, family status or disability."[8] The code then went on to define *age* for the purpose of section 5(1) as "an age that is eighteen years or more and less than sixty-five years."[9] In other words, employers were free to legally treat workers under 18 and those 65 and older in discriminatory ways: to pay them less, to terminate their employment, and more. This is why there is a lower minimum wage for employees under the age of 18. The most significant way in which employers treated those 65 and older was to terminate the employment of anyone who reached that age, regardless of the employee's performance and willingness to work.

When the human rights laws were initially written, legislators thought that individuals aged 65 and over would already be retired, and therefore not in need of human rights protection. Moreover, programs such as Old Age Security and pensions were available for those who attained that age, causing politicians to believe that older individuals would not need to work to earn income. Last, until recently there were few older workers and many young workers, because of the large "baby boom" generation born between 1946 and 1965. Politicians were of the view that limiting employment after 65 was reasonable public policy, as doing so would create more jobs for younger people. In any case, few people would be affected by mandatory retirement and the majority of those who reached 65 wanted to retire in any case.

The relatively few individuals who wanted to continue in their job past age 65 had no legal recourse, as the human rights laws (explained above in regard to employees in Ontario) were clear. However, the lack of legal recourse for those who were forced into involuntary retirement solely because of their age changed in the mid-1980s, when the Canadian Charter of Rights and Freedoms became law. As noted in the introduction of this chapter, section 15 of the Charter (enacted in 1982, but not in force until 1985) guarantees equality rights: "Every individual is equal before and under the law and has the right to the equal protection and equal benefit of the law without discrimination and, in particular, without discrimination based on race, national or ethnic origin, colour, religion, sex, age or mental or physical disability."[10]

As analyzed in other chapters in this volume, a momentous effect of the Charter was a substantial expansion and protection of individual rights with regard to same-sex marriage and sexual orientation. It seemed apparent that it was only a matter of time until the Supreme Court of Canada, using section 15 of the Charter, would also end arbitrarily forcing workers to retire at age 65 for no other reason than that they had reached that age. The Charter compels that all laws in Canada comply with its provisions, which the human rights laws such as Ontario's, at least with respect to employment, clearly did not.[11]

In the mid-1980s a group of university professors in Ontario who were being forced into retirement because they had reached the age of 65 initiated a constitutional or Charter challenge of mandatory retirement. They argued that the mandatory retirement policies of their universities, as allowed by the Ontario Human Rights Code, were contrary to section 15 of the Charter, which prohibited discrimination based on age. In other words, they argued that the specific wording of the Ontario code excluding those 65 and over from human rights protection was unconstitutional.

In 1990, in a startling decision, the Supreme Court of Canada ruled that, although the Ontario Human Rights Code was discriminatory on the basis of age, the law was justified by section 1 of the Charter as a "reasonable limit." Section 1 allows for limits on equality rights if they "can be demonstrably justified in a free and democratic society."[12] The majority of the judges on the Court argued that mandatory retirement at 65 was a feature of modern society and "part of the very fabric of the organization of the labour market in this country."[13] Moreover, the majority concluded that age discrimination is unlike other types of discrimination because "there is a general relationship between advancing age and declining ability," whereas no such correlation exists with any of the other specified grounds (race, colour, religion).[14] The judges argued that it is acceptable for politicians making laws to balance the competing needs of different generations, in this case to provide jobs for younger workers while stripping jobs from older workers.[15]

However, not all the judges on the Supreme Court agreed. The dissenting voices (the two female justices) took issue with the majority opinion. One wrote that mandatory retirement "operates to perpetuate the stereotype of older persons as unproductive, inefficient and lacking in competence … reinforcing the stereotype that older employees are no longer useful members of the labour force and their services may therefore be freely and arbitrarily dispensed with."[16] The other judge stated that mandatory retirement "is inconsistent with the fundamental values enshrined in [the Charter]: the protection and enhancement of human dignity, the promotion of equal opportunity, and the development of human potential based upon individual ability."[17] Interestingly, the average age of the Supreme Court judges who made this ruling was 65, and three were older than that, as the mandatory retirement age for Supreme Court judges is 75.

The ruling that age discrimination in employment, in the form of mandatory retirement at age 65, was legal could not be further appealed, as decisions of the Supreme Court are final. Therefore, mandatory retirement continued to be practised by nearly all employers in Canada. The only possibility for change, as the Supreme Court pointed out in its decision, was for politicians to rewrite human rights and employment legislation to protect the rights of workers 65 and over.[18]

By the late 1990s, as the first cohort of baby-boomers was reaching their 50s, more and more stories about mandatory retirement, similar to the one illustrated below, appeared in the mass media and public domain.

> A woman returned to employment in her 50s, after having raised a family, as a result of marital breakdown. Her employer did not have a mandatory retirement policy; however, one was instituted as she was approaching age 65. She retired on a very inadequate pension and her request to keep working in a situation that would enable her to still contribute to the pension was denied. However, after retirement, she returned to work with the same employer on a contract basis. She was no longer entitled to contribute to her pension, is no longer eligible for paid vacation and has no job security.[19]

The United Nations declared 1999 the International Year of Older Persons, in recognition of worldwide demographic trends that showed an aging population in many countries, the result of families having fewer children than in the past and people living longer. In 2000 a Canadian federal government review of human rights legislation recommended that mandatory retirement be further studied and that changes be made to the legislation.[20] The Ontario Human Rights Commission, after an extensive study in 2001, recommended elimination of compulsory retirement at age 65 and extension of protection from discrimination based on age to workers 65 and older.[21] Also in 2001, the British Columbia Court of Appeal called on the Supreme Court of Canada to reconsider its landmark 1990 decision. The British Columbia court observed that "the extent to which mandatory retirement policies impact on other equality rights, and on the mobility of the workforce, have become prominent social issues."[22]

Starting in Ontario in 2005, provincial legislators across Canada began passing amendments that extended full human rights protection to employees of 65 and over. This was done by simply deleting a few words in the human rights code. For example, in Ontario the human rights code definition of *age* as "an age that is eighteen years or more and less than sixty-five years" was changed to read "'age' means an age that is 18 years or more."[23] This banned mandatory retirement at age 65, because employers could no longer treat workers 65 and older differently from those aged 18 to 64. When the Ontario government introduced the change in legislation, it stated that the reason was to

> give all citizens the right to choose when they want to leave the workplace. This legislation is a simple acknowledgement of what we already know: Skills, ability, commitment and drive do not suddenly evaporate when somebody turns 65. In fact, in many cases employees are forced to leave a long-time job they love, only to take their years of experience and skills to a new and unfamiliar employer or organization. There have been many cases in Ontario where organizations and educational facilities have lost valued employees through this long-standing and, let's face it, rather archaic policy.[24]

Workers in industries under federal jurisdiction, such as commercial airlines, were the last for whom contractual mandatory retirement was outlawed. Under the Canadian Human Rights Act it was "not a discriminatory practice if an individual's employment is terminated because that individual has reached the normal age of retirement for employees working in positions similar to the position of that individual."[25] However, in 2011 the federal government deleted the quoted portion of the Act, which eliminated mandatory retirement for workers under its jurisdiction; the change came into effect in December 2012. During debate on the change in the House of Commons, the government noted:

> We are eliminating the mandatory retirement age for federally regulated employees in order to give older workers the option of staying in the workplace. We know that Canadians are healthier and they are living longer than ever before in our history. In economically difficult times, older workers sometimes want to choose to stay working for another year or two and make some extra money for their families or for themselves in their retirement. This contributes to economic growth. Older workers have a great deal to contribute and our government is giving them the go-ahead.[26]

The long and tortuous process of eliminating arbitrary age-based discrimination in employment in Canada, which had started in the mid-1980s, was at last completed after more than a quarter century.[27]

A worry about abolishing forced retirement raised by some younger people was that youth unemployment would increase, with recent graduates finding it more difficult to make the transition from school to work. That is, by increasing protection for older workers and permitting those who wished to be employed longer to keep working, there would be fewer jobs available for younger workers. A similar argument was used to resist the entry of large numbers of women into the labour market for fear that they would take jobs from men. Another variation of this argument claims that immigrants arriving in Canada reduce the number of jobs available for those already in the country because immigrants take jobs away from non-immigrants.

However, the assertion that an older person's remaining in a job results in denying a job to a younger person is referred to as the "lump of labour" fallacy—an assumption that the number of jobs in an economy is finite.[28] In fact the opposite happens: having more people employed creates more jobs in the economy. For example, having more women employed resulted in the economy's creating many new jobs, from daycare workers to auto mechanics, because women earning employment income spent the money they earned on goods and services. In the same manner, newly arrived immigrants and their children create new jobs for teachers and many others.

The Organisation for Economic Co-operation and Development (OECD) has concluded that "The idea that public policy can re-shuffle a fixed number of jobs between workers of different ages is simply not true."[29] Nevertheless, the argument that older workers keep jobs from youth continues to have currency among many, especially since it has intuitive appeal. This argument also highlights (as the Supreme Court of Canada noted) that because everyone grows old, there is a tendency to see age-related questions not in terms of individual rights—such as the right of a worker to retain her job—but rather in terms of group rights and claims.

The events recounted above illustrate that banning age-based discrimination in employment in the form of mandatory retirement was undertaken by politicians largely for reasons that have little relation to human rights. Rather, they revised the laws because of political and demographic pressures: more older people than ever before (most of whom vote), who did not want to be told to retire at age 65, and comparatively fewer younger people (who are less likely to vote). In other words, politicians were reacting to the demands and interests of voters, a large number of whom were growing older. Moreover, legislators acted to initiate more flexible retirement policies, conceived by the OECD as part of a broader "ageing society strategy" that allows people as they grow older to lead productive lives, make choices, and enjoy economic freedom.[30]

Although most Canadians no longer face an arbitrary employer-imposed retirement date, this does not mean that employers cannot influence retirement decisions. Employers can offer legal incentives, such as a one-time bonus ("Here's $10,000 if you retire this year!") that workers can obtain only if they retire. For instance, an employer could provide a bonus for employees who retire at age 62 but not for those who retire at 63 or later. In addition, as has always been the case, those who are self-employed face no imposed retirement age.

Finally, employers still have recourse to setting a mandatory retirement age when it is integral to the duties of a job. This is called a "good faith occupational qualification" or "bona fide occupational requirement." To set a specific age for retirement, employers have to demonstrate that the age-based requirement or qualification is integral to the job and that an employee could not be accommodated without causing undue hardship to the employer. For example, since 1957 Air Canada has required its pilots to retire at 60, a policy that was supported by the union representing the pilots. This age was set because older pilots were thought to be unable to fly safely. As a result, Air Canada pilots who reached 60 would often then begin employment with airlines based in the United States or other nations that set 65 (or higher) as the mandatory retirement age, sometimes flying the same routes as Air Canada.

A long-standing legal dispute, which lasted more than eight years, began in 2006, pitting Air Canada and its pilots' union against a group of pilots who had their employment terminated as a result of reaching the age of 60.[31] The legal case was still underway as of late 2014, although the revision of the Canadian Human Rights Act in 2012 meant that the airline and the union had to make reforms.[32] At present there must be at least one pilot under 60 in the cockpit at all times, but the other pilot may be above that age; most important, pilots over 65 cannot fill the position of captain.[33] This too may change as further human rights tribunal and court cases challenge these age-based rules, especially since all Air Canada pilots 40 and over undergo medical exams twice a year and annual flight-simulator testing.

A few employers continue to enforce mandatory retirement at age 65, couching this as a "voluntary" policy. Most notably, Unifor—Canada's largest private-sector union—requires that its employees (not the workers it represents) retire at age 65, on the flawed assumption that doing so ensures generational change.[34] When Unifor employees who are forced to retire at 65 take a complaint to a human rights tribunal, the union settles privately, before a legal judgement is made. In this way it retains an archaic and discriminatory practice that would be found unconstitutional if a human rights tribunal or court were to rule on it.

A few employment positions in Canada continue to have bona fide occupational retirement ages. Judges must retire at 70 or 75, depending on the court, while members of the Senate of Canada must retire at age 75. Elected politicians do not face mandatory retirement. Firefighters may also have a mandatory retirement age, usually 60, legally imposed on them.[35] Other occupations that continue to have age-based retirement rules include police officers, school bus drivers, and certain members of the armed forces.

Last, the Supreme Court of Canada recently ruled that partners in a business, such as a law firm or accounting office, can be forced to retire at a predetermined age. The case arose when a partner at a law firm in Vancouver refused to retire at the age of 65, as required by his firm's mandatory retirement policy. The Supreme Court stated that partners are not employees but rather part-owners of a business, and thus are not protected from discrimination in employment under human rights laws. In other words, only employees are protected, not owners (or part-owners).[36]

The review above illustrates that although discrimination based on age, with regard to retirement, has been considerably reduced in the past decade and more rights of older individuals are protected, debates continue. Human rights and protection from discrimination are not set in stone; rather they evolve over time as broad trends in society change, such as demographics, attitudes, and political pressures, as well as judicial decisions.

Illegal Discrimination and Ageism

As outlined in the previous section, until the past decade the most common form of legal age discrimination in the workplace in Canada was mandatory retirement at age 65. More prevalent, however, both in the workplace and beyond—and far harder to observe—is illegal discrimination. This type of discrimination often arises from ageism. Ageism is the "process of systematic stereotyping and discrimination against people because they are old, just as racism and sexism accomplish this for skin colour and gender."[37] In other words, ageism is the construction of negative images of and attitudes toward older people, based solely on chronological age, which then results in discrimination.

Ageism works in three steps. First, prejudicial attitudes arise toward aging or older persons, the aging process, and old age. Second, these attitudes result in discriminatory practices against aging and older people. Last, the practices are institutionalized (made part of everyday policies, rules, and laws), which then perpetuates the stereotypes against older people. For example, in 2013 the police force in the city of Sudbury, Ontario, urged residents to anonymously report poor driving by senior citizens, as part of a safe-driving initiative. Critics quickly pointed out that driving ability is a matter of skill, not age, and that targeting older drivers was unfair. That is, the police force appeared to have a stereotypical view of older drivers as being more prone to accidents or careless driving than other drivers. Responding to the criticisms, the police apologized and amended the initiative to target all drivers rather than focusing solely on the elderly.

Ageist attitudes arise when all people who have reached a particular milestone such as retirement or a specific age (such as 65) are seen as substantially different from younger individuals. The result is negative stereotypes about the skills, roles, and lifestyles of older and retired people, expressed in policies such as mandatory retirement. Prejudicial attitudes can arise from the mass media and popular culture, such as in portrayals of older people and advancing age on birthday cards, the roles given to older actors in Hollywood films, or widely held views about older people and driving.

In employment environments, older workers as a group are often viewed as being not technology-savvy, unwilling to learn, and less physically attractive. Negative stereotyping of older persons as rigid, incapable of learning, or lacking creativity has an impact on how they are perceived by managers and colleagues.[38] These attitudes translate into behaviours by employers (and younger co-workers) such that older workers are denied the same opportunities as younger people, forced to retire before they are ready, rejected for employment on the basis of their age, and streamed into lower-paid, short-term temporary or volunteer jobs. Negative stereotypes of older workers are further fuelled by mass media stories that focus on intergenerational conflict, such as "greedy geezers" selfishly staying longer in jobs at the expense of younger workers.[39]

Illegal age discrimination is, by its very nature, difficult to observe and thus to bring to light. For instance, a group of older female workers who were hired to hand out samples in stores made a human rights complaint alleging that they were let go from their jobs to make way for younger female workers.[40] In such cases it can be impossible to obtain evidence in organizational records and documents that the employer's decision was due to ageism. Similar obstacles arise when attempting to prove ageism in hiring, promotion, scheduling of hours, training, and other aspects of the employer–employee relationship.

To combat ageism and the negative stereotyping of older persons, emphasis has shifted to changing attitudes in the first instance, rather than behaviours. For example, the World Health Organization (WHO) launched an "active aging" campaign to showcase aging as "a positive experience."[41] Active aging policies are meant to safeguard older people's participation in the social, labour market, economic, cultural, spiritual, and civic spheres.

Canadian governments have embraced active aging in policy shifts such as eliminating age-based retirement. A criticism of the active aging policies is that although they are designed to combat ageism, over time they could generate detrimental stereotypes that older people must remain active and make contributions to society. In other words, passivity and inactivity, and even relaxation and leisure, would be seen as wasteful and unhealthy.[42] Such a stereotype could stigmatize older persons who remain largely at home, who are disabled, or who may have no interest in being active (as defined by the active aging paradigm).

Besides active aging policies, the rights of older persons are receiving more attention than ever before. This is often referred to as a rights-based approach to aging. The WHO, the United Nations, and national organizations—such as AARP (formerly the American Association of Retired Persons) in the United States and CARP (formerly the Canadian Association of Retired People) in Canada—are increasingly advocating for the rights of older people. In 2002 the United Nations adopted a plan that commits governments around the world to link aging to social and economic development and human rights.[43] The Office of the High Commissioner for Human Rights (part of the United Nations) and other groups underscore that age discrimination is a reality in the lives of many older people. Moreover, these groups also stress that age-related discrimination is often compounded by other discrimination, such as that based on disability, sex, socioeconomic status, or ethnicity.

The recent emphasis on the human rights of and legal protection for older individuals is partly explained by demographic trends. More people, especially those that are part of the baby-boom generation, are reaching their 60s and are thus more likely to experience age discrimination, or at least to become aware of aging-related matters. The baby-boom generation is also a group that over the past several decades has led the fight for rights and equality in regards to gender, race, ethnicity, and sexual orientation. Consequently, it is not surprising that the baby-boomers will be especially active in combatting ageism.

Social Exclusion and an Age-Based Rights Movement

The most extreme (but not uncommon) form of ageism is social exclusion: deprivation and lack of access to social activities and networks, causing reduced or poor quality of life for people of a particular age group. Older individuals are particularly prone to lacking social relationships—contact with family and friends—along with having limited access to services and activities such as health care, finance, and cultural outlets.

In 2012 the Law Commission of Ontario concluded that some laws contain stereotypes of older persons and sometimes fail to consider the experience of older adults.[44] Its report notes that ageist and paternalistic attitudes are a cause of elder abuse both within families and in institutions such as long-term care facilities. The Commission found in its research that for many individuals, a heightened sense of insecurity was associated with aging:

> This insecurity was associated with a sense of diminished control over circumstances. Individuals expressed anxiety about their finances once an exit from the labour force reduced their ability to respond to losses or increased needs, their ability to maintain independence as their health and abilities declined, their ability to retain control over their life and maintain dignity in the face of well-intended paternalism or serious illness, and whether they would continue to be treated with respect and consideration as age advanced.[45]

To combat social exclusion, there are calls for an age-based or elders' civil rights movement, which would lessen such insecurity.[46]

The rise of a rights-based movement echoes other civil rights movements of the past 60 years that reduced discrimination based on gender, race, and sexual orientation.[47] Such a movement recognizes that because of the unique features of aging, age discrimination is "often treated differently, and more negatively, as opposed to the other grounds of unlawful discrimination, such as sex, race and disability."[48] The differential treatment of "old age," or "age discrimination," under human rights laws extends well beyond Canada. For example, the United Nations Universal Declaration of Human Rights does not include age as a legally prohibited distinction. Other seminal UN documents, such as the International Bill of Human Rights, also fail to mention older people.

The UN has adopted conventions (binding in international law) to protect particular groups, such as the 2006 Convention on the Rights of Persons with Disabilities, the 1979 Convention on the Elimination of All Forms of Discrimination Against Women, and the 1965 International Convention on the Elimination of All Forms of Racial Discrimination. There is currently ongoing discussion—but by no means agreement—that a United Nations (that is, international) convention or treaty to protect the human rights of older people is needed. In 2014 the United Nations appointed its first independent expert on the human rights of older persons. This was recognition of the 700 million people in the world aged 60 years and over in 2014, a number that will double by 2025. The argument for a UN convention on the rights of older people is that it "would establish touchstones for legal protection of the rights of older people which are routinely violated."[49] To be effective, especially in protecting the right to employment for older workers, such a convention would need to

> recognize the rights of older workers by including: heightened protections against age discrimination; recognition of the contribution of older workers; heightened job protection to prevent older people from being pushed out of the workplace through harassment; the right to ongoing education and on-work training to allow older workers to adapt to changing technologies and working environments; and flexible and part-time working rights to accommodate sickness or disability.[50]

International treaties would help to align the laws across countries to prevent age discrimination, which currently vary considerably from nation to nation, especially with regard to employment.[51] For example, in some nations such as South Korea, employees can be involuntarily retired, for no reason other than chronological age, at almost any age an employer chooses, even in their mid-40s. Until recently it was legal in South Korea for employers to refuse to hire workers who were older than their early 30s. Similar practices—some legal, others not, but widely practised—are found in other nations.

However, the focus on the rights of older people (whose numbers are increasing) should not obscure the fact that in some cases children and young people are also not protected from discrimination based solely on their age. For example, the Criminal Code of Canada states "Every schoolteacher, parent or person standing in the place of a parent is justified in using force by way of correction toward a pupil or child, as the case may be, who is under his care, if the force does not exceed what is reasonable under the circumstances."[52] In 2004, in response to a constitutional challenge to this section of the Code (which allows adults to strike children), the Supreme Court of Canada ruled that it does not violate the Canadian Charter of Rights and Freedoms.[53] The majority of the Court concluded that the law as written does not infringe on a child's rights to security of the person or to equality, and does not constitute cruel and unusual treatment or punishment.[54] Not all nine justices agreed, however; one wrote that the law "encourages a view of children as less worthy of protection and respect for their bodily integrity based on outdated notions of their inferior personhood."[55]

The degree to which children should be treated differently under human rights legislation, and other laws, is complex. Most people would agree "with the principle that children should, say, benefit from extra safeguards against sexual exploitation because of their specific vulnerability in respect of capacity and consent. On the other hand, when does different treatment unjustifiably interfere with a child's rights?"[56] For example, why should workers under the age of 18 have a lower minimum wage and fewer human rights protections in the workplace than those 18 and over? Similarly, should the voting age be lowered to 16, on the grounds that youth are well able to participate in the electoral process, and indeed should do so to ensure their rights are protected?[57] The case of Canada's corporal punishment legislation raises difficult questions about age discrimination, not unlike those discussed earlier in this chapter about mandatory retirement and laws affecting older persons.

Conclusion

As this chapter has outlined, age shapes how others are perceived and treated, such as how they are addressed, or assumptions about their knowledge of popular culture or technology, or even how loudly one speaks to them.[58] Age is not the only characteristic that influences attitudes toward others. For instance, gender, ethnic background, religion, and other attributes of individuals and groups are important in shaping interactions as well. However, age is different, as pointed out by the Supreme Court of Canada, in that (barring an early death) all individuals will enter the state of old age. That is, old age "is a characteristic that, if we are fortunate, will come to each of us."[59] The same is not the case for other characteristics or markers of personal identity, in that not all individuals will become female or pregnant or members of a particular racial, religious, or ethnic group.

Like other forms of discrimination, discrimination based on age reveals multifaceted aspects of modern societies. Ageism and age discrimination are increasingly important public policy matters in Canada, and in other nations, because of rapid population aging. The "age-quake" or "silver tsunami" caused by the large baby-boom generation entering old age will certainly raise more and more human rights matters related to age discrimination, ageism, and social exclusion. Many of these questions and associated debates, as this chapter has proposed, will raise complex questions about intergenerational equity and claims to resources such as health care by members of different generations.

Although ageism is widespread, a focus on the rights of only one age group, such as the elderly, is improper and will only reinforce intergenerational tensions. Rather, as this chapter suggests, the rights of children and youth, and indeed those of other age groups, must also be considered and protected. Age will remain a fundamental characteristic of individuals throughout their life course; this very fact, if no other, demands that age discrimination and ageism receive increased attention from legislators, judges, and citizens.

Takeaway Messages

- Age discrimination is a complex issue, and so is the manner in which legislators and the courts must balance conflicting rights and claims, especially in the context of rapid population aging.
- Age discrimination has to a large extent been treated differently by the courts, in contrast to discrimination based on other grounds such as race, because aging is something that everyone experiences.

Study Questions

- Is age discrimination different from discrimination based on other grounds, such as disability, gender, or ethnic background? Why?
- In making laws, legislators are guided by the preferences of voters as expressed at the ballot box. With a rapidly aging population in Canada, do you think politicians will pass laws that favour the elderly (for example, by granting this group more rights and services) at the expense of the young? Would any such laws represent a violation of human rights?

Issues for Debate or Roundtable

- If you were hiring a new employee, would you choose a person aged 25, 45, or 65? Why?
- You are hiring a new employee and have a choice between two candidates with equal skills and qualifications. Which of the following characteristics will put one candidate at a disadvantage? Why?
  - the candidate's age
  - the candidate's skin colour or ethnic origin
  - the candidate's physical disability
  - the candidate's expression of religious belief (such as wearing a visible religious symbol)
  - the candidate's gender
  - the candidate's sexual orientation
- Do you agree that "elder rights" is the next civil rights movement? Why?

Additional Reading

Cotter, Anne-Marie Mooney. *Just a Number: An International Legal Analysis on Age Discrimination*. Aldershot, UK: Ashgate, 2008.

Posthuma, Richard A., and Michael A. Campion. "Age Stereotypes in the Workplace: Common Stereotypes, Moderators, and Future Research Directions?"

Journal of Management 35, no. 1 (26 October 2007): 158–88. http://dx.doi.org/10.1177/0149206308318617.

Scharf, Thomas, and Norah C. Keating, eds. *From Exclusion to Inclusion in Old Age: A Global Challenge*. Bristol, UK: Polity Press, 2012. http://dx.doi.org/10.1332/policypress/9781847427731.001.0001.

Websites

Advocacy Centre for the Elderly. http://www.advocacycentreelderly.org/.

CARP (formerly Canadian Association of Retired People). http://www.carp.ca/.

Debate.org. http://www.debate.org/opinions/should-there-be-a-maximum-age-restriction-for-licensed-drivers.

Ontario Human Rights Commission. http://www.ohrc.on.ca/en/code_grounds/age.

Notes

1. The author is most grateful to Devika Goberdhan, an MA candidate at York University, for her assistance in completing this chapter.
2. In most provinces in Canada, only people 16 and over can get married, and those under 18 need written consent from both parents. The minimum age at which individuals can purchase and consume alcohol is 19 in all provinces but Alberta, Manitoba, and Quebec, where it is 18. The voting age in Canada is 18.
3. In Canada the age of consent for sexual activity is 16 years (it was raised from 14 years in 2008). However, 14- or 15-year-olds can consent to sexual activity with a partner, as long as the partner is less than five years older and there is no relationship of trust, authority, or dependency or any other exploitation of the young person. Moreover, 12- and 13-year-olds can consent to sexual activity with another young person who is less than two years older and with whom there is no relationship of trust, authority, or dependency or other exploitation of the young person.
4. Canadian Charter of Rights and Freedoms, s. 2, Part I of the Constitution Act, 1982, being Schedule B to the Canada Act 1982 (UK), 1982, c. 11.
5. Ibid.
6. These requirements apply in the province of Ontario; other provinces have similar regulations. Some provinces, such as Alberta, British Columbia, and Manitoba, allow a child of at least 12 years of age to work and require written consent from the parent or guardian. For more details, see J. Lewko, K. Hall, G. Egeh, et al., *Current Health and Safety Policies Protecting Young Workers in Canada* (Sudbury: Center for Research in Human Development, Laurentian University, 2011). http://onf.org/system/attachments/49/original/Young_Worker_Policy_Review.pdf.
7. Saskatchewan introduced Canada's first human rights act in 1947, with the remainder of provinces doing so between 1962 (Ontario) and 1975 (Quebec). The federal government introduced the Canadian Human Rights Act in 1977.
8. Ontario Human Rights Code, RSO 1990, c. H.19.
9. Ibid., s. 9(a) [now 10(a)].
10. Charter of Rights and Freedoms, s. 2.

11. M.D. Lepofsky, "The Canadian Judicial Approach to Equality Rights: Freedom Ride or Roller Coaster?" *Law and Contemporary Problems* 55, no. 1 (1992): 167–99.
12. Charter of Rights and Freedoms, s. 2.
13. Supreme Court of Canada, *McKinney v. University of Guelph*, [1990] 3 S.C.R. 229, at 235.
14. Ibid., at 97.
15. T.R. Klassen and T. Gillin, "Legalized Age Discrimination," *Journal of Law and Social Policy* 30, no. 2 (2005): 35–51.
16. Supreme Court of Canada, *McKinney*, at 413.
17. Ibid., at 424.
18. Specifically the Court wrote that to find mandatory retirement in violation of the Charter would be to "impose on the whole country a regime not forged through the democratic process but by the heavy hand of the law"; *McKinney*, at 238.
19. Ontario Human Rights Commission, *Time for Action: Advancing Human Rights for Older Ontarians* (Toronto: Ontario Human Rights Commission, 2001), 30.
20. Canadian Human Rights Review Panel, *Promoting Equity: A New Vision* (Ottawa: Canadian Human Rights Review Panel, 2000).
21. Ontario Human Rights Commission, *Time for Action.*
22. British Columbia Court of Appeal, *Greater Vancouver Regional District Employees' Union v. Greater Vancouver Regional District*, (2001) B.C.C.A. 435, at 127.
23. Ontario Human Rights Code, s. 9(a) [now 10(a)].
24. Bill 211, An Act to Amend the Human Rights Code and Certain Other Acts to End Mandatory Retirement, 2d sess., 38th Legislature, 2005, S.0. 2005, C.29.
25. Canadian Human Rights Act, R.S.C. 1985, ch.15.
26. Canada, *House of Commons Debates*, 5 October 2011.
27. Mandatory retirement now applies only to employees in New Brunswick who are members of a pension plan.
28. J.R. Kesselman, "Challenging the Economic Assumptions of Mandatory Retirement," in *Time's Up: Mandatory Retirement in Canada*, ed. C.T. Gillin, D. MacGregor, and T.R. Klassen (Toronto: James Lorimer, 2005), 161–89.
29. Organisation for Economic Co-operation and Development [OECD], *Pensions at a Glance: Retirement-Income Systems in OECD and G20 Countries* (Paris: OECD, 2011).
30. OECD, *Reforms for an Ageing Society* (Paris: OECD, 2000), 126.
31. See Fly Past 60, http://www.flypast60.com/about.htm.
32. Air Canada is regulated by the federal government rather than by a province, hence the case falls under federal human rights jurisdiction.
33. Vanessa Lu, "Air Canada Pilots Can Continue Flying Past Age 60 under New Rules," *Toronto Star*, 24 January 2013, http://www.thestar.com/business/2013/01/24/air_canada_pilots_can_continue_flying_past_age_60_under_new_rules.html.
34. Unifor Constitution, 7, www.unifor.org/sites/default/files/attachments/unifor_constitution.pdf.
35. See, for example, *Corrigan v. Mississauga (City)*, 2013 H.R.T.O. 1313.
36. *McCormick v. Fasken Martineau DuMoulin LLP*, 2014 SCC 39, [2014] 2 S.C.R. 108.
37. R.N. Butler and M. Lewis, *Aging and Mental Health: Positive Psychosocial Approaches* (Oxford: C.V. Mosby, 1973), 34.
38. H. Dennis and K. Thomas, "Ageism in the Workplace," *Generations* 31, no. 1 (2007).

39. M. Powell, "What Do Newspapers Say about Older Adults in the Workforce?" in *Ageism and Mistreatment of Older Workers: Current Reality, Future Solutions*, ed. P. Brownell and J.J. Kelly (New York: Springer, 2013), 49–68.
40. S. Pigg, "Women File Age Discrimination Complaint against Metro, Sample Company," *Toronto Star*, 20 August 2012, http://www.thestar.com/business/2012/08/20/women_file_age_discrimination_complaint_against_metro_sample_company.html.
41. World Health Organization [WHO], *Active Ageing: A Policy Framework* (Geneva: WHO, 2002), 12.
42. D.J. Ekerdt, "The Busy Ethic: Moral Continuity Between Work and Retirement," *Gerontologist* 26 (1986): 239–44.
43. Adopted at the Second World Assembly on Ageing, Madrid, Spain, April 2002; see United Nations, *Political Declaration and Madrid International Plan of Action on Ageing*, http://undesadspd.org/Portals/0/ageing/documents/Fulltext-E.pdf.
44. Law Commission of Ontario, *A Framework for the Law as It Affects Older Adults: Advancing Substantive Equality for Older Persons Through Law, Policy and Practice* (Toronto: Law Commission of Ontario, 2012).
45. Ibid., 59.
46. See, for example, N.A. Kohn, "The Lawyer's Role in Fostering an Elder Rights Movement," special issue, *William Mitchell Law Review* 49 (2010).
47. N.A. Kohn, "Keynote Address. Elder Rights: The Next Civil Rights Movement," *Temple Political and Civil Rights Law Review* 21, no. 2 (2012): 321–28.
48. M. Sargeant, "Ageism and Age Discrimination," in *Age Discrimination and Diversity: Multiple Discrimination from an Age Perspective*, ed. M. Sargeant (Cambridge: Cambridge University Press, 2011), 10.
49. I. Doron, B. Brown, and S.B. Somers, "International Protection for the Human Rights of Older People: History and Future Prospects," in *Ageism and Mistreatment of Older Workers: Current Reality, Future Solutions*, ed. P. Brownell and J.J. Kelly (New York: Springer, 2013), 175.
50. Ibid., 177.
51. J.N. Lahey, "International Comparison of Age Discrimination Laws," *Research on Aging* 32, no. 6 (2010): 679–97.
52. Criminal Code of Canada, s. 43.
53. *Canadian Foundation for Children, Youth and the Law v. Canada (Attorney General)*, [2004] S.C.C. 4.
54. The Supreme Court stated that the use of force must be sober and reasoned and used to restrain or express symbolic disapproval. Furthermore, force cannot be used with children under the age of two or those with particular disabilities. Force cannot be used when a child is 13 or over, cannot involve objects such as rulers or belts, and cannot be applied to the head. The Court also specified that the use of force must be transitory, must not harm or degrade the child, and must not be based on the gravity of the wrongdoing. Last, the ruling stated that corporal punishment is unreasonable in schools but teachers can use force to remove students from classrooms or secure compliance with instructions.
55. *Canadian Foundation for Children, Youth and the Law v. Canada (Attorney General)*, [2004] S.C.C. 4, at para. 232.
56. S. Flacks, "Youth Justice Reform: Redressing Age Discrimination Against Children?" *Youth Justice* 12 (2012): 31.

57. A number of countries have lowered the voting age to 16, including Argentina, Austria, and Brazil, while proposals to do so are on the agenda in several other nations.
58. A.J.J. Cuddy and S.T. Fiske, "Doddering but Dear: Process, Content, and Function in Stereotyping Older Persons," in *Ageism: Stereotyping and Prejudice Against Older Persons*, ed. T. Nelson (Cambridge, MA: MIT Press, 2004), 3–26.
59. Sargeant, "Ageism and Age Discrimination," 7.

9
Aboriginal Rights: The Right to Self-Government versus the Right to Self-Determination

GORDON DIGIACOMO AND TRACIE SCOTT

Learning Objectives

- To learn the difference between the right of self-government and the right of self-determination
- To learn the details of a leading Canadian example of Aboriginal self-government

In one of his post–prime ministerial writings, Pierre Trudeau wrote, "Throughout our negotiations with the aboriginal peoples, we refused to talk about 'self-determination,' and only envisaged the possibility of 'self-government' on condition that a heterogeneous population might still live in a given territory."[1] Trudeau thus distinguished between self-government and self-determination and stressed that Canada could accommodate Aboriginal demands to the extent that they were consistent with the meaning of self-government. But what is self-government, and how does it differ from self-determination? These are the questions that this chapter tries to address.

The chapter unfolds as follows: After this introduction, it briefly discusses Aboriginal rights and treaty rights. The next sections focus on the meaning of self-determination and of self-government. The final section, by far the lengthiest, provides a detailed explanation of and commentary on what may be considered a leading example of Aboriginal self-government in Canada, namely the agreement negotiated by the federal government, the Government of British Columbia, and the Nisga'a Nation of BC.

Aboriginal rights are protected by sections 25 and 35 of the Constitution Act, 1982. Section 25, which is part of the Charter of Rights and Freedoms, ensures that nothing in the Charter can abolish or detract from the Aboriginal or treaty rights set out in the Royal Proclamation of 1763 or that now exist in treaties or land claims agreements or that may be acquired in new land claims agreements. Section 35, which is outside the Charter, affirms what is contained in section 25, defines who Aboriginal people are, and makes clear that Aboriginal and treaty rights are guaranteed to both male and female persons. It also provides that Aboriginal representatives have the right to participate in federal–provincial discussions on proposed constitutional amendments that may affect them. Because section 35 is outside of the Charter, it is not subject to section 1, the provision that allows governments to restrict rights in a reasonable way if they can advance a demonstrable justification.

Aboriginal Rights and Treaty Rights

Aboriginal rights are "rights held by aboriginal peoples, not by virtue of Crown grant, legislation or treaty, but 'by reason of the fact that aboriginal peoples were once independent, self-governing entities in possession of most of the lands now making up Canada.'"[2] More specifically, *Aboriginal rights* refers to activities that are based on the practices, customs, or traditions that, prior to European contact, were integral to the distinctive culture of the Aboriginal group claiming the right.

Thomas Isaac defines treaty rights as "those rights expressly set out in treaties and agreements, or subsequently inferred as a result of judicial interpretation, between Aboriginal people and the Crown."[3] Section 35 of the Constitution Act, 1982, recognizes existing Aboriginal and treaty rights. Further, the section recognizes treaty rights that may be acquired by way of land claims agreements. Examples of treaty rights include the right to hunt, fish, and trap. Because of the constitutional reform in 1982, treaty rights are legally enforceable and cannot be unilaterally altered by the federal government. The difference between Aboriginal rights and treaty rights is summed up by Patrick Monahan as follows: "Whereas Aboriginal rights flow from the historic use and occupation of land by Aboriginal peoples, Treaty rights are those contained in official agreements between the Crown and Aboriginal peoples."[4] So, while Aboriginal rights may be very similar to treaty rights, the source of the rights differs.

When we talk about Aboriginal and treaty rights, we are talking mostly about the relationship between Aboriginal peoples and the land. And when we talk about this relationship, the issue of Aboriginal title arises. As former chief justice Antonio Lamer wrote in *Van der Peet*, "Aboriginal title is a sub-category of Aboriginal rights which deals solely with claims of rights to land."[5] *Aboriginal title* refers to the right to use and occupancy of land historically occupied by an Aboriginal group. Justice Lamer elaborated in *Delgamuukw*: "Aboriginal title is a right in land and, as such, is more than the right to engage in specific activities which may be themselves Aboriginal rights. Rather, it confers the right to use land for a variety of activities, not all of which need be aspects of practices, customs and traditions which are integral to the distinctive cultures of Aboriginal societies."[6]

So if an Aboriginal group can show that it occupied an area as an organized society prior to European contact, it can claim Aboriginal title. If the group was nomadic, it need only show that some activity or practice or tradition taking place on the land was integral to its culture. It will then have demonstrated an Aboriginal right to engage in that practice or custom. Aboriginal title is recognized in the Royal Proclamation of 1763. It was also recognized by the Supreme Court of Canada, in the *Calder* ruling,[7] as well as in *R. v. Guerin*.[8] In *Delgamuukw*, the Supreme Court identified the criteria needed to claim Aboriginal title:

1. prior to the British assertion of sovereignty, the land must have been occupied by the ancestors of the Aboriginal group claiming title;
2. continuity between existing and pre-sovereignty occupation must be demonstrated when existing occupation of lands in question is being offered as proof of pre-sovereignty occupation; and
3. at the time of sovereignty, the occupation by the Aboriginal group must have been exclusive.[9]

It should be noted that, even if an Aboriginal title claim is demonstrated, this does not mean that the land in question is beyond the reach of the federal and provincial governments. Both levels may infringe Aboriginal rights, including Aboriginal title, if the infringement is "in pursuit of a valid legislative objective that is compelling and substantive" and if the infringement is consistent with the fiduciary or trust relationship that the federal and provincial governments have with the Aboriginal nations.[10]

The Right of Self-Government and the Right of Self-Determination

Many commentators use the terms *self-government* and *self-determination* interchangeably. When some commentators and writers say "self-government," they actually mean self-determination, while others do the reverse.[11] This chapter makes a distinction, since the objectives of the exercise of each right are quite different.

In a nutshell, self-government is what, for instance, the provincial governments of Canada possess and exercise. Self-determination, on the other hand, is what a secessionist party such as the Parti Québécois seeks. A politically self-governing people possesses an array of powers that enable their political leaders to make decisions on issues of key importance to the

Figure 9.1 Continuum of Power

self-government	self-determination

people who elected them. However, that self-governing people remains subject to the constitution, including its bill of rights, of the larger entity.

Self-determination, on the other hand, refers to independence, to complete sovereignty, to the power of political leaders to make decisions on all matters. The entity does not share power with another jurisdiction (unless it chooses to), and its sovereignty is recognized internationally. We may think of self-government and self-determination as being at the opposite ends of a continuum of power, as expressed in Figure 9.1. The more a government moves to the right side of the continuum, the more power and jurisdiction it acquires.

The Right of Self-Determination

In recent years there has been renewed scholarly interest in the right of self-determination and the right of secession, a development that Donald Horowitz also noted in a 2003 article.[12] Further, there appears to be an emergent scholarly tolerance for the secessionist option. For instance, Gregory P. Marchildon, a prominent scholar based at the University of Regina and a former senior public servant in the government of Saskatchewan, has referred to Canada, Belgium, Spain, and the United Kingdom as postmodern federations; one of the characteristics of postmodern federations, in his view, is that they are constantly struggling to construct alternatives to secession, partition, and violence. He writes that "there are no guarantees concerning the future and it seems possible, perhaps even likely, that certain sub-states in these postmodern federations will eventually attain the status of associated states if not fully independent states in the future."[13]

Similarly, Gagnon and Iacovino write "Multinational democracies must live with the prospect of potential secession because of the imperative of self-government rights (self-determination), the dictates of popular sovereignty and democracy, and the fact that citizens are entitled to debate the boundaries of their political communities."[14] In yet another article, Susanna Mancini, a scholar of international law at the University of Bologna, discusses the right of secession and the relationship between it and constitutionalism. Her basic argument is that, whatever one may think of the right of secession, it is prudent for states to develop a constitutional procedure for secession in order to avoid its worst excesses and possibilities. She speculates that international law may be "moving toward the legitimization of the 'secessionist option,' albeit only if it is compatible with democratic standards."[15]

These authors speak of secession in somewhat facile terms. They do not offer legitimate justifications for the breakup of an existing state, nor do they elaborate on the enormous difficulties associated with secession, including the possibility that a secessionist province or state may itself have to face secessionist pressures.

For some Aboriginal leaders, the key objective was—and perhaps still is—self-determination. For instance, a former national chief of the Assembly of First Nations, Ovide Mercredi, once stated, "We will not allow some other society to decide what we can do and determine the limits of our authority."[16] It is not hard to understand why some Aboriginal leaders (and others) would hold to this position and seek to exercise the right of self-determination. As Jennifer Dalton notes, "prior to Crown sovereignty, Aboriginal peoples were treated as sovereign nations capable of governing themselves according to their own laws and customs."[17]

Realistically speaking, no government of Canada could accept the kind of relationship that is suggested in Mercredi's comment and that would flow from Dalton's observation. And, in fact, support for an Aboriginal right to self-determination—meaning sovereignty—is not substantial. Peter Russell puts the issue this way:

> Though it is difficult to see a principled reason for denying that an Aboriginal nation's right to self-determination includes the right to secede and form its own independent state, as a practical matter there are few Aboriginal leaders or groups with separatist aspirations. Most of those Canadians who have a strong identity with an Aboriginal people also have a Canadian identity. The attachment of Aboriginal peoples to Canada may be based as much on economic prudence as patriotic sentiment, still it means they should be able to satisfy their demand for autonomy within the Canadian nation-state.[18]

The vast majority of Aboriginal communities tend to support some sort of self-government arrangement.

However, prominent scholar Kiera Ladner, a political science professor at the University of Manitoba, takes a harder line than many people, including many Aboriginal leaders. Ladner believes in Aboriginal peoples' right to self-determination. And by self-determination, she does in fact mean full sovereignty for Aboriginal nations. Ladner espouses what she calls "treaty federalism," or what James Tully called "treaty constitutionalism." Treaty federalism, Ladner writes, "is an agreed on framework for the mutual co-existence of two sovereign entities within the same territory."[19] Treaty federalism is different from the kind of federalism that governs Canada: "Treaty federalism, as distinct from provincial federalism, refers to the federal (nation-to-nation) relationships established in the treaties and the division of powers that emerged from these agreements."[20]

Ladner goes on to say that

> modern treaty federalism envisions a renewed nation-to-nation relationship, and a re-constitution of Indigenous polities as sovereigns within their own spheres of influence and jurisdiction and as co-sovereigns within their traditional territories. This is not significantly different from what was agreed to in the treaties, for no First Nation ever agreed to cede, abdicate, or share their internal sovereignty with the representatives of the Crown. Rather, the Crown agreed that it would not interfere with the "Indian way of life," except to provide assistance in the areas stipulated by the treaty.[21]

Ladner espouses this type of arrangement because "Indigenous peoples are not citizens of Canada, they are citizens of nations with the powers and jurisdiction implicit in nationhood."[22] Further, she argues, "Indigenous peoples are nations; they are not subordinate levels of government. Canadian governments cannot dictate the terms and conditions of Aboriginal governance, just as Indigenous peoples cannot dictate the terms and conditions of Canadian governance."[23] Current self-government agreements and models, in her view, perceive Aboriginal governments as inferior or subordinate governments exercising a limited array of delegated powers. For Ladner, agreements on power-sharing should be seen as agreements between sovereign nations.

The Right of Self-Determination in International Human Rights Instruments

Canada is a signatory to numerous international treaties, two of which are the International Covenant on Civil and Political Rights (ICCPR) and the International Covenant on Economic, Social, and Cultural Rights (ICESCR). Article 1 of the ICCPR states, "All peoples have the right of self-determination. By virtue of that right they freely determine their political status and freely pursue their economic, social and cultural development." Article 3 states, "The States Parties to the present Covenant [...] shall promote the realization of the right of self-determination, and shall respect that right, in conformity with the provisions of the Charter of the United Nations." Articles 1 and 3 of the ICESCR are identical to those of the ICCPR.

Adopted in the mid-1960s, the Covenants, through articles 1 and 3, were intended to support the independence movements of colonized peoples, particularly those in Africa. However, they were not adopted to encourage the dismemberment of existing states. Thus, at the 1993 World Conference on Human Rights, organized by the UN and held in Vienna, the delegates affirmed the right of self-determination of peoples but also declared that the right "shall not be construed as authorizing or encouraging any action which would dismember or impair, totally or in part, the territorial integrity or political unity of sovereign and independent States [...] possessed of a Government representing the whole people belonging to the territory without distinction of any kind" (Part 1, art. 2).

Article 3 of the UN Declaration on the Rights of Indigenous Peoples affirms that "Indigenous peoples have the right to self-determination. By virtue of that right they freely determine their political status and freely pursue their economic, social and cultural development." But here too a caveat was inserted. Article 46 states, "Nothing in this Declaration may be interpreted as implying for any State, people, group or person any right to engage in any activity or to perform any act contrary to the Charter of the United Nations or construed as authorizing or encouraging any action which would dismember or impair, totally or in part, the territorial integrity or political unity of sovereign and independent States." In other words, the Declaration supports the Aboriginal pursuit of self-government but denies that self-government means secession or full sovereignty.

In its Secession Reference the Supreme Court of Canada discussed the scope of the right of self-determination. It surveyed several international instruments, including the two international covenants referred to earlier. The Court concluded,

> The international law principle of self-determination has evolved within a framework of respect for the territorial integrity of existing states. The various international documents that support the existence of a people's right to self-determination also contain parallel statements supportive of the conclusion that the exercise of such a right must be sufficiently limited to prevent threats to an existing state's territorial integrity or the stability of relations between sovereign states.[24]

Using the terms *internal* and *external* self-determination, the Court determined further that

> the recognized sources of international law establish that the right to self-determination of a people is normally fulfilled through *internal* self-determination—a people's pursuit of its political, economic, social and cultural development within the framework of an existing state. A right to

> *external* self-determination [...] arises in only the most extreme of cases and, even then, under carefully defined circumstances.[25]

The Supreme Court went on to point out that the right of self-determination—that is, external self-determination—can be legitimately exercised only by those under colonial rule; by those who are oppressed, for example, under foreign military occupation; or "where a definable group is denied meaningful access to government to pursue their political, economic, social and cultural development."[26]

It would be hard to deny that Canada's Aboriginal peoples had been oppressed and denied access to government.[27] However, given the enormous political progress of Aboriginal peoples since the early 1970s, the insertion of sections 25 and 35 into the Canadian constitution, the slow but definite progress on land claims, the 1995 federal acknowledgment of the inherent Aboriginal right of self-government—not to mention the apparent preference of Aboriginal peoples themselves—it is arguable that the case for access to the right of external self-determination may not have the force it once had.

The Inherent Aboriginal Right to Self-Government

The issue of Aboriginals' inherent right to self-government has been on their agenda since the 1982 constitutional reforms. The right is described as "inherent" because, as Isaac points out, it is not "based on any express constitutional provision or agreement"; rather, it "inheres in Aboriginal peoples' residual sovereignty."[28]

The case for this right received support from the first chief justice of the US Supreme Court, John Marshall. He wrote,

> Indian nations [have] always been considered as distinct, independent political communities, retaining their original natural rights. ... The very term, "nation," so generally applied to them, means "a people distinct from others" ... The words "treaty" and "nation" are words of our own language, selected in our diplomatic and legislative proceedings, by ourselves, having a definite and well-understood meaning. We have applied them to other nations of the earth. They are applied to all in the same sense.[29]

Marshall was also quoted with approval by the Supreme Court of Canada in *R. v. Sioui*, as follows:

> Such was the policy of Great Britain towards the Indian nations inhabiting the territory from which she excluded all other Europeans; such her

> claims, and such her practical exposition of the charters she had granted: she considered them as nations capable of maintaining the relations of peace and war; of governing themselves, under her protection; and she made treaties with them, the obligation of which she acknowledged.[30]

Unfortunately for the American Indian tribes, Marshall's assessment of the policy of Great Britain did not lead him to conclude that they were beyond the reach of the American state. This was evident from his opinion in *Cherokee v. Georgia* (1831). Here, Ward Churchill writes, Marshall conceded that argumentation "intended to prove the character of the Cherokees as a state, as a distinct political society, separated from others, capable of governing itself, has ... been completely successful." And yet Marshall concluded, "It may well be doubted whether those tribes which reside within the acknowledged boundaries of the United States can, with strict accuracy, be denominated foreign nations. They may, more correctly, perhaps be denominated domestic dependent nations."[31] Since then the American judiciary and Congress have asserted jurisdiction over American Indian tribes, although, as Martin Papillon writes, "In a number of policy areas, including environmental protection, land management, and criminal justice, tribes have reestablished their authority through the adoption of policies and legislations that reflect their interests and priorities."[32]

In Canada, while the Supreme Court of Canada recognized that Aboriginal nations lived in organized, self-governing societies prior to contact, it also declared, through Justice La Forest in *Mitchell v. Peguis Indian Band*, that "The historical record leaves no doubt that native peoples acknowledged the ultimate sovereignty of the British Crown, and agreed to cede their traditional homelands on the understanding that the Crown would thereafter protect them in the possession and use of such lands as were reserved for their use."[33] What the Court appears to be saying is that Aboriginal nations are able to exercise the right of self-government, not self-determination, and the parameters of exercising that right are subject to negotiation with the federal and provincial governments.

In 1995 the government of Prime Minister Jean Chrétien announced its policy on Aboriginal self-government. Through this document, the federal government recognized "the inherent right of self-government as an existing Aboriginal right under section 35 of the *Constitution Act, 1982*." Further, it stated that "recognition of the inherent right is based on the view that the Aboriginal peoples of Canada have the right to govern themselves in relation to matters that are internal to their communities, integral to their unique cultures, identities, traditions, languages and institutions, and with respect to their special relationship to their land and their resources."

The document emphasized that "Aboriginal governments and institutions exercising the inherent right of self-government will operate within the framework of the Canadian Constitution." It emphasized also that

> the inherent right of self-government does not include a right of sovereignty in the international law sense, and will not result in sovereign independent Aboriginal nation states. On the contrary, implementation of self-government should enhance the participation of Aboriginal peoples in the Canadian federation, and ensure that Aboriginal peoples and their governments do not exist in isolation, separate and apart from the rest of Canadian society.[34]

Because self-government agreements must be subject to the constitution, the Canadian Charter of Rights and Freedoms applies to all Aboriginal governments and institutions.

Among the areas that could be transferred to the jurisdiction of Aboriginal governments are the establishment of governance structures, internal constitutions, elections, and leadership selection processes; education; health and social services; policing and enforcement of Aboriginal laws; property rights; agriculture; housing; local transportation; management of group assets; and regulation of businesses on Aboriginal lands. The document also makes provision for negotiation of financial arrangements for Aboriginal governments. The issues that would be subject to Aboriginal self-governance are considerably more numerous than those now decided by band councils. There are several other issues that Aboriginal governments could decide on, but in the event of a conflict with federal or provincial law, the latter would prevail.

The Aboriginal self-government model is not universally applauded. The conservative political scientist Thomas Flanagan, a former advisor of Prime Minister Harper, has argued that the emphasis on Aboriginal self-government is pointless at a time when more and more Aboriginal citizens are choosing to integrate into mainstream Canadian society. "Forty-two per cent of registered Indians live off reserve; this proportion has been increasing and will soon exceed 50 per cent."[35] Flanagan further observes, "As more aboriginal people pursue formal education and acquire remunerative employment, a somewhat different class cleavage between haves and have-nots is also emerging, but it is strongly affected by the tendency of more prosperous Indians to live off reserve. Even the activists in the aboriginal political movement, unless they are band chiefs, tend to live in towns and cities, where they work as lawyers, professors, administrators, and consultants."[36] In addition, Flanagan suggests that the explosion of Aboriginal entrepreneurship will deepen and broaden Aboriginal ties to white society. This, it would seem, will lead to further Aboriginal movement into mainstream Canada.

Both Flanagan and Margaret Moore point to the small size of many Aboriginal communities, and "so [they] have limited governing capacities."[37] More precisely, they lack financial resources and skilled personnel. Moore proposes that these small communities join together as federations to deliver services, an idea that Flanagan worries about, given the kinship nature of Aboriginal politics and the possibilities of cultural conflict.

Flanagan also criticizes the model for encouraging "aboriginal people to withdraw into themselves, into their own 'First Nations,' under their own 'self-governments,' on their own 'traditional lands,' within their own 'aboriginal communities.'"[38] Acknowledging that the present system cannot be dissolved overnight, he proposes three reforms to current Aboriginal self-governance. First, Aboriginal self-governments need to become more accountable. For Flanagan, that means less reliance on government transfers and more on "self-funding" through taxation. (Moore also makes this argument.) Second, "the concentrated power of elected band councils" needs to be dismantled. "No small group of elected politicians should have control simultaneously of people's land, housing, schools, jobs, and social assistance."[39] This would involve dispersal of power so that the managers of those offices were independent of the band council. Third, "a regime of individual property rights" would need to be introduced, beginning with housing but eventually extending to other areas as well. For Flanagan, collective ownership means de facto ownership by the band council, which has resulted in a variety of governance pathologies in Aboriginal communities.

The section on the Nisga'a settlement that follows shows, among other things, how it addresses the reforms proposed by Flanagan and Moore. This agreement is one of a number of self-government agreements negotiated by Aboriginal communities and the federal and provincial governments. Among them are the Cree-Naskapi settlement (1984) negotiated by the Cree-Naskapi of Quebec and the Quebec and federal governments; the 1995 umbrella agreement negotiated by the Council for Yukon Indians and the Yukon and federal governments; and the 1986 agreement negotiated by the Sechelt Indian Band and the BC and federal governments.[40]

The Nisga'a Final Agreement

The Nisga'a Final Agreement[41] is the product of more than a hundred years of Nisga'a activism, legal manoeuvring, and political negotiation. As early as 1887, Nisga'a chiefs were demanding recognition of their title to their lands.

In 1913 Nisga'a chiefs petitioned the Privy Council to establish their continuing rights and powers over their lands. The *Calder* case, launched in 1968, was the Nisga'a Nation's legal attempt to establish their ongoing Aboriginal title and right to self-government.[42] The decision in this case, handed down in 1973, recognized that continuing Aboriginal title could exist, but the court was divided as to Nisga'a rights over the land. Shortly after this decision, in 1976 the Canadian government began negotiating with the Nisga'a Nation.

It would not be until 1995—years after section 35 was included in the constitution—that the government officially adopted a general policy of negotiating comprehensive land agreements and self-government treaties. This "inherent rights policy" recognized that Aboriginal self-government is an inherent right of Aboriginal peoples that is recognized by section 35 of the constitution. The Nisga'a had already been negotiating with the Canadian government for nearly 20 years when this policy was adopted; they reached an agreement in principle in 1996—one year later. While the Nisga'a Final Agreement (NFA) was not the first comprehensive land claims and self-government agreement, it was one that blazed a trail for implementation of First Nations self-government powers.

The Nisga'a negotiated a wide-ranging and inclusive self-government treaty that established very specific powers and rights over land, resources, and governance. In contrast to the early numbered treaties, and even previous comprehensive land claims treaties, it represented an attempt to provide a comprehensive basis for Nisga'a rights and powers. The resulting treaty is not without its detractors, however, and the future success of the Nisga'a Nation as a result of this treaty is still an open question. It is important, nevertheless, to understand that the Nisga'a ultimately sat at the table negotiating this treaty and ultimately ratified it, though even that process did not go unchallenged.[43]

The treaty focuses on several key areas: title to land, rights over key resources, and jurisdiction over certain governmental areas.[44] Before discussion of the specific provisions, it is important to consider some basic principles included in the treaty that form a structural basis for the new relationships between the Canadian government, the province of British Columbia, and the Nisga'a Nation. Prior to the treaty the Nisga'a were subject to federal jurisdiction, as were all Indians and lands reserved for Indians under the Constitution Act, 1867, section 91(24). The Final Agreement, however, transfers the Nisga'a out from under section 91(24) and creates a new constitutional arrangement. In relation to land, this generally means that the NFA will apply rather than federal law, notably through the Indian Act's (R.S.C., 1985, ch. I-5) no longer applying.[45]

In the preamble, the agreement is described as "[setting] out Nisga'a section 35 rights inside and outside of the area that is identified in this Agreement as Nisga'a Lands." This means that the Nisga'a Nation's section 35 rights are now defined by the treaty rather than by any general legislation or case law applying to Aboriginal peoples. While the treaty becomes the defining instrument for Nisga'a section 35 rights, the agreement recognizes that nothing contained therein alters the Canadian constitution, including the division of powers between the province and the federal government, the status of the Nisga'a as Aboriginal peoples of Canada, and sections 25 and 35 of the constitution. Section 9 also ensures that "the *Canadian Charter of Rights and Freedoms* applies to Nisga'a Government in respect of all matters within its authority, bearing in mind the free and democratic nature of Nisga'a Government as set out in this Agreement." Therefore, while the treaty is to be the foundation of the relationship between the Nisga'a Nation and the respective governments, the Charter and the constitution are recognized. As the late president of Nisga'a Lisims government, Nelson Leeson, described, "we wanted to negotiate our way into Canada, not out of it."

The "land question," as members of the Nisga'a government call it,[46] has always been a vital aspect of First Nations' struggle with the Canadian government. It is a result of this issue that the treaty adopted a modified rights approach that sets out existing Nisga'a Aboriginal rights rather than surrendering them and having the Crown reissue them through treaty. There is a misnomer, however, in calling it "negotiation for land title." *Title*, within the Canadian legal framework, refers to fee-simple title, or ownership. Fee-simple ownership is what individual landholders purchase when they buy a house or a piece of land. This is the largest bundle of rights that an individual can acquire over land; it includes the right to possess, devise, derive income, and dispose of the property for an unlimited time. There are limits, however, on what an individual can do with his or her land. An individual cannot, for example, construct an office tower in a suburban neighbourhood; municipalities, by way of planning restrictions, limit the uses to which land can be put.

There are even more basic limitations on fee-simple landowners, including taxes, police powers, expropriation, and escheat. Taxes are fairly straightforward: governments can impose fees and levies on owners of land. Police powers are also familiar; people cannot with impunity violate the criminal law on their land, though there are some protections against police search and seizure on private property. Expropriation is the government's right to deprive persons of their land. Current legislative schemes regulate this right insofar as the government is required to compensate landowners for the fair market value of their property. Escheat is the mechanism by which land, if not devised or devolved to another, reverts to the government—the ultimate owner of the land. A home may be one's castle, but it is a castle that is still subject to the fees, rules, and regulations of the Queen.

While the Nisga'a Nation was recognized as "fee simple" owner of what in the treaty is called "Nisga'a Lands" (for the purposes of clarity we will refer to these as "core" Nisga'a lands), a closer examination of the agreement demonstrates broader powers than mere individual ownership. The lands amount to 1,992 square kilometres located mainly around four villages in the Nass Valley: Gingolx, Gitlaxt'aamiks, Gitwinksihlkw, and Laxgalts'ap. The treaty states that "the Nisga'a Nation owns Nisga'a Lands in fee simple, being the largest estate known in law. This estate is not subject to any condition, proviso, restriction, exception, or reservation set out in the Land Act, or any comparable limitation under any federal or provincial law. No estate or interest in Nisga'a Lands can be expropriated except as permitted by, and in accordance with, this Agreement."[47] While this provision appears to provide ownership rights equivalent to those of an ordinary purchaser, it may appear that the Nisga'a did not do very well in the negotiation, considering that their traditional territory is approximately 22,000 square kilometres. Indeed, from this limited perspective, it hardly seems that the Nisga'a won a victory. As with many legal constructions, however, it is always the details that count.

Upon closer examination, the first distinguishing feature that arises from the treaty is the collective ownership of core Nisga'a Lands. The treaty recognizes the entire Nisga'a Nation as the owner of the land, not individual members. The definition of "Nisga'a Nation" in the treaty is "the collectivity of those Aboriginal people who share the language, culture and laws of the Nisga'a Indians of the Nass Area, and their descendants."[48] As such, the ownership may be fee simple in language, but it is collective ownership in effect. Indeed, collective ownership is one of the main distinguishing features of Aboriginal landholding that has been recognized in Canadian jurisprudence. In *Delgamuukw*, the three aspects of *sui generis* Aboriginal title were established: (1) Aboriginal title is communally held; (2) Aboriginal title cannot be alienated to anyone except the Crown; and (3) the source of Aboriginal title is "the prior occupation of Canada by Aboriginal peoples."[49]

If we look at the second feature articulated in *Delgamuukw*, Nisga'a ownership of core lands reveals itself as not an ordinary interest. Aboriginal title cannot be alienated to anyone except the Crown. While on one hand the NFA allows the Nisga'a Nation to "dispose of its estate in fee simple on any parcel of Nisga'a Lands to any person,"[50] "a parcel of Nisga'a Lands does not cease to be Nisga'a Lands as a result of any change in ownership of an estate or interest in that parcel."[51] As a result, the Nisga'a can sell a fee simple in the Nisga'a Lands, but the land continues to be core Nisga'a land for other purposes such as taxation and land regulation. Thus, while the land is alienable, it can never truly be outside Nisga'a jurisdiction. Finally, the Nisga'a Nation retains the right of escheat. With ordinary land, if there were no heirs to the land it would revert to the Crown. In the Nisga'a Final Agreement, this Crown right of reversion is avoided by a provision stating that any Nisga'a Land that escheats to the Crown will be transferred, with no charge, to the Nisga'a government.[52] In this way the Nisga'a Nation assumes powers traditionally exercised by the Crown—that of ultimate heir.

Finally, one cannot assess the impact of the core Nisga'a land provisions in isolation from the other sections of the treaty, particularly the taxation and government chapters. Nisga'a Lands do not simply represent the boundaries upon which Nisga'a ownership was established, but also an important demarcation of Nisga'a government jurisdiction. The NFA recognizes the Nisga'a government's jurisdiction to "make laws in respect of direct taxation of Nisga'a citizens on Nisga'a Lands in order to raise revenue for Nisga'a Nation or Nisga'a Village purposes."[53] There is also a provision for negotiation of Nisga'a government powers of direct taxation over persons other than Nisga'a citizens.[54] The chapter on governance also demonstrates the qualitative difference between Nisga'a ownership and ordinary fee-simple ownership. The Nisga'a government has the recognized jurisdiction to provide conditions in its constitution under which Nisga'a lands can be alienated, in whole or in part, or divested through the creation of lesser interests.[55] Therefore, while the NFA has provided that Nisga'a Lands can be alienated, the Nisga'a government retains the power to restrict such alienation if it so chooses. As such, the NFA allows for individual property rights to be created in Nisga'a lands if the Nisga'a Nation chooses. And indeed, the Nisga'a Lisims government passed the Nisga'a Landholding Transition Act in 2009[56] and the Nisga'a Land Title Act in 2012,[57] allowing Nisga'a Nation members to hold title in fee simple.[58]

Core Nisga'a Lands are not the only land dealt with in the treaty. There are vast swathes of territory where the Nisga'a Nation's "usufructuary" rights are recognized. While full "fee simple" was recognized over core lands, large areas of Nisga'a territory are of fundamental importance for traditional (and not so traditional) resources. Traditional resources such as wildlife, migratory birds, fish, timber, and other forest products also require Nisga'a rights over land. The NFA deals with these resources in separate chapters of the treaty that delineate Nisga'a entitlements to these resources in certain areas. For example, in the approximately 16,000 square kilometres of the Nass Wildlife Area, the Nisga'a have co-management and hunting rights over the territory. They also have fishing rights over approximately 26,000 square kilometres.

Indeed, as Neil Sterritt has argued in "The Nisga'a Treaty: Competing Claims Ignored!"[59] the NFA recognized Nisga'a rights even over areas where there were competing First Nations claims.

The Agreement recognizes Nisga'a citizens' "right to harvest wildlife throughout the Nass Wildlife Area."[60] This right is subject to measures necessary for conservation and public safety. There is a system of allocations determined by a Wildlife Committee, created by the NFA to undertake the management and conservation responsibilities. The Wildlife Committee is composed of nine members; four each are from the Nisga'a Nation and the Province of British Columbia, while the government of Canada will appoint the final member. This provision, and others, ensures that Nisga'a representation is involved in any decisions that affect the area. While the Nisga'a right to wildlife is described as the right to harvest for domestic purposes, Nisga'a citizens have the "right to trade or barter among themselves, or with other aboriginal people, any wildlife or wildlife parts harvested under [the] Agreement."[61] Export or sale of wildlife parts, including meat, will still be regulated under federal or provincial law.[62] Therefore, internally there is a right to maintain a trade economy, even with other Aboriginal groups. Externally, however, the sale of wildlife products must conform to the relevant provincial or federal rules.

Similarly, the Nisga'a have recognized fishing rights over 26,000 square kilometres. Nisga'a fish entitlements are held communally by the Nisga'a Nation and are inalienable by them under the treaty.[63] Nisga'a citizens are not required to have provincial or federal licences or to pay fees or royalties for their entitlement.[64] The treaty includes an initial harvest allocation in relation to salmon—a fish in commercial demand—amounting to 13 per cent of the allowable catch for Nass sockeye salmon and 15 per cent of the allowable catch for Nass pink salmon. This is not properly part of the treaty but rather an initial allocation for 25 years, "replaceable at the discretion of the Nisga'a Nation every 15 years for a further 25 years."[65] This is just one example of the detailed negotiations that went into the NFA in relation to vital resources; other fish and ocean resources are also dealt with separately. One interesting feature of this chapter is the distinction between how commercially viable fisheries are negotiated, with specific allocations, and access to other ocean animals and plants that do not have such a high general commercial value, which are dealt with less finely. For example, the entire harvest allocation of oolichan, a fish vital to the Nisga'a Nation but not particularly sought after in commercial terms, is governed by Nisga'a laws alone.

Theory and Practice: The Nisga'a Final Agreement and Implementing Self-Government

International treaties have enshrined the right of self-determination: people's right to "freely determine their political status and freely pursue their economic, social and cultural development."[66] As was explained earlier, though, these rights are not unconditional. The right to self-determination does not authorize or encourage "any action which would dismember or impair, totally or in part, the territorial integrity or political unity of sovereign and independent States ... possessed of a Government representing the whole people belonging to the territory without distinction of any kind."[67] The UN Declaration on the Rights of Indigenous Peoples also incorporates this language, stating that the Declaration should not be "construed as authorizing or encouraging any action which would dismember or impair, totally or in part, the territorial integrity or political unity of sovereign and independent States."[68]

Sovereignty is therefore the elephant in the room that simply cannot be avoided, even among the aspirational statements of international treaties. The Nisga'a Final Agreement demonstrates that this may not be simply the result of an overzealous attachment to the outmoded notion of unchallengeable national sovereignty, but perhaps a reflection of some cold, hard political realities. The majority of the treaty is not made up of statements on Nisga'a nationalism but concerned with the more mundane but important details of who is to create the standards for forest management practices, who is responsible for fighting forest fires. The NFA is interested in the provision of health and medical care and the licensing of marriage commissioners. The Nisga'a did not need a treaty to constitute themselves as a nation—they were already one, but one that was not recognized within the broader Canadian framework. The function of the treaty is therefore less about international or even national recognition than it is about clearly defining the Nation's tangible rights and powers vis-à-vis the provincial and federal governments.

The struggle of First Nations for recognition within the Canadian state may have grown out of the uniquely Canadian experience. Drawing on some international examples, however, it should be seen as representative of a larger international political shift emerging from globalization. If we consider the level of integration of global commerce; the increasing political, military, and economic integration across Europe through the European Union; the development of enforceable international criminal law through the International Criminal Court; and the international cooperation in security efforts to combat terrorism, to name a few, the sovereignty of *Leviathan* begins to look like an antiquated, idealized notion no longer relevant to the modern world.[69]

If we consider the spectrum between self-government and self-determination, it is difficult to name any nation that might fall at the extreme end of self-determination. Even the most powerful nation in the world, the United States of America, is inexorably intertwined with the fate of its neighbours and counterparts. It may be, then, that the NFA can be seen as recognizing the political realities of a globalized world, where legislative powers over membership and territory will ultimately be restrained by relationships with neighbours and economic partners. In this new paradigm, the success of the treaty depends on an ongoing relationship with the provincial and federal governments, as well as other international partners. The Agreement does not ultimately define every right and power, but it sets up a framework for ongoing negotiation of Nisga'a entitlements. Continued commitment to this relationship will therefore determine whether the treaty is a success or a failure. But it can also be said that the success of most countries depends on a continued commitment to developing relationships with their neighbours, partners, and allies.

Takeaway Messages

- Self-government differs from self-determination in that the former provides for a limited array of powers for the entity in question, while the latter means independence and full sovereignty.
- In 1995 the federal government acknowledged that section 35 of the Constitution Act, 1982, includes an inherent Aboriginal right to self-government.

Study Questions

- In your view, how is the Nisga'a Final Agreement deficient?
- Which vision of Canadians' relationship with Aboriginal peoples appeals to you the most: the federal "self-government" vision, the Thomas Flanagan version, or the vision indicated by Kiera Ladner? Why?

Issue for Debate or Roundtable

- Following on the comment made by Peter Russell, is there a principled reason why Canadians should not accept that Aboriginal nations have a right of self-determination and ought to be able to exercise it?

Additional Reading

Anaya, S. James. *International Human Rights and Indigenous Peoples*. New York: Aspen, 2009.

Engle, Karen. *The Elusive Promise of Indigenous Development: Rights, Culture, Strategy*. Durham, NC: Duke University Press, 2010. http://dx.doi.org/10.1215/9780822392965.

McCabe, J. Timothy S. *The Law of Treaties Between the Crown and Aboriginal Peoples*. Markham, ON: LexisNexis Canada, 2010.

Scott, Tracie Lea. *Postcolonial Sovereignty? The Nisga'a Final Agreement* (Saskatoon, SK: Purich, 2012).

Steinman, Erich. "Sovereigns and Citizens? The Contested Status of American Indian Tribal Nations and Their Members." *Citizenship Studies* 15, no. 1 (February 2011): 57–74. http://dx.doi.org/10.1080/13621025.2011.534927.

Websites

Assembly of First Nations. http://www.afn.ca.
Nisga'a Lisims Government. http://www.nisgaanation.ca.

Notes

1. P.E. Trudeau, "The Values of a Just Society," in *Towards a Just Society: The Trudeau Years*, ed. T.S. Axworthy and P.E. Trudeau (Markham, ON: Penguin, 1990), 366.
2. See P. Hogg (quoting B. Slattery), *Constitutional Law of Canada*, student ed. (Toronto: Thomson Reuters Canada, 2009), 636.
3. T. Isaac, *Aboriginal Law: Commentary, Cases and Materials*, 3rd ed. (Saskatoon, SK: Purich, 2004), 71.
4. P. Monahan, *Constitutional Law*, 3rd ed. (Toronto: Irwin Law, 2006), 447–48.
5. *R. v. Van der Peet*, [1996] 2 S.C.R. 507, at para. 74.
6. *Delgamuukw v. British Columbia*, [1997], 3 S.C.R. 1010, at para. 111.
7. *Calder v. Attorney-General (BC)*, [1973], S.C.R. 313.
8. *R. v. Guerin*, [1984], 2 S.C.R. 335.
9. Isaac, *Aboriginal Law*, 19.
10. Ibid., 20. The Supreme Court of Canada again elaborated on Aboriginal title and the rights accompanying Aboriginal title in two decisions in 2014, *Tsilhqot'in Nation v. British Columbia* and *Grassy Narrows First Nation v. Ontario.*
11. To confuse matters further, some use the terms *internal self-determination* and *external self-determination* to convey what we mean by self-government and self-determination respectively.
12. D. Horowitz, "The Cracked Foundations of the Right to Secede," *Journal of Democracy* 14, no. 2 (April 2003): 5.
13. G. Marchildon, "Postmodern Federalism and Sub-State Nationalism," in *The Ashgate Research Companion to Federalism*, ed. A. Ward and L. Ward (Burlington, VT: Ashgate, 2009), 452.

14. A.-G. Gagnon and R. Iacovino, "Canadian Federalism and Multinational Democracy: 'Pressures' from Quebec on the Federation," in *Canadian Federalism: Performance, Effectiveness, and Legitimacy*, ed. H. Bakvis and G. Skogstad (Toronto: Oxford University Press, 2008), 351.
15. S. Mancini, "Rethinking the Boundaries of Democratic Secession: Liberalism, Nationalism, and the Right of Minorities to Self-Determination," *International Journal of Constitutional Law* 6, no. 3–4 (2008): 575.
16. Quoted in S. Brooks, *Canadian Democracy*, 6th ed. (Toronto: Oxford University Press, 2009), 468.
17. J. Dalton, "Aboriginal Self-Determination in Canada: Protections Afforded by the Judiciary and Government," *Canadian Journal of Law and Society* 21, no. 1 (2006): 24.
18. P. Russell, "Indigenous Self-Determination: Is Canada as Good as It Gets?" in *Unfinished Constitutional Business? Rethinking Indigenous Self-Determination*, ed. B.A. Hocking (Canberra, Australia: Aboriginal Studies Press, 2005), 175.
19. K. Ladner, "Treaty Federalism: An Indigenous Vision of Canadian Federalisms," in *New Trends in Canadian Federalism*, ed. F. Rocher and M. Smith, 2nd ed. (Peterborough, ON: Broadview Press, 2003), 178. It is not clear why Ladner uses the word *federalism*. Federalism is a mechanism for unification, which does not appear to be what she is advocating.
20. Ibid., 174.
21. Ibid., 180.
22. Ibid., 186.
23. Ibid., 190.
24. *Reference re Secession of Quebec*, [1998] 2 S.C.R. 217, at para. 127.
25. Ibid., at para. 126, emphasis in original.
26. Ibid., at para. 138.
27. First Nations citizens of Canada acquired voting rights only in 1960.
28. Isaac, *Aboriginal Law*, 453.
29. *Worcester v. Georgia*, [1832] U.S.S.C. 515, at 559–60.
30. Ibid., at 548–49; quoted in *R. v. Sioui*, [1990] 1 S.C.R. 1025, at 1053–54.
31. W. Churchill, "The Tragedy and the Travesty: The Subversion of Indigenous Sovereignty in North America," *American Indian Culture and Research Journal* 22, no. 2 (1998): 28.
32. M. Papillon, "Adapting Federalism: Indigenous Multilevel Governance in Canada and the United States," *Publius* 42, no. 2 (2012): 296.
33. *Mitchell v. Peguis Band*, [1990] 2 S.C.R. 85, at 130.
34. Aboriginal Affairs and Northern Development Canada, "The Government of Canada's Approach to Implementation of the Inherent Right and the Negotiation of Aboriginal Self-Government," http://www.aadnc-aandc.gc.ca/eng/1100100031843/1100100031844.
35. T. Flanagan, *First Nations? Second Thoughts*, 2nd ed. (Montreal: McGill-Queen's University Press, 2008), 110.
36. Ibid., 99.
37. M. Moore, "An Historical Argument for Indigenous Self-Determination," in *Secession and Self-Determination*, ed. S. Macedo and A. Buchanan (New York: New York University Press, 2003), 105.
38. Flanagan, *First Nations?*, 195.

39. Ibid., 198. Similarly, Moore worries about "local self-interested elites who use their authority to preserve and maintain their power base"; Moore, "Historical Argument," 107.
40. Isaac, *Aboriginal Law*, 462–69.
41. Canada, British Columbia, and Nisga'a Nation, Nisga'a Final Agreement [NFA] and Appendices, http://nisgaalisims.ca/the-nisgaa-final-agreement.
42. *Calder v. Attorney-General (BC)*, [1973], S.C.R. 313.
43. See *House of Sga'nisim, Nisibilada v. Canada*, 5 April 2000, [2000] B.C.J. No. 831 (Q.L.), affirmed by the British Columbia Court of Appeal on 20 April, [2000] B.C.J. No. 821.
44. For a detailed analysis of the treaty, see T. Scott, *Postcolonial Sovereignty? The Nisga'a Final Agreement* (Saskatoon, SK: Purich, 2012).
45. NFA, ch. 2, s. 10 states that, "There are no 'lands reserved for the Indians' within the meaning of the Constitution Act, 1867 for the Nisga'a Nation, and there are no 'reserves' as defined in the Indian Act for the use and benefit of a Nisga'a Village, or an Indian band referred to in the Indian Act Transition Chapter, and, for greater certainty, Nisga'a Lands and Nisga'a Fee Simple Lands are not 'lands reserved for the Indians' within the meaning of the Constitution Act, 1867, and are not 'reserves' as defined in the Indian Act."
46. The Nisga'a have always referred to their negotiations with the government as the "land question," because calling it a claim would suggest that they somehow had to establish their entitlement to their land. They have always been of the view that they maintained title to their land and the government had simply not recognized it.
47. NFA, ch. 3, s. 3.
48. Ibid., 12.
49. *Delgamuukw v. British Columbia*, [1997], 3 S.C.R. 1010, at para. 113.
50. NFA, ch. 3, s. 4(a).
51. Ibid., ch. 3, s. 5.
52. Ibid., ch. 3, s. 7.
53. Ibid, ch. 16, s. 1.
54. Ibid., ch. 6, s. 3.
55. Ibid., ch. 11, s. 9.
56. Nisga'a Lisims Government, Nisga'a Landholding Transition Act, NLGSR 2009/02, http://www.nisgaanation.ca/sites/default/files/legislation/2009-02%20-%20Nisga%27a%20Landholding%20Transition%20Act%20-%202009-10-01.pdf.
57. Nisga'a Lisims Government, Nisga'a Land Title Act—Unofficial Consolidation, NLGSR 2010/06, http://www.nisgaanation.ca/sites/default/files/legislation/Nisga%27a%20Land%20Title%20Act%20-%20Unofficial%20Consolidation.pdf.
58. See Nisga'a Nation Knowledge Network, "Nisga'a Individual Landholding Project," http://nnkn.ca/content/nisgaa-individual-landholding-project.
59. N. Sterritt, "The Nisga'a Treaty: Competing Claims Ignored!" *BC Studies* 120 (Winter 1998–99): 73–97.
60. NFA, Ch. 9, s. 1.
61. Ibid., ch. 9, s. 68.
62. Ibid., ch. 9, s. 70.
63. Ibid., ch. 8, s. 1.

64. Ibid., ch. 8, s. 7.
65. Ibid., ch. 8, s. 22(b).
66. UN General Assembly, *International Covenant on Economic, Social and Cultural Rights*, G A Res. 2200A (XXI) (1976), Article 1. Also found in the UN General Assembly, United Nations Declaration on the Rights of Indigenous Peoples, G A Res. 61/295 (2007), Article 3.
67. UN General Assembly, Declaration on the Occasion of the Fiftieth Anniversary of the United Nations, G A Res. 50/6 (1995), Article 1.
68. UN General Assembly, United Nations Declaration on the Rights of Indigenous Peoples, G A Res. 61/295 (2007), Article 46.
69. Thomas Hobbes, *Leviathan* (Peterborough, ON: Broadview, 2002).

10
DisAbling Human Rights? Moving from Rights to Access and Inclusion in Daily Life

DEBORAH STIENSTRA

Learning Objectives

- To understand the legislative framework of disability rights
- To learn about some of the gaps between legislation of disability rights and the lived experiences of people with disabilities
- To learn how public discussions can shape and be affected by disability rights

Disability takes us to the heart of humanity and human rights. Most people will experience disability at some point in their lives. Many fear the perceived dependency and lack of independent capacity, and some argue fiercely for measures to avoid those situations. Disability is an unwanted status, often perceived as a lack rather than a recognized or positive part of human existence. As a result, the experiences of people with disabilities—and for some their very existence—push societies to consider what we mean by "being human" and by "human rights." How do societies reflect the diversity of human bodies and of ways of doing things? How can human rights move from including people with disabilities in able-bodied societies toward transformed societies that enable multiple ways of doing things, all of which are recognized as part of humanity?

In this chapter we consider the landscape of disability rights in Canada in terms of key areas of rights, including access to education, employment, health, legal capacity, transportation, information technologies, and end of life. Despite significant human rights protections, people in Canada with disabilities continue to experience disproportionately high levels of poverty and exclusion. Women, children and youth, and Aboriginal people with disabilities experience even greater marginalization. We ask why this disparity exists between lived experiences and human rights standards, and the extent to which human rights can be used to address this gap.

We argue that Canada has a strong framework of disability rights, embedded in the equality rights section of the Charter of Rights and Freedoms and complemented by human rights, accessibility, employment equity, transportation, and communications legislation. These rights protections are barebones and have required (and received) some significant interpretations to flesh them out, especially through Supreme Court rulings in the areas of health, education, employment, and transportation. But because disability remains understood as a lack and therefore unwanted by most Canadians, the human rights of people with disabilities remain fragile. These rights require vigilant monitoring and intervention through complaints and litigation by people with disabilities and their organizations.

The capacity to undertake this monitoring and intervention has been substantially eroded by cuts to federal funding for the Court Challenges Program and cuts to organizational funding for disability organizations in 2014–15. In addition, the persistent belief among Canadians that it would be better to be dead than to live with disability has fuelled public debate and legislation that may challenge life itself for some people with disabilities. With a framework based in complaints, there is little capacity to respond proactively to promote inclusion of all members of society and to address the chronic poverty and persistent marginalization and exclusion of people with disabilities.

In the following sections, we outline the legislative framework of disability rights and key Supreme Court cases in education, health care, transportation, and information and communications technologies that have increased access and inclusion for people with disabilities. Using the example of employment, we consider how disability rights have failed to make systemic social changes, which results in inability to address the chronic poverty and marginalization of people with disabilities. We illustrate, using the public discussions around assisted suicide, how fragile disability rights are in a world that wants to avoid the loss and dependence associated with disability. Finally, we consider how ongoing discussions around legal capacity offer an example of the transformative potential of disability rights in Canada.

A Strong Legislative Framework of Disability Rights

Disability rights exist at different levels for Canadians with disabilities. At the most general level, section 15 of the Canadian Charter of Rights and Freedoms, which came into force on 17 April 1985, says, "Every individual is equal before and under the law and has the right to the equal protection and equal benefit of the law without discrimination and, in particular, without discrimination based on … mental or physical disability." Having those rights entrenched in the Charter was a challenging task that took concerted lobbying and advocacy by people with disabilities and their allies.[1]

Both the Canadian Human Rights Act and the provincial human rights acts reinforce that discrimination on the basis of disability is not acceptable in Canada. Indeed, the majority of cases that come before the Canadian Human Rights Commission are related to complaints of discrimination based on disability.[2]

The Canadian government reaffirmed its commitment to ensure the human rights of people with disabilities when it ratified the United Nations Convention on the Rights of Persons with Disabilities (UNCRPD) during the Vancouver 2010 Paralympic Games. The Convention provides a more global framework for disability rights. By April 2015, 154 countries had ratified the Convention. Countries are required to report regularly on what they have done to implement the Convention, and Canada submitted its first report in 2014.[3] A committee of international experts reviews these reports and raises any concerns and questions. In addition, non-governmental organizations can submit an alternative, or "shadow," report to the committee reviewing the government's report. These shadow reports provide an opportunity for critique and a different perspective from that of the government. The committee will likely review Canada's next report in 2016; non-governmental organizations, led by the Council of Canadians with Disabilities (CCD), intend to develop and submit a shadow report.

A series of cases before the Supreme Court of Canada have clarified the extent of protections under the Charter and other acts. One key case, in which the Court interpreted how to understand section 15 equality rights, is *Andrews v. Law Society of British Columbia*.[4] In *Andrews*, the Court argued for a vision of substantive equality, recognizing that not all discrimination is intended and that responses need to address both intended and unintended barriers.[5]

Provincial governments are increasingly taking action to enshrine in legislation particular protections for people with disabilities. Ontario led the way in 2001 with the Ontarians with Disabilities Act and the follow-up Accessibility for Ontarians with Disabilities Act (AODA) in 2005. The AODA is changing the landscape for people with disabilities, with its requirements and standards to ensure access in the public and private sectors. Accessibility standards are in place or being developed for transportation, websites, information and communications, design of public spaces, buildings, and customer service. The Manitoba government adopted the Accessibility for Manitobans Act in 2013. The goal of this Act, similar to that of the AODA, was to ensure access for everyone in public services and places. In addition, Manitoba's act shifted from targeting people with disabilities to recognizing that access is an issue for everyone. In June 2014, Nova Scotia announced the appointment of an Advisory Panel on Accessibility Legislation, with the goal of achieving accessibility legislation by 2016.[6]

Some people have suggested that Canada needs an act for persons with disabilities at the federal level, despite wide-ranging human rights protections and the provincial measures.[7] While provincial accessibility acts address areas under provincial jurisdiction, there are several existing rights protections under federal jurisdiction related to employment, communications, and transportation.

Since the mid-1980s, Canadian law has increasingly recognized the barriers to employment faced by people with disabilities and has created tools to assist in removing those barriers. Employment equity and the duty to accommodate are seen as ways to ensure that the Canadian labour force is more inclusive of people with disabilities. The Employment Equity Act covers four groups—women, Aboriginal people, people with disabilities, and members of visible minorities—and has two goals: to achieve equality in the workplace and to correct conditions that lead to disadvantage for members of these groups. Employers, including the federal public service, federally regulated private companies in areas such as banking and transportation, Crown corporations, and federal contractors, must report on their employment of people in these groups, review and identify any barriers to employment, and develop a plan for how they will remove the barriers. Eligible people with disabilities under the Act are defined as having "a long term or recurring physical, mental, sensory, psychiatric or learning impairment and: considers himself/herself to be disadvantaged in employment by reason of that impairment; or believes that an employer or potential employer is likely to consider him/her to be disadvantaged in employment by reason of that impairment."

Workplace accommodations are the proving grounds of employment equity for people with disabilities. The Canadian Human Rights Act and the Employment Equity Act apply to employers, unions, and all employees, and require employers to demonstrate that they have taken every reasonable step, short of undue hardship, to accommodate a worker with disabilities. When workers feel they have not been accommodated, their recourse is to lay a complaint through the Canadian Human Rights Commission, which can be a lengthy and demanding process.

The Canadian Radio-television and Telecommunications Commission (CRTC) regulates telecommunications and broadcasting in Canada. Through the Telecommunications Act and the Broadcasting Act, the CRTC has the responsibility of ensuring access to telecommunications and broadcasting, including through preventing discrimination in the provision of telecommunications services as specified in section 27(2) of the Telecommunications Act.[8] The Canadian Transportation Agency (CTA) is responsible for air and rail transport, interprovincial buses, and marine ferries, and the Canadian Transportation Act ensures accessible transportation for persons with disabilities. The CTA responds to complaints from individuals and develops regulations and standards for accessibility.

Together, these acts and agencies form the legislative framework for disability rights in Canada. While they recognize the possibilities of discrimination based on disability and have complaint processes for when discrimination occurs, this framework results in incremental and often ad hoc implementation of disability rights. In addition, in 2006 the federal government closed the Court Challenges Program, a key program that supported cases addressing issues raised in the Charter. In 2015 the federal government ended funding for disability organizations through the Social Development Partnerships Program—Disability, except for projects approved in a competitive process.[9] These two measures by the federal government substantively reduce the capacity of people with disabilities and their organizations to make complaints or challenge inequality. Few individuals have sufficient income to hire a lawyer to take on their cases of discrimination, and the public resources put into legal aid have been reduced.

In responding to complaints rather than proactively promoting inclusion of all members of society, this framework has limited capacity to respond systematically to chronic poverty among, and marginalization and exclusion of, people with disabilities. The provincial accessibility laws, however, are exceptions; they have the potential for shifting from a complaint-based system to one based on creating access for all members of society. Unfortunately, there will be no comprehensive coverage until more provinces address these issues.

Interpreting Disability Rights

This framework of disability rights is, as argued earlier, barebones, and it has required both complaints and interpretation for its implementation. Over the three decades since the adoption of the Charter of Rights and Freedoms, Canadians have seen significant forward movement in identifying what disability rights look like, especially in the areas of education, transportation, health care, and telecommunications. Each of these decisions helped to put flesh on the bones of the framework and give us a better understanding of what is inclusion of people with disabilities in Canadian society.

Education

One of the foundations of an inclusive and accessible society is access to education. Yet for many children and youth with disabilities in Canada, access to education remains elusive because of physical and attitudinal barriers, lack of disability-related supports, additional costs, and their own invisibility in the curriculum and structures of education.[10] In a ground-breaking decision in 2012, the Supreme Court of Canada, in *Moore v. British Columbia (Education)*, argued that students with disabilities are entitled to receive the accommodation measures they need to access and benefit from public education, since accommodation measures provide a ramp by which students with disabilities can access education.[11]

Jeffrey Moore had been diagnosed with severe learning disabilities and received remedial assistance through the public school board until grade three. Then the school board closed the centre where he received assistance, and Jeffrey's parents sent him to a private school to ensure that he got the assistance he needed. His father filed a complaint with the British Columbia Human Rights Tribunal on his behalf, arguing that Jeffrey was unable to access education that was publicly provided. The Supreme Court agreed that a commitment to access to education is a right for all children in British Columbia, and that this right had been breached in Jeffrey Moore's case by the lack of special education accommodation measures.

This decision is in contrast to an earlier Supreme Court decision, in *Eaton v. Brant County Board of Education* (1997). In that case the Court overturned an Ontario court decision to include Emily Eaton in her local school rather than have her attend a segregated school. The Ontario court argued that "unless the parents of a child who has been identified as exceptional by reason of a physical or mental disability consent to the placement of that child in a segregated environment, the school board must provide a placement that is the least exclusionary from the mainstream and still reasonably capable of meeting the child's special needs."[12] The Supreme Court Decision in *Eaton* took an approach to disability rights of "separate but equal," and in so doing perpetuated segregation and inferior status for people with disabilities. Dianne Pothier argues that this decision fails to adequately take diversity into account and thus undermines the equality of students with disabilities:

> The Supreme Court of Canada's rejection of a presumption of integration amounts to the adoption of a hierarchy of difference, which is inconsistent with the equality guarantee of section 15 of the Charter. A bare presumption in favour of integration is, however, insufficient to satisfy section 15. Integrated education only meets the dictates of section 15 if it is genuinely inclusive and addresses the actual needs of disabled students. ... Compliance with section 15 requires fundamental transformation of the traditional mainstream classroom.[13]

The 2012 *Moore* decision rejected this earlier approach of "separate but equal" in education, arguing instead that special education is a means to the end of achieving access to education for all students, including students with disabilities:

> To define special education as the service at issue risks descending into a kind of "separate but equal" approach. Comparing J only with other special needs students would mean that the District could cut all special needs programs and yet be immune from a claim of discrimination. If J is compared only to other special needs students, full consideration cannot be given to whether he had meaningful access to the education to which all students in British Columbia are entitled. This risks perpetuating the very disadvantage and exclusion the [Human Rights] Code is intended to remedy.[14]

While the *Moore* case offers an integrative approach to special education within the public education system, a proactive approach is required to ensure full inclusion in education. New Brunswick has taken a proactive approach to ensuring inclusive education for all students, with a policy that addresses the heart of the *Moore* decision. In September 2013 the New Brunswick government adopted an inclusive education policy that builds on the principles that every child can learn and that every child requires a common learning environment that is respectful of diversity, universal, and individualized and has the practical supports necessary to implement it.[15] This policy is one of the first of its kind in the world and serves as a model for other jurisdictions in how to implement inclusive public education. Given that New Brunswick is one of the poorer provinces in Canada, it will be interesting to follow how this policy is being implemented and the extent to which it is protected over the longer term from neoliberal cost-cutting measures.

Health Care

Like most Canadians, people with disabilities rely on Canada's publicly funded health-care system, but they meet physical, attitudinal, systemic, and expertise barriers in their access to health care.[16] Health care is complicated for people with disabilities because of the assumptions held by many that disability means something wrong or missing in bodies that we need health-care providers to fix. This is called the "medical model" of disability and assumes that some bodies are normal while others are abnormal. Disability advocates prefer to speak of a "social model" of disability, in which diverse bodies with varying needs are accommodated in our society; we remove barriers for those whose bodies cannot be accommodated in society as it is now.

In 1997 the Supreme Court, in the *Eldridge v. British Columbia (Attorney General)*[17] decision, recognized disability rights in health care. The Court ruled that a British Columbia hospital that had failed to provide sign-language interpretation for a deaf individual was discriminating, with the effect that deaf people did not benefit equally from health services.[18] Barriers to health care remain for most people with disabilities. Despite their high usage of the health-care system, people with disabilities are three times more likely to have unmet health-care needs than people without disabilities.[19] While the *Eldridge* decision has the potential to remove some barriers to access of health care, the persistent unmet needs of people with disabilities suggest that more is needed—including disability-related education for physicians, inclusive design of health-care facilities, and better collaboration between different health- and home-care providers—to ensure inclusion in and access to the health-care system for people with disabilities.

Transportation

Transportation is part of the infrastructure required to lead an ordinary life in Canada, including public transportation within and between cities and in rural and remote areas. Since 2007 the interprovincial transportation infrastructure has become increasingly accessible, especially as a result of two key Supreme Court rulings. Urban transportation systems remain a hodgepodge, with some cities modelling inclusive and accessible transportation and others with little access. Accessible urban transportation has emerged partly in response to provincial human rights and accessibility legislation, as well as to the increasing presence of seniors and people with disabilities. People with disabilities who live in rural and remote communities continue to have much more limited access to public transportation.

As a result of long-sustained advocacy by organizations of people with disabilities and particularly the CCD, the Supreme Court ruled in 2007 that VIA Rail had to ensure that train cars were accessible to people with disabilities.[20] A year later, the Court supported a Canadian Transportation Agency ruling that airlines could not charge a second fare to passengers who required a seat for an attendant, a policy that has been called "one person, one fare."[21] The CCD had been arguing for "one person, one fare" since the early 1980s and had been fighting VIA Rail about inaccessible railcars since 2000. Barriers continue to exist in interprovincial transportation, including the use of small planes that cannot accommodate wheelchairs and scooters, and touch-screen-controlled entertainment systems.[22]

Urban public transportation often includes a parallel system of door-to-door service for some people with disabilities and a mainstream service. Many mainstream systems are increasingly including low-floor buses, accessible stations and stops, tactile way-finding, and online trip-planning and route information. Some accessibility features, such as calling out the stops, have resulted from the advocacy of individuals like David Lepofsky in Toronto. He is a blind transportation user and a lawyer who made a complaint about the inaccessibility of the Toronto Transit Commission (TTC) to the Ontario Human Rights Commission in 2005; the ruling ordered the TTC to call out all stops. While this is a positive step forward, making a human rights complaint is a time-consuming process and often addresses only a particular part of the barrier.

The Accessibility for Ontarians with Disabilities Act has helped to address barriers and set standards for accessibility in Ontario. But despite these legislative requirements for accessibility, removing barriers can become a game of political football between municipal and provincial governments. For example, in 2014 the TTC argued that it could not meet its timeline to make all the subway stations accessible, because the province had not provided sufficient funds.[23]

People with disabilities who live in more rural or remote parts of the country have significantly less access to public transportation. They must rely on private vehicles, interurban buses, or small airplanes. In many parts of the country these services may be under attack as overly expensive and without sufficient customers to justify the expense, if indeed accessible transportation is even provided. For example, since 2010 Greyhound has been reducing or eliminating many of its northern and remote bus routes in Ontario, Manitoba, Alberta, and British Columbia, leaving people with disabilities with fewer options for travel, including to medical appointments in urban locations.

Access to transportation is getting easier in some parts of Canada as a result of human rights and accessibility legislation and the determined advocacy of many people with disabilities. But the transportation systems, especially outside and between major urban centres, continue to impose many barriers and fail to ensure inclusion for all.

Information and Communications Technologies

The Internet, with its social media, websites, and online services, shapes much of our world. These information and communications technologies have brought greater access for some people with disabilities and erected additional barriers to accessibility for others. Some key decisions since 2009 illustrate a greater movement toward access and inclusion in this area.

In 2009 the CRTC adopted a policy on accessibility in broadcasting and telecommunications, recognizing that its policies should be consistent with the Charter of Rights and Freedoms.[24] This came after years of complaints about barriers to telecommunications by consumers with disabilities, including those who were blind and deaf. In response to those complaints, the CRTC required telecommunications companies, for example, to make payphones accessible, to make some telephone equipment accessible to people who were blind, and to ensure that relay operators were available to allow deaf people to communicate with those who used hearing to communicate.

The fast pace of change in telecommunications has rendered many of those decisions irrelevant. But the requirement to ensure access to telecommunications was reinforced in the 2009 policy. One important change as a result of the policy was the introduction of texting for emergency services through 911 calls.[25] This major national initiative increases access for those who do not use oral communications, but it requires users to register first before they can access the system.

In 2008, several telecommunications companies were required to set aside a separate fund, called a "deferral accounts fund," for providing greater access for people with disabilities.[26] Bell Canada had approximately $24 million and Telus $8.43 million to use in that fund, while other telecommunications companies had less. To date, the deferral accounts funds have been used to significantly advance accessibility in some areas of telecommunications.[27] For example, the telecommunications companies, together with organizations of deaf and hard-of-hearing people, created an Internet-based relay system and, in 2015, launched a video relay service for deaf individuals.[28] This meant that deaf people could communicate with hearing people through online relay operators rather than only through a telephone system; once the video relay is in place, they will be able to use sign language to communicate over the Internet.

Other initiatives have resulted in the development of accessible handsets, other mobile devices, and applications, including those that can work with screen-reading programs. The telecommunications companies have used the deferral accounts funds to increase the accessibility of their own websites and to provide training for their staff about accessibility. The deferral accounts decision also required that telecommunications companies consult with disability advocacy organizations around the use of those funds. In Bell Canada's case, this has resulted in a productive collaboration that enhanced Bell's accessibility initiatives.[29]

The Broadcasting Act also has provisions related to disability rights; section 3(1)(p) states that "programming accessible by disabled people should be provided within the Canadian broadcasting system as resources become available for that purpose." This has led to limited closed captioning of television, which was extended in duration and quality by the 2009 CRTC policy. The 2009 policy also provides for audio descriptions and descriptive video.[30]

Accessibility in broadcasting made a significant advance when, following the acquisition of CTV by Bell Canada Enterprises (BCE) in 2011, the CRTC ruled that an independent broadcasting accessibility fund of $5.7 million be created, to be directed by people with disabilities and representatives of disability advocacy groups. The Broadcasting Accessibility Fund represents a variety of stakeholder groups and considers funding proposals.[31]

Another key decision in the area of telecommunications related to the accessibility of websites. In May 2012 the Federal Court of Appeal ruled that the federal government had a responsibility to ensure that access to information included access to online information and services for those who were visually impaired. The argument made in the case brought by Donna Jodhan was based on section 15 of the Charter. Specifically, the decision noted that Jodhan "had been denied equal access to, and equal benefit from, government information and services provided online to the public on the Internet, and that this constitutes discrimination against her on the basis of her physical disability, namely, that she is blind. Accordingly, she has not received the equal benefit of the law without discrimination based on her physical disability and that this constitutes a violation of subsection 15(1) of the Charter."[32] While this decision illustrates the importance of disability rights in ensuring access to information and services online, it required the persistence of one woman who was willing to fight for her rights. Also, the decision was limited to the Treasury Board and did not cover other federal government departments.

Progress has been made in implementing disability rights in telecommunications and broadcasting, but progress has not been easy or reliable. The deferral accounts funds have served as a useful way of educating telecommunications companies about what is required to ensure accessibility in this area, and there has been significant progress. The broadcasting accessibility fund has the potential to increase accessibility. The necessary education and advocacy to implement these initiatives have come from disability organizations with sufficient technical knowledge and the capacity to engage. To ensure inclusion in and access to information and communications technologies will take persistence and education, including of those people who imagine, develop, and manage new technologies.

The disability organizations continue to fight to ensure that disability rights are the basis for understanding by all service providers, including those who provide information and communications technologies, that they are obliged to provide services that can be used by all, including people with disabilities.

Ineffective Disability Rights

Employment is essential to the inclusion and full participation of people with disabilities in Canadian society. Yet, despite long-standing disability employment rights such as employment equity and a duty to accommodate, there remain significant differences between the employment, income, and inclusion in the labour force of people with and without disabilities. As Michael Prince argues, working-age women and men with disabilities

> have a lower level of labour force participation and a higher level of unemployment than Canadians without disabilities, and considerable underemployment; they are more likely to experience social barriers and workplace discrimination; and they have a higher level of poverty and greater dependence on welfare than other citizens. In 2010, the labour force participation rate for people with disabilities was 57.1 percent compared to 80.5 percent for people without disabilities; and among those in the labour force, people with disabilities experienced a higher level of unemployment (11.4 versus 7.0 percent).[33]

The employment situation of women and men with disabilities is also complicated by their earnings and by the type of work they do. Women with disabilities earn less than women without disabilities and less than men with disabilities.[34] While women in general experience precarious or insecure work,[35] women with disabilities disproportionately experience precarious work and have additional barriers to their participation in the workforce as a result of the precarious nature of their work.[36]

In this challenging context, what effect have disability rights had on changing the poverty, marginalization, and exclusion of people with disabilities? Employment equity has not been successful in ensuring that people with disabilities enter the workforce in representative numbers. For example, in the 2013 Employment Equity Act report, people with disabilities represented 2.6 per cent of the regulated workforce, in spite of their availability rate of 4.9 per cent.[37] In addition, the report noted that the number of terminations of disabled people exceeded their hires in 2011 and 2012. While the federal public service has succeeded in having people with disabilities represented above their availability in the labour force, there is some concern that "federal departments and agencies may be reaching their employment equity targets for persons with disabilities through reliance on the demographics of aging, rather than seeking to actively recruit them."[38] People with disabilities continue to have a low rate of applying to and being hired in the public service. The high termination rates in the private and public sectors suggest that disabled people are not being adequately accommodated in the workplace.

Between 2001 and 2006 there was a significant decline in workplace accommodations. Statistics Canada distinguishes between two types of accommodations: those that are physical or structural (handrails, modified workstations, accessible washrooms) and those that are resource-specific (job redesign, modified work schedule, computer aids). The 2009 *Federal Report on Disability* states, "In 2006, 70.2% of employed working-age adults with disabilities with requirements had all of their resource-specific workplace modification needs met, compared to 79.9% in 2001. In contrast, 49.1% of those with physical/structural modification requirements indicated that all of their needs were met in 2006, a decrease from 76.1% in 2001."[39]

Given this situation, it is not surprising that employment of people with disabilities is identified in its first report on the UNCRPD as an area for action by the federal government.[40] The government has tried a number of initiatives, including federal–provincial labour market agreements specific to people with disabilities, which implement programs specific to local provincial environments, and the Enabling Accessibility Fund, which supports making physical and structural modifications for accessibility. The 2013 report on private-sector employment of people with disabilities suggests that the large number of educated unemployed people with disabilities is an untapped pool of resources for the private sector.[41] With so little success in enabling the employment of people with disabilities, and the significant poverty among people with disabilities that often results from lack of employment,[42] this remains a significant area in which disability rights have yet to be implemented.

Life-Threatening Disability Rights

One of the most contentious areas of disability rights relates to the end of life or, more accurately, deciding who determines when or what end of life is for people with disabilities. This issue became a topic of public discussion in the early 1990s, when Sue Rodriguez, a woman with amyotrophic lateral sclerosis (ALS), asked for physician assistance in committing suicide. At that time the Supreme Court ruled to uphold the prohibition against assisted suicide.[43] Its decision rested in part on the equality rights in section 15 of the Charter, arguing that the section could not be applied to the prohibition. The majority argued that to allow assisted suicide for Rodriguez, even though she might be able to make the decision, would place others in a more vulnerable position, raising the possibility of their deaths being hastened or assisted without their consent or against their will.

The murder of Tracy Latimer in 1993 by her father also raised the issue of who gets to decide when people with disabilities die and under what circumstances.[44] Robert Latimer was charged with first-degree murder and sentenced to 10 years in jail. He took his case to the Supreme Court of Canada, asking it to recognize his act as "compassionate homicide," and thus justified and warranting a reduced sentence. In 2001 the Court upheld his conviction and sentence.[45]

In both of these deaths, females with disabilities challenged Canadians to think about the ways in which disability rights shape and are shaped by discussions of euthanasia and assisted suicide. Their deaths raise important questions about disability rights: how do perceptions of disability as suffering or lack prevent us from seeing life with disabilities as possible or positive? How do our laws protect those whose lives rely on the care of others, including caregivers who may think it necessary to end those lives? How are the views and decisions of physicians affected by public discourses that say it is better to be dead than disabled?[46] How do we as a society address the vulnerability and disparities around end of life between people with and without disabilities?

The public discussion on euthanasia and assisted suicide in Canada continues to be robust, moving toward increasing access to physician-assisted death. In June 2014, Quebec became the first jurisdiction in Canada to allow physicians to assist people who have requested to die.[47] While the Quebec legislation contains provisions to support palliative care, it also allows physicians to provide terminal sedation leading to death.

In February 2015, the Supreme Court of Canada ruled in *Carter v. Canada (Attorney-General)* that parliament had one year to address physician-assisted death through legislation. The Court argued that the current prohibition against physician-assisted suicide went against section 7 of the Charter (the right to life, liberty, and security of the person), was overly broad, and, as a result, infringed on the rights of people who did not need protection:

> The object of the prohibition is not, broadly, to preserve life whatever the circumstances, but more specifically to protect vulnerable persons from being induced to commit suicide at a time of weakness. Since a total ban on assisted suicide clearly helps achieve this object, individuals' rights are not deprived arbitrarily. However, the prohibition catches people outside the class of protected persons. It follows that the limitation on their rights is in at least some cases not connected to the objective and that the prohibition is thus overbroad.[48]

The Court's decision has divided the disability and medical communities and moved public discussion and policy much closer to enabling physician-assisted death. In 2014, prior to the decision, the Canadian Medical Association updated its policy on euthanasia and assisted suicide, reinforcing the requirement that physicians not participate in euthanasia and assisted suicide. However, more recent commentary suggests that physicians, including those who provide palliative care, are deeply divided.[49]

For many people with disabilities these changes mark greater threat and uncertainty, including a sense that their lives as disabled people are not valued and may be at risk in a world where physician-assisted death is legal. The CCD and the Canadian Association for Community Living (CACL) argue that the decision imposes an obligation on the state to provide assisted dying, but not to provide palliative care.[50] They suggest that the arguments used to justify assisted suicide—including requiring assistance to eat, toilet, or carry on other activities of daily life—undermine the value of those who are living with disabilities and may justify their deaths.

Disability rights in this area are very much rights about life and death and who gets to decide. Decisions made about assisted dying will provide an indicator of the extent to which disability rights (and disabled people) are an integral part of Canadian society or something considered less valuable than other rights, and may undermine forward movement on disability rights in general.

Disability Pushes the Boundaries of Human Rights

Disability rights require not only the inclusion of people with disabilities in society as it is now, but also the transformation of society to enable the inclusion of all people. One area where disability rights push the boundaries of current understandings of human rights is legal capacity. UNCRPD articles 12 and 13 break new ground when they assert that people with disabilities not only have the equal status of persons under the law and legal capacity, but also that there should be supports in place to ensure they can exercise that legal capacity. This suggests that people with disabilities, including those with intellectual disabilities, mental health disabilities, cognitive impairments, and others, have the right to make decisions about their own lives and be supported in making those decisions. This notion of supported decision-making challenges much of the legal understanding of *capacity* in Canada's laws.

As a result of the UNCRPD and advocacy from people with disabilities, there is an emerging shift in Canadians' understanding of legal capacity and the decision making of people with disabilities. In 2014 the Law Commission of Ontario released a significant discussion paper outlining the existing system, its barriers, and possible ways forward. The paper argues that the dominant approach to understanding legal capacity "is functional and cognitive. It focuses on the ability to make a specific decision or type of decision, at the time the decision is to be made, and in particular on the reasoning process involved in making decisions. This includes the abilities to understand, retain and evaluate the information relevant to the decision (including its likely consequences) and to weigh that information in the balance to reach a decision."[51]

The Law Commission's paper recognizes that the current legislative system in Ontario could be seen to be at odds with a disability rights perspective, because it assumes that capacity is associated with particular cognitive abilities and thus excludes those without those abilities. The dominant approach invokes an "understand and appreciate" test that "creates a threshold for who can and cannot make decisions for themselves based on cognitive abilities. Thus, although it is not a disability–based test, it will have a disproportionate effect on individuals whose disability affects their cognitive abilities, such as persons with intellectual, mental health or neurological disabilities."[52] While this recognition of the exclusionary nature of the dominant concept of capacity is an important step forward, change in this area will require significant movement away from the link between cognitive ability and capacity. This is one of the areas where people with disabilities are pushing the boundaries of human rights. They challenge reason or cognition as the basis for defining who is human and therefore who has human rights.

This approach to understanding legal capacity as linked to cognitive function is closely linked with ensuring that substitute decision makers are in place for those who are deemed incapable of making their own decisions. The UNCRPD challenges states to think beyond a system of substitute decision makers to one of supported decision makers. The Law Commission of Ontario suggests that both supported decision making and co-decision making offer alternatives to the current system of guardianship and substitute decision making, but they require further development in practice: "These approaches represent a fundamental shift in approaches to the law, and have significant implications for almost every aspect of this area of the law.... These newer approaches to decision-making are closely related to the shifts in conceptions of capacity ... and have their basis in a social model of disability and a human rights critique of existing approaches to legal capacity, decision-making and guardianship."[53]

The approach to legal capacity and decision making in Canada's legal system has created systematic barriers for women and men with disabilities, including access to justice and abuse by substitute decision makers. The DisAbled Women's Network of Canada (DAWN Canada) has been at the forefront of identifying barriers for women with disabilities, including an inability to tell their own stories of violence and abuse before the courts—because some were deemed not credible witnesses as a result of being labelled with an intellectual disability. In February 2012 the Supreme Court, in *R. v. D.A.I.*, ruled that people with intellectual disabilities are able to testify and tell their own stories if they promise to tell the truth.[54] The case was of a woman with intellectual disabilities who said she had been repeatedly sexually assaulted. Previous courts had decided that she not be allowed to testify, and as a result the accused was acquitted. The Supreme Court overturned those rulings and argued that the previous courts had set the bar too high in terms of who could provide evidence, and in so doing undermined the victim's access to justice. This case is especially important because of the significant presence of violence in the lives of women with disabilities and the high number of women with disabilities who do not report violence.[55]

People with disabilities also experience barriers to access to justice as a result of lack of information about their rights, abuse and violence from their care providers and substitute decision makers, and barriers resulting from lack of access to transportation and physical access and difficulties communicating. One area that we know little about is why there is a significant presence of men and women with disabilities among criminal offenders, including those with mental health disabilities[56] and cognitive impairments such as fetal alcohol spectrum conditions, and the barriers they face in the context of the justice system. One question that arises is, how do our assumptions about mental illness and cognition shape how we understand criminal intent or activity?

Addressing disability rights in legal capacity and access to justice is one area where assumptions about disability have systemically excluded some people with disabilities. To ensure that people with disabilities have full legal capacity, with the necessary supports and access to justice, will require transformation of our understanding of human rights in this area.

Conclusion

Canada has a strong framework of disability rights embedded in the Charter of Rights and Freedoms and complemented by human rights and other legislation. This framework is increasingly implemented through a range of Supreme Court decisions that use that framework to reinforce disability rights. Several provincial governments have recognized that one aspect of disability rights is legislation that can more proactively create access and inclusion for its citizens. Yet apart from the provincial accessibility laws, most of Canada's disability rights framework is complaint- or case-driven, focused on addressing existing discrimination and identifying barriers. Federal government cuts to the Court Challenges Program and to disability organizations reduce the capacity of people with disabilities and their representative organizations to engage with this system and may, over the longer term, inhibit the development of case law related to disability rights.

Three major areas herald significant shifts in disability rights. The ongoing low employment rate and chronic poverty among people with disabilities suggest that employment-related disability rights are not effective in ensuring the inclusion and access of people with disabilities in Canada's employment system. We need to ask pointed questions about why employment equity legislation is not working effectively for people with disabilities. Why do people with disabilities in the federal public service leave at a faster rate than they are hired? Do people with disabilities receive the workplace accommodations they require in order to remain? Are we signalling as a society that we are unwilling to make the changes necessary to our workplaces and to our own attitudes to ensure that people with disabilities get and keep jobs? Or do we assume that people with disabilities should be recipients of social assistance rather than contributors to our economy and society?

The second area of disability rights, related to end of life and assisted suicide, is also disturbing. The end-of-life discussions that have engaged the Canadian public are framed largely around the right to have ease in our dying and to be afforded comfort when we experience pain, and an unwillingness to accept bodily care and dependence as an aspect of human life rather than something to be avoided at all costs. While the Supreme Court rejected calls to remove the prohibitions on assisted suicide in 1993 and rejected leniency for Robert Latimer in the murder of his disabled daughter in 2001, the Court also rejected a broad ban on assisted dying in 2015 and called on parliament to legislate in this area. That decision and parliament's response will shape the terrain of disability rights for years to come.

Finally, Canadian human rights are being challenged to recognize the ways in which exclusion on the basis of disability is structured into our dominant understandings of legal capacity and is provoking changes in our understanding and practices related to capacity and decision making. Depending on the response to the Ontario Law Commission's 2014 discussion paper, Canadian human rights may become more positively "disabled."

The terrain of disability rights in Canada is dynamic and fragile, requiring action and interpretation as well as proactive transformation to ensure inclusion and access for all Canadians.

Takeaway Messages

- In responding to complaints rather than proactively promoting the inclusion of people with disabilities, the disability rights legislative framework is unable to effectively address systemic issues such as poverty.
- Disability rights require not only the inclusion in society of people with disabilities as it stands now, but also the transformation of society to enable the inclusion of all people.

Study Questions

- What are three key Supreme Court decisions addressing disability rights, and why are they important?
- How do discussions of assisted suicide affect disability rights?
- How does the dominant view of legal capacity challenge the implementation of disability rights, and what needs to be changed in this area?

Issues for Debate or Roundtable

- Agreement to allow assisted suicide will endanger the lives of people with disabilities.
- Employment of people with disabilities in Canada cannot be addressed through legislated disability rights.

Additional Reading

McColl, Mary Ann, and Lyn Jongbloed, eds. *Disability and Social Policy in Canada*. 2nd ed. Toronto: Captus Press, 2006.

Titchkovsky, Tanya. *The Question of Access: Disability, Space, Meaning*. Toronto: University of Toronto Press, 2011.

Titchkovsky, Tanya, and Rod Michalko, eds. *Rethinking Normalcy: A Disability Studies Reader.* Toronto: Canadian Scholars' Press, 2009.

Websites

Canadian Disability Policy Alliance. http://www.disabilitypolicyalliance.ca/.
Council of Canadians with Disabilities. http://www.ccdonline.ca/en/.
DisAbled Women's Network of Canada. http://www.dawncanada.net/.

Notes

1. Y. Peters, "From Charity to Equality: Canadians with Disabilities Take Their Rightful Place in Canada's Constitution," in *Making Equality: History of Advocacy and*

Persons with Disabilities in Canada, ed. D. Stienstra and A. Wight-Felske (Toronto: Captus Press, 2003), 119–36.

2. D. Stienstra, *About Canada: Disability Rights* (Black Point, NS: Fernwood, 2012).
3. Canada, *Convention on the Rights of Persons with Disabilities: First Report of Canada* (Ottawa: Canadian Heritage and Official Languages, 2014).
4. *Andrews v. Law Society of British Columbia*, [1989] 1 S.C.R. 143.
5. Y. Peters, "Twenty Years of Litigating for Disability Equality Rights: Has It Made a Difference?" Council of Canadians with Disabilities, 2004, http://www.ccdonline.ca/en/humanrights/promoting/20years#45.
6. Nova Scotia Department of Community Services, "Panel Will Help Make Province More Accessible," news release, 24 June 2014.
7. M. Prince, *Absent Citizens: Disability Politics and Policy in Canada* (Toronto: University of Toronto Press, 2010).
8. E. Varney, *Disability and Information Technology: A Comparative Study in Media Regulation* (Cambridge: Cambridge University Press, 2013).
9. Canada, CRPD Report, para. 21.
10. Stienstra, *About Canada*.
11. *Moore v. British Columbia (Education)*, 2012 SCC 61.
12. *Eaton v. Brant County Board of Education*, [1997] 1 S.C.R. 241.
13. D. Pothier, "*Eaton v. Brant County Board of Education*," *Canadian Journal of Women and the Law* 18 (2006): 141–42.
14. *Moore v. British Columbia (Education)*, 2012 SCC 61.
15. New Brunswick Department of Education and Early Childhood Development, "Policy 322: Inclusive Education," September 2013, www2.gnb.ca/content/dam/gnb/Departments/ed/pdf/k12/policies-politiques/e/322A.pdf.
16. Stienstra, *About Canada*, 74.
17. *Eldridge v. British Columbia (Attorney General)*, [1997] 3 S.C.R. 624.
18. Peters, "Twenty Years."
19. Stienstra, *About Canada*, 74.
20. *Council of Canadians with Disabilities v. VIA Rail Canada, Inc.*, [2007] 1 S.C.R. 650, 2007 SCC 15.
21. Canadian Transportation Agency, "Decision No. 6-AT-A-2008," 10 January 2008, https://www.otc-cta.gc.ca/eng/ruling/6-at-a-2008.
22. Council of Canadians with Disabilities [CCD], "CCD Comments on Regulatory Proposal to Amend the Air Transportation Regulations (SOR/88-58)," 30 January 2013, http://ccdonline.ca/en/transportation/air/regulations-30jan2013.
23. CityNews (Toronto), "$240M Shortfall Means TTC Can't Make All Subway Stations Accessible," 16 June 2014, www.citynews.ca/2014/06/16/240m-shortfall-means-ttc-cant-make-all-subway-stations-accessible/.
24. Canadian Radio-television and Telecommunications Commission [CRTC], "Broadcasting and Telecom Regulatory Policy CRTC 2009-430," 21 July 2009, http://www.crtc.gc.ca/eng/archive/2009/2009-430.htm.
25. Canadian Wireless Telecommunication Association, TEXT with 9-1-1, http://textwith911.ca/.
26. D. Stienstra, "Swimming Upstream: Accessibility and Telecommunications Policy," in *The Internet Tree: The State of Telecom Policy in Canada 3.0*, ed. M. Moll and L.R. Shade (Ottawa: Canadian Centre for Policy Alternatives, 2011), 153–60.

27. Annual reports from the telecommunications companies on their deferral account initiatives can be found on the CRTC website, http://www.crtc.gc.ca/PartVII/eng/2009/8678/c12_200905557.htm.
28. CRTC, "Video Relay Service (VRS)," 23 January 2015, http://www.crtc.gc.ca/eng/vrs-srv.htm.
29. Bell Canada and Bell Mobility, *2015 Annual Report on Accessibility Initiatives Approved in Decision 2014–527*, 8 April 2015.
30. Varney, *Disability and Information Technology*, 55–62.
31. Broadcasting Accessibility Fund, http://www.baf-far.ca/.
32. *Canada (Attorney General) v. Jodhan*, 2012 FCA 161 (CanLII).
33. M. Prince, "Locating a Window of Opportunity in the Social Economy: Canadians with Disabilities and Labour Market Challenges," *Canadian Journal of Nonprofit and Social Economy Research* 5, no. 1 (2014): 7.
34. D. Galarneau and M. Radulescu, "Employment among the Disabled," in Statistics Canada, *Perspectives on Labour and Income* (Ottawa: Statistics Canada, 2009).
35. L. Vosko, *Precarious Employment: Understanding Labour Market Insecurity in Canada* (Montreal: McGill-Queen's University Press, 2006).
36. K.M. Shuey and E. Jovic, "Disability Accommodation in Nonstandard and Precarious Employment Arrangements," *Work and Occupations* 40, no. 2 (1 May 2013): 174–205; A. Vick and E. Lightman, "Barriers to Employment among Women with Complex Episodic Disabilities," *Journal of Disability Policy Studies* 21, no. 2 (1 September 2010): 70–80.
37. Employment and Social Development Canada, *Employment Equity Act: Annual Report 201* (Ottawa: Government of Canada, 2014).
38. Senate Standing Committee on Human Rights, *Employment Equity in the Federal Public Service: Staying Vigilant for Equality* (Ottawa: Parliament of Canada, 2013), 18.
39. Human Resources and Skills Development Canada, *2009 Federal Disability Report* (Ottawa: Government of Canada, 2009).
40. Canada, , CRPD Report, 17.
41. Employment and Social Development Canada, "Rethinking DisAbility in the Private Sector: Report from the Panel on Labour Market Opportunities for Persons with Disabilities," http://www.esdc.gc.ca/eng/disability/consultations/rethinking_disabilities.shtml.
42. C. Crawford, *Looking into Poverty: Income Sources of Poor People with Disabilities in Canada* (Toronto: Institute for Research and Development on Inclusion and Society and CCD, 2013).
43. *Rodriguez v. British Columbia (Attorney General)*, [1993] 3 S.C.R. 519.
44. Stienstra, *About Canada*, 33–35.
45. *R. v. Latimer*, [2001] 1 S.C.R. 3, 2001 SCC 1.
46. H.M. Chochinov, "Dignity and the Essence of Medicine: The A, B, C and D of Dignity Conserving Care," *British Medical Journal* 335, no. 7612 (28 July 2007): 184–87.
47. Quebec, Bill 52, An Act Respecting End of Life Care, 4 June 2014.
48. *Carter v. Canada (Attorney General)*, 2015 SCC 5.
49. Canadian Medical Association, "Euthanasia and Assisted Suicide (Update 2014)," https://www.cma.ca/Assets/assets-library/document/en/advocacy/EOL/CMA_Policy_Euthanasia_Assisted%20Death_PD15-02-e.pdf; J. Downie, "*Carter*

v. Canada: What's Next for Physicians?" *Canadian Medical Association Journal* 187 (21 April 2015): 481–82.

50. CCD and Canadian Association for Community Living, "Commentary on SCC Assisted Suicide Judgment in *Carter v. Canada*: Key Concerns," 6 February 2015, http://www.ccdonline.ca/en/humanrights/endoflife/media-release-key-concerns-6Feb2015.
51. Law Commission of Ontario, "Legal Capacity, Decision-Making and Guardianship: Discussion Paper," May 2014, 4.
52. Ibid., 5.
53. Ibid., 8.
54. *R. v. D.A.I.*, 2012 SCC 5, [2012] 1 S.C.R. 149.
55. DAWN Canada, "Factsheet: Women with Disabilities and Violence," http://www.dawncanada.net/main/wp-content/uploads/2014/03/English-Violence-January-2014.pdf.
56. M. Sinha, "An Investigation into the Feasibility of Collecting Data on the Involvement of Adults and Youth with Mental Health Issues in the Criminal Justice System," Statistics Canada, 2009.

11
The Politics of Women's Rights

CAROLINE ANDREW

Learning Objectives

- To learn more about the ways in which different institutions, groups, and individuals in Canada have understood the principal obstacles to women's equality and their choice of tools to advance women's equality
- To better understand the extent to which the women's movement in Canada has integrated the practices of intersectionality
- To better understand the possibilities of more coordinated approaches to violence prevention across levels of government, across civil society organizations, and across government–civil society links

Women's rights have been one of the major dimensions of human rights in Canada over the past 50 years. The intent of this chapter is to examine women's rights legislation and judicial decisions in order to do two things: evaluate their impact and understand how the interplay of laws and politics allows us to understand that impact.

This chapter is organized into four major sections. It starts with this introduction, which sets the context for the beginning of the period covered by the chapter, followed by an overview of the period itself. Following this, two sections cover two policy areas: employment and safety/violence against women. The employment section is subdivided into four areas: Ontario pay equity legislation, the federal Employment Equity Act, the Canadian Human Rights Act, and the politics of intersectionality. The third section, on safety/violence against women, looks at government action and civil society interventions. It describes the Canadian Panel on Violence Against Women and the Manitoba experience with specialized services in the criminal justice and social services sectors, and then looks at the Canadian Network of Women's Shelters and Transition Houses and Women in Cities International.

The analysis of women's rights is a particularly interesting and complex one because the second wave of the feminist movement emerged, flourished, and perhaps diminished (we will return to this) in the same period, so the influence of law on politics and of politics on law was front and centre during this time. It was a period of innovation in human rights legislation in Canada and the most active moment of one of the major social movements of the twentieth century. At the same time—and, indeed, the main theme of this chapter—the issue of women's rights became increasing complex because of recognition during this period of the claims of multiple identities of women and the challenges that this has posed, both in law and certainly in politics. Therefore the major theme of this chapter is the ways in which intersectionality has made an impact on the politics and laws of women's equality.

To state it in its simplest form, intersectionality can be understood as the study of intersections between forms or systems of oppression, domination, or discrimination. It originates as a word, and as a concept, from black feminist thought in the United States, making the point that for black women in the US, the impacts of being black and of being a woman were not two separate challenges but one interrelated challenge.[1] In the period covered by this chapter, the issue of intersectionality has been front and centre in the politics of women's rights and, increasingly, in the legal system. One of the early Canadian writings on intersectionality in the legal system is an article by Nitya Iyer, "Disappearing Women: Racial Minority Women in Human Rights Cases," first presented at a conference to mark the twentieth anniversary of the Royal Commission on the Status of Women;[2] it made the point that human rights legislation at that time was not able to deal with multiple identities. Since then there has grown up an abundant literature on intersectionality and an evolving engagement with different dimensions of intersectionality, both by governments and by the women's movement. However, our focus in this chapter is specifically to indicate how this issue has profoundly complicated both the politics and the laws of women's rights. We will now return to the beginning of this period and try to capture the climate of the time for the pursuit of women's rights.

Canadians and Women's Rights, 1975–95

The adoption of the Charter of Rights and Freedoms in 1982 can be considered the iconic moment. It was a law conceived by the prime minister of the day, but section 28—the equality of women—was gained by political pressure from the women's movement. And, in turn, the Charter illustrates all the ambiguities of the politics of women's rights. It has been a beacon of entitlement for the equality of women, there have been ambivalent indications of its actual impact on women's equality, and there have been numerous indications that some of the younger generation of women feel that women's equality was achieved by the Charter and they do not have to be concerned or involved in political action. All these reactions coexist, sometimes in different sectors of the population and sometimes within the same individual.

It is also important, right from the start, to take account of the very strong interrelationship between the international context and the Canadian context of women's rights. Once again, this period was one of activism, including international activism in the field of women's rights. From Mexico in 1975 to the UN Convention on the Elimination of Discrimination Against Women (CEDAW) in 1979 to Beijing in 1995—in all cases, Canadians were there. And these Canadians came back to Canada bringing the international message: doing public education, lobbying governments, and creating organizations. To give only one example, Match International (now the MATCH International Women's Fund) was the first Canadian international organization to establish the issue of women's rights and empowerment as central to successful and sustained development in the global South. It was founded in 1976 by two Canadian women, Norma E. Walmsley and Suzanne Johnson-Harvor, who had been inspired by the women they met at the United Nation's First World Conference on Women, in Mexico City the year before.

This was still the internationalist period of Canadian policy, Canadian imagination, and Canadian programs. The leading role that the Canadian International Development Agency (CIDA) played in the early years in making women's equality one of the key elements in Canadian development policy was seen by Canadian feminists as a normal, and admirable, extension of domestic policy. Like many Canadians, I went abroad on CIDA-funded projects, first on a program to ensure a strong gender-equality component in the creation of a master's degree in urban planning in Hanoi Technical University. I worked with professors at the university to develop community-based research to increase women's participation in the management of local markets, an area that was dominated by men despite the fact that the vast majority of sellers and buyers were women.

I later returned to Vietnam to do gender training for the members of the Social Affairs Committee of the National Assembly of Vietnam, again a CIDA-funded project. It was very exciting to see Vietnam adopting legislation on the equality of women and on elimination of violence against women. At the same time I was aware of the ambiguities that existed in Canada in relation to the limits on achieving equality through the adoption of laws, admirable as those laws might be. Questions arose of implementation, of administrative capacity, of public hesitation and/or resistance; it certainly wasn't that we didn't know about these challenges from living with them in Canada, and Vietnam was no different. At the time we didn't feel that we were imposing Western feminism (perhaps we were), but this was masked by the enthusiasm and commitment of our Vietnamese audiences, and certainly by our naivety. We felt that we were working collaboratively with allies in a worldwide struggle for women's equality.

At about the same time, I was also involved in creating an NGO, Women in Cities International (Femmes et villes international), based in Montreal but acting both internationally and domestically to create safe and inclusive cities for the full diversity of women and girls. I did not consider myself to be doing international development as in Vietnam, but to be working for the equality of women through the variety of opportunities offered to me, locally, across Canada, and internationally. I will come back later to one of the Canadian projects of Women in Cities International, but I refer to it here as one illustration of what seemed to me a period when the work that Canadian women were doing internationally felt more in line with, if not part of, the work of Canada internationally.

Employment: Policy and Politics

There are a multitude of policy areas that can usefully be examined to explore the politics of women's rights and the interrelations among human rights legislation and the politics of equality. I have chosen to limit my analysis to two areas: employment and safety. These are two crucial areas for women's equality, and they capture, I believe, an evolution in the dominant paradigm of the strategy to achieve women's equality. The period of the Royal Commission on the Status of Women was heavily influenced by Simone de Beauvoir's *Le Deuxième Sexe*, in which it is posited that full-time paid employment (in good jobs) is the key to women's equality. At a later stage the issue of violence against women took on much greater significance as a crucial barrier to women's equality and therefore as an area for political action, creating services, and adopting legislation such as the Human Rights Act. We will come back to the politics of violence prevention after looking at the measures put in place to assure women's equality in employment. At the same time, and in line with the major theme of this chapter, both employment and safety are areas where debates about intersectionality have been clearly present.

Equal Pay for Work of Equal Value

A major event in the realm of employment was legislation positing that women should be paid equally for work of equal value. This was a huge advance on the earlier formulation of equal pay for equal work, as women and men were not always employed in the same sectors and it was therefore too easy to simply say that the work was not equal and therefore equal pay did not apply. Equal pay for work of equal value was clearly more relevant, but of course it led to enormous bureaucratic and political efforts to articulate a process of determining how the value of work could be calculated. Pat Armstrong's analysis of the Ontario Pay Equity Act of 1987[3] describes the process, whereby women had first to establish that they were members of a female job class and then find a male job class they could be compared with. Then the comparison was made in terms of "the skill, effort and responsibility normally required in the performance of the work and the conditions under which it is normally performed."[4]

Armstrong's conclusion is worth quoting at length, in that it raises our central question about the political and legal ambiguities of gender as a single category: "The pay-equity legislation in Ontario can be seen as one of the last gasps of a welfare state prepared to recognize both systematic inequality that has an impact on women as a group and the responsibility of the state to intervene on their behalf. It has improved the wages of many women and transformed the attitudes of many others, even though it has not served to end wage inequality between women and men or among women."[5]

The Employment Equity Act

The pay-equity legislation adopted in Ontario applied to both the public and private sectors. During approximately the same period, in 1986 the federal government adopted the Employment Equity Act, which was designed to ensure "that no person shall be denied employment opportunities or benefits for reasons unrelated to ability and, in fulfillment of that goal, to correct the conditions of disadvantage in employment experienced by women, Aboriginal peoples, persons with disabilities and members of visible minorities."[6] The Act applies to, among others, federally regulated private-sector employers with 100 or more employees. These employers are required to file data annually and the data are published in the annual report of the Employment Equity Act.

The data in the 2013 annual report illustrate the basis for the politics of intersectionality. Interestingly (or depressingly), the representation of women has been decreasing over the past decade in relation to their labour market availability (LMA); from 44.9 per cent in 2001, the representation rate for women in 2012 had fallen to 40.9 per cent.[7] Even more depressing are the figures for women within the other designated groups: Aboriginal peoples, persons with disabilities, and members of visible minorities.[8] One way of illustrating this is with the percentages of men and women in each category who earned more than $60,000 annually in 2012 (Table 11.1).

Table 11.1 Percentage of Men and Women Earning over $60,000 per Year, 2011 and 2012

	Men (%)		Women (%)	
	2011	2012	2011	2012
All	49.9	51.5	33.6	35.7
Aboriginals	46.4	44.6	25.4	27.2
Persons with Disabilities	47.2	48.9	29.0	32.5
Visible Minorities	43.5	45.3	31.8	34.1

Source: Employment and Social Development Canada, *Employment Equity Act: Annual Report 2013*, 7, 9, 11, 13.

These figures clearly speak to the multiple facets of inequality, and how legislative measures mandating equal pay for work of equal value have benefited women marginalized only by gender more than women who are doubly marginalized. This has led to the creation of specific policies, programs, and activities on the part of governments and, within civil society, to the creation of organizations mobilizing around the claims for equality of specific groups.

The Canadian Human Rights Act

The federal government enacted the Canadian Human Rights Act in 1977, its intent to extend the laws in Canada that proscribe discrimination. Sections 3 and 3.1 define the prohibited grounds of discrimination: "race, national or ethnic origin, colour, religion, age, sex, sexual orientation, marital status, family status, disability and conviction for an offence for which a pardon has been granted or in respect of which a record suspension has been ordered."[9] "For greater certainty, a discriminatory practice includes a practice based on one or more prohibited grounds of discrimination or on the effect of a combination of prohibited grounds."[10]

The Act does envisage that discrimination can be the result of a combination of prohibited grounds, but the politics of the women's movement have been far more tumultuous than "a combination of prohibited grounds." In a much earlier text I wrote that "It is the simultaneous recognition of gender and ethnicity that has, rather like the collision of two stars, led to a stunning, exhilarating and almost cataclysmic fragmentation of identities. The recognition of these specific fragmentations had been the most salient politically, with class as the perennially less visible definer of political position and political practice in Canada."[11]

The Politics of Intersectionality

Mary-Jo Nadeau has written about the challenges to the traditional organization and leadership of the National Action Committee on the Status of Women (NAC) as being a white, middle-class organization;[12] at the same time a number of new organizations were being created. The Native Women's Association of Canada (NWAC) "is founded on the collective goal to enhance, promote, and foster the social, economic, cultural and political well-being of First Nations and Métis women within First Nation, Métis and Canadian societies. NWAC is an aggregate of thirteen Native women's organizations from across Canada and was incorporated as a non-profit organization in 1974."[13]

DAWN/RAFH—the DisAbled Women's Network of Canada/Réseau d'action des femmes handicapées du Canada—was founded in 1987, following an initial meeting of 17 women in 1985. DAWN/RAFH Canada's mission is to end the poverty, isolation, discrimination, and violence experienced by women with disabilities and deaf women. It has worked to make more visible the conditions of disadvantage of women with disabilities in Canada, both to the public at large and to all levels of government.[14]

In terms of organizations representing racialized women, the National Organization of Immigrant and Visible Minority Women of Canada (NOIVMWC) was active for more than two decades. NOIVMWC was one of the many women's organizations that initially received core funding from Status of Women Canada but then had its funding withdrawn. It appears to be relatively inactive at present.

There is a huge literature on the reasons for women's lower pay and lower representation at the higher levels of management, both public and private. These commentaries can be seen partly as a debate about the relative influence of laws as compared to politics and policies, but also, and very importantly, about patterns of socialization, attitudes, and/or cultural traditions. The literature around the "glass ceiling" refers to the influence of organizational behaviour, attitudes, and cultural understandings.

One recent article on this question comes from the *Harvard Business Review* of March 2014, titled "Manage Your Work, Manage Your Life: Zero In on What Really Matters."[15] The authors describe what they call "intriguing" gender differences: "In defining professional success, women place more value than men do on individual achievement, having passion for their work, receiving respect, but less value on organizational achievement and ongoing learning and development. A lower percentage of women than of men list financial achievement as an aspect of personal or professional success."[16] The role in the family reinforces what we could consider as patterns of socialization and/or cultural understandings: "Men still think of their family responsibilities in terms of breadwinning, whereas women often see theirs as the modelling for their children."[17] And more: "Many women said that the most difficult aspect of managing work and family is contending with cultural expectations about mothering."[18]

Our conclusion on this first policy area, employment, does show the interplay of laws and politics. The laws were extremely important, but certainly so too were the politics of intersectionality and the organizing, policies, and practices of a much more diverse women's movement. A large variety of organizations lobbied and put pressure on governments to create programs for employment training and employment enhancement. Many women's groups were involved in skills development and training with links to possible employment, and new groups were created to establish employment and pre-employment programs. At the same time, this was not the primary focus of the work of a great number of women's organizations that were more centred on delivering services, public education, self-esteem, empowerment, and/or advocacy.

Our look at the organizations created during this period gives some sense of their employment focus, but in general it is clear that for most of these groups employment was not the primary focus. One typical example comes from an Ottawa group, the City for All Women Initiative (CAWI), and its training for animators. I have described this program in a recent article[19] and will simply summarize the employment component of various activities of CAWI. The organization has been centred on training women from community-based women's groups to learn how to engage with the City of Ottawa, how to put forward their issues and make an impact on city-level decisions. At a particular point in time CAWI was not able to access funds to continue this engagement training; instead it began to do facilitator training to equip community-based women with animation skills, a field with employment potential in Ottawa. However, this remains a very small part of CAWI's overall activity and is very much dependent on being able to obtain project funding.

Safety: Policy and Politics

We will come back to the current state of women's organizations and their funding challenges, but in turning to the issue of safety and violence against women, we go back to the recommendations from the Royal Commission on the Status of Women that relate to the creation of government machinery for women's equality. To the Royal Commission, government was seen to be the implementer of social change, of using the incentives of policy, legal obligation, money, and information, and often using these tools of government in partnership with civil society organizations. The Canadian Advisory Committee on the Status of Women (CACSW) was created in 1973, following one of the recommendations from the Royal Commission. It was made up of 3 full-time members and 15 regionally representative part-time members with a mandate to advise the government and inform the public on issues relating to women's equality. The CACSW was disbanded on 1 April 1995.

It was the CACSW that did the first study on the extent of violence against women. When the results were announced in the House of Commons, the laughter this inspired from some federal MPs triggered a huge political reaction from women, furious at this blatant sexism. Violence against women began to be taken more seriously by the government, pushed by the groundswell of pressure from women's groups and individual women, and programs to finance shelters and transition houses were put into place.

One of the characteristics of policy relating to women's equality, for employment and perhaps even more clearly for violence prevention, is the fact that it takes place at all levels of government and all levels of civil society. In order to illustrate this we will highlight two mini case studies from government—the federal government's Canadian Panel on Violence Against Women in 1993 and the work of Manitoba in the criminal justice system and social services—and two case studies of action by civil society—the Canadian Network of Women's Shelters and Transition Houses arguments for a national action plan on violence against women, and Women in Cities International, a Montreal-based NGO that has worked both with Canadian municipalities and internationally to create secure and inclusive cities for the full diversity of women and girls. What is particularly useful for this chapter is that all these case studies include explicit reflections about the interrelationships of law, policy, and politics, about bottom-up and top-down approaches, and about the relationship between the women's movement and the state. This is partly a reflection of the fact that these events took place somewhat later than our earlier laws and programs, and because the fragmenting of the women's movement that we have just described has led to a more critical relationship with the state, at least for a significant part of the women's movement.

Canadian Panel on Violence Against Women

The Panel on Violence Against Women was created in 1991 as a result of a recommendation that same year from a report of the House of Commons Subcommittee on the Status of Women, *The War on Women*. The Panel published its final report, *Changing the Landscape: Ending Violence—Achieving Equality*, in 1993.[20] Its introduction makes the argument that violence against women is both a cause and an effect of women's inequality. The Panel believed that inequality increases women's vulnerability to violence and limits their choices in all aspects of their lives. In turn, women cannot achieve full equality while they are subjected to violence in their daily lives.[21] Its report then identifies the two goals of the Panel: achievement of women's equality and elimination of violence against women. It describes the areas where governments should renew their commitment to women's equality and then, in terms of the elimination of violence, introduces the idea of zero tolerance and a policy framework for its implementation.

There are therefore two sections to the Report: an Equality Action Plan and a Zero Tolerance Policy. The Equality Action Plan starts with a discussion of the benefits of legal commitments, stating "Canada already has a strong, stated commitment to gender equality and a legacy of statutory measures aimed at achieving equality.... In addition to its domestic measures, Canada has made clear and unequivocal international commitments to achieving equality for women by signing a number of international conventions and declarations."[22] Right away, the text juxtaposes our commitments and the reality: "We believe that concrete, practical fulfilment of these commitments along with significant change in key areas of women's lives would make a critical difference in achieving women's equality in our society, thereby reducing women's vulnerability to violence."[23]

The second part of the Panel's message is the Zero Tolerance Policy. It begins by describing the context, including that "male violence against women is at a crisis level in Canada and must be urgently addressed"; "violence against women is one of the crucial social mechanisms by which women are forced into a position subordinate to men"; and "violence against women is an abuse of power and a betrayal of trust."[24] The text then goes on to discuss intersectionality:

> Violence against women includes various types of abuse—psychological, financial, verbal, sexual and physical. It affects all women but with different consequences for Aboriginal and Inuit women, young women, elderly women, women of colour, immigrant women, refugee women, domestic workers, women with disabilities, women from different linguistic backgrounds, women living in rural, northern and isolated communities and lesbians.[25]

In the further description of the Zero Tolerance Policy, reference is made to gender, race, and class rather than to the long list quoted above, but throughout the document the issue of intersectionality is fundamental. The Zero Tolerance Policy was intended to be a framework for the entire Canadian society, "equally relevant to support groups, non-governmental organizations, services, corporations and government institutions."[26] It included an accountability framework with criteria for zero tolerance, steps to be taken in implementation, and a model for organizations to use in implementing a zero tolerance policy.

The Panel is an interesting example of a government-led initiative that made very sweeping recommendations that went far beyond the jurisdiction of the federal government, setting up models of behaviour and accountability for the entire Canadian society. However, the Panel was highly contested by parts of the women's movement and by service providers for not establishing a clear path toward implementation of concrete measures, so the impact of the report was minimal. It remains an interesting document, demonstrating the high point of federal government interest in formulating broad policies to end violence against women, and in a way that first linked elimination of violence against women to achieving equality for women in all major spheres of activity. It is also noteworthy in that the Panel attempted to reconcile the impact of violence on all women, showing a concern for intersectionality and recognition of the differing consequences of violence for different groups of women.

Specialized Services in Manitoba

Manitoba was the first province to set up specialized judicial services for dealing with family violence against women. This government action started in the early 1980s when the province funded a committee on wife abuse. Then, in 1983, the attorney general of Manitoba directed police to lay charges in all reported cases of spousal abuse when police believed that abuse had taken place.[27] Prior this decision, in general the victim had to request that charges be laid, and often this did not happen. In 1990 the Family Violence Court was established to deal with all issues of family violence: spousal abuse, child abuse, and elder abuse. According to the pre- and post-outcome research, this specialization led to increases in victim reporting, conviction rates, probation supervision, jail sentences, and court-mandated treatment.[28]

The second stage of the Manitoba government's initiatives related more to social services, and this led to conflict between the Manitoba Committee on Wife Abuse and the provincial government. The Committee felt that it, as a group made up of community members active in the anti-violence movement, should be the body to decide on appropriate services for battered women.

Jane Ursel, in her analysis of this period of increase in services and programs for battered women, argues that the surge in government activity was a result of lobbying by the women's movement, and particularly that part of it mobilized around violence against women. However, this had led to a debate within the women's movement: "On the one side of the debate are women who view the increased involvement of the state as having the positive outcome of increasing services to battered women and their children, and increasing penalties for battering. On the other side are women who argue that increased involvement of mainstream institutions results in cooptation, distortion, and depoliticization of the issue."[29]

As the Manitoba government moved not only to increase services but also to establish a government wife-abuse office, this led to increased conflict with those parts of the women's movement that saw government activity as necessarily suspect. This was certainly the view of the Manitoba Committee on Wife Abuse in the first years of government activity. It typifies a period of relations between the state and the women's movement that was very influenced by a vision of the state as "fundamentally and irretrievably patriarchal. The policy implications of this perspective are to approach the state apprehensively, with the expectation that whatever the state touches will be turned to patriarchal purposes."[30]

This was an important moment in the history of the women's movement during the period we are describing. As stated at the beginning of the chapter, one of the complexities of this analysis is the evolution of the women's movement during the period, and the conflicts described in the Manitoba case can be seen as one reaction to the increase in government services to victims of violence against women. For some this was a reaction to loss of control over the direction of service provision; when this was linked with a view of governments as being unable to act in women's interests, conflict was inevitable. However, as Ursel points out, the fact that government's role has largely been one of funding community-based services, the result was community-based activity that is better funded and therefore able to offer more and better services.

The early 1980s to the 1990s was a period of considerable expansion of services. Using only the Manitoba example, in 1982 the provincial government spent $52,000 to fund two community-based woman-abuse programs; by 1995 there were 30 programs supported by $6 million in provincial funding.[31] In general, one can say that the hostility within the women's movement to the state as funder has been replaced more recently by hostility toward the state, particularly (but not only) the Harper federal government, for reducing its funding, cutting off organizations that it does not approve of, refusing to fund advocacy, and supporting services rather than empowerment. What follows is a depressing (and incomplete) list of women's organizations that have lost their funding from the federal government:

- Action travail des femmes du Québec
- Alberta Network of Immigrant Women
- Association féminine d'éducation et d'action sociale (AFEAS)
- Canadian Research Institute for the Advancement of Women
- Conseil de l'intervention pour l'accès des femmes au travail (CIAFT)
- Feminists for Just and Equitable Public Policy (FemJEPP), Nova Scotia
- MATCH International
- National Association of Women and the Law (NAWL)
- Native Women's Association of Canada (NWAC)
- Ontario Association of Interval and Transition Houses (OAITH)
- Réseau des tables régionales de groupes de femmes du Québec
- Riverdale Women's Centre, Toronto
- South Asian Women's Centre, Toronto
- Womanspace Resource Centre, Lethbridge, Alberta
- Women's Innovative Justice Initiative, Nova Scotia[32]

More recent opposition to the federal government has often been expressed in personal terms, in the sense of referring to individual politicians rather than to concerns about the nature of the state or the particular ideology of some specific government, although both exist. However, the most common activity is trying to influence particular government actions; our next mini case study gives one illustration of this type of activity.

The Canadian Network of Women's Shelters and Transition Houses

The Canadian Network of Women's Shelters and Transition Houses is a relatively recent creation, established to bring together on a national level the women's sheltering organizations that exist at different levels: provincial, territorial, regional, and Aboriginal. In 2009, 14 of these organizations came together to form the Network.[33] One of their early projects was inspired by international debates—something that we have indicated is one of the constants in Canadian policy on women's equality. In this case the spark was the UN Secretary-General's UNiTE to End Violence Against Women and the importance given by this campaign to the adoption of national action plans (NAPs) on violence against women (VAW). The Network started with the Mapping VAW Policy and Opportunities Project, which was to identify all existing programs that would be impacted by or could serve as a basis for a NAP for Canada.

In 2013 the Network published a report entitled *The Case for a National Action Plan on Violence Against Women.* Its conclusions made the case for a NAP for Canada:

> While some important advancements have been made by various levels of government in Canada to respond to and prevent VAW, far more must be done. As found by this report, many current policies, legislation, strategies, and action plans across Canada lack effective coordination of efforts, conflict with one another, and/or have unintended (negative) consequences. A National Action Plan on VAW that follows the guiding principles laid out in the UN Handbook for National Action Plans on VAW could help address such deficiencies.[34]

The report contains a number of key conclusions that support the call for a national action plan, including that women's safety is compromised by government underfunding of social services, social housing, and supports for women affected by violence; that the focus on the federal level is on gender-neutral victims of crime and family violence; that a change in orientation is needed for service provision to Aboriginal women; and that legal systems across Canada are costly, inaccessible, and fragmented and must be improved in order to better address VAW and to benefit survivors.[35]

This report is an interesting illustration of recent work being done by service providers, using international guidelines and engaging the services of a team of research consultants. The Network is urging more and better government action and using evidence-based recommendations to make the case. The passion and commitment of the service providers has not diminished, but now there is more realization that the political context calls for new strategies of engagement with governments.

Women in Cities International: Practising Intersectionality

Women in Cities International/Femmes et villes international (WICI/FEVI) is, as mentioned earlier, a small NGO based in Montreal that works to foster secure and inclusive cites for the full diversity of women and girls. It has used and adapted women's safety audits[36] both internationally and within Canada. The project I will describe here is one that was built explicitly on the principles of intersectionality, in that it involved working with four communities and four women's organizations, each of which worked with a specific group of women: Aboriginal women in Regina, recent immigrant women in Peel, elderly women in Gatineau, and disabled women in Montreal. The report on the full study is titled *Together for Women's Safety: Creating Safer Communities for Marginalized Women and Everyone.*[37]

The project involved working in the communities to help build partnerships with the local municipality and other community-based groups, and assisting the local group with carrying out the safety audits. But it also involved bringing together the four groups in Montreal to discuss their experiences. This was an extremely valuable part of the project; it led each of the individual projects to become more intersectional after they experienced learning first-hand about the concrete life challenges of other groups in danger of marginalization. It was an example of practising intersectionality, clearly at a very small scale, but in a very real way.

It was more challenging to build ongoing relationships with the local municipality, and this is of course one of the challenges of project funding. A three-year project can only begin the process of building relationships, and once the project has ended, there are no resources to continue developing the relationship.

An interesting addition to the municipal level of activity around women's equality and to the question of violence against women is the recent report by Kate McInturff, of the Canadian Centre for Policy Alternatives: *The Best and Worst Place to Be a Woman in Canada.*[38] The report uses indicators of health, education, political participation, economic security, and personal safety. Of the 20 largest metropolitan areas, Quebec City was ranked first, with the lowest rates of police-reported intimate partner violence against women and police-reported sexual assaults (although, as the report states, we know that only a small percentage of gender-based violence is ever reported) and relatively high salary levels, because of public-sector dominance of the city's economy. Looking again at the WICI/FEVI study, it is depressing to note that Regina has the highest per capita rate of police-reported intimate partner violence against women. That report can be read to reinforce the issue of multiple levels of government and non-government action interrelating but often lacking coordination, a concern that is also highlighted in the report of the Canadian Network of Women's Shelters and Transition Houses, described above.

Conclusion

The major theme in this chapter has been the increasing complexity over the period examined of our understanding of women's human rights, largely because of the growing importance of intersectionality and the multiplicity of identities. As indicated above, there has been an evolving engagement with different dimensions of intersectionality. I would argue that a dimension only being touched upon at the moment is that of sexual identity, particularly the issue of trans identities, but this goes beyond the framework of this chapter and would require a fuller treatment than can be given here.

This growing complexity of women's equality in a context of intersectionality is a result of the interplay between laws and politics, the changes in the women's movement but also in the nature of legislation. I end this chapter with one last illustration, a particularly interesting example of this complexity: the recent debate around the laws on prostitution. This issue was brought to the forefront of public discussion in Canada by a decision of the Supreme Court that struck down existing laws and gave the federal government one year in which to enact new legislation. There has been intense online debate over this issue, but here I simply offer a local example of very different views held, all arguing for the equality of women but from the viewpoints of differently positioned women.

Crime Prevention Ottawa organized a local conference, "Sex Trade and Crime Prevention." Given the strong differences among the groups and positions represented, the conference committee worked to develop common messages. These messages included defining safety as "feeling safe in one's environment—and not feeling fear"; wanting to work together with individuals, groups, and neighbourhoods to promote and ensure safety for those working in the sex trade and for the broader community; and finally, ensuring that resources spent must focus on the safety of sex-trade workers and the broader community. Three groups of women—all of whom have human rights as women—were very differently positioned on this issue: sex workers who worked inside, street sex workers (many of whom were Aboriginal, poor, and often in poor health), and women who lived in neighbourhoods with active street sex workers.

The federal government has acted on legislation and there has been much analysis of the likelihood of this issue coming back before the courts. One could debate which group or groups of women gained from the legislation in terms of their safety and which group or groups lost. But as the Ottawa crime prevention conference experience suggests, the politics and partnerships of community-level decision making can mitigate the impact of the federal legislation. We end as we began: there have been advances in women's human rights over the past half century, but our greater inclusion and understanding of intersectionality has certainly added complexity to the working out of women's human rights.

Takeaway Messages

- Positive social change takes place through tensions between pressure from civil society organizations and policy formulation by government, so conflicts and contestation are part of creating social change.
- Most individuals in Canadian society are included in certain dimensions of intersectionality and excluded in other dimensions.

Study Questions

- Which dimensions of intersectionality are you included in and which others are you excluded from?
- Using the example of the three groups of women differently positioned in terms of the sex trade, how would you evaluate the new legislation that the federal government has introduced? Who gains, and who loses?
- What kinds of actions do you think are most appropriate in trying to reduce salary differentials between women with disabilities and men with disabilities?
- Examine one of the women's groups that has been defunded by the federal government. Determine if it has managed to survive, and if so, what strategies has it used and how successful has it been?

Issues for Debate or Roundtable

- In terms of the long list of missing and murdered Aboriginal women and girls, discuss whether this is more a reflection of violence against women or a reflection of women's inequality.
- Discuss the truth of the following statement: One of the main reasons for women's lower representation in upper management positions is the unequal division of household tasks.

Additional Reading

Boyd, Susan B., ed. *Challenging the Public/Private Divide: Feminism, Law, and Public Policy*. Toronto: University of Toronto Press, 1997.

Brodie, Janine, and Linda Trimble, eds. *Reinventing Canada: Politics of the 21st Century*. Toronto: Prentice-Hall, 2003.

Johnson, Holly, and Myrna Dawson. *Violence Against Women in Canada: Research and Policy Perspectives*. Toronto: Oxford University Press, 2011.

Sheehy, Elizabeth A. *Defending Battered Women on Trial: Lessons from the Transcripts*. Vancouver: UBC Press, 2014.

Whitzman, Carolyn, Crystal Legacy, Caroline Andrew, Fran Klodawsky, Margaret Shaw, and Kalpana Viswanath, eds. *Building Inclusive Cities: Women's Safety and the Right to the City*. Abingdon, UK: Routledge, 2013.

Websites

City for All Women Initiative/Initiative: Une ville pour toutes les femmes (CAWI/IVTF). http://www.cawi-ivtf.org/.

DisAbled Women's Network (DAWN) Canada. http://www.dawncanada.net/.
Native Women's Association of Canada (NWAC). http://www.nwac.ca/.
Women in Cities/Femmes et villes International (WICI). http://www.femmesetvilles.org/index.php/en/.

Notes

1. K. Crenshaw, "Demarginalizing the Intersection of Race and Sex: A Black Feminist Critique of Antidiscrimination Doctrine, Feminist Theory and Antiracist Politics," *University of Chicago Legal Forum 1989*, 139–67.
2. N. Iyer, "Disappearing Women: Racial Minority Women in Human Rights Cases," in *Women and the Canadian State*, ed. C. Andrew and S. Rodgers (Montreal: McGill-Queen's University Press, 1997), 241–61.
3. P. Armstrong, "Pay Equity: Not Just a Matter of Money," *Women and the Canadian State*, ed. C. Andrew and S. Rodgers (Montreal: McGill-Queen's University Press, 1997), 122–37.
4. Ibid, 128.
5. Ibid, 137.
6. Canada, Employment Equity Act (S.C. 1995, c. 44), s. 2.
7. Employment and Social Development Canada, *Employment Equity Act: Annual Report 2013* (Ottawa: Government of Canada, 2014), 2.
8. Members of visible minorities are defined by the Canadian Employment Equity Act as "persons, other than Aboriginal people, who are non-Caucasian in race and non-white in colour"; Employment Equity Act, s. 3.
9. Canada, Canadian Human Rights Act (R.S.C., 1985, C. H-6), s. 3.
10. Ibid, s. 3.1.
11. C. Andrew, "Ethnicities, Citizenship and Feminisms: Theorizing the Political Practices of Intersectionality," *Nationalism and Ethnic Politics* 1, no. 3 (1995): 1–3, 65.
12. M.-J. Nadeau, "Rebuilding the House of Canadian Feminism: NAC and the Racial Politics of Participation," in *Opening Doors Wider*, ed. S. Bashevkin (Vancouver: UBC Press, 2009), 33–50.
13. Native Women's Association of Canada, http://www.nwac.ca/.
14. DAWN-RAFH Canada, "Our Mission and Vision" and "Our History," http://www.dawncanada.net/.
15. B. Groysberg and R. Abrahams, *Harvard Business Review*, March 2014, 58–66.
16. Ibid., 60.
17. Ibid., 61.
18. Ibid., 62.
19. C. Andrew, F. Klodawsky, and J. Siltanen, "Soft Skills and Hard Prejudices: Pathways to Improve the Life Chances of Recent Immigrant Women in Ottawa, Canada," *Diversities* 15, no. 1 (2013): 67–78.
20. Canadian Panel on Violence Against Women, *Changing the Landscape: Ending Violence—Achieving Equality* (Ottawa: Minister of Supply and Services Canada, 1993).
21. Ibid, 3.
22. Ibid., 5.
23. Ibid.
24. Ibid., 23.

25. Ibid.
26. Ibid., 25.
27. J. Ursel, "Considering the Impact of the Battered Women's Movement on the State: The Example of Manitoba," in *Women and the Canadian State*, ed. C. Andrew and S. Rodgers (Montreal: McGill-Queen's University Press, 1997), 155–79.
28. Ibid., 171–76.
29. Ibid., 155.
30. Ibid., 178.
31. Ibid., 176.
32. D. Gruending, "Stephen Harper's Hit List: Organizations Whose Funding Has Been Cut or Ended," http://www.dennisgruending.ca/2011/03/stephen-harpers-hit-list/.
33. Canadian Network of Women's Shelters and Transition Houses [CNWSTH], "About Us," http://endvaw.ca/about-us.
34. CNWSTH, *The Case for a National Action Plan on Violence Against Women*, (Ottawa: CNWSTH, 2013), 39, http://endvaw.ca/our-work/the-case-for-a-national-plan-on-violence-against-women-and-girls.
35. Ibid., 6.
36. A tool created by METRAC, an anti-violence organization in Toronto, and used around the world; www.metrac.org. See also Women in Cities International, *Women's Safety Audits: What Works and Where?* (Nairobi: UN-HABITAT, 2008), http://www.femmesetvilles.org/images/Publications/womens%20safety%20audits%20what%20works%20en.pdf.
37. Women in Cities International, *Together for Women's Safety: Creating Safer Communities for Marginalized Women and Everyone* (Montreal: WICI, 2010), http://www.femmesetvilles.org/images/Publications/together%20for%20womens%20safety%20en.pdf.
38. K. McInturff, *The Best and Worst Places to Be a Woman in Canada 2015* (Ottawa: Canadian Centre for Policy Alternatives, 2015), https://www.policyalternatives.ca/sites/default/files/uploads/publications/National%20Office/2015/07/Best_and_Worst_Places_to_Be_a_Woman2015.pdf.

12
"All Manner of Wickedness Abounds": Reconciling Queer Rights and Religious Rights

KAREN BUSBY[1]

Learning Objectives

- To learn about some of the reforms used to achieve legal equality for queer (non-heterosexual) people
- To understand, apply, and evaluate how the Canadian Charter of Rights and Freedoms and human rights legislation help to protect rights to equality and non-discrimination for queer people and religious freedom for believers
- To explore and evaluate how Canadian law reconciles religious rights claims and queer equality rights claims

> If a man also lie with mankind, as he lieth with a woman, both of them have committed an abomination: they shall surely be put to death; their blood shall be upon them.
>
> —*Leviticus 20:13*

> Come on people, wake up! It's time to stand together and take whatever steps are necessary to reverse the wickedness that our lethargy has authorized to spawn. Where homosexuality flourishes, all manner of wickedness abounds. ... These activists ... are perverse, self-centred and morally deprived individuals who are spreading their psychological disease into every area of our lives.
>
> —*Rev. Stephen Boissoin, letter published in the Red Deer Advocate, 17 June 2002*

A 2013 Pew Research Poll asked people in 39 countries, "Should society accept homosexuality?" The Spaniards surveyed were the least likely to respond no (11 per cent), while Nigerians were the most likely to respond no (98 per cent). This study noted that "there is a strong relationship between a country's religiosity and opinions about homosexuality. There is far less acceptance of homosexuality in countries where religion is central to people's lives—measured by whether they consider religion to be very important, whether they believe it is necessary to believe in God in order to be moral, and whether they pray at least once a day."[2] This correlation is reflected in law: Spain was one of the first countries to permit same-sex marriage, whereas same-sex sexual activity is criminally prohibited in Nigeria and a convicted person could be subject to the death penalty. The percentage of Canadians who responded that homosexuality is unacceptable is low but not insignificant: 14 per cent.

While some claim that "arguments against equality claims for lesbians and gays are almost exclusively religious in nature,"[3] stereotypical thinking associating homosexuality and pedophilia/sexual abuse of children often emerges as the justification used by politicians and others for anti-gay laws. In early 2014 the Ugandan government passed new laws that criminally prohibited queer sex and required everyone to report suspected homosexuals to the police. Ugandan president Yoweri Museveni justified these draconian laws by pointing to the "arrogant and careless Western groups that are fond of coming into our schools and recruiting young children into homosexuality and lesbianism."[4] President Vladimir Putin attempted to reassure those going to Russia for the 2014 Winter Olympics that they had nothing to fear from recently passed Russian anti-gay laws, stating, "We aren't banning anything, we aren't rounding up anyone, we have no criminal punishment for such relations unlike many other countries. One can feel relaxed and at ease, but please leave the children in peace."[5]

Such thinking may also still have purchase in the United States; 43 per cent of those surveyed in an American Gallup poll in 2005 opined that homosexuals should not be hired as elementary schoolteachers, an outcome that suggests an underlying belief that queer people may harm children. Canada is not immune from these opinions either. Two very recent Canadian cases, discussed later in this chapter, *Boissoin* and *Whatcott*, concern religiously motivated opinions on proposed anti-homophobia initiatives in public schools that, among other things, conflate homosexuality and child sexual abuse.

Given the correlation between social acceptance of homosexuality and both the degree of religiosity and the persistence of unfounded fears of child abuse by gay men,[6] it is interesting to explore how Canadian law reconciles religious rights claims and queer (non-heterosexual) equality rights claims, paying some attention to arguments for the protection of children. I start this chapter by surveying some of the constitutionally and statutorily protected rights in Canada of equality and non-discrimination for queer people (those with non-heterosexual sexualities) and religious freedom for believers, and then I explore the interplay between these two rights claims. Following this, I focus on two questions that help to deepen our understanding of this interplay. First, if one feels compelled by religious belief to speak out against homosexuality, as did both Whatcott and Boissoin, should such statements be immune from hate-expression laws? Second, should religiously mandated schools be compelled to permit gay–straight alliance groups to form and meet on their premises?

A word on methodology: my survey of religious and queer rights law cannot be comprehensive in this short chapter. For example, regarding queer rights, I look at criminal law, relationship recognition, expressive rights, and gay–straight alliances, but I do not discuss laws relating to violence against queer people; access to assisted human reproduction and protection of the autonomy of queer families; HIV/AIDS-related issues; police harassment; or trans people. Moreover, as a legal scholar, I focus mainly on what judges say about law, describing settled law or forecasting how new law might develop out of established precedents (legal scholars also critique law or suggest reforms, often relying on insights from other disciplines). The focus on judgements and law reform may leave readers with the mistaken impression that social change is transcendent, that it happens because of brilliantly strategic lawyers and some enlightened judges. As well, readers might believe that reforms to law have immediate impacts for the new rights-bearers. Law reform happens in tandem with other social change; sometimes it leads and sometimes it follows. But without on-the-ground, active, and committed public interest groups, none of the legal changes described herein would have been possible.

Queer People and the Right to Equality

Criminal Law

In 1967 the Supreme Court of Canada (SCC) upheld the finding that Everett Klippert was a dangerous sexual offender who could be imprisoned indeterminately under preventive detention.[7] No one had made a complaint against Klippert; rather, a gross indecency charge had resulted after police happened to ask him about his sexual activities while conducting another investigation. He, perhaps naively, disclosed sexual liaisons with other men. There was no evidence of violence or coercion in those relationships, but the sexual activities (including anal penetration) he described were, at the time, criminal offences. Moreover, since he had stated that he intended to continue to pursue sexual relationships with men, the SCC held that the dangerous offender criterion—a likelihood of reoffending—was met.

The *Klippert* majority (three of five SCC judges hearing the case) held that "whether the criminal law, with respect to sexual misconduct of the sort in which the appellant has indulged for nearly twenty-five years, should be changed to the extent to which it has been recently in England, by the Sexual Offences Act 1967, c. 60, is obviously not for us to say; our jurisdiction is to interpret and apply laws validly enacted."[8] The two dissenting judges, in contrast, suggested that the law should be repealed because lifetime incarceration for consensual homosexual activity was too harsh. In part because this decision was seen as unfair, federal politicians called for decriminalization of sexual activity between consenting adults of the same sex.

Although then federal justice minister Pierre Trudeau exhorted shortly after the *Klippert* decision, "There's no place for the state in the bedrooms of the nation," the absolute prohibition against anal penetration did not change until 1969. Klippert was not released from prison until 1971. Curiously, anal penetration is still a criminal offence if more than two people are present or if one of the participants is under 18, unless the participants are married to each other. No other sexual crime concerns the number of people present, and the age of consent for most other sexual activity is 16. The anal-penetration provisions have been declared unconstitutional by two appellate courts (Ontario and Quebec) and one superior court (Alberta).[9] However, as the provisions have not been repealed and its constitutionality has not been challenged before the SCC, the provisions remain "on the books" in most Canadian jurisdictions.

Relationship Recognition

Since the adoption of the Canadian Charter of Rights and Freedom in 1982, judges are no longer bound by restrictions, as was the *Klippert* court, to simply "interpret and apply laws validly enacted." Now they can also determine whether laws or other government actions violate rights and freedoms—such as the rights to equality and to religious freedom—and whether governments can justify interference with rights and freedoms if they show that the interference is "demonstrably justified in a free and democratic society" (as this provision is in section 1 of the Charter, it is often referred to as a "section 1 analysis").

The equality rights section (section 15), which came into force in 1985, states "Every individual is equal before and under the law and has the right to the equal protection and equal benefit of the law without discrimination and, in particular, without discrimination based on race, national or ethnic origin, colour, religion, sex, age or mental or physical disability." The precise test for determining whether section 15 equality rights have been violated has been subject to debate and dissension among SCC judges. The current test is this: does the distinction established by the law under challenge create a *disadvantage* by perpetuating stereotypes or prejudice on the claimant because of his or her membership in an *enumerated or analogous group*?[10] If a law perpetuates pre-existing disadvantage, fails to correspond with actual needs and characteristics, or has a severe impact on access to an important interest or social good, there is a good chance that the "disadvantage" part of the test will be satisfied.

Sexual orientation is not expressly enumerated in section 15 as a prohibited ground of discrimination. However, the SCC held that it was analogous to the enumerated grounds and therefore an additional prohibited ground.[11] But in early cases, the Court was reluctant to give section 15 a robust interpretation that would protect queer people. In *Egan v. Canada* (1995), for example, the SCC found that public pension legislation that benefited only heterosexual married and common-law spouses was not discriminatory. It stated that the "ultimate *raison d'être* ... [is] the biological and social realities that heterosexual couples have the unique ability to procreate, that most children are the product of these relationships, and that they are generally cared for and nurtured by those who live in that relationship. In this sense, marriage is by nature heterosexual."[12]

The SCC reasoned that queer people were not being discriminated against because of their sexuality; rather, they did not fit into the procreative social unit that parliament sought to support. However, in *M. v. H.* (1999),[13] the Court turned away from its reasoning in *Egan*. It held that the Ontario Family Law Act, by defining *spouse* as a partner in a heterosexual conjugal relationship and excluding partners in homosexual conjugal relationships from spousal support on the breakdown of a relationship, discriminated without justification on the basis of sexual orientation. More particularly, the Act perpetuated historic prejudices about the existence and worthiness of queer relationships and failed to take into account the needs of queer families, which are functionally similar to non-queer families, and therefore violated the Charter-protected right to equality.

Following *M. v. H.*, most provinces and the federal government conducted legislative audits and amended many acts that touched on relationship obligations and benefits, to ensure conformity with equality rights. In Manitoba, for example, three omnibus acts—An Act to Comply with the SCC Decision in *M. v. H.*, the Charter Compliance Act, and the Common Law Partners' Property and Related Amendments Act[14]—amended some 70 acts ranging from the Anatomy Act (defining the "preferred claimant" of a deceased's remains) to the Vital Statistics Act (effectively permitting two lesbian mothers to be named on a birth certificate), in order to more fully respect the equality rights of queer people. As will be discussed in more detail later on, lawsuits were filed across the country claiming the right to same-sex marriage, and ultimately, in 2005, the federal government passed legislation permitting same-sex marriage.

Human Rights Codes

The Charter only applies to "government action"; it does not apply to private action. However, human rights codes prevent both government and private actors—such as private-sector employers, retail businesses, and landlords—from engaging in discrimination and harassment on enumerated grounds (including religion and sexual orientation) in employment and the provision of services or accommodation. Without human rights code protection, queer people could be (and were) fired simply because they were gay or suspected of being gay.[15] In 1977, Quebec was the first province to amend its human rights code to prohibit discrimination on the basis of sexual orientation. Other provinces, the territories, and the federal government followed suit, although Alberta's legislation was originally amended by judicial fiat in the 1998 *Vriend* case,[16] not by legislative action.[17] It was not until 2009 that Alberta finally amended its human rights legislation to include sexual orientation as a prohibited ground. Only a few jurisdictions have changed their human rights codes to specifically include gender identity—the Northwest Territories (2002), Ontario (2012), and Manitoba (2012)—although every human rights commission in Canada states that it will accept gender-identity discrimination claims.[18]

Sexual Expression

Sexual expression is subject to various prohibitions and regulations in Canada. Under the Criminal Code,[19] the sale or distribution of "obscene" materials is a crime punishable by up to two years in prison. The Code also criminalizes the production, sale, and possession of child pornography. Sexual representations in advertising are regulated by the Canadian Code of Advertising Standards and Gender Portrayal Guidelines.[20] The Code of Advertising Standards prohibits gender discrimination, while the accompanying guidelines advise against sexual exploitation and violent domination of either gender. Sexual expression is also regulated in the film industry, through classification and licensing regimes. Rating standards, which are determined provincially, place special emphasis on nudity and sexual explicitness. In Manitoba the Amusements Act[21] controls not only the ratings of films but also the sale and public accessibility of films that have sexual content.

Restrictive sexual-expression laws have been used to suppress access to information about being queer.[22] Vancouver-based bookstore Little Sister's, which caters to the queer community, sued the federal government in 1984 because almost every shipment to the store was being seized and inspected by Canada Customs (now the Customs and Revenue Agency), which purported to be looking for obscene materials. Canada Customs had (and still has) the power to seize materials when they cross over a border into Canada if they suspect that the materials may be "obscene" under the Criminal Code. Some shipments to Little Sister's were detained for up to a year, rendering them commercially unusable. Only 20 per cent of the seized materials were predominantly photographs or other images; 80 per cent were text-based. During the rise and height of the AIDS/HIV pandemic (mid-1980s to mid-1990s), Canada Customs would not permit any materials into the country that described or depicted anal penetration, thereby inhibiting access to information on HIV transmission prevention and treatment. Fifteen years after Little Sister's started its lawsuit, the Supreme Court of Canada held that the procedures used by Canada Customs agents had denied the equality rights of queer people. But the Court upheld the obscenity law and most aspects of its implementation through border controls, confident that better training for customs officials would solve the problems.[23]

The Little Sister's litigation revealed deep tensions in queer communities over whether and how to control sexual expression. Some lesbian activists, along with many other feminists, believed that "porn is the theory, rape is the practice," and therefore sought legal and other prohibitions and restrictions on sexually explicit materials. Others wanted to celebrate sexual diversity or did not think prohibition or regulation of sexually explicit materials was an effective way to address its underbelly.[24]

Egale Canada (formerly Equality for Gays and Lesbians Everywhere), one of the country's leading national queer organizations, has struggled with whether and how to regulate expression. It settled on supporting the use of criminal law to suppress particularly harmful (hateful) expression, but not the use of law to suppress other homophobic expression. Egale Canada participated as an intervener before the Supreme Court in the *Little Sister's* case. While Egale Canada and other queer-sensitive interveners (the Women's Legal Education and Action Fund [LEAF] and the HIV-AIDS Network) supported the Little Sister's claim of discriminatory treatment by Canada Customs officials, none of these interveners supported the argument that the Criminal Code obscenity provisions should be struck down.[25] A few years later, Egale Canada supported amending criminal laws prohibiting the public promotion of hatred to include, as an "identifiable group," people distinguished by their sexual orientation.[26] On the other hand, as will be discussed, it never took a position either for or against anti-hate-expression laws in human rights codes, intervening in only one case, *Whatcott* (2013), on a fairly narrow point.[27]

Rights to Religious Freedom

Minority Catholic and Protestant believers in Canada have enjoyed constitutionally protected education rights in some provinces, and many provinces permit and partially fund religiously mandated schools. Governments have made some efforts to protect religious beliefs in other ways, such as promising to respect conscientiously objecting Mennonites who refused military service.[28] But most religious minorities have faced some religious suppression or interference from both governmental and private actors at various points in Canadian history. While many examples of state suppression of religious expression could be cited, I will mention just two, pre-Charter examples.

Colonization brought the suppression of many forms of expression of indigenous spirituality and the intrusion of Christian ideology. Ceremonies such as the Sun Dance and the potlatch were prohibited, and residential schools were systematically used as a tool to eradicate indigenous cultures and beliefs.[29] The second example is from 1959, when the Supreme Court of Canada addressed the religious freedom of Jehovah's Witnesses in *Roncarelli v. Duplessis.*[30] Frank Roncarelli, a long-time restaurant owner, had provided bail for Jehovah's Witnesses who were arrested for street-corner proselytizing, contrary to a provincial law. Upon discovering the source of the bail securities, Maurice Duplessis, who was both attorney general and premier of Quebec, ordered permanent revocation of Roncarelli's liquor licence. The Supreme Court found that Duplessis, in his public capacity, had unjustly revoked Roncarelli's licence as punishment for his religious actions.

Religious Expression

People in Canada have a Charter-protected right to freedom of religion and of conscience. Freedom of religion is "the right to entertain such religious beliefs as one chooses, the right to declare religious beliefs openly and without fear of hindrance or reprisal and the right to manifest belief by worship and practice, or by teaching and dissemination."[31] In *R. v. Big M Drug Mart Ltd* (1985), the Supreme Court of Canada held that the federal Lord's Day Act, which required most businesses to close on Sundays, violated Charter-protected religious rights because the primary purpose of the law was to compel Sabbath observance, regardless of a business owner's beliefs. The Court opined that "the

Act creates a climate hostile to, and gives the appearance of discrimination against, non-Christian Canadians. It takes religious values rooted in Christian morality and, using the force of the state, translates them into a positive law binding on believers and non-believers alike."[32]

More particularly, a religious practice is protected when a person holds the belief that the particular practice represents a nexus to the divine or is experientially religious in nature. Such beliefs are protected even if they are not generally held by co-religionists; individual belief is all that is required.[33] Nor does the claimant need to assert that the practice is mandatory, only that it enhances the connection to the divine. That a practice has been observed for only a short time is not relevant unless an opponent can demonstrate that the belief is insincere, fictitious, or artifice. Thus, for example, a Muslim woman's assertion that wearing a face-covering brings her closer to the divine supports protection against interference with her right to wear a face-covering, even if she (or others) does not believe that wearing a face-covering is mandatory, even though most Muslim women do not follow this practice, and even if she has only recently adopted the practice.[34] Finally, the right is protected only if the interference is more than trivial.

Canadian courts, however, have consistently said that the Charter does not provide absolute protection for religious freedom, and that in some cases it must yield to larger public interests such as an important legislative objective or undue interference with the fundamental rights and freedoms of others. Most of the religious freedom cases asserting that legislative regimes violate the Charter involve situations where the effect (but not the objective) of the rule is religious discrimination or preference. For example, mandatory photo licence requirements are not enacted to prevent people who hold religious beliefs from driving, but if individuals believe that they are forbidden by divine law from being photographed, the effect may be to render them ineligible to drive because they cannot get a driver's licence.[35] Less often, the government's intent is to interfere with a religious rights claim, such as Sunday closing laws, prohibitions against Mormon "celestial marriages" (polygamy), and state decision making when Jehovah's Witness minors (or their parents) refuse blood transfusions.[36] Regardless of whether the interference is on purpose or only in effect, as part of the section 1 analysis the government has to show that the law has a pressing and substantial objective, and that the means used to achieve the objective are proportional to the interference. Intentional interference is less likely to meet the "pressing and substantial objective" requirement.

The recent *N.S.* case is another example of a situation where Charter-protected religious rights gave way to a strong competing interest: the constitutionally protected right of the accused to make full answer and defence.

N.S. alleged that she had been sexually assaulted from a young age by her uncle and cousin. She was ordered to remove her face-covering (a niqab) while testifying at the preliminary inquiry. She refused, and ultimately the matter was heard by the Supreme Court. A majority of the judges held that "the need to accommodate and balance sincerely held religious beliefs against other interests [in this case, a defendant's right to full answer and defence] is deeply entrenched in Canadian law." Therefore there can be no hard-and-fast rule about whether a face-covering must be removed. Rather, the Court held that, once it was determined that there was in fact a conflict between the rights of the individuals involved, such that upholding the rights of one would infringe on the rights of the other, two additional questions should be asked: Is there a way to accommodate both rights and avoid the conflict between them? If no accommodation is possible, do the salutary effects of requiring the witness to remove the niqab outweigh the deleterious effects of doing so?

The Court did not weigh the salutary and deleterious effects in the *N.S.* case. Instead it ordered that this determination be made by a lower-court judge presiding at a new preliminary inquiry. However, the Court noted that niqab removal was unlikely to be necessary if a witness's evidence was uncontested or credibility was not at issue, implying that otherwise, removal might be necessary. As the dissenting Supreme Court judges noted, "the majority's conclusion that being unable to see the witness's face is acceptable from a fair trial perspective if the evidence is 'uncontested,' essentially means that sexual assault complainants, whose evidence will inevitably be contested, will be forced to choose between laying a complaint and wearing a niqab." It was not surprising, then, that the judge presiding at the second preliminary inquiry held that N.S. must remove her veil for precisely those reasons.[37] Ultimately N.S. removed her veil and testified at the preliminary inquiry after the judge restricted who could see her face. On the eve of the trial, the Crown withdrew the charges, stating that, based on new evidence, there was no reasonable prospect of conviction.

Religious Rights in the Marriage References

Canadian governments have the power to refer important legal questions to courts for advisory opinions. In the 2000s, three separate references concerning marriage, each with religious dimensions, were referred to courts for opinions. In each case the judges held that constitutional equality rights prevailed over religious rights.

As noted earlier, following the *M. v. H* case, same-sex couples filed lawsuits across the country asserting the right to equal marriage. When appeal courts started finding in favour of the couples, the federal government asked the Supreme Court of Canada for an advisory opinion on draft legislation permitting same-sex civil marriage. The strongest opposition to the draft came from religious organizations, which argued that marriage was fundamentally a religious institution available only to opposite-sex couples and that the institution of marriage would be devalued if queers could marry. The Supreme Court rejected these arguments, noting that "the mere recognition of the equality rights of one group cannot, in itself, constitute a violation of the s.15(1) rights of another.... Although the right to same-sex marriage conferred by the proposed legislation may potentially conflict with the right to freedom of religion if the legislation becomes law ... It has not been demonstrated in this reference that impermissible conflicts ... will arise."[38] However, the Court also held that the Charter's religious freedom guarantee "is broad enough to protect religious officials from being compelled by the state to perform civil or religious same-sex marriages that are contrary to their religious beliefs."[39]

In *Reference re Marriage Commissioners*, the Saskatchewan Court of Appeal had to consider whether a proposed law that would allow marriage commissioners (people licensed to perform civil marriages) to refuse to perform same-sex marriages violated the constitutionally protected equality rights of queer people. The court stated that "putting gays and lesbians in a situation where a marriage commissioner can refuse to provide his or her services solely because of their sexual orientation would clearly be a retrograde step—a step that would perpetuate disadvantage and involve stereotypes about the worthiness of same-sex unions." But it also recognized that requiring all marriage commissioners to perform same-sex marriages could prove a substantial interference with their religious rights. On balance, the court held that queer equality rights had to be upheld. Specifically, "the state serves everyone equally without providing better, poorer or different services to one individual compared to another by making distinctions on the basis of factors like race, religion or gender. ... Persons who voluntarily choose to assume an office, like that of marriage commissioner, cannot expect to directly shape the office's intersection with the public so as to make it conform with their personal religious or other beliefs."[40]

For years the government of British Columbia struggled with whether to prosecute members of a Mormon sect that practised polygamy in the belief that multiple or "celestial" marriages would confer certain benefits in the afterlife. Rather than initiating a criminal prosecution, it referred the question of whether this law violated the right to religious freedom to the Supreme Court of British Columbia for an opinion.[41] The court advised that the Criminal Code prohibition of polygamy triggered a violation of religious beliefs sincerely held by Muslims, Mormons, and Wiccans. However, it also advised that the law was justified as a reasonable limit, because polygamy was harmful to women and children.

Accommodation of Difference

Most human rights code religious rights claims—that is, claims related to employment or the provision of goods and services in both the public and private sectors—can be resolved by using the well-established human rights principles concerning accommodation of difference in employment and services. In a nutshell, unless the accommodation of a religious practice imposes undue hardship on an employer or service provider (including cost, safety, or security), the accommodation must be made. Thus, for example, a Seventh-Day Adventist working in retail must be given Saturdays off for the Sabbath; Sikh can wear turbans instead of the traditional Stetsons worn by members of the Royal Canadian Mounted Police, and they can carry ceremonial knives in most situations where there are no heightened security concerns (such as on airplanes); Jews may build small temporary structures (*sukkot*) on their balconies as part of a religious observance, even where their condo by-laws prohibit such structures for aesthetic reasons;[42] and many workplaces and educational institutions have smudging policies to facilitate observance of indigenous spiritual practices and accommodate requests by Muslims for private places in which to offer prayers.

What happens when there are competing anti-discrimination claims, for example, when a service provider's religious right claim conflicts with a queer person's right to service without discrimination? Religious organizations such as churches and schools have the ability to discriminate. For example, they can determine, free from anti-discrimination norms, who can serve as clergy or teaching staff, those for whom they will conduct marriage ceremonies, whether to expel students for violating sexual norms, and to whom they will rent a church hall.[43]

Where an enterprise does not primarily serve co-religionists, discrimination is much less likely to be allowed by human rights tribunals. In other words, service providers or employees who hold religious beliefs cannot refuse to provide employment, services, or accommodation to queers. For example, an organization with a faith mission to provide services to people living with mental disabilities could not terminate an employee who "came out" as a lesbian, because the clientele it served was identified by their disability, not by their religious beliefs; religious functions were not part of her job.[44] In another case, a landlord failed to convince a human rights panel that his eviction of a gay couple was justified because of his right to religious freedom under the Charter.[45]

Most recently, another human rights tribunal found that business owners who refused bed-and-breakfast accommodations to a homosexual couple had discriminated on the basis of sexual orientation and could not justify their actions based on freedom of religion.[46] The tribunal held, like others before it, that a church or religious organization may hold a bona fide and reasonably justified reason for discrimination in the provision of religious services, such as a religious school's requirement that employees be believers.[47] However, independent business owners, while they may have religious beliefs, cannot rely on those beliefs to deny non-faith-based services to the public when those services are not otherwise restricted to co-religionists.

Can we draw any conclusions from this review of religious rights? Judges are protective of religious freedom, especially if the asserted right can be accommodated. But if the asserted right interferes with an important legislative objective or unduly interferes with the fundamental rights and freedoms of others, the religious right probably will not prevail. In particular, Canadian courts take the view that believers are free to hold and express their views, but they cannot prevent others from holding and acting on their own beliefs or discriminate against them if they do.

Religious Expressive Rights and Queer Equality Rights

Let's start with a quick review. The essence of religious freedom is "the right to *declare* religious beliefs openly and without fear of hindrance or reprisal, and the right to manifest religious belief by worship and practice or by *teaching and dissemination*."[48] Equality rights are violated when a distinction established by a law creates a disadvantage by perpetuating stereotypes or prejudice on the claimant because of his or her membership in an enumerated or analogous group. We now turn to two case studies where these rights may be difficult to reconcile. Two questions are at issue: first, if one feels compelled by religious belief to speak out against homosexuality, is such expression immune from hate-expression laws? Second, should religiously mandated schools be compelled to permit gay–straight alliance groups to form and meet on their premises?

Hateful Expression

In 2002, Reverend Stephen Boissoin wrote in a letter published in the *Red Deer Advocate* that "homosexual rights activists and those who defend them" were criminals and were brainwashing children through anti-homophobia initiatives in public schools.[49] He asserted that "my banner has now been raised and war has been declared so as to defend the precious sanctity of our innocent children and youth," and, as noted in the epigraph of this chapter, "It's time to stand together and take whatever steps are necessary to reverse the wickedness that our lethargy has authorized to spawn. Where homosexuality flourishes, all manner of wickedness abounds." Dr. Darren Lund complained to the Alberta Human Rights Commission that the letter was hate speech and therefore sanctionable under the province's Human Rights, Citizenship and Multiculturalism Act,[50] which provides that

> 3. (1) No person shall publish … any statement … or other representation that …
> (b) is likely to expose a person or a class of persons to hatred or contempt because of the race, religious beliefs, colour, gender, physical disability, mental disability, age, ancestry, place of origin, marital status, source of income or family status of that person or class of persons.[51]
> (2) Nothing in this section shall be deemed to interfere with the free expression of opinion on any subject.

While the Human Rights Commission found the letter to be discriminatory, the Alberta Court of Appeal unanimously ruled that it was not hate speech under the Alberta act. Despite the offensive and demeaning tone of the letter, the Court justified Boissoin's message as an appropriate part of a greater political debate and as an opinion protected under section 3(2). The Court held that Boissoin had merely exercised his right to express his opinion.

In 2013, shortly after the *Boissoin* case was decided, the Supreme Court heard a similar hate-speech case, *Saskatchewan Human Rights Commission v. Whatcott*.[52] Four hate-speech complaints were made after William Whatcott distributed flyers that condemned the inclusion of queer literature in public schools and promoted civil law discrimination against queer individuals. Whatcott, like Boissoin, wrote that gay men are predisposed to sexually abuse children. The Court observed that the flyers

> seek to vilify those of same-sex orientation by portraying them as child abusers or predators. Examples of this in Flyers D and E would include: "Our children will pay the price in disease, death, abuse …"; "Sodomites are 430 times more likely to acquire Aids & 3 times more likely to sexually abuse children!"; and "[o]ur acceptance of homosexuality and our toleration [*sic*] of its promotion in our school system will lead to the early death and morbidity of many children."[53]

The relevant provisions of the Saskatchewan Human Rights Code are similar to those of the Alberta act, with the important exception that the Saskatchewan act references not just statements that expose people to "hatred" but also statements that "ridicule[s], belittle[s], or otherwise affronts the dignity of" a class of people.[54] Whatcott argued in his defence that "sexual conduct has long been a topic of religious discussion and debate," and "many religious people also believe that they are obligated to do good and warn others of the danger."[55] He asserted "that the prohibition of speech of the type contained in his flyers will force people like himself to choose between following their conscience by preaching about same-sex sexual practices or following the law." The Christian Legal Fellowship argued that the law "limits the free expression of every religious adherent whose beliefs on sexuality or other controversial topics do not conform to those of mainstream society and allows those with minority views to be silenced through the operation of law."[56]

Although *Boissoin* was decided prior to *Whatcott*, the Supreme Court's decision did not mention the Alberta court's ruling. Arguably, the language used in the Boissoin letter is more inflammatory than that of the Whatcott flyers, but Boissoin's writing did not violate human rights law, whereas some of Whatcott's writing did. The two decisions, less than six months apart, are in conflict with one another in other material ways. While the Supreme Court ruling in *Whatcott* likely overrode many aspects of the Alberta Court of Appeal ruling in *Boissoin*, it is worth exploring the differences between these two decisions in how they balance queer rights and religious rights. A key difference between the two cases is that Boissoin did not challenge the Charter validity of the Alberta act. Rather, the case was argued solely on the language, including the defences contained in the Alberta act, whereas Whatcott's defence rested on Charter claims.

The first conflict between *Boissoin* and *Whatcott* is whether a distinction can be made between homosexuals and homosexuality. In *Boissoin*, the Alberta Court of Appeal found that the letter could not be defined as hate speech because the "subject and perceived target of the speech was sexual behavior; i.e., homosexuality, rather than homosexuals."[57] The distinction, the Court decided, was justified by the opening paragraphs of Boissoin's letter: "The following is not intended for those who are suffering from an unwanted sexual identity crisis. For you, I have understanding, care, compassion and tolerance. I sympathize with you and offer you my love and fellowship."[58]

The court found that Boissoin intended to communicate that homosexual acts were morally reprehensible, not that homosexuals were. The "love the sinner, hate the sin" argument also arose in *Whatcott* but was rejected. As an intervener in *Whatcott*, Egale Canada argued that if the Supreme Court were to allow a distinction between the act and the actor, human rights would be placed within an unjust hierarchy.[59] Individuals who found themselves inseparable from their race or religion would be afforded full protection, while the rights of queer individuals would be given lesser recognition. In rejecting the "love the sinner, hate the sin" argument in *Whatcott*, the Court stated, "If expression targeting certain sexual behaviour is framed in such a way as to expose persons of an identifiable sexual orientation to what is objectively viewed as detestation and vilification, it cannot be said that such speech only targets the behaviour. It quite clearly targets the vulnerable group."[60]

Boissoin's letter was published in a newspaper, a forum traditionally used for discussion of public interest matters. When determining whether or not the letter was hate speech, the Alberta court decided that the context within which it was presented was of paramount importance. The Court stated, "Whether offensive or not, the letter was perceived to stimulate and add to an ongoing public debate on matters of public interest, as distinct from hate propaganda, which serves no useful function and has no redeeming qualities. A certain amount of public debate concerning such an issue must be permitted, even if some of it is offensive, to make the general public aware that such type of thinking is present in the community and to allow for its rebuttal."[61]

The Alberta court determined that, when the letter was viewed within the context of the newspaper and the then current socio-political climate, a reasonable person would not understand it to expose homosexuals to hatred or contempt, but would merely see it as an "overstated and intemperate opinion" and a "polemic on a matter of public interest."[62] In *Whatcott*, the Supreme Court acknowledged the importance of context in determinations of hate speech, but it rejected the proposition that an otherwise hateful statement should be protected expression simply because it was made within the context of ongoing political discourse. As *Whatcott* seems to overrule *Boissoin* on this point, language that exposes a group or individual to detestation or vilification can no longer be justified by being part of a moral debate or public discourse.

The *Whatcott* court also considered whether the Bible was at risk of being considered as hate speech. Here the Court stated that, "while use of the Bible as a credible authority for a hateful proposition has been considered a hallmark of hatred, it would only be unusual circumstances and context that could transform a simple reading or publication of a religion's holy text into what could objectively be viewed as hate speech."[63] As legal scholar Richard Moon has observed, the Supreme Court has avoided directly repudiating the religious view that homosexuality is sinful because it does not want to enter debates on religious dogma.[64]

The Supreme Court asked whether the infringement of freedom of religion and expression authorized by the Saskatchewan act could be "demonstrably justified in a free and democratic society" and therefore could not be saved by section 1. (Remember that section 1 of the Charter protects laws that infringe Charter-protected rights if a strong justification for the infringement is established.) The Court found that hate speech—that is, an extreme manifestation of detestation and vilification—is not justifiable even if the individual producing the hate speech may have an honest and sincere belief in its truth. It was irrelevant whether hate-speech provisions merely infringed on the individual's freedom of expression or the speech originated from a sincerely held religious belief and infringed on the Charter-protected right to religious freedom. All individual beliefs, whether based on morality, religion, or other personal preference, were equally subject to the hate-speech restrictions contained in the legislation. The Court stated,

> It is sufficient here to say that if the sincerity of a religious belief would automatically preclude the finding of a contravention of s.14(1)(*b*), the s.1 analysis would be derailed with no balancing of the competing rights.
>
> Apart from that concern, the fact that a person circulates a hate publication in the furtherance of a sincere religious belief goes to the question of the subjective view of the publisher, which is irrelevant to the objective application of the definition of hatred. Allowing the dissemination of hate speech to be excused by a sincerely held belief would, in effect, provide an absolute defence and would gut the prohibition of effectiveness.[65]

However, the Court found that while the Saskatchewan act's prohibition on hateful expression could be justified, the prohibition against speech that "ridicules, belittles or otherwise affronts the dignity of" persons included more speech than was necessary to achieve constitutionally permissible restrictions on expressive or religious rights. The Court held that expression that "ridicules, belittles or otherwise affronts the dignity of" persons, while repugnant and offensive, did not incite the level of abhorrence, delegitimization, and rejection that risks causing discrimination or other harmful effects. These prohibitions therefore were constitutionally invalid.

The *Whatcott* Court found that two of the four flyers violated section 14(1)(a) of the Saskatchewan act in that they exposed or tended to expose queer people to hatred, in part because the flyers vilified queer people, relying on the prejudicial stereotype of gay men as child abusers or predators. However, as the Court had effectively excised the words "ridicules, belittles or otherwise affronts the dignity of" from the act, the other two flyers, while offensive, were not found to have exposed homosexuals to "detestation and vilification." Notably, neither of those two flyers made assertions concerning queer people and child abuse.

So if one feels compelled by religious belief to speak out against homosexuality, is such expression immune from hate-expression laws?

When freedoms of expression or religion clash with other rights, Canadian courts have traditionally afforded major protection to the expressive and religious rights of the Charter.[66] Internal limits on these rights allow individuals to exercise them freely, up to the point where they expose another person or group of persons to hatred, contempt, or vilification. People in Canada "are free to preach against same-sex activities, to urge its censorship from the public school curriculum and to seek to convert others to their point of view. Their freedom to express those views is unlimited, except by the narrow requirement that they not be conveyed through hate speech."[67]

Stereotypical portrayals of gay men as child sexual abusers are likely to satisfy the hatred test. While context is important in determining whether or not language reaches the point of causing contempt and vilification, hate speech cannot be justified simply because it is presented within public debate or based on a religious belief. Even language that may have great social or political merit cannot be protected if any part of it contains hate speech.[68]

Gay–Straight Alliances in Religious Schools

In a case that mesmerized the country in 2002, school officials forbade Marc Hall from attending his Catholic high school prom with his boyfriend, stating that they could not be seen to be encouraging or condoning any interactions between same-sex romantic couples, as such interactions were contrary to Catholic teachings.[69] A judge on the Ontario Superior Court of Justice ordered the school to permit the couple to attend on the ground that the prom was not an event of religious significance. Other arguments were made in the case—such as that the school could not dictate that extracurricular activities conform to religious teachings—but the Court decided the case on a simple, narrow ground and left other arguments for another day.

In the decade since the *Hall* case was decided, human rights tribunals and courts have held that public schools must provide a discrimination-free environment for queer students. Thus corrective action was justified when a school failed to take action to stop homophobic bullying; when a school board refused to permit its libraries to collect books depicting queer families; when a librarian refused to catalogue queer books and a school guidance counsellor was unapologetic after homophobic letters he wrote were published in a local paper.[70] In contrast, however, the Supreme Court of Canada sided with Trinity Western University, a private evangelical Christian school that required students not to engage in queer sex, by nullifying the provincial teacher-accreditation body's decision to refuse to recognize its graduates. It held that

> absent concrete evidence that training teachers at [Trinity Western University] fosters discrimination in the public schools of B.C., the freedom of individuals to adhere to certain religious beliefs while at TWU should be respected. Acting on those beliefs, however, is a different matter. If a teacher in the public school system engages in discriminatory conduct, that teacher can be subject to disciplinary proceedings before the BCCT. In this way, the scope of the freedom of religion and equality rights that have come into conflict can be circumscribed and thereby reconciled.[71]

While many schools have adopted safe(r) school policies that are intended to further anti-discrimination goals, high school students still report alarming rates of discrimination. A 2013 study by Catherine Taylor and her team of social scientists found that, among other things,

- 70 per cent of students participating in the study, LGBTQ and non-LGBTQ, reported hearing expressions such as "that's so gay" every day in school and almost half (48%) reported hearing remarks such as "faggot," "lezbo," and "dyke" every day in school.
- More than one in five (21%) LGBTQ students reported being physically harassed or assaulted due to their sexual orientation.
- Almost two-thirds (64%) of LGBTQ students and 61 per cent of students with LGBTQ parents reported that they feel unsafe at school.[72]

In the past few years, some provincial governments have passed legislation requiring all schools, including schools operating under a religious mandate (such as independent faith-based schools and constitutionally protected separate schools), to permit gay–straight alliances (GSAs) to form and meet on their premises.[73] Such clubs are created, usually on the initiative of a group of students, so that students can talk and learn about issues related to sexual orientation and gender identity. Membership is open to all interested students; often, but not always, a supportive teacher is assigned to the club. According to one website, "GSAs play a vital role in making schools safer for LGBTQ students by providing supportive and accepting spaces as well as doing broader organizing work against homophobia and transphobia in school."[74]

Research undertaken by legal scholar Donn Short demonstrates that GSAs are an important initiative, but only an initial step in reducing the homophobic climate that queer students endure. He observes, "Current conceptions of safety are insufficiently robust and must be re-conceptualized so that safety comes to be viewed as incorporating a pursuit of equity and social justice."[75] Thus he concludes, among other things, that "queer realities must be reflected in course content and in school culture" and

> heterosexual students must be implicated in schooling processes and the regimes of silence, invisibility, and oppression of the official and unofficial curricula and general school life. Curriculum content must not be merely a presentation of information about queer students received by heterosexual and nonqueer students in their normative positions. Inclusive education alone is inadequate. The general school life must include and celebrate queer youth and friendships between heterosexual and queer students.[76]

The debates around the passage of legislation mandating openness to GSAs in all high schools generated vociferous opposition from some religious and political leaders, on the basis that religious freedom was again under attack. One leader argued that the proposed law was "the greatest challenge facing Canadian churches" and "part of a hidden agenda to destroy Christianity."[77] One city council passed a resolution asserting that the new law "would undermine [schools'] ability to uphold their faith perspective."[78] Without doubt, Short's call for "celebrating queer youth" would raise even more ire. (Curiously absent, however, from the commentary in the Manitoba debate was the linking of homosexuality and child sexual abuse.)

Is there merit to the claim that requiring all schools—including religiously mandated schools—to permit student-led GSAs to meet on school property infringes or interferes with anyone's religious freedom? Two recent Supreme Court decisions, *L.S. v. Commission scolaire des Chênes* and *Loyola v. Quebec (Attorney General)*,[79] are useful though perhaps contradictory on this point. In *L.S.* the Court considered whether a provincially mandated curriculum requiring all students to take a course on ethics and religious culture (ERC) interfered with the religious freedom of some students or their parents (the course replaced denominationally specific courses on morality and religious doctrine). The Court rejected the argument that such a course interfered with parents' right to transmit a particular faith to their children. But in *Loyola*, the Court held that a Catholic school could not be required to teach a course that was neutral on Catholic doctrine. The *Loyola* court rationalized this departure from *L.S.* by stating,

> the collective manifestation and transmission of Catholic beliefs through a private denominational school—are a crucial part of Loyola's claim. In *S.L.*, this Court held that the imposition of the ERC Program in public schools did not impose limits on the religious freedom of individual

> students and parents. This case, however, can be distinguished from *S.L.* because Loyola is a private religious institution created to support the collective practice of Catholicism and the transmission of the Catholic faith. The question is not only how Loyola is required to teach about other religions, but also how it is asked to teach about the very faith that animates its character and the comparative relationship between Catholicism and other faiths. The Minister's decision therefore demonstrably interferes with the manner in which the members of an institution formed for the very purpose of transmitting Catholicism, can teach and learn about the Catholic faith. This engages religious freedom protected under s. 2(a) of the Charter.[80]

So how does the reasoning in these two cases inform an opinion on the constitutionality of GSAs in religious schools? Religious freedom is violated only when there is substantial interference with a religious practice. It could be argued that the existence of GSAs cannot be considered as any kind of substantial interference; simple exposure to a different way of being in the world does not infringe religious rights. No one is required to do anything that is contrary to their faith: no one has to go meetings or events; no one has to make supportive statements; no one is prevented from expressing a view on the mission of a GSA. Providing students with a room to meet in and allowing them to announce their events does not in any material way interfere with the religious rights of those who do not attend the meetings.

But the *Loyola* court was concerned about the collective aspects of the school's enterprise. Can it be argued that the school's religious culture—if this culture is, in fact, protected by the reasoning in *Loyola*—is compromised by the existence of a GSA? The *L.S.* Court observed that "the suggestion that exposing children to a variety of religious facts in itself infringes their religious freedom or that of their parents amounts to a rejection of the multicultural reality of Canadian society and ignores the Quebec government's obligations with regard to public education."[81] (Remember too that in the *Reference re Same-Sex Marriage* the Court held that "the mere recognition of the equality rights of one group cannot, in itself, constitute a violation of the s.15(1) rights of another.")[82] Thus, exposure to ideas that do not comport with the dominant ethos is far from being a problem; rather, the Court insinuates that, given Canadian pluralism, exposure to various cultures (among which I would include queer cultures) is an obligation. The tricky question is whether permitting a GSA represents more than simple "exposure" and is rather an infringement of the collective manifestation of Catholic beliefs.

The case law reconciling religious and equality rights—especially the *Trinity Western* case[83]—does not require that queer people be treated with equal respect, much less affirmed or celebrated. As legal scholar Richard

Moon has observed, the Supreme Court wants to avoid wading into questions of religious doctrine and therefore must "avoid repudiating directly the religious view that homosexuality [is] sinful."[84] Administrators, teachers, and students at religious schools who believe that homosexuality is religiously condemned are, in the end, required only to be tolerant of queer people in their midst.

Conclusion

Less than 50 years ago, queer people could be incarcerated indefinitely for participating in sexual activities with people whose genitals resembled their own. Criminal laws changed, and in the next two decades, human rights codes were amended to prohibit discrimination against queers. More recently, queer people have successfully challenged governments for discriminatory law-enforcement practices around sexual expression and have overcome objections to the idea that queer families should enjoy state and private benefits and obligations. Moreover, people whose religious beliefs include that homosexuality is sinful cannot, in relying on this belief, refuse to provide goods and services they otherwise make available to the public. But, until and unless the Supreme Court of Canada is willing to comment on religious doctrine, more specifically repudiating the religious view that homosexuality is sinful, bastions of discriminatory thinking will not be dismantled by law anytime soon. People who hold religious beliefs equating homosexuality with sin will remain free to espouse this view as long as their expression does not amount to hate speech, and schools will be required to tolerate but not to affirm queer students.

Takeaway Messages

- The Charter of Rights and Freedoms applies to government action, whereas human rights legislation applies to both public- and private-sector activities.
- The essence of religious freedom is "the right to *declare* religious beliefs openly and without fear of hindrance or reprisal, and the right to manifest religious belief by worship and practice or by *teaching and dissemination*." Equality rights are violated when a distinction established by a law creates disadvantage by perpetuating stereotypes or prejudice on the claimant because of his or her membership in an enumerated or analogous group.
- Rights are not absolute. Sometimes governments can justify interference with a right, and when rights collide with one another—as religious rights and queer rights often do—either the parties must mediate a solution (usually relying on established norms) or the courts will impose one.

Study Questions

- Have courts struck a fair balance between religious rights and queer rights? Discuss with reference to specific situations.
- Donn Short calls for schools to adopt anti-homophobia policies that "pursue equity and social justice." Concretely, what would be included in such policies?
- Are courts too quick to find that government interference with a religious right can be justified under section 1 of the Charter as a "reasonable limit in a free and democratic country"?
- People who do not identify with the sex assigned to them at birth (usually based on the appearance of their genitals) face various legal conundrums. For example, should the public health-care system pay for gender-reassignment therapies such as surgeries, counselling, and drug treatments? How should the issue of sex markers be dealt with on government-issued documents such as passports and birth certificates?

Issues for Debate or Roundtable

- If a school is operating under a religious mandate, should it be required to permit GSAs to meet on its premises? Should they be required to do more than merely tolerate queer students?
- Queer families now have the same legal rights as straight families. Has this achievement compromised sexual freedom or autonomy claims? Does this recognition fit uncomfortably with neoliberal ideas about personal responsibility?
- If a faith-based university requires students to promise not to engage in sex outside of heterosexual marriage, and students risk being expelled for such conduct, should law societies refuse to consider for admission to practice students who graduate from such programs? Are religious freedom rights infringed by the law societies' decisions? Are equality rights denied by the university's decision? (Research tip: Go to the Canadian Legal Information Institute's website, at https://www.canlii.org/en/, and search "Trinity Western" and "law school.")

Additional Reading

Brooks, Carellin. *Every Inch a Woman: Phallic Possession, Feminity, and the Text.* Vancouver: UBC Press, 2007.

Janoff, Doug. *Pink Blood: Homophobic Violence in Canada.* Toronto: University of Toronto Press, 2005.

Kelly, Fiona. *Transforming Law's Family: The Legal Recognition of Planned Lesbian Motherhood.* Vancouver: UBC Press, 2011.

Rayside, David, and Clyde Wilcox, eds. *Faith, Politics, and Sexual Diversity in Canada and the United States.* Vancouver: UBC Press, 2011.

Warner, Tom. *Never Going Back: A History of Queer Activism in Canada.* Toronto: University of Toronto Press, 2002.

Zylan, Yvonne. *States of Passion: Law, Identity, and Social Construction of Desire.* New York: Oxford University Press, 2011.

Websites

Canadian Legal Information Institute. http://www.canlii.org/en/.
Egale Canada. http://egale.ca/.
Evangelical Fellowship of Canada. http://www.evangelicalfellowship.ca/.
Supreme Court of Canada. http://www.scc-csc.gc.ca/home-accueil/index-eng.aspx.

Notes

1. Miranda Grayson provided invaluable research assistance in the preparation of this paper. Diana King, Ellen Henry, and Helen Fallding provided feedback on earlier iterations, and the University of Manitoba's Centre for Human Rights Research and the Legal Research Institute provided financial support.
2. Pew Research, "The Global Divide on Homosexuality: Greater Acceptance in More Secular and Affluent Countries," 4 June 2013, http://www.pewglobal.org/2013/06/04/the-global-divide-on-homosexuality/#fn-27120-2.
3. B. MacDougall and D. Short, "Religion-Based Claims for Impinging on Queer Citizenship," *Dalhousie Law Journal* 32, no. 2 (2010): 135.
4. As quoted by T. McConnell, "Uganda's New Anti-Gay Law: Part of a Broader Trend in Africa," *National Geographic*, 28 February 2014.
5. Associated Press, "Vladimir Putin Tells Gays in Sochi to Leave Children Alone: Russian President Emphasizes Ban on Homosexual 'Propaganda' among Minors," 17 January 2014, http://www.cbc.ca/news/world/vladimir-putin-tells-gays-in-sochi-to-leave-children-alone-1.2500331.
6. "The empirical research does *not* show that gay or bisexual men are any more likely than heterosexual men to molest children. This is not to argue that homosexual and bisexual men never molest children. But there is no scientific basis for asserting that they are more likely than heterosexual men to do so"; G. Herek, "Facts about Homosexuality and Child Molestation," http://psychology.ucdavis.edu/faculty_sites/rainbow/html/facts_molestation.html.
7. *R. v. Klippert*, [1967] S.C.R. 822.
8. Ibid., at 831.
9. *R. v. C.M.*, 1995 CanLII 8924 (ON C.A.); *R. c. Roy*, 1998 CanLII 12775 (QC C.A.); *R. v. Roth*, 2002 ABQB 145.
10. *Withler v. Canada (Attorney General)*, 2011 SCC 12; *Quebec (Attorney General) v. A.*, 2013 SCC 5.
11. *Egan v. Canada*, 1995 SCC 98.
12. Ibid., at 538.

13. *M v. H.*, 1999 SCC 686.
14. *An Act to Comply with the SCC Decision in* M. v. H., S.M. 2001, c. 37; *The Charter Compliance Act*, S.M. 2002, c. 24; *The Common-Law Partners' Property and Related Amendments Act*, S.M. 2002, c. 48.
15. G. Kinsman and P. Gentile, *The Canadian War on Queers: National Security as Sexual Regulation* (Vancouver: UBC Press, 2009).
16. *Vriend v. Alberta*, 1998 SCC 816.
17. *Alberta Human Rights Act*, RSA 2000, c. A25.5.
18. *Human Rights Act* (Northwest Territories), S.N.W.T. 2002, c. 18; *Human Rights Code* (Ontario), R.S.O. 1990, c. H19; *Human Rights Code* (Manitoba), C.C.S.M. 1987, c. H175.
19. *Criminal Code*, R.S.C., 1985, c. C46, ss. 163–69.
20. Advertising Standards Canada, "The Canadian Code of Advertising Standards," 1963, amended 2010, http://www.adstandards.com/en/standards/canCodeOfAdStandards.aspx; Advertising Standards Canada, "Gender Portrayal Guidelines," 1993, http://www.adstandards.com/en/standards/genderportrayalguidelines.aspx.
21. *The Amusements Act*, C.C.S.M., 1988, c. A70.
22. See J. Fuller and S. Blackley, *Restricted Entry: Censorship on Trial*, 2nd ed. (Vancouver: Press Gang, 1996).
23. *Little Sisters Book and Art Emporium v. Canada (Minister of Justice)* 2000 SCC 69.
24. See, for example, C.A. MacKinnon and A. Dworkin, eds., *In Harm's Way: The Pornography Civil Rights Hearing* (Cambridge, MA: Harvard University Press, 1997); and B. Cossman, S. Bell, L. Gotell, and B.L. Ross, *Bad Attitude/s on Trial: Pornography, Feminism and the Butler Decision* (Toronto: University of Toronto Press, 1997).
25. See K. Busby, "The Queer Sensitive Interveners in the *Little Sisters* Case: A Response to Dr Kendall," *Journal of Homosexuality* 47, nos. 3/4 (2004): 129–50; C.N. Kendall, "Educating Gay Male Youth: Since When Is Pornography a Path Towards Self-Respect?" *Journal of Homosexuality* 47, nos. 3/4 (2004): 83–128.
26. Egale Canada, "EGALE Submissions to the House of Commons Standing Committee on Justice and Human Rights," 1 January 1970, http://egale.ca/all/egale-submissions-to-the-house-of-commons-standing-committee-on-justice-and-human-rights/.
27. *Saskatchewan Human Rights Commission v. Whatcott*, 2013 SCC 11 (Factum of the Intervener Egale Canada Inc.). See also the text accompanying notes 64–67.
28. Order-in-Council 1873-959, http://www.collectionscanada.gc.ca/databases/orders/001022-119.01-e.php?&sisn_id_nbr=9708&page_sequence_nbr=1&interval=20&&page_id_nbr=28293&&&PHPSESSID=6rifo16m1k9vs1mgsodg8bdgu1.
29. R. Dussault and G. Erasmus, "Looking Back, Looking Forward," *Report of the Royal Commission on Aboriginal Peoples*, vol. 1 (Ottawa: Royal Commission on Aboriginal Peoples, 1996).
30. *Roncarelli v. Duplessis*, 1959 SCC 105.
31. *R. v. Big M Drug Mart Ltd*, 1985 SCC 69, at para. 99.
32. Ibid., at para. 97.
33. *Syndicat Northcrest v. Amselem*, 2004 SCC 47; *Alberta v. Hutterian Brethren of Wilson Colony*, 2009 SCC 37.
34. *R. v. N.S.*, 2012 SCC 72.
35. *Alberta v. Hutterian Brethren of Wilson Colony.*

36. *Big M Drug Mart*; *Reference re Section 293 of the Criminal Code of Canada*, 2011 BCSC 1588 (the "Polygamy Reference"); *A.C. v. Manitoba (Director of Child and Family Services)*, 2009 SCC 30.
37. *R. v. M-d. S. and M-l. S*, reasons for decision issued 24 April 2013 by J. Weisman (on appeal).
38. *Reference re Same-Sex Marriage*, 2004 SCC 79, introductory note in judgement.
39. Ibid.
40. *Marriage Commissioners Appointed under the Marriage Act (Re)*, 2011 SKCA 3, at para. 97.
41. *Alberta v. Hutterian Brethren of Wilson Colony*.
42. *Ontario Human Rights Commission and O'Malley v. Simpsons-Sears Ltd*, [1985] 2 S.C.R. 536; *Multani v. Commission scolaire Marguerite-Bourgeoys*, [2006] 1 S.C.R. 256; *Syndicat Northcrest v. Amselem*.
43. *Caldwell et al. v. Stuart et al.*, [1984] 2 S.C.R. 60; *Reference re Same-Sex Marriage*; *Trinity Western University v. British Columbia College of Teachers*, 2001 SCC 31; *Smith v. Knights of Columbus*, 2005 BCHRTD 544.
44. *Ontario Human Rights Commission v. Christian Horizons*, 2010 ONSC 2105.
45. *Robertson v. Goertzen*, 2010 NTHRAP 1.
46. *Eadie and Thomas v. Riverbend Bed and Breakfast and Others (No. 2)*, 2012 BCHRT 247.
47. *Schroen v. Steinbach Bible College*, Manitoba Human Rights Tribunal (D. King, adjudicator), 1999, http://www.manitobahumanrights.ca/publications/legal/schroen.html#VI.
48. *R. v Big M Drug Mart Ltd*.
49. *Lund v. Boissoin*, 2012 ABCA 300, at para. 4.
50. *Human Rights, Citizenship and Multiculturalism Act*, RSA 2000, c H14. The Alberta act was renamed the Alberta *Human Rights Act* in 2009. Human rights codes in the Northwest Territories, British Columbia, Alberta, and Saskatchewan have provisions that permit human rights tribunals to sanction hate speech. Until recently, hate speech was also regulated by the federal *Canadian Human Rights Act*, but these provisions, which governed electronic expression, including the Internet, were repealed in 2013; *Canadian Human Rights Act*, R.S.C. 1985, c. H6. Finally, anyone who incites or wilfully promotes hatred against an identifiable group is guilty of a criminal offence and is liable to up to two years of imprisonment; *Criminal Code*, s. 319.
51. Sexual orientation was read into the Alberta legislation as a result of the decision in *Vriend*.
52. *Saskatchewan Human Rights Commission v. Whatcott*, 2013 SCC 11.
53. Ibid., at para. 189.
54. *Saskatchewan Human Rights Code*, S.S. 1979, c. S24.1.
55. *Whatcott*, at para. 152.
56. Ibid., at para. 156.
57. *Boissoin*, at para. 73.
58. Ibid., at para. 4.
59. Egale Canada, "EGALE Submissions."
60. *Whatcott*, at para. 24.
61. Ibid., at para. 70.
62. Ibid., at para. 77.
63. Ibid., at para. 199.

64. R. Moon, "The Supreme Court of Canada's Attempt to Reconcile Freedom of Religion and Sexual Orientation Equality in Public Schools," in *Faith, Politics, and Sexual Diversity in Canada and the United States*, ed. D. Rayside and C. Wilcox (Vancouver: UBC Press, 2011), 32.
65. *Whatcott*, at para. 142–43.
66. Ibid., at para. 153–54.
67. Ibid., para. 174.
68. Ibid.
69. *Hall (Litigation Guardian of) v. Powers*, (2002) 59 D.L.R. (3d) 423,
70. *School District No. 44 (North Vancouver) v. Jubran*, 2005 BCCA 201 (CanLII); *Chamberlain v. Surrey School District No. 36*, 2002 SCC 86; *Chiang v. Vancouver Board of Education*, 2009 BCHRT 319; *Kempling v. British Columbia College of Teachers*, 2004 BCSC 133.
71. *Trinity Western University*, headnote.
72. C. Taylor, T. Peter, et al., *Every Class in Every School: The First National Climate Survey on Homophobia, Biphobia, and Transphobia in Canadian Schools. Final Report* (Toronto: Egale Canada Human Rights Trust, 2011).
73. Manitoba, Ontario, and Alberta have made these amendments. The *Ontario Education Act* (as amended by the *Accepting Schools Act*, 2012 S.O. 2012 C.5) provides for the following:

    303.1 (1) Every board shall support pupils who want to establish and lead activities and organizations that promote a safe and inclusive learning environment, the acceptance of and respect for others and the creation of a positive school climate, including,

    (a) activities or organizations that promote gender equity;
    (b) activities or organizations that promote anti-racism;
    (c) activities or organizations that promote the awareness and understanding of, and respect for, people with disabilities; or
    (d) activities or organizations that promote the awareness and understanding of, and respect for, people of all sexual orientations and gender identities, including organizations with the name gay-straight alliance or another name.

    (2) For greater certainty, neither the board nor the principal shall refuse to allow a pupil to use the name gay-straight alliance or a similar name for an organization described in clause (1)(d).

74. GSA Network, *GSA Advisor Handbook* (San Francisco: National Association of GSA Networks, 2011), http://www.gsanetwork.org/advisor-handbook.
75. D. Short, *"Don't Be So Gay!" Queers, Bullying and Making Schools Safe* (Vancouver: UBC Press, 2013), 12.
76. Ibid., 13.
77. A recording of Pastor Ray Duerksen's sermon can be found at *Winnipeg Free Press*, "Southland Church Sermon Targets Bill 18," video, 4:47, posted 7 March 2013, http://www.winnipegfreepress.com/local/sermon-rips-anti-bullying-bill-195817061.html.
78. For the full resolution, see CBC News, "Anti-Bullying Bill Like 'Persecution' in Steinbach," 7 March 2013, http://www.cbc.ca/news/canada/manitoba/anti-bullying-bill-like-persecution-in-steinbach-1.1340156.

79. *L.S. v. Commission scolaire des Chênes*, 2012 SCC 7; *Loyola High School v. Quebec (Attorney-General)*, 2015 SCC 12.
80. *Loyola High School v. Quebec (Attorney General)*, 2015 SCC 12.
81. Ibid., headnote.
82. *Reference re Same-Sex Marriage*.
83. *Trinity Western University*, headnote.
84. Moon, "Supreme Court of Canada's Attempt."

13
The Arab Spring and Human Rights: Discarding the Old Clichés

MAHMOOD MONSHIPOURI AND KELLEY O'DELL

Learning Objectives

- To understand that striking an equilibrium between freedoms and economic and political stability is the key to successful transition to democracy and safeguarding human dignity
- To understand the ways in which Western neoliberal economic programs and policies adversely affect local and specific conditions of the Middle East and North Africa

The 2011 uprisings in the Middle East and North Africa (MENA) provided a unique opportunity for local voices that have long been suppressed and silenced under authoritarian regimes to be heard by the rest of the world. These rising voices of dissension manifested themselves in uprisings of unprecedented significance that shook the foundations of authoritarian regimes, at the same time upending long-held beliefs that the people and cultural traditions of the MENA region were resigned to a destiny of autocratic rule. The region's engagement with the human rights idea has become apparent in local demands and claims, discrediting the cliché that "this region is a region of monolithic identities at odds with notions of human rights and other pluralistic, democratic ideas."[1]

Increasingly, however, the euphoria of the Arab Spring has given way to the realities of political transition. In some cases, such as Bahrain and Yemen, human rights became the first casualties of the peaceful uprisings. In other cases, such as Tunisia and Egypt, despite peaceful democratic transitions, the process has been vexatious and difficult, to say the least. Regime transition often presents crises of governability, rooted in the turbulence that permeates political and social change. This is especially true of transitions born of violent uprising, which typically involve disruptions to the state, economy, and social relations. Even democratic transitions, which tend to produce legitimate authority and respect for the rule of law and human rights, result in upheaval, uncertainty, and counterrevolutionary resistance to reform.

Transitional periods and processes raise essential and unresolved questions regarding the viability of the democratic process. A long view of history demonstrates that repression is never an adequate mechanism of political control, nor one of the most effective tools of governing.[2] Yet it is equally true that combatting authoritarianism, deeply embedded patronage, endemic corruption, and mismanagement of the economy in frail fledgling democracies is no easy task, and that the possibility of backsliding into a new form of illiberal democracy or traditional authoritarianism usually remains. The struggling democracies of the post–Arab revolts era have found themselves entangled in such a historical trajectory.

This chapter reviews the major barriers to protecting and promoting human rights in this transitional period, as well as ways to implement programs for the betterment of human rights conditions. To illustrate the difficulties surrounding democratic transition in the MENA region, we highlight several cases in which democratic transitions are underway and propose potentially manageable strategies that could mitigate some of the obstacles the region faces in this regard. Our central argument is that the Arab peoples' power, efforts, and sacrifices that generated the 2011 uprisings throughout the region are potent and capable of reshaping local and national politics. Serious and daunting challenges lie ahead, however, given the intensity, scope, and pace of drastic change unfolding in the region. Although the historical and contemporary contexts within which human rights abuses must be tackled vary from one country to another, in large part because of the varying obstacles each country faces, the fact remains that progress toward human rights becomes sustainable only if it is institutionalized. Another, equally difficult task is protecting women's rights, especially in the context of neoliberal economic policies.

The Impact of the Information Revolution

The prevailing use of modern communication technologies has undoubtedly given human rights struggles an unprecedented jolt and momentum. The free flow of information has created a new generation that is plugged in and proactive, less conformist, and more cognizant of the outside world. This combination has made younger generations far more receptive to internationally recognized modern ideas of human rights. At the same time, international borders have become more porous in this era of globalization than at any time in the past, thanks in large part to cyberspace.

Although views differ about the effectiveness of human rights norms and institutions, human rights issues today merit particular attention, as they have become a dominant framework for many political struggles within and across national boundaries. It is in this context that we turn our attention to the uprisings in the MENA region. The aspirations of the people in this region for basic human rights, articulated in universal terms, are emblematic of a yearning for the same basic civil and political liberties that Westerners have sought both conceptually and institutionally. As the entire region experiences an "Arab awakening," the political parlance is changing. The notion of *sha'b* ("the people") has become a decisive marker of identity in Tunisia, establishing itself as the pertinent signifier of consensus.[3] The social movement that has transpired since 2011 has had a profound impact on the country's political consciousness, turning individuals from people into citizens.

Struggles for Dignity and Justice

Arguably, these uprisings were "about dignity and justice, not collective self-pity. It is very unlikely that a za'im [leader] claiming to have miraculous healing powers will be able to seduce Tunisians, who are advocating a politics of justice, not compassion."[4] To merely translate people's economic woes into unrest misses a larger point. Ordinary Arabs themselves depict the heart of this movement as a revolution for dignity. Eating bread is no longer enough; liberty and dignity equally drive their revolts.[5] Through their uprisings, as one expert notes, Egyptians have created a more favourable terrain in which their power relative to the state has increased.[6]

Youth and their demands for human rights and dignity overwhelmed Egypt's Morsi presidency, a presidency that seems to have failed to connect with young people—a requisite for solidification of the country's fragile democracy. The Morsi administration faced many protests, indigenous and local in nature and propelled largely by lack of hope for economic recovery and political order. One of the most crucial challenges that undermined Morsi's administration was the absence of proper and effective economic and political structures to drive democratic changes forward.

An alternative view holds that the spontaneous nature of the street protests proved to be an asset for such youth movements, by offering them a political voice, even one outside traditional democratic mechanisms. This possibility, along with the decentralization of information in the Internet age, rendered the poorly run and mismanaged Morsi government vulnerable to wider public criticism and unrest. To be sure, the Egyptian people have invested heavily in the transition process and are prepared to deal with all its attendant uncertainties. Questions continue, however, about the pace of change and the extent to which such a transformation may provoke violence. Violence and further social discord are likely to occur over the issue of separation of powers, as well as the role of security forces and the military in post-revolutionary Egypt. As noted above, democratic transitions can easily get derailed, leading to non-democratic actions, processes, and outcomes, especially in their early stages.

Few transitional democracies have remained insulated from the political and socioeconomic shocks of unfolding changes, wherever they may have occurred. Moreover, democratic transitions in the developing world may not always culminate in liberal capitalist democracy. If this is indeed the case, one should not be overly troubled. Egypt's transition from revolution to democracy may take much longer than expected, but the initial democratization experiments in France, Germany, and Italy also proved to be lengthy, drawn-out, and at times bloody. Similarly, despite two decades of democratization in Eastern Europe since the early 1990s, the prospects for establishing full-fledged and genuine democratic systems are still far from positive.

However, Egypt's transition to post-revolutionary democracy has been marred by the trials of 43 employees of foreign non-profit groups, including 16 Americans, who have been convicted of receiving illegal funds from abroad and operating unlicensed organizations.[7] These harsh verdicts raise questions about the judiciary's accountability and its unpredictability, while displaying yet another symptom of Egypt's lack of transitional justice. In this sense, experts note, "it is even more of a concern when the same judge issues harsher penalties to defenders of democracy than to those accused of killing protesters."[8]

Egypt: Crisis of Governability

Egypt's first democratically elected president, Mohammad Morsi, faced the difficulties of governing a country going through a democratic transition. He ruled over a fractured and polarized society, and his management of the country's economy and politics proved to be woefully inconsistent and inadequate. Morsi's support for the 2013 draft constitution invited much controversy, as the draft was largely a reformulation of the 2012 constitution, based on the negotiations that had transpired between special interests and groups. The 2013 draft failed to offer a new vision for the state, or protection for the underprivileged and vulnerable. Article 31, for example, indicated that the state was required to preserve the "security of information space," which was widely regarded as a function of national security. Details regarding this function were left to the legislative branch. Similarly, article 204 stated, "Civilians can be tried before military courts for crimes against the military"—crimes that could conceivably involve limitations on free speech. The limitations remained both unclear and non-comprehensive.[9] Some would no doubt argue that excluding organizations such as the Muslim Brotherhood from authority is a worthwhile objective. The problem with that approach, however, is that it has left Egypt's many other concerns unattended to, including its desperate need for social justice.

As economic and political pressures accumulated over Morsi's head, attending to the country's well-being posed new challenges for his regime's survival. Finally, on 3 July 2013, he was deposed in a soft coup engineered by the Supreme Council of Armed Forces (SCAF). Before the July coup, many observers had warned about such an eventuality. Nabil Abdel-Fattah, director of Al-Ahram Center for Social and Historic Studies, wrote that, given Egypt's dire economic predicament, there was danger of an eruption among the most underprivileged sectors of the population. In fact, Abdel-Fattah noted that a "revolution of the hungry" was imminent, given the growing impoverishment of the urban and rural poor.[10] A currency decline raised concerns over the government's ability to stabilize the economy. The 2011 Arab Spring uprisings came at a time when Egypt was saddled with a huge debt ($35 billion), accumulated during Hosni Mubarak's regime. The country's reserves have since dropped to $15 billion, in large part a result of the government's attempts to avert further currency woes.[11]

Politically, Morsi's blatant attempts to shore up executive power came under great scrutiny when he faced vociferous opposition to the nation's draft constitution in late 2012. His constitutional declaration of December 2012 gave him more power than even ousted president Hosni Mubarak, and Morsi exempted himself from any independent review. Moreover, he dismissed the prosecutor general, a clear violation of article 14, section 1 of the International Covenant on Civil and Political Rights (ICCPR), which states that dismissal of judges by the executive is incompatible with an "independent and impartial tribunal established by the law."[12]

Following protests on the anniversary of the Port Said incident in which 74 people were killed in a soccer stadium, Morsi's imposition of martial law on the cities of Suez, Ismailiya, and Port Said pointed to a turn toward adoption of authoritarian governance to maintain order and security. This shift of policy exposed the glaring contradictions of Morsi's government, which supported policies not broadly favoured by the Egyptian public while at the same time claiming to have built inclusive economic and political institutions.

In the face of the political turmoil and uncertainty generated by the rush to fill the power vacuum, draft a new constitution, marginalize the opposition, and consolidate its power, the Morsi administration was unable to fulfill any of its big promises. This is very typical, as some experts remind us, of Islamists who enter the power arena: "Their commitments to promoting social justice, reducing subsidies in order to provide more fiscal space in budgets, attacking cronyism, and eliminating waste in bloated bureaucracies have not been realized thus far."[13]

The events in post-coup Egypt have left the country deeply polarized and its human rights conditions progressively deteriorating, with state media portraying members and supporters of the Muslim Brotherhood as terrorists and youth movements as foreign-inspired traitors. The state of human rights suffered yet another major setback when the country's interim government supported a new law against public protests, one requiring a permit to hold any demonstration. Youth and secular activists openly denounced this law, claiming that it allows authorities to broaden their crackdown on protests while largely targeting Islamist supporters of ousted president Mohamed Morsi.

On balance, as Heba Morayef notes, human rights activists and other pro-democracy political forces in Egypt—who in 2011 believed they could reform state institutions and legislative structures—grossly miscalculated their power. One lesson learned was the need to institutionalize reform during the earlier part of an uprising, when public sentiment generates unprecedented momentum and there is a political will within the regime to effectively respond to protesters' demands. "Today," Morayef points out, "human rights groups find themselves with few allies and very limited access to subservient media."[14]

Since 2014, when Abdel Fatah el-Sisi won the presidential elections, the SCAF has gone on the offensive, accusing the April 6 Youth Movement of being foreign agents. Increasingly, human rights organizations have failed to solidify the constituencies they gained in earlier months, although many of them have restructured their activities and strategies to move in that direction.[15] While it is true that the uprisings reconfigured relations between citizen-subjects and their states, as Ellen Lust argues, the post-uprising elections have also become a tool that authoritarian regimes use in various ways to try to maintain their hold on power. In some cases, such as Egypt, Libya, Tunisia, and Yemen, elections have become an arena of contestation in the post-rupture transitions. The extent to which elections contribute to the struggle over the state after leaders fall—and bolster the possibility of establishing democratic institutions—turns on how drastically the transitional regime has extricated itself from the former elites and how developed multi-party elections were in the past.[16] On both of these accounts, the prospect of Egypt's transition to democracy remains doubtful, if not ominous.

Since the 2011 uprisings, women have paid a heavy price for demanding their rights. Sexual violence has noticeably increased. According to testimonies compiled by the Egypt-based New Woman Foundation, Nazra for

Feminist Studies, and the El-Nadeem Center for Rehabilitation of Victims of Violence and Torture, more than 20 women were attacked on 25 January 2013 while demonstrating in and around Cairo's Tahrir Square. This surge in gender-based violence occurring in public during political protests has been alarming. Such acts of violence are a blatant violation of international human rights instruments—including the International Covenant on Economic, Social, and Cultural Rights (ICESCR), to which Egypt is a party—which call for the prevention of violence against women and promotion of equality between men and women.[17]

Four years after the 2011 uprisings, one journalist writes, the great hopes for change have been dashed. What was once viewed as the first move toward establishing democracy in the Arab world's largest country instead led to a military coup, political uncertainty and chaos, and intense polarization. The Islamists, who won office through popular election, have been outlawed. The country is ruled by an army general. Opposition figures, journalists, and activists have been jailed. Economic conditions have progressively deteriorated, leaving millions of people much worse off. Perhaps most significantly, the broadly shared passion for political change has dimmed completely, and widespread optimism that something better is around the corner has considerably subsided. In short, the years since the Arab Spring have yielded nothing of what Egyptians were hoping for.[18]

There is no doubt that the new constitutional document (after amendment of the suspended 2012 constitution)—approved in January 2014 by 98 per cent of voters, in a turnout of only 39 per cent—contains both progressive and regressive elements. Some articles reflect the progressive side of the new version. Among others can be cited the articles covering these issues: the right to strike (15), health care (18), education (19), academic independence (21), human dignity (51), torture (52), personal freedom (54), due process (55), freedom of belief (64), freedom of thought (65), and freedom of the press (70).

There are, however, also many contradictions in the new constitution. A quick glance at the preamble of the new version reveals this sentence: "We are now drafting a Constitution that completes the building of a modern democratic state with a civilian government."[19] One interpretation of this is that the term *civilian rule* or *civilian government* means that military personnel and religious clerics are prevented from participating in the cabinet. Article 201, however, stipulates "the Minister of Defense is the Commander in Chief of the Armed Forces and is appointed from among its officers."[20] This means that although authority has been granted to the president to appoint the minister of defence, the president is obligated to choose this minister from among the ranks of the military.[21]

Another example that illustrates yet another contradiction in the new constitution is article 55, pertaining to due process. It stipulates, "All those who are apprehended, detained or have their freedom restricted shall be treated in a way that preserves their dignity. They may not be tortured, terrorized, or coerced. They may not be physically or mentally harmed, or arrested and confined in designated locations that are appropriate [*sic*] according to humanitarian and health standards. The state shall provide means of access for those with disabilities."[22] Likewise, article 96 relates to due process: "The accused is innocent until proven guilty in a fair court of law, which provides guarantees for him to defend himself. The law shall regulate the appeal of felony sentences. The state shall provide protection to the victims, witnesses, accused and informants as necessary and in accordance with the law."[23]

The above statutory and constitutional provisions appear fundamentally sound. Yet in practice, there is no denying that the rising popularity of the military has rendered limiting military powers in the constitution politically difficult, if not impossible. Consider, for example, article 204, on the military judiciary, which defines a broad spectrum of crimes as within the competencies of the military judiciary. Many civilians have been tried by military courts in the past without much regard to due process, and the power of the military to subject civilians to military trials has remained largely unaltered in this new constitution.

Tunisia: New Challenges

Tunisia is known as the birthplace of the recent democratic uprisings in the Middle East and North Africa and the country that offered the best prospects for democratization of all the Arab countries. However, the assassination of two prominent secular leaders there has led to widespread concern that the kind of zero-sum politics that has come to define the post–Arab Spring tumult in Egypt, Libya, and Syria will also transpire in Tunisia. The violent acts and the slaying of politicians and fierce critics of Tunisia's ruling Islamic party portend rumblings of discontent and instability throughout the country, posing serious threats to the democratic process underway.

The first slaying, in February 2013, was of Chokri Belaid, secretary-general of the Unified Democratic Patriots Party and general coordinator of the People's Front, an outspoken critic of the Islamist party Ennahda. The second assassination, on 25 July 2013, was of the founder and former leader of the People's Movement, Mohamed Brahmi, whose movement had won two seats in the 2011 Constituent Assembly elections. Both killings led to renewed outbursts of violence and turmoil in the country, the likes of which had not been seen since the ouster two years before of the autocratic leader Zine el-Abidine Ben Ali.

With Tunisia descending into chaos and further political violence in the ensuing weeks and months, two key questions were raised: Would further tumult irreversibly affect Tunisia's democratic transition? And would Islamists and secularists enter into an agreement on mutual terms? A political deal was reached on 15 December 2013, between Beji Caid Essebsi, a former prime minister who now led the new, secular-minded political party Nidaa Tounes, and Rachid Ghanouchi, spiritual leader of the Islamist party Ennahda. It meant that the Islamists agreed to step back from political power in exchange for a permanent place in Tunisian politics and not being outlawed, as the Muslim Brotherhood has been in Egypt.[24] Under the new deal, the members of the National Constituent Assembly returned to work and passed the constitution, appointed an election commission, and passed an electoral law.[25] With the constitution completed, the Islamist-led government stepped down and transferred power to a caretaker government that would hold office until elections were held later in 2014.

While some elements of the new Tunisian constitution provide a sound legal basis for equality, others clearly invite controversy. A reassuring example is article 46, pertaining to gender parity, which states "The state guarantees equal opportunities between men and women in the bearing of all the various responsibilities in all fields. The state seeks to achieve equal representation for women and men in elected council (parity). The state takes the necessary measures to eliminate violence against women."[26]

One article that has prompted legitimate concerns about whether some freedoms may be subject to misinterpretation, manipulation, or abuse is article 6, "Incitement to Violence," which stipulates "The state protects religion, guarantees freedom of belief and religious practices, protects sanctities, and ensures the neutrality of mosques and places of worship away from partisan instrumentalization. The state is committed to spreading the values of moderation and tolerance, and to protect the sacred and prevent it from being attacked, and is also committed to prohibit charges of *takfir* and incitement to hatred and violence, and to combat them."[27] This article, experts observe, poses both potential and actual threats not only to freedom of religion but also to freedom of expression. Hip-hop musicians and rappers, for example, will be subject to extraordinary scrutiny by the secret police and government officials as part of a broader crackdown on freedom of speech in the name of combatting terrorism.[28]

It is worth noting that, under pressure from Western governments and civil society groups, Ennahda made several concessions that made forging a consensus for the constitution possible, even though those concessions created divisions within the party. It dropped, for example, its initial goal of establishing Tunisia as "an Islamic state and declaring the supremacy of *Shari'ah* law."[29] Surprisingly, the 2014 parliamentary elections gave secularists the upper hand in forming Tunisia's new government, compelling the Islamists to retreat from the nation's high politics. The secular Nidaa Tounes party won 85 seats in the elections, defeating its main rival, Ennahda—a party that only three years before had swept to power as Tunisians celebrated the collapse of a dictatorial regime—which won 69 seats.[30]

Subsequently, Beji Caid Essebsi's victory over incumbent Moncef Marzouki in the presidential elections, held on 23 November 2014, brought a justifiable degree of optimism to the country, making it the only Arab country to have moved from authoritarian rule to democracy since the 2011 uprisings swept the region. No less significant was the fact that President Essebsi's party, Nidaa Tounes, had won the largest number of seats in the previous parliamentary elections.[31]

On 18 March 2015, terrorist attacks on Tunisia's Bardo National Museum claimed the lives of 20 tourists and 3 Tunisians, casting a shadow over the last ray of hope from the Arab Spring. These attacks on civilians demonstrated that Tunisia's pathway to democracy is fraught with difficulties. Equally disturbing is the fact that Tunisia has contributed the largest number of fighters to radical movements such as the Islamic State in Iraq and Syria (ISIS), a global jihadist group bent on stoking sectarian tensions and violence in the region.[32] There are also concerns that the chaos in Libya may spill over into neighbouring countries such as Tunisia and Algeria, given the permeable borders between these states.

Bahrain: Sectarian Strife or Social Justice?

A key internal source of political divisiveness in the Arabian Peninsula is the Shia–Sunni split. With the exception of Bahrain, where Shi'ites make up almost 70 per cent of the population, in the rest of Arab states of the Persian Gulf, Shia constitutes an important minority. Despite their substantial population and centuries of presence in the region, most of the current Sunni regimes view Shi'ites as a threat to political stability and social cohesion. This accounts for the systematic and widespread discrimination against Shia citizens by the state apparatuses in most Gulf Cooperation Council (GCC) countries (Bahrain, Kuwait, Oman, Qatar, Saudi Arabia, and the United Arab Emirates). Too often Shi'ites are treated as second-class citizens and are denied proper representation in the civilian and military institutions of the majority of GCC countries.[33]

The Saudi government pursues a deliberate policy of discrimination against its Shia subjects, denying them the freedom to practise many of their religious ceremonies. A 2009 report by Human Rights Watch listed several examples of institutional discrimination against the Saudi Shia minority. These include, among others, the dominance of Sunni tribunals over the only three Shia courts and the prevalence of teaching exclusively Sunni Islam to students at Saudi schools.[34] The persistent alienation of Shia citizens within most GCC countries has noticeably undermined the political legitimacy of the rulers and the social cohesion of their societies. These sectarian rifts were most acute in Bahrain and Saudi Arabia after the 1979 Iranian revolution, but they have become even more pronounced since the 2011 Arab uprisings.[35]

The 14 February 2011 uprisings in Bahrain were met with fierce reaction from the al-Khalifa regime, leading to a suffocating political atmosphere characterized by attacks on dissenters and opposition groups. On 14 March 2011, at the invitation of the Bahraini regime, Saudi tanks and troops entered Bahrain to suppress the opposition forces. The Bahraini regime unleashed a comprehensive campaign of repression and intimidation that collectively punished virtually the entire Shia majority.[36] This campaign involved, among other things, a sectarian crackdown on opposition activists, newspapers editors, bloggers, and anyone else representing independent media. Doctors were convicted and imprisoned for treating wounded protestors, including some 20 doctors sentenced to 15 years in prison last fall for treating protestors. Likewise, students and faculty were dismissed from universities for the vaguest of associations with the protest movement.[37]

A fictitious view of sectarian strife, coloured by an authoritarian perspective, portrayed the opposing social movements as intensely religious and parochial. To deepen the divide between the Shia and Sunni communities, the Bahraini government ordered the destruction of a number of Shi'ite religious buildings. According to one source, at least 28 mosques and Shi'ite religious institutions have been demolished since the crackdown. Although the justice ministry claimed the reason for the demolitions was lack of a licence, the timing of these acts left no doubt in the minds of Shi'ites about the repressive nature of the action.[38]

Fearing loss of its power, the Bahraini regime deployed every possible repressive measure. However, the fact remains that the Shi'ites were not demanding a Shia government; they were (and still are) demanding rule of law and a constitutional monarchy, not looking to Iran as an example. (The type of Shi'ism practised in Bahrain is different from that in Iran. Iranians practise Usuli Shiism, which is predicated on control of the government by Shia clerics, while in Bahrain the most common type is Akhbari, which opposes the clergy's control of government.) The protestors have asked for the release of political prisoners; creation of a more representative and empowered parliament; establishment of a constitution written by the people; and a new, more representative cabinet. They have also strongly demanded that the prime minister, Khalifa bin Salman al-Khalifa—the king's uncle, who has been in office for the past 40 years—step down.

Abdullahdi al-Khawaja, a prominent human rights activist sentenced to life imprisonment, was on a 110-day hunger strike until 17 March 2013. He had not been taken to a hospital for the simple reason that he refused to wear a prison uniform, asserting that he deserved not to be treated as a criminal. And Bahrain has increasingly become known as the "Republic of Tear Gas." Twenty people have died from tear gas inhalation since November 2011, and opposition leaders say that tear gas has caused a total of 30 deaths.[39]

Syria: An Unpredictable Future

It is generally argued that the sectarian dividing line in the MENA region, particularly in Iraq since the US invasion of that country, is drawn by power and money, not a dispute over the nature of Islam.[40] The sectarian split in Syria is not the whole story either. The lingering sectarian tensions in Syria result partly from an internal sectarian divide but are provoked largely by internal power struggles between different minorities (Alawite, Druze, and Christian) on the one hand and the majority Sunnis on the other. These tensions, which are fuelled and magnified by regional competition among Sunni-led movements and Shi'ite-inspired unrest, have led to a civil war with devastating results: enormous loss of life, streams of refugees, and virulent violence from both the Assad regime and its opposing forces.

The civil war in Syria has led to a grave humanitarian crisis. One-third of the country's population has been displaced. More than two million refugees have fled to neighbouring countries, particularly Jordan and Lebanon; more than four million people are displaced inside the country. Food and medical aid are not regularly distributed within the country. With millions of lives at risk, United Nations officials have called for greater humanitarian access to all parts of Syria, as well as more aid from the global community.[41] The complexity of the situation, coupled with outsider interventions, has rendered options for a negotiated transition difficult. Intense regional and international competition, as the experts point out, has further exacerbated domestic Syrian dynamics. The banality of violence, the proliferation of weapons, and the radicalization of some elements within the opposition have made the situation in Syria extremely difficult to resolve in the foreseeable future.[42]

The lack of cohesion and the political and structural weaknesses of the Syrian political opposition, as well as the rise of a radical Islamist militia, are likely to significantly complicate their shared aim of toppling the Assad regime. With Syrian uprisings morphing into a zero-sum civil war predicated on a military victory against the Assad regime, the human costs in coming years will be horrendous.[43] Likewise, the reluctance of Western states to intervene in Syria and the risks of humanitarian intervention in yet another Arab country, along with questions regarding the legality of such action, have prevented activation of the concept of responsibility to protect (R2P). Adopted by the UN General Assembly in 2005, R2P calls for collective action to prevent or end "genocide, war crimes, ethnic cleansing, and crimes against humanity."[44]

The resurgence of jihadists in Syria's chaos has led to a revival of fears of Al-Qaeda in the region. Some analysts and American officials have argued that the rise of such a threat might force US policy makers to revert to counterterrorism as the guiding focus of their policy toward the region. "We need to start talking to the Assad regime again about counterterrorism and other issues of shared concern," writes Ryan C. Crocker, a veteran diplomat who served in Syria, Iraq, and Afghanistan.[45] This, Crocker continues, "will have to be done very, very quietly. But bad as Assad is, he is not as bad as the jihadis who would take over in his absence."[46] These types of tactical adjustments seek expedient solutions that fall far short of addressing the human rights situation. As of this writing, the prospects for any improvement in human rights conditions in Syria appear bleak.

The Political Economy of Unrest

Modern-day dictators in the MENA region have used food subsidies to ensure obedience, prolong dependence on the state, and maintain power, from Egypt's Gamal Abdel Nasser, who used subsidies as a means of managing and controlling society, to Saddam Hussein's self-serving and corrupt use of the UN's oil-for-food program and the food subsidies that for many years helped shore up Egypt's Hosni Mubarak. But in 2008, when grain prices rose, a wave of bread riots spread throughout the region, forcing governments to respond by increasing subsidies, raising wages, or simply lavishing cash grants on their people.

By 2010 Egypt had become by far the world's largest wheat importer, spending nearly $3 billion a year on food subsidies. When prices soared even higher in 2010, Mubarak and other rulers in the region responded by announcing a new round of handouts. This strategy, however, could no longer subdue the unrest, as the rioters were demanding something more than just bread; they were asking for freedom, justice, and security.[47] Human rights had entered Arab street discourse with a vengeance. As one commentator aptly put it, "Human progress comes in moral stages, usually each higher than the last one."[48]

Increasingly, youth in the MENA region tend to articulate their demands largely in internationally recognized human rights terms. The younger members of Egypt's Muslim Brotherhood are attempting to articulate a new vision sensitive to the new reality of the region, rejecting the group's old conservative platform that bars women and Coptic Christians from becoming head of state.[49]

Several aspects of US foreign policy toward the Middle East and North Africa, a region handicapped by conflicting agendas and paradoxes, need to be reconsidered in these changing and challenging times. The policy of quiet diplomacy has not borne fruit in some cases, but neither has supporting the status quo in the name of long-term geostrategic considerations. In the face of the social unrest and protests now spreading across the Arab world, the need for a US foreign policy for the MENA region that represents a new strain of thinking is aptly captured by Tom Malinowski, Washington director of Human Rights Watch: "If we bet on the stability of authoritarian states, we will be right most of the time, but wrong at the crucial time."[50] Both George W. Bush's crusading moralizing and Barack Obama's policy of engagement failed to convince Hosni Mubarak to lift Egypt's state of emergency and permit international observers to monitor the 2005 and 2010 parliamentary elections. In both cases Mubarak turned the other way, using the bogeyman of the Muslim Brotherhood and takeover by Islamic militants.[51] There is a need for different policies to help us navigate a new path in this critical region.

Arguably, the outcomes of these uprisings may dovetail nicely with the long-term strategic interests of the West more generally and the United States in particular. These youth-led revolutions are driven more by the secular demands of human dignity, jobs, rule of law, economic prosperity, and participation in national affairs than by grand ideological statements.[52] What the recent popular movements in the MENA region, such as Iran's Green Movement and the Arab revolts, have in common is an unprecedented desire to achieve social justice, human rights, and democratic governance. "We may be witnessing," Asef Bayat observes, "the coming of a post-Islamist Middle East, in which the prevailing popular movements assume a post-national, post-ideological, civil, and democratic character."[53] The young people and their political organizations (the "Facebook generation") have created a new centre in Egypt—aligned with neither the Mubarak regime nor the Muslim Brotherhood—where the focus of US foreign policy should be. Aligning interests with values should become the task of US foreign policy makers, recognizing that their national interest is no longer reducible to geopolitics and power alone.

While demands for democracy and political involvement are on the rise in MENA countries, the West should consider the economic desperation of the post-revolutionary states and not take for granted poverty-stricken populations' desire for economic stability. Such desires threaten to arouse nostalgia for the deceptive stability of autocratic regimes, which in reality absorb huge portions of MENA economies for state and military control, operating with little to no transparency and making transition to a more liberal economy nearly impossible.

For example, in Egypt, when the Muslim Brotherhood assumed the reins of a broken economy, the West offered virtually no useful monetary assistance other than a $4.8-billion loan from the International Monetary Fund (IMF). In the Middle Eastern context, this loan was typical IMF fare, demanding dramatic subsidy cuts and tax increases and furthering cutbacks in state-owned industries. Moreover, the contingent reform policies were gender-blind, failing to take into consideration their dramatic negative effects on Egyptian women.

IMF policies facilitate the patriarchal policies of MENA governments. In Egypt and elsewhere, IMF policies employ a trickle-down theory by expanding export-oriented industries. They hold that, if states follow IMF steps to restructure to an export-oriented economy, increased well-being of women will naturally follow. The IMF fails, however, to identify why employers in private export industries are so eager to hire women. In truth, these enterprises tend to pay low wages and provide few protections, so only jobless women are desperate enough to apply for employment.[54] In a free-market system, such industries thrive on exploiting MENA's vast pool of disenfranchised women; they can easily deny benefits to a woman, secure in the guarantee that another is willing to take her place.

When IMF policies demand a transition from public to private industry, women are invariably hit the hardest. Throughout the MENA region, state-owned economic sectors have historically been most hospitable to women, attracting female workers with generous maternity and childcare benefits even when public-sector wages have fallen because of government spending cuts.[55] Since public-sector "redundant labour" jobs are thus dominated by females, women are the first to go when the state-owned sector shuts down inefficient departments. They are given two options: either accept a paltry early retirement package from the government or risk being fired one day by a private-industry employer, without welfare provisions or unemployment benefits.[56]

These acts are clearly a violation of article 2 of the Convention on the Elimination of All Forms of Discrimination Against Women (CEDAW), which states that state parties should take all appropriate measures to eliminate discrimination against women by any person, organization, or enterprise. Meanwhile, in countries such as Egypt, the export-oriented private sector has not generated enough jobs to absorb these unemployed women. According to Alan Richards and John Waterbury, "Labor-intensive manufactured exports continue to respond sluggishly and there has been no great inflow of foreign direct investment."[57]

Accordingly, adoption of the IMF's technique of slashing public-sector industries and employee benefits in Egypt was tantamount to political suicide, in effect forcing Morsi to abandon an already struggling population. No wonder he put off accepting the politically crippling but seemingly inevitable IMF loan. Because of the West's unforgiving economic pressures, the Muslim Brotherhood experienced an ironic turning of the table: the very IMF restructuring policies that had fostered discontent with Mubarak during the neo-liberalization era tied the hands of Morsi's nascent government as demands for bread superseded demands for democracy.

Today's international negotiations in the Middle East often give precedence to economic interests at the expense of human rights. However, such a preference is inherently contradictory, as successful implementation of economic policies has much to gain from social support, and much to lose from lack thereof. This form of social support can be ensured only when economic stability is coupled with the provision of human rights—the two factors are absolutely co-dependent. This is why the West has much to learn from its mistakes in Egypt, where General Sisi gained domestic support by spurning IMF negotiations in favour of a $12-billion parcel promised by the Gulf states that favoured the Muslim Brotherhood's ouster.[58]

With these billions, Sisi can continue to postpone economic and humanitarian reform and retain his corrupt hold on Egypt's economy, of which the Egyptian military owns a speculated share of up to 40 per cent.[59] Gulf handouts can only prolong Egypt's corruption, intensify class stratification, and worsen already poor working conditions in a system where women have access to the fewest protections. Meanwhile, if economic aid from Gulf countries is contingent on exclusion of the Muslim Brotherhood from power, will the Egyptian population choose democracy over economic stability?

IMF loans and restructuring policies in Egypt and the greater MENA region have been fundamentally short-sighted, in that they attempt to make dramatic "quick fixes" to the economy without taking into account the long-term effects of human suffering, or the extent to which these policies disproportionately affect women. Such oversights ultimately place huge strains on MENA governments and natural resources, strains that post-revolutionary governments simply cannot shoulder. A more long-sighted policy would avoid indiscriminate across-the-board cutbacks in spending and instead invest in strategic areas such as education, employment, and poverty relief. Such investments might decelerate the process of deficit reduction, but in the long run they would decrease, rather than increase, the number of poor, government-dependent citizens in MENA countries, ultimately reducing the governments' huge spending obligations to the people.[60]

Democratic Values and Economic Reform

It is now widely believed that support for democracy and economic development are the most effective policy tools to fight terrorism. Because of the democratic deficit in the Middle East, one expert notes, the streets became the political and emotional outlets for the masses. Osama bin Laden spoke in the vivid language of popular Islamic preachers and built on a deep and widespread resentment against the West and the local ruling elites identified with it. The lack of formal outlets for expressing opinion on public concerns created the democracy deficit in much of the Arab world, and this made it easier for terrorists such as bin Laden to act in the name of religion to hijack the Arab street.[61]

A growing consensus is emerging that helping the region's countries to educate their youth will not just eradicate the culture of violence by mitigating poverty and ignorance but will also advance the cause of long-term economic development.[62] As an antidote to Islamic militancy, the recent Arab revolutions in Egypt, Tunisia, Libya, and Yemen and the significant upheavals in Syria, Jordan, and Bahrain serve as a potent counter-commentary to Islamic radicalism. While bin Laden preached hate and violence under Islam, it was street youth who called for peaceful protest and universal democratic ideals. In this vein, it seems that a pan-Arab identity that accounts for a broad religious, ethnic, and political swathe in the Middle East better drives the protest movements in the Arab street.

Some scholars have warned against the reductionism of focusing on religion as the main cause of conflicts between Muslim and Christian communities. "There are many perspectives in the Muslim community," J. Dudley Woodberry points out, "and even these are changing, and conflicts between Muslim and Christian communities in places like Indonesia and Sudan have ethnic, economic, and political, as well as religious, roots."[63] The Muslim world has in recent years seen rising (and encouraging) voices of moderation, religious tolerance, democratic social movements, and human rights. Arguing that the United States could benefit from supporting the call for open societies and the rule of law in the Muslim world, one observer cautions, "It will be highly imprudent, even reckless, to treat the Middle East and neighboring

Muslim societies, with a population of half a billion, merely in terms of their available energy resources and strategic values."[64]

In the post–Cold War era the Muslim world has seen an internal struggle over the role of Islam in public life, in which the forces of change and continuity have clashed with those of the status quo. This struggle has taken the form of a self-critical approach in the aftermath of the 9/11 tragedy, becoming in the process a struggle for the soul of Muslims. At the heart of this political and cultural struggle lie two key questions: Whose Islam? And what Islam? The first question has to do with who should lead or decide in Islamic societies: elected or unelected officials? The second question concerns whether to restore past doctrines and laws or to reinterpret and reformulate laws in light of the new realities of contemporary society.[65] The real issue is if and when this trend will lay the groundwork for a Muslim Reformation, a development whose encouragement should be an important objective of US policy.[66]

The Obama administration was wise to allow the Arab protestors to wrest authority from their autocracies, although its support could have come much sooner and with greater force. However, the deficit of dignity in the Middle East has become palpable. The Arab street feels monopolized and abused by foreign interests. The protests did indeed need to become a revolution for Arabs and by Arabs, whatever the outcome. The region now faces a war of ideas that also must be waged from within.

Al-Jazeera ("the peninsula"), the independent all-Arab television news network based in Qatar, popularized investigative reporting and freedom of information around the Muslim/Arab world during the events following the 9/11 attacks and the subsequent war waged in Afghanistan. The official slogan of Al-Jazeera—*al-rai wa rai al-akar* ("the opinion and the opposite opinion")—has virtually become a political slogan for many Arabs who favour presenting wide-ranging ideas and discussing them peacefully.[67] Its impact on the struggle for a free press and freedom of public opinion in the Arab world has been dramatically visible. For the first time, the Arab public is getting a taste of a free journalism.[68]

The September 11 tragedy also vividly illustrated that the growth of Islamic radicalism poses a huge threat to the existing Middle Eastern regimes and leaders. Hence the Saudis' peace initiative amid the intensification of the second *intifada*, and hence the argument that US public diplomacy should foster genuine avenues for political participation that would create space for moderate and reform-minded Muslim leaders, scholars, lawyers, and journalists and other beleaguered liberals to freely express their views.[69] The policy of supporting democratic movements and regimes offers not only better prospects for stability but also long-term credibility for US foreign policy in the region.

Conclusion

MENA nations have endured a state of economic crisis and political corruption for decades, producing a social climate in which demands for economic stability often supersede demands for liberty. Now post-revolutionary states struggle with the dual inheritance of exhausted economies and social cleavages, both remnants of corrupt authoritarian regimes. Many, if not all, of these states will fail in their immediate transitions to democracy, while the West watches, weary with skepticism. As Sheri Berman asserts, "This skepticism is as predictable as it is misguided ... it is the pathologies inherent in authoritarianism that help cause the underlying problems in the first place."[70] These post-revolutionary experiments in democracy may fail, but they will provide invaluable experience for MENA populations' social memories, and very likely will facilitate future transitions to democratic systems. This is why the West, if it hopes to promote human rights in the Middle East, should be conscious that its strategic political and economic interests in the region cannot be served in the long term without popular support from MENA civilians.

Though it is difficult for international actors to pressure MENA governments to promote human rights and embrace gender equity policies, the perpetuation of economic inequality and poverty allows MENA leaders to prioritize economic crises over the provision of basic human rights. So long as the region's people cannot afford to put bread on the table, they will naturally be willing to put off demands around issues such as women's rights and will instead favour the more pressing priority of day-to-day survival. Thus, by pursuing policies that impoverish citizens without providing economic security fallback, the West perpetuates an atmosphere whereby the population will support a government that can provide economic security at any price. It is time for the IMF and the international community at large to acknowledge that stability cannot thrive for long on the sacrifices of the vulnerable people they leave behind, and to shape their loans and economic policies accordingly.

Takeaway Message

- The maintenance of political stability to the exclusion of basic human rights entails enormous costs—in terms of both human suffering and negative political consequences—for the Middle East and North Africa region. In addition, the pursuit of neoliberal economic programs is likely to intensify class stratification, deepen gender inequality, and further aggravate the already poor economic conditions of the most underprivileged members of the society. Economic stability and prosperity should not be pursued to the detriment of basic human rights. There is clearly a disconnect between the persistence of authoritarianism and economic development.

Study Questions

- Why did the 2011 uprisings occur in the Middle East and North Africa?
- What was the most important driver of the people's demands—economic incentives or the goal of justice and freedom for all?
- What role can the outside world—especially the West—play in supporting such democratic uprisings?
- Why should the outside world espouse such popular movements, given that the consequences of these uprisings remain uncertain for the foreseeable future?

Issue for Debate and Roundtable

- The flaws of the authoritarian rulers of the Middle East and North Africa have been exposed, thanks to the information explosion and social media. A myriad of crises reflects far deeper socioeconomic and political problems that these societies are facing. This means that the Western world must rethink its policy options toward these rapidly changing and troubled societies. Internally, local and national governments must come to grips with the imperative of providing justice, freedom, and economic security all at the same time. Given these new realities, one key question persists: what should be the roles of the state, NGOs, the private sector, and international financial institutions?

Additional Reading

Akyol, Mustafa. *Islam Without Extremes: A Muslim Case for Liberty*. New York: W.W. Norton, 2011.

Brynen, Rex, Pete W. Moore, Bassel F. Salloukh, and Marie-Joëlle Zahar. *Beyond the Arab Spring: Authoritarianism and Democratization in the Arab World*. Boulder, CO: Lynne Rienner, 2012.

Merlini, Cesare, and Olivier Roy, eds. *Arab Society in Revolt: The West's Mediterranean Challenge*. Washington, DC: Brookings Institution Press, 2012.

Sadiki, Larbi, Heiko Wimmen, and Layla Al-Zubaidi, eds. *Democratic Transition in the Middle East: Unmaking Power*. New York: Routledge, 2013.

Websites

Arab Foundation for Freedom and Equality. http://www.afemena.org/.
6 April Movement. http://6aprilmove.blogspot.ca/.
New Internationalist: People, Ideas and Action for Global Justice. http://newint.org/books/reference/world-development/case-studies/social-networking-in-the-arab-spring/.

Notes

1. A.T. Chase, *Human Rights, Revolution, and Reform in the Muslim World* (Boulder, CO: Lynne Rienner, 2012), 188.
2. A. Richards, J. Waterbury, M. Cammett, and I. Diwan, *A Political Economy of the Middle East*, 3rd ed. (Boulder, CO: Westview Press, 2014), 419.
3. N. Marzouki, "From People to Citizens in Tunisia," *Middle East Report 259: North Africa* 42, no. 2 (Summer 2011): 16–19, especially 17–18.
4. Ibid., 18.
5. R. Marquand, "Dignity Drives Arab Revolts," *Christian Science Monitor*, 14 March 2011, 10.
6. S. Mokhtari, "Cairo Optimism: The People Are Now Part of the Equation," openDemocracy, 24 June 2012, https://www.opendemocracy.net/shadi-mokhtari/cairo-optimism-people-are-now-part-of-equation.
7. B. Hubbard, "Egypt Convicts Workers at Foreign Nonprofit Groups, Including 16 Americans," *New York Times*, 5 June 2013, A4.
8. N. Messieh, "INSIGHT: NGO Verdict Revives Calls for Reevaluating US Assistance to Egypt," *Middle East Voices*, 6 June 2013, http://middleeastvoices.voanews.com/2013/06/insight-ngo-verdict-revives-calls-for-reevaluating-us-assistance-to-egypt-47654/?from=mevlister.
9. Z. al-Ali, "Egypt's Missed Constitutional Movement," *Foreign Policy*, 17 December 2013, http://foreignpolicy.com/2013/12/17/egypts-missed-constitutional-moment/.
10. *Al-Ahram*, 10–16 January 2013, 9.
11. Reuters, "Egypt Foreign Reserves Fall Below $15 bln, Highlight Need for IMF Deal," 5 February 2013, http://www.reuters.com/article/2013/02/05/egypt-reserves-idUSL5N0B58LD20130205.
12. Center for the Study of Human Rights, *Twenty-Four Human Rights Documents* (New York: Columbia University, 1992), 21.
13. M. Cammett and I. Diwan, *The Political Economy of the Arab Uprisings* (Boulder, CO: Westview Press, 2014), 28.
14. H. Morayef, "Re-examining Human Rights Change in Egypt," Middle East Research and Information Project, 17 April 2015, www.merip.org/mer/mer274/reexamining-human-rights-change-egypt?ip_login_no_cache=30da42077c337905d9c01e95cfe0445e.
15. Ibid.
16. E. Lust, "Elections," in *The Arab Uprisings Explained: New Contentious Politics in the Middle East*, ed. M. Lynch (New York: Columbia University Press, 2014), 229, 239.

17. Equality Now, "Egypt: Stop Sexual Violence Against Women Demanding Their Rights," 11 April 2013, http://www.equalitynow.org/take_action/discrimination_in_law_action382.
18. L. Loveluck, "The Revolution That Wasn't?" *Christian Science Monitor Weekly*, 20 January 2014, 18–20.
19. *Daily News Egypt*, "The 2014 Egyptian Constitution: Without Accountability, Checks or Balances," 24 March 2014, http://www.dailynewsegypt.com/2014/03/24/2014-egyptian-constitutionwithout-accountability-checks-balances/#sthash.dcoeIDiN.dpuf.
20. Ibid.
21. Ibid.
22. The Arab Republic of Egypt, Draft Constitution, 2013: New Constitutional Document after Amending the Suspended 2012 Constitution, 2 December 2013, 23, http://www.constitutionnet.org/files/final_constitution_-idea-_english-2_dec_2013-signed.pdf.
23. Ibid., 33.
24. C. Gall, "A Political Deal in a Deeply Divided Tunisia," *New York Times*, 17 December 2013, A1, A11.
25. C. Gall, "Three Years after Uprisings, Tunisia Approves Constitution," *New York Times*, 27 January 2014, A5.
26. A. Macmanus, "Tunisia's Constitution (and View to Egypt)," Tahrir Institute for Middle East Policy, 13 February 2014, http://timep.org/commentary/tunisias-constitution-and-a-view-to-egypt.
27. Ibid.
28. Ibid.
29. Gall, "Three Years after Uprisings."
30. C. Gall, "Islamist Party in Tunisia Concedes to Secularists," *New York Times*, 27 October 2014, http://www.nytimes.com/2014/10/28/world/africa/nidaa-tounes-ennahda-tunisian-parliamentary-election.html?_r=0.
31. BBC News, "Tunisia Election: Beji Caid Essebsi Sworn in as President," 31 December 2014, http://www.bbc.com/news/world-africa-30639792.
32. K. Sullivan, "Tunisia, after Igniting Arab Spring, Sends the Most fighters to Islamic State in Syria," *Washington Post*, 28 October 2014, http://www.washingtonpost.com/world/national-security/tunisia-after-igniting-arab-spring-sends-the-most-fighters-to-islamic-state-in-syria/2014/10/28/b5db4faa-5971-11e4-8264-deed989ae9a2_story.html.
33. M. El-Katiri, *The Future of the Arab Gulf Monarchies in the Age of Uncertainties* (Carlisle, PA: Strategic Studies Institute and US Army War College Press, 2013), 14.
34. Ibid., 15. The results of the 2009 Human Rights Watch report are cited in this study.
35. Ibid., 16–17.
36. M. Lynch, *The Arab Uprising: The Unfinished Revolutions of the New Middle East* (New York: PublicAffairs, 2012), 138.
37. Ibid.
38. F. Khosrokhavar, *The New Arab Revolutions That Shook the World* (Boulder, CO: Paradigm, 2012), 128.
39. *New York Times*, 23 April 2012, A6.
40. D. Murphy, "Briefing: What's Behind Iraq Violence?" *Christian Science Monitor Weekly*, 27 January 2014, 13.

41. L. Mason, "World's Largest Civilian Disaster: Can World Ignore it?" *Christian Science Monitor*, 9 December 2013, 36.
42. E. Hokayem, *Syria's Uprising and the Fracturing of the Levant* (London: International Institute for Strategic Studies, 2013), 16–17.
43. Ibid., 102.
44. Ibid., 165–66.
45. Quoted in R.F. Worth and E. Schmitt, "Jihadist Groups Gain in Turmoil Across Mideast," *New York Times*, 4 December 2013, A1, A8.
46. Ibid., A8
47. A. Ciezadlo, "Eat, Drink, Protest: Stories of the Middle East's Hungry Rumblings," *Foreign Policy* 186 (May/June 2011), 79.
48. C. Jones, "The Slap Heard Round the World," *Christian Science Monitor*, 14 March 2011, 31.
49. A. Bayat, "Arab Revolts: Islamists Aren't Coming," *Insight Turkey* 13, no. 2 (Spring 2011): 14.
50. T. Malinowski, "Did Wikileaks Take Down Tunisia's Government?" in *Revolution in the Arab World: Tunisia, Egypt, and the Unmaking of an Era*, ed. M. Lynch, S.B. Glasser, and B. Hounshell (Washington, DC: Foreign Policy, 2011), 61.
51. J. Traub, "RIP, Engagement," in *Revolution in the Arab World: Tunisia, Egypt, and the Unmaking of an Era*, ed. M. Lynch, S.B. Glasser, and B. Hounshell (Washington, DC: Foreign Policy, 2011), 171.
52. F. Zakaria, "How Democracy Can Work in the Middle East, *Time*, 3 February 2011, http://content.time.com/time/magazine/article/0,9171,2046038,00.html.
53. Bayat, "Arab Revolts," 14.
54. K. Pfeifer and M.P. Posusney, "Arab Economies and Globalization: An Overview," in *Women and Globalization in the Arab Middle East: Gender, Economy and Society*, ed. E.A. Doumato and M.P. Posusney (Boulder, CO: Lynne Rienner, 2003), 49.
55. M.P. Posusney and E.A. Doumato, "Introduction: The Mixed Blessing of Globalization," in *Women and Globalization in the Arab Middle East: Gender, Economy and Society*, ed. E.A. Doumato and M.P. Posusney (Boulder, CO: Lynne Rienner, 2003), 6.
56. Pfeifer and Posusney, "Arab Economies," 48.
57. A. Richards and J. Waterbury, *A Political Economy of the Middle East*, 3rd ed. (Boulder, CO: Westview Press, 2007), 251.
58. A. Malik and T. McCormick, "Egypt's Economy of Dependence," *New York Times*, 6 August 2013, http://www.nytimes.com/2013/08/07/opinion/global/egypts-economy-of-dependence.html?_r=1&.
59. Ibid.
60. J. Olmstead, "Reexamining the Fertility Puzzle in MENA," in *Women and Globalization in the Arab Middle East: Gender, Economy and Society*, ed. E.A. Doumato and M.P. Posusney (Boulder, CO: Lynne Rienner, 2003), 91.
61. D.F. Eickelman, "Bin Laden, the Arab Street, and the Middle East's Democracy Deficit," *Current History* (January 2002): 36–39.
62. J. Stern, "The Protean Enemy," *Foreign Affairs* 82, no. 4 (July/August 2003): 27–40.
63. J.D. Woodberry, "Terrorism, Islam, and Mission: Reflections of a Guest in Muslim Lands," *International Bulletin of Missionary Research* (January 2002): 6.

64. A. Amanat, "Empowered Through Violence: The Reinventing of Islamic Extremism," in *The Age of Terror: America and the West after September 11*, ed. S. Talbott and N. Chanda (New York: Basic Books, 2001), 50.
65. J.L. Esposito, *Unholy War: Terror in the Name of Islam* (New York: Oxford University Press, 2002), 147–60.
66. G.E. Fuller, "The Future of Political Islam," *Foreign Affairs* 81, no. 2 (March/April 2002): 59.
67. L.Y. Bahry, "The New Arab Media Phenomenon: Qatar's Al-Jazeera," *Middle East Policy* 8, no. 2 (June 2001): 88–99.
68. M. el-Nawawy and A.I. Farag, *Al-Jazeera: How the Free Arab News Network Scooped the World and Changed the Middle East* (Boulder, CO: Westview Press, 2002).
69. A.W. Hawthorne, "Promoting Religious Freedom in the Arab World, Post–September 11," *PolicyWatch* 586, 7 December 2001, http://www.washingtoninstitute.org/policy-analysis/view/promoting-religious-freedom-in-the-arab-world-postseptember-11.
70. S.G. Jones, "The Mirage of the Arab Spring: Deal with the Region You Have, Not the Region You Want," *Foreign Affairs* (January/February 2013), https://www.foreignaffairs.com/articles/libya/2012-12-03/mirage-arab-spring.

14
Freedom of Religion: A Change in Perspective?

MELANIE ADRIAN

Learning Objectives

- To be able to situate religious freedom within the modern human rights movement
- To understand the interconnections between religious rights, pluralism, and democracy
- To identify the main legal treaties that outline the right to religious freedom
- To be able to articulate some important differences in the way religious freedom is understood at the United Nations and in Europe, the Americas, and Africa
- To be able to cite three landmark European legal cases that are examples of how religious freedom is currently being adjudicated

The development of the modern human rights system was in large part a reaction to the events that occurred during the Second World War. The rise of absolutist forms of government that suppressed the rights of individuals and targeted—en masse—specific groups such as Jews, homosexuals, and those non-compliant with state policies, shocked the moral conscience of humankind. How could we have allowed this to happen? How can we stop such tragedy from occurring again? The answer, many thought, was a more rugged global system that stressed international cooperation, state responsibility, and human rights. That system is what we call the United Nations (UN); it is a forum in which states can come together to debate and agree (or disagree) on issues of international security, rights, and the obligations of governments and individuals.[1]

Freedom of religion was (and remains) an important right that was debated and included in one of the first human rights treaties signed under UN auspices, the Universal Declaration of Human Rights (UDHR). In that treaty, religion and also non-religious belief, thought, and expression were incorporated as discussed below. Ensuring a diversity of thoughts and ideas, it was held, would lead to pluralism.[2] The idea of pluralism remains a key factor in the debate around human rights generally and religious liberty specifically. In simplistic terms, pluralism—the existence of a diversity of ethnic, cultural, political, or religious groups—is an important strengthening agent of democracy. Democracy in turn is thought to uphold human rights, which, it is held, keep the power of states in check. The legacy of the Second World War is palpable.

In the past 20 years the rights movement has made important strides in establishing itself as an accepted legal, political, and social system. More and more, individuals and groups, particularly religious communities, are demanding their rights.[3] This has forced governments to think about their relationship with minority groups and to understand the boundaries and nuances of, for example, a multicultural society such as Canada. Questions arise: should government workers be allowed to wear a veil? Should young Sikhs be permitted to wear the *kirpan* (ritual dagger) in public schools? More generally, how do we ensure that minority groups integrate adequately into "Canadian life," thus preventing a strongly fractionalized society?[4]

For religious groups, and Muslim communities in particular, tensions around religious freedom have shifted since the events of 11 September 2001. Data show that discrimination in housing, education, and the workplace has increased for religious minorities.[5] Muslims' ability to successfully claim their rights has significantly decreased. In fact, some argue that in the world's most developed human rights court, the European Court of Human Rights (ECHR), judgements in cases involving Islam have become predictable: states are generally found not to be in violation of the articles protecting religious freedom and thus are able to curtail the rights of religious people.[6] This trend is highly problematic for many reasons, foremost among them that it endangers the important role rights play in maintaining pluralism and democracy. No longer is religious freedom helping to maintain diversity and democracy, as the drafters of the UDHR imagined. In too many cases, religious freedom is being curtailed for the sake of upholding the rights of the majority and empowering states.[7]

In the following pages, I will show that the drafters of the UDHR had it right: we need freedom in order to build and maintain strong, pluralistic societies that protect everyone's right to religious freedom. Restricting this right may give states powers that are dangerously far-reaching and have a major impact on the way in which diversity can flourish (or not).

The chapter proceeds in the following way: I give the reader a sense of the importance of religious freedom by showing how that right has been delineated at the UN, as well as by regional human rights systems in Europe, the Americas, and Africa.[8] Next I contextualize how this freedom has been protected and challenged in Europe. This includes a discussion of how restrictions have been understood and how margin of appreciation has been applied. I then introduce three prominent cases that take up religious manifestation (through veiling) in elementary schools in Switzerland (*Dahlab v. Switzerland*), in universities in Turkey (*Şahin v. Turkey*), and on the streets of France (*S.A.S. v. France*). These cases show that the ECHR demonstrates a bias in the way it widely allows restrictions to religious freedom and applies the margin of appreciation concept. This is contrary to what the drafters of the UDHR and subsequent interpreters of the applicable conventions intended: that the right to religious freedom be interpreted generously and restrictions narrowly understood. A contrary trend endangers rights, pluralism, and democracy.

The Importance of Religious Freedom

At the United Nations

The Universal Declaration of Human Rights was the first declaration to be formulated under the new United Nations in the late 1940s.[9] In the UDHR, article 18 spells out what it means to have a right to religious freedom: "Everyone has the right to freedom of thought, conscience and religion; this right includes freedom to change his religion or belief, and freedom, either alone or in community with others and in public or private, to manifest his religion or belief in teaching, practice, worship and observance."[10]

The UDHR, together with the Declaration on the Elimination of All Forms of Intolerance and of Discrimination Based on Religion or Belief, passed by the UN General Assembly in 1981, reflects the most comprehensive internationally agreed-upon expression of religious freedom. The negotiations around the drafting of the Declaration forced a conversation about the definitions of *religion*, *belief*, and *intolerance*, among other concepts. Article 2 of the Declaration forbids discrimination by any state, institution, group, persons, or person on the grounds of religion or other beliefs. It states in part that, "for the purposes of the present Declaration, the expression 'intolerance and discrimination based on religion or belief' means any distinction, exclusion, restriction or preference based on religion or belief and having as its purpose or as its effect nullification or impairment of the recognition, enjoyment or exercise of human rights and fundamental freedoms on an equal basis."[11] The point here is that no religion or religious person shall be excluded or treated differently on the basis of religious preference or practice. This sentiment is further supported by a General Assembly resolution passed in 1998, the Declaration on the Elimination of All Forms of Religious Intolerance, which urges states to treat religious freedom with the seriousness it warrants.[12]

In addition to the two Declarations and the Resolution, the UN has used its interpretive arms to uphold and support the right to religious freedom. One of the main human rights institutions at the United Nations, the former Commission on Human Rights, was one such arm. The Commission was mandated to examine and report on human rights abuses and to adopt resolutions on matters of import.[13] Now known as the Human Rights Council, it passed two resolutions at its thirty-ninth meeting in April 1998. One emphasized that "freedom of thought, conscience, religion and belief is *far-reaching and profound*."[14] The second resolution passed in the 1998 session concerns the rights of persons belonging to national or ethnic, religious, and linguistic minorities. It states, "Religious minorities contribute to political and social stability" and reaffirms the obligation of states to ensure that persons belonging to such minorities may "exercise fully and effectively all human rights and fundamental freedoms without any discrimination and in full equality before the law."[15] This supports the original intention of the rights community, which underscores rights as promoting diversity. These examples show that protection of religious freedom has long been an important concern of the international community at the United Nations.

Outside of the declarations and resolutions, arguably the most significant convention in relation to religious rights is the International Covenant on Civil and Political Rights (ICCPR). Article 18 of that Covenant states in full:

> 1. Everyone shall have the right to freedom of thought, conscience and religion. This right shall include freedom to have or to adopt a religion or belief of his choice, and freedom, either individually or in community with others and in public or private, to manifest his religion or belief in worship, observance, practice and teaching.
>
> 2. No one shall be subject to coercion which would impair his freedom to have or to adopt a religion or belief of his choice.
>
> 3. Freedom to manifest one's religion or beliefs may be subject only to such limitations as are prescribed by law and are necessary to protect public safety, order, health, or morals or the fundamental rights and freedoms of others.
>
> 4. The States Parties to the present Covenant undertake to have respect for the liberty of parents and, when applicable, legal guardians to ensure the religious and moral education of their children in conformity with their own convictions.[16]

We can see that much of the wording of the Declaration's article 18 is contained in this section, and that the limitations, contained in paragraph 3, are public safety, order, health, morals, and protection of the freedom of others. We will discuss these restrictions in the pages that follow.

The Human Rights Committee of the ICCPR, established to monitor implementation of the Covenant and its Protocols[17] in the territories of states party to it, has made two important contributions. The first emphasizes that restrictions of rights are to be strictly interpreted and that they must be applied "only for purposes for which they are prescribed and must be directly related and proportionate to the specific need on which they are predicated."[18] Thus limitations on the right to religious freedom are to be narrowly understood, and proportional if the right is restricted.

The second contribution made by the Human Rights Committee occurred in 2005 and involved a case brought before it by Raihon Hudoyberganova, an Uzbek national. In brief, Hudoyberganova, a student in the Islamic Affairs Department at the Tashkent State Institute for Eastern Languages, submitted a complaint to the Committee because she was prohibited from wearing a hijab, which she wore in accordance with her Muslim beliefs. The problems began in 1997, and in 1998 she was excluded from the Institute, which had adopted regulations prohibiting the wearing of religious garb. On 15 May 1998 a national law was passed in Uzbekistan that prohibited all citizens from wearing religious dress in public places and expelled students from classes upon non-compliance.[19] After exhausting all national legal remedies, Hudoyberganova took her complaint to the United Nations.

The Human Rights Committee ruled in her favour by holding that there was a violation of article 18(2) of the ICCPR.[20] Uzbekistan was expected to change its domestic laws to comply with this ruling and to allow Hudoyberganova and others to wear religious head-coverings. I highlight this case not only to show that religious freedom generally is recognized and further understood as a central right, but also because the Committee's ruling was in favour of a young woman who insisted on her right to wear the hijab at university. This contrasts sharply with the judgements in similar cases brought before the European Court of Human Rights.[21]

To conclude this discussion of the importance of religious freedom at the UN, let us take stock of the important declarations, conventions, resolutions, and comments that define and refine the right to religious freedom. The right is expressed in the following documents:

- Universal Declaration of Human Rights (1948)
- Declaration on the Elimination of All Forms of Intolerance and of Discrimination Based on Religion or Belief (1981)
- General Assembly Resolution on the Elimination of All Forms of Religious Intolerance (1998)
- two Resolutions of the Commission on Human Rights (1998)

- International Covenant on Civil and Political Rights, article 18 (1966)
- Human Rights Committee, Comment 22 (1993)
- the Uzbekistan case brought before the Human Rights Committee (2005).[22]

These documents and judgements go some way toward showing that the right to religious freedom is a consistently articulated norm within the human rights community, and they demonstrate the deliberate way in which it has been expressed. Restrictions of this right can be applied only in narrow, proportional ways.

Let us now turn to how the regional human rights systems understand the articulation of religious freedom.

In the Regional Systems[23]

Europe

The European Convention for the Protection of Human Rights and Fundamental Freedoms, signed in 1950, enshrines religious freedom in article 9. The article states that

> 1. Everyone has the right to freedom of thought, conscience and religion; this right includes freedom to change his religion or belief and freedom, either alone or in community with others and in public or private, to manifest his religion or belief, in worship, teaching, practice and observance.
>
> 2. Freedom to manifest one's religion or beliefs shall be subject only to such limitations as are prescribed by law and are necessary in a democratic society in the interests of public safety, for the protection of public order, health or morals, or for the protection of the rights and freedoms of others.[24]

This article protects freedom of thought, conscience, and religion much like article 18 of the ICCPR. In fact, the second paragraph is almost identical to the paragraph 3 of article 18, in which "limitations as are prescribed by law and are necessary to protect public safety, order, health, or morals or the fundamental rights and freedoms of others."

In contrast to the ICCPR, in which the right to religious freedom is non-derogable, article 15 of the European Convention lists the right to religious freedom as a derogable right. This means that in times of war or other public emergency, contracting states "may take measures derogating from its obligations under this Convention to the extent strictly required by the exigencies of the situation."[25]

The Americas

The ninth annual Conference of the Americas adopted the American Declaration of the Rights and Duties of Man in 1948. An underappreciated fact about the Americas is that it was the first regional system to adopt a human rights treaty.[26] The Inter-American Conference adopted the Declaration of the Rights and Duties of Man while the UDHR was still being formulated.[27]

The context of the Americas differs significantly from that of Europe. Democracy is not always assured and governments are often hostile to the international Human Rights Commission and Court. In addition to protracted monetary issues, lengthy dictatorships have affected the development and power of the Inter-American Court of Human Rights.[28] Nevertheless, the American Convention on Human Rights followed the Declaration in 1960. Also known as the Pact of San José, the Convention was signed under the auspices of the Organization of American States (OAS) and entered into force in 1978.[29] In the Convention, religious freedom is guaranteed in article 12:

> 1. Everyone has the right to freedom of conscience and of religion. This right includes freedom to maintain or to change one's religion or beliefs, and freedom to profess or disseminate one's religion or beliefs, either individually or together with others, in public or in private.
>
> 2. No one shall be subject to restrictions that might impair his freedom to maintain or to change his religion or beliefs.
>
> 3. Freedom to manifest one's religion and beliefs may be subject only to the limitations prescribed by law that are necessary to protect public safety, order, health, or morals, or the rights or freedoms of others.
>
> 4. Parents or guardians, as the case may be, have the right to provide for the religious and moral education of their children or wards that is in accord with their own convictions.

Under the American human rights system, religious freedom is non-derogable.

Africa

The Organization of African Unity (OAU), now the African Union, which brings together African states, adopted the African Charter on Human and Peoples' Rights in 1981.[30] What is immediately striking about this document is the title, which includes a distinction between *human* and *peoples*. This difference engrains both the importance of an individual's right and the recognition that rights are often practised as a collectivity or group.[31]

This distinction harkens back to Africa's colonial past, seeking to empower Africans with complete liberation.[32]

Like the American Convention on Human Rights, the African Charter focuses not just on rights but on duties as well, outlining 26 rights and 3 duties, which focus on family, society, and respect for others.[33] As the preamble to the Charter states, "The enjoyment of rights and freedoms also implies the performance of duties on the part of everyone." It goes on to say "it is henceforth essential to pay a particular attention to the right to development and that civil and political rights cannot be dissociated from economic, social and cultural rights in their conception as well as universality and that the satisfaction of economic, social and cultural rights is a guarantee for the enjoyment of civil and political rights." In this way the Charter is unique, because it brings together all types of rights—civil and political rights on one hand and economic, cultural, and social rights on the other—within the context of development.[34] It is an important advancement in the way that we think about the nature of human rights, as encompassing the entirety of the individual.

In terms of freedom of religion, the Charter protects the right in article 8, which states, "Freedom of conscience, the profession and free practice of religion shall be guaranteed. No one may, subject to law and order, be submitted to measures restricting the exercise of these freedoms." This article protects freedom of conscience and religion, but not thought. Since there is no derogation clause in the Charter (as opposed to all the other human rights agreements mentioned above), freedom of religion can be restricted by law and order but not by public emergency or war.[35]

To conclude this section of the chapter, we have seen that religious freedom is a consistently defined and legally articulated international right, at the level of the United Nations and in the regional human rights systems of Europe, the Americas, and Africa. The contexts differ widely between the continents, of course, and this affects the way in which rights are understood generally, and religious freedom more specifically. The examples highlight, however, the importance of religion as a critical right to ensure diversity, pluralism, and the protection of minorities.

In order to ascertain how the right to religious freedom is protected, we consider the European Court of Human Rights (ECHR), because it has the most developed human rights case law of all the systems, particularly in regards to religious freedom. This law not only pertains to Europe but also sets precedents worldwide. Let us now look at what religious freedom means in practice. Here we will discuss how religious freedom can be restricted and contrast it to how this has manifested in practice. I argue that, contrary to the sense that the UN outlines—that limitations to religious freedom should be narrowly interpreted—states are being given wide leeway to restrain religious freedom.

Religious Freedom in the European Context

Let us recall that the Human Rights Council of the UN emphasized, "freedom of thought conscience, religion and belief is far-reaching and profound."[36] In addition, the Human Rights Committee has emphasized that restrictions of rights are to be narrowly understood and proportional if the right is restricted. This raises a question: in what circumstances can religious freedom be limited? Let us take the case of Europe as an example.

Restrictions on Religious Freedom

The limitations clause of article 9 of the European Convention on Human Rights is as follows: "(2) Freedom to manifest one's religion or beliefs shall be subject only to such limitations as are prescribed by law and are necessary in a democratic society in the interests of public safety, for the protection of public order, health or morals, or for the protection of the rights and freedoms of others." The clause lays out three general tests by which restrictions on the right to religious freedom can be examined. The first asks if the manifestation in question is "prescribed by law." The second urges adjudicators to ask if the restriction is necessary in a democratic society. The last test looks at the aim of the restriction: is it for the protection of public safety, order, morals, or health and protection of the rights and freedoms of others?[37]

Javier Martínez-Torrón, a legal scholar, looks at each test in some detail and points to four interpretive principles that have been employed by the European Court of Human Rights to adjudicate limitations on freedom of religion. The first principle is that the freedoms protected by article 9(1) are to be understood in their widest sense, and that the limitations are to be understood in a narrow way. That is, rights need to be given the utmost protection and limited only when necessary. This makes sense, Martínez-Torrón observes, because the article is "aimed at protecting pluralism, without which—as the Court has repeatedly emphasized—democracy cannot exist."[38] Thus giving a wide scope to religious freedom helps protect pluralism and democracy.

The second principle is that any limitation on religious freedom must be "prescribed by law" and "necessary in a democratic society." In terms of how it is prescribed, legal certainty must be respected, and this is why any law must be accessible, precise, and predicable to all citizens.[39] "Necessary in a democratic society" is defined as "a society based upon the guarantee of pluralism and upon the supremacy of law," where "necessary" means that there has to exist a *pressing social need* that must be evaluated according to the facts at hand.[40]

The third principle involves the doctrine of margin of appreciation. A complex and controversial doctrine, margin of appreciation is basically the idea that each country is entitled to a certain leeway in which to adjudicate individual rights and national interests vis-à-vis universal values. There is recognition that states must have some scope for discretion between competing values, and this doctrine ensures that flexibility.[41] The doctrine is seen as important because it allows national value adjudication, so that states may remain true to their domestic history while still being part of extra-national systems such as the European Union and the United Nations.

The fourth principle is that the aims under article 9(2) must be proportionate to the action.[42] That is, there must be a proportional relationship between the restriction and the act. The aim of this principle is to balance rights and limitations in a fair way.

These four principles taken together mean that the right to freedom of religion is wide in its scope and narrow in its limitations; that laws must be open, precise, and predictable; that limitations must meet a pressing social need; that a margin of appreciation is allowed to each state; and that the aim of the restriction must be proportionate. These are the key issues the Court considers when evaluating a possible restriction on the freedom of religion in each case brought before it.

The problem we are finding is that in cases dealing with religious freedom, the Court is granting states a wide margin of appreciation. The following three examples show how the ECHR has decided cases dealing with religion, and women's head-coverings in particular. We will see that restrictions (rather than rights) have been widely interpreted and a wide (rather than narrow) margin of appreciation given to states; the letter of the law has not been questioned; pressing social need has not been adequately demonstrated; and thus proportionality has not been sufficiently addressed.

Dahlab v. Switzerland

The case of *Dahlab v. Switzerland* (2001) involved a young elementary schoolteacher who was a convert to Islam and who believed that her faith required her to dress modestly and cover her head with a scarf. Lucia Dahlab, a Swiss national, began teaching in Geneva in 1990 and started covering her hair at the end of the 1990–91 school year. A meeting was held in 1996 with the heads of the school and the district, wherein Mrs. Dahlab was requested to stop wearing the hijab. Although no grievances had been made by other teachers or parents, it was felt that the headscarf contravened section 6 of the Public Education Act and constituted "an obvious means of identification imposed by a teacher on her pupils, especially in a public, secular education system."[43] Her appeal was denied at the cantonal and federal levels. She thus took her case to the ECHR, where her application was dismissed.

Dahlab's case was dismissed because the Court believed that the headscarf had an undue influence on students at a "tender age" and that it violated Switzerland's principle of secularism. Using the three-pronged test discussed above, the Court had to show that the restriction was prescribed by law, necessary in a democratic society, and required for the protection of public safety, order, morals, or health and the rights and freedoms of others.[44]

The Court agreed with the Swiss state that the restrictive measure was laid out clearly by law. Swiss schools are non-denominational, a fact laid out in article 27(3) of the Federal Constitution of the Swiss Confederation, as well as in section 6 of the Public Education Act. The Constitution and the Education Act establish the principle of neutrality in public schools. The ECHR agreed with the state on this point without questioning the connections the state was making between the manifestation of religious symbols, the school system, and neutrality. The state argued that teachers who do not show their religious affiliation preserve the neutrality of schools. The ECHR could have argued that it is what is taught in the schools that preserves the neutrality of the system, not what a teacher wears on her head. Furthermore, the Court could have linked Dahlab's hijab with the positive promotion of pluralism, given that no one had objected to her headscarf and it did not, according to the case file, affect her teaching in any way. Instead, the state argued—and the ECHR agreed—that neutrality demanded the scarf be removed. Pluralism, it seems, had to be restricted in the educational realm.

The second test asks if the measure taken is necessary in a democratic society. Here the Court ruled that the state had a right to restrict Dahlab's use of the headscarf because the law was intended to preserve denominational neutrality. The judgement states that "the interference with the applicant's freedom to manifest her religion was justified by the need, in a democratic society, to protect the right of State school pupils to be taught in a context of denominational neutrality."[45]

In the third and final test, the restriction must be intended to protect public safety, order, morals, or health and the rights and freedoms of others. The question in this case did not focus on public health or safety but rather the rights and freedoms of the students. Here the ECHR drew on the idea of margin of appreciation to allow the Swiss state to make this decision.[46] In addition, the judges argued that it is very difficult to determine the nature of a hijab's influence on children as young as those in question, and that it was better not to allow it. Furthermore, the Court stated, the headscarf was difficult to understand in light of gender equality, and therefore also tolerance and respect, which are values that teachers in a democratic society must communicate to their students. The judgement is worth quoting at length:

> The Court accepts that it is very difficult to assess the impact that a powerful external symbol such as the wearing of a headscarf may have on the freedom of conscience and religion of very young children. The applicant's pupils were aged between four and eight, an age at which children wonder about many things and are also more easily influenced than older pupils. In those circumstances, it cannot be denied outright that the wearing of a headscarf might have some kind of proselytising effect, seeing that it appears to be imposed on women by a precept which is laid down in the Koran and which, as the Federal Court noted, is hard to square with the principle of gender equality. It therefore appears difficult to reconcile the wearing of an Islamic headscarf with the message of tolerance, respect for others and, above all, equality and non-discrimination that all teachers in a democratic society must convey to their pupils.[47]

It seems rather careless for the Court to make such unfounded and illogical connections between the hijab and its proselytizing effect on young people, the hijab and gender equality, the hijab and (in)tolerance, equality, and non-discrimination. None of these assertions are based on scientific data and were taken from the arguments of the Swiss state, which are also not based on any scientific data. The connections are shaky at best and incorrect at worst, particularly if one is reading in the field of social science.[48]

Şahin v. Turkey

Let us now consider the case of *Şahin v. Turkey* to assess whether the *Dahlab* judgement was a one-off on the part of the Court or evidence of a trend in regard to Islam specifically and freedom of religion more generally. Along with *S.A.S. v. France* (discussed below), *Şahin* is one of the groundbreaking cases of our time involving religious freedom—the Grand Chamber of the ECHR decided the case. While in *Dahlab* the issue revolved around the hijab in elementary schools, this case involved the right of university students to wear the headscarf on campus property.

Leyla Şahin was a young Muslim woman who claimed a right to wear her headscarf at the University of Istanbul.[49] She had studied medicine for four years without incident at the University of Bursa and had transferred to Istanbul in 1997. In 1998 the University of Istanbul issued a regulation that prohibited students from covering their heads or sporting beards.[50] After she declined to take off her headscarf, Şahin was refused access to classes and examinations. After exhausting domestic remedies, she took her case to the European Court of Human Rights.

The Grand Chamber of the ECHR found no violation of Şahin's right to religious freedom. In light of the circumstances of the case, and according to the standard three-pronged test, the Court held that the measure was prescribed by law (Turkey had domestic law to this effect); that it had a legitimate aim, because it was necessary in a democratic society and upheld the principles of secularism and equality; and that it was proportionate to the aim it sought.[51] We will examine each in turn.

The first test seeks to ascertain if the measure is prescribed by law. According to the Turkish state, the measure was laid out on 23 February 1998 in a university-issued circular that forbade head-coverings and beards.[52] In addition, it argued that Turkey is a secular state, according to article 2 of its constitution.

Şahin questioned the legal provisions in light of the consideration that its judicial and university systems had been established by successive coups d'état. Part of the reason for this verdict, she herself mentions, is that the Court understood the history of secularism in Turkey exclusively from the point of view of the state. It never considered that the laws banning head-coverings were made during times of military rule and thus imposed on the population, and that those rules are generally relaxed during periods of democratic action in Turkey. Jeremy Gunn demonstrates this clearly by showing that in fact the "long standing tradition" of banning the headscarf, which the Court accepted without critique, is based on long years of military rule rather than on democratic initiatives.[53] Thus, taking the Turkish government's position on the hijab at face value undermines the principles of democracy the Court is vested to uphold.

The second test seeks to ascertain if the measure taken was necessary in a democratic society. We have just seen that the Court accepted Turkey's version of history, thereby sidelining the way in which these laws came to be—without principles of democracy. Therefore, the position the Court took on this aspect of the case already undermined democratic tenets. At any rate, it held that the banning of the hijab was necessary for democracy, and deferred to the margin of appreciation to make its case. The judgement states that "where questions concerning the relationship between State and religions are at stake, on which opinion in a democratic society may reasonably differ widely, the role of the national decision-making body must be given special importance."[54]

The final test involves showing that a restriction is for the protection of public safety, order, morals, or health and the rights and freedoms of others. Here is where the judgement gets particularly interesting. The Court states that rights are a balancing act between those of groups and those of the individual. Using this sentiment, the Court accepted that the Turkish state could restrict the right of Şahin to wear the hijab:

> Pluralism and democracy must also be based on dialogue and a spirit of compromise necessarily entailing various concessions on the part of individuals or groups of individuals which are justified in order to maintain and promote the ideals and values of a democratic society … these "rights and freedoms" … it must be accepted that the need to protect them may lead States to restrict other rights or freedoms likewise set forth in the Convention. It is precisely this constant search for a balance between the fundamental rights of each individual which constitutes the foundation of a "democratic society."[55]

The Court subsequently used the *Dahlab* case to support its reasoning in regard to the perceived problem of the hijab. In fact, it used the same wording in its judgement.[56]

The *Dahlab* case, which I have shown is problematic at best, has now become one of the standards in how the hijab is understood in international law. Precedents are being set on this basis that restrict the freedom to wear a headscarf in particular and the right to religious freedom more generally. This is true not only in Europe but more generally. As *Dahlab* demonstrated, young students should not be exposed to the hijab for fear of influencing them; such a head-covering, it was argued, is not a symbol of gender equality and does not promote tolerance. The *Şahin* case showed that university-age adults should also not be allowed to wear the hijab, because it is a threat to secularism and democracy.

These cases clearly demonstrate how Islam and the hijab have been stripped of their diversity of meaning and construed in unhelpful, incorrect, and superficial ways. The Court did not allude to the range of meanings behind the hijab and did not take into consideration the contexts that shape constructions of covering the head or perceptions of history. Furthermore, connections between veiling and equality and toleration, for example, are not proven but merely assumed. The ECHR has, seemingly without question, adopted these assumptions that were made by domestic legislatures.

This leads us to a larger problem. By granting states a wide margin of appreciation in cases dealing with religious freedom and by understanding restrictions widely, more and more states are limiting religious manifestation.

We saw this particularly keenly when in 2011 France banned veils covering the face from all public spaces. *Dahlab*, *Şahin*, and *S.A.S.* have set legal precedents that apply in all states party to the UN Conventions. As we have seen, religious freedom is an important right that is closely linked with pluralism and democracy. The danger, therefore, is not only in regards to this particular right but also to the way in which we understand our larger social and political contexts. Let us examine the final case, *S.A.S. v. France,* which is the most recent case taken up by the Grand Chamber. We will see that in this case the Court ultimately supported France and upheld the restriction on the right to religious freedom, but, in an interesting twist, debunked some of its previous statements about veiling and equality and security.

S.A.S. v. France

The case of *S.A.S. v. France* is named after a French national who was born in Pakistan and who brought the case forward in response to a law passed in 2011 that banned the Muslim face veil from all public spaces (except religious ones) across the country.[57] The law means that any woman who covers her face risks a fine and/or may be asked to enroll in a citizenship course if she is seen on the street or in a bus, government building, hospital, or daycare centre.[58]

In terms of the first of the Court's three-pronged tests, there was no disagreement that the restriction was prescribed by law, as the French government had passed a law banning face veils. Thus the restriction was prescribed by law. The Court then went on to consider the question of legitimate aim, along with what is necessary in a democratic society, thereby folding the second and third tests into one.

On the question of the legitimate aim of the law, the Court considered the issue of safety first. Did covering the face pose a security threat? Here the French government argued that banning the face veil was necessary to ensure public safety. The Court, however, was not persuaded by this argument, and held that the restriction might have been warranted if there had been a real danger to safety. Since there was no imminent threat from women wearing the veil (or a more general threat), the law, the Court held, was too heavy-handed: "as to the women concerned, they are thus obliged to give up completely an element of their identity … whereas the objective alluded to by the Government could be attained by a mere obligation to show their face and to identify themselves where a risk for the safety of persons and property has been established."[59]

In regard to the question of necessity in a democratic society, the government argued that three values underlie an open and democratic society (notice the use of the term *open*), including equality of men and women, respect for human dignity, and respect for the minimum requirements of life in society. In a surprising turn of events, the Court denied that the face veil indicated gender inequality. How could it be, when women such as the applicant argued to wear it? The judgement reads, "The Court takes the view … that a State Party cannot invoke gender equality in order to ban a practice that is defended by women."[60] Thus, if a woman argues that she is equal while wearing the face veil, the Court will accept this as equality.

On the issue of dignity, the government argued that wearing a face veil essentially "effaced" women from the public sphere. The government stated that, no matter whether this type of eradication of women from public was chosen or imposed, "it was necessarily dehumanising and could hardly be regarded as consistent with human dignity."[61] The Court disagreed and held that, although some might find the clothing "strange," it introduced an expression of cultural diversity that added to the pluralism necessary in democracy.[62]

As we can see, in its reasoning on all three of these issues—security, equality, and dignity—the ECHR defended the right of the individual to religious manifestation (even in light of security arguments), ensured diversity, and emphasized pluralism. It challenged the government on each of its arguments and made the point that restricting religious freedom is a limitation on the identity of the individual that ultimately endangers pluralism (as related to a healthy democracy). Given these opinions, it is odd that the ECHR then changed tracks and argued that the law should be upheld.

Ultimately the Court was convinced by the government that respect for an open and democratic society demands that one see the face. The government argued, and the ECHR accepted, that "the face plays an important role in social interaction."[63] Furthermore,

> It can understand the view that individuals who are present in places open to all may not wish to see practices or attitudes developing there which would fundamentally call into question the possibility of open interpersonal relationships, which, by virtue of an established consensus, forms an indispensable element of community life within the society in question. The Court is therefore able to accept that the barrier raised against others by a veil concealing the face is perceived by the respondent State as breaching the right of others to live in a space of socialisation which makes living together easier. That being said, in view of the flexibility of the notion of "living together" and the resulting risk of abuse, the Court must engage in a careful examination of the necessity of the impugned limitation.[64]

It is somewhat perplexing to read this paragraph, the tone of which changes quite substantially from that of the first part of the decision. Having called the practice of face veiling "strange," the ECHR nevertheless held that the expression of identity and protection of pluralism were more important matters than the seemingly bizarre nature of the practice. Yet here the Court is arguing that the principle of respect for the minimum requirements of life in society, as the French government argued, was part of "protection of the rights and freedoms of others." The argument is thus that individuals in an open society have a right to carry on interpersonal relationships with others that include visual identification of the face. The ECHR is concerned that if the face were hidden, this would compromise life—an open life—in the community.[65]

In the paragraph from the judgement above, the ECHR makes a number of unfounded assumptions. Two in particular will be addressed here: the effect of the face veil on interpersonal relationships and the concept of "living together."

Regarding the effect of the face veil on relationships, the more precise concern driving this issue seems to be the effect of the veil on communication and how that changes the dynamics of interpersonal relationships. The underlying assumption is that for women who wear the face veil the possibility of sustaining open interpersonal relationships is impeded. But what does *open* mean? Given that the veil does not muzzle women who wear it and that they can speak and respond as they choose and move their bodies, hands, and heads, this seems a gross overgeneralization about its effect. At issue are the visual cues given by the nose, mouth, cheeks, and chin.

Here the ECHR might take note of a case decided at the Canadian Supreme Court, *R. v. N.S.*, in which dissenting justice Rosalie Abella argued that the importance of the "demeanour package," as she referred to it, is overemphasized at best. There is no question that seeing someone's face (or not) makes a qualitative difference in the way communication is experienced. But how different this is from communicating with others whose facial expressions are difficult or impossible to read—such as those affected by a stroke, burn victims, or those suffering from facial disfigurement—is questionable.

In terms of the importance of seeing the face as a central measure of "living together," as the French government argued and the ECHR accepted, the concept is so vague as to make any attempt to define it as a legal term impossible. What does "living together" mean legally? This is a concept so ambiguous that it is not useful in the law. In the words of dissenting judges Nussberger and Jaederblom, who held strong reservations to the judgement in *S.A.S. v. France,* the term is "vague" and "far-fetched."[66]

These two assumptions that the ECHR made about the effect of the face veil on interpersonal relationships and the concept of "living together"—and ultimately its decision to uphold the law—are detrimental to the free expression of religious identity. What the ECHR and French government are advocating is a narrow idea of what it means to belong in French society: the face must be uncovered in order to meet the basic standards of an open and democratic society. What about the question of pluralism and the right not to enter into discourse with others—the right to be an outsider?[67] They prescribe not only the degree to which a woman can be covered but also the nature and quality of her interpersonal relationships. This seems overly deterministic. In fact, now that women who veil cannot be seen in public spaces, they belong to France only in the quiet refuges of their homes—to the detriment of discussion, debate, and lived pluralism.[68]

In supporting the French government in this case, the ECHR made assumptions about the effect of the face veil on interpersonal relationships and the concept of "living together" at the expense of personal religious expression, continuing dialogue, and pluralism. This decision, although somewhat more open to issues around security, equality, and dignity, is in line with the decisions made in *Dahlab* and *Şahin* that restrict religious freedom.

Conclusion

This chapter has taken up the right to religious freedom. I have shown that this is a central right at the United Nations as well as in the regional human rights systems of Europe, the Americas, and Africa. Religious freedom is guaranteed and protected across the globe and can be challenged only in restricted and narrowly defined ways, according to the declarations, conventions, resolutions, and opinions discussed above.

Yet, as we have seen, religious freedom has been challenged in Europe. This chapter explored three cases involving Muslim women who wished to cover their head or face in public: one dealt with the right of an elementary school teacher in Switzerland to wear the hijab (*Dahlab v. Switzerland*); the second took up wearing the hijab in universities in Turkey (*Şahin v. Turkey*); and the third discussed wearing of the face veil in public spaces in France (*S.A.S. v. France*). These cases show that the European Court of Human Rights is biased in the way restrictions are widely allowed and margin of appreciation applied. I have argued that this is contrary to what the drafters of the Universal Declaration of Human Rights and subsequent interpreters of the applicable conventions intended. The problem with restricting religious freedom in this way is that it does not just imperil this central right, it also jeopardizes other rights, pluralism, and democracy.

Takeaway Messages

- Religious freedom is an internationally protected right of long standing.
- Religious freedom shares important interconnections with pluralism and democracy.
- Increasingly the right to religious freedom is being narrowly interpreted and states are being given a wide margin of appreciation.
- *Dahlab v. Switzerland*, *Şahin v. Turkey*, and *S.A.S. v. France* are landmark European legal cases that exemplify how religious freedom is currently being adjudicated.

Study Questions

- What are the three general tests laid out in the restrictions clause of article 9 of the European Convention on Human Rights (ECHR)?
- According to legal scholar Javier Martínez-Torrón, what are the four interpretive principles for article 9(2) of the ECHR? Why are they important?
- Name one difference among the ways religious freedom is understood in Europe, the Americas, and Africa.

Issues for Debate or Roundtable

- Argue for or against the following statement: Given the political realities of our time, religious manifestation should be increasingly restricted.
- Debate the validity of the following statement: Democracy rests on a robust pluralism that demands a wide interpretation of religious manifestation.

Additional Reading

Bowen, John Richard. *Why the French Don't Like Headscarves: Islam, the State, and Public Space*. Princeton, NJ: Princeton University Press, 2007. http://dx.doi.org/10.1515/9781400837564.

Boyle, Kevin. "Human Rights, Religion and Democracy: The Refah Party Case." *Essex Human Rights Journal* 1, no. 1 (2004): 1–16.

Cesari, Jocelyne. *Why the West Fears Islam: An Exploration of Muslims in Liberal Democracies*. New York: Palgrave MacMillan, 2013. http://dx.doi.org/10.1057/9781137121202.

Websites

African Union. http://www.au.int/.

European Court of Human Rights. http://www.echr.coe.int/Pages/home.aspx?p=home.

Organization of American States. http://www.oas.org/en/topics/human_rights.asp.
United Nations. http://un.org/en/.

Notes

1. The United Nations was not the first international forum of this kind; it was preceded by the League of Nations. For the similarities and differences between the two systems, see H.J. Steiner and P. Alston, *International Human Rights in Context: Law, Politics, Morals*, 2nd ed. (Oxford: Oxford University Press, 2000), 93–126.
2. Morsink points this out, particularly in regard to article 18 of the ICCPR; J. Morsink, *The Universal Declaration of Human Rights: Origins, Drafting and Intent* (Philadelphia: University of Pennsylvania Press, 1999), 260.
3. A good example here is the recent events in the Middle East known as the Arab Spring. See Human Rights Watch, "World Report 2012: Strengthen Support for 'Arab Spring,'" 22 January 2012, https://www.hrw.org/report/2012/01/22/world-report-2012/events-2011.
4. See Will Kymlicka's lecture on multiculturalism in Canada, in which he characterizes religious rights as the third wave of multiculturalism; W. Kymlicka, "The Three Lives of Multiculturalism," Laurier Institution Multicultural Lecture, 2008, podcast, 53:59, http://thelaurier.ca/lecturepodcasts/.
5. See European Monitoring Centre on Racism and Xenophobia [EUMC], *Muslims in the European Union: Discrimination and Islamophobia* (Vienna: EUMC, 2006), http://fra.europa.eu/sites/default/files/fra_uploads/156-Manifestations_EN.pdf.
6. H. Elver, "The Headscarf Controversy: Secularism and Freedom of Religion," in *Religion and Global Politics*, ed. J.L. Esposito (New York: Oxford University Press, 2012), 83–84.
7. See, for example, *Şahin v. Turkey* or *Dahlab v. Switzerland*, discussed below.
8. I will not take up the Arab human rights system, as that is largely dormant, nor that proposed for Asia, as it is not yet developed.
9. For a comprehensive look at the UDHR and its drafting process, see Morsink, *Universal Declaration of Human Rights*, 281–95.
10. I. Brownlie, *Basic Documents in International Law*, 4th ed. (Oxford: Oxford University Press, 1995), 258.
11. As reproduced in N. Lerner, *Religion, Beliefs, and International Human Rights* (Maryknoll, NY: Orbis Books, 2000), 137.
12. A/RES/52/122, 23 February 1998.
13. The UN Commission on Human Rights was replaced by the Human Rights Council. According to its website, it is "an inter-governmental body within the UN system made up of 47 States responsible for strengthening the promotion and protection of human rights around the globe. The Council was created by the UN General Assembly on 15 March 2006 with the main purpose of addressing situations of human rights violations and make [*sic*] recommendations on them"; United Nations Human Rights Council, http://www.ohchr.org/EN/HRBodies/HRC/Pages/AboutCouncil.aspx.
14. Implementation of the Declaration on the Elimination of All Forms of Intolerance and of Discrimination Based on Religion or Belief, Commission on Human Rights Resolution 1998/18 (emphasis added).

15. Rights of Persons Belonging to National or Ethnic, Religious and Linguistic Minorities, Commission on Human Rights Resolution 1998/19, para. 2.
16. Brownlie, *Basic Documents*, 284.
17. A protocol is a supplementary agreement to a convention. The ICCPR has two additional protocols; the first allows for individual communications and the second seeks to abolish the death penalty.
18. Declaration on the Elimination of All Forms of Intolerance, 3.
19. United Nations, Human Rights Committee of the ICCPR, Communication No. 931/2000: "Uzbekistan," CCPR/C/82/D/931/2000, 2005.
20. Ibid., para. 6.2.
21. See, for example, *Leyla Şahin v. Turkey*, European Court of Human Rights (Grand Chamber), Application No. 44774/98, 10 November 2005.
22. This is not an exhaustive list.
23. The Arab world has created a human rights system that is largely non-functioning. Asia has proposed one but it is not yet developed. See H.J. Steiner, P. Alston, and R. Goodman, *International Human Rights in Context: Law, Politics, Morals*, 3rd ed. (Oxford: Oxford University Press, 2008), 780.
24. Brownlie, *Basic Documents*, 332.
25. T. Stahnke and J.P. Martin, *Religion and Human Rights: Basic Documents* (New York: Center for the Study of Human Rights, Columbia University, 1998), 141.
26. The 21 original signatories to the Declaration included Argentina, Bolivia, Brazil, Chile, Colombia, Costa Rica, Cuba, Dominican Republic, Ecuador, El Salvador, Guatemala, Haiti, Honduras, Mexico, Nicaragua, Panama, Paraguay, Peru, United States of America, Uruguay, and Venezuela. Canada joined the Organization of American States, and thus became party to the Declaration and subsequent treaties, in 1990.
27. There are 10 articles setting out duties.
28. Steiner, Alston, and Goodman, *International Human Rights*, 868.
29. Organization of American States, Department of International Law, American Convention on Human Rights "Pact of San Jose, Costa Rica" (B-32), http://www.oas.org/juridico/english/treaties/b-32.html/.
30. African Union, African (Banjul) Charter on Human and Peoples' Rights, adopted 27 June 1981, OAU Doc. CAB/LEG/67/3 rev. 5, 21 I.L.M. 58 (1982), entered into force 21 October 1986, http://www.au.int/en/sites/default/files/banjul_charter.pdf.
31. Only individual rights are protected by conventions. However, there is a long-standing debate within the rights world around the rights of groups. See, for example, C. Sistare, L. May, and L. Francis, eds., *Groups and Group Rights* (Lawrence: University Press of Kansas, 2001).
32. See, in particular, the preamble to the Charter, which states in part, "Conscious of their duty to achieve the total liberation of Africa, the peoples of which are still struggling for their dignity and genuine independence, and undertaking to eliminate colonialism, neo-colonialism, apartheid, Zionism and to dismantle aggressive foreign military bases and all forms of discrimination, particularly those based on race, ethnic group, color, sex, language, religion or political opinions." See also M. Mutua, *The African Human Rights System: A Critical Evaluation* (New York: UNDP, 2000), 5.
33. See chapter 2, art. 27, 28, and 29.

34. The separation of these rights was brought about by the political circumstances of the Cold War. For this reason there is a distinction between civil and political rights on the one hand and economic, social, and cultural rights on the other.
35. Mutua, *African Human Rights System*, 8.
36. Declaration on the Elimination of All Forms of Intolerance.
37. Brownlie, *Basic Documents*, 333.
38. J. Martínez-Torrón, "Limitations on Religious Freedom in the Case Law of the European Court of Human Rights," *Emory International Law Review* 19, no. 2 (2005): 595. However, he also notes that in the case of freedom of religion, the Court has tended to construe the rights protected under article 9(1) more narrowly and thus have found no need to consider a restriction at all. He states, "It is possible to observe in the Strasbourg case law … a certain tendency to construe restrictively the scope of protection of Article 9(1) … which implies a lesser resource to the limitation concepts contained in Article 9(2)."
39. Ibid., 597–98.
40. Ibid., 599.
41. E. Benvenisti, "Margin of Appreciation, Consensus, and Universal Standards," *International Law and Politics* 31 (1999): 843–44. Benvenisti goes on to point out that in reality there exists a double margin of appreciation: one given to local authorities to evaluate the necessity of the act and then to the Court, which evaluates if those acts were compatible with the Convention. Also, the margin of appreciation varies: (1) the more objective the restrictive measure, the less discretion the national authorities have; (2) when the restriction applies to an individual's private life and not so much to the community, the margin of appreciation is less than if it applied to the whole community (601).
42. I will say more about proportionality below.
43. *Lucia Dahlab v. Switzerland*, European Court of Human Rights, Application No. 42393/98, 2001, Part A.
44. J. Martínez-Torrón, "The Permissible Scope of Legal Limitations on the Freedom of Religion or Belief: A Comparative Perspective," *Global Jurist Advances* 3, no. 2 (2003).
45. *Dahlab v. Switzerland*, Part B.
46. Interestingly, the Court first lays out its command over margin of appreciation by stating, "as to whether the measure was 'necessary in a democratic society,' the Court reiterates that, according to its settled case-law, the Contracting States have a certain margin of appreciation in assessing the existence and extent of the need for interference, but this margin is subject to European supervision, embracing both the law and the decisions applying it, even those given by independent courts"; *Dahlab v. Switzerland*.
47. Ibid.
48. On the veil, see L. Ahmed, *Women and Gender in Islam: Historical Roots of a Modern Debate* (New Haven, CT: Yale University Press, 1992); and L. Ahmed, *A Quiet Revolution: The Veil's Resurgence, from the Middle East to America* (New Haven, CT: Yale University Press, 2011). On the meaning of piety, women, and veil, see S. Mahmood, *Politics of Piety: The Islamic Revival and the Feminist Subject* (Princeton, NJ: Princeton University Press, 2012). On women's equality, see F. Mernissi, *The Veil and the Male Elite: A Feminist Interpretation of Women's Rights in Islam* (Reading, MA: Addison-Wesley, 1991). On Islam and tolerance and

modernity, see A. Al-Azmeh, *Islams and Modernities* (London: Verso, 1996). For another legal opinion, see J.T. Gunn, "Fearful Symbols: The Islamic Headscarf and the European Court of Human Rights," paper presented at Forum on Freedom of Religion or Belief, Strasbourg, 2005). On gender and justice in Islam, see O. Safi, *Progressive Muslims: On Justice, Gender, and Pluralism* (Oxford: Oneworld, 2003).

49. *Şahin v. Turkey*.
50. Ibid., at 15.
51. Ibid., at 98, 99, 100, 104.
52. Ibid., at 15.
53. Gunn, "Fearful Symbols."
54. *Şahin v. Turkey*, at 109.
55. Ibid., at 108.
56. *Dahlab v. Switzerland*, at 111.
57. *S.A.S. v. France*, European Court of Human Rights (Grand Chamber), No. 43835/11, 1 July 2014, at 10, 76.
58. Ibid., at 28.
59. *S.A.S. v. France*, at 139.
60. Ibid., at 119.
61. Ibid., at 82.
62. The ECHR notes that "respect for human dignity cannot legitimately justify a blanket ban on the wearing of the full-face veil in public places. The Court is aware that the clothing in question is perceived as strange by many of those who observe it. It would point out, however, that it is the expression of a cultural identity which contributes to the pluralism that is inherent in democracy"; ibid., at 120.
63. Ibid., at 122.
64. Ibid.
65. "Consequently, having regard in particular to the breadth of the margin of appreciation afforded to the respondent State in the present case, the Court finds that the ban imposed by the Law of 11 October 2010 can be regarded as proportionate to the aim pursued, namely the preservation of the conditions of 'living together' as an element of the 'protection of the rights and freedoms of others.'"; ibid., at 157.
66. Ibid., dissenting opinion, at 4, 5.
67. Ibid., at 8.
68. Dissenting judges Nussberger and Jaederblom also worry about this issue; ibid., at 21.

PART FOUR

15
Whither Economic and Social Rights? Assessing the Position of Economic and Social Rights in the Neoliberal, Post-Crisis Context

SUSAN KANG AND JENNIFER RUTLEDGE

Learning Objectives

- To understand the unique nature and challenges of economic and social rights
- To understand the key international legal foundations of economic and social rights
- To understand how judicialization, at both the national and regional levels, creates opportunities to enforce and protect economic and social rights

Recent decades have created two contradictory trends in economic and social rights. On the one hand, there was a reaffirmation of the importance of economic and social rights as post-transitional countries created constitutional rights guarantees and countries in the global North began to incorporate rights protections through European Union directives and other agreements. On the other hand, financial crises, instability, and market forces have resulted in states that are unwilling or unable to intervene to protect such rights. Considering the tension inherent in these two trends, how do states, international institutions, and rights advocates construct state responsibility to these rights during a time when states feel greater economic pressures to conform to market prerogatives?

This chapter answers this question by investigating recent legal and institutional developments at the regional, domestic, and international levels in global North and South contexts. We first outline the scope of the issue, including definitions of economic and social rights as typically understood within international law, and then turn to an analysis of recent developments regarding these rights. The second section focuses on economic and social rights in the global North, with particular attention to the Canadian Charter of Rights and Freedoms and the European Community and the Council of Europe in the post-crisis austerity era. The third section focuses on the global South, with particular attention to the constitutionalization of such rights and resulting jurisprudence. We conclude by considering the possibilities for rights protection in a post–financial crisis world and argue that rights fulfillment is possible as increasing institutionalization brings attention and legitimacy to those rights.

The Scope of Economic and Social Rights

Economic and social (E/S) rights are fundamental human rights that, if fulfilled, allow one to live a life of human dignity.[1] These rights—which include the right to health, family, education, standard of living, housing, and science and culture—are found within the text of the Universal Declaration of Human Rights (UDHR) and were legally codified by the International Covenant on Economic, Social, and Cultural Rights (ICESCR) in 1966. Through the ICESCR, these rights were given the same legal force as the rights included under the International Covenant on Civil and Political Rights (ICCPR), and thus signatories are obligated to respect, protect, and fulfill these rights. However, because the ICESCR includes the principle of progressive realization, some observers claim that it lacks the legal force of the ICCPR.

The principle of progressive realization, in article 2 of the ICESCR, states, "Each State Party to the present Covenant undertakes to take steps, individually and through international assistance and co-operation, especially economic and technical, to the maximum of its available resources, with a view to achieving progressively the full realization of the rights recognized in the present Covenant by all appropriate means, including particularly the adoption of legislative measures." This article implies that state signatories may be unable to fulfill these rights because of resource constraints. Unlike the ICCPR, which obligates states to take immediate action, the parties to this Covenant are only obliged to take steps toward fulfillment of these rights. The principle of progressive realization has often been thought to render the Covenant useless, particularly for developing countries where resource constraints are an issue.

A view of the ICESCR as ineffective is strengthened by the weak enforcement mechanisms of the Covenant. For instance, while the Optional Protocol to the International Covenant on Civil and Political Rights specifies a quasi-judicial procedure to examine complaints and has been in effect since 1976, the Optional Protocol to the ICESCR came into effect only on 5 May 2013, has only 10 participating state parties, and is a complaint and inquiry mechanism. Furthermore, while the UDHR states that "everyone has the right to an effective remedy by the competent national tribunals for acts violating the fundamental rights granted him by the constitution or by law" (art. 8), the ICESCR, unlike the ICCPR, contains no provision requiring or even encouraging judicial remedies. Because international remedies for E/S rights are weak, national governments are largely responsible for holding themselves accountable for rights violations.

One of the chief remedies for any rights violation is through the courts,[2] but it seems likely that the lack of importance ascribed to judicial remedies for E/S rights as opposed to civil and political rights has encouraged many governments to believe that judicial remedies are inappropriate or impractical in this area.[3] However, the ESCR Committee, in General Comment No. 9 (1998), argues that such a distinction between the types of rights and the efficacy of courts is not warranted. In particular, it points out that separation-of-powers arguments—which see legislatures responsible for making policy and courts responsible for adjudicating disputes—ignore the reality of many courts' involvement in areas that have implications for resource allocation, as well as curtailing the courts' ability to make decisions to protect the most vulnerable.

Further, this view ignores the reality of the many countries that have explicitly made socioeconomic rights justiciable by including them in constitutions. The waves of democratization in the twentieth century created constitutions that enshrined more rights than ever before. A review conducted for this paper of 188 available constitutions showed that 25 countries include a broad standard of living right in their constitution, 34 specifically include the right to housing, and 8 specifically include the right to food. One constitution mentions the rights to food and housing while ignoring the other standard-of-living rights, and another includes a standard-of-living right for children. Turning to education, 139 countries specifically mention the right to education and 104 mention the right to health. A further 106 countries specifically mention the right to a family. This review clearly demonstrates that specific E/S rights are enshrined in constitutions, giving citizens claims for the protection of these rights.

The inclusion of rights within the constitution is particularly useful when a country has granted its courts the power of judicial review. Judicial review gives "courts the explicit power to overrule acts of the legislature as being in violation of the Constitution,"[4] which allows the court to protect values of democracy over the will of elected legislatures. Judicial review goes hand in hand with constitutions that focus on laying out basic rights, as it functions to protect those core rights. While the origin of judicial review is usually located in *Marbury v. Madison* (1803) in the United States, courts were seldom granted the power of judicial review until after the Second World War. The turn toward empowering courts with judicial review emerged rapidly following the war and Europe's experience with democratically elected fascist regimes prior to and during the war. Since then, new constitutions have often included checks on the legislature, and judicial review has become a prominent feature written into constitutions in most new democracies.[5] At this point in time, 64 non-OECD countries have power of judicial review. The remainder of this chapter examines the use of judicial and quasi-judicial instruments for protecting and promoting E/S rights in Canada, Greece, South Africa, and Brazil.

Economic and Social Rights in the Global North

This section discusses economic and social rights in the global North, with a particular focus on Canadian and European-level courts. E/S rights hold a complicated position in these more economically developed countries. On the one hand, the countries enjoy strong state capacity and revenue-generating economies, resources necessary to protect E/S rights. On the other hand, global North countries have been strongly influenced by economic minimalist ideologies such as neoliberalism,[6] and thus states can be reluctant to intervene for more equitable social and economic outcomes. These tensions have led to an unclear consensus among human rights scholars about the role that E/S rights play in the "West" (broadly defined).[7] However, with increasing threats to E/S rights, global North activists have begun to promote these rights through an array of domestic and transnational institutions. For example, Canadian activists, similarly to activists within global South contexts, have argued that the Canadian Charter of Rights and Freedoms includes protections for E/S rights, and European activists have used the Council of Europe's recent Collective Complaints Procedure under the European Social Charter to demand greater state respect for a broad range of E/S rights.

Canada

Canada demonstrates how competing political ideologies have resulted in a lack of consensus on the position of E/S rights as fundamental rights. Initially Canada took a stance similar to the rest of the Western world during negotiations over the United Nations Declaration of Human Rights. In addition, fearing threats to parliamentary sovereignty,[8] the Canadian government took a reluctant stance toward E/S rights during the ECOSOC meetings of the UN. The Canadian Special Joint Committee on Human Rights and Fundamental Freedoms met 10 times in 1948 to clarify Canada's UN human rights obligations. The Canadian delegation made strong statements against the inclusion of social, economic, and cultural rights, considering them to be mere "responsibilities" that lacked the status of civil and political rights.[9] After Canada signed the Universal Declaration, a national discussion began on how to best conceptualize and codify human rights in Canada.[10] During the postwar period, Canada's human rights identity began to shift as the country developed a stronger sense of social citizenship.

There is evidence that Canada was supporting E/S rights by the 1970s, since it ratified the International Covenant on Economic, Social, and Cultural Rights in 1976. Indeed, it did so only after every province had written its commitment to those rights into its laws. Further, Margot Young argues, key Canadian programs that clearly promote E/S rights—such as national health care, social assistance, a national pension, and unemployment insurance—are "defining features of Canadians' national identity."[11] Despite this domestic support, E/S rights were not explicitly included in the text of the Canadian Charter of Rights and Freedoms in 1982.[12] The Special Joint Committee of the Senate and the House of Commons on the Constitution of Canada considered including this international commitment in the Constitution Act of 1982. However, civil society and human rights organizations preferred an expansive understanding of rights, such as the right to equality, to include E/S factors.[13] This lack of codification may have led to setbacks in the legal protection of E/S rights; Canada's political axis has shifted since the 1990s with the spread of conservatism, austerity, and increased political support for an unregulated market.[14]

Despite Canada's increasing conservatism, the nation's human rights commitments provide the possibility of domestic judicial enforcement. While Canada's international human rights obligations (including E/S rights) are not self-executing, the Supreme Court of Canada has interpreted the Charter in the context of Canada's human rights commitments. In the 1989 *Slaight Communications* decisions, the Court referenced the ICESCR in emphasizing the existence of an "interpretative presumption," meaning that the Charter is presumed to provide protection similar to Canada's international human rights ratifications.[15] Similarly, the Court stated in *Reference re Public Service Employee Relations Act (Alberta)*, a 1987 Charter challenge relating to domestic labour rights, that international norms "provide a relevant and persuasive source for interpretation of the provisions of the Charter, especially when they arise out of Canada's international obligations under human rights conventions."[16]

Thus there is a possibility that the Supreme Court of Canada could interpret social and economic obligations under the Charter. As Justice Claire L'Heureux-Dubé wrote in the *Ewanchuk* decision, "Our Charter is the primary vehicle through which international human rights achieve a domestic effect … In particular, s. 15 and s. 7 embody the notion of respect of human dignity and integrity."[17] Section 7 protects the right to life and security of the person and section 15 specifies equal protection under the law. The Court interpreted a broad, internationally recognized right of workers' freedom of association and protection of collective bargaining, in the 2007 *Health Services* case, from the simple clause on "freedom of association."[18] However, just as the jurisprudence on workers' collective bargaining rights remained unclear for many years, the Supreme Court's jurisdiction has not necessarily progressed on more E/S rights–sensitive interpretations of sections 7 and 15, but it has not definitively ruled against such interpretations either.[19]

In several cases the Supreme of Court of Canada failed to take an activist role in expanding Charter rights to include E/S rights components. For example, in *Gosselin v. Quebec* (2002), a class-action lawsuit claimed that a 1984 Quebec law severely curtailed social assistance payments to recipients under the age of 30, in violation of sections 7 and 15(1) of the Canadian Charter of Rights and Freedoms. The section 15 claim was dismissed, as there was no evidence of age discrimination. The Supreme Court upheld the lower courts' decision that section 7 (security of persons) did not create any positive obligations on the state but merely limited the state from depriving people (through its justice system) of their rights to life, liberty, and security.[20]

The *Gosselin* case was politically significant, particularly for those in the legal activism community who saw the case as a potential tool in the struggle against widespread austerity and cutbacks in social programs throughout Canada. It was the first poverty-based Charter challenge at the Supreme Court.[21] The justices were clearly split, with five in the majority and four dissenting. However, the Court's decision left the door open for a broader obligation, finding that "the circumstances of this case do not warrant a novel application of S. 7 as the basis for a positive state obligation to guarantee adequate living standards."[22] Justice Beverley McLaughlin stated in a concurring opinion that "the question therefore is not whether S. 7 has ever been—or will ever be—recognized as creating positive rights. Rather the question is whether the present circumstances warrant a novel application of S. 7 as the basis for a positive obligation to guarantee adequate living standards. I conclude that they do not." The dissenting judges, in an opinion written by Justice Louise Arbour, argued that section 7 includes "positive dimensions," stating that the majority narrow view of section 7 "is of little consolation to those who, like the claimants in this case, are faced with the daily struggle to meet their most basic bodily and psychological needs. To them, such a purely negative right to security of the person is essentially meaningless: theirs is a world in which the primary threats to security of the person come not from others but from their own dire circumstances."[23]

The Supreme Court has argued for some positive state obligations to E/S rights but generally remains reluctant to do so. In *Schachter v. Canada* (1992) the Court stated that section 15 was a "hybrid" right because it created both positive and negative duties for the state (section 15 encourages social programs such as assistance for mothers).[24] Sometimes the Court has ordered positive policy changes to provide certain types of assistance and benefits such as security of tenure and human rights legislation.[25] In *Eldridge v. British Columbia* (1997) the Court rejected the Court of Appeal's earlier decision that section 15 did not require positive obligation on the government to ensure availability of services to promote equality of outcome, despite claims of budgetary pressures.[26] Similarly, the Court also found that the government has a positive obligation to promote equality, in *Vriend v. Alberta* (1997).[27] But in *Egan v. Canada* (1995) the majority of the Court ruled that excluding a homosexual partner from spousal benefits under the Old Age Security Act did not constitute a violation of section 15 (on non-discrimination). L'Heureux-Dubé's dissenting opinion stated that "economic prejudices or benefits" are relevant to section 15, particularly as they relate to offending "inherent human dignity."[28]

While Canada certainly has a strong commitment to E/S rights as evidenced in social policy compared to its southern neighbour, the position of these rights remains unclear. While Charter protections as determined by the Supreme Court remain ambiguous, some provincial-level protections exist. For instance, because the federal Human Rights Act protects Canadians from a host of discriminatory practices, advocates, including the Canadian Human Rights Act Review Panel, have argued that social condition should be an included protected category as a way to ensure economic and social rights, and a number of jurisdictions have begun including social condition in their own legislation. For example, the Quebec Charter of Rights and Freedoms includes some protections for economic and social rights as well as protections against discrimination based on "social condition."[29] Similarly, the human rights laws of New Brunswick and the Northwest Territories include well-defined protections of social condition, and Manitoba's Human Rights Code includes protection for "social disadvantage."[30] But broader economic and social rights protections have not been instituted, through either statutory or judicial means, at the federal level. The possibly landmark *Gosselin* case resulted in a noncommittal decision from a deeply divided Court, perhaps reflecting a lack of a clear consensus within broader Canadian society. However, activists may continue to bring Charter challenges under sections 7 and 15 and perhaps an appropriate case will lead to a decision, much like the unexpected 2007 *Health Services* decision, which allowed for the broader interpretation that human rights groups had originally hoped for in the initial Charter negotiations.

Europe

The widespread adoption of austerity policies since the 2008 financial crisis throughout Europe has had clear negative effects. While there is a range to the severity of cuts, a recent report commissioned by the European Trade Union Commission found that budget cuts have been concentrated in social protection expenditures, and that tax burden increases (usually through indirect taxes) have not been equitable.[31] While most states still claim respect for their E/S rights obligations, nearly all European countries have imposed austerity policies in the name of public indebtedness. These cuts include reductions in health care, pensions, family benefits, and other forms of social security across Europe. The Council of Europe's Parliamentary Assembly passed Resolution 1884 in 2012, stating that European countries' harmful austerity programs, whether or not externally imposed by the European "troika"—the International Monetary Fund, the European Commission, and the European Central Bank—would likely worsen the social effects of the crisis and negatively affect the social rights of those already economically marginalized.[32]

Social rights in Europe are protected primarily by the 1961 European Social Charter (revised in 1966), a document of the Council of Europe, and the European Community's 1989 Community Charter of Fundamental Social Rights of Workers.[33] However, since the Community Charter is focused largely on employment-related rights, this section focuses on the European Social Charter, which covers a broader range of E/S rights (including housing, education, health, social protection, non-discrimination, and social security) and creates a dual monitoring regime based on country reporting and a collective complaints procedure. In addition to the original 1961 document, several additional protocols have expanded the rights and created new monitoring mechanisms. In particular, the 1995 Additional Protocol created the Collective Complaints Procedure, allowing international organizations of employers and trade unions, other international NGOs with consultative status with the Council of Europe, and national employer and trade union organizations to bring complaints against state parties.[34] State parties to the 1995 Additional Protocol may respond to the complaint and the Committee of Independent Experts later reviews its merits, which may lead to a hearing and a report to the Committee of Ministers, which votes on a recommendation to the state involved.

The Collective Complaints Procedure came into force in 1998, when the minimum of five state parties had joined;[35] as of 2012, 15 states had become party to the procedure. Between 1998 and 2015 the European Committee of Social Rights received 115 complaints.[36] Unlike European Court of Human Rights rulings, decisions of the European Committee on Social Rights must be referred to the Committee of Ministers for "definitive disposal," and it cannot demand settlement, remuneration, or other forms of provisional measures in cases of violations.[37] This reflects the bifurcated, perhaps second-class, status of social rights even within the Council of Europe's bodies. Likewise, the Committee of Ministers may not always endorse or adopt the Committee of Social Rights' findings but simply pass resolutions noting its decisions. While this regime lacks the stronger legal basis of the European Convention of Human Rights and its protection through the European Court of Human Rights (specifically the individual-based complaints admission to the Court),[38] the Social Charter is accessible to "social partners" and NGOs in order to criticize state practices, making it a relatively accessible institution.[39]

The Collective Complaints Procedure has created transnational legal opportunities for activists to challenge states in their protection of E/S rights. The digest of collective complaints, limited to those found admissible by the Committee from 1998 to 2012, demonstrates the diversity of cases. Since trade unions have the ability to bring complaints, most of the collective complaints are related to workplace standards, such as overtime, dismissal, and union rights. Most of the non-workplace-related collective complaints brought to the Committee related to possible E/S rights violations of highly vulnerable groups, such as Roma, Travellers, persons with disabilities, children, and migrants who lack legal status. Rights violations focus largely on housing, education, health care, and other social assistance.[40] However, since the creation of austerity measures following the financial crisis, new groups have brought collective complaints under the European Social Charter. Given the intense scrutiny of Greece during the recent financial crisis, this section will explore activists' use of the complaint procedure to challenge neoliberal curtailing of pensions and social security systems in Greece since 2010.

Greece and Austerity

Through a series of several related cases, the Committee of Independent Experts found Greece to be in violation of its obligations to the Social Charter. The Committee first expressed its concerns about problems with Greece's protection of E/S rights after reviewing the country's 2009 reports on articles 3, 4, and 11–14 of the Charter.[41] Greek civil society and workers' organizations brought a number of related collective complaints to the European Committee on Social Rights in 2012 (complaints 76–80).[42] Trade unions and organizations of retirees and pensioners complained that recent legislation—namely "Act No. 3845 of 6 May 2010, Act No. 3847 of 11 May 2010, Act No. 3863 of 15 July 2010, Act No. 3865 of 21 July 2010,

Act No. 3896 of 1 July 2011 and Act No. 4024 of 27 October 2011"—violated articles 12(3), the right to social security and states' related obligation "to endeavour to raise progressively the system of social security to a higher level," and 13(1), the right to social and medical assistance, including access for those without adequate resources through the social security system, of the 1961 European Social Charter. The laws in question increased workers' contributions to both public and private pension schemes, changed the age of retirement, and limited the resulting pension contributions. Some of these reductions represented up to 40 per cent of prior benefit levels, and holiday bonuses were also reduced.

The Greek government justified these policies passed by the national parliament "as necessary for the protection of public interests," following the requirements of the troika's 2010 bailout conditions. Furthermore, as the government had accepted a high-level consultative visit from the International Labour Organization in 2011, it argued that the pension-system reform respected international standards. In addition, the government claimed that the new laws allowed for exemptions for the "most vulnerable social groups," and asked the European Social Committee to reject the complaint.[43]

The Committee of Ministers had already advised Greece not to reform its social security system in such a way as to push pensioners and workers below the poverty line, and to maintain its responsibilities to the European Code of Social Security. The Committee had also urged the government to create a statistical system to monitor poverty and to coordinate its social security policies with its tax, wage, and other industrial policies. In its response to the collective complaint, the Committee stated that changes to the pension system did not necessarily constitute a violation of the European Social Charter. However, it found that the "cumulative effect" of the legal changes would be "bound to bring about a significant degradation of the standard of living and the living conditions of the pensioners concerned."[44]

The Committee argued that the government had not done sufficient research and analysis to measure the impact of those changes on vulnerable members of society; they had also not involved these populations in any discussion or consultation about alternative policies that might have limited the negative effects on vulnerable pensioners. As a result, the Committee found that the Greek government hadn't met its requirements under article 12(3) to "maintain a sufficient level of protection for the benefit of the most vulnerable members of society, even though the effects of the adopted measures risk bringing about a large scale pauperisation of a significant segment of the population, as has been observed by various international organisations."[45]

While the Committee's decision was not legally binding on the Greek government, it has been publicized by trade unions and human rights organizations as evidence of how the troika-imposed reforms violate human rights. For example, the European Trade Union Confederation immediately published the Committee's findings on its website, as did the International Labour Organization.[46] Further, the decision provides an international standard on how to consider E/S rights requirements during times of economic crisis. While the long-term effect of this decision in Greece is yet to be determined, the Committee's condemnation may influence others, leading to such actions as the European Parliament's recent condemnation of the troika's policies in Portugal, Ireland, Greece, and Spain (sometimes referred to as the PIGS) as a violation of the European Community's fundamental rights.[47]

The Global South

Given the poverty and lack of resources in the global South, it is difficult to have high expectations for the enforcement E/S rights, particularly given the principle of progressive realization. However, the inclusion of E/S rights within many national constitutions in the global South allows citizens to promote these rights via judicial review. For instance, the Indian Supreme Court has, since the late 1970s, taken an aggressive role in expanding India's E/S rights obligations; the Court has declared a right to education, the right to shelter, and the right to childhood as inherent to the right to life, one of the fundamental rights protected by its constitution. Through these declarations, the Court has made these rights enforceable. India is often used as a classic example of an activist court using its power to protect and promote E/S rights.[48]

Another classic example of an activist system is Colombia, which is considered a "striking example of judicial review regarding health rights."[49] In Colombia, court interventions were aided by the 1991 constitution, which enshrined a number of new rights and procedures, including the *tutela* system, which allowed individual petitioners to bring actions to the Constitutional Court regarding fundamental rights violations. Between 1999 and 2008, 674,612 actions for the protection of health rights were filed before the courts. Similarly, in Brazil and South Africa new constitutions solidified E/S rights and created a new role for the judiciary. This section explores Brazil and South Africa in some detail to assess E/S protection by courts.

South Africa

In 1996, as South Africa transitioned out of apartheid, its legislature began the work of constructing a new constitution, one that was designed explicitly to address the impact of apartheid's racist legacy and to build a society focused on social justice and the improvement of citizens' lives. During the lead-up to the 1996 constitution, a number of political parties and civil society organizations agreed that E/S rights should be included in order to meet the transformative goals of the constitution. One of the leading arguments for inclusion of these rights was that E/S rights in the Bill of Rights would support "redistributive state measures to ensure equitable access to resources and social services"[50] that would address the legacy of apartheid. Thus the constitution includes major E/S rights, to adequate housing, health care, education, food and water, labour, and social security.[51] Importantly, and following the model of the ICESCR, these rights are qualified by a progressive realization clause, which suggests that the state must meet these rights according to its available resources.

Following passage of the constitution, the Constitutional Court, as well as the provincial High Courts and the Supreme Court of Appeal, began to hear E/S cases. A number of landmark cases have been decided that established the Court's jurisprudence on E/S rights. The most far-reaching in their implications include *Soobramoney v. Minister of Health, SwaZulu-Natal, Minster of Health and Others v. Treatment Action Campaign and Others*, and *Government of the Republic of South Africa v. Grootboom.*[52]

The *Soobramoney* case was the first to consider the enforcement of E/S rights. It was a response to a petition from a man who wanted a positive order to make the local hospital provide him with dialysis, as he was in the last stages of renal failure and could not afford treatment at a private hospital. When the case reached the Constitutional Court, it upheld the ruling of the High Court that the applicant did not meet the medical standards for treatment and that the guidelines for access to treatment had been applied fairly and rationally.[53] Further, the Court's ruling emphasized that the right to health does not obligate the state to provide everything to everyone, particularly when there are limited resources.[54] Instead, the state should focus on greater threats to public health rather than lesser threats to individuals.

In the second landmark health case, the Treatment Action Campaign (TAC) contended that the state's response to the need for preventing mother-to-child transmission of HIV was too limited and lacking under constitutional obligations. The Campaign argued that limiting distribution of the antiretroviral drug nevirapine was unreasonable, and that there was no national campaign or program to prevent mother-to-child transmission. Both the High Court and the Constitutional Court upheld the Campaign's claim that the government was violating the right to access health-care services.

Grootboom involved a claim for housing from a group of people who had been evicted from private land and were unable to build shelter, as usable materials had been destroyed during the eviction. In this case the Court found the government in violation of its E/S rights obligations. However, it was a nuanced ruling that provided a framework for many future rulings: it stressed that the state did not have to provide housing for anyone, but it should create conditions of access to housing for all, with particular attention to the poor.[55] In addition, the Court ruled that the government needed to create and implement a plan to deal with the problem.

While relatively few E/S cases have reached the Constitutional Court at this time, these three cases demonstrate the willingness of the judiciary to enforce E/S rights.[56] The Constitutional Court has used the judgements in *Grootboom* and *Soobramoney* in particular to develop a model of "reasonableness review" to determine the positive duties imposed by E/S rights. Under this model the Court works to determine whether the chosen means will reasonably "facilitate the socio-economic rights in question."[57] It does not prescribe policy solutions but allows the government to determine policy on its own, within resource constraints. The Court is thus able to be flexible in its adjudication and the government flexible in its solutions.

However, the reasonableness standard and the attention given to creation of government programs rather than individual claims means that vulnerable groups in South Africa often find their E/S rights unprotected, despite the Constitutional Court's singling out of the poor as a vulnerable group in need of special protection. In addition, although the Court has wide remedial powers—including the power to issue declaratory and mandatory orders, as well as to exercise supervisory jurisdiction—it has largely relied only on declaratory orders. This is a weak remedy and demonstrates reluctance on the part of the Court to hold the state accountable.

Ultimately, while in some cases enforcement has worked well, such as in the TAC case, which led to a comprehensive national HIV/AIDS program that includes the use of antiretroviral drugs, enforcement in many other cases has been less successful. For instance, the housing program required by the *Grootboom* case took four years for the government to develop, and its implementation has been slow and uneven. Irene Grootboom, the main plaintiff, never did acquire access to housing as required by the constitution, and died homeless in 2008. A detailed review of 32 Constitutional Court cases by Jonathan Berger finds that the vast majority have been unsuccessful at improving the lives of those affected by the ruling.[58]

The successful cases seem to have one of two items in common. One circumstance in which cases are resolved successfully seems to be when they are supported by well-organized civil society organizations (such as the Treatment Action Campaign) that are willing to organize, advocate, and litigate repeatedly. Right now there is a larger civil society organized around health issues than around the other rights that have seen litigation—housing, social security, and education[59]—so it is likely that those other rights will continue to be marginalized.

The second instance in which cases are successful is when the ascribed remedy does not cost the government very much. For instance, the TAC case, which is regarded as wildly successful, was certainly helped by the fact that drug companies agreed to pay for use of the drug, rather than the government having to foot the bill.[60] The Court has consistently found against individually enforceable rights to health, education, housing, and social assistance, which would put a resource burden on the state, and instead has focused on a reasonableness approach that asks the state to begin creating plans for extending benefits. This is ultimately a cautious approach and preserves a traditional deference to elected bodies.

Brazil

The Brazilian constitution, like the South African, is considered a transformational constitution. Emerging from a post-dictatorship consensus in 1988, it establishes human dignity as the centrepiece of the country's legal framework.[61] The constitution includes human rights as fundamental rights and lists them in the untouchable part of the constitution; it also incorporates human rights treaties as constitutional provisions. Importantly, E/S rights are included as fundamental rights; the rights to education, health, work, housing, leisure, security, social security, and protection of motherhood and childhood are included in article 6. Unlike the Indian and South African constitutions, the Brazilian constitution also lays out guidelines and rules for state programs and policies. For instance, the rights to health and education in the constitution are given specific budgetary allocations; municipalities, for instance, are required to spend at least 25 per cent of their tax revenues on education.

The inclusion of E/S rights in the fundamental clauses makes it clear that these rights are justiciable in Brazil. In addition to the regular mechanisms of writs of *habeas corpus* and *mandamus* and a petition for a people's action to protect public property, the 1988 constitution created a new type of remedial right: a writ of injunction that ensures "the immediate exercise of constitutional rights should a regulatory provision be lacking and direct action for unconstitutionality on the basis of omission."[62] These provisions drastically increased the potential for the courts to play a strong role in protecting and fulfilling Brazil's obligations of E/S rights.

In addition to the structure of the constitution, the structure of the judiciary in Brazil is important to its success in fulfilling E/S rights. The judiciary is entirely independent. The most important actor is the Federal Supreme

Court (STF), which is both the final appeals court and a specialized constitutional review court. The four federal superior courts and the courts at the federal and state levels can also make decisions on constitutionality. Decisions made by these courts do not set formal binding precedent, which means that every judge in any case can interpret the law anew, even when the cases have similar factual bases. This has led to both a large number of cases and a high success rate for cases that request individual remedies, particularly for health issues. For instance, a 2004 study found that in the state of Rio de Janeiro in 1991 there was exactly one right to health care, while there were 1,444 in 2002.[63] This type of increase in seen in the other states as well.

While the conditions for successful judicial enforcement of E/S rights were laid out in the constitution, initially the courts took a deferential role toward the political branches, mostly finding that E/S rights were programmatic norms and required the legislature to create programs to fulfill those rights.[64] This changed dramatically when the effects of the AIDS pandemic began to be felt in Brazil in the mid-1990s. Beginning in 1996, some plaintiffs were successful with claims that the constitutional right to health created an obligation on the state to provide expensive AIDS-treatment drugs. These decisions were largely injunctive orders that required the state to provide treatment for the individual plaintiffs. Once these cases began to be successful, the number rose rapidly.

While there are no precedent-setting cases in Brazil, it does seem that most right-to-health cases regarding access to medicine rely on reasoning provided in two STF cases.[65] In both of these cases, in which individuals were requesting the HIV drug Invirase, the state countered with a resource limitation claim; in both cases this was dismissed by the STF. In the first case the STF dismissed the resource limitation claim completely and found that the state was remiss in upholding its obligations to provide medication for individuals unable to afford it, as required in specific legislation. In the second case the court did acknowledge the resource argument but dismissed it as a secondary concern for the state, holding that the right to live and therefore the right to health were the primary interests of the state. This decision became de facto precedent in the thousands of other right-to-health cases. In the area of health, at least, the judiciary has largely created a system in which individual cases will be supported over the economic interests of the state.

Despite the high success rate in the courts, enforcement of these orders tends to be more sporadic and dependent on which state the plaintiff resides in. Similarly, there are large state-by-state differences in who can access the courts: people in richer states are more likely to pursue litigation than those in poorer states. Thus, despite an active judiciary, comprehensive fulfillment of Brazil's rights obligations is dependent on other factors as well.

Conclusion: A Role for Courts

Looking at the cases in the global North and the South might present a dismal picture of the role of courts in protecting and promoting socio-economic rights, and certainly a less positive role than that hoped for by proponents of judicial review and rights protection. However, we argue that these cases simply tell us that, under certain conditions, courts will be ineffective at protecting socioeconomic rights, while under other conditions, they can prove very effective at protection. Like all institutional mechanisms, domestic courts and international quasi-judicial institutions are merely one of many tools available to social and economic rights activists.

The Supreme Court of India (SCI) demonstrates the mixed nature of court efficacy. A survey of cases beginning in 1950 reveals that in India there have been 209 cases regarding the right to health and 173 cases regarding the right to education, and that plaintiffs have won 81 per cent of these cases nationwide.[66] While this is a remarkable success rate, an analysis of the efficacy of their rulings provides a more mixed picture. For instance, the judiciary was responsible for a number of new policies but in many cases was unable or unwilling to enforce those policies. In part this is due to the weak remedies issued by the SCI, such as declaration of a right without suggested remedies or provisions that require the government to develop plans.[67] For instance, the SCI has favoured the creation of supervising authorities or committees that are required to report back to the court periodically, or court-monitored implementation that left it to the petitioners to return to court of their own volition if there was no redress.[68] In some cases these weak remedies have rendered the activist nature of the case decisions less promising for fulfillment of social and economic rights in India.

However, in some cases where an active and engaged petitioner regularly returned to court and thus kept media attention on the issue at hand, the Court has delivered sweeping social change. For instance, in the 2001 *Mid-Day Meals* case, the People's Union for Civil Liberties returned again and again to the SCI in order to keep Court, media, and government attention on the lack of a school meals program that had been promised in a 1995 legislative act. The interactive and iterative nature of the court process in India worked to change social conditions in the country and led to the populace's beginning to demand fulfillment of the right to food.[69] In this case the Court was an important player in the protection and promotion of socioeconomic rights.

Canada, India, Colombia, South Africa, and Brazil demonstrate that courts are not the only answer to socioeconomic rights protection, but rather that they can be an important component of rights protection, depending on the independence and strength of the court. In particular, the legal opportunity structure created by a constitution can open up new possibilities for rights protection. In addition, an active and engaged civil society can play a large role in forcing courts to engage with socioeconomic rights issues. In conjunction with a willing legislature, courts are an important part of the national and international framework for the protection of socioeconomic rights. Similarly, international quasi-judicial institutions such as the European Social Rights Committee can play a role in bringing attention to issues and providing legitimacy for the positions of petitioners; much like domestic courts, regional institutions can provide support for positions that the state is unwilling to engage with or take seriously.

Judicial and quasi-judicial institutions are only one part of a long-term strategy for rights fulfillment. It can take a long time for cases to be brought to trial, and decisions can be slow. Further, court orders are dependent on budget constraints for implementation, which can further hinder their efficacy. Because of these shortcomings, court orders are usually unable to alleviate short-term suffering, but they should be regarded as one of the tools available for human rights activists. Judicial and quasi-judicial institutions can provide strong support for activist positions and bring attention to human rights issues, but they are unable to create effective social and economic rights regimes on their own. The creation of such regimes requires continuous activist pressure and mobilization. This chapter demonstrates that when domestic political and legislative institutions are hostile to economic and social rights, activists can turn to judicial and quasi-judicial institutions to promote their causes. While economic and social rights may lack strong political support, these institutions are often one of the most powerful venues in which activists can press for their protection.

Takeaway Messages

- Economic and social (E/S) rights often lack the same broad "consensus" of civil and political rights and thus are often given secondary status for political reasons.
- E/S rights are often characterized as an economic burden on the state, and thus are quickly discarded or derogated in times of economic "stress" or "crisis."
- Newer constitutional arrangements, especially in post-transitional global South countries, have created some legal protections for E/S rights; thus, given difficult political circumstances, E/S rights activists have turned to the courts.

Study Questions

- What are the similarities and differences in the ways that E/S rights differ in Canada and in various global South countries?
- What are the practical implications of including E/S rights in a state constitution?
- Under what conditions will E/S rights be successfully protected?

Issues for Debate or Roundtable

- How could the international community better protect E/S rights? Through new treaties? New incentives? Other mechanisms?
- Should economic and social rights be protected in times of economic crisis?

Additional Reading

Hertel, Shareen, and Lanse Minkler. *Economic Rights: Conceptual, Measurement, and Policy Issues*. Cambridge: Cambridge University Press, 2007. http://dx.doi.org/10.1017/CBO9780511511257.

Howard-Hassmann, Rhoda, and Claude E. Welch, eds. *Economic Rights in Canada and the United States*. Philadelphia: University of Pennsylvania Press, 2009.

Jung, Courtney, and Evan Rosevear. *Economic and Social Rights in Developing Country Constitutions: Preliminary Report on the TIESR Dataset*. Draft for comment, 26 January 2011.

O'Connell, Paul. *Vindicating Socio-Economic Rights: International Standards and Comparative Experiences*. London: Routledge, 2012.

Websites

Center for Economic and Social Rights. http://www.cesr.org.

Economic and Social Rights Empowerment Initiative. http://www.serfindex.org.

European Committee of Social Rights (ECSR). http://www.coe.int/t/dghl/monitoring/socialcharter/ecsr/ecsrdefault_EN.asp

National Economic and Social Rights Initiative. http://www.nesri.org/human-rights/economic-and-social-rights.

Notes

1. J. Donnelly, *Universal Human Rights in Theory and Practice*, 2nd ed. (Ithaca, NY: Cornell University Press, 2003).
2. C. Epp, *The Rights Revolution: Lawyers, Activists, and Supreme Courts in Comparative Perspective* (Chicago: University of Chicago Press, 1998).

3. P. Alston and R. Goodman, *International Human Rights in Context: Law, Politics, Morals: Text and Materials* (Oxford: Oxford University Press, 2008), 313.
4. T. Ginsburg, *Judicial Review in New Democracies: Constitutional Courts in Asian Cases* (New York: Cambridge University Press, 2003), 6.
5. Ibid., 9.
6. In this chapter we understand neoliberalism as an economic orthodoxy that includes both an ideological component (in which individual human freedom and happiness require minimal economic regulation and intervention) and a policy component (promotion of free trade, individualism, liberal monetary policy, privatization, property rights, importance of attracting capital, attacks on trade unions and the welfare state, and retrenchment of the regulatory state). See D. Harvey, *A Brief History of Neoliberalism* (Oxford: Oxford University Press, 2005).
7. See D.J. Whelan and J. Donnelly, "The West, Economic and Social Rights, and the Global Human Rights Regime: Setting the Record Straight," *Human Rights Quarterly* 29, no. 4 (2007): 908–49; A. Kirkup and T. Evans, "The Myth of Western Opposition to Economic, Social, and Cultural Rights? A Reply to Whelan and Donnelly," *Human Rights Quarterly* 31, no. 1 (2009): 221–37; S.L. Kang, "The Unsettled Relationship of Economic and Social Rights and the West: A Response to Whelan and Donnelly," *Human Rights Quarterly* 31, no. 4 (2009): 1006–29.
8. C. Maclennan, *Toward the Charter: Canadians and the Demand for a National Bill of Rights, 1929–1960* (Montreal: McGill-Queen's University Press, 2003), 71.
9. Ibid., 77.
10. Ibid., 83.
11. M. Young, "Introduction," in *Poverty: Rights, Social Citizenship, and Legal Activism*, ed. M. Young, S.B. Boyd, G. Brodsky, and S. Day, 1–22 (Vancouver: UBC Press), 7.
12. This replaced the much weaker 1960 Canadian Bill of Rights, which had many shortcomings, including its limited scope to only the federal government; F.L. Morton, "The Political Impact of the Canadian Charter of Rights and Freedoms," *Canadian Journal of Political Science / Revue canadienne de science politique* 20, no. 1 (1987): 32.
13. B. Porter and M. Jackman, "Canada," in *Social Rights Jurisprudence: Emerging Trends in International and Comparative Law*, ed. M. Langford, 209–29 (Cambridge: Cambridge University Press, 2008).
14. E. Broadbent, "The Rise and Fall of Economic and Social Rights: What Next?" Canadian Centre for Policy Alternatives, 2010, http://www.policyalternatives.ca/sites/default/files/uploads/publications/reports/docs/Rise_and_Fall_of_Economic_and_Social_Rights.pdf.
15. Porter and Jackman, "Canada," 215.
16. *Reference re Public Service Employment Relations Act (Alberta)*, [1987] S.C.R. 313, at 60.
17. *R. v. Ewanchuk*, [1999] 1 S.C.R. 330, at para. 73.
18. *Health Services and Support—Facilities Subsector Bargaining Assn v. British Columbia*, 2007 SCC 27.
19. Porter and Jackman, "Canada."
20. *Gosselin v. Quebec (Attorney General)*, [2002] 4 S.C.R. 429, 2002 SCC 84.
21. Young, "Introduction."
22. *Gosselin v. Quebec*.
23. Ibid., at para. 80–82.

24. *Schachter v. Canada*, [1992] 2 S.C.R. 679.
25. Porter and Jackman, "Canada," 6.
26. G. Brodsky and S. Day, "Beyond the Social and Economic Rights Debate: Substantive Equality Speaks to Poverty," *Canadian Journal of Women and the Law* 14 (2002): 212. The Court argued that even with budgetary constraints, there were many ways in which British Columbia could have upheld its obligations to the deaf plaintiffs, and it had failed to meet that need.
27. *Vriend v. Alberta*, (1997) 151 D.L.R. (4th) 577 (SCC).
28. It should be noted that this decision laid the legal foundation for Charter protection against discrimination based on sexual orientation, resulting in a federal guarantee of such protection.
29. L. Arbour and F. Lafontaine, "Beyond Self-Congratulations: The Charter at 25 in an International Perspective," *Osgoode Hall Law Journal* 45 (2007): 268.
30. D. Adams, "Social Condition in Canadian Human Rights Legislation," BC Human Rights Coalition, 2013; W. McKay and N. Kim, "Adding Social Condition to the *Canadian Human Rights Act*," Canadian Human Rights Coalition, 2009, http://www.chrc-ccdp.ca/sites/default/files/sc_eng.pdf.
31. S. Theodoropoulou and A. Watt, "Withdrawal Symptoms: An Assessment of the Austerity Packages in Europe," Working Paper 2001.02 (Brussels: European Trade Union Institute, 2011). There have been exceptions, however; both France and Luxembourg have relied on income taxes to raise government revenues.
32. Council of Europe, "Austerity Measures: A Danger for Democracy and Social Rights," Parliamentary Assembly Resolution 1884 (2012), http://assembly.coe.int/nw/xml/XRef/Xref-XML2HTML-en.asp?fileid=18916&lang=en.
33. Kenner argues that this deliberate choice excludes the rights of European citizens who are not workers, ignoring general social security, public health, and education provisions and focusing more on labour market concerns relating to the Common Market rather than social and economic rights by themselves. J. Kenner, "Economic and Social Rights in the EU Legal Order: The Mirage of Indivisibility," in *Economic and Social Rights under the EU Charter of Fundamental Rights: A Legal Perspective*, ed. T.K. Hervey and J. Kenner (Portland, OR: Hart, 2003), 1–24.
34. Council of Europe, *European Social Charter Collective Texts*, 6th ed. (Brussels: Council of Europe, 2008), 41–42, http://www.coe.int/t/dghl/monitoring/socialcharter/presentation/ESCCollectedTexts_en.pdf.
35. R.R. Churchill and U. Khaliq, "The Collective Complaints System of the European Social Charter: An Effective Mechanism for Ensuring Compliance with Economic and Social Rights?" *European Journal of International Law* 15, no. 3 (June 2004): 423.
36. Council of Europe, Directorate General of Human Rights and the Rule of Law, "The European Social Charter's Procedure of Collective Complaints" (Strasbourg: Council of Europe, May 2012).
37. Churchill and Khaliq, "Collective Complaints System," 347.
38. Ibid., 433.
39. Council of Europe, "Procedure of Collective Complaints."
40. European Committee of Social Rights, *Collective Complaints Procedure: Summaries of Decisions on the Merits, 1998–2012*, 30 May 2013, http://www.aedh.eu/plugins/fckeditor/userfiles/file/DESC/Federation%20on%20employed%20pensioners%20of%20Greece%20_%20Greece.pdf. Greece is a state party to the

1961 Social Charter and has accepted 67 of the 72 paragraphs. While it signed the Revised Charter, it has not ratified it. Greece did ratify the Additional Protocol, allowing for participation in the system of collective complaints. See Council of Europe, Directorate General of Human Rights and the Rule of Law, Department of the European Social Charter and the European Code of Social Security, "Greece and the European Social Charter," 2012, http://www.coe.int/t/dghl/monitoring/socialcharter/Complaints/Complaints_en.asp.

41. Greece is a state party to the 1961 Social Charter and has accepted 67 of the 72 paragraphs. While it signed the Revised Charter, it has not ratified it. Greece ratified the Additional Protocol, allowing for participation in the system of collective complaints. See Council of Europe, Directorate General of Human Rights and the Rule of Law, Department of the European Social Charter and the European Code of Social Security, 2012.
42. The complainants included the Federation of Employed Pensioners, Panhellenic Federation of Public Service Pensioners, Pensioners' Union of the Athens-Piraeus Electric Railways, Panhellenic Federation of Pensioners of the Public Electricity Corporation, and Pensioner's Union of the Agricultural Bank of Greece. See European Committee of Social Rights, *Collective Complaints Procedure*.
43. European Committee of Social Rights, *Federation of Employed Pensioners of Greece (IKA-ETAM) v. Greece*, European Social Charter, Council of Europe, complaint no. 76/2012, 2012, http://www.coe.int/t/dghl/monitoring/socialcharter/Complaints/Complaints_en.asp.
44. Ibid.
45. Ibid.
46. European Trade Union Confederation, "Greece: Pension Austerity Measures Violate Fundamental Social Rights," 17 August 2012, http://www.etuc.org/press/greece-pension-austerity-measures-violate-fundamental-social-rights#.UwzzG840-LA; International Labour Organization, "European Committee of Social Rights Says Greek Labour Reforms Violate International Law," 8 November 2012, http://www.ilo.org/brussels/WCMS_192951/lang--en/index.htm.
47. V. Pop, "Bailout Troika 'In Breach' of EU Fundamental Rights Laws," EU Observer, 29 January 2014, http://euobserver.com/social/122899; The Press Project, "European Parliament Committee: Troika Responsible for High Unemployment in Memorandum Countries," Reportage: European Economy, 15 January 2014, http://www.thepressproject.net/article/54598/European-Parliament-Committee-on-Employment-Troika-responsible-for-high-unemployment-in-Memorandum-countries.
48. S.P. Sathe, *Judicial Activism in India: Transgressing Borders and Enforcing Limits* (New Delhi: Oxford University Press, 2002); J. Kothari, "Social Rights and the Indian Constitution," *Law, Social Justice and Global Development Journal* 2 (2004); M. Khosla, "Addressing Judicial Activism in the Indian Supreme Court: Towards an Evolved Debate," *Hastings International and Comparative Law Review* 32 (2009): 55.
49. A.E. Yamin and O. Parra-Vera, "Judicial Protection of the Right to Health in Colombia: From Social Demands to Individual Claims to Public Debates, *Hastings International and Comparative Law Review* 33 (2010): 431.
50. S. Liebenberg, "South Africa: Adjudicating Social Rights under a Transformative Constitution," in *Social Rights Jurisprudence: Emerging Trends in International and Comparative Law*, ed. M Langford (Cambridge: Cambridge University Press, 2008), 76.

51. In addition, children's rights, the socioeconomic rights of detained people, environmental rights, language and cultural rights, and property rights focused on the duty of the state to foster access are all included.
52. Other accounts list other cases as landmark cases, commonly including *Minister of Public Works v. Kyalami Ridge*, another housing case; *Khosa v. Minister of Social Development* and *Mahlaule v. Minster of Social Development*, both of which dealt with equality; and *President of RSA v. Modderklip ABoerdery (Pty) Ltd*, which dealt with access to courts. We focus on the three above because of their importance for the substance of E/S rights litigation in South Africa.
53. One of the medical criteria to access the dialysis program was that the patient needed to be eligible for a kidney transplant; this patient, because he was in the late stages of the disease, was not.
54. J. Berger, "Litigating for Social Justice in Post-Apartheid South Africa: A Focus on Health and Education," in *Courting Social Justice: Judicial Enforcement of Social and Economic Rights in the Developing World*, ed. V. Gauri and D. Brinks (New York: Cambridge University Press, 2008), 54.
55. Ibid., 48.
56. Far more cases have been decided by the provincial High Courts and will perhaps eventually make their way to the Constitutional Court.
57. Liebenberg, "South Africa," 83.
58. Berger, "Litigating for Social Justice."
59. Ibid.
60. O.L.M. Ferraz, "The Right to Health in the Courts of Brazil: Worsening Health Inequities?" *Health and Human Rights Journal* 11, no. 2 (August 2013): 33–45.
61. F. Piovesan, "Brazil: Impact and Challenges of Social Rights in Courts," in *Social Rights Jurisprudence: Emerging Trends in International and Comparative Law*, ed. M. Langford, 182–91 (Cambridge: Cambridge University Press, 2008), 182.
62. Ibid., 184.
63. Ferraz, "Right to Health."
64. O.L.M. Ferraz, "Between Usurpation and Abdication? The Right to Health in the Courts of Brazil and South Africa," August 2009, http://dx.doi.org/10.2139/ssrn.1458299.
65. RE242.859/RS and RE/AgR271.286-RS; Ferraz, "Right to Health."
66. Shankar and Mehta, 2008.
67. Tushnet, 2009.
68. S. Shankar and P.B. Mehta, "Courts and Socioeconomic Rights in India," in *Courting Social Justice: Judicial Enforcement of Social and Economic Rights in the Developing World*, ed. V. Gauri and D. Brinks (New York: Cambridge University Press, 2008), 174.
69. J.G. Rutledge, "Courts as Entrepreneurs: The Case of the Indian Mid-Day Meals Programme," *Asian Politics and Policy* 4, no. 4 (2012): 527–47.

16
Business and Human Rights: Challenges in Accessing Remedy and Justice

SARA SECK AND KIRSTEN STEFANIK

Learning Objectives

- To understand international efforts to address the challenges associated with corporate accountability for international human rights violations
- To identify and understand judicial and non-judicial mechanisms available for victims to seek remedy from transnational business
- To develop a familiarity with the 2011 United Nations Guiding Principles for Business and Human Rights

This chapter is about human rights violations committed by transnational corporations[1] or associated with their operations, and the mechanisms, judicial and non-judicial, that could provide victims with a remedy. First the chapter provides an overview of the nature of the problem, including the structure of the transnational corporation, and briefly introduces early international efforts to confront it. Next the chapter examines the debates over corporate criminal liability in the international criminal law context, notably in relation to drafting of the Statute of the International Criminal Court. The challenges of accessing private law remedies through transnational civil litigation in Canadian and US courts will then be explored. The chapter then turns to the 2011 United Nations "Protect, Respect and Remedy" Framework and Guiding Principles on Business and Human Rights, a polycentric governance framework that identifies the state's duty to protect human rights, the corporate responsibility to respect human rights, and the need for access to remedy for victims of human rights violations. The chapter concludes with reflections on the role of non-judicial mechanisms, including alternative justice and healing mechanisms, as well as the possibility of a binding international treaty.

The Rise of the Transnational Corporation

The international community has changed dramatically in the past hundred years: states, traditionally the sole actors on the international stage, have been joined by a vast array of non-state actors, including international organizations, nongovernmental organizations, transnational corporations (TNCs), and individuals.[2] In particular, TNCs have taken on an expansive role in the global community, with transnational operations, extensive financial resources, substantial power and influence, and a correspondingly significant impact on society, including human rights and the environment. Yet the institutions and tools for accountability for violations of human rights have not evolved at the same pace as the dynamic of the international community.

Globalization and the ever-increasing interconnectedness of world economies have contributed to this rapid increase in the number of TNCs. In fact, "some of the most powerful and sophisticated actors on the world stage are companies, not governments."[3] On that point, the revenues of ExxonMobil in 2011 were equivalent to the entirety of the economy of Norway! And the workforce of one of the world's largest employers, Walmart, is second in size only to the American and Chinese armed forces.[4] Undoubtedly, TNCs have achieved a powerful position in the international community.

With this vastly increased presence around the world—perhaps, at least in part, as a result of a preoccupation with profit maximization[5]—has come an increasing number of reports about corporate involvement in the perpetration of human rights violations. The most serious of allegations include accusations of torture, rape, summary execution, forced displacement, forced labour, environmental crimes, and genocide. Other common contemporary concerns include allegations of violations of indigenous rights and environmental rights by extractive companies,[6] labour and health and safety rights by manufacturers,[7] and freedom of information and privacy rights by Internet technology companies.[8] While some allegations are concerned with the conduct of the TNC itself, others arise from conduct associated with TNC operations, including that of the host state government, military or police forces, or those in a contractual relationship with the TNC. Some allegations concern crimes under international and national laws, while others claim less egregious violations—but violations nonetheless—of international human rights law. Yet the ability of those whose rights have been violated to seek remedy and to hold TNCs accountable for violations of internationally recognized human rights remains underdeveloped.

The Corporation as Legal Entity

In most domestic legal contexts a corporation is considered a "legal person," that is, it has its own legal existence separate from the legal existence of the individuals who incorporated (essentially, created and registered) the company. As such, once the corporation is created and legally incorporated, "it must be treated like any other independent person with rights and liabilities appropriate to itself."[9] While the people who work for and own the corporation—employees, managers, directors, officers—all have roles, rights, responsibilities, and, often, legal duties in their capacities, they themselves are not the corporation. The corporation is a separate legal entity unto itself.[10]

Only in the rarest of circumstances, where there is proof of fraud or intentional civil (as opposed to criminal) wrongs on the part of a company's directors, shareholders, or employees, or where the company in question is merely an undercapitalized shell unable to meet its reasonable financial needs, will a court "pierce the corporate veil" and look to the individuals behind the corporation to assign liability.[11] A TNC consists of multiple corporate entities that are affiliates of a parent company, whether subsidiaries or associates.[12] However, the social understanding of the TNC is of the corporate enterprise as a whole.[13]

International Recognition of the Problem

Chartered trading companies played a key role in the history of colonial expansion, through entities such as the East India Company and the Hudson's Bay Company, but the perception of TNCs in the early twentieth century was relatively benign. During the 1970s, however, TNCs were feverishly attempting to capitalize on markets outside their domestic sphere and "had become synonymous, around the world, with power and wealth and, to many, a potent symbol of ... economic and political domination" by powerful developed states.[14] With the expansion of TNC operations came concerns about "national sovereignty, democracy and diversity," particularly in newly independent developing host countries.[15] Until the 1970s, very few international regulations were placed on TNCs, particularly on those that were expanding into developing nations, where governments were eager to access capital and technology through foreign direct investment.

As a result of concerns about capitalism's global expansion, during the mid-1970s governments and international organizations began to advocate an international regulatory solution. For example, in 1974, the UN Commission on Transnational Corporations (UNCTC) was established in order to draft a "code of conduct." The text of the draft it produced mandated that TNCs "respect human rights and fundamental freedoms in the countries in which they operate." However, in 1992 the project was abandoned.[16]

In 1977 the International Labour Organization (ILO) released its Tripartite Declaration Concerning Multinational Enterprises and Social Policy, aimed at TNCs as well as governments, employers, and workers organizations. Subsequently amended to incorporate the 1998 ILO Declaration on Fundamental Principles and Rights at Work, the Declaration sets out principles in a range of employment-related areas, including industrial relations, non-discrimination, child labour, workplace conditions, and security of employment, and recommends that these principles be observed on a voluntary basis.[17] The normative standards developed by the ILO continue to be influential both for host state legal reform and as a reference point for TNCs.

In 1976 the Organisation for Economic Co-operation and Development (OECD) released its Guidelines on Multinational Enterprises as an annex to the OECD's Declaration on International Investment and Multinational Enterprises. Adhering states are required to promote the OECD Guidelines to TNCs for voluntary compliance.[18] The Guidelines span many topics from consumer protection to the environment, and have been revised and updated several times; the most recent revision (2011) for the first time explicitly incorporates human rights.[19] Notably, since 2000, each participating country is required to establish a "national contact point" (NCP) charged with contributing to resolution of disputes arising from implementation of the Guidelines. The effectiveness of the NCP process varies considerably depending on the structure of the mechanism, a topic to which we return below in the discussion of non-judicial grievance mechanisms.[20]

International Corporate Criminal Accountability

As noted earlier in this chapter, TNCs may be implicated in egregious rights violations that rise to the level of international crimes. These crimes often occur in the context of countries and communities that are undergoing transitional justice processes after a period of armed conflict. Little advancement has been made in developing mechanisms aimed at holding corporations, as a collective, criminally accountable when they are the perpetrators or aiders and abettors of these crimes.

The traditional international legal system was largely state-centric: states were the creators of international law and states were its subjects. The Nuremberg Military Tribunal after the Second World War represented a momentous shift in this traditional rubric, by making individuals the subjects of international criminal accountability. While this may have appeared to open the door to a broader spectrum of subjects under international criminal law, the list has remained the same since Nuremberg—individuals. Geoffrey Robertson attributes this focus on the prosecution and accountability of individuals to the decision at Nuremberg to prosecute "select individuals as 'representatives' of corporations"[21] rather than impose corporate criminal liability. He suggests that it created a mindset in which we do not necessarily appreciate the fact that individual liability is not always the most effective means of achieving justice. As Mark Drumbl argues, "There are limits to the ability of judicialized determinations of individual criminal culpability to attain postconflict and transitional justice."[22]

In a context where only a few individuals acting outside the scope of their employment have committed crimes, individual liability may be appropriate. However, when TNCs violate human rights, it is more often the case that we need to "address the business corporation as a whole rather than targeting specific individuals,"[23] since it is often difficult, and/or insufficient, to target merely one or a few individual members of the corporation and hold them accountable.

TNCs have elaborate structures consisting of numerous employees, multiple officers and directors, and complicated operating procedures. This means that it can be particularly challenging to identify the individual who possessed the "controlling mind" behind corporate action in a specific operation. The human rights abuses, rather than being the product of the acts or decisions of a single individual, are the product of the corporation as a whole, separate from the individuals behind it—very much in line with the way it is often legally defined (see above). It is also possible that there are "situations where, while a corporation may be to blame for a corporate crime, no individual deserves such blame."[24]

Where factors such as these are at play and a liable individual cannot be found, it is abhorrent if the international (or national) system simply does nothing. Such inaction likely serves only to create a sense of impunity among many TNCs. Where there remains this mentality that an individual can take the fall while business continues as usual, it seems apparent that individual liability is not providing a sufficient deterrent. On this point Joanna Kyriakakis notes, "If deterrence is a key concern,... punishment of the corporate entity directly, as opposed to individuals therein, is more likely to create lasting results."[25] In addition, targeting the corporation as a whole may motivate corporations to improve their internal accountability mechanisms.[26] And pursuing corporations as a whole provides the additional benefit of greater access to financial resources when awarding monetary restitution. Ultimately, if we are truly going to achieve accountability for the human rights abuses in question and seek to address and redress them, then we will often need to turn away from traditional individual-targeted processes and look at the accountability of the corporation as a whole.

As the international community worked to negotiate and draft the Statute for the International Criminal Court (ICC), corporate criminal accountability featured as a point of debate and controversy. Should the Court have jurisdiction over corporations as legal persons, or should its jurisdiction be limited to natural persons—individuals—as had been the practice at the Nuremberg trials and later international tribunals for crimes committed in the former Yugoslavia and Rwanda?[27] Supporters of including corporate liability included France, the United States, and Tanzania.[28] These three supporters are interesting, as they represent different geographic locales, developed and developing nations, and common law and civil law jurisdictions. France was a very strong supporter of criminal jurisdiction over "legal persons,"[29] despite the fact that, as a civil law country, it comes from a legal tradition that historically does not recognize criminal liability for corporations and other legal persons.[30] Meanwhile, Tanzania's memories of "companies that had used their profits to purchase, store and distribute arms that were used in the perpetration of the Rwandan genocide" were still fresh, motivating its support for the inclusion of corporate criminal liability.[31] Finally, the United States, despite strong reservations about creation of the Court as a whole, supported the inclusion of corporate liability throughout treaty negotiations; however, it announced in 2002 that it did not intend to ratify and accept binding legal obligations stemming from ratification of the treaty.[32]

Ultimately, an agreement on including corporations in the ICC's jurisdiction could not be reached by the states participating in treaty negotiations at the Rome Conference. Article 25(1) of the Rome Statute of the International Criminal Court limited the Court's jurisdiction to "natural persons" (that is, individuals).[33] Christina Chiomenti attributes the failure to reach consensus on ICC jurisdiction over corporate crimes to the understanding of many states (and their representatives) as to the distinction between civil and criminal liability: civil liability being seen as a means to redress the situation and criminal liability being seen as seeking to deter.[34] Another obstacle was that some delegations saw little need to go after corporations when they could simply prosecute individuals within the corporation, an argument already evaluated above.[35]

The *redress* versus *deter* argument, while generally accurate as to the aims of civil and criminal liability, does not hold up. While the punishment imposed under criminal law would likely be the same as under civil law in cases of corporate criminal accountability—financial remuneration and recognition of wrongs committed—criminal law carries an additional stigma that is not found in civil lawsuits.[36] Further, it is difficult to see how the crimes at issue do not warrant the deterrent weight of criminal conviction. Rape, torture, genocide, and forced labour are no less criminal and no less abhorrent when committed by a corporation than when they are committed by an individual.

Kai Ambos articulates a further reason for the rejection of corporate criminal liability by the states negotiating the ICC Statute: "there are not yet universally recognized common standards for corporate liability; in fact, the concept is not even recognized in some major criminal law systems."[37] This is indeed true. For instance, the German legal system does not recognize corporate criminal liability, and at the time of the drafting of the ICC Statute, neither did Italian law.[38] However, since the 1998 drafting, corporate criminal accountability has increasingly been recognized in domestic laws.[39] For instance, in 2001 Italy passed a statute creating corporate criminal liability.[40] While national approaches to corporate criminal liability can and do vary,[41] the increasing recognition and incorporation of the concept in national legal systems over the past 15 years suggests a shift in international sentiment, and perhaps potential for renewed debate over bringing the concept into the international legal system.

A focus on international criminal liability for corporations, as opposed to national criminal liability, is crucial because the former does not prevent domestic efforts to hold corporations criminally accountable, while also offering some distinct benefits that a merely national approach does not provide. States do have legal responsibilities to prevent corporations in their jurisdiction from perpetrating violations of human rights.[42] Unfortunately, when it comes to corporations, there are many disincentives to actually enforcing respect for human rights norms. As Matt Phillips notes, "Some governments, to remain competitive in the international marketplace, have become reluctant to unilaterally introduce rules corporations might consider unattractive."[43] If some countries introduce tougher criminal accountability—or even only tougher civil liability—for corporations, there is potential for them to lose much valued foreign investment. International, as opposed to national, criminal liability creates an even playing field, with no additional risk of losing investment to a nation with less stringent standards.[44]

Nonetheless, the decision to exclude legal persons, and thus corporations, from the jurisdiction of the ICC has not stopped states from leaving open the possibility of domestic jurisdiction for international crimes committed by corporations. For example, Canada's Crimes Against Humanity and War Crimes Act, passed in 2000, does not rule out the possibility of trying corporations in Canada for crimes against humanity and war crimes.[45]

There is a strong case for the Statute of the ICC to be amended at a future review conference, to include jurisdiction over crimes committed by corporations. Alternatively, there is a strong case for the creation of a new forum charged with holding corporations accountable for international crimes. Indeed, Geoffrey Robertson has commented on the illogicality of an international system that fails to apply to transnational corporations "whose global activities generate more product and greater influence than many UN member states will ever possess."[46] As TNCs are now broadly recognized as actors in international law, it is necessary for international criminal law to catch up with this recognition and accordingly recognize that corporations have international obligations, and can and should be held accountable for violations of those obligations and violations of international law.

Challenges in Accessing Judicial Remedy

An alternative to the prosecution of TNCs for international crimes or other violations of international human rights laws is a private-law civil action. These are brought directly by the victims in civil (as opposed to criminal) courts, where a damage award is the usual remedy. This section illustrates the challenges of accessing judicial remedy through transnational civil litigation in Canadian courts as well as those in the United States.

Civil Litigation in Canada

It can be challenging for litigants to bring civil actions against Canadian corporations for wrongdoings outside of Canada. In 1997 a public interest group filed a claim against Cambior Inc. for contamination from mine tailings in the Essequibo River in Guyana. However, the Quebec Superior Court dismissed the action because of the doctrine *forum non conveniens*, stating that the courts of Guyana were better suited to deal with the lawsuit.[47] In the case of *Yassin v. Green Park International Inc.*,[48] the Quebec Court of Appeal was hesitant to pass judgement with respect to occupancy of land that was not in Canada, despite the claim that the Canadian construction company was aiding and abetting the State of Israel in building settlements in the occupied territories, in violation of international law. Instead the Court held that an Israeli court was a more appropriate forum for resolution of the dispute.[49]

Attempts to bring novel claims that do not raise jurisdictional issues can also prove challenging. In 2011 plaintiffs from Ecuador brought a civil claim in the Ontario Superior Court of Justice against Copper Mesa Mining Corporation and individual directors resident in Ontario, as well as the Toronto Stock Exchange, "alleging that they suffered injuries, death threats and other intimidation by private security forces hired by [the corporation]."[50] The Ontario Court of Appeal dismissed the case, affirming the lower court's decision that the plaintiffs had failed to seek redress "against proper parties, based on properly pleaded and sustainable causes of action."[51]

On the other hand, in 2013 an Ontario court held that negligence claims against Hudbay Minerals arising from mining operations in Guatemala could proceed to trial in Ontario.[52] The allegations included claims by 11 Q'eqchi' Maya women that they had been gang-raped by mining company security personnel, police, and the military during forced removal from their village. Additional claims related to the death and wounding of two community leaders opposed to the mine.[53] In determining the preliminary motion to strike, the court held that "it was not plain and obvious" that the negligence claims of the plaintiffs were untenable, and that the plaintiffs had "properly pleaded the elements necessary to recognize a novel duty of care."[54] The case is proceeding to trial, and similar cases are increasingly being brought forward in Canada.

Civil Litigation in the United States

In the United States, lawyers creatively revived a statute from 1789 to allow civil claims to be brought on behalf of victims of corporate human rights abuses. The Alien Tort Claims Act (ATCA) reads "The district courts shall have original jurisdiction of any civil action by an alien for a tort only, committed in violation of the law of nations or a treaty of the United States."[55] It was originally drafted to address issues of piracy but was first revived in the 1980s to bring suits against torturers living in the United States or dictators travelling to or through the US.[56] In *Filártiga*, the court read "law of nations" to mean "customary international law" and stated that within customary international law there was a group of human rights and fundamental freedoms, which, for the purposes of the case before them, included a prohibition on torture.

More recently, the ATCA has been employed in attempts to seek accountability and restitution for human rights abuses perpetrated by corporations. Often cases do not involve direct perpetration of crimes by corporations. Rather, the corporations are frequently alleged to have been complicit in or to have aided and abetted the commission of violations of human rights committed by other parties.[57]

Burma: Unocal

Unocal, a California oil and gas company, invested in a project in Burma to build a pipeline to transport gas to Thailand. At this time Burma was a known "military dictatorship accused of violating the human rights of the Burmese people."[58] The Burmese military was contracted by the corporation to provide security for the project. During the course of the project there were reports from international human rights organizations that "the Burmese army was using forced labor and brutalizing the Karen population to provide 'security' for Unocal workers and equipment."[59] In October 1996, members of a Burmese minority group who "alleged that they or their family members had been subjected to relocation, forced labor, torture, murder, and rape on the Yadana pipeline project filed a class action suit against Unocal in a U.S. federal court."[60] The case was ultimately settled out of court.

Nigeria: Wiwa v. Shell

Royal Dutch Shell has spent decades in oil production in Nigeria. As local opposition grew in the area of operation, it was alleged that Nigerian soldiers used deadly force to suppress peaceful protests by the Ogoni people, at the request of Shell and with Shell's assistance.[61] It was further alleged that Shell colluded with the Nigerian military regime in a "strategy that resulted in the executions of nine Ogoni leaders who were working for environmental justice and human rights."[62] A civil case was brought against Shell in the United States under the ATCA by the surviving family members of some Ogoni leaders. In 2009 a settlement was reached in which Shell agreed to pay $15.5 million to the families of environmental activists Ken Saro Wiwa and others who had been tortured and killed by the Nigerian government.[63]

Sudan: Talisman Energy

Talisman Energy, a Canadian oil and gas corporation, participated in oilfields projects in southern Sudan from 1998 to 2003, a period that overlapped with the country's long-running civil war. During this conflict the government of Sudan and its allies "committed well-documented human rights abuses, bombing and strafing villages with gunships, and engaging in raids on civilian populations perceived to be sympathetic to rebel militias."[64] In 2001 a civil lawsuit was brought against the company in the United States under the ATCA, alleging the "company's complicity in the Sudanese Government's human rights abuses against non-Muslim Sudanese living in the area of Talisman's oil concession in southern Sudan and that these abuses amounted to genocide."[65] Talisman, with the support of the Canadian government, unsuccessfully tried to get the case dismissed to Canadian courts.[66] The New York case was ultimately dismissed on the basis of insufficient evidence.[67]

Nigeria: Kiobel v. Shell

This litigation arose from similar facts to those in the *Wiwa v. Shell* case described above, but with different plaintiffs. The result was strikingly different.

Rather than settling the case, Shell chose to litigate, arguing in part that corporations cannot directly violate international law, and therefore could not be subject to the ATCA.[68] Ultimately the United States Supreme Court, rather than determining this question, sought rehearing on the question of whether the ATCA itself violated the presumption against extraterritoriality under US domestic law. The majority of the Court found that it did, as the intention of the drafters of the ATCA was not to provide a forum for resolution of disputes that occurred outside the territory of the United States.[69]

The full fallout of the *Kiobel* decision remains to be seen, but it has considerably circumscribed the potential for the ATCA to be used as a tool for civil remedy of violations of international human rights norms, including against corporate actors. The arguments made by lawyers for Shell in *Kiobel* led John Ruggie, author of the UN's "Protect, Respect and Remedy" Framework and Guiding Principles on Business and Human Rights (described below), to question whether Shell's expansive litigation strategy was consistent with its corporate social responsibility obligations.[70]

Beyond the ATCA: Remedy in State Courts

Despite the attention given to the ATCA in the US context, it is important to recognize that some cases have been brought in state courts under traditional private international law principles, where the law to be applied to settle the dispute is the foreign law rather than international law. An example is the litigation arising from a mining tailings dam spill in the Philippines, originally brought in the courts of Nevada against Placer Dome, a Canadian company, by the Philippine province of Marinduque.[71] After Barrick Gold acquired Placer Dome, the case continued, surviving an attempt to dismiss it to Canadian courts.[72] Settlement negotiations have been attempted, so far unsuccessfully.[73]

Further UN Initiatives

There have been several attempts in the early twenty-first century to address the ongoing problem of TNCs and human rights through the United Nations. In 1999, former UN secretary-general Kofi Annan asked business leaders at the World Economic Forum in Davos to embrace and enact a global compact.[74] The UN Global Compact was established in 2000 with the intent to act as a "strategic platform for participants to advance their commitments to sustainability and corporate citizenship."[75] It comprises "ten universally accepted principles in the areas of human rights, labour, environment and anti-corruption."[76] Because it is a non-binding set of recommendations, adherence to the principles by business participants has been criticized.[77] For example, some corporations are alleged to have repeatedly violated the Compact's principles yet are still able to advertise their commitment to it,[78] as expulsion is the consequence of failure to communicate progress in accordance with the reporting policy.[79] An alternative view of the Global Compact is that its intention is to serve as a learning network rather than a corporate accountability tool. Viewed in this light, participation in the Global Compact helps businesses in all sectors and all parts of the world to better understand what they must do to prevent harm, including human rights violations, with attention to local context provided by local networks.[80]

In 2003, the UN Sub-Commission on the Promotion and Protection of Human Rights approved a draft set of Norms on the Responsibilities of Transnational Corporations.[81] The Norms have been described as a translation of existing state obligations under international human rights law for TNCs.[82] The Sub-Commission recommended the Norms to the UN Commission on Human Rights for further study, but they were rejected and described as having "no legal standing."[83] One notable difference between the UN Norms and other initiatives is the distinction drawn between TNCs and "other business enterprises," a more expansive phrase that includes TNCs.[84] To limit their applicability, the Norms were intended to apply to an enterprise only if it "had any relation with a transnational corporation, if the impact of its activities is not entirely local, or if the activities involve violations of the right to security of persons."[85] An additional distinction between the Norms and other initiatives was the position that TNCs have an obligation to *protect* human rights. As noted by Clapham, this implies that the Norms combined "the obligation to respect rights with an obligation to contribute to their realization by others."[86]

The "Protect, Respect and Remedy" Framework and Guiding Principles on Business and Human Rights

The 2005 appointment of Harvard professor John G. Ruggie as UN Special Representative on Business and Human Rights (SRSG) was designed to move beyond divisive discussions of the merit of the draft Norms. In June 2008, the "Protect, Respect and Remedy" Framework[87] was unanimously welcomed by the UN Human Rights Council, and the SRSG was given a renewed mandate to provide concrete and practical recommendations for its implementation. Both "Protect, Respect and Remedy" and the Guiding Principles on Business and Human Rights, unanimously endorsed by the Human Rights Council in June 2011, were the subject of extensive multi-stakeholder consultations all over the world.[88] Importantly, the Guiding Principles describe their normative contribution as lying "not in the creation of new international law obligations but in elaborating the implications of existing standards and practices for States and businesses; integrating them within a single, logically coherent and comprehensive template; and identifying where the current regime falls short and how it should be improved."[89]

"Protect, Respect and Remedy" and the Guiding Principles apply to all human rights and are designed to "assist all social actors—governments, companies, and civil society—to reduce the adverse human rights consequences of [institutional] misalignments."[90] There are three "differentiated but complementary responsibilities": (1) the state duty to protect against human rights abuses by business enterprises; (2) the corporate responsibility to respect human rights; and (3) the need for greater access by victims to effective remedies. While the state duty to protect is described as lying "at the very core of the international human rights regime," the corporate responsibility to respect is described in non-legal terms as "the basic expectation society has of business in relation to human rights."[91] However, access to remedy by victims is also essential, because "even the most concerted efforts cannot prevent all abuse."[92]

The Guiding Principles follow the template of "Protect, Respect and Remedy," with each pillar described as "an essential component in an inter-related and dynamic system of preventative and remedial measures."[93] Two foundational principles underlie the state duty to protect. Principle 1 provides that "[s]tates must protect against human rights abuse within their territory and/or jurisdiction by third parties, including business enterprises. This requires taking appropriate steps to prevent, investigate, punish and redress such abuse through effective policies, legislation, regulations and adjudication."

According to principle 2, "[s]tates should set out clearly the expectation that all business enterprises domiciled in their territory and/or jurisdiction respect human rights throughout their operations." This principle was highly contested because of disagreement over whether home states are obligated under international human rights law to regulate and adjudicate transnational corporate conduct, or whether, at the other extreme, it is impermissible for them to do so because of the prohibitive jurisdictional rules of public international law.[94]

The operational principles of the state duty to protect are elaborated in principles 4 to 10, within four overarching themes that touch upon both regulation and policy; they include specific guidance on "supporting business respect for human rights in conflict-affected areas" (principle 7)[95] and the need for states to maintain "adequate domestic policy space" and regulatory ability to meet their own human rights obligations, even when pursuing investment treaties or contracts with other states or business enterprises (principle 9).

The corporate responsibility to respect rights is presented in foundational principle 11: "Business enterprises should respect human rights. This means that they should avoid infringing on the human rights of others and should address adverse human rights impacts with which they are involved." It is described as a "global standard of expected conduct for all business enterprises wherever they operate" that is independent of the ability or willingness of states to "fulfil their own human rights obligations." It is also "over and above compliance with national laws and regulations protecting human rights." Importantly, "[b]usiness enterprises should not undermine States' abilities to meet their own human rights obligations, including by actions that might weaken the integrity of judicial processes."[96] The responsibility to respect applies to all "internationally recognized human rights," while the specific rights implicated will depend in part on industry and country context (principle 12).

Under principle 13, the responsibility requires business enterprises to: "(a) Avoid causing or contributing to adverse human right impacts through their own activities, and address such impacts where they occur; (b) Seek to prevent or mitigate adverse human rights impacts that are directly linked to their operations, products or services by their business relationships, even if they have not contributed to those impacts." Importantly, *business relationships* is "understood to include relationships with business partners, entities in its value chain, and any other non-State or State entity directly linked to its business operations, products or services."[97] Moreover, unlike the draft Norms discussed above, principle 14 indicates that the responsibility to respect "applies to all enterprises regardless of their size, operational context, ownership and structure." The "policies and processes" that business enterprises should have in place are a policy commitment, a "human rights due-diligence process," and processes to remediate human rights impacts that the enterprise "caused" or to which it "contributed" (principle 15). Operational principles then expand upon these requirements.[98]

Access to remedy, the third pillar, is informed by a foundational principle 25, which provides as part of the duty to protect that "States must take appropriate steps to ensure, through judicial, administrative, legislative or other appropriate means, that when such abuses occur within their territory and/or jurisdiction those affected have access to effective remedy."

Remedies may include "apologies, restitution, rehabilitation, financial or non-financial compensation and punitive sanctions (whether criminal or administrative, such as fines), as well as the prevention of harm through, for example, injunctions or guarantees of non-repetition." The term *grievance* is defined as "a perceived injustice evoking an individual's or a group's sense of entitlement."[99]

Five operational principles elaborate access to remedy. Principle 26 addresses the need for states to reduce legal and other barriers that "prevent legitimate cases from being brought before the courts" and the need to ensure that the "legitimate and peaceful activities of human rights defenders are not obstructed."[100] Brief reference is also made to the problem of legal barriers created through attribution of responsibility to separate members of a corporate group." Principle 27 suggests that "alongside judicial mechanisms," states should "provide effective and appropriate non-judicial grievance mechanisms ... as part of a comprehensive State-based system for ... remedy."[101]

Access to remedy also includes "non-state-based grievance mechanisms." Principle 28 highlights that states should play a role in facilitating access to effective mechanisms: first, those "administered by a business enterprise alone or with stakeholders, by an industry association or a multi-stakeholder group,"[102] and second, "regional and international human rights bodies," which have at times dealt with a state's failure to meet its own duty to protect.[103] Principle 28 thus highlights that remedy may be sought against the state as well as or instead of the business enterprise.[104] However, by categorizing regional and international human rights mechanisms as non-state-based grievance mechanisms rather than enforcers of international law, the Guiding Principles appear to equate such mechanisms with private company or industry grievance mechanisms, which are discussed in further detail in principles 29 and 30. Finally, principle 31 outlines "effectiveness criteria for non-judicial grievance mechanisms," which should be legitimate, accessible, predictable, equitable, transparent, rights-compatible, and a source of continuous learning.

While "Protect, Respect and Remedy" and the Guiding Principles have been commended for reaching a global consensus on business and human rights for the first time, they have also been the subject of critique, on both process and substantive grounds. For example, Surya Deva is critical of the consensus-based approach taken to inform the substance of the Guiding Principles, suggesting that it has undermined the normative value of human rights through the use of terminology such as *social expectations*, *risk*, and *due diligence*. As a result, the aim of ensuring TNC legal accountability for human rights violations is sacrificed in the interest of securing business support. Deva also criticizes the Guiding Principles for limiting businesses to a responsibility to respect rights, rather than extending to the protection and fulfillment of rights. Finally, he and others are critical of the decision to frame the business principle as a responsibility rather than a duty, with the deliberate intention of avoiding the possibility that it could be construed as a direct legal obligation under international law.[105]

On the other hand, Karin Buhmann's study of the development of the Guiding Principles suggests that business participants were not the only non-state stakeholders whose voices were influential. According to Buhmann, a "discursive strategy that evolved during the process" may be seen to have led to "effective adoption of international policy and law on issues that require a multi-stakeholder approach for their solution," with system-specific language used to appeal to different participants.[106] In her view, this was necessary in order to allow non-state actors whose voices are not directly represented at the Human Rights Council to "contribute expertise, question assumptions and make proposals."[107]

Corporate lawyers were influential in the development of the Guiding Principles, including through a project designed specifically to engage them in mapping the relationship between corporate and securities law and human rights.[108] Ultimately, despite the clear distinction in the Guiding Principles between obligations under international law and the responsibility to respect, scholars such as Peter Muchlinski suggest that domestic legal implications will inevitably flow from the due diligence processes under the responsibility to respect, whether or not this was the understanding of those who endorsed the Guiding Principles.[109] This binding domestic legal status is likely to emerge in many forms, including through directors' duties under corporate law and as part of the standard of care to which businesses are held in domestic private law tort actions such as the *Hudbay* case, noted above.

It remains to be seen how much influence the Guiding Principles will ultimately have. There are signs that an increasing number of TNCs are adopting human rights policies and engaging in human rights due diligence, steps that, if properly undertaken, will help to prevent future human rights violations from occurring. Moreover, the legal profession has begun to take notice, realizing that the responsibility to respect has implications for their role when advising business clients.[110] However, while the Guiding Principles have value as a preventive tool, the quest for corporate accountability for violations of human rights remains. The ultimate challenge will be for businesses and their lawyers to take seriously the importance of not undermining the ability of states to protect human rights, including the right of access to remedy.

Non-Judicial Remedies and Grievance Mechanisms

The challenges of accessing judicial remedy and accountability have been discussed above. "Protect, Respect and Remedy" and the Guiding Principles highlight that non-judicial remedies, including company-level mechanisms, are equally important to consider. These may take many forms, and they have met with mixed success to date.[111] Commonly cited examples include state-based processes such as the national contact point (NCP) for the OECD Guidelines, briefly noted above,[112] and Canada's Corporate Social Responsibility Counsellor for the Extractive Industries Operating Internationally,[113] as well as non-state-based mechanisms such as the International Finance Corporation's compliance advisor ombudsperson.[114] Many of these instruments have been updated to reflect the new expectations for human rights due diligence incorporated in the Guiding Principles.[115]

The relationship between these processes and state law is complex and as yet not fully explored, but there are signs that effective transnational non-judicial grievance mechanisms may have a positive influence on host-state compliance with international human rights law.[116] For example, even though the outcome of an OECD NCP process cannot compel a company to comply with the violated guideline, a finding of non-compliance by a foreign NCP may spur a host state's domestic court to take seriously allegations it might otherwise ignore (to date there is only anecdotal evidence of this link). Nevertheless, it is clear that this type of influence can arise only if the structure of the non-judicial mechanism is itself sufficiently strong. To date this has not been the case with regard to Canadian mechanisms, which are frequently criticized as weak and overly reliant on voluntary participation.[117]

One of the most innovative aspects of the Guiding Principles is the discussion of operational-level grievance mechanisms. The Principles are clear that for them to be effective they should be "[b]ased upon engagement and dialogue: consulting the stakeholder groups for whose use they are intended on their design and performance, and focusing on dialogue as the means to address and resolve grievances."[118] Furthermore,

> For an operational-level grievance mechanism, engaging with affected stakeholder groups about its design and performance can help to ensure that it meets their needs, that they will use it in practice, and that there is a shared interest in ensuring its success. Since a business enterprise cannot, with legitimacy, both be the subject of complaints and unilaterally determine their outcome, these mechanisms should focus on reaching agreed solutions through dialogue. Where adjudication is needed, this should be provided by a legitimate, independent third-party mechanism.[119]

Examples of company-level grievance mechanisms, as well as company-funded but independent remedy mechanisms, are increasingly emerging as shared learning encourages new attempts.[120] However, how to reconcile the outcomes of these non-judicial, non-state, non-law mechanisms with the rule of state law is contested, highlighted by controversy over requirements to sign legal waivers to prevent future civil claims as a condition of accessing non-judicial remedy.[121]

Truth and Reconciliation Commissions and Citizens' Tribunals

The remedy mechanisms identified in "Protect, Respect and Remedy" and the Guiding Principles are not the only possibilities. Two additional ideas to consider are truth and reconciliation commissions (TRCs) and citizens' tribunals.

TRCs are a non-judicial mechanism for redressing mass violations of human rights in a state over a period of time. While they are created by the state and their mandate is provided by the state, once established, they operate relatively independently from the state. They examine diverse human rights violations over time with an emphasis on collecting victim testimonies in an effort to develop an accurate account of the violations that occurred. Ultimately a TRC prepares a report outlining the truth it has discovered through its fact-finding mission and offers recommendations on reforms, reparations, and steps needed to avoid recurrence of human rights violations and to allow society to move forward. While uncommon, a few, including the South African TRC, have looked at corporate involvement in human rights violations.[122] Unfortunately, their recommendations regarding corporations have achieved very limited results.[123]

Citizens' tribunals have emerged as a grassroots form of non-judicial remedy designed to provide a creative way to address the need of victims and communities to tell their stories and find judgement, albeit non-legal, against TNCs that they allege have perpetrated human rights violations. According to Craig Borowiak, they "originate with a judgment that states and/or international organizations have failed to meet their normative and legal obligations to uphold justice."[124] In the face of these failures, citizens band together to adopt "the juridical form of a trial or commission, with the presentation of evidence through public testimonies followed by an analysis by a 'jury' … or 'panel of experts.'"[125] Through the use of public hearings and publicity they attempt to bring attention not only to the harms they have suffered but also to the failure of national and international law to address those harms. These tribunals have no official mandate or sponsorship; rather, they are a realization of grassroots community efforts to find solutions that meet people's personal justice needs in the circumstances in which they exist. The tribunals do ultimately pass judgement on the entities they accuse of perpetrating the harms, as well as (sometimes) the national and international entities that have failed to take official action.[126]

A citizens' tribunal was held in Guatemala in July 2012 to address human rights violations allegedly perpetrated against the community of San Miguel Ixtahuacá and stemming from operations at the Marlin Mine by a subsidiary corporation of the Canadian company Goldcorp. The community formed the tribunal and conducted public hearings over two days, featuring testimony from community members and expert witnesses, including doctors, health experts, academics, human rights advocates, and experts on mining and the environment. Testimonies were delivered before a panel of 13 judges: laypeople from the fields of human rights, environmental advocacy, science, medicine, and anthropology. A written judgement was produced that found Goldcorp guilty of human rights abuses. The verdict was published online and copies were delivered to the Guatemalan government and the Canadian embassy in Guatemala. Goldcorp's offices in Guatemala and Canada refused to accept a copy of the verdict.[127]

A Treaty?

Despite the consensus that appeared to exist with the wide endorsement of the UN's "Protect, Respect and Remedy" and Guiding Principles for Business and Human Rights, there has been increasing pressure to pursue a traditional international law route to address the ongoing problem of transnational corporate accountability—a binding treaty on business and human rights. A binding multilateral agreement does exist, mandating state parties to ensure the prosecution of anti-bribery and anti-corruption offences involving foreign officials, although enforcement was weak in Canada until very recently.[128]

In 2013 the Government of Ecuador proposed that a legally binding treaty be developed within the United Nations system, a proposal that led to endorsement of a resolution at the UN Human Rights Council in June 2014 to explore whether such an instrument could be negotiated.[129] At the same time, John Ruggie, who was responsible for developing the Guiding Principles, urged caution, saying that the treaty route could "end in largely symbolic gestures, of little practical use to real people in real places."[130] It is not surprising that Ecuador has taken the lead role in proposing a binding treaty, given the notorious, long-standing and still unresolved civil dispute over oil pollution in the Amazon associated with operations by Texaco (now Chevron).[131] The possible outcome of the treaty track is unclear at this time.

Proposals have also been made recently for establishment of a World Court of Human Rights, which would be responsible for hearing cases arising under 21 UN human rights treaties, including cases against TNCs that chose to be subject to its jurisdiction.[132] However, the logistics and practicality of such a proposal remain contested.[133]

Conclusion

This chapter has explored the nature of the transnational corporation, United Nations efforts to develop a code of conduct for TNCs, and debates over international corporate criminal liability in drafting of the Statute of the International Criminal Court. The challenges of accessing remedy through transnational civil litigation in Canadian and US courts were then explored. The three pillars of the "Protect, Respect and Remedy" Framework and Guiding Principles on Business and Human Rights were outlined in detail. The chapter concluded with reflections on the role of non-judicial remedy mechanisms, alternative justice and healing tools, and proposals for a binding international treaty.

The recent proposal to seek a multilateral treaty to ensure corporate accountability for human rights abuses perpetrated by TNCs reflects a tendency to seek a single, overarching solution to a very complex problem. TNCs operate with ease across the territorial boundaries of nation-states but in the human rights context often appear immune from liability and accountability, both at home and abroad as well as directly under international law. While dependent for their existence on the contents of the statutory laws that give them legal personality, TNCs are often very powerful—some even more powerful than some states.

Ultimately it remains to be seen whether businesses, including powerful TNCs, and their lawyers will fully embrace the responsibility to respect identified in the Guiding Principles. To do so would require not only implementing human rights policies and conducting human rights due diligence but also grappling with the imperative of not undermining the ability of the state to embrace its own duty to protect rights, including the right of victims to access judicial remedy and seek accountability for wrongdoing. While at first glance it may seem hopelessly idealistic to suggest that powerful TNCs might choose to operate as social enterprises,[134] this ideal may seem less unreachable if we remember that TNCs are made up of individuals who engage collectively in the business enterprise.

Takeaway Messages

- The UN Guiding Principles have created a normative expectation that businesses respect international human rights by implementing a policy, undertaking human rights due diligence, and enabling remedy for victims.
- Currently there is no international criminal legal forum in which to hold TNCs accountable for egregious human rights violations, and states appear reluctant to prosecute allegations of TNC misconduct, including the aiding and abetting of host-state violations in conflict-affected areas.
- Access to civil remedy for violations of international human rights by businesses is challenging, no matter what the nature of the allegations. Lack of access to legal remedy has led to a proliferation of non-judicial grievance and remedy mechanisms, including company-level and citizens' tribunals.

Study Questions

- What are the three pillars of the UN Guiding Principles? What should states do? What should businesses do?
- Why are businesses not subject to the International Criminal Court's jurisdiction? Should they be?
- What challenges do victims face in seeking remedy against TNCs for violations of their human rights? Can non-judicial remedies adequately address these harms?

Issues for Debate or Roundtable

- To meet their responsibility to respect human rights, businesses must undertake due diligence that may require conducting a human rights impact assessment (HRIA). Is it possible for a human rights impact assessment to undermine respect for human rights? Is it inevitably a useful tool? Compare these two experiences: Nestlé, the global food and beverage giant, in 2008 formed a partnership with the Danish Institute for Human Rights to assess its overall human rights compliance in the countries where it operates.[135] Goldcorp, a global mining TNC, conducted an HRIA of a mine in Guatemala as a result of a shareholder proposal from a group of socially responsible investors;[136] it was subject to criticism for not having adequately incorporated the perspective of the affected communities into the HRIA process itself.[137]

- A business's responsibility to respect is said to be independent of a host state's compliance with its own duty to protect rights. Should home-state regulation of TNCs play an important role in filling the "governance gaps" left by host-state incapacity or unwillingness to regulate? Or will corporate power and lobbying inevitably undermine efforts to extend home-state law to address TNC violations internationally? Consider the Canadian experience with the failure of Bill C-300,[138] a bill designed to ensure that Canadian mining companies operating internationally respect human rights or risk the loss of taxpayer-supported benefits.

Additional Reading

Simons, Penelope, and Audrey Macklin. *The Governance Gap: Extractive Industries, Human Rights, and the Home State Advantage*. London: Routledge, 2013.

Kerr, Michael, Richard Janda, and Chip Pitts. *Corporate Social Responsibility: A Legal Analysis*. LexisNexis, 2009.

Ratner, Stephen. "Corporations and Human Rights: A Theory of Legal Responsibility." *Yale Law Journal* 111, no. 3 (2001): 443–545. http://dx.doi.org/10.2307/797542.

Baxi, Upendra. "Mass Torts, Multinational Enterprise Liability, and Private International Law," *Recueil des cours* 276 (1999).

Websites

Business and Human Rights Resource Centre. http://business-humanrights.org/.

OHCHR, "Business and Human Rights." http://www.ohchr.org/EN/Issues/Business/Pages/BusinessIndex.aspx.

Global Business Initiative on Human Rights. http://www.global-business-initiative.org/.

Notes

1. The term *transnational corporation* (TNC) is here used interchangeably with *multinational corporation* (MNC), *multinational enterprise* (MNE), and *transnational business*.
2. A. Clapham, *Human Rights Obligations of Non-State Actors* (Oxford: Oxford University Press, 2006).
3. C. Albin-Lackey, "Without Rules: A Failed Approach to Corporate Accountability," in Human Rights Watch, *World Report 2013: Events of 2012* (New York: Human Rights Watch, 2013), 29–40, http://www.hrw.org/sites/default/files/reports/wr2013.pdf.
4. Ibid.
5. L.E. Strine, Jr., "Our Continuing Struggle with the Idea That For-Profit Corporations Seek Profit," *Wake Forest Law Review* 47 (2012): 135.
6. UN Human Rights Committee, *Report of the Special Rapporteur on the Rights of Indigenous Peoples, James Anaya: Extractive Industries and Indigenous Peoples*, UN Doc A/HRC/21/41 (Geneva: UNHRC, 2013).

7. For examples of responses to health and safety concerns arising from the recent Bangladesh garment factory fires, see Bangladesh Accord Foundation, Accord on Fire and Building Safety in Bangladesh, 2013, http://www.bangladeshaccord.org/wp-content/uploads/2013/10/the_accord.pdf; and Alliance for Bangladesh Worker Safety, "About the Alliance for Bangladesh Worker Safety," 2013, http://www.bangladeshworkersafety.org/who-we-are/about-the-alliance.
8. See, for example, R. Deibert, J. Palfrey, R. Rohozinski, and J. Zittrain, eds., *Access Denied: The Practice and Policy of Global Internet Filtering* (Cambridge, MA: MIT Press, 2008).
9. R. Yalden, J. Sarra, P. Paton, et al. *Business Organizations: Principles, Policies, and Practice* (Toronto: Emond Montgomery, 2008), 133–35.
10. *Salomon v. A. Salomon & Co. Ltd* (1896), [1897] AC 22 HL (Eng), quoted in ibid., 135–47.
11. Yalden et al., *Business Organizations*, 167–68.
12. See C.D. Wallace, *The Multinational Enterprise and Legal Control: Host State Sovereignty in an Era of Globalization* (The Hague: Kluwer Law, 2002), 102–3.
13. L.C. Backer, "Multinational Corporations as Objects and Sources of Transnational Regulation," *ILSA Journal of International and Comparative Law* 14, no. 2 (2008): 509–21.
14. J.A. Zerk, *Multinationals and Corporate Social Responsibility* (Cambridge: Cambridge University Press, 2011), 9. See also A. Anghie, *Imperialism, Sovereignty and the Making of International Law* (Cambridge: Cambridge University Press, 2005), 67–69; and R. Vernon, *Sovereignty at Bay: The Multinational Spread of US Enterprise* (New York: Basic Books, 1971).
15. Zerk, *Multinationals*, 9–10, 244.
16. Ibid., 245–48. See also United Nations Intellectual History Project, "The UN and Transnational Corporations," Briefing Note no. 17, July 2009, http://www.unhistory.org/briefing/17TNCs.pdf.
17. Zerk, *Multinationals*, 254–57. See, generally, International Labour Organization, Tripartite Declaration of Principles Concerning Multinational Enterprises and Social Policy (Geneva: ILO, 2006), http://www.ilo.org/wcmsp5/groups/public/---ed_emp/---emp_ent/---multi/documents/publication/wcms_094386.pdf.
18. Zerk, *Multinationals*, 248–54.
19. Organisation for Economic Co-operation and Development, *OECD Guidelines for Multinational Enterprises, 2011 Edition* (Washington, DC: OECD, 2011), http://www.oecd-ilibrary.org/governance/oecd-guidelines-for-multinational-enterprises_9789264115415-en.
20. OECD Watch, "Performance of National Contact Points and the Implementation of the OECD Guidelines in the 2012–2013 Implementation Cycle," June 2013, http://oecdwatch.org/publications-en/Publication_4080/.
21. G. Robertson, *Crimes Against Humanity: The Struggle for Global Justice* (London: Penguin, 2006), 187.
22. M.A. Drumbl, "Collective Responsibility and Post-Conflict Justice," in *Accountability for Collective Wrongdoing*, ed. T. Isaacs and R. Vernon (Cambridge: Cambridge University Press, 2011), 24.
23. A. Voiculescu, "Changing Paradigms of Corporate Criminal Responsibility: Lessons for Corporate Social Responsibility," in *The New Corporate Accountability:*

Corporate Social Responsibility and the Law, ed. D. McBarnet, A. Voiculescu, and T. Campbell (Cambridge: Cambridge University Press, 2007), 399.
24. Ibid., 407–8. This could arise when the directors and officers responsible for developing blameworthy policy were no longer with the company, for example.
25. J. Kyriakakis, "Corporations and the ICC: The Complementarity Objection Stripped Bare," *Criminal Law Forum* 19 (2008): 149.
26. Ibid.
27. Ibid. See also C. Chiomenti, "Corporations and the International Criminal Court," in *Transnational Corporations and Human Rights*, ed. O. de Schutter (Portland, OR: Hart, 2006), 287.
28. Kyriakakis, "Corporations and the ICC," 143–44. See also Chiomenti, "Corporations and the International Criminal Court," 290.
29. K. Ambos, "Article 25: Individual Criminal Responsibility," in *Commentary on the Rome Statute of the International Criminal Court*, ed. O. Triffterer (Baden-Baden, Germany: Nomos, 1999), 477.
30. S. Tully, "International Criminal Law," in *International Corporate Legal Responsibility*, ed. S. Tully (The Hague: Kluwer Law, 2012), 452.
31. Kyriakakis, "Corporations and the ICC," 143–44; Chiomenti, "Corporations and the International Criminal Court," 290.
32. US Department of State, "International Criminal Court: Letter to UN Secretary General Kofi Annan," news release, 6 May 2002, http://2001-2009.state.gov/r/pa/prs/ps/2002/9968.htm.
33. UN Diplomatic Conference of Plenipotentiaries on the Establishment of an International Criminal Court, Rome Statute of the International Criminal Court, 1998, UN Doc. A/CONF. 183/9.
34. Chiomenti, "Corporations and the International Criminal Court," 293.
35. Kyriakakis, "Corporations and the ICC," 148.
36. R.C. Slye, "Corporations, Veils, and International Criminal Liability," *Brooklyn Journal of International Law* 33 (August 2007): 970–72.
37. Ambos, "Article 25," 478.
38. Tully, "International Criminal Law," 452.
39. See, generally, M. Pieth and R. Ivory, eds., *Corporate Criminal Liability: Emergence, Convergence, and Risk* (Dordrecht, Netherlands: Springer, 2011).
40. Voilescu, "Changing Paradigms," 421–22.
41. Pieth and Ivory, *Corporate Criminal Liability*, 39.
42. Kyriakakis, "Corporations and the ICC," 145.
43. M. Phillips, "Global Rules for Corporate Accountability: The Proposal to Establish a Corporate Accountability Convention," *Multinational Monitor* 23, no. 10 (October/November 2002).
44. Kyriakakis, "Corporations and the ICC," 148.
45. See, for example, W.C. Wanless, "Corporate Liability for International Crimes under Canada's Crimes Against Humanity and War Crimes Act," *Journal of International Criminal Justice* 7, no. 1 (2009).
46. Kyriakakis, "Corporations and the ICC," 186.
47. *Recherches Internationales Québec c. Cambior Inc.*, [1999] RJQ 1581 (Qc Sup Ct), at para. 10.
48. *Yassin c. Green Park International Inc.*, [2010] RJQ 15646 (Qc CA).

49. Ibid., at para. 75–80. For another case with different facts but a similar result, see *Anvil Mining Ltd. c. Association canadienne contre l'impunité*, [2011] RJQ 6588 (Qc CA), accepting jurisdiction to hear the case, but see *Anvil Mining Ltd c. Association canadienne contre l'impunité*, [2012] RJQ 368 (Qc CA), determining that the case cannot be heard in Québec.
50. *Piedra v. Copper Mesa Mining Corp.*, 2010 ONSC 2421, aff'd 2011 ONCA 191.
51. *Piedra v. Copper Mesa Mining Corp.*, 2011 ONCA 191, para. 99.
52. *Choc v. Hudbay Minerals Inc.*, 2013 ONSC 1414.
53. Ibid., at para. 4–7. See also the summary of the lawsuits on the plaintiffs' website, http://www.chocversushudbay.com/about#Summary%20of%20Choc.
54. *Choc v. Hudbay Minerals*, at para. 75. See also Business and Human Rights Resource Center, "Nevsun Lawsuit (re Bisha Mine, Eritrea)," http://business-humanrights.org/en/nevsun-lawsuit-re-bisha-mine-eritrea; and "Tahoe Resources Lawsuit (re Guatemala)," http://business-humanrights.org/en/tahoe-resources-lawsuit-re-guatemala.
55. Alien Tort Statue, 28 USC sec. 1350 (1789).
56. See, for example, *Filártiga v. Peña-Irala*, 630 F (2d) 876 (2d Cir 1980).
57. See, for example, International Commission of Jurists, *Report of the ICJ Expert Legal Panel on Corporate Complicity in International Crimes: Corporate Complicity and Legal Accountability,* vol. 2, *Criminal Law and International Crimes* (Geneva: ICJ, 2008), http://www.refworld.org/docid/4a78423f2.html.
58. *Doe v. Unocal Corp*, 395 F (3d) 932 (9th Cir 2002), opinion vacated and rehearing *en banc* granted, 395 F (3d) 978 (9th Cir 2003), as discussed in M. Velasquez, "Unocal in Burma," Markkula Center for Applied Ethics, Santa Clara University, 3 November 2004, http://www.scu.edu/ethics/practicing/focusareas/business/Unocal-in-Burma.html.
59. Velasquez, "Unocal in Burma."
60. Ibid.
61. See EarthRights International, "Wiwa v. Royal Dutch Shell," http://www.earthrights.org/legal/wiwa-v-royal-dutchshell/; Center for Constitutional Rights, *Wiwa et al. v. Royal Dutch Petroleum Company et al.*: Complaint, 2006, http://dg5vd3ocj3r4t.cloudfront.net/sites/default/files/legal/Wiwa-Original-Complaint_0.pdf.
62. EarthRights International, "Wiwa."
63. Ibid. The settlement was made without admission of wrongdoing.
64. EarthRights International, "Amicus Brief in *Presbyterian Church of Sudan v. Talisman Energy*," http://www.earthrights.org/publication/amicus-brief-presbyterian-church-sudan-v-talisman-energy.
65. Business and Human Rights Resource Centre, "Talisman Lawsuit (re Sudan)," 18 February 2014, http://business-humanrights.org/en/talisman-lawsuit-re-sudan#c9318.
66. *Presbyterian Church of Sudan v. Talisman Energy, Inc.*, (30 August 2005), New York No. 01 Civ 9882 (DLC) (SD NY 2005), at 1, discussing a diplomatic note from the Canadian embassy to the US government; Brief of Amicus Curiae: The Government of Canada in Support of Dismissal of the Underlying Action, *Presbyterian Church of Sudan v. Talisman Energy Inc.*, No. 01-9882 (2nd Cir 8 May 2007).
67. *Presbyterian Church of Sudan v. Talisman Energy Inc.*, 582 F (3d) 244 (2nd Cir 2009), upholding dismissal on summary judgement motion. The plaintiffs petitioned

for writ of *certiorari* to the US Court of Appeals, 2nd Circuit, in October 2010, which was denied.

68. *Kiobel v. Royal Dutch Petroleum Co.*, 621 F (3d) 111 (2nd Cir 2010), aff'd, 133 S Ct 1659 (2013).
69. *Kiobel v. Royal Dutch Petroleum* 569 US (2013). See also L.C. Backer, "Sara Seck on '*Kiobel* and the E-word: Reflections on Transnational Environmental Responsibility in an Interconnected World,'" *Law at the End of the Day* [blog], 5 July 2013, http://lcbackerblog.blogspot.ca/2013/07/sara-seck-on-kiobel-and-e-word.html; Business and Human Rights Resource Centre, "Kiobel Case: US Supreme Court Review of Alien Tort Claims Act," http://www.business-humanrights.org/Documents/SupremeCourtATCAReview.
70. J.G. Ruggie, "Kiobel and Corporate Social Responsibility," issues brief, 4 September 2012, John F. Kennedy School of Government, Harvard University, http://www.hks.harvard.edu/content/download/66095/1237190/version/1/file/KIOBEL+AND+CORPORATE+SOCIAL+RESPONSIBILITY%281%29.pdf.
71. M. Harrison, "Barrick Gold Using Coercive Settlement Provisions to Perpetuate Legacy of Environmental Harm," EarthRights International, 31 March 2014, http://www.earthrights.org/blog/barrick-gold-using-coercive-settlement-provisions-perpetuate-legacy-environmental-harm.
72. *Provincial Gov't of Marinduque v. Placer Dome Inc.*, 582 F (3d) 1083 (9th Cir 2009), reversing dismissal on *forum non conveniens* and act-of-state doctrine.
73. Harrison, "Barrick Gold."
74. Clapham, *Human Rights Obligations*, 218.
75. United Nations Global Compact, "Participation," https://www.unglobalcompact.org/participation.
76. UN Global Compact, "About the UN Global Compact," https://www.unglobalcompact.org/about.
77. Clapham, *Human Rights Obligations*, 225.
78. S. Deva, "Treating Human Rights Lightly: A Critique of the Consensus Rhetoric and the Language Employed by the Guiding Principles," in *Human Rights Obligations of Business: Beyond the Corporate Responsibility to Respect?* ed. S. Deva and D. Bilchitz (London: Routledge, 2012), 92.
79. UN Global Compact, "Expelled Participants," https://www.unglobalcompact.org/participation/report/cop/create-and-submit/expelled.
80. A. Rasche and D.U. Gilbert, "Institutionalizing Global Governance: The Role of the United Nations Global Compact," *Business Ethics: A European Review* 21, no. 1 (2012): 100–14; A. Rasche, S. Waddock, and M. McIntosh, "The United Nations Global Compact: Retrospect and Prospect," *Business and Society* 52, no. 1 (2012): 6–30.
81. UN Sub-Commission on the Promotion and Protection of Human Rights, *Norms on the Responsibilities of Transnational Corporations and Other Business Enterprises with Regard to Human Rights*, UN Doc E/CN.4/Sub.2/2003/12/Rev.2 (New York: UN Economic and Social Council, 2003); D. Weissbrodt and M. Kruger, "Norms on the Responsibilities of Transnational Corporations and Other Business Enterprises with Regard to Human Rights," *American Journal of International Law* 97 (2003): 901.
82. Zerk, *Multinationals*, 261.

83. Commission on Human Rights, *Report on Sixtieth Session*, UN Doc E/4/2004/73/Rev.1 (New York: UNHCR, 2004), para. (c).
84. Ibid., para. 20.
85. Ibid., para. 21.
86. Clapham, *Human Rights Obligations*, 231.
87. UN Human Rights Council, "Promotion and Protection of All Human Rights, Civil, Political, Economic, Social and Cultural Rights, Including the Right to Development [Protect, Respect, Remedy]," 7 April 2008, UN Doc A/HRC/8/5.
88. UN Human Rights Council, "Report of the Special Representative of the Secretary-General on the Issues of Human Rights and Transnational Corporations and Other Business Enterprises, John Ruggie [Guiding Principles]," 21 March 2011, UN Doc A/HRC/17/31, paras. 7–8, 12. See also three addenda: "Piloting Principles for Effective Company/Stakeholder Grievance Mechanisms," 24 May 2011, UN Doc A/HRC/17/3/Add.1; "Human Rights and Corporate Law," 2011, UN Doc A/HRC/17/31/Add.2; and "Principles for Responsible Contracts," 2011, UN Doc A/HRC/17/31/Add.3. See, further, Business and Human Rights Resource Centre, "UN Secretary-General's Special Representative on Business and Human Rights," http://business-humanrights.org/en/un-secretary-generals-special-representative-on-business-human-rights.
89. Guiding Principles, para. 14.
90. Protect, Respect, Remedy, paras. 7, 17.
91. Ibid., paras. 9, 55.
92. Ibid., para. 82.
93. Guiding Principles, para. 6.
94. See, further, S.L. Seck, "Canadian Mining Internationally and the UN Guiding Principles for Business and Human Rights," *Canadian Yearbook of International Law* 49 (2011): 107–12.
95. See, further, J. Ruggie, "Report of the Special Representative of the Secretary-General on the Issue of Human Rights and Transnational Corporations and Other Business Enterprises," 27 May 2011, UN Doc A/HRC/17/32.
96. Guiding Principles, Commentary on Principle 11.
97. Ibid., commentary on principle 13. See, further, principle 17(a) on human rights due diligence.
98. Ibid., principles 16–21. Notably, human rights due diligence is said to go beyond risks to the company to include "risks to rights-holders," and it is distinguished from legal liability; commentary on principle 17.
99. Ibid., commentary on principle 25. A grievance may be based on "law, contract, explicit or implicit promises, customary practice, or general notions of fairness of aggrieved communities."
100. Ibid., commentary on principle 26.
101. Ibid., principle 27. Notably, judicial remedy "is not always required; nor is it always" the approach favoured by claimants "even where judicial systems are effective and well-resourced." Consequently, there is an "essential role" for "[a]dministrative, legislative, and other non-judicial mechanisms" as a complement and supplement to judicial mechanisms.
102. Ibid., principle 28 and commentary. According to the commentary, non-state-based grievance mechanisms administered by business enterprises offer potential

benefits, including "transnational reach." The commentary also notes that non-state-based grievance mechanisms are "non-judicial, but may use adjudicative, dialogue-based or other culturally appropriate and rights-compatible processes."

103. Ibid., commentary on principle 28.
104. S.L. Seck, "Collective Responsibility and Transnational Corporate Conduct," in *Accountability for Collective Wrongdoing*, ed. R. Vernon and T. Isaacs (Cambridge: Cambridge University Press, 2011), 158–59: discussing with respect to Protect, Respect, Remedy.
105. See, especially, Deva, "Treating Human Rights," 78–104; and P. Simons, "International Law's Invisible Hand and the Future of Corporate Accountability for Violations of Human Rights," *Journal of Human Rights and the Environment* 3, no. 1 (2012): 5.
106. K. Buhmann, "Navigating from 'Train Wreck' to Being 'Welcomed': Negotiation Strategies and Argumentative Patterns in the Development of the UN Framework," in *Regulating Corporate Human Rights Violations: Humanizing Business*, ed. S. Deva and D. Bilchitz (London: Routledge, 2012), 55–56.
107. Ibid., 57.
108. S.L. Seck, "Corporate Law Tools and the Guiding Principles for Business and Human Rights," in *Business and Human Rights*, ed. M.K. Sinha (London: Sage, 2013), 93–130. Co-author Sara Seck contributed to this aspect of the Ruggie mandate, co-convening a multi-stakeholder consultation on the subject in Toronto in 2010.
109. P. Muchlinski, "Implementing the New UN Human Rights Framework: Implications for Corporate Law, Governance and Regulation," *Business Ethics Quarterly* 22, no. 1 (2012): 145–77.
110. International Bar Association, "Business and Human Rights Guidance for Bar Associations," working draft, 2014, http://www.ibanet.org/Article/Detail.aspx?ArticleUid=f906f28f-a2ee-4adc-a0a6-e5dc19032271.
111. E. Morgera, *Corporate Accountability in International Environmental Law* (Oxford: Oxford University Press, 2009), chs. 10 and 11.
112. See Foreign Affairs, Trade and Development Canada, "Canada's National Contact Point (NCP) for the Organisation for Economic Co-operation and Development (OECD) Guidelines for Multinational Enterprises (MNEs)," http://www.international.gc.ca/trade-agreements-accords-commerciaux/ncp-pcn/index.aspx?lang=eng&menu_id=1&menu=R.
113. See Seck, "Canadian Mining," 79–85; Foreign Affairs, Trade and Development Canada, "Canada's Enhanced Corporate Social Responsibility Strategy to Strengthen Canada's Extractive Sector Abroad," 2014, http://www.international.gc.ca/trade-agreements-accords-commerciaux/topics-domaines/other-autre/csr-strat-rse.aspx?lang=eng.
114. Morgera, *Corporate Accountability*, 216–22; Compliance Advisor Ombudsman, "Our Mandate," http://www.cao-ombudsman.org/. The CAO references the International Finance Corporation (IFC) Sustainability Framework, including its Performance Standards, compliance with which may be a contractual requirement for access to financing; International Finance Corporation, *IFC Performance Standards on Environmental and Social Sustainability*, 1 January 2012, http://www.ifc.org/wps/wcm/connect/c8f524004a73daeca09afdf998895a12/IFC_Performance_Standards.pdf?MOD=AJPERES.

115. For example, the OECD MNE Guidelines and IFC Sustainability Performance Standards were both updated in 2011. See OECD, *2011 Update of the OECD Guidelines for Multinational Enterprises: Comparative Table of Changes Made to the 2000 Text* (Washington: OECD, 2011), http://www.oecd.org/en/daf/inv/mne/49744860.pdf.
116. L.C. Backer, "Governance Without Government: An Overview," in *Beyond Territoriality: Transnational Legal Authority in an Age of Globalization*, ed. G. Teubner, J. Zekoll, and P. Zumbansen (Leiden: Martinus Nijhoff, 2012), 133–38, describing the relationship between the UK's NCP process and the courts and government of India with regard to the Vedanta Mine proposal. For more, see Business and Human Rights Resource Centre, "Vedanta Resources Lawsuit (re Dongria Kondh in Orissa)," http://business-humanrights.org/en/vedanta-resources-lawsuit-re-dongria-kondh-in-Orissa.
117. See Seck, "Canadian Mining," 79–85; OECD Watch, "Performance of National Contact Points."
118. Guiding Principles, principle 31.
119. Ibid., commentary on principle 31.
120. See, for example, ACCESS Facility, "About ACCESS," http://www.accessfacility.org/. It is described as "an independent platform for a broad range of stakeholders to learn, explore, share ideas, forge relationships, and find solutions that work for them." The site's "Case Study Library" (http://www.accessfacility.org/case-stories) contains 185 entries featuring a wide variety of non-judicial grievance mechanisms, including both state- and non-state-based.
121. C. Coumans, "Brief on Concerns Related to Project-Level Non-Judicial Grievance Mechanisms" (Ottawa: MiningWatch Canada, 2014), http://www.miningwatch.ca/sites/www.miningwatch.ca/files/brief_on_njgms_access_meeting_april_2014_final.pdf. See also Office of the High Commissioner for Human Rights, "Re: Allegations Regarding the Porgera Joint Venture Remedy Framework" (Geneva: OHCHR, 2013), http://business-humanrights.org/sites/default/files/media/ohchr-porgera-joint-venture-letter-aug-2013.pdf.
122. See S. Michalowski, ed., *Corporate Accountability in the Context of Transitional Justice* (New York: Routledge, 2013).
123. See C. Sandoval and G. Surfleet, "Corporations and Redress in Transitional Justice Processes," in *Corporate Accountability in the Context of Transitional Justice*, ed. S. Michalowski (New York: Routledge, 2013), 93.
124. C. Borowiak, "The World Tribunal on Iraq: Citizens' Tribunals and the Struggle for Accountability," *New Political Science* 30, no. 2 (2008): 165.
125. Ibid.
126. Ibid., 166–67.
127. Health Tribunal Project, http://healthtribunal.org/.
128. OECD, Convention on Combating Bribery of Foreign Public Officials in International Business Transactions, 1997, Doc. No. DAFFE/IME/BR(97)20, 37 I.L.M. 1 (entered into force 15 February 1999); Seck, "Canadian Mining," 78.
129. See Business and Human Rights Resource Centre, "Binding Treaty," http://business-humanrights.org/en/binding-treaty.
130. J.G. Ruggie, "A UN Business and Human Rights Treaty Update," Business and Human Rights Resource Centre, 1 May 2014, http://business-humanrights.

org/sites/default/files/media/documents/ruggie-un-business-human-rights-treaty-update-1-may-2014.pdf.

131. Compare Amazon Watch's ChevronToxico, http://chevrontoxico.com/, and EarthRights International, "Amicus Briefs in Chevron/Ecuador Litigation," http://www.earthrights.org/publication/amicus-briefs-chevron-ecuador-litigation, with Chevron Corporation, "Ecuador Lawsuit: Facts about Chevron and Texaco in Ecuador," http://www.chevron.com/ecuador/.
132. M. Scheinin, *Towards a World Court of Human Rights* (Geneva: Geneva Academy of International Humanitarian Law and Human Rights, 2009), http://www.eui.eu/Documents/DepartmentsCentres/AcademyofEuropeanLaw/CourseMaterialsHR/HR2009/Scheinin/ScheininClassReading1.pdf.
133. P. Alston, "Against a World Court for Human Rights," Public Law Research Paper no. 13-71, School of Law, New York University, 2013.
134. See Social Enterprise Canada, "What Is a Social Enterprise?" http://www.socialenterprisecanada.ca/en/learn/nav/whatisasocialenterprise.html.
135. Nestlé and Danish Institute for Human Rights, *Talking the Human Rights Walk: Nestlé's Experience Assessing Human Rights Impacts in Its Business Activities* (Vevey: Nestlé, 2013), http://www.nestle.com/asset-library/documents/library/documents/corporate_social_responsibility/nestle-hria-white-paper.pdf.
136. On Common Ground Consultants, *Human Rights Assessment of Goldcorp's Marlin Mine* (Vancouver: Steering Committee for the Human Rights Impact Assessment of the Marlin Mine, 2010), http://csr.goldcorp.com/2011/docs/2010_human_full_en.pdf.
137. A. Dhir, "Shareholder Engagement in the Embedded Business Corporation: Investment Activism, Human Rights, and TWAIL Discourse," *Business Ethics Quarterly* 22, no. 1 (2012): 99.
138. Seck, "Canadian Mining," 62–75.

17
Human Rights and Climate Change

SAM ADELMAN

Learning Objectives

- To become familiar with the relationships between human rights, ethics, politics, and climate justice
- To understand and discuss the limits and potential of human rights in addressing climate change
- To understand the links between climate justice, social justice, and global justice

This chapter addresses the relationship between human rights and climate change. It begins with a discussion of the impacts of anthropogenic global warming on human rights such as the right to life and the right to health, based on the scientific consensus in the fifth assessment report of the Intergovernmental Panel on Climate Change. This is followed by an analysis of the possibilities and limits of using human rights to address a problem that James Hansen has described as a planetary emergency. I discuss the campaign to overcome the limits of human rights by making ecocide the fifth crime against peace under the Rome Statute of the International Criminal Court.

My central argument is that although human rights enjoy a relatively high level of legitimacy, finding solutions to climate change is ultimately a matter of politics and economics. The following section contrasts arguments in favour of the right to emit greenhouse gases with substantive rights such as the right to a clean and healthy environment. The chapter concludes with three brief case studies: the 2005 Inuit petition to the Inter-American Commission on Human Rights, the lack of human rights protection for climate refugees, and the emergence in Latin America of legal protections of the Rights of Nature.

The Impact of Climate Change on Human Rights

In 2014 the Intergovernmental Panel on Climate Change (IPCC) reiterated the overwhelming scientific consensus that the impacts of anthropogenic climate change will be "severe, pervasive and irreversible."[1] In stark and unequivocal language, the report indicates that climate change will be one of the biggest threats confronting humanity in the twenty-first century. In the words of its chairman, Rajendra Pachauri, "Nobody on this planet is going to be untouched by the impacts of climate change."[2] The report confirms James Hansen's assertion that humanity is facing a planetary emergency in which every human right in the International Bill of Rights will be violated somewhere soon, including the right to life—the precondition for all other rights.[3] The poor and vulnerable—women, children, the elderly, and the weak—will suffer most, particularly in less developed countries that are least responsible for the problem but have the fewest resources and limited resilience and adaptive capacity.

The right to life is threatened by systemic risks due to extreme weather events, leading to breakdowns in infrastructure and critical services such as electricity, water supply, and health and emergency services. The IPCC expresses "very high confidence" that injuries, diseases, and deaths will increase because of more intense heat waves and fires, and "high confidence" that under-nutrition will result from diminished food production in poor regions. The right to health will be undermined by increased risks from food-, water-, and vector-borne diseases.

The right to private and family life and the right to culture will be affected as increasing warming puts some ecosystems at risk of abrupt and irreversible changes, which will slow economic growth and poverty reduction, erode food security, and trigger new poverty traps, particularly in urban areas and emerging hunger hotspots. The IPCC predicts with high confidence that hundreds of millions of people will be displaced by land loss from coastal and inland flooding, which will increase the risks of death, injury, severe ill-health, and disrupted livelihoods in low-lying coastal zones and small island developing states (SIDS) due to storm surges and rising sea levels.

The right to food will be threatened by the breakdown of food systems due to warming, drought, flooding, and desertification. All aspects of food security are likely to be affected, not least access to food. Rural livelihoods and income will be undermined by insufficient access to drinking and irrigation water and reduced agricultural productivity, especially for farmers and pastoralists with minimal capital in semi-arid regions. In Africa "between 75 million and 250 million people are projected to be exposed to increased water stress" by 2020.[4]

Climate change will compromise the right to peace and security through "significant impacts on forms of migration that compromise human security." It will indirectly increase "risks from violent conflict in the form of civil war, inter-group violence, and violent protests by exacerbating well-established drivers of these conflicts such as poverty and economic shocks."[5]

Using human rights to address anthropogenic climate change is necessary because politicians have failed to deal with the problem under the 1992 UN Framework Convention on Climate Change (UNFCCC) and the now-expired Kyoto Protocol, neither of which specifically links human rights and climate change. Unwilling to constrain the ecocidal rapaciousness of global capitalism, politicians have instead placed their faith in the putative power of efficient, self-regulating markets, but if markets were going to solve the problem, they would presumably have done so by now. Human rights are not designed to prevent dangerous anthropogenic warming, but they can be used to ameliorate and perhaps prevent some of its impacts.

Possibilities and Limits

The International Bill of Rights came into existence before the dangers of anthropogenic climate change were understood, and few subsequent human rights instruments contain provisions on environmental protection. No human right against climate change has been formulated and there is little prospect of a climate rights convention or a protocol to the UNFCCC. Climate change has seldom been conspicuous in international environmental law.[6] It is only relatively recently that inclusion of environmental rights has become the norm in new or amended constitutions such as those of South Africa, Ecuador, and Kenya. Following first-generation civil and political rights and second-generation economic, social, and cultural rights, environmental rights comprise part of the third generation of collective developmental and solidarity human rights.[7] There is no generally accepted definition of environmental rights, but they clearly include rights derived from human rights law and international environmental law.[8] In addition, there is no agreed standard for addressing environmental issues under human rights law.

Stephen Humphreys considers it puzzling, given the scale and urgency of the problem, that until relatively recently there has been a resounding silence on human rights in mainstream climate literature and debates, despite the IPCC's repeated observations about food, water, and health. This is partly explained by difficulties with enforcing certain rights (such as those of migrants) establishing extraterritorial responsibility and local accountability, the extent to which emergency conditions limit the application of human rights, and conflicts between rights.[9]

The persistent failure of the largest emitting states to accede to a viable and legally binding successor to the Kyoto Protocol is a sign of the dysfunctionality of contemporary international governance. Human rights are a way of demanding that sovereign states cease pursuing economic policies that increase greenhouse (GHG) emissions rather than promoting the use of renewable energy and adhere to the obligations they accepted under the Kyoto Protocol.[10] Caney argues that "persons have fundamental interests in health, subsistence and supporting themselves and that the duty to protect these interests from dangerous climate change is not unreasonably demanding on the appropriate would-be duty bearers."[11]

There is a long history of using human rights to address global injustices such as apartheid, racism, gender and sexual discrimination, and poverty. Framing climate change in this way links the idea of an inherent minimum human dignity, based on equality and universality, to the personal suffering caused by GHG emissions, by arousing compassion and empathy about a problem that is not always readily apparent and whose human agency is obscured. Whereas environmental law tends to treat ecological destruction in cost-benefit terms, as an externality, human rights concentrates attention on the impacts on individuals caused by those most responsible for emitting and benefiting from the use of fossil fuels—mainly states and corporations. Using human rights highlights the inextricable connection between human and environmental well-being.

Human rights have broad public appeal and greater legitimacy than many other ethical, legal, and political discourses. David Bollier and Burns Weston argue that human rights trump other legal obligations because "they are juridically more elevated," making it possible to challenge the sovereign prerogatives of states and the parochial agendas of private elites.[12] A further advantage is that international human rights tribunals often require lower standards of proof than domestic courts, and the burden of proof is often on the state as the primary duty-bearer under international human rights law.

Finally, human rights make it possible to defend the interests of future generations. In a decision concerning the use of forests, the Indian Supreme Court held that "the present generation has no right to deplete all the existing forests and leave nothing for the next and future generations."[13] The Brundtland Commission's definition of sustainable development as "development that meets the needs of the present without compromising future generations to meet their own needs" has been widely incorporated into treaties, constitutions, and national legislation, although the nature and extent of the right remain contentious.[14] The principle of intergenerational equity is recognized in the preamble and article 3 of the UNFCCC. The Preamble states the parties' determination "to protect the climate system for present and future generations." Article 3 urges states to take "precautionary measures to anticipate, prevent or minimize the causes of climate change and mitigate its adverse effects."[15]

Human rights are of limited use unless they create corresponding duties on other actors to protect or refrain from violating them and provide remedies enforceable in courts or other tribunals.[16] Human rights must be justiciable to enable victims to establish liability, seek remedies, and claim compensation for loss and damage caused by anthropogenic climate change.[17] Koivurova correctly observes that "[w]e are still living in a time when legal liability in the international community is largely defined on the basis of the compensation principles of general international law and these ... are difficult to apply to the consequences of climate change."[18]

We should, however, be wary of asking human rights to do what they were not designed for, and of placing too much faith in an idea that has not always delivered what it promises. Wendy Brown warns that we should be aware of what rights discourse does *not* say about itself. Human rights discourse is a form of politics that seeks to organize political space, "often with the aim of monopolizing it. It also stands as a critique of dissonant political projects, converges neatly with the requisites of liberal imperialism and global free trade, and legitimates both as well."[19]

Human rights may be part of the solution, but they are generally used retrospectively, and rarely to confront underlying structures of domination and exploitation. Demands for climate justice and an end to the use of fossil fuels represent a dissonant political project that is provoking a massive backlash from vested interests such as states and hydrocarbon energy companies. Liberal conceptions of human rights prioritize civil and political rights over economic, social, and cultural rights and place particular emphasis on property. Focusing on individual suffering may obscure structural and systemic violations of human rights—the maldistribution of resources and forms of production and consumption that cause climate change and inhibit adaptation and mitigation strategies.

Upendra Baxi argues that human rights emerge from the suffering of impoverished and rightless people. He describes the sustained attempt by neoliberal capitalism to appropriate rights, through construction of a regime of trade-related, market-friendly human rights designed to supplant the Universal Declaration of Human Rights (UDHR) perspective with a new paradigm that

> seeks to demote, even reverse, the notion that universal human rights are designed for the attainment of dignity and well-being of human beings and for enhancing the security and well-being of socially, economically and civilizationally vulnerable peoples and communities. The emergent paradigm insists upon the promotion and the protection of the collective human rights of global capital, in ways which "justify" corporate well-being

> and dignity even when it entails continuing gross and flagrant violation of human rights of actually existing human beings and communities.[20]

Using human rights ipso facto perpetuates anthropocentric perspectives, which are compounded by Eurocentric worldviews that implicitly view humanity as detached from and superior to nature.

A conspicuous limitation is the extent to which the enforcement of human rights depends on states, which have historically been the most consistent and egregious violators of them. Since states are the primary duty-bearers under human rights law and climate law, corporations have no direct obligations or liabilities for anthropogenic climate change. Companies such as Shell in Ogoniland and Chevron in the Ecuadorean Amazon have consistently evaded responsibility for environmental destruction and human rights violations while greenwashing their activities. Transnational corporations have funded climate denial while moving to protect their rights as "corporate legal humanity."[21]

Polly Higgins is leading a campaign to fill this lacuna in seeking to pre-empt, prevent, and prohibit ecocide by making it the fifth crime against peace under the Rome Statute, which established the International Criminal Court (ICC).[22] State and non-state actors would have strict liability under international criminal law, with the aim of deterring individuals in positions of responsibility—including legislators, policy makers, company directors, and investors—from engaging in or permitting large-scale environmental destruction. Ecocide is already a war crime under article 8(2) of the Rome Statute.

"An international law of Ecocide where intent was a necessary component of the crime opens up the legal loophole of sidestepping responsibility on the basis that mass damage or destruction was not intended. Most corporate ecocide is not intended; often it is deemed collateral damage or an accident."[23] Higgins proposes the following amendment to the Rome Statute: "Ecocide is the extensive damage to, destruction of or loss of ecosystem(s) of a given territory, whether by human agency or by other causes, to such an extent that peaceful enjoyment by the inhabitants of that territory has been severely diminished."[24]

Criminalizing ecocide offers a way of partially overcoming the limits of human rights law, environmental law, and tort law, and hopefully preventing human rights violations. However, it is not certain that the 86 states required to amend the Rome Statute will agree to do so. As with human rights, the crime of ecocide would become operative only retrospectively. Criminalizing ecocide during peacetime would be a welcome step that could decrease ecological devastation, but it is not evident that it can be used to reduce GHG emissions.

A mock trial was held in the Supreme Court of England and Wales in September 2011.[25] The chief executive officers of two fictional fossil fuel companies were found guilty of causing ecocide through the extraction of oil from the Athabasca tar sands, in a demonstration of how a law against ecocide could work in practice. A further harbinger of the possible establishment of an international climate court was the inaugural session of the Ethics Tribunal on the Rights of Nature and Mother Earth, in Quito in January 2014.[26] In 2010 the World People's Conference on Climate Change and the Rights of Mother Earth in Cochabamba, Bolivia, had demanded "creation of an International Climate and Environmental Justice Tribunal that has the legal capacity to prevent, judge and penalize States, industries and people that by commission or omission contaminate and provoke climate change."[27] The 2014 Tribunal held that the nine cases it considered were all in contravention of the Universal Declaration of the Rights of Mother Earth, or Ecuador's constitution. The Tribunal will sit permanently and hear cases from around the world.

Using Human Rights

Humphreys observes that existing approaches to climate change "mobilise human rights rhetoric to underpin a just global climate regime; they do not examine specific human rights violations resulting from climate change or seek to inject human rights principles into climate change law. At bottom, they invoke human rights in order to spur action on climate change rather than advocating climate change action in order to prevent human rights consequences."[28]

The first clear articulation of the link between human rights and the environment came in the 1972 Stockholm Declaration on the Human Environment.[29] The preamble recognizes that a healthy environment is necessary for the enjoyment of human rights. Principle 1 states, "Man has the fundamental right to freedom, equality and adequate conditions of life, in an environment of a quality that permits a life of dignity and well-being, and he bears a solemn responsibility to protect and improve the environment for present and future generations." In 1990 the UN General Assembly declared "that all individuals are entitled to live in an environment adequate for their health and well-being."[30]

In November 2007, small island developing states (SIDS) adopted the Malé Declaration on the Human Dimension of Global Climate Change, which included a request to the UN Human Rights Council to convene a debate on climate change and human rights. This resulted in a report by the Office of the High Commissioner for Human Rights, which concluded that climate change threatens the enjoyment of numerous rights but does not necessarily violate them; nevertheless it called for greater involvement by human rights expert bodies in the UNFCCC.[31] The UN Security Council has scarcely addressed the issue, apart from a discussion on the impacts of climate change on peace and security in 2007.

As I have argued elsewhere, climate change can be addressed by invoking or adapting existing rights or formulating new ones.[32] The latter may be formulated in positive or negative terms: as a right, for example, *to* a clean and healthy environment or subsistence emissions, or *against* violations of one or more human rights.[33] The use of existing substantive rights is promoted by the expansion theory, which advocates the extension of human rights to new problems. Leib argues that the theory is of limited use because of the difficulty facing plaintiffs in establishing a causal connection between environmental harm and the alleged rights violation, not least by GHG emissions from activities that are not illegal.[34] There is clear evidence of a link between slow-onset impacts such as the inundation of SIDS and desertification, but it is more difficult to attribute extreme weather events exclusively to anthropogenic warming or to ascribe the effects of climate change to specific defendants, "partly because damage occurring now is a result of emissions in the past and particularly because any individual emitter will only be responsible for a very small percentage of overall GHGs."[35]

Leib describes additional difficulties in using human rights to defend non-anthropocentric interests such as future generations, animals, or nature, and because "reliance on existing rights lacks the consistency necessary to the recognition of new rights, which impedes the transformation of this practice into a principle of customary international law."[36] She contrasts the expansion theory to the environmental democracy theory, which aims to mobilize the use of procedural and civil and political rights by demonstrating the essential conceptual link between environmental protection and democratic values and practices. In addition, she outlines the genesis theory, which constructs the argument for a new human right on the basis that environmental rights are the foundation for all other human rights. The biggest advantage of environmental rights resides in the ability to use them to stop pollution or other destructive activities, although they may have a strong deterrent value as well: "From a legal perspective, the importance of environmental rights lies in facilitating injunctive relief, rather than merely providing compensatory damages to victims."[37]

The following sections discuss two divergent human rights issues: the right to emit and the right to a clean and healthy environment.

Emissions Rights

Most theories of climate justice take an ethical approach to climate change. They focus on the criteria for determining responsibilities for global warming and the duties to which they give rise. The three main criteria are the historical responsibility of developed countries for GHG emissions (some of which remain in the atmosphere for more than a hundred years),[38] the benefits they have accrued from fossil-fuelled industrialization, and their ensuing ability to discharge their ecological debts by providing the resources needed by developing countries for adaptation and mitigation.[39] Climate justice is thus intertwined with broader questions of distributive and social justice, gender justice, the global justice concern with impoverishment, and environmental justice.

There is a mutually reinforcing negative relationship between global justice and climate justice, in that climate change increases poverty, which in turn reduces resilience and adaptive capacity.[40] When the income of the 85 richest persons on Earth exceeds that of the poorest 3.5 billion, and when some individuals are richer than entire countries,[41] it is not surprising that less developed states lack adequate resources for adaptation and mitigation. Liberal theories tend to elide the tight connections between climate change, capitalism, and poverty; they take the promises of sustainable development and green economy at face value while generally disregarding ecofeminist and ecosocialist perspectives and subaltern and indigenous rights, knowledges, and epistemologies.

Sands argues that sustainable development is based on three principles in addition to intergenerational equity: intra-generational equity or equitable use, the principle of sustainable use, and the principle of integration.[42] It is also based on the concepts of needs and limitation. Promising a virtuous combination of economic growth, environmental protection, and social justice, sustainable development appears to provide an ideal legal basis for dealing with climate change. In reality, however, it has proved to be an oxymoron, with unconstrained fossil-fuelled economic growth almost invariably taking precedence over environmental protection and justice.[43]

Given the scale and urgency of climate change, it may seem both logical and urgent to assert a right to a clean atmosphere or right against GHG emissions. Advocating a right to emit seems at the very least antithetical to the idea of human rights as a possible solution to climate change. They are proposed primarily as a means of survival, but Humphreys notes that when atmospheric rights were proposed in early climate change debates, "they were consistently treated as fundamental, universal and inalienable. Yet, the legal incarnation of use-rights to the atmosphere has instead taken the very different form of exclusive tradable commodities."[44]

There are two forms of emissions rights: a human right to equal per capita emissions and a right to subsistence emissions. The notion of a right to equal per capita emissions that treats the atmosphere as a collective good to which everyone should have equal access, is ethically objectionable.[45] It is unclear whether its proponents believe that an equal entitlement to emit should be based on the carbon footprint of the average Chinese or American[46] or, absurdly, that the needy should have a right—which they are unable to exercise—to emit as much as the opulent.[47] Promoting equal emissions rights is surely the wrong approach when urgent action is required to reduce GHG stocks if the world is to have any chance of preventing dangerous anthropogenic warming.[48]

The idea of a right to subsistence emissions is based on Henry Shue's distinction between basic and non-basic rights and his contention that security and subsistence are basic rights, indispensable to each other and to all other rights.[49] Shue argues that the rich should be required to sacrifice some of their non-basic rights in order to protect the subsistence rights of the poor to "unpolluted air, unpolluted water, adequate food, adequate clothing, adequate shelter, and minimal preventative health care."[50] It might be argued that a right to subsistence emissions is a corollary of the right to development, but there is a touch of irony in asserting that those most vulnerable to the effects of greenhouse gases have the right to emit them.[51]

Nevertheless, a right to subsistence emissions is consistent with the principle of common but differentiated responsibility at the heart of the UNFCCC. The principle reflects general principles of equity in international law in placing primary responsibility on developed countries to act first to reduce emissions, while allowing developing countries to follow more slowly. The principle operates retrospectively by focusing on historical responsibility for past emissions stocks. Although all countries had a common responsibility to mitigate climate change under the Kyoto Protocol, developed countries had binding commitments to cut GHG emissions, provide financial resources, and transfer technologies to assist developing countries in adapting to and mitigating the effects of climate change. In contrast, developing countries were permitted to increase emissions in order to produce the economic growth needed to alleviate poverty.

Rights Against Climate Change

An alternative approach is to formulate human rights against global warming.[52] Anthropogenic climate change threatens the human right to "physical security"[53] and the rights to life, health, and subsistence.[54] Caney argues that global warming jeopardizes the individual human right to development and possibly a human right not to be forcibly evicted that could be asserted by SIDS.[55] In Vanderheiden's view, "a stable climate may be considered as among the most basic rights" because of the seriousness of the threat climate change poses to "the maintenance of an adequate environment."[56] Building on Hayward's support for a human right to "an environment adequate for (human) health and well-being,"[57] he argues,

> The right to an adequate environment is intended to encompass a broad range of anthropocentric duties of environmental protection, and the right to climatic stability appears to be an obvious corollary of such a right. While climate change is only one of many ongoing threats to the maintenance of an adequate environment, it must be regarded as among the most serious threats. Therefore, the duty to maintain climatic stability, or to refrain from excessive GHG emissions, is a necessary but insufficient condition for meeting the general obligation to maintain an adequate environment, making this a subsidiary right to the general right sketched above.[58]

There is no international right to a clean and healthy environment, but more than a hundred constitutions incorporate environmental rights.[59] By 2002, 53 constitutions recognized the right to a clean and healthy environment and 92 imposed a duty on national governments to prevent harm to the environment.[60] The increasing prevalence of a right to a clean and healthy environment is a welcome development, but it is unclear to what extent such a right can be effectively deployed against climate change. The transboundary nature of climate change makes it difficult to use domestic courts to control the GHG emissions of other states, to impose liability on actors who do not fall under the jurisdiction of constitutional courts, or to provide remedies for those whose rights are infringed.

Weston and Bollier argue that a human right to environment in general is juridically recognized in three ways: as an entitlement derived from other recognized rights such as the rights to life and health, as an entitlement autonomous unto itself, and as a cluster of procedural entitlements.[61] They make the right to a clean and healthy environment the centrepiece of a new rights-based paradigm of green governance independent of the "state market." Human rights must be understood as embodied in active social practice and not merely confined to formal law, even if their "corporeal and tangible substance … is not always readily visible. Human rights are not to be seen as mere abstractions that may or may not be honoured by administrative agencies, legislatures, and courts." They argue that the right to a clean and healthy environment is the only means by which individuals and civil society can address climate change internationally and that it facilitates political mobilization on environmental issues domestically, especially where the right has been incorporated into the law. Above all, it "provides a powerful narrative and means for envisioning and bringing about an effective, socially rooted system of ecological governance."[62]

Case Studies

Indigenous Rights: The Inuit Petition

Indigenous peoples have been in the vanguard of attempts to link climate change and human rights. Westra describes the impact of climate change on Inuit culture and society as an eco-crime.[63] The IPCC warns, "It is very likely that the Arctic sea ice cover will continue to shrink and thin and that Northern Hemisphere spring snow-cover will decrease during the 21st century as global mean surface temperature rises."[64] The indigenous peoples of the Arctic depend on snow and ice for food and income, which are in turn contingent upon the traditional activities of hunting, fishing, and reindeer herding.

In 2005 the Inuit population in the Canadian Arctic brought a petition before the Inter-American Commission on Human Rights that, in effect, demanded a right to be cold. The petition alleged that

> the impacts of climate change, caused by acts and omissions by the United States, violate the Inuit's fundamental human rights protected by the American Declaration of the Rights and Duties of Man and other international instruments. These include their rights to the benefits of culture, to property, to the preservation of health, life, physical integrity, security and a means of subsistence and to residence, movement, and the inviolability of the home.[65]

These rights are protected by the American Declaration of the Rights and Duties of Man as well as the International Bill of Rights.[66] The Commission declined to assess the merits of the petition because the information provided did not enable it "to determine whether the alleged facts would tend to characterize a violation of rights protected by the American Declaration," but allowed the petitioners to place their argument on record in a "Hearing of a General Nature."

Since the United States is not a party to the Declaration, there was no possibility that it would be held liable. In addition, the Inuit were confronted by the other legal hurdles that confront most attempts to use human rights to deal with climate change. These include rules of standing and causation. It is a general requirement that complainants must be directly affected by the rights violation they are alleging in order to be able to bring a case before a court or tribunal. This is relatively easier in jurisdictions that permit social action litigation, such as India (where it originated, at the prompting of activist lawyers) and South Africa (where it is part of the constitution).[67] As Westra points out, the "procedural blockage of any consideration of human rights violations is a constant aspect of litigation involving environment, human rights and the US courts."[68]

Greenhouse gases do not respect borders. This creates two problems. First, it is difficult to establish a causal link between particular environmental harms and the emissions of particular states or companies. Second, GHG emissions may not be the only cause of the harm.[69] It may be relatively easy to link slow-onset climate change impacts, such as desertification or sea level rise, to an increase in mean global temperature due to emissions, but climate scientists caution against ascribing extreme weather events to global warming, despite mounting evidence to that effect. It was therefore almost impossible for the Inuit to link US emissions to the rights under threat. They did not expect to win the case, but they did succeed in reframing what had previously been viewed as an environmental law problem as a human rights issue caused by climate change.[70] Sheila Watt-Cloutier, the Inuk leader who presented the petition, accepted that a "declaration from the commission may not [be] enforceable, but it has great moral value. We intend the petition to educate and encourage the United States to join the community of nations in a global effort to combat climate change."[71] The Inuit case is a good example of the degree that ethics, law and politics, and human rights overlap.

Climate Migrants

Article 15 of the UDHR provides the right not to be arbitrarily deprived of one's nationality, but no right exists to the ground beneath one's feet. There is no obligation on other countries to accept the inhabitants of small island states such as Palau, Kiribati, Tuvalu, and the Maldives, who will be forced to relocate as their homes are inundated, and little prospect of an international agreement to protect them.[72]

The International Organization for Migration estimates that 20 million people were displaced by extreme weather events in 2008. Forecasts of the number of climate-induced migrants by the middle of the century vary from "25 million to 1 billion people with a figure of 200 million being the most widely cited estimate."[73] Climate change will force people to move temporarily or permanently, but only those who cross borders fall within the ambit of the definition in the 1951 Convention Relating to the Status of Refugees—of a refugee as someone with a well-founded fear of persecution on the grounds of "race, religion, nationality, membership of a particular social group or political opinion."[74] Some SIDS policymakers are resistant to this solution because they view refugee status as a form of disempowerment.

Decisions to migrate commonly have more than one motivation, making it likely that developed states reluctant to admit refugees will refuse entry to victims of climate change on the pretext that they are economic migrants. Poverty does not constitute a form of persecution under the 1951 Convention, and there is little likelihood that an exception will be made for climate refugees, despite the ecological debt owed by developed countries. In 2013 the New Zealand High Court rejected a Kiribati man's application for political asylum on the grounds that he was trying to escape rising seas and the environmental risks caused by climate change. The court ruled that his claim did not meet the criteria of the 1951 Convention and held that, "[b]y returning to Kiribati, he would not suffer a sustained and systemic violation of his basic human rights such as the right to life ... or the right to adequate food, clothing and housing."[75]

The limits of human rights lead McAdam to ask whether the plights of SIDS are better addressed through a rights-based approach or one that prioritizes needs. She argues,

> While it may be possible to reach general international agreement on overarching normative principles, based on human rights law, the duty to cooperate, and general international law principles of humanity and dignity, the detail and implementation of responses will need to be crafted for particular circumstances. Localized and/or regional responses may be better able to respond to the particular needs of affected populations in determining who should move, when, in what fashion, and with what outcome.[76]

The rights of those prompted to cross borders could be protected in a variety of ways: through a climate treaty along the lines of the 1951 Convention, regional agreements, or bilateral treaties. Their rights will not be specifically protected if they are treated as victims of "natural" disasters and given assistance on an ad hoc basis channelled through the United Nations Office for the Coordination of Humanitarian Affairs.[77] There is little prospect of a dedicated international treaty on climate refugees or additional protocols to the 1951 Convention or the UNFCCC. Regional solutions of the kind advocated by McAdam for SIDS in the Oceania region are more feasible because of cultural ties that facilitate integration into diaspora communities in Australia and New Zealand—the most likely destinations.

In September 2011, Palau and the Marshall Islands announced their intention to seek an Advisory Opinion from the International Court of Justice to establish the obligations of states in relation to climate change, including guidance on application of the "no harm" principle in international environmental law. Palau president Johnson Toribiong told the UN General Assembly, "The case should be clear. The ICJ has already confirmed that customary international law obliges States to ensure that activities within their jurisdiction and control respect the environment of other States."[78] Unfortunately, advisory opinions are persuasive but not binding, like much "soft" international environmental and human rights law.

Rights of Nature (Pachamama)

The deficiencies of the UNFCCC framework and international environmental law have led to a growing crescendo of calls for alternative conceptions and uses of law. One example is the nascent field of "Earth jurisprudence," which prioritizes the rights of nature rather than human rights. A leading figure is Cormac Cullinan, who trenchantly criticizes environmental law for treating nature as property and facilitating managed degradation of the environment.[79]

There is growing support in Latin America for ecocentric approaches—based on the worldviews of indigenous Andean cultures—that counter the inherent anthropocentrism of human rights by using law to protect the rights of "Mother Earth" (Pachamama). These approaches reject the fetishization of economic growth in favour of the guiding moral/ethical principle of *buen vivir*. Roughly translated as "good living" or "collective well-being," this principle envisages a communal model of development based on harmony and solidarity, in contrast to the competitive individualism of Eurocentric thinking and neoliberal capitalism. In Andean spiritual worldviews, human well-being is possible only within a community in harmony with nature, according to principles of reciprocity, complementarity, and relationality rather than a nature/society dualism. Nature is viewed as an essential and constitutive element of social life rather than an external environment, and is valued for itself rather than as natural capital. Natural resources must be protected against utilitarian instrumentalism, and economic objectives must be reconciled with social justice.

Buen vivir was incorporated into the 2008 Ecuador constitution and codified in the Law of the Rights of Mother Earth in Bolivia in 2011.[80] The Ecuador constitution was the first to codify the rights of nature. Articles 10 and 71–74 recognize the inalienable rights of ecosystems to exist and flourish, create a right to petition on behalf of ecosystems, and oblige the state to remedy violations of those rights. Article 71 provides that nature—where life is reproduced and occurs—has the right to integral respect for its existence and for maintenance and regeneration of its life cycles, structure, functions, and evolutionary processes.

Whereas Ecuador's recognition of the inherent rights of nature is designed to promote an alternative developmental regime, Bolivia has adopted this worldview as a guiding moral/ethical principle in a plurinational state, linked to other principles such as unity, equality, dignity, freedom, reciprocity, and gender equity.[81] And whereas Ecuador's constitution declares the right of Mother Nature to be respected integrally in its existence, management, and regeneration of its vital cycles, structures, functions, and processes, the Bolivian constitution does not recognize any intrinsic rights of nature. It does, however, declare a right (albeit anthropocentric) to a healthy, protected, and fair environment for citizens of present and future generations, as well as for other living beings, to exist and develop normally and permanently (art. 33). Article 34 creates the possibility of civil legal actions in defence of the environment.

Despite these developments, the legal systems of both countries are still based largely on Western conceptions of law that privilege individual rights. The Law of the Rights of Mother Earth enumerates seven rights to which Mother Earth and her constituent life systems, including human communities, are entitled: life, the diversity of life, water, clean air, equilibrium, restoration, and to live free of contamination. *Buen vivir* has been criticized as a form of romanticism, but Gudynas points out that it presents clear proposals for reforms to the law, environmental accounting, and tax reforms, as well as the dematerialization of economies.[82] In 2008, Ecuador gave all its forests, lakes, and waterways rights equivalent to human rights.[83]

Constitutionalizing the rights of Mother Earth does not guarantee that environmentally friendly policies will result. The Yasuni National Park contains an estimated 846 million barrels of oil, about 20 per cent of Ecuador's reserves. In 2007 Ecuador launched the so-called Yasuní-ITT (Ishpingo-Tambococha-Tiputini) initiative, under which it was willing to refrain from exploiting the oil and to protect the forest if other countries paid compensation—amounting to half the anticipated income of US$7.2 billion—into a trust fund administered by the UN Development Programme, with a board that included representatives of indigenous peoples, local communities, and academics. Revenue from the trust fund would be used to support renewable energy sources, reforestation, and social development. Ecuador was prepared to sacrifice the market value of the oil despite the large contribution of this natural resource to its GDP, so long as this was reflected in the collective willingness of the international community to address the problem of climate change. The national heritage minister, Maria Fernanda Espinosa, declared, "We need to change the logic, we need to change the way we do things."[84]

In August 2013, Ecuador abandoned the plan because of lack of foreign support. The trust fund had received $13 million of the US$3.6 billion target. The project collapsed amid recriminations that the confused strategy of President Rafael Correa had deterred potential contributors, and suspicions that he had been negotiating a deal with PetroOriental, part-owned by the Chinese state company SINOPEC, to exploit the oil reserves in an adjacent area. Indigenous peoples, peasants, and ecologists called for a referendum to decide the issue.[85] There were suspicions that the initiative had failed because it did not conform to market ideology, but Norway cited the novelty of the scheme as the reason for its refusal to participate. The Yasuní project raises the question whether *buen vivir* is no more than a "discursive tool and co-opted term, functional to the state and its structures and with little significance for real intercultural, interepistemic, and plurinational transformation."[86]

Conclusion

Human rights inevitably promote an anthropocentric view of the relationship between human beings and nature that facilitates anthropogenic climate change. In the absence of geo-engineering fixes (which are ethically problematic) and the failure of politics and markets, it is likely that victims of climate change will turn increasingly to the law in general and human rights in particular in search of remedies and compensation. Human rights provide an elevated language of ethics and dignity, capable of transcending ordinary law and politics, but it is not simple to deploy them at the international level in a state-centric system. Likewise, their efficacy at the domestic level is contingent upon the degree to which states respect them, the willingness of courts to admit cases, and above all on the degree to which they are incorporated into constitutions or legislation and thereby made justiciable. Nevertheless, we should expect attempts to use existing rights and formulate new ones to increase as the impacts of climate change intensify demands for climate justice, especially for those least responsible for it—the poor, the weak, and the vulnerable. The optimum solution would be a dedicated climate convention or, failing that, an additional human rights protocol to the UNFCCC, but this is unlikely in light of the dysfunctional nature of international governance.

Comprehending the scale of the planetary emergency confronting humanity, environmental groups, social movements, students, and individuals are seeking a new, progressive, and ecocentric politics and an end to the neo-liberal dystopia of conspicuous consumption and endless growth. Lawyers are responding with innovative ideas for using human rights, some of which appear utopian. Human rights focus on people rather than profit. Human rights are ends in themselves and, in relation to climate change, potentially a means of saving the planet. They are utopian by nature in that they postulate an end to discrimination and exploitation.

For decades it was difficult to envisage an end to apartheid, a system now declared a crime against humanity. The struggle against apartheid provides two other lessons. The first is that human rights can play an important role in framing a problem and garnering support to end it, but they are not a substitute for a politics of climate and distributive justice. The second lesson is that the end of apartheid was hastened by sanctions and boycotts. There is a growing disinvestment movement on campuses in North America and the United Kingdom demanding that universities, municipalities, and cultural institutions cut their ties to the fossil-fuel industry. Burning fossil fuels is unethical, unsustainable, and tantamount to a crime against humanity. Archbishop Desmond Tutu has called for an apartheid-style boycott to save the planet.[87]

Wendy Brown argues that if "the global problem today is defined as terrible human suffering consequent to limited individual rights against abusive state powers, then human rights may be the best tactic against this problem."[88] We may agree with her that there is no quarrel to be had if human rights do no more than alleviate suffering, but that we must demand more of them even as we acknowledge that other forms of politics may offer more appropriate remedies to the depredations of unrestrained capitalism.[89]

Takeaway Messages

- Climate change is perhaps the single biggest threat facing humanity in the twenty-first century. Reducing the use of fossil fuels is therefore imperative and urgent.
- Climate change is fundamentally a political issue. Human rights are a form of politics rather than a substitute for it.

Study Questions

- What are the advantages and limitations of using human rights to address climate change?
- What is the relationship between climate justice and human rights?

Issues for Debate or Roundtable

- Is it acceptable to circumscribe the human rights of some individuals in order to reduce greenhouse gas emissions?
- Would a global tax on fossil fuels violate human rights?
- Is it necessary to address inequality in order to deal with climate change?
- What other actions should be taken to deal with climate change, and by whom?

Additional Reading

Gardiner, Stephen M. *A Perfect Moral Storm: The Ethical Tragedy of Climate Change.* New York: Oxford University Press, 2011. http://dx.doi.org/10.1093/acprof:oso/9780195379440.001.0001.

Klein, Naomi. *This Changes Everything: Capitalism vs the Climate.* London: Penguin, 2015.

Simms, Andrew. *Ecological Debt: Global Warming and the Wealth of Nations.* London: Pluto Press, 2009.

Websites

350.org. http://350.org/.
Eradicating Ecocide. http://eradicatingecocide.com/.
The Guardian. http://www.theguardian.com/uk/environment.
Pachamama Alliance. http://www.pachamama.org/.
Zunia Knowledge Exchange. http://zunia.org/cat/environment.

Notes

1. The facts in this section are taken from the International Panel on Climate Change (IPCC) unless otherwise stated. Under the onslaught of climate deniers, climate scientists have erred on the side of caution in predicting the impacts of global warming. For scientific terminology, the fifth assessment report's language is akin to panic. IPCC, *Climate Science 2013: The Physical Science Basis* (Cambridge: Cambridge University Press, 2013), 14.
2. M. McGrath, "Climate Impacts 'Overwhelming'—UN," BBC News, 31 March 2014, http://www.bbc.co.uk/news/science-environment-26810559.
3. Common Dreams, "'Planetary Emergency': New Data Elevates Climate Change Alarm," 20 September 2012, http://www.commondreams.org/news/2012/09/20/planetary-emergency-new-data-elevates-climate-change-alarm. The International Bill of Rights comprises the non-binding 1948 Universal Declaration of Human Rights and the two 1966 covenants, the International Covenant on Civil and Political Rights, with its two Optional Protocols, and the International Covenant on Economic, Social, and Cultural Rights.
4. M.L. Parry and IPCC, *Climate Change 2007: Impacts, Adaptation and Vulnerability* (Cambridge: Cambridge University Press, 2007), 13.

5. IPCC, *Climate Change 2014: Impacts, Adaptation, and Vulnerability: Summary for Policymakers* (31 March 2014): 11, 12, https://ipcc-wg2.gov/AR5/images/uploads/IPCC_WG2AR5_SPM_Approved.pdf.
6. For example, the substantial handbook edited by Bodansky et al. does not contain a chapter specifically on climate change; D. Bodansky, J. Brunnée, and E. Hey, ed., *The Oxford Handbook of International Environmental Law* (Oxford: Oxford University Press, 2007). See also P. Sands, *Principles of International Environmental Law* (Cambridge: Cambridge University Press, 2003).
7. These include the right to self-determination and the right to development.
8. D. Shelton, "Environmental Rights," in *Peoples' Rights*, ed. P. Alston (Oxford: Oxford University Press, 2001); S. Humphreys, *Human Rights and Climate Change* (Cambridge: Cambridge University Press, 2010).
9. Humphreys, *Human Rights and Climate Change*, 2ff.
10. On one level, the history of human rights since 1948 is an account of a succession of attempts, from the Nuremberg war crimes trials to the establishment of the International Criminal Court (ICC), to circumscribe the power of sovereign states. In June 2015 the District Court in The Hague upheld a complaint by the Urgenda Foundation, a citizens' platform, against the Netherlands government for its failure to decrease emissions consistent with its obligations under the Kyoto Protocol. Urgenda used a combination of tort and human rights law; case number C/09/456689/HA ZA 13-1396 24-06-2015.
11. S. Caney, "Human Rights, Climate Change, and Discounting," *Environmental Politics* 17, no. 4 (2008): 539.
12. D. Bollier and B.H. Weston, "The Human Right to a Clean and Healthy Environment," Corporate Social Responsibility Newswire, 20 December 2013, http://www.csrwire.com/blog/posts/1157-the-human-right-to-a-clean-and-healthy-environment.
13. *State of Himachal Pradesh v. Ganesh Wood Products* (1995) 6 SCC 363, at para. 46.
14. World Commission on Environment and Development (WCED), *Our Common Future* (Oxford: Oxford University Press, 1987), 43. The constitutional right to a balanced and healthful ecology (art. 2, s. 16, 1987 Constitution) was relied upon in *Minors Oposa et al. v. Secretary of the Environment and Natural Resources Fulgencio Factoran*, 33 ILM 173 (1994), in which the Philippines Supreme Court held that rights extend to future generations. The broad conception of legal standing adopted in this case enabled citizens and environmental groups to represent present and future generations without having to prove that they themselves had been directly affected by environmental harm.
15. The precautionary principle states that where there are threats of serious or irreversible damage, a lack of scientific certainty should not be used as a reason to postpone cost-effective measures to prevent environmental degradation. There are divergent views on its content and definition and what obligations it imposes on whom. Suffice it to note that it has not prevented the inexorable rise in GHG emissions.
16. See Sen's assertion that human rights are first and foremost ethical demands, and Baxi's riposte on the error of distinguishing between them as either legal/juridical or ethical. A. Sen, "Elements of a Theory of Human Rights," *Philosophy and Public Affairs* 32, no. 4 (2004): 315–56; U. Baxi, *Human Rights in a Posthuman World: Critical Essays* (New Delhi: Oxford University Press, 2007).

17. Insistent demands by developing countries for compensation for loss and damage led to adoption of the Warsaw International Mechanism at the 19th Conference of the Parties to the UN Framework Convention on Climate Change in Warsaw, December 2013. If the mechanism proves to be viable it could provide a significant source of compensation for human rights violations.
18. T. Koivurova, *Introduction to International Environmental Law* (Abingdon, UK: Routledge, 2014), 173.
19. W. Brown "'The Most We Can Hope for …': Human Rights and the Politics of Fatalism," *South Atlantic Quarterly* 103, no. 2/3 (2004): 461.
20. U. Baxi, *The Future of Human Rights* (New Delhi: Oxford University Press, 2006), 234. Baxi's prescience was vindicated by the bizarre decision of the US Supreme Court that corporations can have human rights, in *Citizens United v. FEC* 130 S. Ct. 876 (2010).
21. A. Grear and U. Baxi, *Redirecting Human Rights: Facing the Challenge of Corporate Legal Humanity* (Basingstoke, UK: Palgrave Macmillan, 2010). For a history of attempts to criminalize ecocide, see P. Higgins, D. Short, and N. South, "Protecting the Planet: A Proposal for a Law of Ecocide," *Crime, Law and Social Change* 59, no. 3 (2013): 251–66, and P. Higgins, *Eradicating Ecocide* (London: Shepheard-Walwyn, 2010), on ecocide in general. Donald Brown has suggested that climate denial could be construed as a crime against humanity; D. Brown, "A New Kind of Crime Against Humanity? The Fossil Fuel Industry's Disinformation Campaign on Climate Change," Rock Ethics Institute, Penn State University, 24 October 2010, http://sites.psu.edu/rockblogs/2010/10/24/a-new-kind-of-crime-against-humanity-the-fossil-fuel-industrys-disinformation-campaign-on-climate-change/.
22. Higgins, Short, and South, "Protecting the Planet," 261.
23. Ibid.
24. Ibid.
25. Details can be found at Eradicating Ecocide, "Mock Trial," http://eradicatingecocide.com/the-law/mock-trial/.
26. On the possibility of an international environmental tribunal, see J. Bentz-Hölzl and M. Brocker, "Climate Change and Global Justice," in *Justice and Conflicts: Theoretical and Empirical Contributions*, ed. E. Kals and J. Maes (Berlin: Springer, 2012), 263–66.
27. World People's Conference on Climate Change and the Rights of Mother Earth, Cochabamba, Bolivia, "Universal Declaration of Rights of Mother Earth," Global Alliance for the Rights of Nature, 22 April 2010, http://therightsofnature.org/universal-declaration/.
28. Humphreys, *Human Rights and Climate Change*, 15–16.
29. Declaration of the United Nations Conference on the Human Environment, June 1972, UN Doc. A/Conf.48/14/Rev. 1(1973); 11 ILM 1416 (1972).
30. UN General Assembly, Resolution on the Need to Ensure a Healthy Environment for the Well-Being of Individuals, 14 December 1990, A/RES/45/94. See also see Human Rights Council [HRC], Resolution 7/23: Human Rights and Climate Change, 28 March 2008, UN Doc. A/HRC/RES/7/23, for which the Council submitted a study on the relationship between climate change and human rights (see note 31, below); and HRC Resolution 18/22, 28 September 2011, UN Doc. A/HRC/18/L.26/Rev.1.

31. UN Human Rights Council (UNHRC), "Report of the Office of the High Commissioner for Human Rights on the Relationship Between Climate Change and Human Rights," 15 January 2009, UN Doc. A/HRC/10/61.
32. S. Adelman, "Rethinking Human Rights: The Impact of Climate Change on the Dominant Discourse," in *Human Rights and Climate Change*, ed. S. Humphreys (Cambridge: Cambridge University Press, 2010).
33. A distinction is regularly made between positive and negative rights. The former require others (usually the state) to take steps to protect them, whereas the latter are characterized by the requirement that others should not interfere with their enjoyment. Climate change jeopardizes both types of rights, such as the right to life and the right to health respectively. The 1993 Vienna Declaration and Programme of Action declared, "All human rights are universal, indivisible and interdependent and interrelated"; UN General Assembly, 12 July 1993, A/CONF.157/23: http://www.refworld.org/docid/3ae6b39ec.html.
34. L.H. Leib, *Human Rights and the Environment: Philosophical, Theoretical and Legal Perspectives* (Leiden: Martinus Nijhoff, 2011).
35. R. Lord, S. Goldberg, L. Rajamani, and J. Brunnée, eds., *Climate Change Liability: Transnational Law and Practice* (Cambridge: Cambridge University Press, 2012), 33–34.
36. Leib, *Human Rights and the Environment*, 158.
37. Ibid., 158–59.
38. Methane is a particularly potent greenhouse gas that persists in the atmosphere for about 12 years, whereas nitrous oxide can last for up to 144 years.
39. J. Moss, "Climate Justice," in *Climate Change and Social Justice*, ed. J. Moss (Melbourne: Melbourne University Press, 2009).
40. See Bell for a discussion on the links between climate justice and global justice; D. Bell, "Climate Change and Human Rights," *Wiley Interdisciplinary Reviews: Climate Change* 4, no. 3 (2013): 159–70.
41. Oxfam, *Working for the Few: Political Capture and Economic Inequality* (Boston: Oxfam International, 2104).
42. Sands, *Principles*, 253. The principle of integration requires that environmental considerations be integrated into economic policies and programs and that development needs to be considered in applying environmental objectives.
43. It was reincarnated at the 2012 Rio+20 UN Conference on Sustainable Development, in the form of green economy in the context of sustainable development and poverty eradication. For a critique see S. Adelman, "Rio+20: Sustainable Injustice in a Time of Crises," *Journal of Human Rights and the Environment* 4, no. 1 (2013): 6–31.
44. Humphreys, *Human Rights and Climate Change*, 15.
45. S. Caney, "Climate Change, Energy Rights, and Equality," in *The Ethics of Global Climate Change*, ed. D.G. Arnold (Cambridge: Cambridge University Press, 2011). In the same volume, Moellendorf argues that the libertarian principle of common atmospheric property rights is more demanding than intergenerational justice; D. Moellendorf, "Common Atmospheric Ownership and Equal Emissions Entitlements," in *The Ethics of Global Climate Change*, ed. D.G. Arnold (Cambridge: Cambridge University Press, 2011).
46. In 2010 the respective figures were 6.2 and 17.6 tonnes of CO_2 per capita; World Bank, "CO_2 Emissions," http://data.worldbank.org/indicator/EN.ATM.CO2E.PC.

China is responsible for a quarter of global CO_2 emissions and the United States for 17 per cent. Emissions almost doubled in the first decade of this century.

47. We can be sure that the rich will claim that their rights are being violated if the yardstick is the emissions of the poor, either nationally or internationally.
48. To prevent dangerous anthropogenic climate change resulting from an increase in average global temperature of more than 2 degrees Celsius, climate scientists calculate that GHG emissions should not exceed 350 ppm; J. Hansen, M. Sato, P. Kharecha, et al., "Target Atmospheric CO_2: Where Should Humanity Aim?" *Open Atmosphere Science Journal* 2 (2008): 217–31.
49. H. Shue, *Basic Rights: Subsistence, Affluence, and U.S. Foreign Policy* (Princeton, NJ: Princeton University Press, 1980).
50. Ibid., 18–19.
51. Renewable energy is now sufficiently cheap and effective to meet global energy needs by 2030, if the political will exists. See M.Z. Jacobson and M.A. Delucchi, "A Path to Sustainable Energy by 2030," *Scientific American*, November 2009, 58–65.
52. S. Caney, "Cosmopolitan Justice, Rights and Global Climate Change," *Canadian Journal of Law and Jurisprudence* 19, no. 2 (2006): 263; S. Caney, "Human Rights, Climate Change," 539; S. Vanderheiden, *Atmospheric Justice: A Political Theory of Climate Change* (Oxford: Oxford University Press, 2008), 246.
53. H. Shue, "Bequeathing Hazards: Security Rights and Property Rights of Future Generations," in *Global Environmental Economics: Equity and the Limits to Markets*, ed. M. Dore and T. Mount (Oxford: Blackwell, 1999), 39.
54. S. Caney, "Human Rights, Responsibilities and Climate Change," in *Global Basic Rights*, ed. C. Beitz and R. Goodin (Oxford: Oxford University Press, 2009), 227–47.
55. S. Caney, "Climate Change, Human Rights and Moral Thresholds," in *Human Rights and Climate Change*, ed. S. Humphreys (Cambridge: Cambridge University Press, 2010), 80.
56. Vanderheiden, *Atmospheric Justice*, 246, 242.
57. T. Hayward, *Constitutional Environmental Rights* (Oxford: Oxford University Press, 2005), 29. Hayward has also argued in favour of a human right to a fair share of "ecological space"; T. Hayward, "Human Rights versus Emission Rights: Climate Justice and the Equitable Distribution of Ecological Space," *Ethics and International Affairs* 21, no. 4 (2007): 445.
58. Vanderheiden, *Atmospheric Justice*, 241–42.
59. A.C. Kiss and D. Shelton, *Guide to International Environmental Law* (Leiden: Martinus Nijhoff, 2007), 238.
60. H. Fadaei, "Human Rights Approaches to Sustainable Development," *NGLS Roundup* 90 (May 2002): 3, http://www.un-ngls.org/orf/pdf/ru90hrsd.pdf. Two international treaties also provide a right to environmental quality; Shelton, "Environmental Rights," 265.
61. B.H. Weston and D. Bollier, *Green Governance: Ecological Survival, Human Rights, and the Law of the Commons* (Cambridge: Cambridge University Press, 2014), 33.
62. Ibid., 28, 29.
63. L. Westra, *Environmental Justice and the Rights of Indigenous Peoples: International and Domestic Legal Perspectives* (London: Earthscan, 2008), 208.
64. IPCC, *Climate Science 2013*, 24.

65. Inuit Circumpolar Council Canada, *Petition to the Inter-American Commission on Human Rights Seeking Relief from Violations Resulting from Global Warming Caused by Acts and Omissions of the United States*, 7 December 2005, http://www.inuitcircumpolar.com/uploads/3/0/5/4/30542564/finalpetitionicc.pdf. The Commission had previously recognized the link between the right to life and environmental degradation in a case brought by the Yanomami community of the Amazon against the Brazilian government; Case of Yanomami Indians, Judgement, 1985, Case 7615 (Brazil), Inter-Am. C.H.R., OEA/Ser.L/V/II.66 doc. 10 rev. 1.
66. Organization of American States, American Declaration on the Rights and Duties of Man, Apr. 1948, OAS Resolution XXX, OEA/Ser.L.V/II.82 doc.6 rev.1.
67. The South African Constitutional Court has been relatively reluctant to embrace public interest litigation.
68. L. Westra, *Environmental Justice and the Rights of Ecological Refugees* (London: Earthscan, 2009), 141.
69. Lord et al., *Climate Change Liability*, 33.
70. H.M. Osofsky, "The Inuit Petition as a Bridge? Beyond Dialectics of Climate Change and Indigenous Peoples' Rights," *American Indian Law Review* 31, no. 2 (2006): 676. Legal rules on causation require a connection between an act and its effects. In order to satisfy the requirements of legal causation, a plaintiff must establish that the harm alleged arose from global warming caused at least in part by the defendant.
71. S. Watt-Cloutier, "The Climate Change Petition by the Inuit Circumpolar Conference to the Inter-American Commission on Human Rights," *presentation at the Inuit Circumpolar Conference Eleventh Conference of Parties to the UN Framework Convention on Climate Change Montreal, 7 December 2005,* http://www.inuitcircumpolar.com/uploads/3/0/5/4/30542564/finalpetitionicc.pdf.
72. For reasons of space, the focus in this section is on climate refugees, that is, those who cross borders in order to highlight a particular human rights problem. This is not to minimize the rights of internally displaced persons, who likely comprise the greatest number of climate migrants and who would be regarded as Convention refugees if they crossed a border. In principle they can be protected by their own states, depending on the extent of climate-change impacts and available resources. The definition and terminology of *climate-induced migration* are contested; J. McAdam, *Climate Change, Forced Migration, and International Law* (Oxford: Oxford University Press, 2012).
73. F. Lazcko and C. Aghazarm, *Migration, Environment and Climate Change: Assessing the Evidence* (Geneva: International Organization for Migration, 2009), 5.
74. This has been extended to include generalized violence, for example, in the Organization of African Unity [OAU] Convention Governing the Specific Aspects of Refugee Problems in Africa, 10 September 1969, 1001 U.N.T.S. 45, and the Cartagena Declaration on Refugees, a non-binding agreement adopted by the Colloquium on the International Protection of Refugees in Latin America, Mexico, and Panama in November 1984.
75. *Ioane Teitiota v. Chief Executive of the Ministry of Business Innovation and Employment*, CIV-2013–404–3528 [2013] NZHC 3125, at para. 54.
76. McAdam, *Climate Change, Forced Migration*, 269.
77. By definition, anthropogenic climate change is not natural.

78. UN News Centre, "Palau Seeks UN World Court Opinion on Damage Caused by Greenhouse Gases," 22 September 2011, http://www.un.org/apps/news/story.asp?NewsID=39710&Cr=pacific+island&Cr1#.UyhVFc4THSg. Tuvalu had earlier threatened to file an action in the ICJ against the United States and Australia for their contribution to global climate change and their failure to accept obligations under the Kyoto Protocol to reduce GHG emissions, but this has not happened to date.
79. C. Cullinan, "The Rule of Nature's Law," in *Rule of Law for Nature: New Ideas and Dimensions in Environmental Law*, ed. C. Voigt (Cambridge: Cambridge University Press, 2013).
80. Legislative Assembly of the Plurinational State of Bolivia, *Law of the Rights of Mother Earth*, passed 21 December 2010 (entered into force 2011). The 2011 case *Wheeler c. Director de la Procuraduria General del Estado de Loja* was the first case in history to vindicate the rights of nature. In October 2012 Bolivia passed Law No. 300, *Mother Earth and Integral Development for Living Well*, which is aimed at achieving complementarity and balance.
81. E. Gudynas, "Buen Vivir: Today's Tomorrow," *Development* 54, no. 4 (2011): 443.
82. Ibid., 446.
83. In 2012, legal identity was conferred on a river for the first time, under the Tūtohu Whakatupua Agreement. The Whanganui River in New Zealand, now known as Te Awa Tupua, will have standing through legal custodians from an *iwi* on the river and the national government, who are designated to bring legal actions to defend its interests as a protected entity.
84. D. Blair, "Ecuador's Novel Plan to Save Rainforest," *Financial Times*, 3 January 2011, http://www.ft.com/cms/s/0/7493ad72-1766-11e0-badd-00144feabdc0.html.
85. M. Löwy, "Ecosocial Struggles of Indigenous Peoples," *Capitalism Nature Socialism* 25, no. 2 (2014): 14–24.
86. C. Walsh, "Development as Buen Vivir: Institutional Arrangements and (De) colonial Entanglements," *Society of International Development* 53, no. 1 (2010): 20.
87. D. Tutu, "We Need an Apartheid-Style Boycott to Save the Planet," *The Guardian*, 10 April 2014, http://www.theguardian.com/commentisfree/2014/apr/10/divest-fossil-fuels-climate-change-keystone-xl. In 2015 *The Guardian* launched a campaign to get the Gates Foundation and the Wellcome Trust to divest their holdings in fossil fuels. This is part of the fastest-growing divestment campaign in history.
88. Brown, "The Most We Can Hope," 461.
89. Ibid., 452, 462.

18
Human Rights and Security: Reflections on an Integral Relation

TREVOR PURVIS

Learning Objectives

- To problematize the apparently common-sense notion that we must simply strike a balance between human rights and security, as though the two exist in a zero-sum relationship
- To see the need for not just the creation of human rights instruments (constitutional guarantees, international treaties) but also for corresponding political institutions and mechanisms dedicated to and capable of their promotion and protection
- To understand that while modern political and legal thought has largely regarded such institutions and mechanisms as limited to the extent and capacities of the sovereign state, an increasingly globalized world has seen the rise of new bases for such protections

Two days after the terrorist attacks of 11 September 2001, the *Economist* had already characterized 9/11 as "the day the world changed."[1] It was a sentiment that would issue from a wide range of actors as the fallout from that day reverberated around the globe: from those who would use it as a vehicle to promote a new, bellicose focus for Western foreign policy to those who saw it simply as a harbinger of incomprehensible new danger, raising the spectre of a chaotic world of equally indeterminate and inexplicable threats. But the speed with which such epochal change was announced was, from the moment of its first utterance, suspect. Such pronouncements may be reasonable with the distance afforded by the passage of time, but in this instance they seemed simply and ominously portentous of the fact that the infamous events of that day would surely be mobilized to change the world.

In the intervening years those events have indeed served as a touchstone for effecting change, and in few areas have those changes been more profound than in reordering the relationship between security and human rights. For more than a decade now, a good deal of academic, popular, and political discussion has been preoccupied with the need to find an "appropriate balance" between human rights and the imperatives of security. Too much freedom, too much privacy, and unqualified respect for the rights of individuals and groups are regarded by many as excesses we can no longer afford in a world affected by terrorism, operating in tandem with the reality of weapons of mass destruction. Security, we are told, rests upon a realistic assessment of possible threats and a willingness to forego the luxuries of excessive freedom to secure our collective and future well-being. Clearly, we are told, we had gotten that balance wrong, at great expense to our security, and in turn, reassessment and adjustment are urgently required in pursuit of a promised safer world.

This was a remarkable *volte-face*. The end of the Cold War a dozen years earlier had been widely celebrated as ushering in the possibility of international peace and justice, governed by an international rule of law and a new-found dedication to the protection of human rights. But since the attacks of that day, sovereignty and the state are back with a vengeance. East and West, North and South, states have gained a new lease on life, not least by investing in the hallmarks of sovereignty: violence and death. In the international fight against the evils of terrorism, a newly renovated logic of security has been mobilized to justify an entrenched retreat from the core elements of the post–Second World War international legal order.

This chapter offers a backdrop against which to assess the current implications of Arendt's assertion of the still central and paradoxical role of the modern state, not simply as the principal threat to human rights but as their principal protector as well.[2] But it also seeks to locate that observation in respect of her equally poignant suggestion that "human dignity needs a new guarantee which can be found only in a new political principle, in a new law on earth, whose validity this time must comprehend the whole of humanity while its power must remain strictly limited, rooted in and controlled by newly defined territorial entities."[3] Still reeling from the devastation of two world wars, the horrors of the recent Holocaust, and the onset of a new, stultifying Cold War, Arendt's prose resonates with weariness and disillusionment with modernity. But more than six decades later, the responsibility of states to their own, and to the community of states more generally, has seen significant changes.

Those changes are both tentative and fragile, and recent events have shattered any basis for complacency about their capacity for development outside of sustained, concerted efforts to resist appropriation of their tenets in the name of imperial intrigue. The post-9/11 retreat from human rights commitments in the name of security, not only internationally but also within (most particularly, developed) nation-states, suggests a dangerous trajectory for the future of human rights and calls out for redoubled commitment to the universality of their protections, the responsibility of state actors for their actualization, and a strenuous effort to shore up the international institutional framework that was the legacy of the Second World War.

Hobbes and Sovereignty: Security *contra* Rights

The very notion of security is integrally related to that of politics generally. Peace, order, public safety, justice—all depend on some variant of security and respond to threats generally associated with "insecurity"—that is, all seek to militate against the sorts of threats that inject existential indeterminacy into our lives. The pursuit of security in some guise or another has been a principal objective of political organization from antiquity, and the fact that "security studies" have been, until quite recently, dominated almost exclusively by a profoundly state-centric realism with a myopic focus on state security does not diminish the link between the existential security of individuals and the myriad non-state-based associations and identities they comprise.

Modernity focused attention squarely on security as the touchstone of a new institutional matrix for the protection of collective interests—the modern state—although in assuming the givens of the parameters and constituents of community, its principal theorists assumed away—via the mythical social contract—a vast field of the political to the notion of its a priori natural constitution. This theoretical move served to naturalize the domain of the political and level the field of plurality and difference that is constitutive thereof. In this regard, two giants of early modern political philosophy, Bodin and Hobbes, deserve particular emphasis. Each was concerned centrally with the violent disorder that wracked their respective worlds, and each opined that the route to an ordered, secure world was through the political-institutional actualization/instantiation of a new principle: sovereignty.[4]

It is often overlooked, however, that both were writing against a backdrop of, and in response to, internal social and political disorder, having each borne witness to the dramatic and violent dissolution of both in their respective historical contexts. Bodin was writing against the backdrop of the religious wars that wracked France during the second half of the sixteenth century. Hobbes's *Leviathan* was a political-philosophical reaction to the problem of violent social upheaval in the English Civil Wars. And while the word itself does not actually appear in its text, novel elements of the concept of sovereignty combined to form the centrepiece of the Peace of Westphalia, an instance of theory become practice par excellence, with the practical instantiation of the concept serving as a plausible response to the internecine belligerence of the Thirty Years' War.

It is in Hobbes that we see the most sophisticated and sustained effort to provide a justification for limiting "natural rights" in the name of realizing the security to be had from pursuit of the common good. Individuals shorn of the protections of political community occupied a state of nature characterized as a "warre of every man against every man"[5] in which life would be "solitary, poore, nasty, brutish and short."[6] In Hobbes, "as long as [the] natural Right of every man to every thing endureth, there can be no security to any man."[7] It was in the quest for peace, security, and a civil life that man would reasonably cede to Leviathan his right to everything that his naturally given capacities would otherwise enable him to acquire. Only under such conditions would the avaricious character of individuals be domesticated and the foundations of orderly social and commercial intercourse secured. This was a pragmatic and (to his mind) necessary response to that character so manifest in the world around him. Submission to Leviathan was the only way to gain genuine lasting existential security.

The war of all against all was not, however, banished from human existence; rather, the internal peace secured by absolute obeisance to Leviathan effectively pushes nature's eternal state of war to the frontier of the sovereign's realm. With respect to external relations, sovereigns—now the embodiment of the lone man in the state of nature, avaricious and jealously independent—look obsessively outward "in the state and posture of Gladiators; having their weapons pointing, and their eyes fixed on one another; that is, their Forts, Garrisons, and Guns upon the Frontiers of their Kingdomes; and continuall Spyes upon their neighbours, which is a posture of War."[8] Fears whose sources were once ubiquitous can, in the security of a commonwealth, be turned squarely abroad.

Liberal Philosophy and the Promise of the Rights of Man

The capacity to give to its subjects the law and a monopoly on violence to enforce it were the hallmarks of Leviathan. Positive law and its enforcement would be the mechanism through which the sovereign would exercise authority, all the while standing above any other as the fount of all legislation and the subject of none. But four decades later, Hobbes's new bourgeois man would firmly claim his right against the absolute authority of Leviathan, with the crystallization of liberal thought in the work of John Locke. After Locke and his followers, civil rights against absolute tyranny would acquire a central place in modern liberal political philosophy, and henceforth the sanctity of the sovereign would depend upon his/her successful fulfillment of obligations to protect property and the functional ordering of civil society.[9] Casting aside Hobbes's bleak anthropology and the absolutism that he saw as its remedy, Locke and his successors crafted a politico-philosophical doctrine whose core elements would be reflected in the founding documents of emerging liberal republics and would drive bourgeois revolutionary impulses for decades to come. Rejecting the tyrannical tendencies of absolute monarchy, liberal republicans envisioned a political world in which ultimate sovereignty resided in the people-nation. Sovereigns unwilling or unable to fulfill their obligation to secure the conditions of life, liberty, and property should rightfully be deposed.

If liberalism split with Hobbes on the question of submission to higher authority, it also did so on the question of right, reasserting the naturalness of specific rights against Leviathan. According to liberals, henceforth

> civil rights—that is the varying rights of citizens in different countries—were supposed to embody and spell out in the form of tangible laws the eternal Rights of Man, which by themselves were supposed to be independent of citizenship and nationality. All human beings were citizens of some kind of political community; if the laws of their country did not live up to the demands of the Rights of Man, they were expected to change them, by legislation in democratic countries or through revolutionary action in despotisms.[10]

If indeed "inalienable" and "natural," however, the Rights of Man were, in reality, markedly circumscribed and anything but self-actualizing. The emancipatory scope of the liberal revolutions of the eighteenth and nineteenth century was initially much narrower than the lofty rhetoric of their chief exponents suggested. If men were indeed "born equal but everywhere in chains" and "endowed with inalienable rights," the revolutions originally contemplated the extension of those rights to a limited number of men. And no sooner were they announced than these eternal, inalienable rights of all *men* were called into question; absent some mechanism(s) to ensure their protection and efforts to secure the conditions under which they might be realized, they would remain little more than "nonsense upon stilts."[11]

To the extent that security of life, liberty, and property had been achieved, it was only so for white males of the propertied classes in bourgeois polities—only they possessed the legal personality requisite to press actionable rights claims. It would take more than a century of bloody oppression and political struggle to abolish slavery and extend the franchise, first to the men of the working classes, and subsequently to women. It would take even longer in many liberal democracies to include (however tenuously and incompletely) people of colour and indigenous peoples within the fold of rights protections. Only then would the promise of the Rights of Man achieve some semblance of their universal application within the all too non-universal confines of the nation-state.

The rhetoric of liberal Enlightenment discourse did, however, quickly acquire an ideological resonance well beyond the bourgeois classes; it was held up as representing a broader set of universalist aspirations for recognition of the common dignity of all human beings.[12] Nevertheless, the lofty aspirations for the Rights of Man remained stubbornly confined to the ambit of the sovereign state. Any effort to claim a binding legal character for such rights beyond those confines would be—according to an increasingly dominant legal positivism—doomed to failure; absent a sovereign, such claims were nothing but positive morality.

The impetus driving practical struggles for the extension of rights to the subordinated masses first arose from their immiseration and its attendant chronic insecurity under the bleak conditions engendered by capitalist industrialization and corresponding urbanization. Central to the eighteenth- and nineteenth-century bourgeois revolutions were civil rights to property and "basic" freedoms such as free expression, freedom of the press, and freedom from unwarranted arrest and detention. The contradictions of industrial capitalism became increasingly manifest in the condition of a rapidly growing urban working class struggling to reproduce their daily existence. Within public discourse, these socioeconomic transformations spurred intensified demands for greater inclusiveness of the social contract, demands that drew urgency and vitality from the threat of revolutionary forces on the ground. The appropriation by and extension of rights to hitherto marginalized and frequently destitute elements of the populations of Western states arose largely out of political struggles to actualize the promises of bourgeois rhetoric (and they remain so to this day).

The twentieth century ushered in remarkable transformations in the discourses and practices of rights, first on the basis of common citizenship[13] and later on that of common humanity. These changes were rooted in questions of security, both broadly and conventionally conceived, and paved the way for efforts to extend the ambit of rights protections beyond the scope of the state to all human beings, on the basis of shared human dignity.

The First World War saw unprecedented mobilization of military, economic, and popular resources by industrialized states toward the war effort. The tremendous toll in human lives and the large-scale destruction of that conflict forced an immediate and dramatic reorganization of political life in some of the states involved, leading to the rise of Bolshevism and the corresponding demise of the Russian empire, the dissolution of the Ottoman and Austro-Hungarian empires, and economic destitution visited upon Germany in punishment for its sins. But when the postwar economic expansion enjoyed by the Western allies collapsed with the great crash of 1929, the connection between "national" and "social" security would acquire a novel palpability.

The sweeping global geopolitical reorganization effected at Versailles laid the foundations for a host of struggles, many of whose dynamics had direct and dire human rights consequences in the decades immediately following, and whose implications resonate to this day. Reflecting upon the massive dislocations and misery resulting from the nationalist consolidations that followed the First World War and the dissolution of empires, Hannah Arendt famously highlighted the emptiness of the promise of human rights absent political institutions capable of enforcing them.

One of most pernicious sources of the ensuing humanitarian crises was practical application of one of the core tenets of the Enlightenment refracted through the reorganization of hitherto multicultural societies: the right of peoples to self-determination. Spurred by its new currency, afforded by both Leninist and Wilsonian doctrines, this right became the cornerstone of a struggle for ethno-national consolidation. It was rendered particularly noxious by its combination with the nationalities principle—the idea that every "nation" must form its own state and that every state must have its own nation. As the nationalities principle had it, those unable to achieve state-national self-determination were destined for the dustbin of history. It was a principle that took deep ideological root in the tumultuous years following Versailles. It spurred discrimination against national minorities, efforts at ethnic purification, and in many cases the complete disenfranchisement of large numbers of people, who as a result were left stateless.

Those who, because of circumstances beyond their own control, found themselves uprooted and adrift in a world of nation-states—people who had lost all connection to "a community willing and able to guarantee any rights"—discovered all too brutally that the so-called Rights of Man were nothing more than the rights of citizens.[14] A human rights principle touted by many as a cornerstone of the "post-imperial," post–First World War politics degenerated rapidly into a premise for, first, the expulsion of minorities from political communities, and subsequently their expulsion from the community of humanity ostensibly contemplated by the so-called Rights of Man.

But this was not the totality of the toxins injected into the geopolitical atmosphere at Versailles. The crippling conditions imposed on vanquished Germany thoroughly undermined the coherence and viability of the Weimar Republic, whose demise cemented the conditions under which Nazi totalitarianism rose. The League of Nations mandates system was developed ostensibly to provide a framework under which the indigenous peoples of former colonial possessions of the now-defunct empires would be tutored to levels of social maturity commensurate with the demands of equal membership in the community of civilized states. In practice it became a vehicle for re-colonization and domination by the European powers, which set about carving up the political map into a shape determined by their own imperial interests, with little or no regard for those of the indigenous populations. Under the guise of preparing the "uncivilized" for conditions of self-determination, the Europeans (particularly the British and French) set about pitting peoples against one another; they crafted a geopolitical landscape that frequently bore little or no relationship to the complex ethno-cultural reality upon which it was imposed.

As for life within the societies of the Allied victors of the Great War, where questions of nationality had been hitherto largely incidental to the masses, things began to change. The obligations of national service imposed by conscription were combined with insecurities arising from deepening social interdependence, rooted in the intensification and increasing complexities of the division of labour and modern urban life. These circumstances introduced a new element in the calculus of citizenship rights. If young men and women were expected to mobilize to the call to arms, and if the totality of national industrial output could be put at the disposal of the machinery of total war, then surely the attendant sacrifices implied a reciprocal obligation upon states. The expanded social contract implied by conscription in the name of *national* security should translate into an obligation on the state to ensure conditions under which those same citizens could enjoy the lives they had fought for: a modicum of *social* security.

While the first decade following the Great War saw little movement on these fronts, the challenges presented by the Bolshevik revolution and fears that similarly radical ideological roots might find fertile ground among the disaffected classes of the West intensified with the economic crash of 1929. Roosevelt's New Deal, a response to the widespread destitution and disaffection engendered by the Great Depression, established a general template for other Western states to address not only the human tragedy that had been precipitated by the economic collapse, but also the political challenge it presented of placating a restless working class and the feared appeal of socialist discourse. If the First World War had underlined the need for state-national security inherent in a world of new technologies designed for human destruction on an unprecedented scale, the forces unleashed by Versailles and the excesses of unfettered markets highlighted the fact that "national security" could fall victim to instability from within.

The Postwar Order: Human Rights in Abeyance

The Second World War laid bare the impoverishment of legal positivism taken to its logical extremes. A three-centuries-old paradigm of juridico-political thought rooted in the imperatives of security, order, and absolute deference to sovereign authority had degenerated into an orgy of killing and destruction that devoured all in its path. Following a particularly tautological mode of reasoning, positivism had divorced law from any moral foundations, suggesting that what is legal is quite simply what the law establishes as such.[15] For positivism, efforts to derive notions of right from any source external to law are doomed to irreconcilably confuse law with morality. In the mid-twentieth century, however, the absolute separation of law from any normative foundations led to "*Arbeit macht frei*" and lent logical credulity to claims by defendants in the dock at Nuremberg of the legal force of superior orders. If, as positive law would have it, the commands of the Führer had the force of law, their actions could not possibly be construed as illegal.

From the ashes of that bloodbath came a solemn commitment from a newly forged international community "to save succeeding generations from the scourge of war" and to create conditions under which human rights might be realized.[16] Two world conflicts had highlighted the profound human insecurity engendered by war. If the promise of human rights was to be realized, humanity could no longer countenance the horrors of warfare. The new, total warfare of the twentieth century had bred hitherto unimaginable savagery and brutality, made possible by modern innovations in killing technologies and wholesale disregard for the lives and well-being of the citizenry of enemy states. In response, international law contemplated introducing a new legal subject: the individual human being, both as a rights-bearer and a bearer of obligations. Guarantees of human rights, hitherto limited to the subjects of individual states, would now theoretically become the province of individuals and groups worldwide, regardless of state affiliation, and with the promise of supra-state institutions to ensure compliance.

The implications of this new commitment were immediately put into play when the perpetrators of gross violations of human rights and "crimes against peace" from the vanquished Axis powers were put on trial at the Nuremberg and Tokyo tribunals. Despite the quite fundamental flaws underpinning these tribunals (no one was tried for the horrendous crimes perpetrated by Allied powers), there was a strong sense in many quarters that a new era for the legal enforcement of human rights was at hand.[17] Out of these trials and the newly minted United Nations Charter came resounding condemnation and recognition of the inherent illegality of the use of aggressive force as an instrument of national policy. The new cosmopolitan ethos suggested that henceforth individuals responsible for the most egregious violations of human rights would be held criminally culpable before international law. Those whose rights had been violated would henceforth have some recourse to a limited justice arising from the criminal responsibility of perpetrators for the violations they had suffered.

International peace and security were to be a central preoccupation of the new order. The prohibition of aggression was widely recognized as having attained *jus cogens* status, a peremptory norm of international law that permitted no derogation. So too with war crimes and massive human rights violations in the form of crimes against humanity, with special focus on the most egregious of the latter, to which the neologism *genocide* was attached. Each such norm not only permitted no derogation but implied a corresponding obligation *erga omnes*—upon all members of the community—to either apprehend and try those suspected of offending against those norms or to extradite them to jurisdictions capable of and willing to do so.

State signatories to a rapidly expanding array of international human rights instruments ostensibly took it upon themselves to be the guarantors of such rights. Their fellow members of the international community would judge their legitimacy as members against the backdrop of their success in creating conditions under which those promises would be realized. The expanding panoply of instruments, with their equally expansive lists of signatories, implied that perhaps—in cases where states were unable to meet all those obligations through lack of adequate resources or crises beyond their control—fellow signatories might even, out of a shared commitment to the equal dignity of all human beings, take on the burden of creating conditions adequate to realizing the human rights of those least able to do so themselves.

The new system was to be a union of sovereign consent and an international rule of law. Sovereignty was ostensibly maintained by virtue of state consent to be bound by these legal obligations. The past excesses of state sovereignty, meanwhile, were to be tamed by an order that would be self-policing on the basis of the core tenets of the new order.

Enlightenment principles finally seemed to have gained at least rhetorical purchase in the postwar international sphere. In the liberal democracies of the West, this project gained new impetus through the universalist pretensions of the Keynesian welfare state and gradual extension of an array of protections and services to all citizens as a condition of the social contract—now squarely under conditions of citizenship, as opposed to the original Hobbesian concept of subjection. Henceforth, full citizenship, in T.H. Marshall's classic formulation, would be realized through dedication to extending civil, political, and social rights to all, with special and novel emphasis on the latter. Social rights were crucial to ensuring citizens' capacity to enjoy the full range of human rights, from "a modicum of economic welfare and *security* to the right to share to the full in the social heritage and to live the life of a civilized being according to the standards prevailing in the society."[18] In contrast to the simple subjection under sovereign rule suggested by Hobbes, this implies something more than simple membership in a collectivity and passive submission to authority. Indeed, the bare subjection contemplated by the Hobbesian relationship between sovereign and ruled is one from which well-being and the fruits of an ordered civil society are enjoyed by dint of the beneficence of Leviathan. The concept of citizenship, however, implies a shift from subjection to subjectivity.

The broad developmental trajectory of the citizen–polity relation reflected a hard-won deepening and extension of the rights of the citizen, launching the concept of social security to the forefront of the fields of public policy and administration. The vicissitudes of life in modern industrial societies could be made more tolerable by institutions designed to militate against the vagaries of markets and the frailty of human life. As Marshall clearly understood, the full flourishing of human potential contemplated by the discourse of rights required attention to creating conditions under which their benefits might be realizable. For what are civil rights to freedom of expression and thought, protection and enforcement of property rights, political rights, and so on, if one's existence is dominated by destitution and chronic existential insecurity? In this sense, social security offered a new, palpable sense that the Rights of Man—human rights—might indeed be realizable.

But again this modified social contract was limited to the ambit of the state, and the capacity for actualizing rights—both collective and individual—depended on the security to be realized by dint of common association in a delimited political space. Outside the territory and protections of the state, the world still looked very much like the one Hobbes envisioned, and the anarchy of that "outside" was frequently invoked to limit and assail rights within.

After the Cold War: New Rights Possibilities

Despite the dramatic proliferation of instruments at the international level, for four and a half decades the promise of the postwar human rights project was held largely in abeyance; Cold War tensions polarized global politics and shaped the specific dynamics of global development. If citizenship rights made significant gains in the context of liberal democracies, the same cannot be said of the newly minted human-rights regime of the postwar international legal order. A new legal order, backed by supranational institutions that might enhance and protect the human rights of all, was beyond the grasp of a world riven by the ideological and geopolitical polarities of the Cold War.

Social security represented a partial bulwark against some of the vagaries of modern life by creating conditions under which fuller enjoyment of human rights might be possible. However, even within liberal democracies, the imperatives of national security were frequently mobilized to justify curtailment and outright violation of some of the most "basic" rights promised by liberalism, such as freedom of thought, association, and conscience. But such assaults on civil and political rights paled in comparison with the inability of human rights pronouncements to bring meaningful relief to the immiserated masses of a rapidly decolonizing world, one that was being drawn equally rapidly into the dynamics of global capitalism. This was a period dominated by marked insecurity in the daily lives of those who populated the margins of the developed world, while those who populated the latter enjoyed security from external threat, paradoxically, through the "logic" of mutually assured destruction.

Similar to 9/11, many regarded the "fall" of the Berlin Wall as another moment when the world changed. With the end of the Cold War, voices on the right were quick to proclaim the fall of communism as the denouement of history, an epochal change that marked the advent of a "new world order."[19] Others saw in the changes a host of possibilities that, despite apparent lines of fracture in the global political landscape, held out new potential for realization of cosmopolitan ideals and the flourishing of human rights.[20] A shrinking world would, of necessity, bind us by our common humanity and interdependence. Everywhere there was talk of globalization, and speculation and prognostications of the end of the state abounded. Sovereignty and the state were making a one-way trip to the dustbin of history—not, as Marx suggested, by dint of the forces of proletarian internationalism, but rather in the face of the revolutionary democratizing forces of liberal capitalism.

In the field of security studies a new concept emerged, challenging the myopic state-centric focus that had dominated the Cold War. Now state security would have to share theoretical and policy space with "human security."[21] Where the Cold War had given rise to an entire academic subdiscipline of "security studies," that field's concern with "security" issues in domestic contexts was restricted to national/state security. Issues related to the security of individual lives, and of non-state associations in which crucial aspects of their plural social subjectivities were rooted, were largely regarded as naive or misguided preoccupations and distractions by those concerned with the heady issues of international affairs.

In a Hobbesian world of states in which the Cold War of all against all might at any time turn nuclear, state security trumped all. Realism reigned hegemonic, with characteristically little time for the niceties of international law and human rights. The world was seemingly safer now from the "scourge of war" and the threat of total annihilation that had held human rights concerns in abeyance for decades. The easing of geopolitical tensions was seen to create conditions under which international institutions and global civil society could finally turn their attention to the other promises outlined in the preamble of the UN Charter: to bolster faith in human rights and the dignity and equal worth of all people everywhere, by establishing conditions under which social progress and better standards of life, and, in turn, justice and respect for the obligations arising from international law, might be realized.

International law had shifted to centre stage; the postwar legal commitment to promoting and protecting human rights and a corresponding willingness to punish the most egregious human-rights violators could finally be realized. Within a decade, a significant majority of states parties to the UN had agreed to finally establish a permanent International Criminal Court (ICC), one that would not, incidentally, eclipse sovereign authority but rather exist alongside it, occupying complementary, not superior, jurisdiction. Thus, perpetrators of the most serious international crimes would be brought before their own national courts or those of other nations (by dint of universal jurisdiction). Only in cases where national courts failed to take action would the new ICC's jurisdiction kick in.

Worthy of mention too is the widespread development of academic and policy discourse about humanitarian intervention and the *right* (even the *obligation*) to intervene in breaches of the sovereign independence of states, in cases where the most egregious violations of human rights and rampant human insecurity were manifest. Following the failure of the international community to respond to massive human rights atrocities in Rwanda and former Yugoslavia in the mid-1990s, the new doctrine sought to counter the principle of non-interference in the internal affairs of sovereign states. Reworking liberal contract theory, the new discourse of "responsibility to protect" suggested that sovereigns who breached the social contract, through massive human rights violations or failure to respond to catastrophic events befalling their subjects, would thereby forfeit rightful claim to sovereignty. In such situations, responsibility would fall on the shoulders of the international community to protect populations, trumping any former rights of sovereign independence.[22] The new doctrine was widely embraced in many quarters and ultimately adopted by the United Nations General Assembly.

But if a new cosmopolitan ethos had squarely taken hold in some quarters, the overwhelming power of capital and the new hegemony of neoliberal thought within the dominant institutions of global capitalism yielded a very different idea as to how the new peace and prosperity might best be pursued. Western governments and the global financial institutions created in the wake of the Second World War were now pursuing radical policies designed to foster conditions under which capital expansion might best flourish, on the flawed assumption that markets, liberated from the constraints of state-imposed regulation, would create the conditions most conducive to realization of human rights. Despite the renewed currency that the end of the Cold War had lent to the discourse of human rights, the ascendancy of neoliberalism ushered in a massive retreat from the universalist pretensions of the Keynesian welfare state, and with it, a significant reversal of the project of full citizenship envisioned by T.H. Marshall in the early postwar years. The collapse of the Soviet economy was met with insistence that shock therapy—dramatic and complete exposure to market forces—would yield the most effective path for integration in the global economy (in contrast to the lessons of Versailles, which so thoroughly informed the Marshall Plan in post–Second World War Europe). Meanwhile, the International Monetary Fund and the World Bank introduced "structural adjustment" imperatives upon recipient states, imposing conditions that decimated public services and enterprises regarded by advocates of human security as central to creating conditions adequate to their ends. Thus the new human rights possibilities, trumpeted in some quarters as a "peace dividend" of a post–Cold War world, were sorely circumscribed from the outset.

After 9/11: Consolidating the Neoliberal Assault on Human Rights

Hopes for a practical flourishing of human rights took a significant blow with the terrorist attacks of 9/11. But however traumatic those events were, the characterization of that day as "the day the world changed" implies too readily that subsequent events arose *ex nihilo*, shaped only by, and in response to, the attacks. It is important to abjure any such oversimplifications, and much more useful to see them as offering a prism through which prominent strains of pre-existing thought and political inertia were refracted; they served, that is, as a tipping point of sorts, just as the fall of the Berlin Wall had been 12 years earlier.

As sudden as it seemed at the time, the "new world order" ushered in by the end of the Cold War similarly served to focus pre-existing strains of thought and action. In that event, the triumphalism of the right was rooted in the conviction that the new laissez-faire capitalism of neoliberal economic and social policies had broken the back of Soviet communism. The new left-liberal internationalism, on the other hand, took inspiration from the Eastern European civil society–based social movements that had played such a crucial role in toppling authoritarian regimes from below. Both seemed to imply a lesser role for states in the future. For one side, markets, unfettered by the state, would deliver long-desired prosperity and personal security. For the other, states and their intrusions into everyday life had been a crucial source of repression against the forces of civil society and rights and freedoms denied by, rather than secured through, state institutions. Transnational solidarity, circumventing the formal institutions of state power, had been integral to the success of these movements and held out a promise of new human rights possibilities.

The events of 9/11 created ideological space for practical consolidation of a radically recalibrated geopolitical calculus, its roots deeply embedded in the neoliberal thinking that had been gaining ascendancy since the 1970s. One aspect of the post-9/11 turn has been a marked reassertion of the "state" as a prominent organizer of social life. In the post–Second World War period, the state took on an interventionist role through promulgation of social policy, in the East through management of command economies and in the West through the provisions of the welfare state. In contrast, today's state has been a site of retreat on these fronts, emerging as a leaner, more directly disciplinary state whose penchant for manifesting violent power seems to grow daily.

Since 11 September 2001, events have revealed a marked retreat from human rights in favour of national security, with a corresponding diminution of the protections implied by the idealism of the human rights order first articulated clearly by the authors of the United Nations Charter and the Universal Declaration of Human Rights. And any hope that the neoliberal assault on and retreat from state involvement in the universal social service provisions envisioned by Marshall would leave the other fields of rights—the civil and political—intact has been equally dashed. Since 9/11 even those rights have come under direct assault in the name of security.

Returning to my opening remarks, it is worth noting just how little has in fact changed for so many after 11 September 2001. The infamous events of that day saw the untimely deaths of some 3,000 people in New York, Washington, and Pennsylvania. Meanwhile, elsewhere in the world, more than 30,000 people died from hunger and poverty-related causes,[23] and roughly the same number have perished every day in the intervening dozen years. To put that number in perspective, the Nazis, even at the height of their brutality, were unable to match such a death rate. Since 9/11, some 130 million people have died of hunger-related causes, about 60 per cent of those children.

Existential insecurity plagues the daily lives of hundreds of millions the world round. Before and after 9/11, the Democratic Republic of the Congo was at the centre of what Africans have referred to as their "world war," a conflict that resulted in the deaths of some 6 million people. In Darfur the genocidal policies of the Bashir regime and its Janjaweed militia carried on apace. In the Middle East, the longest-lasting and largest refugee problem of the twentieth century remains unresolved: approximately 5.5 million Palestinians remain stateless 65 years after their expulsion, all while Western governments hesitate at (or outright obstruct) efforts at lasting resolution of their plight. The principal reason—security. For so many people, with respect to their "security," nothing at all has changed.

Of course, much in fact *has* changed. Wars fought in the name of our security have caused massive death and insecurity for others while prominent voices shilling for such action have sought partial justification in "responsibility to protect," regardless (or in spite of) international legal prohibitions.[24] Millions have been displaced and live as refugees, while others confront the reality of death by violence daily. In the name of our security, innocents in other lands are regularly caught in the crosshairs of Hellfire missiles aimed, we are told, at terrorists—just so much "collateral damage" of attacks ostensibly commensurate with the logic of "zero-casualty warfare." Detainees captured in the "War on Terror" have been subjected to torture and other cruel and degrading attacks on their human dignity, often at the hands of the forces of Western states. Sometimes they are simply refouled (sent back) to states that—often working in conjunction with Western security apparatuses—violate the supposed peremptory norm of international law that prohibits such acts. The citizens of Syria remain mired in the violence and insecurity of a brutal civil war while Western politicians and pundits wring their hands about the brutality of the Syrian regime. It is worth recalling that Syria recently played a useful role in the extension of national security for those same Western interests, as a willing, cooperative participant in the post-9/11 torture archipelago contrived by the United States and its allies.

Migrants who, fleeing the insecurity of chronic poverty, war, and destitution, attempt to reach the West were once simply referred to as "economic migrants" (with pejorative connotations of false refugee claims or "queue jumping"). Now they are increasingly spoken of as "security threats," even as possible terrorists, and interned "accordingly." In direct violation of international human rights obligations, many of these "security threats" are refouled to their home states, where they often face torture and persecution, some never to be heard of again. When they do arrive safely in the West, they become objects of suspicion based on their appearance, dress, or religious affiliation, or simply the sound of their name. As such they have been swept up in dragnets and/or placed under surveillance by state security apparatuses.

In parts of the United States, itself an immigrant society, this has reached absurd proportions that recall totalitarian practices: if an individual even looks as though he or she might be an illegal immigrant, police have cause to insist on identification proving citizenship, which, if not on hand, can lead to detention. Citizens of Western states have been subjected to "extraordinary rendition" to torture by, or with the direct complicity of, Western states, again in the name of our collective security. This dramatically calls into question both the "who" in *our* and the supposed equality of status associated with citizenship.

Some aspects of the new security regime are refreshingly not premised on racial, ethnic, or religious profiling. It appears that the principle of equality extends not only to rights but to their negation as well, as the assault on human rights contemplated by the new security regime goes much deeper still. In the name of national security, the privacy rights of individual citizens—rights of free expression, freedom of assembly, freedom of the press, freedom of thought and religion, due process, and *habeas corpus*—have all come under direct assault. Recent revelations about the activities of Western security apparatuses via Wikileaks have shed light on the depth and scope of licence those institutions have assumed in the post-9/11 era.

There is a strange irony in all of this, one that highlights a crisis of contemporary liberal democracies as much as a crisis of human rights more generally. If the most basic of liberal rights are now compromised in the name of "our" collective security, the promise of the liberal project that saw extension of a range of rights, including first the nationals of Western states as citizens and then all of humanity more generally, then that project seems to have stalled, if not failed. Strangely, it's as though the social contract we created with Leviathan has turned back on us, casting us into some sort of perverse postmodern state of nature.

Conclusion

Hannah Arendt once (in)famously characterized Adolf Eichmann's "thoughtlessness" with respect to the genocide he orchestrated as representing the "banality of evil."[25] What Arendt was getting at was that evil is not necessarily perpetrated by monsters, by people with wicked intent and awful power. It is, rather, able to operate through the everyday actions of "thoughtless" individuals: people who fail to reflect upon the ethical implications of their everyday actions. While they are not driven by ill intentions, it would be wrong to attribute to such individuals the idea of good intentions, for their intentions are generally limited to their own "security," absent consideration of the insecurity those actions simultaneously create for others.

In a world in which human capacity is adequate to the task of resolving most of the conditions that result in the untimely deaths of more than 10 million people annually—roughly the same death rate as the Second World War, including those deaths manufactured in the concentration camps of Nazi Germany—something is terribly awry. In a world in which Western governments actively permit, indeed perpetrate—in direct violation of supposedly non-derogable principles of international law—daily violations of human dignity on a scale that subjects entire nations to degrading indignities and undermines the foundations of individual security, all in the name of higher security imperatives, something seems dreadfully amiss.

In an important respect, the recent assault upon human rights in the anarchic world of international relations has been mirrored by an assault on human rights and civil liberties in Western liberal democracies. To suggest that these processes mirror one another is not to simply highlight their simultaneity but rather to emphasize their intimate connection. For all the talk of the forces of globalization drawing humanity closer together, the increasing abstraction of social relations characteristic of late-modern life has enabled an ethical distancing that, despite so much talk of human rights, seems at least as profound as that of the past, when knowledge of horrors elsewhere was often scant, even non-existent. In a context dominated by egocentric neoliberal ideology and in which fear and loathing of the Other have become central elements of popular political discourse, attention to human rights must, we are told, be balanced with concern for security. Whatever truth there may be in such arguments, it is to be found in a narrowly defined concept of security that sees the two as existing in a tense zero-sum relationship. And in this tense relationship, the new "balance" is located markedly far from human rights in favour of security.

Such formulations, however, ask too much of us. They suggest that after three and a half centuries we have not really moved beyond Hobbes, and that today all rights must be subject to the whims of a Leviathan that, like Hobbes's, knows no superior. Whatever rights we think we enjoy are illusory, as they are always potentially subject to unilateral revocation in our supposed "security interests." Rule by exception—unencumbered by law when the constraints of law become too inconvenient to the designs of power—seems to have become a defining feature of political life since 9/11. The rule of law, arguably the most powerful ideal bequeathed by liberalism, is readily cast to the wind. Law—both domestic constitutional law and international law—appears so pliable and indeterminate as to make a mockery of contentions that law rules at all, other than as a thinly veiled midwife to raw power.

Hobbes and his liberal successors recognized the profound measure of security to be derived from relative determinacy in social intercourse. For Hobbes this security would be secured by dint of Leviathan's absolute authority to dictate the conditions of such intercourse, but liberals injected a reflexive loop into the equation that would mediate not only social behaviour generally but the conduct of the sovereign as well. That loop is rooted in what we have come to speak of as "the rule of law." And if the law that was to rule did so originally in the interest of a narrowly conceived community of bourgeois men, the promise of the Rights of Man was gradually, in response to the legitimatory demands of broader publics, extended to capture the interests of those increasingly plural populations. This process lent greater determinacy, and in turn security, to the lives of those broader populations, simultaneously securing the legitimacy required for law—not, *pace* Hobbes, fear and awe—to rule.

A similar set of developments has unfolded in the realm of international relations. Where, in the interests of a nascent global capitalism, Europeans lorded over a global world with violence and force through centuries of colonialism and imperialism, an increasingly complex world gradually called for alternative modes of governance that would supplant violence and fear as mechanisms to gain cooperation and compliance in pursuit of an increasingly greater interest. If today's institutions of global capitalism require the security derived from determinacy afforded by global regulation, realization of human rights holds out the promise of injecting an enhanced level of determinacy into the lives of the globe's immiserated masses that occupy the margins of growth, both within developing economies and among the growing ranks of the disenfranchised populating the developed world.[26]

As Arendt noted more than a half century ago, human rights are of no value to those who are seeking their realization, absent a political society whose institutions are capable of enforcing them and through which they might press claims for such enforcement. Even today, after so much development of human rights discourse and proliferation of instruments and institutions dedicated to their protection, human rights continue to rely on forms of institutionalized political life, most particularly states, for their actualization and the existential security that arises therefrom. The great paradox remains: while states continue to represent a crucial collective institutional substratum within which dynamics of social power are played out (and thus remain critical guarantors of human rights), they remain as much as ever their greatest source of threat. In an era when the exception is too regularly invoked in response to security concerns and rights guarantees are readily disregarded, it seems that efforts to secure conditions under which human rights might flourish must also entail enhancing a wider range of institutions best suited to those ends. Some solace is to be found in the fact that the state no longer exhausts that range.

Today, institutions dedicated to human rights promotion and protection operate in spheres that transect the boundaries of political life, which were until recently ossified in a rigidly conceived Westphalian system of states conceived of as exhausting the realm of the "realistically" political. The lived experience of rights—the capacity for individuals and collectivities not only to claim but also to realize the benefits to be derived from successful recognition of those claims—has historically taken shape within, and has in turn shaped, the localized distillation of social power that structures the specific dynamics of political action and possibility. Once dominated almost exclusively by the state, new fields of political action have emerged. In an increasingly globalized world, new institutions have arisen that are irreducible either to states or their corresponding populations. These represent a fragile and tentative potential bulwark against states as the principal threats to human rights; they represent loci in and through which political power and struggle irreducible to the state may be played out, militating against states and state actors that hitherto acted with impunity grounded in absolute sovereignty. They have not, however, supplanted the power of states and the status of citizenship as providing the contexts most likely capable of attending to the specific, dynamic shape of human rights realities.

Human rights realities will always be shaped by struggles to institutionalize social and economic relations in a fashion that aims to create more just conditions of life. Any measure of the justice of specific matrices of relations will always be contestable, relatively contextually determined, and, in turn, political. Those contexts are in turn plural, both spatially—local, state-national, transnational, and, increasingly, global—and substantively shaped by social, economic, and political specificities. In an important respect, the modern quest for security has sought, if not consistently, then persistently to quash elements of those pluralities via politics: to domesticate and subdue the political impulse; to dominate, dedifferentiate, and level what is inherently multiple, varied, and uneven; and to narrow their foci. But if the state in its myriad guises has been (and remains) the principal institutional matrix through which politics operate, the sources of political action arise from social pluralities that are in no way exhausted by its reach.

State security has been, at least since Bodin and Hobbes, premised upon an intrinsic concept of human security, and the conventional Hobbesian and liberal variants of the social contract view the dynamic between the two as integral to social order and peace. The problem of each, however, is that it is premised upon an a priori fixing of the political field in a move that supposes genuine *in*security is, by dint of the social contract, banished to the margins of the state's territory. Moreover, each contemplates a characterization of the individual human and his or her interests as conceivable outside the common institutions and relations—institutions and relations that actually raise human beings out of the fundamentally nonhuman conditions that Giorgio Agamben has so starkly captured with his concept of "bare life."[27] It would not be inappropriate to characterize the long march of modern politics as a contest for the assertion of rights so forcefully banished by Hobbes.

While cast in terms of legality, human rights are fundamentally and simultaneously social, economic, and political and rely upon the field of political action for their realization. The meaning ascribed to specific human rights claims and struggles will always be refracted through the specific contexts in which the distribution of social power is contested and in which rights claims are enunciated.[28] Absent acknowledgement of these characteristics, the substantive content of those rights and any measure of their efficacy becomes unintelligible. This is as true for rights of citizenship conceived conventionally, as a status arising from membership in a political specific community defined by a state, as it is for human rights more generally.

While human rights discourse has been mobilized in the pursuit of ends that have resulted in egregious human rights violations, often in direct contravention of international law (the US war against Iraq stands as a particularly poignant case), such is the nature of rights discourse generally. It does not condemn rights but rather highlights their very political nature. In recent years, neoliberal individualism has coupled with a particular breed of liberal cosmopolitanism to acquire dominance over human rights discourses and practices; they have combined to bolster a new imperial ethos that is equally scornful of individual and collective human rights when those contradict its imperatives.[29] Spurred by "necessities" ushered in by the threat of global terrorism, these combined strains—not wholly unlike Hobbes's move to negate individual rights in favour of the security arising from submission to Leviathan—have placed imperial right and an antisocial individualism above the rights of states and the potential protections afforded by citizenship, with global and regional hegemons all too frequently setting aside core elements of international and domestic law in favour of exceptional action.[30]

A nascent and fragile international politics, not of force but of law, must assiduously resist the return to a politics of might and claim for human dignity a politics of *right*. To this end, the pursuit of human rights and the security to be derived from their realization must be bolstered by redoubled commitment to the rule of law and foursquare rejection of the type of exceptionalism that has been such a prominent characteristic of the post-9/11 era. The contention that human rights must be balanced against security concerns has, in short, been misleading. The relationship between the two is integral, not oppositional. Absent human rights, there is simply no security.

Takeaway Messages

- Human rights require both dedicated institutions and corresponding political commitment and action adequate to their realization.
- The enjoyment of human rights depends upon conditions of existential security, often spoken of today in terms of "human security."
- Existential or human security depends not simply on conventional institutions dedicated to state/national security but rather on a broader panoply of institutions, dedicated to securing life conditions under which individuals and groups may realize full enjoyment of their human rights.

Study Questions

- The suggestion that we must strive to achieve a workable balance between human rights and security implies that the two exist in a zero-sum relationship. Why might such a formulation be particularly problematic from a human rights perspective?
- In much modern legal and political theory and practice, security of the state has been regarded as enjoying a necessary primacy over other social and political concerns. From a human rights perspective, in what ways are such formulations both problematic and compelling today?

Issues for Debate or Roundtable

- Do recognizing and struggling to enhance the human rights of others (people who do not share our national citizenship) necessarily imply that we must relinquish aspects of our own security?
- Are there some elements of our rights we should be willing to forego in the name of our collective security? If so, which ones? And whose security are we speaking of when we refer to our collective security?

Additional Reading

Booth, Ken. *Theory of World Security*. Cambridge: Cambridge University Press, 2007. http://dx.doi.org/10.1017/CBO9780511840210.

Dunne, Tim, and Nicholas Wheeler. "'We the Peoples': Contending Discourses of Security in Human Rights Theory and Practice." *International Relations* 18, no. 1 (2004): 9–23. http://dx.doi.org/10.1177/0047117804041738.

Habermas, Jürgen. "The Kantian Project of the Constitutionalism of International Law: Does It Still Have a Chance?" In *Multiculturalism and the Law: Critical Debates*, ed. O.P. Shabani. Cardiff: University of Wales Press, 2007.

Isaac, Jeffrey C. "A New Guarantee on Earth: Hannah Arendt on Human Dignity and the Politics of Human Rights." *American Political Science Review* 90, no. 1 (1996): 61–73. http://dx.doi.org/10.2307/2082798.

Websites

Amnesty International. http://www.amnesty.org/en/.

Human Rights Watch. http://www.hrw.org/.

Office of the United Nations High Commissioner for Human Rights. http://www.ohchr.org/EN/Pages/WelcomePage.aspx.

United Nations Trust Fund for Human Security. http://un.org/humansecurity/.

Notes

1. *The Economist*, "America Attacked: The Day the World Changed," 13 September 2001, http://www.economist.com/node/780341.
2. H. Arendt, *The Origins of Totalitarianism* (New York: Harcourt, Brace, Jovanovich, 1968), 267–302.
3. Ibid., ix.
4. J. Bodin, *On Sovereignty: Four Chapters from "The Six Books of the Commonwealth,"* ed. R. Geuss (Cambridge: Cambridge University Press, 1992); T. Hobbes, *Leviathan*, ed. R. Tuck (Cambridge: Cambridge University Press, 1991).
5. Hobbes, *Leviathan*, 90.
6. Ibid., 89.
7. Ibid., 91.
8. Ibid., 90.
9. J. Locke, *Two Treatises of Government*, ed. R. Guess, Q. Skinner, and R. Tuck (Cambridge: Cambridge University Press, 1988).
10. Arendt, *Origins of Totalitarianism*, 293.
11. J. Bentham, "Anarchical Fallacies; being an examination of the Declaration of Rights issued during the French Revolution," in *Nonsense upon Stilts: Bentham, Burke and Marx on the Rights of Man*, ed. J. Waldron, 46–69 (London: Methuen, 1987), 53.
12. See, for instance, Olympe de Gouges and Mary Wollstonecraft and their respective calls for extension of the "rights of man" to women. O. de Gouges, "The Declaration of the Rights of Woman [1791]," in M.R. Ishay, *The Human Rights Reader: Major Political Essays, Speeches and Documents from the Bible to the Present* (New York: Routledge, 2007); M. Wollstonecraft, *A Vindication of the Rights of Woman*, ed. M. Brody (London: Penguin, 1992).
13. T. Purvis and A. Hunt, "Citizenship versus Identity: Transformations in the Discourses and Practices of Citizenship," *Social and Legal Studies* 8 (1999): 457–82.
14. Arendt, *Origins of Totalitarianism*, 297.

15. As Hersch Lauterpacht has suggested, "Whatever may have been its merits in the past history of International Law, rigid positivism can no longer be regarded as being in accordance with existing international law"; cited in A.M. de Zayas, "International Law and Mass Population Transfers," *Harvard International Law Journal* 16 (1975): 208.
16. See the preamble to the Charter of the United Nations.
17. Cf. Q. Wright, "The Law of the Nuremberg Trial," *American Journal of International Law* 41 (1947): 38–72.
18. T.H. Marshall, "Citizenship and Social Class," in *Citizenship and Social Class*, ed. T. Bottomore (London: Pluto Press, 1992), 11 (emphasis added).
19. F. Fukuyama, "The End of History?" *National Interest* (1989): 3–18; F. Fukuyama, *The End of History and the Last Man* (New York: Avon Books, 1992); G.H.W. Bush, "Address before a Joint Session of the Congress on the Persian Gulf Crisis and the Federal Budget Deficit," 11 September 1990, http://bush41library.tamu.edu/archives/public-papers/2217.
20. For an excellent sampling of some of the burgeoning literature on post–Cold War cosmopolitan possibilities, see G.W. Brown and D. Held, *The Cosmopolitanism Reader* (Cambridge, MA: Polity Press, 2010).
21. The idea of human security first gained prominence in the United Nations Development Programme's *Human Development Report 1994* (New York: Oxford University Press, 1994).
22. Cf. International Commission on Intervention and State Sovereignty, "Responsibility to Protect: Report of the International Commission on Intervention and State Sovereignty" (Ottawa: International Development Research Centre, 2001).
23. This is likely a conservative estimate. UNICEF's website suggests that in 2002, roughly 29,000 children under the age of five died every day, mainly from preventable causes, a majority of whom succumbed to "six causes: diarrhoea, malaria, neonatal infection, pneumonia, preterm delivery, or lack of oxygen at birth." UNICEF, "Goal: Reduce Child Mortality," http://www.unicef.org/mdg/childmortality.html.
24. M. Ignatieff, "The Burden," *New York Times Magazine*, 2003; D. Reiff, "R2P, R.I.P.," *New York Times*, 7 November 2011. It should be noted that the legitimacy of the new ICC, touted at its inception as ushering in an end to impunity and a triumph for the rule of law at the international level, has been sorely tested by post-9/11 realities. All its indictments to date have been issued against Africans, many of whose alleged crimes, however ghastly, pale by comparison with the human rights outcomes arising from pursuit of the "War on Terror," executed by the United States and its allies in violation of peremptory norms of international law. As a result, the Court confronts a debilitating crisis of legitimacy. See K. Roth, "Africa Attacks the International Criminal Court," *New York Review of Books*, 6 February 2014.
25. H. Arendt, *Eichmann in Jerusalem: A Report on the Banality of Evil* (New York: Viking, 1964), 280ff.
26. T. Purvis, "Looking for Life Signs in an International Rule of Law," in *Empires Law*, ed. A. Bartholomew (London: Pluto Press, 2006).
27. G. Agamben, *Homo Sacer: Sovereign Power and Bare Life*, trans. D. Heller-Roazen (Stanford, CA: Stanford University Press, 1998). This echoes Marx's critique of the "Robinsonades," the classical liberal political economists who took as their

point of departure a Robinson Crusoe–like character, cast up on the shores of social and economic life but whose humanity is somehow, and nonsensically, separable therefrom. See K. Marx, *Grundrisse: Foundations of the Critique of Political Economy*, ed. Q. Hoare, trans. M. Nicolaus (Harmondsworth, UK: Penguin, 1973), 83–85.

28. A. Woodiwiss, *Human Rights* (London: Routledge, 2005), 4.
29. J.L. Cohen, "Sovereign Equality v. Imperial Right: The Battle over the 'New World Order,'" *Constellations* 13, no. 4 (2006): 485–505.
30. A point equally evident in US incursions in Afghanistan and Iraq as in Russian irredentist intrigue in the Crimea.

19
Now You See Me: Privacy, Technology, and Autonomy in the Digital Age

VALERIE STEEVES

Learning Objectives

- To become familiar with the range of national and international instruments designed to protect privacy
- To understand the ways in which the bureaucratic desire to maximize efficiency and the commercial monetization of personal information have constrained human rights protections for privacy
- To understand current privacy issues around national security surveillance, the corporate collection of data, and social media in a human rights context

"Privacy Is Over"[1]

As the following examples illustrate, the past few years have been difficult ones for privacy. Edward Snowden's revelations about the Five Eyes[2] disturbed citizens and government leaders alike, especially after it was revealed that the United States was routinely listening in on phone conversations of the heads of state of its allies. German Chancellor Angela Merkel, whose own conversations had been surreptitiously monitored by the US National Security Agency (NSA), responded by saying that "spying among friends" was "unacceptable."[3] Merkel also compared the NSA to Stasi, the ultra-repressive East German security agency, which had collected detailed dossiers on virtually all its citizens during the Cold War.[4]

Google released its Google Glass[5] for beta testing by 8,000 "explorers." Literally with a blink of the eye, Google Glass wearers can activate a video function and record whatever they happen to see. Moreover, this information can be automatically shared with Google, adding to the growing digital footprint we leave behind us as we surf the Internet, interact with various corporations, and—if Google has its way—walk by someone wearing Glass. The first to ban the device was the 5 Point Café, a Seattle dive bar. The bar's owner, Dave Meinert, argued that Glass's ability to constantly record the wearer's experiences violated the expectations of other people in the bar, because a bar was "kind of a private place." Casinos, educational institutions, and some municipalities soon followed suit. As privacy lawyer Timothy Toohey noted, "This is just the beginning … Google Glass is going to cause quite a brawl."[6]

North of the border, Canada joined a growing number of countries criminalizing "revenge porn," in which disgruntled ex-partners—almost always men—post intimate pictures of their former girlfriends on the Web as a form of social shaming.[7] Tacked on to the Canadian legislation were provisions that greatly expanded the police's ability to collect information about citizens from Internet service providers without a warrant. These so-called lawful access provisions had been defeated in parliament on three previous occasions, the last time after more than 150,000 Canadians signed a petition condemning police online spying.[8] Both the mother of Amanda Todd, a British Columbia teen who committed suicide after a partially nude picture of her was distributed online, and Ontario's Information and Privacy Commissioner, Ann Cavoukian, called on the government to stop using child victims of crime as a smokescreen behind which to invade people's privacy.[9] The legislation passed nonetheless.

Developments such as these have led many to conclude that privacy is dead. However, in spite of the recurring obituaries, people continue to push back against new surveillance practices, for a variety of reasons. Critics worry that overzealous national security initiatives such as Five Eyes threaten to upset the democratic balance between citizen and state. Commercial practices such as Google Glass, which collectively record up to 75,000 individual data points on each consumer per day,[10] can constrain our ability to make choices for ourselves, especially when people are sorted into categories for preferential or discriminatory treatment based on their demographics. And constant monitoring of the intimate and mundane details that we post on social media challenges the traditional divide between our private lives and our public personas. As Canadian teens put it, all this surveillance is just plain creepy.[11]

This chapter examines the ways in which emerging information technologies—and the bureaucratic and commercial agendas behind them—have shaped and constrained our experience of privacy since the United Nations first enshrined a right to privacy in the Universal Declaration of Human Rights (UDHR) in 1948. We explore how, with the advent of mainframe computing in the 1960s and 1970s, new methods of collecting, storing, and using personal information raised serious concerns about privacy. However, the same period was marked by growth of government bureaucracy in Europe and the monetization of personal information in North America.

I argue that those two factors worked to reframe privacy protection, through the creation of regulatory mechanisms designed to legitimize the ways in which both the public and private sector use increasing amounts of information about us for their own purposes. Privacy was accordingly recast as a matter of individual control over the collection, use, and disclosure of personal information and the broader links to human dignity and personality in the UDHR were subsumed in the procedural mechanisms of informational control.

A Brief History of Privacy

Discussions of privacy often start by noting that privacy has been an elusive concept to define. Privacy advocates seek to protect privacy because, as a fundamental human right and an essential part of democracy, it is a good in itself. However, communitarians and information collectors such as governments and corporations often argue that privacy detracts from other legitimate social goals, such as government efficiency, economic growth, and the creation of knowledge. Bennett notes that "over thirty years of semantic and philosophical analysis ... leaves [one] with the overwhelming sense that privacy is a deeply and essentially contested concept," grounded in "questionable assumptions" about the individual, civil society, and the state, and "it is those very assumptions that require careful interrogation if the 'politics' of privacy are to be unearthed."[12]

Certainly over the past century, much of the political struggle around privacy has been triggered by new technologies. Warren and Brandeis, who popularized the classic definition of privacy as "the right to be let alone" in 1890, were writing in response to their concerns that the newspaper industry was using the new technology of photography to capture and publish images of private individuals. By the mid-1960s, concerns about the effect of other new technologies on privacy had again come to the forefront and were generating what Regan calls a "literature of alarm."[13] A plethora of popular literature of the day worried that communication technologies, such as listening devices and telephone taps, enabled the state to eavesdrop on conversations that were previously protected by the physical barriers between private and public spaces. The information management capacities of computerized databases also raised concerns that the ability of governments and corporations to monitor large populations would inexorably erode democratic governance and individual autonomy.

Privacy protection accordingly took to the legislative stage in most developed countries in the 1970s. Legislators sought to enact a set of procedural protections based on Alan Westin's popularization of privacy as individuals' right "to determine for themselves when, how and to what extent information about them is communicated to others."[14] Westin's definition was subsequently taken up by more than 85 countries,[15] and his set of data protection principles[16] now dominates privacy law worldwide.[17]

However, the concerns of the time were rooted not in technological change but in the events that had occurred 25 years earlier. Europeans in particular were sensitive to the ways in which central recordkeeping had facilitated the identification and exportation of Jewish people during the Nazi occupation of Europe. Accordingly, the promise of faster, more efficient computerized recordkeeping raised the spectre of mass deportation and oppressive social control.[18] In his seminal work on the history of data protection, Flaherty provides an interesting window on the attitudes of the day: "the development of computer and data banks has aroused elemental anxieties. In England in particular, such sentiments are fuelled by the presence of individuals who have lived under totalitarian regimes and who fear the potential abuse of data banks by governments or invading forces … [Abuse of population registries] is a common fear in European countries that suffered under Nazi occupation, or were seriously threatened by it."[19]

Because of the legacy of the Second World War, the postwar international community concluded that "disregard and contempt for human rights … resulted in barbarous acts which have outraged the conscience of mankind,"[20] and came together through the United Nations to adopt the Universal Declaration of Human Rights, on 10 December 1948. The Declaration expressly provides for protection of privacy. Article 12 declares "No one shall be subjected to arbitrary interference with his privacy, family, home or correspondence, nor to attacks upon his honour and reputation. Everyone has the right to the protection of the law against such interference or attacks."

Privacy is also indirectly protected through provisions guaranteeing the right to life, liberty, and security of the person and to freedom of thought, conscience, and religion. The right to freedom of religion expressly includes the right to practise a religion or belief in public or private. The Declaration also lays the groundwork for respect of privacy as a social right tied to the right to free development of personality.

When the Council of Europe first passed the European Convention for the Protection of Human Rights and Fundamental Freedoms in 1950, it incorporated similar privacy rights in articles 8 and 9, subject to such limitations "as are prescribed by law and are necessary in a democratic society in the interests of public safety, for the protection of public order, health or morals, or for the protection of the rights and freedoms of others." And when the United Nations adopted the International Covenant on Civil and Political Rights in 1966, once again protections for privacy that mirrored the provisions of the UDHR were included. The language used in these instruments created a broad legal right to privacy and cast that right as an essential element of human dignity, freedom, and the democratic process. Thus legal protections for privacy that flowed from the experiences of the Second World War recognized privacy as a fundamental human right, and protected it accordingly.

When legislators again picked up the privacy portfolio in the 1970s, they placed their concerns about new information technologies in this context. The 1973 report of the US Department of Health, Education, and Welfare Secretary's Advisory Committee on Automated Personal Data Systems is typical:

> Most of the advanced industrial nations of Western Europe and North America share concerns about the social impact of computer-based personal data systems ... The discussions that have taken place in most of the industrial nations revolve around themes that are familiar to American students of the problem: loss of individuality, loss of control over information, the possibility of linking databases to create dossiers, rigid decision making by powerful, centralized bureaucracies.[21]

Accordingly, early interest in privacy legislation on the part of the public, the United Nations, and the Council of Europe focused on socio-democratic issues, such as the impact of new technologies on individuality and freedom, and on the exercise of bureaucratic or governmental power. These concerns were shared by scholars who were "motivated by a desire to build institutional and cultural barriers against the comprehensive monitoring of private life that appeared—before the Second World War and later, during the Cold War years—as a necessary condition for the functioning of totalitarian or authoritarian regimes."[22]

However, data protection was not necessarily a good fit with broader concerns about dignity, autonomy, and the promotion of human rights. In fact, the first jurisdiction to enact data protection legislation, the German state of Hesse, was motivated by a very different set of concerns. Under German constitutional law, state and federal laws are administered by local authorities. State governments were using computers to centralize their information gathering and processing, and local governments worried that this centralization would in effect transfer the power and influence traditionally held by local authorities to the state bureaucracy. For its part, the state legislature was concerned that data processing would enhance the executive's power, especially if the legislature were cut off from information held in computers owned and operated by the state bureaucracy.[23]

Data protection laws were accordingly introduced in Hesse in 1970, not to protect privacy but to settle an ongoing dispute between bureaucrats and politicians over which level of government would enjoy the power that came with computerized control of citizens' information. Data protection was accordingly seen as a tool to enhance state power and control; the various levels of government competed for access to data processing to enhance their own effectiveness and wished to set out basic ground rules to protect administrative turf. Citizen concerns about confidentiality and privacy remained an important thread as the fabric of the legislative program was woven. However, the Hesse act demonstrates that data protection laws were enacted because they are consistent with bureaucratic and political interests in safeguarding their respective spheres of power. The rights of a citizen to access and correct his or her data are also consistent with the administrative need for data integrity: citizen oversight of records safeguards the data itself and helps ensure that the information used for policy making and administration is indeed accurate.

When Sweden became the first national government to pass data protection legislation, three years later, it was both the most computerized country in the world and the country with the most extensive routine surveillance in Europe. Flaherty called it "the model surveillance society in the Western world, because of its high degree of automation, the pervasiveness of personal identification numbers to facilitate record linkages, and the extent of data transfers between the public and private sectors."[24] He concluded that "Sweden illustrates the kind of surveillance society that results when record linkages are so easy to accomplish that the power holders cannot resist using them to try to solve real and alleged social problems."[25]

Although citizen concerns about automation of the 1970 census raised questions about privacy, the Swedish government's interest in data protection was rooted in a desire to protect Sweden's national sovereignty against the possibility of its automated population registers falling into the hands of a foreign power. A study published in 1976 by the Swedish Ministry of Defence summarized these concerns well:

> A possible aggressor, who is trying to gain effective and complete control of the population when engaged in acts of war on Swedish territory, may find it necessary to have access to population registers. This assumption is confirmed by experience from the Second World War … Sweden has ten or so computerized central population registers. In most cases these registers contain very detailed information which would be extremely valuable for a possible aggressor aiming to establish control of Swedish territory.[26]

Moreover, data protection was seen by Swedish authorities as a way to ensure that data would continue to flow to the state, by quelling citizen concerns about the privacy of automated census data. As the National Tax Board put it, "coming under surveillance is a privilege,"[27] and "the population should themselves feel that there is a good reason for being recorded in the population registration system ... that [it] simplifies life for them and is an efficient support in achieving a correct distribution of social rights and obligations."[28] From this perspective, data protection was a tool to legitimize state collection of information—to advance ongoing state surveillance more than to protect privacy.

When the Council of Europe (COE) enacted privacy rules two months after Sweden passed its legislation, it returned to the human rights roots underlying citizen concerns. The Resolution of the Protection of the Privacy of Individuals vis-à-vis Electronic Data Banks in the Private Sector (the "Private-Sector Resolution") was its response to an earlier report by the Council's Committee of Experts on Human Rights, which concluded that the law of the time did not provide sufficient protection for citizens against intrusions by technical devices, especially because international covenants applied only to public authorities and did nothing to restrict intrusive practices on the part of private organizations. Although the COE resolution adopted a set of data protection principles, those principles were contextualized by broader statements rooted in the Council's commitment to human rights. For example, the annex to the Private-Sector Resolution states that information about intimate private life should not be collected, because it might lead to unfair discrimination, and the explanatory report suggests that member states should enact provisions to limit the types of data that can be collected.

The COE's primary interest in filling the gap in the law to restrict the negative effects of surveillance technologies was bracketed by competing interests in greater political integration across Europe and administrative modernization. Nonetheless, the Private-Sector Resolution subordinated managerial imperatives—to collect and use large amounts of information to manage risk—to the need to protect individual privacy and autonomy.

Interestingly, when the COE passed its Resolution on the Protection of the Privacy of Individuals vis-à-vis Electronic Data Banks in the Public Sector (the "Public-Sector Resolution") the next year, concerns about privacy as a human right were notably absent. The preamble to the Public-Sector Resolution did not mention the need to protect individuals from potential abuses. Instead it expressly stated that the Resolution was intended to promote greater political integration among member states, by contributing to "public understanding and confidence with regard to new administrative techniques which public authorities in the member states are using in order to ensure the optimal performance of the tasks entrusted to them." The "problems" the Resolution sought to resolve were no longer grounded in historical memory of the Holocaust; instead it was intended to allay public anxiety about new technologies so that governments could continue to use these technologies as they emerged:

> Public anxiety has arisen not because many abuses of information technology have actually been discovered but rather from the possibility of abuse … the discussion is apt to flare up on the occasion of each new project for the use of information technology. In this connection, it should be kept in mind that the success with which computers can be used to public affairs will depend very much on the degree of confidence the public is willing to give to their use.[29]

The Public-Sector Resolution accordingly took on a pedagogical role, seeking to allay public concerns by "sufficiently informing" citizens about new technologies in order to manufacture public trust in emerging administrative practices. In other words, data protection laws were less about protecting people from growing surveillance and more about legitimizing that surveillance through the adoption of procedural rules. As the preamble stated, data surveillance "should be regarded as a positive development. The purpose of the present resolution is not to oppose such use but to reinforce it with certain guarantees."

This shift away from a human rights perspective of privacy, to a focus on managerial efficiency and the legitimacy of surveillance practices, did not occur in a vacuum. As Burkert writes, "Right from the outset, the concept of data protection in Europe was not merely a European affair. American international companies and their subsidiaries … conveyed the American view on regulation and on privacy regulation in particular."[30] From the American perspective, any restriction on the flow of personal information constitutes a trade barrier. American policy is accordingly shaped less by the managerialism evident in the European Union and more by a desire to free technological innovation and trade from cumbersome regulatory mechanisms.

Subsequent international efforts to protect privacy have been heavily influenced by this position. For example, the influential Organisation for Economic Co-operation and Development (OECD)'s Guidelines on the Protection of Personal Privacy and Transborder Flows of Personal Data, passed in 1980, contains a set of data protection principles. The Guidelines also ask member states to "take all reasonable and appropriate steps to ensure that transborder flows … are uninterrupted and secure" and to avoid passing domestic legislation "in the name of the protection of privacy and individual liberties, which would create obstacles to transborder flows of personal data that would exceed requirements for such protection."

The importance of the uninterrupted flow of information in the international marketplace was later underlined in the OECD's Declaration of Transborder Flows in 1985. The Declaration states that these flows are "an important consequence of technological advances and are playing an increasing role in national economies." Since "computerized data and information now circulate, by and large, freely on an international scale" and this circulation brings "social and economic benefits resulting from access to a variety of sources of information and of efficient and effective information services," OECD member states agreed to "promote access to data and information and related services, and avoid the creation of unjustified barriers to the international exchange of data and information."

Thus the OECD Guidelines were at least in part intended to promote the flow of personal data between states to enhance trade and promote efficiencies. Again data protection was perceived to be consistent with these goals. Indeed, the admonition in section 18—to avoid laws "in the name of the protection of privacy and individual liberties" that would obstruct the flow of personal data—implies that data protection was adopted because it minimizes the risk to economic and bureaucratic goals that could be posed by privacy legislation based on a perspective other than data protection.

In 1981 the Council of Europe opened its Convention for the Protection of Individuals with Regard to Automatic Processing of Personal Data for ratification. Although the Convention applies only to the automated processing of personal data, its provisions are very similar to the OECD Guidelines. In addition, both processes were influenced by the American perspective. As a member of the OECD, the United States took an active role in drafting the Guidelines, and the COE Convention "received special wording to provide for the unlikely event that the US would join."[31]

The Convention again enacts a set of data protection principles in an express attempt to "reconcile" the "fundamental value" of privacy with the "fundamental value of … the free flow of information" (preamble). Although the Convention does not suggest that an organization has a right to access an individual's personal information that is co-equal with the individual's right to privacy, it does imply that organizational access is a competing interest of equal importance. This is inconsistent with the COE's strong statements in 1973 against managerial practices that create dangers to privacy, and shows how the Council's original concerns about the potential negative impact on individual autonomy and human rights had been eclipsed by managerial demands and commercial imperatives to access data, regardless of citizen expectations of privacy.

This "process of forgetting" is also evidenced by the priority that the Convention gives to the free disclosure and exchange of personal information. Article 12(2) provides that "[a] party shall not, *for the sole purpose of the protection of privacy*, prohibit or subject to special authorization transborder flows of personal data going to the territory of another Party" (emphasis added). This is a surprising statement from a human rights perspective, as it implies that a state is prohibited from restricting the flow of data to a fellow signatory to the Convention solely because the restriction is required to protect privacy. And, like the other instruments we have examined, the Convention builds in significant exceptions to data protection requirements for the purposes of security, public safety, crime control, statistics, and scientific research. However, the Convention's list of exceptions in article 9 also includes data required to promote "the monetary interests of the state." It is difficult to conceive of restrictions being placed on other human rights—such as the right to free speech or security of the person, for example—justified solely on the basis of fiscal benefits.

The importance of commercial surveillance continued to shape privacy policy after the 1981 Convention. By the late 1980s the European Union had become concerned that lack of a uniform approach to privacy across Europe could impede the free flow of personal data across borders and make trade more difficult, both within Europe and between Europe and North America. Accordingly, when the EU enacted its Directive on the Protection of Personal Data with Regard to the Processing of Personal Data and on the Free Movement of Such Data in 1995, it called on member states to adopt data protection laws as a way of promoting trade.

The Directive was also a key part of a policy structure developed to support the "information superhighway," and as such it sought to create social and political conditions conducive to the adoption and mass implementation of new technologies. Like the Council of Europe before it, the EU was concerned that consumers would not adopt e-commerce unless they were confident that there were rules protecting their personal information. The Directive reflected the "perception, enunciated from the highest circles of government and inter-governmental policy-making, that trust and trustworthiness were key elements of the climate in which [e-commerce] initiatives would flourish."[32] Once again privacy policy took on a pedagogical role; instead of reflecting citizen concerns about the protection of privacy as an essential part of human dignity and autonomy, it became a tool with which to reconstitute those concerns and make them conducive to the prerogatives of bureaucratic efficiency and technological innovation.

As we see below, both of these trends—promoting managerial efficiency and freeing up trade and innovation—have influenced Canada's approach to privacy. They have, in turn, constrained the full protection of privacy as a human right.

Privacy in the Canadian Context

Although Canada played a key role in the drafting of the UDHR, human rights protections for privacy within Canada have been patchy at best. Canada is a signatory to the UN conventions discussed above, but the Canadian Charter of Rights and Freedoms does not contain a specific provision protecting privacy. The Supreme Court of Canada has attempted to fill the gap by using section 8 of the Charter (the right to be free of unreasonable search and seizure) to protect citizens from police surveillance when they have a "reasonable expectation of privacy." For example, the police cannot place a hotel room under surveillance unless they first obtain a warrant, because a warrantless search would violate the occupant's reasonable expectation of privacy. On the other hand, the police may use video surveillance in a public washroom because the courts have said that people using the washroom do not have an expectation of privacy.

Part of the problem lies in the fact that, with the advent of new technologies, the police do not need to watch what occurs in private spaces; they can instead collect data about those spaces and use that data as a proxy to determine what is happening inside. For example, in *R. v. Tessling* (2004), the Supreme Court allowed the police to fly over Walter Tessling's house and use a forward-looking infrared camera to take a picture of heat escaping from the house. Although the police would not have been able to obtain a warrant to enter the house, because they only suspected that Tessling was operating a grow-op, they were able to "look into" the house to see how many lights were on and where they were located. The Court allowed this because the heat pattern was only "information" about the house. Unlike bodily and territorial privacy, which are given a high level of protection by the courts, informational privacy is protected only if it involves a biographical core of personal information that the citizen would not wish the state to have access to. Information about heat escaping from lights does not meet that test, even though the house itself and the activities within it would have been protected if the police had entered the house.

But privacy has also lost ground. As data protection legislation diffused throughout many parts of the world, Canadian legislators also created laws that privileged managerial efficiency and trade over the broader meaning of privacy as a human right. Canada's Privacy Act, which was passed in 1982, governs collection, use, and disclosure of personal information by the public sector. Although the Act gives Canadians rights to access and correct information held about them, section 4 indicates that information can be collected for any purpose that "relates directly to an operating program or activity of the [government] institution." Moreover, the ability to control the collection is limited by vague language and exceptions to the general rules. Under section 5, the individual must be advised of the purpose for collection, but only when the information is collected directly; indirect collection is allowed whenever direct collection is not possible. However, neither requirement applies when it *might* "result in the collection of inaccurate information" or "defeat the purpose or prejudice the use for which information is collected." Thus the government can legally collect personal information without the individual's knowledge or consent, and the test to determine whether or not it even has to notify the individual is the mere possibility that notice might prejudice the use of the data as defined by the government.

The case of *Smith v. Attorney General of Canada* (2001) is a good example of how this can defeat a broader understanding of privacy as a human right and the link between privacy and human dignity and autonomy. Smith was accused of committing fraud because her data showed up in both the employment insurance database and the customs database. The government was routinely matching the data between the two in an attempt to catch "cheaters" who were travelling outside the country while collecting employment insurance benefits. The Privacy Commissioner of Canada argued that this constituted unreasonable search and seizure because it treated every Canadian traveller like a criminal suspect, in effect allowing the state to place citizens under surveillance on the off-chance that they were committing an offence. The Supreme Court disagreed and held that any reasonable expectation of privacy on the part of a traveller did not outweigh the government's need to ensure that people are complying with the law.

The most interesting aspect for our purposes is that the government had consulted with the Privacy Commissioner before beginning the data-matching program. The Commissioner had indicated that the practice would have serious implications for privacy, because that kind of "fishing expedition"—traditionally viewed as an abuse of power—potentially impairs the citizen's dignity and autonomy. The government rejected the Commissioner's advice because the matching program was a highly efficient tool for bureaucrats administering the employment insurance program and complied with the narrow data protection provisions included in the Privacy Act. This, in effect, privileged the government's desire to access personal data because it was an efficient way of administering a government program and ignored broader concerns about privacy as a human right.

The same concerns about bureaucratic efficiency drove much of the discussion when Canada passed its data protection legislation for the private sector. However, the Personal Information Protection and Electronic Documents Act (PIPEDA), which was enacted in 1999, was also a direct response to the EU's Directive on the Protection of Personal Data with Regard to the Processing of Personal Data and on the Free Movement of Such Data. The absence of data protection rules was seen as a barrier to trade with Europe, and PIPEDA was pursued as a way to both open up trade and build consumer trust on the part of Canadians. For example, the discussion paper that preceded the legislation argued that data protection laws were needed to "strike the right balance between the *business need* to gather, store, and use personal information and the *consumer need* to be informed about how that information will be used." Data protection was accordingly seen as an essential element "of building the consumer trust and the market certainty needed to make Canada a world leader in electronic commerce."[33] In addition, PIPEDA itself was based on the results of negotiations among industry, government, and consumer group stakeholders. Like the Privacy Act before it, PIPEDA contains a long list of exceptions to ensure that the data protection rights given to consumers do not reduce the efficiency of conflicting goals, such as policing, research, administration, or e-commerce.

In this chapter I have argued that the desire to promote these conflicting goals has reconstructed the strong protections for privacy first articulated in the UDHR as a set of procedural protections that give individuals limited rights to access and correct the information that governments and corporations use to make decisions about them. The proof may be in the pudding. As the report *Transparent Lives: Surveillance in Canada* makes clear, surveillance has grown exponentially in Canada since PIPEDA was enacted.[34] The report also notes that the line between the public and private sectors is becoming increasingly blurred: information that cannot be legally collected by governments (because to do so would violate section 8 of the Charter) is routinely collected by corporations and then shared with governments, without warrants or any other kind of accountability mechanism. Moreover, privacy is increasingly constrained by "smart" technologies like the camera that captured the heat patterns of Tessling's house, technologies that record the GPS locations of our cellphones, our use of electronic bus passes, the photos and comments we post on social media, and our faces as they are captured on closed-circuit television security cameras. And all of this information is collected so that others—governments and corporations—can make decisions about the kinds of benefits and services we are entitled to enjoy.

Back to the Beginning: Protecting Privacy as a Human Right

Our brief review of the history of privacy protection indicates that privacy rights as set out in the UDHR were expressly linked to human dignity and autonomy. The UDHR also acknowledged the important role that privacy plays in allowing us to enjoy other human rights; it is hard to exercise our freedom of speech or association when everything we say and do is routinely and constantly monitored and then shared with governments and corporations.

Ironically, when the government first began talking about the need for PIPEDA in the late 1990s, a parallel process was initiated by the House of Commons Standing Committee on Human Rights and the Status of Persons with Disabilities (HURAD) that expressed privacy protection firmly in the human rights language of the UDHR. HURAD conducted hearings and public consultations to explore legislative options that could account for the effect of new technologies; it concluded that, although data protection legislation was "clearly a critical part of the spectrum of privacy interest, in a world of increasingly intrusive technologies, it is by no means the only game in town."[35] HURAD argued that truly effective privacy protection can be sustained only if the value of privacy as a human right is given greater weight than the bureaucratic efficiencies and economic benefits of an unconstrained flow of personal information. To do this, it recommended that the government enact a privacy rights charter with quasi-constitutional status and require all federal laws to respect everyone's "physical, bodily and psychological integrity and privacy; privacy of personal information; freedom from surveillance; privacy of personal communications; and privacy of personal space."[36]

The proposed charter was intended to be "umbrella legislation" that would help guide the development and application of all federal laws, including data protection legislation. By giving the charter precedence over the latter, HURAD hoped to "capture the full breadth of privacy, like a wide angle lens taking in a panoramic view, as opposed to the data protection framework … that focuses, like a close-up lens, tightly on informational privacy rights."[37] In making its recommendations, HURAD drew expressly on the early work of the United Nations and the Council of Europe: "Ultimately, [the privacy charter] is about taking privacy seriously as a human right. To do that, we must invoke recent history and remind ourselves *why* the right to privacy was entrenched in the UDHR and subsequent human rights instruments. Otherwise, we may be seduced into believing that privacy is simply a consumer rights issue that can be fixed by a few codes of conduct and some new, privacy enhancing technologies."[38]

A Privacy Rights Charter modelled on HURAD's recommendations was introduced in the Senate of Canada by Senator Sheila Finestone in 2000. However, the Charter died on the order table after the government refused to support it, because of fears that legal recognition of privacy as a human right would place many of the government's information practices in jeopardy. The Department of Justice's senior general counsel for public law policy, Elizabeth Sanderson, told the Senate Standing Committee on Social Affairs, Science, and Technology at the time, although the government was "sympathetic" to the Charter, legally protecting privacy as a human right "would create a good deal of uncertainty and quite possibly may pose obstacles to many government programs and policy":

> Let me give you a concrete example where the [Charter] could affect departmental legislation and operations. Citizenship and Immigration Canada (CIC) collects a great deal of personal information relating to immigration applications and to the enforcement of deportation orders and immigration offences. [The Charter] would potentially require CIC to defend its information gathering and sharing activities in court ... In conclusion, while [the Charter] can be praised as intending to enhance the privacy of Canadians, the devil may be in the detail. Changes could come *at the expense of certainty, public safety, operational efficiency and fiscal responsibility.*[39]

Ongoing Conflicts Between Efficiency and Innovation and Privacy

So whither the human right to privacy? Canada remains a signatory to the UDHR, but its domestic legislation largely ignores the human rights impact of new surveillance technologies. Public policy continues to promote bureaucratic efficiency and trade over privacy, and legal reforms to data protection legislation, both PIPEDA and its provincial counterparts, have only added to the long list of exceptions that allow organizations to sidestep the procedural protections that data protection offers.

Most recently, the government proposed changing the law to enable organizations to voluntarily disclose personal information to any other organization for the purpose of investigating a breach of an agreement, and to protect organizations from legal liability for releasing personal information.[40] Both of these changes would make it easier for organizations to share personal information without the individual's knowledge or consent. What is perhaps most perplexing about these amendments is that they were proposed at a time when citizen concerns about privacy were at an all-time high, especially after it was revealed that, even without the amendments, the government asks telecom companies to voluntarily release personal information about their subscribers approximately 1.2 million times each year. As Geist notes, "It is not Canadians who have given up on privacy. It is the Canadian government."[41]

However, a number of advocacy groups continue to challenge these kinds of practices by using human rights language to frame the issues. For example, the International Campaign Against Mass Surveillance was launched in 2005 by more than a hundred civil-society groups, including the American Civil Liberties Union, the International Civil Liberties Monitoring Group, and Statewatch. The campaign declaration calls on governments to "stop the wholesale, indiscriminate collection and retention of information on citizens, including the acquisition of databanks from private companies," because they "erode or are contrary to existing data protection, privacy and other human rights laws and standards."[42] From this perspective, the fact that data collection conforms to procedural rules is not enough to legitimize it; the test is whether or not it complies with the human rights obligations articulated in international instruments such as the UDHR. As Ursula Franklin notes, the choice of language is particularly important:

> When human rights informs the language in which the discussion among you and the general public and Parliament takes place, you speak then, rightfully about citizens and all that comes with that. On the other hand, if the emphasis is primarily on the protection of data, one does look at a market model, one does look at an economic model, and all the things you've heard about the new economy. Then it is the language of the market that informs your discourse.[43]

Let's return to the three examples set out at the beginning of this chapter to see how human rights language opens up opportunities for legal responses that go beyond data protection and take human dignity and autonomy into account more fully.

Five Eyes surveillance has been universally condemned in the press as invoking Big Brother politics—precisely the kind of thing the drafters of the UDHR were concerned about—but spy agencies continue to maintain that their practices are legal. The broad exemptions contained in data protection legislation certainly enable companies to cooperate with government spying programs. Nonetheless, when Edward Snowden was defending his actions as a whistleblower, he called on

> Article 12 of the Universal Declaration of Human Rights, and numerous statutes and treaties [that] forbid such systems of massive, pervasive surveillance.

> While the US Constitution marks these programs as illegal, my government argues that secret court rulings, which the world is not permitted to see, somehow legitimize an illegal affair. These rulings simply corrupt the most basic notion of justice—that it must be seen to be done. The immoral cannot be made moral through the use of secret law.[44]

Canadian Federal Court Judge Richard Mosley agrees. In November 2013 he lambasted the Canadian Security Intelligence Service (CSIS) for deliberately misleading the Court so it could use Canadian warrants to get other members of the Five Eyes to spy on Canadians on foreign soil. One month later, the General Assembly of the United Nations passed the Resolution on the Right to Privacy in the Digital Age. In it, the Assembly states that it is

> [d]eeply concerned at the negative impact that surveillance and/or interception of communications, including extraterritorial surveillance and/or interception of communications, as well as the collection of personal data, in particular when carried out on a mass scale, may have on the exercise and enjoyment of human rights ... [and] calls upon states to respect and protect the right to privacy, including in the context of digital communications [and] to take measures to put an end to violations of those rights and to create the conditions to prevent such violations, including by ensuring that relevant national legislation complies with their obligations under international human rights law.

Google Glass continues to be a subject of controversy, especially because it underlines how pervasive commercial data collection has become. Google Glass illustrates how "smart" environments, replete with sensors, create a leaky environment. The platforms on which we play, work, and shop and the devices we carry share information about us promiscuously on an ongoing basis, often in the background and outside our control. Moreover, private-sector interests in marketing and the commodification of online social interactions, on the one hand, and public-sector concerns about efficiency and risk reduction, on the other, have combined to create a system in which decisions about us are routinely made on the basis of data collected about us. These "data shadows" are used to profile us, both for benefits and as risks, in essence automating discrimination in new and disturbing ways.

Data protection rules have been insufficient to curb this because they fail to examine the purposes of the collection. Although organizations are required to collect and use data only for the purposes they specify, broad and largely meaningless "purposes" such as "optimizing your user experience" have consistently been accepted by data protection regulators. Once collection is legitimated by a transparent goal of this type, any discrimination based on how the data is used to profile the individual recedes into the algorithm; it becomes increasingly difficult to challenge the kinds of disadvantages that are reinforced by the sort.

In order to challenge this practice, in May 2014 a group of privacy advocates issued the Ottawa Statement on Mass Surveillance in Canada. They noted "[t]hat there is extensive targeting and profiling of individuals and groups on grounds of race and ethnicity, political and religious views, social class, age, gender, sexual preference and disability; [and that] Canadian privacy and data protection laws and regulations are regularly bypassed, undermined or broken, and are inadequate for dealing with information and privacy rights in the age of big data and ubiquitous surveillance."[45] To rectify the situation, they called upon government to "fully respect the Canadian Charter of Rights and Freedoms including the right to privacy, freedom of thought and expression, freedom of association and peaceful assembly, and security against unreasonable search and seizure."[46]

"Revenge porn" illustrates how information available on networked media can cause harm to a person's reputation, even when the information is true. Online providers such as Google typically resist deleting this kind of content. However, in 2014 the Court of Justice of the European Union held in favour of a Spanish man who was embarrassed by online references to social security debts he had incurred in 1998. The Court determined that individuals are entitled to have irrelevant or excessive information about them excluded from the Internet giant's search results, unless there is a public interest that militates against it.[47] Within one day of making the service available, Google received 12,000 requests to block information.

Conclusion

In each of the above cases, the language of human rights was used to expand upon the protections offered by data protection and to reassert the importance of privacy to the democratic process and to human dignity and autonomy. Human rights instruments were referenced to challenge the bureaucratic and commercial imperatives that lie at the base of many government and corporate information practices. Meeting the challenges posed by networked technologies will not be easy. However, the "panoramic lens" of human rights can help us move beyond narrow procedural rules and consider more deeply the kind of society we want to be. Data protection is a part of the puzzle, but it is privacy as a human right that will provide the big picture.

Takeaway Messages

- Privacy rights are central to individual autonomy and dignity.
- Effective privacy protection must go beyond data protection and interrogate the impact of surveillance practices on privacy as a human right.

Study Questions

- Privacy has been variously defined as the right to be let alone, the right to control what personal information others know about you, and the right to a private life. Which definition is the most compelling to you, and why?
- Google collects every email you send or receive through Gmail and uses it for a variety of purposes, including selling information about you to advertisers. Does this practice violate your privacy? Why or why not?

Issues for Debate or Roundtable

- Given the popularity of social media, is privacy something that people continue to value?
- The right to ask a search engine to delete links to irrelevant or excessive information about oneself is sometimes called "the right to be forgotten." Is there a public interest in providing people with ongoing access to such information? Does deleting the links to the information violate the poster's right to free expression?

Additional Reading

Humphreys, Stephen. *Navigating the Dataverse: Privacy, Technology, Human Rights.* Geneva: International Council on Human Rights Policy, 2011.

Solove, Daniel J. *Understanding Privacy*. Cambridge, MA: Harvard University Press, 2008.

Websites

Canadian Internet Policy and Public Interest Clinic. https://www.cippic.ca/.
Electronic Privacy Information Centre. https://epic.org/.
OpenMedia. https://openmedia.ca/.
Privacy International. https://www.privacyinternational.org/.

Notes

1. T.L. Friedman, "Four Words Going Bye-Bye," *New York Times*, 20 May 2014, http://mobile.nytimes.com/2014/05/21/opinion/friedman-four-words-going-bye-bye.html?from=mostemailed&_r=0.
2. "Five Eyes" refers to the United States, the United Kingdom, Canada, Australia, and New Zealand, which have signed a multilateral agreement to cooperate in signals-intelligence gathering. Edward Snowden released documents indicating that the Five Eyes countries circumvent laws that restrict their ability to spy on their own citizens by asking one of the other members to do it for them, and that American and Canadian intelligence agencies routinely collect telephone and Internet records en masse from corporations such as Google, Facebook, and Verizon.
3. L. Baker and A. Rinke, "Merkel Frosty on the U.S. over 'Unacceptable' Spying Allegations," *Reuters*, 24 October 2013, http://news.yahoo.com/germany-france-unite-anger-over-u-spying-accusations-094005929.html.
4. I. Traynor and P. Lewis, "Merkel Compared NSA to Stasi in Heated Encounter with Obama," *The Guardian*, 17 December 2013, http://www.theguardian.com/world/2013/dec/17/merkel-compares-nsa-stasi-obama.
5. A pair of glasses without lenses but with a tiny computer attached to the frame that can access networked media and record sound and video.
6. D. Streitfeld, "Google Glass Picks up Early Signal: Keep Out," *New York Times*, 6 May 2013, http://www.nytimes.com/2013/05/07/technology/personaltech/google-glass-picks-up-early-signal-keep-out.html.
7. Bill C-13, *Protecting Canadians from Online Crime Act*, 2nd Session, 41st Parliament, 62–63 Elizabeth II, 2013–2014.
8. OpenMedia, https://openmedia.ca.
9. M. Geist, "From Toews to Todd: The Unravelling of the Government's Online Privacy Laws," *Huffington Post*, 26 May 2014, http://www.huffingtonpost.ca/michael-geist/carol-todd-privacy-bill_b_5393244.html.
10. J. Gerstein and S. Simon, "Who Watches the Watchers? Big Data Goes Unchecked," *Politico*, 14 May 2014, http://www.politico.com/story/2014/05/big-data-beyond-the-nsa-106653.html.
11. V. Steeves, *Young Canadians in a Wired World, Phase III: Experts or Amateurs? Gauging Young Canadians' Digital Literacy Skills* (Ottawa: MediaSmarts, 2012), 64.
12. C. Bennett, "The Political Economy of Privacy: A Review of the Literature," paper prepared for the DOE Human Genome Project, Center for Social and Legal Research, University of Victoria, BC, 1995, 2.
13. P. Regan, *Legislating Privacy* (Chapel Hill: University of North Carolina Press, 1995), 13.
14. A. Westin, *Privacy and Freedom* (New York: Atheneum, 1967), 7.
15. G. Greenleaf, "Global Data Privacy Laws: 89 Countries, and Accelerating," *Privacy Laws and Business International Report* 115 (February 2012).
16. Data protection principles require that organizations collecting personal information be accountable for their handling of the information; identify the purpose for collection and use; obtain the information with the data subject's knowledge and/or consent; collect only information that is relevant to the purpose; use the information only for the stated purpose; retain the information only for as long

as is needed for the stated purpose; ensure that the information is accurate; keep the information secure; be open about their information practices; and provide the data subject with access to the information it has collected about him or her. Data protection laws require organizations to comply with some or all of these practices; C. Bennett and C. Raab, *The Governance of Privacy: Policy Instruments in Global Perspective* (Cambridge, MA: MIT Press, 2006).

17. Bennett and Raab, *Governance of Privacy.*
18. D. Flaherty, *Privacy and Government Data Banks: An International Perspective* (London: Mansell, 1979), 44; H. Burkert, "Privacy—Data Protection: A German/European Perspective," in *Governance of Global Networks in the Light of Differing Local Values*, ed. C. Engel and K.H. Keller (Baden-Baden, Germany: Nomos, 2000), 60.
19. Flaherty, *Privacy and Government Data Banks*, 44.
20. United Nations, Universal Declaration of Human Rights, preamble.
21. US Department of Health, Education and Welfare, Secretary's Advisory Committee on Automated Personal Data Systems, *Records, Computers and the Rights of Citizens* (Washington, DC: HEW, 1973), appendix B.
22. Bennett and Raab, *Governance of Privacy*, 23.
23. Burkert, "Privacy—Data Protection," 44–45.
24. Flaherty, *Privacy and Government Data Banks*, 4.
25. Ibid., 94.
26. Sweden, Ministry of Defence, *Secretariat for National Security Policy and Long Range Defence Planning Report* (Stockholm, 1976).
27. G. Persson, "Computerized Personal Registers and the Protection of Privacy," *Current Sweden* 344 (1986): 2.
28. Sweden, National Tax Board, "Population Registration in Sweden," brochure (Stockholm: National Tax Board, 2003).
29. Council of Europe, Resolution on the Protection of the Privacy of Individuals vis-à-vis Electronic Data Banks in the Public Sector, (74) 29, Explanatory Memorandum, para. 5.
30. Burkert, "Privacy—Data Protection," 65–66.
31. Ibid., 66.
32. Bennett and Raab, *Governance of Privacy*, 79.
33. Industry Canada and Department of Justice, Task Force on Electronic Commerce, *Building Canada's Information Economy and Society: The Protection of Personal Information* (Ottawa: Public Works and Government Services Canada, 1998): 3 (emphasis added).
34. C.J. Bennett, K.D. Haggerty, D. Lyon, and V. Steeves, *Transparent Lives: Surveillance in Canada* (Edmonton: Athabasca University Press, 2014).
35. Canada, House of Commons Standing Committee on Human Rights and the Status of Persons with Disabilities, *Privacy: Where Do We Draw the Line?* (Ottawa: Public Works and Government Services Canada, 1997), 24.
36. Ibid., 45.
37. Ibid, 44–45.
38. Ibid., 72.
39. Canada, Proceedings of the Standing Senate Committee on Social Affairs, Science and Technology, Issue 25: Evidence, 20 September 2001, 25 (emphasis added).

40. See Parliament of Canada, Bill S-4, *Digital Privacy Act*, and Bill C-13, *Protecting Canadians from Online Crime Act*, 2nd Session, 41st Parliament, 62–63 Elizabeth II, 2013–2014.
41. M. Geist, "Why Has the Canadian Government Given Up on Protecting Our Privacy?" *Toronto Star*, 30 May 2014, http://www.thestar.com/business/2014/05/30/why_has_the_canadian_government_given_up_on_protecting_our_privacy.html.
42. American Civil Liberties Union, "Campaign Declaration: International Campaign Against Mass Surveillance," https://www.aclu.org/technology-and-liberty/campaign-declaration-international-campaign-against-mass-surveillance.
43. Cited in House of Commons Standing Committee on Human Rights and the Status of Persons with Disabilities, *Privacy*, 34.
44. E. Snowden, "Edward Snowden's Statement to Human Rights Groups in Full," *The Telegraph*, 12 July 2013, http://www.telegraph.co.uk/news/worldnews/europe/russia/10176529/Edward-Snowdens-statement-to-human-rights-groups-in-full.html.
45. "Transparent Lives: Surveillance in Canada, Ottawa Statement on Mass Surveillance in Canada," 10 May 2014, http://www.surveillanceincanada.org/node/32.
46. Ibid.
47. *Google Spain SL and Google Inc. v. Agencia Española de Protección de Datos (AEPD) and Mario Costeja González*, Case C-131/12, Court of Justice of the European Union, 13 May 2012.

Concluding Discussion: The Effectiveness of Rights Instruments

GORDON DIGIACOMO

The several chapters in this book have discussed a broad range of human rights-related concerns and, in the process, sought to make students aware of the key rights instruments that affect Canadians—the Canadian Charter of Rights and Freedoms, the provincial human rights codes, and the United Nations human rights treaties. Some readers may have found the sprawling content of the volume unwelcoming. Others will have found it an intellectual feast from which they could not be easily pulled away. Still others will agree that it is justified because of the dearth of such books in Canada. In any case, it is our hope that readers found the chapters to be written in a clear and engaging style and the arguments presented in a comprehensible way.

In addition, we would like readers to note that human rights matters are not the preserve of the legal profession, that the protection of rights depends to a substantial degree on the design of political institutions and on the work of NGOs and other elements of civil society. We hope too that readers will see that states are not the only perpetrators of rights abuses: the corporate sector must also be held to account for the times when it treats people's rights in an abusive fashion. We hope that readers will look at globalization not only from an economic perspective but also from a rights perspective, and demand from their leaders a more critical approach to free trade. We would like our readers to have gained a better understanding of the human rights issues facing particular communities. And we believe that the chapters will help them come to an informed opinion about such contemporary concerns as ageism, environmental rights, privacy rights, the rights of migrant workers, religious freedom, and the efforts of the state to deal with security concerns.

In this the book's final discussion, we look briefly at the effectiveness of rights instruments. More specifically, we consider three questions: first, is litigation an effective way to advance rights protection and to stimulate social change? Second, has the Charter of Rights and Freedoms made a difference in the lives of Canadians? And third, have international human rights treaties had any success in protecting and promoting the rights of people around the globe, particularly in states with oppressive regimes?

Litigation, Rights Protection, and Social Change

In a provocative book, Gerald Rosenberg argues that the ability of human-rights litigation to effect substantial social reform is very limited. He examines litigation efforts in several areas, including the American civil rights movement, the women's rights movement, and the same-sex marriage issue, and concludes that court victories contributed only marginally to the achievement of substantial reform in those areas. When litigation is effective, it is only because it has been embedded in a basic strategy of political mobilization. "In the end," Rosenberg writes, "there is no substitute for political action."[1]

Similarly, Hirschl and Rosevear point out that, four years after the well-known *Grootboom* decision in South Africa (in which the South African Constitutional Court upheld the right of homeless people to adequate housing), the lives of those involved had changed little. They quote from the South African *Sunday Times*: "Squatters' precedent-setting victory in the Constitutional Court has gained them only stinking latrines. ... Leaking sewage and piles of rotting rubbish smell so bad in Grootboom that you can actually taste the stench."[2] In this case, the homeless people's victory in the courts had a limited shelf life.

On the other hand, the role played by the courts in making social change possible was indispensable for some citizens. Consider, for instance, the gay and lesbian community in Canada. It is widely agreed that they benefited significantly from adoption of the Charter of Rights and Freedoms and the ensuing litigation. This certainly was the assessment of Miriam Smith in her exhaustive analysis of the achievement of lesbian and gay rights in Canada and the United States.[3] Four judicial decisions, all rendered since adoption of the Charter, are seen to be especially important. In *Egan v. Canada* (1995), a majority of the Supreme Court held that sexual orientation, which is not listed in section 15 as a prohibited ground of discrimination, is an analogous ground. According to Justice La Forest, sexual orientation "falls within the ambit of s. 15 protection as being analogous to the enumerated grounds." Thus sexual orientation was read into section 15 of the Charter. In *Vriend v. Alberta* (1998), the Supreme Court unanimously held that the Alberta government's omission of protection from discrimination based on sexual orientation was contrary to the Charter, and it read sexual orientation into the Alberta human rights code. In the third decision, *M. v. H.* (1999), the Court ruled that "the limitation of support provisions in Ontario's family law legislation to opposite-sex partners was an unjustified violation of section 15 of the Charter."[4]

The fourth decision dealt with same-sex marriage. In 2002–03, courts in British Columbia, Ontario, and Quebec held that the opposite-sex requirement for marriage was discrimination based on sexual orientation. As a result of these decisions and a Supreme Court Reference decision, the federal government introduced legislation that changed the definition of marriage to "the lawful union of two persons to the exclusion of all others," thus including marriages of people of the same sex.

Smith repeatedly refers to the important part played by the courts in advancing gay and lesbian rights. She concludes unequivocally that "In the area of lesbian and gay rights, courts have played a critically important role in shaping policy. This study drives home the point that courts are more likely to recognize lesbian and gay rights than other political actors."[5] This was especially the case during the 1990s, the Chrétien era. In her view, the Chrétien government would have stalemated on gay and lesbian rights and ignored the issue "had it not been for the impact of judicial empowerment."[6] She argues further that the Chrétien government had not wanted even to add sexual orientation to the federal Canadian Human Rights Act "and did so only after a pattern of lower court decisions made it clear that the Supreme Court would inevitably force the government to do so."[7] Clearly the Charter and the court actions it made possible resulted in huge advances for gays and lesbians in Canada.

Siri Gloppen, a political scientist and human rights specialist based at the University of Oslo, has studied the "social transformation performance" of courts and offers comments that are relevant here, particularly in relation to the roles of the law and of politics in effecting social change. She defines social transformation as "the altering of structured inequalities and power relations in society in ways that reduce the weight of morally irrelevant circumstances, such as socio-economic status/class, gender, race, religion or sexual orientation."[8] Courts' contributions to social transformation lie in the altering of structured inequalities and in the way they make possible social inclusion of marginalized groups. The contributions range from providing legal redress for marginalized groups to "passively serving as a public platform where claims can be articulated. As a focal point for mobilization and publicity this may have important political effects even in the absence of a judgment acknowledging the claim."[9]

That said, Gloppen declares flat out that "ensuring social equality is mainly a task for elected politicians," and that democratic decision making by elected bodies must be accorded sufficient political space.[10] With respect to the role of the courts, she writes,

> In a democratic system, judges are obliged to protect all citizens' rights and to ensure that "collective decisions be made by political institutions whose structure, composition, and practices treat all members of the community, as

> individuals, with equal concern and respect." Courts should repair the malfunctioning of the democratic process when the latter systematically impairs the interests of marginalized groups. But this does not preclude a role for the other branches of power.[11]

Gloppen stresses that the social transformation potential of court decisions depends on factors outside the legal system: "even where the courts make pro-transformation judgments, factors beyond their control may undermine their decisions. These are related to the fundamentals of the political and economic context, the level of state formation and the government's capacity to implement rulings."[12] By "political context" Gloppen means, above all, "the balance of power between the competing political forces (whether there is a dominant party that can afford to ignore court decisions, or a more balanced political situation where overruling or ignoring court decisions may be politically costly)."[13] Essentially, what Gloppen is arguing is that the advancement of citizens' rights depends not only on responsive courts but also on rights-conscious political parties and an active civil society.

Has the Charter Made a Difference?

In Canada the amount of research undertaken on the effectiveness of the Charter is not great. While there is not space here to take on such a project, it is possible to show that communities that campaigned vigorously for a comprehensive Charter won many victories in the courts, and that, while one may argue whether those victories brought about dramatic social change, they hold enormous significance for the communities concerned. The discussion above of the victories of the gay and lesbian community provides a case in point, but we can also point to the victories of minority-language communities, Canadians with disabilities, Aboriginal peoples, and those involved in the criminal justice system.

Minority-Language Groups

In their volume on the Charter, Robert Sharpe and Kent Roach agree that the official-language minorities, particularly French-language minorities, have done well since adoption of the Charter. They acknowledge that "The recognition and protection of language rights was significantly enhanced under the *Charter of Rights and Freedoms*."[14] The Supreme Court of Canada has given the "minority language education rights in section 23 … a generous interpretation."[15] Three decisions are particularly noteworthy. The first of these is *Mahé v. Alberta* (1990). Here the Court ruled that the right to receive instruction in minority-language education facilities includes the right to control and manage such facilities. In *Doucet-Boudreau v. Nova Scotia* (2003), the Supreme Court upheld a ruling by a superior court judge in which he not only ordered the construction of several French-language schools but also declared that the court would retain jurisdiction, in order to receive reports on the government's compliance with his order.

And the Supreme Court's decision in *R. v. Beaulac* (1999) is seen to be important because of its elaboration of the concept of substantive equality for official-language communities. The justices wrote, "The principle of substantive equality ... provides in particular that language rights that are institutionally based require government action for their implementation and therefore create obligations for the State.... It also means that the exercise of language rights must not be considered exceptional or as something in the nature of a request for an accommodation."[16] In the assessment of Muscati and Rouleau, "Governments are responding. Provincial governments erected the minority-language education structure that will allow official language minorities to survive, grow and flourish."[17]

Persons with Disabilities

With respect to persons with disabilities, the inclusion in the Charter of mental or physical disability as a prohibited ground of discrimination made Canada unique. For more than a decade, Canada was the only state in the world that constitutionally protected persons with disabilities.[18] The Charter accelerated a shift in thinking about disability: from the medical or charity model to the rights or social model of disability. However, no one would suggest that because of the Charter, the struggle for equality is over for Canadians with disabilities. Indeed, Deborah Stienstra's chapter in this volume makes exactly that point. But clearly the insertion of disability into the Charter was seen by disability rights activists as being essential to their cause. The several court victories of Canadians with disabilities impelled a leading disability rights activist to declare, "Persons with disabilities have clearly succeeded in laying down some important footings on which to demand that Canadian society begin to restructure its institutions to be inclusive and respectful of disability equality rights.... It is law reform that will ultimately create a world that is welcoming and respectful of the equality rights of persons with disabilities. The highest court of Canada has prescribed a number of foundational principles on which to base this process."[19] In this sense, the Charter can be said to be making a difference.[20]

Aboriginal Peoples

Aboriginal peoples campaigned vigorously for inclusion of Aboriginal and treaty rights in the Charter during the parliamentary hearings of 1980–81. As a result, section 25 and section 35 were inserted to protect those rights.[21] More recently, the former chief of the Assembly of First Nations, Shawn Atleo, and a leading Aboriginal rights lawyer, David Nahwegahbow, have commented on the effectiveness of section 35. The message of both is that the section has changed the legal landscape, affording substantial protection for Aboriginal and treaty rights that, before 1982, had little or no protection. For Nahwegahbow, "s. 35 has made Canada a more democratic society, but it has not yet completely fulfilled the promise of reconciliation.... s. 35 has given additional protection for aboriginal and treaty rights."[22] For Atleo, "We do have positions of strength to build on—and I believe that section 35 remains a key cornerstone of this work."[23]

Aboriginal peoples have had several victories in the courts since 1982. Nahwegahbow argues that among the most significant are the Supreme Court's judgements in *Haida Nation v. British Columbia (Minister of Forests)* (2004) and *Mikisew Cree First Nation v. Canada (Minister of Canadian Heritage)* (2005). The key issue in these cases was the government's duty to consult Aboriginal peoples when their lands are affected. "These cases have given significant leverage because the duty to consult and accommodate gives First Nations a say in developments within their traditional lands and the potential for economic benefits, like resource revenue-sharing."[24]

Another important Supreme Court decision came in the case of *Tsilhqot'in Nation v. British Columbia*. Here the justices agreed that the Tsilhqot'in Nation had established Aboriginal title over an area of land in BC. Aboriginal title, the Court stated, "confers the right to use and control the land and to reap the benefits flowing from it." In addition, "The right to control the land conferred by Aboriginal title means that governments and others seeking to use the land must obtain the consent of the Aboriginal title holders." If the government wants to act in spite of an Aboriginal group's wishes, it must demonstrate "(1) that it discharged its procedural duty to consult and accommodate; (2) that its actions were backed by a compelling and substantial objective; and (3) that the governmental action is consistent with the Crown's fiduciary obligation to the group."[25] Not surprisingly, this firm and clear declaration of support for the concept of Aboriginal title was welcomed by Aboriginal leaders.[26]

It should also be mentioned here that section 35 made possible another important victory for Aboriginal peoples: the 1995 Government of Canada recognition that the section embraces the inherent right of First Nations to self-government. As it has been for persons with disabilities, no one could possibly conclude that the adoption of constitutional rights has radically improved the living conditions of Aboriginal citizens. Many continue to live in appalling circumstances. But it clearly has struck at the kind of structured inequality that Siri Gloppen refers to in her definition of social transformation. It has strengthened considerably the position of Aboriginal peoples in their interactions with the Canadian state.

Some scholars, such as Kiera Ladner and Michael McCrossan, take a harder line. The focus of their critique is the Supreme Court's interpretation of sections 25 and 35 of the Charter. They deny that Aboriginal peoples ever ceded their sovereignty and they contend that Aboriginal nations have their own traditions of rights and individualism that "are extremely different from, and are quite incompatible with" Western, Eurocentric traditions. They argue that the Supreme Court's assumption of Crown sovereignty has diminished the possibilities for a "decolonized relationship" between Canada and the Aboriginal nations:

> Six years after *Sparrow*, writing for a majority of the Court in *R. v. Van der Peet*, then Chief Justice Antonio Lamer argued that the purpose behind recognizing and affirming Aboriginal rights in section 35(1) of the *Constitution Act, 1982*, was to achieve a "reconciliation of the pre-existence of Aboriginal societies with the sovereignty of the Crown." Such an understanding of section 35 undermined its potential for decolonization as it served to naturalize Crown sovereignty and take it as a given rather than as a power of the Crown whose legitimacy over Aboriginal people had yet to be determined.[27]

Realistically speaking, it is difficult to imagine a high court in a sovereign state rendering a decision that recognized the sovereignty of a community within that state.

Criminal Justice

With respect to the Charter's impact on those tangled up in the criminal justice system, it appears generally to have been positive. This would be the overall evaluation of Marc Rosenberg, currently a judge on the Ontario Court of Appeal, who assessed the Charter on five criteria: wrongful convictions, access to justice, privacy and security, speedier justice, and sentencing. Rosenberg concludes that the Charter has contributed to the prevention of wrongful convictions.[28] Further, it "has proved a success in increasing our personal sense of privacy and security against unwarranted state intrusion."[29]

With respect to speedier justice, it has prevented trial delays from "spinning totally out of control," although it has not yet made a significant contribution toward actual reduction in trial delays.[30]

On access to justice, Rosenberg concludes that, "on balance ... the Charter cannot be considered a great success in the context of access to justice for the accused, at least as measured by the guarantee to the right to counsel."[31] However, women and children have been accorded greater protection as victims and as witnesses. With respect to sentencing, the Charter's impact has been negligible. However, as a result of certain decisions, it seems unlikely that the death penalty will ever be returned to Canada. For Rosenberg this represents "one unequivocal advance in the administration of criminal justice attributable to the Charter, an advance that mitigates all pessimism and doubts about the importance and value of the Charter in our criminal justice system."[32]

Women's Rights

For women in Canada, the Charter is said not to have had a significant impact. This is the view of Sharpe and Roach, who conclude that "while women's groups were among the most active in lobbying for a powerful equality guarantee, the gains to women from equality litigation have been modest." On the other hand, they acknowledge that "general public acceptance of and respect for gender equality has been enhanced by the Charter."[33] Anne Forrest, director of women's studies at the University of Windsor, is more enthusiastic about the Charter. She states that its "particular mix of individual and minority rights and interpretive flexibility" is a "combination" that has served the interests of women and other historically disadvantaged groups, "because justice is now read against the standard of substantive equality" rather than only formal equality.[34]

From the foregoing, it can be reasonably concluded that the Charter has made a difference for many Canadians who historically had found themselves in a vulnerable position.

International Rights Instruments

Doubts about the effectiveness of rights instruments extend to the international instruments. The leaders of many nations around the globe regularly and flagrantly violate human rights to such an extent that one wonders if the international treaties have had any impact at all. A number of scholars have attempted to address the question of whether human rights treaties have been effective. Tony Evans does not set out to address the issue, but he does argue that rights treaties are completely inadequate, that they are the wrong tool to get at the source of many human rights violations.

As indicated in this book's introduction, Evans uses globalization theory to investigate and critique the international human rights regime and its implementation. His argument is essentially that "the structures of the global political economy, and the interests that these structures support" may be the causes of many human rights violations. Such causes may, for example, include "large-scale engineering projects that displace tens of thousands of people against their wishes"; "the ease with which governments overlook the violations of human rights perpetrated by important trading partners"; and "the continued supply of military equipment to strategic allies regardless of their human rights record."[35] But, he writes, "Instead of asking why violations of human rights continue to occur on a global scale, which would include an assessment of structural causes of violations, attention is focused on the sites of violations and identifying those responsible for atrocities. Social, economic and political practices are rarely factored into the analysis of human rights violations, which leaves those who benefit from these practices free of all moral responsibility."[36] In a scathing denunciation of the role of international law, Evans argues that "it has little to contribute to challenging an order that constitutes a major source of human rights violations."[37] Nevertheless, when political leaders see rights abuses persisting, they respond by determining that "we need even more international law to correct earlier shortcomings."[38]

Beth Simmons is more optimistic about the possibilities of international law, an optimism doubtless given a boost by the findings discussed in her book *Mobilizing for Human Rights.* Simmons examines international compliance with four treaties: the International Covenant on Civil and Political Rights and its Optional Protocol on the Death Penalty; the Convention on the Elimination of All Forms of Discrimination Against Women; the Convention Against Torture and Other Cruel, Inhuman or Degrading Treatment or Punishment; and the Convention on the Rights of the Child and its Optional Protocol Relating to Children in Armed Conflict. Simmons found that human rights treaties have in fact made a positive contribution to the realization of rights throughout the world. Her principal conclusion is that international human rights treaties have an impact for the better—not in countries that can be described as stable democracies, nor in countries she calls stable autocracies, but in the "in-between" countries, countries that are transitioning to democracy. In those countries there is a degree of political space that allows for some democratic activity and mobilization. There are also citizens with the capacity and motivation to mobilize. She calls her theory to explain treaty compliance in these transitioning countries the "domestic politics theory of treaty compliance." In brief, the theory holds that treaties help to shape the national policy agenda, influence legal decision making, and encourage rights NGOs to mobilize.[39]

Notwithstanding the findings of Simmons and others, the fact remains that large segments of the globe's population are led by authoritarian governments that have little interest in complying with the provisions of the UN's nine principal human rights instruments and the five regional human rights treaties, even if they have signed and ratified them. Eric Posner has looked at several studies on the effectiveness of international human rights law and concludes that "Understood in the best possible light, these studies suggest that a small number of treaty provisions may have improved a small number of human rights outcomes in a small number of countries by a small, possibly trivial amount.... Realistically, one can have little confidence that the treaties have improved people's lives."[40]

This unhappy situation exists because there is very little that the international community can do to influence internal human rights practices. One of the tools available is the system of treaty bodies created by the UN to monitor implementation of the nine treaties. The committees and the treaties monitored are set out in Table C.1.

The treaty bodies perform a number of tasks, as set out in the treaties that created them. These include considering state parties' periodic reports, addressing individual complaints, conducting country investigations, and interpreting treaty provisions.[41] These methodologies constitute what Rhona Smith has called "light touch" monitoring mechanisms.[42] In reality, the treaty bodies are powerless in the face of an authoritarian regime—or any regime—that is determined to violate the rights of its citizens. Even Canada, as supportive of the UN and its treaties as a country can be, nevertheless was able to ignore with impunity the Human Rights Committee's determination that an Ontario government decision to fund Catholic schools and not those of other religions was in fact a violation of article 26 of the International Covenant on Civil and Political Rights.

The weaknesses of the international human rights legal system are well known. Numerous proposals to strengthen the system have been offered, but they all bump up against international politics and the principles of national sovereignty and non-intervention in the internal affairs of sovereign states.[43] As a result, the likelihood of a spike in the near future in levels of compliance with human rights law is low. On the other hand, it is perhaps an indicator of the presumptuousness of the generations born after the Second World War that we would expect to see, in the space of 60 years or so, a global order based on the rule of human rights law. The protection afforded

Table C.1

Committee	Treaty Monitored
Human Rights Committee	International Covenant on Civil and Political Rights (ICCPR) and its optional protocols
Committee on Economic, Social, and Cultural Rights	International Covenant on Economic, Social, and Cultural Rights (ICESCR)
Committee on the Elimination of Racial Discrimination	International Convention on the Elimination of All Forms of Racial Discrimination
Committee on the Elimination of Discrimination Against Women	Convention on the Elimination of All Forms of Discrimination Against Women and its optional protocol
Committee Against Torture	Convention Against Torture and Other Cruel, Inhuman or Degrading Treatment
Sub-committee on Prevention of Torture and Other Cruel, Inhuman or Degrading Treatment or Punishment	Optional Protocol of the Convention Against Torture
Committee on the Rights of the Child	Convention on the Rights of the Child and its optional protocols
Committee on Migrant Workers	International Convention on the Protection of the Rights of All Migrant Workers and Members of Their Families
Committee on the Rights of Persons with Disabilities	International Convention on the Rights of Persons with Disabilities
Committee on Enforced Disappearances	International Convention for the Protection of All Persons from Enforced Disappearance

by the international rights instruments may not yet be available to everyone, but it seems clear that the world would be a different place were those treaties not in place. Even Eric Posner, who is among the more pessimistic analysts of human rights law, acknowledges in his latest book that the percentage of "free countries" in the world increased from 29 per cent in 1973 to 42 per cent in 1991 to 46 per cent in 2012. In 2013, of 194 countries on the planet, 90 were described by Freedom House as "free."[44] It is not unreasonable to suggest that the international rights architecture is at least partially responsible for that growth, however slow it may be.

The work of ensuring rights protection for everyone must and will go on. Everyone must be able to feel the self-respect that comes with the knowledge that there is a legal order and there are political institutions created to protect one's right to exist, to belong, and to flourish, regardless of the morally irrelevant category into which that person falls.

Notes

1. G. Rosenberg, *The Hollow Hope: Can Courts Bring about Social Change?* 2nd ed. (Chicago: University of Chicago Press, 2008), 431.
2. R. Hirschl and E. Rosevear, "Constitutional Law Meets Comparative Politics: Socio-economic Rights and Political Realities," in *The Legal Protection of Human Rights: Sceptical Essays*, ed. T. Campbell, K.D. Ewing, and A. Tomkins (Oxford: Oxford University Press, 2011), 218.
3. M. Smith, *Political Institutions and Lesbian and Gay Rights in the United States and Canada* (New York: Routledge, 2008).
4. R. Sharpe and K. Roach, *The Charter of Rights and Freedoms*, 4th ed. (Toronto: Irwin Law, 2009), 336.
5. Smith, *Political Institutions*, 185.
6. Ibid., 105.
7. Ibid., 183. Interestingly, gays and lesbians in Canada at the time were not well mobilized for political action. According to Smith, "the movement in Canada is very poorly organized and resourced compared to the professionalism, organizational variety, depth and skill of U.S. lesbian and gay organizations"; ibid., 190.
8. S. Gloppen, "Courts and Social Transformation: An Analytical Framework," in *Courts and Social Transformation in New Democracies: An Institutional Voice for the Poor?* ed. R. Gargarella, P. Domingo, and T. Roux (Burlington, VT: Ashgate, 2006), 37–38.
9. Ibid., 38.
10. Ibid., 39–40.
11. Ibid., 39.
12. Ibid., 54.
13. Ibid., 55.
14. Sharpe and Roach, *Charter of Rights and Freedoms*, 371.
15. Ibid., 367.
16. Quoted in S. Muscati and N. Rouleau, "The Future of Canada's Official-Language Minorities," in *Official Languages of Canada: New Essays*, J.E. Magnet (Markham, ON: LexisNexis Canada, 2008), 386.
17. Ibid.
18. R.D. Kelemen and L. Vanhala, "The Shift to the Rights Model of Disability in the EU and Canada," *Regional and Federal Studies* 20, no. 1 (March 2010): 8.
19. Y. Peters, "Twenty Years of Litigating for Disability Equality Rights: Has It Made a Difference?" Council of Canadians with Disabilities, 26 January 2004, http://www.ccdonline.ca/en/humanrights/promoting/20years#introduction. Among the most important of the disability rights cases is *Eldridge v. British Columbia (A.G.)* (1997). At issue was the BC government's refusal to provide sign-language interpretation to enable deaf patients to communicate effectively with their health-care providers. Peters writes, "The [Supreme] Court ruled that the failure to provide sign language interpretation constituted adverse effect discrimination against deaf persons. It argued that the notion that governments should be entitled to provide benefits to the general population without ensuring that disadvantaged members of society have the resources to take full advantage of those benefits 'bespeaks a thin and impoverished vision of s. 15(1).'"

20. On 17 April 2012, the thirtieth anniversary of the Charter of Rights and Freedoms, the Council of Canadians with Disabilities issued a press release in which the chairperson of the Council stated, "CCD celebrates the anniversary of the Charter and all those who have been using it to remove barriers to the full and equal participation of people with disabilities. April 17 is an important anniversary which we must celebrate every year." Presumably the Council believes the Charter's birth ought to be celebrated because it has been beneficial to Canadians with disabilities; Council of Canadians with Disabilities, "Constitutional Equity Rights: People with Disabilities Still Celebrating 30 Years Later," press release, 17 April 2012, http://www.ccdonline.ca/en/humanrights/promoting/charter-press-release-17apri2012.
21. Section 35 is not in the Charter itself.
22. D. Nahwegahbow, "The Promise of Reconciliation," *National*, March 2012, http://www.nationalmagazine.ca/Articles/May-2012/The-promise-of-reconciliation.aspx.
23. S. Atleo, "National Chief Speaking Notes—Thirty Years Later: Section 35 Still Necessary Path Forward," Assembly of First Nations, http://www.afn.ca/index.php/en/national-chief/highlights-from-the-national-chief/national-chief-speaking-notes-thirty-years-later-section-35-still-nece.
24. Nahwegahbow, "Promise of Reconciliation."
25. *Tsilhqot'in Nation v. British Columbia*, [2014] 2 S.C.R. 256, at paras. 2, 76–77.
26. See Assembly of First Nations, "Assembly of First Nations Congratulates Tsilhqot'in National Government on Landmark Legal Victory at Supreme Court of Canada, Calls on Federal Government to Work with First Nations on New Approaches to Support Real Reconciliation with First Nations," press release, 26 June 2014, http://www.afn.ca/index.php/en/news-media/latest-news/assembly-of-first-nations-congratulates-tsilhqotin-national-government.
27. K. Ladner and M. McCrossan, "The Road Not Taken: Aboriginal Rights after the Re-imagining of the Canadian Constitutional Order," in *Contested Constitutionalism: Reflections on the Canadian Charter of Rights and Freedoms*, ed. J. Kelly and C. Manfredi (Vancouver: UBC Press, 2009), 272.
28. M. Rosenberg, "Twenty-Five Years Later: The Impact of the *Canadian Charter of Rights and Freedoms* on the Criminal Law," Court of Appeal for Ontario, www.ontariocourts.ca/coa/en/ps/publications/twenty-five_years_later.htm.
29. Ibid., 10.
30. Ibid., 12.
31. Ibid., 7.
32. Ibid., 12.
33. Sharpe and Roach, *Charter of Rights and Freedoms*, 354. In a similar vein, Diana Majury writes in a 2002 article that "the Charter is full of problems, of analysis and of results. At the same time, there have been some positive decisions, some good equality analysis, and some statements that take my breath away coming from the top court in the country." She thinks clear-cut victories for women have come in the areas of reproduction and violence against women. The "most troubling" concern is the Court's unwillingness or the Charter's inability to deal with socioeconomic disparities; D. Majury, "The Charter, Equality Rights, and Women: Equivocation and Celebration," *Osgoode Hall Law Journal* 40, no. 3/4 (2002), 335.

34. A. Forrest, *No Birthday Party for Our Charter of Rights and Freedoms*, University of Windsor Women's Studies, http://www1.uwindsor.ca/womensstudies/no-birthday-party. The comments of former Supreme Court justice Louise Arbour and her colleague Fannie LaFontaine are worth noting here. They have described the Charter as "a catalyst for positive social change in Canada" and "a solid instrument of social progress in Canada"; L. Arbour and F. LaFontaine, "Beyond Self-Congratulation: The Charter at 25 in an International Perspective," *Osgoode Hall Law Journal* 45, no. 2 (2007): 244–45.
35. T. Evans, *The Politics of Human Rights: A Global Perspective* (Ann Arbor, MI: Pluto Press, 2005), 28.
36. Ibid., 64.
37. Ibid., 69.
38. Ibid., 71.
39. B. Simmons, *Mobilizing for Human Rights: International Law in Domestic Politics* (New York: Cambridge University Press, 2009), 114.
40. E. Posner, *The Twilight of Human Rights Law* (New York: Oxford University Press, 2014), 78. For Simmons's response to Posner, see B. Simmons, "What's Right with Human Rights," *Democracy: A Journal of Ideas* 35 (Winter 2015), www.democracy-journal.org/35/whats-right-with-human-rights.php. See also Simmons's reply to Posner's column of 25 November 2014: "Twilight or Dark Glasses? A Reply to Eric Posner," openDemocracy, 23 December 2014, https://www.opendemocracy.net/openglobalrights/beth-simmons/twilight-or-dark-glasses-reply-to-eric-posner.
41. UN Office of the High Commissioner for Human Rights, "Monitoring the Core International Human Rights Treaties," www.ohchr.org/EN/HRBodies/Pages/WhatTBDo.aspx.
42. R.K.M. Smith, "Human Rights in International Law," in *Human Rights: Politics and Practice*, ed. M. Goodhart (Oxford: Oxford University Press, 2009), 42.
43. For a discussion and evaluation of some of the reform proposals that have been advanced, as well as presentations of her own, see E. Hafner-Burton, *Making Human Rights a Reality* (Princeton, NJ: Princeton University Press, 2013), 117–33, and *Forced to Be Good: Why Trade Agreements Boost Human Rights* (Ithaca, NY: Cornell University Press, 2009). Hafner-Burton is director of the Laboratory on International Law and Regulation at the University of California, San Diego.
44. Posner, *Twilight*, 4.

Appendix A: International Human Rights Treaties

Tables A.1 and A.2 below identify formal treaties. Not included are declarations, which are non-binding. The three not listed are the Universal Declaration of Human Rights, approved by the United Nations in 1948; the American Declaration on the Rights and Duties of Man, adopted in 1948 by the states that created the Organization of American States that year; and the ASEAN Human Rights Declaration, adopted in 2012 by the member states of the Association of Southeast Asian Nations.

Table A.1 Core United Nations Human Rights Treaties

Instrument	Entry into Force	Ratification by Canada
International Covenant on Civil and Political Rights, 1966	March 1976	May 1976
Optional Protocol to the International Covenant on Civil and Political Rights, 1966	March 1976	May 1976
Second Optional Protocol to the International Covenant on Civil and Political Rights, 1989	July 1991	November 2005
International Covenant on Economic, Social and Cultural Rights, 1966	March 1976	May 1976
Optional Protocol to the International Covenant on Economic, Social and Cultural Rights, 2008	May 2013	Not ratified
International Convention on the Elimination of All Forms of Racial Discrimination, 1965	January 1969	October 1970
Convention on the Elimination of All Forms of Discrimination Against Women, 1979	September 1981	December 1981
Optional Protocol to the Convention on the Elimination of All Forms of Discrimination Against Women, 1999	December 2000	October 2002
Convention Against Torture and Other Cruel, Inhuman or Degrading Treatment or Punishment, 1984	June 1987	June 1987
Optional Protocol to the Convention Against Torture and Other Cruel, Inhuman or Degrading Treatment or Punishment, 2002	June 2006	Not ratified

Table A.1 Core United Nations Human Rights Treaties

Instrument	Entry into Force	Ratification by Canada
Convention on the Rights of the Child, 1989	September 1990	December 1991
Optional Protocol to the Convention on the Rights of the Child on the Involvement of Children in Armed Conflict, 2000	May 2002	July 2000
Optional Protocol to the Convention on the Rights of the Child on the Sale of Children, Child Prostitution and Child Pornography, 2000	January 2002	September 2005
Optional Protocol to the Convention on the Rights of the Child on a Communications Procedure, 2011	April 2014	Not ratified
International Convention on the Protection of the Rights of All Migrant Workers and Members of Their Families, 1990	July 2003	Not ratified
Convention on the Rights of Persons with Disabilities, 2006	May 2008	March 2010
Optional Protocol to the Convention on the Rights of Persons with Disabilities, 2006	May 2008	Not ratified
International Convention for the Protection of All Persons from Enforced Disappearance, 2006	December 2010	Not ratified

Table A.2 Regional Human Rights Treaties

Treaty	Parties
European Convention for the Protection of Human Rights and Fundamental Freedoms (came into force 1953)	all 47 member states of the Council of Europe
European Social Charter (came into force 1965)	ratified by 43 of 47 member states of the Council of Europe
African Charter on Human and Peoples' Rights (came into force 1986)	ratified by 53 of 54 member states of the African Union
American Convention on Human Rights (came into force 1978)	ratified by 23 of 35 member states of the Organization of American States (not ratified by Canada)
Arab Charter on Human Rights (came into force 2008)	ratified by 17 of 22 member states of the League of Arab States

Appendix B: Simulation Exercise

This simulation exercise is one that I have used in several of my courses. The following was used in a fourth-year political science class, Politics of Human Rights. Variations of it have been used in other courses where human rights or constitution-making was a key theme.

Before the simulation, students should be guided through several rights instruments, including the Canadian Charter of Rights and Freedoms, the UN human rights treaties, and the various regional (continental) rights instruments. They should also have learned about constitutions and rights and political institutions and rights.

Introduction

East Rodan has just seceded from Rodan. The transitional government wishes to place the new country securely on the path of democracy. Like the leadership of most newly independent states, it sees as its first step the drafting of a constitution, and toward this end it recently held elections for a 200-member interim parliament. The interim parliament then created a 100-member constituent assembly (CA), some members of which were elected members of the interim parliament and some appointed from outside the interim parliament.[1]

The CA comprises members with a variety of backgrounds: professionals, businesspeople, workers, farmers, human rights activists, former politicians, academics, students, clergy, members of the military, and police personnel. It is generally representative of the country's regions, its major ethnic, religious, and linguistic communities, and its demographics. The membership is also ideologically diverse, and substantial differences exist among the members on how the East Rodan state should be configured.

Collectively, the class is a committee of the CA, the Human Rights Committee, and its membership is as varied as that of the CA. Your concerns are human rights and your mandate is to address these questions: Should the constitution of East Rodan contain a charter of rights? If so, what should be in such a charter? And what political and judicial institutions will protect rights most effectively?

The New Country

The new country is situated in Eastern Europe. It is not an impoverished country but it is also not wealthy, and there is a huge gap between rich and poor. The population is about 10 million. People under 24 years old are a rapidly growing segment of the population. By European standards, it is a geographically large country. One of the countries bordering East Rodan is Bosnia-Herzegovina.

The country has just come to the end of a 20-year period of ethnic strife, culminating in independence on [insert date]. There is great animosity between the French-speaking majority and the Muslim minority within the country from which East Rodan has just achieved independence. On a number of occasions violence has broken out. The Muslim community has long felt systematically shut out of the mainstream of economic, social, and political life in Rodan. The Aboriginal community is socially and economically marginalized in both East Rodan and Rodan proper. The Aboriginals harbour a deep anger and a deep sense of grievance.

The larger country of Rodan may be described as an illiberal democracy. For instance, there have been elections, using a system similar to that used in Canada, but the elections were very flawed events, often accompanied by violence. Rights protection is very weak. The federalism that it practises is far from exemplary. The government is highly authoritarian and provincial leaders are frequently branded "warlords." Corruption is characteristic of governance at both levels. However, liberal democratic impulses were much stronger in the East Rodan region; hence the drive for independence. It was one of the better-off regions of Rodan, sustained by a robust sense of entrepreneurship among the people.

- *Languages:* About 40 per cent of the citizens of East Rodan claim French as their mother tongue, about 30 per cent Arabic, and about 20 per cent English.
- *Religions:* About 30 per cent of the citizens of East Rodan are practising Muslims and about 20 per cent are practising Christians. The remaining 50 per cent consists of citizens who are Jewish, Buddhists, Hindus, or Sikhs; who subscribe to a non-traditional religion; or who do not practise any religion.
- *Ethnic Communities:* About 10 per cent of the population consists of Aboriginal citizens, half of whom live in the north of the country. The Muslim population, composed largely of citizens with origins in Lebanon, Egypt, Pakistan, Bosnia, Iran, and Libya, is concentrated in

the southern part of the country. The French-speaking and English-speaking populations are scattered throughout East Rodan.

- *Economy:* The economy is based on forestry. A few multinational corporations dominate the forestry industry, but there are numerous small firms that cut and harvest logs. A furniture-manufacturing sector is starting to emerge. At this point the industry is dominated by one transnational corporation, but again there are several smaller firms.
- A vigorous information technology industry has emerged and is soon expected to be a major player in the economy.
- Labour unions are a growing force in the country and represent about 10 per cent of the workforce. They are growing not only in numbers but also in militancy. The gap between East Rodan's economic elite and the working class is very wide and is a deeply annoying issue for the unions.
- *Civil Society:* Civil society in East Rodan cannot be said to be well-developed. There is a strong belief among citizens in the importance of family. Associations representing the ethnic and linguistic communities are active. Organized religion is very strong throughout the country.
- Advocacy groups are scarce, although a few international environmental groups have set up offices in the new country. The media, with a few exceptions, are very weak.
- While more political parties are starting to emerge, political life is dominated by a couple of ethnically based parties. A workers' party has emerged and has the support of the labour unions.
- *Education:* There is a high rate of illiteracy in East Rodan, as well as a high dropout rate among secondary school students. There is one university. Internet use is not high but it is increasing. There are few publications and few libraries.

Committee Co-Chairs

Two student co-chairs, elected by the class, will provide leadership of the Committee. As two of East Rodan's leading legal scholars, educated in Canadian and European universities, the two co-chairs have immense credibility and are hugely respected by the other Committee members. This credibility gives the co-chairs a generous amount of latitude. Their primary task is to prepare a final report, based mostly *but not entirely* on sub-committee reports. They will also make appointments to the sub-committees, ensuring that each has varied representation. To do this, the co-chairs should consult with each sub-committee member and together come up with a background for each.

The co-chairs also preside over meetings of the Committee, monitor the work of the sub-committees, meet periodically with representatives of the sub-committees, and help to resolve difficulties and disputes. The co-chairs may also want to consult with experts, such as other professors and representatives of human rights NGOs.

Sub-Committees

1. Bill of Rights Sub-Committee I
2. Bill of Rights Sub-Committee II
   - These two sub-committees have to settle the question of whether East Rodan should have a bill of rights at all. If it should, the sub-committees will then have to determine if the bill should be inserted into East Rodan's constitution or be simply a statutory bill.
   - If a bill of rights, either constitutional or statutory, is thought to be desirable, the sub-committees will then have to decide what should go into the bill of rights, being sure to explain why some rights have been included and others left out. They will determine whether the bill of rights should be comprehensive or minimal, whether there should be a Supreme Court with the power to strike down legislation, how appointments to the Supreme Court should be made, and how the independence of the Court should be assured.
   - What other rights-focused judicial or quasi-judicial institutions should be created, if any?
   - Representatives from each Sub-Committee, along with the Co-Chairs, will have to meet to sort out the work load of each.
3. State Structure Sub-Committee
   - Should the country have a federal system or a unitary system of government? Which safeguards rights the best? If federal, what kind—centralized or decentralized?
   - If federal, what is the role of the sub-national governments in rights protection? And if federal, how should the provinces be determined? If unitary, should there be some sort of alternative decentralization method?
   - Also, whether federal or not, how should the government (or governments) incorporate international human rights treaties into East Rodan's domestic law?
   - Should the parliament be unicameral or bicameral? Which protects rights best?

4. Political Institutions Sub-Committee
   - This sub-committee will make recommendations on which kind of electoral system the new country should have. Which safeguards rights the best? Should there be reserved seats? Should the electoral system be entrenched in the constitution?
   - What type of executive—parliamentary or presidential—best protects rights? What role should the parliament and legislatures have in rights protection?
   - The sub-committee will also consider the role of political parties in protecting rights. What can be done, if anything, to ensure that political parties do their part in rights protection? Should political parties be constitutionally required to have a national focus?

Note: Students may wish to create a fifth committee: a research committee tasked with finding out what kinds of institutions other countries, particularly those at a stage of development similar to that of East Rodan, have established to protect rights. The instructor should leave this up to the co-chairs and the sub-committees.

Formal Meetings

The purpose of the formal meetings of the Committee is to discuss and debate the reports of the sub-committees and to come to an agreement on the recommendations that the Committee will present to the entire CA. Obviously much discussion will have to occur before the formal meetings: between the sub-committees, within the sub-committees, and between the co-chairs and each sub-committee.

The co-chairs will determine what percentage of the Committee's membership will be required to approve adoption of the recommendations of each sub-committee.

Note: In doing their work, including in the meetings of the sub-committees and the Committee as a whole, students are expected to engage with each other. That means clearly conveying disagreement, asking for explanations and clarifications, proposing alternatives, and even confronting and challenging one another. In real life, the work that CA members are asked to do is complex; it can and does easily arouse strong emotions. Some newly democratizing countries spend months simply discussing how the CA members will be determined. For the citizens of East Rodan, much is at stake. In short, the Human Rights Committee is not a place for easy agreement, excessive cordiality, or vows of silence.

Grading

Sub-Committees

1. *Report Outline:* Worth 10 per cent of the simulation mark, it should be at least three double-spaced pages in length and submitted mid-term. It should briefly describe what issues the report will deal with and how it will unfold. It should identify the major sources to be used, as well as the duties of each member. The document will require some research in order to determine what issues the report will address. One copy should be given to the instructor and one to the co-chairs.
2. *Sub-Committee Report:* Worth 30 per cent of the simulation mark, the sub-committee report should be at least 25 double-spaced pages in length. One copy should be sent to the instructor, one to the co-chairs, and one to each of the other sub-committees.
3. *Peer Assessment:* 10 per cent of the simulation mark will come from student peer assessments.

Co-Chairs

1. *Student Assessment:* 15 per cent of each co-chair's simulation mark should be based on the assessments of the students.
2. *Progress Report:* One progress report, worth 5 per cent, should be submitted to the instructor by the Committee co-chairs. It should be at least three double-spaced pages in length and should contain information on the work of the sub-committees as well as the work of the co-chairs.
3. *Final Report:* 30 per cent of the co-chairs' simulation mark should be based on the final report that they prepare. The report will be derived mostly, but not exclusively, from the sub-committee reports and from the agreements reached during the meetings. It should contain both analysis and recommendations. A draft of the final report should be circulated to the sub-committees and their feedback sought before it is submitted.

Note

1. For more on the creation of constituent assemblies, see L. Miller, ed., *Framing the State in Times of Transition: Case Studies in Constitution Making* (Washington, DC: US Institute of Peace Press, 2010).

Glossary

Aboriginal title—the right of Aboriginal people to exclusive use and occupancy of land, based on historic occupancy and relationship to that land.

Accessibility—the ability of all to use, engage with, belong to, participate in, and benefit from a product, space, website, community, policy, and so on.

Accession—A state may sign an international treaty but it is not bound by it. The treaty is usually subject to future ratification, acceptance, or approval, all of which are described as accession. Only then can a country be described as being a party to a treaty, rather than merely a signatory.

Accommodations for persons with disabilities—adjustments or arrangements made to typical ways of doing that allow those with disabilities to participate. Some examples are increased flexibility in work hours; written materials provided in alternative formats, including digitized text, Braille, or large print; sign-language interpreters or real-time captioning provided for persons who are deaf or hard of hearing; automatic entry doors; and accessible washrooms.

Accommodation of difference—employers, service providers, and others are required to accommodate differences that arise on prohibited grounds of discrimination unless the accommodation is "undue."

Active aging—ensuring that, as they age, individuals remain in charge of their own lives for as long as possible and, where possible, can contribute to the economy and society.

Ageism—discrimination against people on the grounds of age, usually referring to discrimination against the elderly. In age discrimination, an individual's chronological age is a factor when making decisions such as offering employment.

Age-based social exclusion—deprivation and lack of access to social activities and networks, causing reduced or poor quality of life for people of a particular age group.

Arab Spring—a series of uprisings initiated in Tunisia in late 2010 and in Egypt in early 2011, caused by lack of freedoms, widespread political repression, crumbling economies, and high unemployment rates, especially among youth. People eventually rejected continuation of past, failed policies and rampant coercive methods, and staged massive demonstrations in the streets of Tunisia, Egypt, Libya, Bahrain, Yemen,

Syria, and other Arab countries. This response to lack of freedom and poor economic conditions was best captured by the catalyst of the Tunisian uprisings: Mohamed Bouazizi's self-immolation in the face of government harassment of his produce stand in Sidi Bouzid, a provincial city in central Tunisia. Waves of protest subsequently swept across the region, leading to rather peaceful change in some areas and violent backlash and turmoil in others.

Austerity—political ideologies and public policies that reduce state expenditures, particularly on social provisions and entitlement programs, with the goal of reducing budget deficits.

Buen vivir—roughly, a moral/ethical principle relating to living well or collective well-being in Andean cosmology; in Kichwa expressed as *sumuk kawsay* (Ecuador), and in Aymara as *suma qamaña* (Bolivia).

Child—according to the UN Convention on the Rights of the Child (art. 1), "every human being below eighteen years."

Civil court—a court that deals with non-criminal cases by applying private law to disputes between litigants. Similarly, a civil lawsuit is a non-criminal court case and civil liability is non-criminal liability. (Note: This should not be confused with a civil-law legal system.)

Common-law and civil-law legal systems—a common-law legal system, such as in English Canada and the United States, is one where the decisions of earlier or higher courts have binding legal value on future decisions. Judges in common-law systems can make law through precedent (earlier decisions). In contrast, in civil-law legal systems, such as in Quebec and France, all law is written down in statutes (codified) and applied by judges; judges do not make law.

Communitarian rights—positive rights that can be said to belong to politically organized ethnic, linguistic, national, racial, religious, and other groups, especially rights of self-government and identity maintenance.

Constituent government—a general term designating the government of a constituent political community.

Constituent political community—a general term describing the political communities that make up a federation, such as cantons in Switzerland, *Länder* in Austria and Germany, provinces in Canada, and states in the United States and Australia.

Constitution—a country's supreme law. All laws must be consistent with it. It sets out the principles on which the government is based, identifies the structures of governance, and defines the limits of government power.

Convention—a treaty, typically of a multilateral nature, that is legally binding on its signatories.

Covenant—an agreement or pact based on voluntary consent and mutual promises between individuals, parties, or peoples, of independent and relatively equal status for purposes of the covenant, to engage in or refrain from certain actions in order to achieve limited or comprehensive joint ends, while respecting and protecting the individual integrities of the covenanting parties.

Corporate accountability—the process that requires a corporation to explain, justify, disprove, or accept culpability for its actions (or omissions) that are alleged to have violated—either directly or indirectly, by complicity or aiding and abetting a third party—the human rights of an individual or individuals. Legal accountability is sought through the judicial system under either criminal or civil law. Non-legal accountability may be had via a non-judicial mechanism such as a truth commission, or through the media and public opinion.

Cultural relativism—a theory defined by a belief in the absence of any hierarchy of values or any exterior standard against which to judge the virtues of particular traditions or beliefs. In the later 1940s, a major cultural relativist critique of the Universal Declaration of Human Rights was mounted on the basis of its pretensions to transcend cultural differences. After a period of relative dormancy, cultural relativism re-emerged as a major critique of universal human rights in the 1970s, rising to prominence in the "Asian values" debate of the late 1980s and 1990s.

Data protection—a set of procedural protections to ensure that individuals know why their personal information is being collected, how it is being used, and if it is accurate.

Declaration—a treaty, typically of a multilateral nature, that is not legally binding on its signatories.

Decree—the power of the executive branch of government to enact laws without action by the legislative branch. The power may be described in the constitution and limits to that power defined.

Democratization—a process that entails democratic transition and a framework for the emergence of opportunities to engage a bottom-up movement for socioeconomic and political change. This process or framework may include, among other things, separation of powers, the rule of law, judicial independence, legitimate governance, and imposition of limits to the body politic on an autocratic state. This process may also be initiated from the top down, leading to similar possibilities for a new synthesis of power, transparency, responsibilities, and accountability to the public at large.

Derogation—the partial repeal of a law, which limits its scope or force.

Disability—the experience of meeting barriers or facing exclusion as a result of living with a certain body or bodily differences.

Eco-centric—a philosophical perspective that places intrinsic value on nature and living organisms, regardless of their perceived usefulness or importance to human beings, in contrast to anthropocentric, or human-centred, value systems.

Economic and social rights—human rights relating to the protection of human dignity through guaranteed protections of basic human needs. Economic and social rights include the rights to adequate food, adequate housing, education, health, social security, water and sanitation, and work.

Enumerated and analogous grounds—specific identities, such as race and sex, as prohibited grounds for discrimination set out in section 15 of the Canadian Charter of Rights and Freedoms. Analogous grounds are prohibited grounds such as sexual orientation and marital status that are not specifically enumerated but which bear similarities to the enumerated grounds.

Entrenched—placed in the constitution.

Epistemic communities—groups or networks of experts with recognized knowledge in a particular issue area.

Federalism—a mode of governance that establishes or maintains unity while preserving diversity, by constitutionally uniting separate political communities in a limited but encompassing political community, wherein power is divided and shared between a general government with certain country-wide responsibilities and constituent governments with autonomous local responsibilities, and wherein both the general and constituent governments have independent authority to make laws for all individuals who reside within their respective territorial spheres of constitutional authority.

Foreign direct investment—investment by a company incorporated (based) in one country in a company in a different country.

Forum non conveniens—a legal doctrine that allow courts to exercise discretionary power to dismiss legal cases on the basis that they are not the most appropriate forum (court or jurisdiction) to hear the case in question.

Freedom of religion—a person's belief that an activity which enhances their connection to the divine is protected by the religious-freedom clause in the Charter of Rights and Freedoms. It does not matter if co-religionists do not share the same belief or if the activity is optional rather than mandated.

Gatekeeper NGO—a non-governmental organization that exerts disproportionate influence on the advocacy network in which it operates. In the field of human rights, gatekeepers include Amnesty International and Human Rights Watch.

GHGs—greenhouse gases responsible for anthropogenic climate change, particularly carbon dioxide, nitrous oxide, and methane.

GONGO—an organization created by a government seeking to extend its influence into the NGO community. Its relationship with the state disqualifies it from being considered an NGO.

Greenwashing—the dissemination of disinformation by an organization in order to present an environmentally responsible public image at odds with its practices.

Hate speech—expression that conveys extreme enmity toward people who experience discrimination by virtue of their race, sexuality, and so on. Prohibitions on hate speech are constitutionally justified, but prohibitions on speech that merely belittles or ridicules are not.

Home state vs. host state—the home state is the state in which a transnational corporation (TNC) is incorporated or headquartered. The host state is a state outside the home state in which the TNC has operations, either directly or through joint ventures or subsidiary corporations.

Human security—the idea that security, conventionally conceived, is too narrow; that genuine security that attends to human rights imperatives must encompass not only state security but the existential security of individuals and groups to enjoy fruitful lives, individually and collectively, even when doing so impinges upon the sovereign rights of states to do as they wish vis-à-vis their own populations and internal affairs. To this end, human security focuses on the creation of conditions under which the flourishing of human beings and the realization of human rights might be achieved.

Inclusion—experiences and practices that value diversity and encourage and enable all to participate and contribute.

Intersectionality—a theory that suggests that (and seeks to examine how) various biological, social, and cultural categories such as gender, race, class, ability, sexual orientation, caste, and other axes of identity interact on multiple and often simultaneous levels, contributing to systemic injustice and social inequality. Intersectionality holds that the classical conceptualizations of oppression within society, such as racism, sexism, homophobia, transphobia, and belief-based bigotry (such as nationalism), do not act independently of one another. Instead, these forms of oppression interrelate, creating a system of oppression that reflects the intersection of multiple forms of discrimination.

Islamists—a term generally used to denote opposition by Islamic-oriented parties or movements, groups, and individuals. Islamists have become the most dynamic political force across the Arab world specifically, and the Middle East and North Africa more generally, in the past half century. While modern Islamist parties have demonstrated willingness to work with secular and centrist parties, classical Islamists have pursued a strictly ideological line, averting such cooperation and fuelling internal instabilities and violence. Islamists can be divided into conservatives, nationalists, and neoliberal factions, all of whom radically differ on the goals of achieving political power, spreading Islamist goals through revolution, political reform, and/or economic development.

Iwi—the largest social units in Maori culture.

Judicialization—the enforcement and creation of rights production through judicial institutions, domestic or transnational.

Justiciability—the ability of courts, domestic or transnational, to rule on specific human rights. Often countries' inclusion of certain human rights in national constitutions allows for the justiciability of those rights in domestic courts.

Labour rights—a group of rights pertaining to relations between workers and their employers that include workers' pay, benefits, safe working conditions, security, and the right to bargain collectively.

Legal capacity—the ability to make decisions, sign contracts, vote, defend rights in court, and be recognized before the law.

Legislatures and parliaments—chambers that represent the legislative branch of government. In Canada it is common to refer to the federal chamber as parliament, comprising the House of Commons, the Senate, and the Crown, and to the provincial chambers as legislatures. *Legislature* and *parliament* can be used interchangeably and as generic terms.

Liberal nationalism—a broad orientation that retains enthusiasm for the nation-state as the guarantor of individual freedom. This nationalism is more often described in terms of values, law, and constitutionalism, without strong racial, linguistic, or religious exclusivity. International cooperation and international institutions were, and remain, highly compatible with this kind of nationalism, as do notions of universal human rights and individual freedom. Its constituent ideals have been discernible since the late eighteenth century, and they persist, broadly, in much of the contemporary democratic world.

Litigant—a person or party that is suing another or being sued. This may be the plaintiff (person/party bringing the lawsuit), the defendant (person/party being sued), the applicant (person/party appealing a lower-court decision), or the respondent (person/party defending in an appeal). It does not refer to a lawyer or a witness.

Litigation—the process of accessing the courts to settle a dispute.

Lower-skilled migrant workers—workers whose educational levels do not exceed a high school (secondary school) diploma or two years of occupation-specific training.

Mandatory retirement—a practice of employers, permitted by human rights legislation, to terminate employment of workers solely for the reason of chronological age.

Naming and shaming—a tactic employed by human rights NGOs to identify violations and their perpetrators, with the express intent of seeking to prevent their recurrence in the future.

Natural rights—the idea that human beings enjoy rights that arise from nature. The concept dates back to antiquity and is rooted in the notion of natural law: that through a process of reasoned reflection, rational beings can arrive at an array of agreed-upon principles that ought to govern the order of all facets of nature, including human relations. Such rights ostensibly pre-exist the establishment of specific political communities, arising, rather, from the basic fact of our shared humanity and human nature.

NGO—a non-governmental organization. This is a contested concept that most often refers to formally organized non-profit, non-violent, non-state actors. NGOs can pursue objectives ranging from improved human rights protections to pro-gun legislation.

Non-judicial remedy—the mechanism by which a right is sought to be enforced and/or by which a violation of a right is to be redressed. A non-judicial remedy is a mechanism by which this is accomplished that does not employ a court of law or other adjudicative body. Whereas judicial remedies emanate from bodies capable of making legally binding rulings (courts, judges, etc.), non-judicial remedies do not have the force of law and, therefore, are not legally binding or enforceable.

Norm entrepreneurs—individuals or organizations that work to raise awareness and build support for their particular issue or cause.

Parliamentary supremacy—the idea that the will of the elected legislature must take precedence over rulings of the judiciary (or decisions of the Crown).

Permanent immigrants—individuals who are admitted by the Canadian government to settle in Canada permanently.

Political institutions—a term that refers to enduring rules and norms that shape behaviour and expectations and constrain activity. The term *political institution* refers to the enduring rules and norms associated with public governance, such as a constitution.

Privacy—the right to be free from arbitrary interference with one's privacy, family, home, or correspondence, and from attacks on one's honour and reputation.

Progressive realization—the concept that because of the resources required to realize economic and social rights, states are obligated to protect only such rights as is possible, given their resource constraints. In article 2 of the ICESCR, states must progressively reach the full realization of the rights through "appropriate means."

Quasi-judicial institutions—specialized tribunals, such as the Canadian Human Rights Commission, that function like courts, although the rules are not as rigid as those of a formal court. The decision makers of a quasi-judicial institution are not judges, but most do have a legal background.

Racialized—a term used to emphasize the fact that racial categories are social constructions that change in time and space and are attributed with status and meaning.

Reasonable expectation of privacy—the expectation that one's communications will not be intercepted by anyone other than the intended recipient.

Restriction—a legal term denoting the limitation or curtailment of a right.

Rights of man—terminology that was the precursor of what today we refer to as "human rights." Originally espoused in founding documents of the French and American Revolutions and informed by the philosophical and political innovations of the Enlightenment, these rights were regarded as natural and inalienable.

Section 1 analysis—section 1 of the Charter of Rights and Freedoms provides that governments can interfere with Charter rights if that interference is "demonstrably justifiable in a free and democratic society." Among other things, governments must show that the legislation has a "pressing and substantial objective" and that the right has been "minimally impaired."

Security—as conventionally conceived in "security studies," those imperatives that arise in defence of the state against threats to its existence, both internal and external.

Self-determination—in the context of this volume, the power of communities or nations to govern themselves without fear of being overruled by a higher authority, unless the community or nation accepts the legitimacy of the higher authority. In other words, the community or nation has complete sovereignty or independence.

Self-government—in the context of this volume, the array of powers that a community or nation possesses that enables it to make decisions on matters that are important to it. However, the constitution of a higher authority still applies and the community or nation cannot violate it.

Social licence to operate—a grant of social permission or legitimacy to conduct business granted by local communities and other stakeholders in which a corporation operates. This community and stakeholder acceptance or approval is essential to ensure the viability of a business project. It is not a one-time grant of social legitimacy but an ongoing grant that must be maintained by the corporation in order to continue its operations in the community. Social licence to operate requires establishing a good relationship, often reliant on building trust, between the corporation and the local community and other stakeholders; open and honest communication between the corporation and the communities in which it is operating; and ongoing management and minimization of the risks of negative impacts from the activities of the corporation.

Social model of disability—an approach that recognizes that diverse bodies with varying needs can be accommodated in our society and works to remove barriers for those whose bodies cannot be accommodated in society as it is now.

Subsidiary and associate companies—subsidiary is a company in which another company (the parent company) has a controlling or majority interest, while an associate is a company in which the parent has a non-controlling, or minority, interest.

Substantive equality—distinguished from formal equality in that formal equality sees only discrimination that occurs directly, while substantive equality sees discrimination that occurs indirectly or systemically. For instance, a law prohibiting women from serving in a police force would be an act of direct discrimination. But a law framed in gender-neutral language that barred persons less than six feet tall from being a police officer would be an act of indirect or systemic discrimination.[1] Substantive equality acknowledges differences among groups; therefore the actual impacts of an impugned law on a group must be investigated, taking into account social, economic, and historical factors. In some cases differential treatment may be seen to be discriminatory, but in other cases it may be required to ameliorate the conditions of a group.

Supported decision making—assistance and supports available to enable a person to exercise her or his legal capacity.

Temporary migrant workers—workers who remain in a destination country for a limited period of time that is stated in a work authorization visa tied to a contract between a specific employer and a worker.

Transgender—the state of one's gender identity (self-identification as a woman, a man, neither, or both) or gender expression not matching one's assigned sex (identification by others as male, female, or intersex, based on physical/genetic characteristics). Transgender is independent of sexual orientation; transgender people may identify as heterosexual, homosexual, bisexual, pansexual, polysexual, or asexual, and some may consider conventional labels of sexual orientation inadequate or inapplicable to them. The precise definition for *transgender* is changing but nevertheless includes "of, relating to, or designating a person whose identity does not conform unambiguously to conventional notions of male or female gender roles, but combines or moves between these."

Transnational corporation (TNC) —a corporation with business operations (facilities, factories, and other assets) located in more than one country. A TNC consists of a web of interconnected parent corporation(s), subsidiaries, affiliates, suppliers, distributors, branches, franchises, joint ventures, and so forth. Well-known examples include Walmart, Nike, Pfizer, and Unilever. *Transnational corporation* is often used interchangeably with *multinational corporation* (MNC) or *multinational enterprise* (MNE).

Universality—in the human rights sphere, the equal application of rights for all people across the world, and, to a lesser extent, their applicability across time. It has been one of the defining features of modern human rights discourse and was apparent at least as early as the debates on the 1789 Declaration of the Rights of Man and the Citizen. Many of the great transformations wrought by human rights have involved expansion of who properly resides within the category of *universal*, from religious dissenters to women to the colonized and the disabled. Most meaningful versions of human rights presuppose universality of some sort.

Ultra vires—outside the jurisdiction of.

Visible minority—a term used by the Canadian government to identify a person or group visibly not one of the majority in a given population. The term is used primarily as a demographic category by Statistics Canada in connection with employment equity policies. The qualifier *visible* is important in the Canadian context, as political divisions have traditionally been determined by language (French vs. English) and religion (Catholics vs. Protestants), which are "invisible" traits.

Note

1. See P. Hogg, *Constitutional Law of Canada* (Toronto: Thomson Reuters Canada, 2009), 1187–88).

Index